V 74

LAND, LAW AND PLANNING

LAW IN CONTEXT
Editors: Robert Stevens (Professor of Law in Yale University)
and William Twining (Professor of Law in the University of
Warwick)

Already published:

Accidents, Compensation and the Law   P. S. Atiyah
Company Law and Capitalism   Tom Hadden
Karl Llewllyn and the Realist Movement   William Twining
Cases and Materials on the English Legal System   Michael Zander
Computers and the Law   Colin Tapper
Tribunals and Government   J. A. Farmer
Government and Law   T. C. Hartley and J. A. G. Griffith
Landlord and Tenant   Martin Partington

Land, Law and Planning

Cases, materials and text

PATRICK McAUSLAN

Professor of Law at the University of Warwick

WEIDENFELD AND NICOLSON

London

To Dorrette

'The real truth is that all this talk about
judicial attitudes to planning is moonshine.
There isn't any planning law, it's all
planning lore, planning mythology.'
R. H. S. Crossman, *Diaries, The Sunday Times*,
23 March 1975

Weidenfeld and Nicolson
11 St John's Hill, London SW11

ISBN 0 297 76880 8 cased
ISBN 0 297 76881 6 paperback

*Printed in Great Britain by Cox & Wyman Ltd,
London, Fakenham and Reading*

CONTENTS

Cases   ix
Statutes   xvii
Acknowledgements   xxiii
Abbreviations   xxiv
Preface   xxv

CHAPTER I   PROLOGOMENA TO PLANNING:
THE CONTINUITY OF PROBLEMS AND LAWS   I
  1   Introduction   I
  2   Procedural problems   6
      (a) *The disparate nature of decisions*   8
      (b) *Changing views and attitudes towards decisions*
           and institutions   9
      (c) *Unintended effects of new structures*   11
  3   Professional problems   12
      (a) *Planners and planning*   12
      (b) *Developers*   26
      (c) *Lawyers*   30
  4   The continuity of laws   33
      (a) *Introduction*   33
      (b) *Pre-Industrial Revolution legislation*   34
      (c) *Post-Industrial Revolution legislation*   37
  5   Judicial regulation of land use via nuisance   48
      (a) *The concept at work*   48
      (b) *Does nuisance go too far or not far enough?*   65
      (c) *Nuisance and public development: the defence of*
           legislative authority   74

CHAPTER 2 DECISION MAKERS, DECISION MAKING AND
PUBLIC PARTICIPATION 77
1 Introduction 77
2 The decision makers 77
   (a) *Central government: structure* 77
   (b) *Central government: functions* 80
   (c) *Local authorities: structure* 82
   (d) *Local authorities: functions* 84
3 Interrelations between central and local government 87
   (a) *Circulars* 90
   (b) *Consultation* 93
   (c) *Adjudicatory functions between local authorities* 94
4 Decision making: an introduction 94
5 Public participation 101
   (a) *What and why?* 101
   (b) *Two vehicles for public participation* 113
   (c) *New institutions of and approaches to participation* 136

CHAPTER 3 CREATING THE PLAN 142
1 Introduction 142
2 Genesis of structure and local planning 142
   (a) *Regional planning* 143
   (b) *The defects of the 1947-style development plan* 154
3 The reforms of 1968 and 1972: towards a
solution? 158
   (a) *Proposed reforms in the planning system and the
debate thereon* 158
   (b) *Proposed reforms in the local government system
and the debate thereon* 171
4 The problems of the solutions 174
   (a) *Local government reorganisation* 177
   (b) *The scope and form of structure planning* 184
   (c) *Are there enough planners to go round?* 210
   (d) *Public participation* 216
   (e) *Is structure planning obsolescent?* 241

CHAPTER 4   DEVELOPMENT AND ITS CONTROL: PRIVATE
LAW   245
 1 Introduction   245
 2 Restrictive covenants running at equity   247
    (a) *Evolution and nature*   249
    (b) *Annexation*   254
    (c) *Assignment*   258
    (d) *The development scheme*   272
 3 Use by public authorities   283
 4 Positive covenants   292
 5 Public control of covenants   302
    (a) *Section 84, Law of Property Acts 1925–69*   303
    (b) *Other controls*   315
 6 The long lease   329
    (a) *General*   329
    (b) *Control by the ground landlord*   330
    (c) *Development and planning of estates*   333
    (d) *The Leasehold Reform Act and its aftermath*   335

CHAPTER 5   DEVELOPMENT AND ITS CONTROL: PUBLIC
LAW   350
 1 Introduction   350
 2 Control at the local planning authority level   354
    (a) *Extent of control*   354
    (b) *Who controls?*   356
    (c) *How is control exercised?*   369
 3 Control at the central government level   449
    (a) *The occasions for ministerial or departmental
        decision-making*   449
    (b) *Types of ministerial or departmental hearing*   452

CHAPTER 6   DEVELOPMENT AND ITS CONTROL: CONTROLS
EXTERNAL TO THE PLANNING SYSTEM   484
 1 Introduction   484
 2 Judicial control: planning law   485
    (a) *Enforcement notices*   486

(b) *Is it development?* 509
(c) *Permitted development* 554
3 Judicial control: administrative law 558
  (a) *General principles of judicial review* 558
  (b) *Locus standi* 566
4 Administrative controls 579
  (a) *The Council on Tribunals* 579
  (b) *The Parliamentary Commissioner for Administration* 590

CHAPTER 7 LAND VALUES AND COMPENSATION 602
1 Introduction 602
2 Land values and planning 603
  (a) *The problem stated* 603
  (b) *Solutions officially proposed or attempted 1942–71* 607
  (c) *Solutions proposed since 1971* 612
3 Compensation 623
  (a) *Is there a right to compensation?* 624
  (b) *When is compensation assessed?* 636
  (c) *The assessment of market value* 641
  (d) *Depreciation and injurious affection* 662
  (e) *Disturbance* 672
  (f) *Defects of market value as a basis of compensation* 678
  (g) *Inverse compulsory purchase* 684
  (h) *Compensation and participation* 696

Notes 700
Index 727

Cases

Abbott's Park Estate, Re [1972] 2 All E.R. 177   348

Agricultural, Horticultural and Forestry Industry Training Board v. *Aylesbury Mushrooms Ltd* [1972] 1 All E.R. 280   715

Alliance Economic Investment Co. Ltd v. *Berton* (1923) 21 L.G.R. 403   **319**

Allnatt London Properties v. *Middlesex C.C.* (1964) 15 P. & C.R. 288   719

Arcade Hotel Pty., Re [1962] V.R. 274   255

Argyle Motors v. *Birkenhead Corporation* [1974] 1 All E.R. 201   **666**

Associated Provincial Picture Houses Ltd v. *Wednesbury Corporation* [1947] 2 All E.R. 680   420, 421, 630

Attorney-General (on the relation of Hornchurch U.D.C.) v. *Bastow* [1957] 1 All E.R. 497   505

Attorney-General v. *Doughty* (1752) 2 Ves. Sen. 453, 28 E.R. 290   250

Attorney-General v. *Smith* [1958] 2 All E.R. 557   **503**, 506

Attorney-General v. *Wimbledon House Estate Co. Ltd* [1904] 2 Ch. 34   505

Attorney-General of the Gambia v. *N'Jie* [1961] 2 All E.R. 504   570, 571

Ayre Harbour Trustees v. *Oswald* (1883) 8 App. Cas 623   317

Ballard's Conveyance, Re [1937] 2 All E.R. 691   265

Baxter v. *Four Oaks Properties Ltd* [1965] 1 All E.R. 906   **273**, 283, 712

Bedford (Duke of) v. *Trustees of the British Museum* (1822) 2 My. & K.552, 39 E.R. 1055   248

Belfast Corporation v. *O.D. Cars Ltd* [1960] 1 All E.R. 65   **624**

Bendles Motors Ltd v. *Bristol Corporation* [1963] 1 All E.R. 578   719

Bentley's case 1723 1 stra. 557, 93 E.R. 698   48

Birmingham Corporation v. *Minister of Housing and Local Government*
   [1963] 3 All E.R. 669   **526**

Birmingham Corporation v. *West Midland Baptist (Trust) Association
   (Incorporated)* [1969] 3 All E.R. 172   **636**, 658, 723

Biss v. *Smallburgh R.D.C.* [1964] 2 All E.R. 543   540

Blackpool Corporation v. *Lockyer* [1948] 1 All E.R. 85   704

Bland v. *Moseley*, cited in (1606) 9 Co. Rep. at p. 58a (Aldred's
   Case)   250

Bolivian Trust Ltd v. *Secretary of State for the Environment* [1972] 3 All
   E.R. 918   **507**

Britt v. *Bucks. C.C.* [1963] 2 All E.R. 175   424

Brookdene Investments Ltd v. *M.H.L.G.* (1970) 21 P. & C.R. 545   **686**

Brooks v. *Glos. C.C.* (1967) 19 P & C.R. 90   547

Brunner v. *Greenslade* [1970] 3 All E.R. 833   712, 713

Bryers & Morris, R (1931) 40 O.W.N. 572   325

Buccleuch (Duke of) v. *Metropolitan Board of Works* (1872) L.R.
   5 H.L. 518   **663**

Burdle v. *Secretary of State for the Environment* [1972] 3 All E.R. 240
   543, 548, **549**, 553, 719

Buxton v. *M.H.L.G.* [1960] 3 All E.R. 408   407, 567, 569, 570, 571,
   572, 577, 702

Caledonian Railway Co. v. *Walker's Trustees* (1882) 7 App. Cas. 259
   667

Calthorpe Estate, Edgbaston, Birmingham, Re, Anstruther-Gough-Calthorpe
   v. *Grey* (1973) 25 P. & C.R. 120   **346**

Camrose (Viscount) v. *Basingstoke Corporation* [1966] 3 All E.R. 161
   644, 660, 661

Cardiff Corporation v. *Secretary of State for Wales* (1971) 22 P. & C.R.
   718   413

Cater v. *Essex C.C.* [1959] 2 All E.R. 213   493

Catt v. *Tourle* (1869) 4 Ch. App. 654   251

Chasemore v. *Richards* (1859) 7 H.L. Cas. 349, 11 E.R. 140   250

Chelmsford Corporation v. *Secretary of State for the Environment* (1971)
   22 P. & C.R. 880   **393**

Chelmsford R.D.C. v. *Powell* [1963] 1 All E.R. 150   **501**

Cheshire C.C. v. *Woodward* [1962] 1 All E.R. 517   **511**

Child v. *Douglas* [1854] 1 Kay 560   257

City of London Corporation v. *Secretary of State for the Environment* (1973) 71 L.G.R. 28   519, **521**

Coleen Properties Ltd v. *M.H.L.G.* [1971] 1 All E.R. 1049   718

Coleshill and District Investment Co. Ltd v. *M.H.L.G.* [1969] 2 All E.R. 525   **92**, 499, 510, **513**, 518

Colonial Sugar Refining Co. Ltd v. *Melbourne Harbour Trust Commissioners* [1927] A.C. 343   629, 722

Commissioner for Local Government, Lands and Settlement v. *Kaderbhai* [1931] A.C. 652   **321**

Cooper v. *Wandsworth Board of Works* (1862) 14 C.B.N.S. 180, 143 E.R. 414   **46**

Cowper Essex v. *Acton Local Board* (1889) 14 App. Cas. 153   663

Crump v. *Lambert* (1867) L.R. 3 Eq. 409   58

Dalton v. *Angus* (1881) 6 App. Cas. 740   250

Davy v. *Leeds Corporation* [1965] 1 All E.R. 753   **646**

De Mattos v. *Gibson* (1858) 4 De G. & J. 276, 45. E.R. 108   251

De Mulder v. *Secretary of State for the Environment* [1974] 1 All E.R. 776   719

Director of Public Prosecutions v. *Ottewell* [1968] 3 All E.R. 153   509

Dolphin's Conveyance, Re [1970] 2 All E.R. 66   **280**

Driscoll v. *Church Commissioners for England* [1956] 3 All E.R. 802   291

East Barnet U.D.C. v. *British Transport Commission* [1961] 3 All E.R. 878   530, 541, 544

East End Dwellings Co. Ltd v. *Finsbury Borough Council* [1951] 2 All E.R. 587   656

East Riding C.C. v. *Park Estate (Bridlington) Ltd* [1955] 2 All E.R. 269   493, 495, 497

Ellis and Ruislip–Northwood U.D.C., Re [1920] 1 K.B. 343   702

Elliston v. *Reacher* [1908] 2 Ch. 374   277, 278, 283

Errington v. *Minister of Health* [1935] 1 K.B. 249   560, 561

Essex Real Estate Co. v. *Holmes* (1930) 37 O.W.N. 392   325

Evans v. *Collins* [1964] 1 All E.R. 808   701

Fawcett Properties Ltd v. *Bucks. C.C.* [1961] A.C. 636   36, **419**, 719

Fitzpatrick Development Ltd v. *M.H.L.G.* (1965) unreported   407

Formby v. *Barker* [1903] 2 Ch. 539   252

Franklin v. *Minister of Town and Country Planning* [1947] 2 All E.R. 289   **562**, 565

Gaunt v. *Finney* (1872) 8 Ch. App. 8   59

Geddis v. *Bann Reservoir Proprietors* (1878) 3 App. Cas. 430   75

Gee v. *The National Trust* (1966) 17 P. & C.R. 7   **289**

Ghey & Galton's Application, Re [1957] 3 All E.R. 164   304

Givaudan & Co. Ltd v. *M.H.L.G.* [1966] 3 All E.R. 696   **464**, 470, 566

Gregory v. *London Borough of Camden* [1966] 2 All E.R. 196   **576**, 578

Hall & Co. Ltd v. *Shoreham-by-Sea U.D.C.* [1964] 1 All E.R. 1   **423**, 429, 719

Halsall v. *Brizell* [1957] Ch. 169   300

Halsey v. *Esso Petroleum* [1961] 2 All E.R. 145   50, **53**, 65, 665

Hamblett v. *Flintshire C.C.* (1961) 11 P. & C.R. 284   540

Hamilton v. *West Sussex C.C.* [1958] 2 All E.R. 174   **392**, 393

Hammersmith and City Railway Co. v. *Brand* (1869) L.R. 4 H.L. 171   662, 671

Hampstead and Suburban Properties Ltd v. *Diomedous* [1969] 3 All E.R. 545

Hartley v. *M. H. L. G.* [1969] 3 All E. R. 1658 **531**, 537

Harvey v. *Crawley Development Corporation* [1957] 1 All E.R. 504   **675**

Hawley v. *Steele* [1898] 2 Ch. 394   268, 269

Hawes v. *Thornton Cleveleys R.D.C.* (1965) 17 P. & C.R. 22   540

Hendy v. *Bristol Corporation* (1974) 72 L.G.R. 405   724

Heywood's Conveyance, R [1938] 2 All E.R. 230   317

Horn v. *Sunderland Corporation* [1941] 1 All E.R. 480   **673**

Howard v. *Secretary of State for the Environment* [1974] 1 All E.R. 644   **500**

Iddenden v. *Secretary of State for the Environment* [1972] 3 All E.R. 882   **498**

Inland Revenue Commissioners v. *Dodwell, O'Mahoney & Co. Ltd* [1952] 1 All E.R. 531   640

James v. *Secretary of State for Wales* [1966] 3 All E.R. 964   431

Jeffs Transfer, Re (No. 2) [1966] 1 All E.R. 937   255, **271**

Jelson Ltd v. *M.H.L.G.* [1969] 3 All E.R. 147   **651**

Johnson & Co. (Builders) Ltd v. *Minister of Health* [1947] 2 All E.R. 395   561

Jubb v. *Hull Dock Co.* (1846) 9 QB 443   724

Kent C.C. v. *Kingsway Investments (Kent) Ltd* [1970] 1 All E.R. 70   716, 717, 719

Keppell v. *Bailey* (1834) 2 My. and K. 517, 39 E.R. 1042   248

Kruse v. *Johnson* [1898] 2 Q.B. 91   424

Lade and Lade v. *Brighton Corporation* (1971) 22 P. & C.R. 737   **694**

Lambe v. *Secretary of State for War* [1955] 2 All E.R. 386   723

Lavender (H) and Son Ltd v. *M.H.L.G.* [1970] 3 All E.R. 871   566

Lawrence v. *South County Freeholds Ltd* [1939] 2 All E.R. 503   278

Leicester (Earl of) v. *Wells-next-the-Sea U.D.C.* [1972] 3 All E.R. 77
316, 565

Lever Finance Co. v. *London Borough of Westminster* [1970] 3 All E.R.
496   439, **443**, 448, 565, 566

Llewellyn v. *Hinson, Llewellyn* v. *Christmas* [1948] 2 All E.R. 65   527

Local Government Board v. *Arlidge* [1915] A.C. 120   11

London C.C. v. *Allen* [1914] 3 K.B. 642   252, 253, 283, 284, 291, 712

London and South-Western Railway Co. v. *Gomm* (1882) 20 Ch. D.
562   249, 252, 257

Luby v. *Newcastle-under-Lyme Corporation* [1964] 3 All E.R. 169   701

Luke of Pavenham (Lord) v. *M.H.L.G.* [1969] 2 All E.R. 1066   **462**,
472, 561

Luker v. *Dennis* (1877) 7 Ch. D. 227   251

McDougall & Waddell, Re [1945] 2 D.L.R. 244   325

McKellen v. *M.L.H.,* Estates Gazette 6/5/66   532

Manchester Corporation v. *Farnworth* [1930] A.C. 171   75

Manchester, Sheffield and Lincolnshire Rly. Co. v. *Anderson* [1988] 2 Ch.
394   267

Mann v. *Stephens* (1846) 15 Sim 377 60 E.R. 665   248

Margate Corporation v. *Devotwill Investments* [1970] 3 All E.R. 864
653

Marriage v. *East Norfolk Rivers Catchment Board* [1949] 2 All E.R.
1021   **74**

Martell v. *Consett Iron Co.* [1955] 1 All E.R. 481   66

Marten v. *Flight Refuelling, Ltd* [1961] 2 All E.R. 696   **259**, 270

Maurice v. *London C.C.* [1964] 1 All E.R. 779   570, 572

Mercian Housing Society Ltd's Application, Re (1971) 23 P. & C.R.
116   **308**, 315

Metropolitan Asylum District v. *Hill* (1881) 6 App. Cas. 193   75

Metropolitan Board of Works v. *McCarthy* (1874) L.R. 7 H.L. 243
666, 667

Millbourn v. *Lyons* [1914] 2 Ch. 231   252

Miller (T.A.) Ltd v. *M.H.L.G.* [1968] 2 All E.R. 633   533

Miller-Mead v. *M.H.L.G.* [1963] 1 All E.R. 459   432, **489**, 497

Mizen Bros. v. *Mitcham U.D.C.* (1929) Estates Gazette Digest, p. 258
674

Moy v. *Stoop* (1909) 25 T.L.R. 262   50

Munnich v. *Godstone U.D.C.* [1966] 1 All E.R. 930   **495**

Murphy (J.) & Sons Ltd v. *Secretary of State for the Environment* [1973] 2 All E.R. 26   406

Myers v. *Milton Keynes Development Corporation* [1974] 2 All E.R. 1096   **658**

Myton Ltd v. *M.H.L.G.* (1963) 61 L.G.R. 1690   **466**, 470

National Trust v. *Midlands Electricity Board* [1952] 1 All E.R. 298 **286**

Neale v. *Del Soto* [1945] 1 All E.R. 191   527

Newton Abbott Co-operative Society Ltd v. *Williamson & Treadgold, Ltd* [1952] 1 All E.R. 279   262, 263, 266

Nisbet and Potts' Contract, Re [1906] 1 Ch. 386   252

Noble & Wolf v. *Alley* [1951] 1 D.L.R. 321   321, **324**

Norfolk C.C. v. *Secretary of State for the Environment* [1973] 3 All E.R. 673   **436**

Northbourne (Lord) v. *Johnston & Son* [1922] 2 Ch. 309   265, 267

Offer v. *Minister of Health* [1936] 1 K.B. 40   720

Official Receiver ex parte, Re *Reed, Bowen & Co.* (1887) 19 Q.B.D.174 570

Patchett v. *Leathem* (1949) 65 T.L.R. 69   704

Penny v. *Penny* (1868) L.R. 5 Eq. 227   638

Petticoat Lane Rentals v. *Secretary of State for the Environment* [1971] 2 All E.R. 793   **534**

Phipps v. *Pears* [1964] 2 All E.R. 35   250

Pointe Gourde Quarrying and Transport Co. Ltd v. *Sub-Intendent of Crown Lands* [1947] A.C. 565   **643**, 644, 645

Pride of Derby and Derbyshire Angling Association Ltd v. *British Celanese Ltd* [1953] 1 All E.R. 179   **65**

Prosser v. *M.H.L.G.* (1969) 67 L.G.R. 109   535, 536

Purkiss' Application, Re [1962] 1 W.L.R. 902   315

Pyx Granite Co. Ltd v. *M.H.L.G.* [1959] 3 All E.R. 1   420, 426, 428, 429, 719

R. v. *Bradford-on-Avon R.D.C.*, ex parte *Boulton* [1964] 2 All E.R. 492   **381**, 385, 560, **573**, 575, 577

R. v. *Chandler* (1702) 1 Salk. 377; 91 E.R. 378   495

R. v. *Electricity Commissioners*, ex parte *London Electricity Joint Committee Co.* (**1920**) *Ltd* [1924] 1 K.B. 171   574

R. v. *Hendon R.D.C.*, ex parte *Chorley* [1933] 2 K.B. 696   560, **561**, 573, 574, 576

R. v. *London Borough of Hillingdon*, ex parte *Royco Homes Ltd* [1974] 2 All E.R. 643   **426**, 430, **573**, 575 716

R. v. *M.H.L.G.*, ex parte *Chichester R.D.C.* [1960] 2 All E.R. 407
685

R. v. *M.H.L.G.*, ex parte *Rank Organisation Ltd* [1958] 3 All E.R.
322   687

R. v. *Surrey Justices* (1870) L.R. 5 Q.B. 466   577

R. v. *Yeovil Corporation*, ex parte *Trustees of Elim Pentecostal Church,
Yeovil* (1972) 70 L.G.R. 142   **433,** 438

Renals v. *Cowlishaw* (1878) 9 Ch. D. 125   257, 258, 277

Ricket v. *Directors etc. of Metropolitan Railway Co.* (1867) L.R. 2 H.L.
175   667

Ridge v. *Baldwin* [1963] 2 All E.R. 66   574, 575

Rogers v. *Hosegood* [1900] 2 Ch. 388   **255**

Rollo v. *Minister of Town and Country Planning* [1948] 1 All E.R. 13
704

Rusell v. *Archdale* [1964] Ch. 38   255

Rylands v. *Fletcher* (1866) L.R. 1 Ex. 265 affd. (1868) LR. 3 H.L. 330
11, 48, 55

Sagnata Investments Ltd v. *Norwich Corporation* [1971] 2 All E.R. 1441
716

St Helen's Smelting Co. v. *Tipping* (1865) 11 H.L.C. 642, 11 E.R.
1483   50, **51**

Shemara Ltd v. *Luton Corporation* (1967) 18 P. & C.R. 520   **388**

Sherwood Close (Barnes) Management Co. Ltd, Re [1971] 3 All E.R.
1283   347, 348

Sidebotham, Re (1880) 14 Ch. D. 458   568, 569, 570

Slattery v. *Naylor* (1888) 13 App. Cas. 446   625

Slough Estates Ltd v. *Slough Corporation* (1970) 68 L.G.R. 669   **431,**
436, 438

South Eastern Railway Co. v. *L.C.C.* [1915] 2 Ch. 252   643

South Eastern Railway Co. and Wiffin's Contract, Re [1907] 2 Ch. 366
317

Southend-on-Sea Corporation v. *Hodgson (Wickford) Ltd* [1961] 2 All
E.R. 46   **440,** 446, 448, 565, 566

Spicer v. *Martin* (1888) 14 App. Cas. 12   277, 278

Stilwell v. *Blackman* [1968] Ch. 508   255

Stourcliffe Estates Co. Ltd v. *Bournemouth Corporation* [1910] 2 Ch.
12   317

Stringer v. *M.H.L.G.* [1971] 1 All E.R. 65   **406, 409,** 565

Stubbs v. *West Hartlepool Corporation* (1961) 12 P. & C.R. 365   **692**

Sussex Caravan Parks Ltd v. *Richardson* [1961] 1 All E.R. 731   432

Tod-Heatly v. *Benham* (1880) 40 Ch. D. 80   64

Trentham (G. Percy) Ltd v. *C.C.* [1966] 1 All E.R. 701   **537, 544,** 552

Tulk v. *Moxhay* (1848) 2 Ph. 774, 41 E.R. 1143   11, **247,** 249, 251, 252, 261, 325

Turner v. *Secretary of State for the Environment* (1974) 28 P. & C.R. 123   **567**

Union of London and Smith's Bank Ltd's Conveyance, Re Miles v. *Easter* [1933] Ch. 611   262, 263, 264, 265

Walter v. *Selfe* (1851) 4 De G. & Sm. 315, 64 E.R. 849   59, 63, 73

Wards Construction (Medway) Ltd's Application, Re, (1973) 25 P. & C.R. 223   **312**

Webb v. *Bird* (1862) 13 C.B. (N.S.) 841, 143 E.R. 332   250

Webb v. *Russell* (1789) 3 T.R. 393, 100 E.R. 639   257

Webber v. *M.H.L.G.* [1967] 3 All E.R. 981   533, **539,** 541, 719

Wellington (Mayor of) v. *Lower Hutt (Mayor of)* [1904] A.C. 773   319

Wells v. *M.H.L.G.* [1967] 2 All E.R. 1041   446, **447,** 448, 451, 472 485

West Ham Central Charity Board v. *East London Waterworks Co.* [1900] 1 Ch. 624   701

Westminster Bank Ltd v. *M.H.L.G.* [1970] 1 All E.R. 734   **627,** 641

White v. *Bijou Mansions Ltd* [1938] 1 All E.R. 546   282

Williams v. *M.H.L.G.* (1969) 67 L.G.R. 109   548

Wilson v. *Liverpool City Council* [1971] 1 All E.R. 628   **644**

Wilson v. *Secretary of State for the Environment* [1974] 1 All E.R. 428 715

Wilson v. *West Sussex C.C.* (1963) 61 L.G.R. 287   436

Wood v. *Conway Corporation* [1914] 2 Ch. 47   61

Wood v. *Secretary of State for the Environment* [1973] 2 All E.R. 404 **545**

Zetland (Marquess of) v. *Driver* [1938] 2 All E.R. 158   288

Statutes

1388 An Act for the punishment of them which cause corruption near city or great town to corrupt the air. 2 Statutes 306

s.2	34	s.4	34
s.3	34		

1589 An act against the erecting and maintaining of cottages. 6 Statutes 409

s.1	35	s.4	35
s.3	35	s.6	35

1667 An Act for Rebuilding the City of London. 8 Statutes 233   44

s.3	35	s.5	36
s.4	36	s.6	36

1845 Land Clauses Consolidation Act (c. 18)

s.18	637		45, 637, 638, 662, 673
s.63	664	s.68	666, 668

1846 Removal of Nuisances Act (c.96) 37, 44

1848 Public Health Act (c.63)   37, 42, 44, 701

1851 Labouring Classes Lodging Houses Act (c.34)   43

1855 Metropolis Local Management Act (c.120)   46

1862 Thames Embankment Act (c.93), s.27   664–5

1863 Alkali Act (c.124)   701

1875 Artizans and Labourers' Dwellings Improvement Act (c.36) 38, 42

Public Health Act (c.55)   44, 625

1890 Housing of the Working Classes Act (c.70)   38, 43

1907 National Trust Act (c.cxxxvi)   286

1909 Housing Town Planning etc. Act (c.44)   33, 38, 39, 453

s.27   319

1919 Acquisition of Land (Assessment of Compensation) Act (c.57)
638, 673
s.1   674   s.2   636, 674, 676
1920 Increase of Rent and Mortgage Interest (Restrictions)
Act (c.17)   528
Government of Ireland Act (c.67), s.5   624, 626
1925 Housing Act (c.14), s.64, Sch. III   673
Town Planning Act (c.16)   561
Law of Property Act (c.20), s.78   258
s.84   271, 290-2, 303-4 s.184 **306**, 312, 315, 318
s.198   267, 270
Land Charges Act (c.22), s.10   267, 287
1926 Smallholdings and Allotments Act (c.32)   317, 422
1930 Housing Act (c.39), s.34   422
1930 London Building Act (20 & 21 Geo. 5 c.clviii)   570
1930 Land Drainage Act (c.44)   74
s.6   74, 75   s.34   74-6
s.12   75   s.38   74-5
1931 Planning and Housing Act (Northern Ireland), s.10   624, 626
1932 Town and Country Planning Act (c.48), s.34   39, 155, 712
1936 Public Health Act (c.49)   41
Housing Act (c.51)   284
s.5   284
s.6   529   s.115   422
                                                 s.148   712
1937 National Trust Act (c.lvii)   291
1939 National Trust Act (c.lxxxvi)   292
1943 Town and Country Planning (Interim Development)
Act (c.29)   39
1944 Town and Country Planning Act (c.47) s.57   732
1946 New Towns Act (c.68)   39, 379, 562
1947 Town and Country Planning Act (c.51)   28, 39, 40, 92, 154-5,
                     319, 393, 419, 426, 503, 505, 573, 610, 611, 617
s.4   707
s.10   720
s.12   511-12, 527-9   s.23   441-2, 491-4, 498
s.14   420, 424   s.36   419
                                                 s.55   723
                                                 s.119   419, 512
s.16   425-6, 466, 568   Sch. 1   707
s.18   503   Sch. 3   516
1947 Electricity Act (c.54), s.1   287
s.2   287   s.3   287
1948 River Boards Act (c.32)   67

1948	Companies Act (c.38)		299
1949	Lands Tribunal Act (c.42)		303
1951	Rivers (Prevention of Pollution) Act (c.54)		67
s.11	66		
1952	Property Law Act (New Zealand) (as amended)		**328**
1953	Town and Country Planning Act (c.16)		611
1954	Landlord and Tenant Act (c.56)		714
1954	Town and Country Planning Act (c.73)		611
1956	Leicester Corporation Act (c.xlix), s.6		**284**
1957	Housing Act (c.56)		116, 646
s.36	529	s.114	422
s.43	648, 718	s.151	**284**
s.105	317	s.165	**318**, 713
1958	Tribunals and Inquiries Act (c.66), s.1		581
1959	Highways Act (c.56), s.72		672–9
1959	Town and Country Planning Act (c.53), s.9		646–8, 723
s.14	723		
s.37	382–4	s.39	693
1960	Caravan Sites and Control of Development Act (c.62), s.3		496
s.17	496	s.33	490–1, 493–4, 501, 527–8
1961	Land Compensation Act (c.33)		116, 642, 651
s.5	642, **645**		
s.6	642, 644, 646, 660	s.17	650, 652–3
s.9	642, **645**	s.18	652
s.14	642, 649, 659, 660	s.22	642, 650, 653
s.15	649, 659, 660	Sch. 1	644, 660, 723
s.16	649, 650, 654, 659		
	Housing Act (c.65)		527
1962	Town and Country Planning Act (c.38)		93, 361, 534
s.4	116		
s.12	515–18, 521–2, 538 540, 687–8	s.45	418, 498, 539
s.13	540	s.129	651, 686–8
s.17	410, 411, 434, 523	s.130	654
s.18	418, 522–3	s.133	651
		s.141	694
s.23	463, 581	s.176	521
s.27	116	s.179	409, 463, 521
s.28	116	s.180	513, 549
s.34	417	s.181	514
s.37	285	s.207	117, 593
s.43	390–1, 447, 472, 514	s.221	514–17
1964	Industrial Training Act (c.16)		715

1965 Control of Office and Industrial Development Act (c.33)   29, 466
      Compulsory Purchase Act (c.56)   662
s.7   **662**   s.10   316, **666**
      New Towns Act (c.59), s.1   117, 189, 379, 658
      Race Relations Act (c.73)   328
      Birkenhead Corporation (Mersey Tunnel Approaches) Act
          (c.xxxviii)   666
1967 Land Commission Act (c.1)   611, 612, 617, 700
      Parliamentary Commissioner Act (c.13)   590
      Civic Amenities Act (c.69)   309, 700
      Leasehold Reform Act (c.88)   299, 329, 335–6, 347–8, 713
s.19   337, **338**, 342, 346
1968 Rent Act (c.23)   428
      Race Relations Act (c.71), s.5   321, **328**
      Town and Country Planning Act (c.72)
      Part I, s.15   498–9
s.16   500, 501   s.18   508
s.17   507–9   s.64   434–5
1969 Local Government Grants (Social Needs) Act (c.2)   208
      Housing Act (c.33) Part II   700, 701
      Law of Property Act (c.59), s.28   303
1970 The Conveyancing and Law of Property Act R.S.O. c.85
      (Ontario) s.22   **328**
1971 Highways Act (c.41), s.47   690
      Tribunals and Inquiries Act (c.62)   236
      Town and Country Planning Act (c.78)   42, 81, 108, 172, 218,
                                                  223, 357, 574
s.4   715–16   s.52   **284**, 285
s.6   **184**, 235, 711   s.53   447, 716–17
s.7   167, **184**, 235   s.63   716
s.8   169, **216**, 234, 703, 707   s.64   716
                          226
s.9   707, 720   s.65   701
s.10   708   s.70   414, 716
s.10B   186, 708   s.77   414, 716
s.10C   178, 703   s.78   414, 716
s.11   **184**, 235, 708   s.79   414, 716
s.12   234   s.80   414, 716
s.13   **236**   s.87   **487**, 718
s.14   **180, 238**, 711, 720   s.88   451, 483, 486, **488**
s.15   178   s.90   **489**, 718
s.19   711   s.94   **506**, 718
s.22   **351**, 541   s.101   704

s.23	**352**	s.127	315, 318
		s.139	694
s.24	**353**	s.164	633
s.26	**371**	s.169	633
s.27	**380**, 384–5	s.177	718
s.29	**403, 414**	s.180	684
s.30	**416**, 716	s.192	690, 725
s.32	**414**	s.194	695
s.33	**414**, 548	s.244	720
s.35	**450**	s.245	571, 720
s.36	**449**	s.246	436, 545
s.41	414, **430**, 716	s.276	703, 717
s.42	414, **430**, 716	s.289	722
s.44	716	Sch. 4	711
s.45	717	Sch. 8	632, 633
s.51	717	Sch. 9	718

1972 Town and Country Planning (Amendment) Act (c.42)   44, 80, 225, 234, 700

s.4	711		

Housing Finance Act (c.47)   42
Deposits of Poisonous Wastes Act (c.21)   36
Industry Act (c.63)   143
Local Government Act (c.70)   41, 81–2, 87, 94, 154, 181, 234–5, 238 359 364

s.101	87, **396**, 714	s.245	704
s.110	704	s.246	704
s.183	704, 708	Sch. 16	**356, 379**

Coventry Corporation Act (c.xxix) s.4   **316**
Devon River Authority (General Powers) Act (c.xxxviii)   **682**

1973 Land Compensation Act (c.26)   635, 662, 689, 697–8, 700

s.1	**668**	s.30	**681**
s.2	669	s.32	**681**
s.3	**669**	s.37	**677**
s.4	**669**	s.38	**678**
s.5	670	s.22	692
s.6	**670**	s.39	**678**
s.7	670	s.68	691
s.8	**670**	s.69	691
s.9	671	s.70	691
s.15	671	s.71	691
s.17	**671**	s.74	692
s.26	**671**	s.75	691
s.29	**680**	s.76	691

1974	Local Government Act (c.7), Part III	721
	Town and Country Amenities Act (c.32)	700
	Control of Pollution Act (c.40)	700
	Housing Act (c.44)	680, 700, 713
1975	Housing Rents and Subsidies Act	701

Acknowledgements

The author and publishers would like to thank the following for permission to reproduce material from their publications:

Allen and Unwin for Peter Hall (ed.) *The Containment of Urban England*, G. McCrone, *Regional Policy in Britain*, J. A. G. Griffith, *Central Departments and Local Authorities* and Dame E. Sharp, *The Ministry of Housing and Local Government*; Sweet and Maxwell for C. H. Preston and G. H. Newsom, *Restrictive Covenants Affecting Land* and for extracts from the *Journal of Planning and Environment Law*; Butterworths for Keith Davies, *Law of Compulsory Purchase and Planning*; the Acton Society Trust for Peter Hall (ed.), *Land Values*; Penguin Books for S. A. de Smith, *Constitutional and Administrative Law*; John Murray for John Betjeman, *Collected Poems*; Faber and Faber for a diagram from J. Brian McLoughlin, *Control and Urban Planning*; the *Journal of the Royal Town Planning Institute*; *Justice*; *New Society*; and *The Spectator*.

Journal Abbreviations

Journal Abbreviations

J.P.L.	Journal of Planning Law (this became the Journal of Planning and Environmental Law in January 1973)
J.R.T.P.I.	Journal of the Royal Town Planning Institute
J.T.P.I.	Journal of the Town Planning Institute. (This became the J.R.T.P.I. in March 1971)
L.G.C.	Local Government Chronicle
L.Q.R.	Law Quarterly Review
M.L.R.	Modern Law Review
P.L.	Public Law
T. & C.P.	Town and Country Planning
T.P.R.	Town Planning Review

Preface

As we move into the last quarter of the twentieth century, the planning, development and control of the use of land assume greater and greater importance in the United Kingdom. More and more people are affected by it, and, of greater importance, more and more people wish to play some part in those planning decisions that affect their lives. Whether looked at as an aspect of land law – what may an individual do with his own land? – or an aspect of public law – how may the authorities control what an individual does with his land and for what purposes? – it would seem to follow that planning and the law that provides for it should be assuming a correspondingly greater and greater role in the lawyer's education for his or her responsibilities in modern British society. Until comparatively recently, however, planning law was not generally regarded as a subject worthy of study in its own right in British law schools. If it appeared at all, it was fitted rather uneasily into the last two or three weeks of a course on land law or as part of the topic of public inquiries in an administrative law course. Of late, there are signs that this approach is changing and courses on planning law are now making their appearance in the ever-increasing lists of 'third-year options' in many law schools. This book is designed to help further the process of making the law of land-use planning as challenging and as central a course in the curriculum of the law school as any of the more traditional ones.

In setting out to create such a course and such a book, I was helped by this absence of a traditional approach to the subject.

There was no standard model in respect of which I had to explain or justify a decision not to follow either to myself or to others. While I derived a great deal of initial help from some of the American works on the subject, particularly J. H. Beuscher's *Land Use Controls* and C. M. Haar's *Land Use Planning*, the design and the contents of this book have been based, in the final analysis, on my perception of the needs and interests of law students studying in an English law school.

It is as well to spell out what my perception is. I believe that law students need to gain from a book and course on planning law an understanding of the different ways in which the use of land can be controlled by public and private agencies and public and private law techniques, and the various conflicts and pressures (by no means all of them legal), that operate within and on the system, if that is what it is, of land-use planning. The book is then an attempt, via the medium of the law, to provide materials for an analysis, discussion and criticism of the decision-making process and some of the policies that lie behind and are implemented by that process in land-use planning in England. This is not the usual purpose of an English law book, but I believe it to be a necessary one for a book on *planning* law. Planning is concerned with the allocation of scarce resources and each decision, within the sphere of planning, even on a minor matter of development control, represents a value judgement about the way a particular resource – usually land – should be used. A lawyer who intends to play a part in the planning process is likely to be able to make a more useful contribution, whatever his or her particular role is, if he or she has had the opportunity, during their education, to think about and discuss what the aims of planning are, how far the process is apt to implement the aims, and what are the ways that the law helps or hinders that process by interposing its own values, assumptions and practices.

There is another set of students for whom a book on planning law, with the perspectives of this one, might be valuable. These are planning students. Virtually all planning courses have some law in them but far too often this is presented in an uncritical manner. For planning students the law is something that exists but is not worth spending very much time on. A few basic rules must be learned, but the legal bases of planning need not be understood in the sense in which the social, economic and political bases of planning and planning techniques must be understood. As a result, there exists throughout the planning profession an incomprehension and resentment of law and lawyers, attitudes which, it must be admitted, are fuelled by many lawyers' equal incomprehension of planning, but which find their way into the planning process to its detriment. I believe that these attitudes need to be changed and that change can begin via the educational process. This book is not a long hymn of praise for law and lawyers, or plans and planners; rather it tries to give a balanced picture of law, planning and the interaction between the two and I hope that some planning students might use it and understand law and its role a little better as a result.

Long though the book is, I am only too conscious of its omissions. As originally submitted to the publishers, the first two chapters were spread over five chapters with more materials on the problems of planning, nuisance, decision-making and public inquiries. The publishers, however, made it clear that they could not publish the book unless it was substantially reduced in size. I reluctantly decided that I had little alternative but to comply with their request and in doing so found it necessary to remove some of the materials from the last five chapters as well, in order to get down to a publishable length. Even as originally submitted, however, the book would have left out many topics. Views will no doubt differ on what should be and should not be in a book on land-use planning, so what must be admitted is that this book presents and could only present 'one view of the cathedral' of the law of land and its use and control in England.

Inevitably, in putting together a book such as this, I have received a great deal of help from many people and organisations and it is my pleasure to be able to record this here. A generous grant from the Nuffield Foundation's Socio-Legal Materials Fund covered the costs of the initial gathering together of the materials, the employment of research assistants and secretarial help and I am very grateful to the Foundation for their help. The editors of this series have been a constant source of encouragement to me in urging me on, in reading through the whole manuscript and, not least, in urging the publishers on.

Within the Law School at the University of Warwick, my debts are many. Neal Roberts, my valued colleague for two years between 1972–4 and now at Osgoode Hall Law School in Toronto, played a valuable part in helping get the materials into some sort of order. He helped me in the putting together of a second draft of the materials and the form of Chapter 7, and to some extent Chapter

6, reflect some of his ideas. The discussions I had with him on planning generally and the use of the materials were both instructive and enjoyable; the text of the book has greatly benefited from them. I would like to thank David Farrier for agreeing to my using part of the text of a joint paper we gave to the UKNCCL Colloquium on Compensation in 1973 in Chapter 7. I would like to thank, too, my two student research assistants, Peter Draper and Mark Pawlowski. Both did very valuable work for me, ferreting out materials and drawing my attention to issues which I would otherwise have missed. I owe an enormous debt of gratitude to successive generations of students in the planning law course who waded through huge masses of undigested materials, but whose enthusiasm rarely flagged and whose acumen and work helped give the final version whatever merit it has. To Geoffrey Wilson and my other colleagues in the Law School, I am grateful for the creation of the kind of intellectual atmosphere in which unorthodoxy can flourish yet never become the orthodox. This is, I should add, a wholeheartedly 'Warwick' book.

Outside the Law School, my debts are equally large. John Pemberton, Jolyon Hall, Elizabeth Anker and Sharon Loughran in the Government Publications and Law sections of the library were ever present and ever helpful. I have learned a great deal about the planning system in practice from my work as a local councillor, first on the now defunct Leamington Spa Borough Council, and now on the Warwick District Council. I have drawn freely from my experiences on those councils and I would like to thank my colleagues on them, in particular on their planning committees, for tolerating me and helping to educate me. Among the officers I would like to thank particularly are Mr R. G. W. Druitt, one-time Borough Engineer and Planner of Leamington Spa and now a Chief Inspector with the Department of the Environment, and Mr C. J. George, Secretary and Solicitor to the Warwick District Council. I would also like to thank Mr H. E. Greening, the Resident Manager of the Edgbaston Estate, Mr F. R. Barlow of the Bournville Village Trust, Mr R. Jones and Mr F. J. Thompson of Wates Ltd and Mr R. Warren-Evans of Bovis Ltd for the help they gave me through interviews and the documents sent to me. I owe, too, a large measure of thanks to the secretaries who typed my text out so expertly, and helped with xeroxing and the like, June Coleby, Margaret Wright, Barbara Savage and Jean Gardner.

Finally, I owe the biggest debt of all to my wife who had to put up for so long with those absences from the family which seem to be inseparable from writing.

I have endeavoured to take account of the published law and policies of planning up to the end of November 1974. In addition, I was able to include some of the recommendations of the *Final Report of the Review of Development Control*, published in February 1975.

Leamington Spa   J. P. W. B. McAuslan
30 November 1974

I

Prolegomena to Planning: The Continuity of Problems and Laws

1. Introduction

The period commencing in 1965 has seen a major series of reports, reforms and innovations in land-use planning. Indeed, the total package of legislative and administrative changes up to the end of 1974 has never been exceeded since land-use control began to be seen as a necessary aspect of administering an industrialised, urbanised state, and has probably been equalled only by the package of reports, innovations and changes between 1940–50. A mere recital of the major reforms will indicate their extent: the ministry dealing with land-use problems has been twice reorganised and has become a major department of state embracing virtually all aspects of land use; the system of local government has been the subject of several thorough investigations culminating in a Royal Commission, and major reorganisation consequent upon those investigations.[1] The regional problem has been the subject of the first official investigation and report[2] since the Barlow Commission[3] reported in 1940, and this, too, has been followed by legislative and administrative action.

Major changes have also taken place in the laws dealing with land-use planning and control. The system of development planning has been completely revamped and fundamental changes have been made in the methods of approving the plans.[4] Legislation on conservation has greatly increased.[5] The control of development has been reorganised and reported on. The policy of housing improvement and the introduction of the Housing Action Area as a meaningful alternative to the Clearance Area has also extended the array of powers available to the planners.[6] During this same period, the problem of pollution control began to be tackled more vigorously through legislative and administrative action.[7] Two attempts were made to tackle the vexed problem of compensation and betterment;[8] that dealing with betterment lasted only for four years; that dealing with compensation is too recent to assess. Finally, in all areas of reform, the idea of public participation has been very much to the forefront; it was virtually unknown in 1965; by 1970 there could hardly have been a planner, an administrator or a minister who did not feel obliged to stress its importance in all facets of planning.

Yet this outburst of legislation and administrative activity, in which both political parties joined with enthusiasm, was not caused by the sudden growth of a series of new problems of the urban environment, but by a realisation that long-standing problems, in existence before any coherent system of land-use planning was brought into being, and more recent problems created by continuing urbanisation, were not susceptible to solution by the then existing system. One of the major issues to which this book addresses itself is the extent to which the problems of the city, both long-standing and more recent, are susceptible to solutions via the new system and the possibility that the new system may itself contribute to the creation of new problems. The changes which have taken place over the last ten years have been changes in the structures and functions of institutions; a question which must be posed at the outset of this book is whether the problems with which planning purports to deal might not need changes in the structures and functions of society?

What are the problems with which the planning system attempts to grapple? What are the problems of the planning system with which the reforms have attempted to grapple? Are there problems of planning which are not soluble within the existing structure of society? These are the general questions which we must constantly keep in front of us. While we cannot survey the whole field of substantive planning problems, one very basic problem which we must refer to at the outset of this book is that of land: are we short of it? Are we converting agricultural land to urban uses at too great a rate? Do we know sufficient facts about the problem to be able to make a preliminary assessment of the efficacy of the system of land-use planning? Best's article helps clarify some of these issues.

Robin Best,[9] 'Laying the Land-use Myths',
New Society, 2 April 1970

... To a remarkable extent, it is becoming apparent that land-use planning in Britain – and in most other countries too – has been built on a very shaky and insecure foundation of illusion rather than reality. Quite a few of the most important tenets in the conventional wisdom about land use in this country can be shown to be false, or extremely suspect, when examined quantitatively. If we set down just four of the more widespread and now almost traditional views held on this subject, it is not difficult to show how inadequately they measure up to the real-world situation.

For a start, we have what is perhaps the most basic and persistent myth: *Each year urban sprawl is engulfing still greater quantities of good land to add to the vast expanse already sterilised by cities and towns; so that, before long, most of our countryside will be completely submerged beneath bricks and concrete.*

This is a very common belief and it lies at the root of many of the restrictive attitudes that are adopted in land-use and conservation policies. Perhaps because so many of us live and work in towns, we seem inevitably to exaggerate, in the mind's eye, the actual amount of urban land around us. A few facts can give a more correct perspective. In 1960, the urban area occupied no more than 11 per cent of the total surface of England and Wales, and little more than 8 per cent of Britain as a whole. In marked contrast, nearly 80 per cent of the land area was still in some form of agricultural use, a large proportion being improved farmland. Another 7 per cent has also to be added to the 1960 rural total as it was under forest and woodland.

But if the urban area is smaller than is generally recognised, its rate of growth is relatively fast. In the first 60 years of this century, urban land actually doubled its extent in England and Wales. The high point in the rate of conversion was reached in the 1930s when over 60,000 acres (25,000 hectares) of farmland a year were being absorbed. At this time, the fortunes of agriculture were at a very low ebb and land could be bought easily and cheaply, with hardly any constraints imposed by land-use planning. After the second world war, however, transfers of farm-land to urban use were cut back to less than 40,000 acres (16,000 hectares) a year on average, largely through the planning controls operated under the Town and Country Planning Act, 1947.

Contrary to popular belief, there has been no sustained increase in the urban growth rate since the second world war. If anything, the trend has been for a slight decline in urban demands and a tightening-up in housing densities, especially in new town development. If the whole of Britain is considered, afforestation rather than urban growth is now the chief absorber of farmland though the land taken is of much lower quality than that normally used for urban purposes.

But in spite of the institutional restrictions on development, urban expansion is taking up a further 1 per cent of the land surface (or thereabouts) each decade. At this rate, by the year 2000 something like 15 or 16 per cent of England and Wales will be covered by cities, towns, villages and transport facilities. This is still not a very substantial portion of the whole landscape, but it is growing steadily and inexorably in magnitude.

Moreover, certain parts of the country are being more severely affected than others; and this circumstance points to a second myth: *Across nearly all of the country, land expropriation by urban and other uses at the expense of agriculture is on a very large scale, and is particularly excessive in south-east England and along the coffin-shaped belt stretching northwestward to Lancashire.*

This concept is again a fallacy, for there are great variations in the rate of urban growth and afforestation in different parts of the country. At one extreme, as many as 21 counties in England and Wales in the 1960s had a rate of change in land use – from agricultural to urban – which was 0·05 per cent or less of the total county area a year. In other words, no more than one acre in 2,000 was affected each year: a very slow turnover by any measure. These areas of sluggish urban expansion lie not only in the upland regions of the country but also along the eastern side, particularly around the Wash, where agricultural output is high.

The fairly rapid urban growth is now concentrated in two main groupings of counties, the so-called 'central urban region' – which comprises mainly the conurbations and the associated areas of northern England and the west midlands – and the London region. These two regions are at present separated by a rather narrow band of only weakly urbanising country. But several large-scale planned developments here, like Milton Keynes and Northampton, will eventually tend to eliminate this predominantly rural divide.

It is important to note how the regional configuration of urban growth has altered. In the years immediately after the second world war, the counties at the core of the London region dominated urban growth, but by the 1960s the situation had changed radically. The most prominent area of urban extension was now, very definitely, parts of the central urban region, where conversion rates reached up to 0·3 per cent a year – i.e., about one acre in 300 went urban each year. The rate of change faded away in the Home Counties as near-saturation of development approached in some districts.

Not only does this latest pattern of regional urban growth run counter to established preconceptions; it is also completely opposed to the trends in population geography, where a south-eastward emphasis is still seen. It is, for instance, most unexpected to find that two counties with very high conversion rates to urban use – Lancashire and Durham – actually had absolute decreases in population.

The explanation of these apparent anomalies lies mainly in changing urban space standards. As the cramped, northern industrial towns renew their physical fabric, people are moving from crowded central areas to lower-density housing on the outskirts. These new estates have more open space and more spacious schools, as well as far fewer houses to the acre. In contrast, many lower-density localities in the London region are being filled in with tighter-built groups of houses and/or flats.

So far I have considered here only the transfer of farmland to urban use. If afforestation is taken into account also, the north-west of England and parts of Wales stand out even more distinctly as the predominant areas of land-use change (by afforestation or urbanisation), as against most of the south and east. And it is, of course, the south and east which is the most productive agricultural part of the country. This brings us to the third major myth: *Agriculture will be gravely endangered, and food shortages a serious possibility, if continuing losses of productive farmland to urban use and afforestation are not soon reduced substantially.*

Again, this is not correct. About 450,000 acres (180,000 hectares) of farmland are lost to urban growth each decade over the whole of Britain, and an even larger area is converted to forest and woodland. But the authorities most closely associated with the agricultural industry are often the least worried on this score.

. . . The most important things that affect the area of land needed for food production are: population growth and composition; the increase in real personal incomes; changing productivity in agriculture; and the balance required between home-produced and imported food products. From a model constructed to take account of these factors, it appears that, over the next 30 years, 'agriculture should be able to accommodate the level of urban growth and afforestation envisaged over this period and make a greater contribution to feeding the population of the United Kingdom than it did in 1965'.

. . . But . . . productivity will also suffer if more fertile agricultural areas are absorbed for development when, as often happens, alternative sites of poorer quality are available.

So planners, too, must share a heavy responsibility for ensuring that agriculture can continue to function efficiently by giving reasonable weight to farming considerations in their decisions. Intense competition for land often seems to be a peculiarly British phenomenon. But do we really compare unfavourably with other countries in this respect? Here is our final myth: *Because of its small size and high degree of urbanisation, Britain is unique in its pattern of land use and in the severity of land competition it experiences.*

A research project, supported by the Social Science Research Council, is now in progress at Wye College on the comparative structure of land use, and the competing demands for land, in several technologically advanced countries. Some of the provisional results already emerging seem destined to provide even more unexpected conclusions than those I have already discussed. Far from taking up a much greater proportion of the land surface than elsewhere, urban land in Britain (8 per cent) is almost matched by the figure in Holland (7 per cent) and exceeded by that in West Germany (10 per cent), which has only slightly below the percentage in England and Wales alone.

As regards urban living space, 91 acres (37 hectares) of urban land for every 1,000 people in Britain is also quite similar to the figure for West Germany. In Holland, however, people are far more tightly crowded together; they have about half this amount of urban space per 1,000 population. The United States is conspicuously different, with an urban area a quarter the density of ours.

The amount of agricultural land per head of population is revealing, too. Britain has easily the largest allocation by comparison with Holland or West Germany, though this includes a lot of poor land. But the proportion of land surface under the most productive farming – the arable – is almost identical in each of the three countries, at between 34 and 37 per cent.

For an industrial nation, it seems, Britain is not particularly exceptional in land use, or in provision of space, compared with some of our European neighbours. But the 1 per cent rural-urban conversion rate over the past ten years in this country is being greatly exceeded in both Holland and West Germany. Britain's stringent planning control appears to be remarkably effective, therefore.

What conclusions are we to draw from all this revised information about the four myths? In the first place, it is evident that our land-use pattern and intensity of the competition for land are far from unique. Other countries of similar socio-economic status have the same, or considerably greater, urban pressures on their rural land. In Britain itself, we appear likely to be able to meet all reasonable demands on our land surface from urban growth and afforestation until the end of the century, without food supplies being affected in any serious way.

But such a conclusion takes little account of the effect on the quality of the environment. Uninspired and poorly executed urban development is only too frequent.

... In the end, it may well be that the breaking point in the continually tightening ratio of man to land will come not from any shortage of surface area for ensuring economic viability, but rather from the growing social and psychological disorders brought about by too many people living close together.

2. Procedural problems

From the perspective of this book, the procedural problems in planning are a major concern and must be introduced here. They may be summed up as follows: (i) the need to create a process of decision making which ensures that relevant information is gathered together; (ii) the need to ensure that decisions are taken without undue delay; (iii) the need to provide that those people likely to be affected by the decisions are given an adequate opportunity to contribute to their final formulation. Within that attempted summary lies a host of difficulties to which we shall be constantly returning in the course of the book.

The difficulties may be classified under three broad headings and discussed via the unifying concept of legitimacy. Stated briefly the three headings are as follows: first, the type of decisions that are taken in the planning field are so disparate that no one solution to the problems outlined above has so far emerged. Second, changing views and ideas of what is right and proper in decision making in this field have led to changing attitudes to the same structure over a period of years so that the structures remain but their functions have gradually changed and broadened. Third, new structures are introduced which have a profound though possibly unintended effect on the decision-making process; new concepts of planning and a new urgency to tackle an old problem also affect the process.

Uniting all these heads, which will be elaborated below, is the concept of legitimacy. For our purposes legitimacy may be taken to involve 'the capacity of a political system to engender and maintain the belief that existing political institutions are the most appropriate or proper ones for the society'.[10] An obvious situation where there are fundamental disputes about the legitimacy of the governmental system is Northern Ireland, particularly since 1969. That is an obvious example because it is extreme; not all crises of legitimacy result in armed conflict and it is not suggested that the issue of the legitimacy of the planning process is likely to engender bitter strife.

The concept is used here to bring out the point that the persistent and widespread dissatisfaction with the planning process may go deeper than just a general feeling that 'things could move faster', or that 'people could be given more of a hearing', or that 'more land should be released for development'. These general feelings have over the years surfaced and been responded to; yet the dissatisfaction with the system remains. Alongside this widespread dissatisfaction is the equally widespread official view that land-use planning is an essential function of modern government, and that the decision-making processes therein are, give or take the odd reform designed to speed things up, fundamentally sound.

It is this official view that needs to be questioned. The concept of legitimacy provides the framework for questioning it. May the dissatisfaction with processes not be a way of expressing dissatisfaction with the existence of the whole system of planning? Before any further alterations of the decision-making process are made, ought we not to try and find out whose interests are being served by the existing processes and whose would be served by any changes? Why has it so readily been assumed that the 27,000 objections received in respect of the Greater London Development Plan and heard at a two-year public inquiry indicated that the system of public inquiries into development plans had broken down and had to be drastically reformed?[11] Is the constant questioning of and alterations to the decision-making process a healthy or an unhealthy sign? Is it likely to increase or destroy the morale of those involved professionally in planning? Does that matter? Is the constant increase in the amount and sophistication of planning resulting in greater or less general acceptance of the usefulness of planning and, if not, what is the purpose behind all this increased planning? The present system of planning dates from 1947; how certain are we that it will still be in existence in the year 2001? It is these and similar questions that must be at the forefront of our thinking now and when we examine in detail in Chapters 3 to 6 the plan-making and development control processes.

(a) The disparate nature of decisions

We may consider now the three heads of concern. First, the type of decisions made in this area. The formal process for reaching a decision on any proposal to develop land is that an application is made either to a local planning authority or to the Department of the Environment, with the local planning authority having an opportunity to comment. Permission is either granted or refused and in the case of a refusal by a local planning authority, there is an appeal to the Minister. This in practice means a public local inquiry heard by an inspector, followed either by a decision taken, on the Minister's behalf, by his civil servants (on a major issue a Minister himself might take the decision) or by a decision taken by the inspector, again on the Minister's behalf.

It is clear that an application to build a garage or extend a house is of a totally different nature from an application to build a power station, or a reservoir, or to redevelop a town centre displacing 200 to 300 inhabitants; yet the framework of decision making in practice is much the same for all these applications. The problem of the large applications is that the amount of capital tied up in them, and the importance of their being completed by a certain date, require that decisions be reached speedily and a timetable adhered to; yet the scale of the development is such that a multitude of objections and comments are usually forthcoming, need to be taken into account, and, unless the whole exercise is to be little more than a charade, may be decisive and so prevent or seriously delay a decision to go ahead with development. Again, the arguments for and against any large-scale development (and we should not over-look the fact that in a village of 2,000 inhabitants, a proposal to build 100 houses is a large-scale development) are much more obviously arguments based on value judgements about the kind of environment, society and future which the protagonists would like to live in; to decide quickly could mean to fail or to be thought to fail to give adequate consideration to both sides of the argument. Are our processes apt to take account of all these points, and, if not, can they be made more sensitive to them? The frustra-tions of public and private developers and conservationists with the normal current procedures, and the considerable swings of the pendulum between the need for public participation and the need for speed, suggest that we are a long way from solving this problem.

Nor must we ignore the small-scale application; it may not affect so many people but it often arouses the same degree of passion. Each year, thousands of these applications are dealt with by local planning authorities; how can we ensure that they are given adequate scrutiny, and that decisions are taken after full considera-tion on the basis of some understanding of the issues involved and not on the basis of prejudice or ignorance? Is the current trend – to devolve power to decide onto the appointed officers of the local planning authorities – the best or only solution? What should be the role of the elected member? Does he or she have any role?

(b) Changing views and attitudes towards decisions and institutions

The second problem area is that of changing attitudes to structures and institutions. Here the focal point is the public local inquiry.[12] This is one of the oldest of administrative devices in the land-use planning field. It has undergone far-reaching changes in response to public concern about its usefulness and its procedures in the last fifteen to twenty years, and is likely to continue to change in response to increased public awareness of planning problems. Whereas once the public local inquiry was seen only as part of the administrative process, now it is also seen as part of the process of public participation. The perception of its functions has changed, and, we shall see in later chapters, this has led to changes in its structure and an alteration of the balance between the citizen and the state. The question of who and what a public local inquiry was for used to be one of the major issues dividing lawyers and planners; we must consider later whether it still does divide them or whether the issue is now more between developers and their various opponents, concerned in different ways to advance the cause of public participation.

Public participation will loom large in this book. This is unavoidable as it looms large in the planning process, affecting both substance and procedure alike. Since it has been a major contributory factor to changing attitudes to the process, this is an opportune time to introduce the subject. In an as yet rather ill-defined and unco-ordinated way, there is an increasing reluctance to accept the planning process as something remote, operated by 'them' against 'us'. Whether it is a middle-class pressure group fighting for conservation, a radical action group fighting against city centre redevelopment, a working-class neighbourhood fighting against pollution or a whole town protesting against a projected major road or airport, there is a demand that structures be reformed in such a way that the views of the planned have much more weight than hitherto in the final decision. How to accommodate this demand within existing structures, indeed whether to accommodate it at all, the extent to which existing structures may have to be or have been changed, the relationship between public participation in planning and a more generalised dissatisfaction with representative democracy and its seeming inability to grapple with major issues are all questions which have come to the forefront of discussions on planning in the last decade. They have however historical antecedents. It would not therefore be misleading to see the present concern with public participation and the present crop of questions to which it gives rise as being in part the latest way of looking at broad issues such as 'Are planning and democracy compatible?' on which F. H. Hayek was writing thirty years ago[13] or 'Are land-use planning and private property compatible?' which has been the subject of debate on and off since the time of Blackstone if not before. In addition, narrower concerns involving the public local inquiry and the role of the local councillor are also in issue here.

(c) Unintended effects of new structures

Thirdly, problems arise from new structures, new concepts and a new sense of urgency. As with the other problems, this is a new variant on an old theme. In the nineteenth century the new concepts associated with the cases of *Tulk* v. *Moxhay*[14] and *Rylands* v. *Fletcher*[15] brought about changes in land-use patterns scarcely foreseen by the judges who decided the cases. The decision in *Local Government Board* v. *Arlidge*[16] on publicity and fairness in the administrative process when applied to the vastly expanded field of land-use control after 1947 had equally far-reaching though unintended effects and led ultimately to major legislative and administrative changes. It is scarcely likely that the protagonists of the early Public Health and Artizans' Dwellings legislation could foresee the growth of the power of local authorities to raze hundreds of acres of their towns and, in partnership with a property developer, rebuild a new city centre; it is even less likely that the early pioneers of the Garden Cities Association could have foreseen Milton Keynes – the new city of 250,000 people.

But today the new type of development plan, the new 'systems approach' to planning espoused by planners, the use of mathematical models and computerised data result in an infinitely more abstract and conceptual approach to land-use planning. They must be looked at both for the contribution they make to a more realistic and useful system of planning now, and for the side effects they have or may have on the decision-making process in the future. Even more so must changes in the organisation and structures themselves be looked at from this point of view. What have been the intended and unintended effects of the creation of the Department of the Environment? What are the intended and what may be the unintended effects of the new local government structure? How likely is it that structure and local plans legislated for on the assumption that both would be produced by the same tier of local government may change their relationship and importance *inter se* if they are made by different tiers of local government?

Finally, is there a new sense of urgency current on land-use problems and what difference does that make to procedures? Each generation assumes that the problems it is grappling with are *the* problems and if they can be solved (and their solution is just round the corner) then the future is assured. A classic illustration of this is the housing problem; in each decade since the 1920s there will be found a housing minister who will say that the housing problem will be solved within the next ten years. Is this generation any different? Our sources of information are greater; we make a more sophisticated use of the information we have; the pace and scale of physical development of all sorts have probably not been equalled this century and the global environmental picture is now part of our consciousness – all this may have contributed to a heightened awareness of the problems facing us, and to changed structures and procedures. Does it bring the solution of the problems any closer? Overall, one question looms in this area, too often unconsidered yet fundamental to the approach adopted here: to what extent do new solutions to old problems themselves throw up new problems no less intractable than the old?

3. Professional problems

The professional problem is a short-hand way of referring to the fact that the planning process is not solely a matter of concepts, procedures and structures but it is also a matter of planners, lawyers and developers, their ideas, their interaction and the use they make of concepts, procedures and structures. This section attempts to introduce planners, planning and developers to lawyers, and law and lawyers' attitudes to planners and planning, in the belief that the ideas and interaction of these persons are an essential part of the planning process and need to be in the forefront of any discussions on the process.

(a) Planners and planning

Taking first the planners and planning, there is a myriad of questions to be considered: who are the planners? what are their skills; what are they trying to do? and how do they try to do it? The professional organisation of the planners is sixty years old,[17] while the planning profession as such could claim to be a good deal older, yet these questions are still as far from an answer in the 1970s as they were in the 1920s; indeed as the scope of planning expands and the problems of the urban environment appear to grow ever more intractable, so the planning profession becomes more ambivalent in its approach to its role, on the one hand beset with doubts, on the other advancing the claim that planners are urban managers, the only urban managers moreover who are aware of the need to be properly trained for that role. That this ambivalence about their role is not new is well brought out by the extracts from Foley's article, which after more than fifteen years remains the best introduction to English planning ideology.

D. L. Foley,[18] 'British Town Planning: One Ideology Or Three?',[19] 1960, *British Journal of Sociology*, vol. 11, p. 211

The ideology of town planning provides a philosophic basis for the activity. It indicates the main goals and approaches. The ideology provides a basic operating rationale. In simplified terms it defines the situation for its participants, particularly specifying the main kinds of problems that the activity is to tackle and the major types of solutions, and the spirit of their application. It characteristically includes a defensive tone, providing the simple replies to criticism or attacks. While town planning also has been developing a sub-culture that specifies in richer detail the behaviour to be expected in varied situations, the ideology stresses the major ideas and approaches.

An ideology tends to build around seemingly self-evident truths and values and, in turn, to bestow a self-justifying tone to its main propositions and chains of reasoning. While the ideology may well contain highly rational arguments, it is characteristically ultra-rational in its overall spirit. It becomes comfortable and protective; and in this way contributes to the emotional security of the participant and to his self-confidence in carrying out the activity. While the ideology thus provides an essential kind of consensus supporting the activity, its self-evident and self-justifying nature may also contribute to a smug and traditional outlook and discourage a healthy self-awareness and sceptical re-examination.

In so far as town planning is a governmental function, the ideology provides a broad and attractive rationale for winning over and maintaining the allegiance of political leaders, appointed officials and citizens. . . .

IDEOLOGY AND PUBLIC POLICY

Before dealing with the substantive features of British town planning ideology and its contextual setting, it may be appropriate very briefly to identify something of the nature and functions of an ideology in a governmental-professional activity such as town planning and to discuss how the ideology of town planning relates to the public policy of town planning. . . .

. . . We are suggesting three substantive propositions as stating, in compressed form, the main ideologies of British town planning. As we stated in our introductory paragraph, these propositions are at once complementary and competitive. We shall first present them in rather general terms, discussing some implications of the relative importance attached to each. We shall then look at the second and third in greater detail, in separate sections below.

(1) *Town planning's main task is to reconcile competing claims for the use of limited land so as to provide a consistent, balanced and orderly arrangement of land*

uses.—This is a sort of budget function, allocating land according to some sense of priorities and working for an overall spatial arrangement that best incorporates this allocation. By itself this ideological proposition carries a sense of neutrality. In political terms it conveys that nice ambiguity that proclaims that a balanced and orderly arrangement of land uses is in the public interest without committing the government to a pre-statement of just what constitutes this balanced and orderly arrangement. It injects civic responsibility, but makes of town planning an umpire type of activity that, in turn, depends upon the wisdom and integrity of elected and appointed officials to act in the public's best interest. It encourages considerable flexibility and adaptability. It ties in well with the central government's fiscal planning, in which commitments must be kept reasonably short-run so as to be able to adapt to new problems or conditions. It also accords well with the authoritativeness that seems to go with Ministerial decisions in Britain. If the Minister judges a planning decision to be in the public interest, that is that. . . .

(2) *Town planning's central function is to provide a good (or better) physical environment; a physical environment of such good quality is essential for the promotion of a healthy and civilized life.*—This ideological view gives to town planning more than a neutral, allocating function. It gives town planning something to champion. This somewhat simplified view of providing a better physical environment most certainly has its own attractions: much of town planning, for example, can then be built around the provision of designated space standards; these coupled with appropriate density controls can be treated in a technical manner in convincingly professional style. The provision of space in its various forms – whether for gardens around houses, for larger parks, for playing fields, or for greenbelts – seems to accord so happily with British values and to provide such a direct and heroic attack on the great villains of overcrowding, congestion, and physical blight that it is readily accepted as an activity of self-evident merit and one with a direct emotional appeal. Similarly, the reconstruction of decrepit structures provides convincing symbolic evidence that 'we are not just sitting around; we are doing something about our problems'. If this can be accompanied by the conviction that new housing will help to rid us of juvenile delinquency, etc., why so much more desirable will the reconstruction seem.

But focusing on a better physical environment also puts town planning in something of a dilemma. Either town planning conceives of this physical environment as sufficiently an end in itself, as a quality to be strived for, while the social-spatial patterns of urban living work themselves out through other mechanisms than town planning: for example, through the market mechanism, through the perpetuation of traditional community patterns, or as the resultant of varied public policies not in themselves necessarily co-ordinated to the point of qualifying as planning. Or town planning openly accepts the better physical environment as merely an intermediate goal in which case the critical question must also be asked: intermediate to what further social goals? As soon as this question gets seriously asked the search for a more complete rationale pushes one rapidly beyond physical planning per se. This leads us to a consideration of the third major view of town planning's function.

(3) *Town planning, as part of a broader social programme, is responsible for providing the physical basis for better urban community life; the main ideals toward which town planning is to strive are (a) the provision of low-density residential areas (b) the fostering of local community life and (c) the control of conurban growth.*—This ideological view accepts, and seems to relate town planning to, the conviction that small, or at the most middle-sized, communities of houses with gardens are to be encouraged. It sees the continued growth of the very large city clusters or conurbations as a distinct threat to various British-held values. Accordingly, town planning, while also including responsibilities for allocating land and improving the physical environment, has as its major challenge the mastery over current urban growth and expansion trends in the interest of preserving or recreating towns and town life. . . .

IMPROVED PHYSICAL ENVIRONMENT AS A GOAL

It may be worth a little fuller examination of the ideological implications of, and support for, the idea of improving the town's physical environment, that we have just identified as the second component philosophic approach in town planning today. Certainly of initial importance is its happy position as an intermediate point of view; it avoids some of the lack of purpose and commitment implicit in the first, neutralist approach, and in providing this possibility of commitment it gains a greater power of attracting support and of providing a sense that one is really working for something worthwhile if engaged in town planning. And yet it seems to avoid the complexities of this being openly an activity involving social planning; it preserves a sort of fiction that this is merely physical planning.

Ideologically the idea of focusing on the physical environment is reasonably simple. For one is able to operate on the assumption that improving the environment is followed by fairly direct and common-sense benefits. Physical environment determinism has always had a fascinating attractiveness. Its products or intermediate ends are readily graspable. A key higher (non-technical) civil servant in a Ministry dealing with town planning is alleged to have asserted some years ago that the greenbelt was the one goal he could readily understand and work toward with conviction!

In a country where a well educated, middle-class elite is induced to take upon itself so much responsibility for concerning itself with public policy, it is undoubtedly a congenial task to insist on a better physical environment as a condition for maintaining civilized living. The empirical evidence as to whether this enlightened middle-class view of what is best for people corresponds with the broad range of citizen reactions is far less clear.

There is also a distinct symbolism in seeking to control and modify the physical environment. It provides wide scope for the notions that individualism has been carried too far and that what we need is a civic architecture, a truly public sense of community arrangement. . . .

The plan itself is an important form of expression. There is no question but that the plan carries its own aesthetics and that plan-preparation indulges in its own brand of tidying up. Putting enough green space on the map, 'cleaning out' some of the mixed uses, and articulating a clear line between different uses and between towns and country – these all must provide a particular satisfaction to certain kinds of persons. How little we really know about this! Similarly, reactions to a plan as being too dictatorial or too utopian may also be involved. In recent years there has been a distinct reaction, apparently, against the broad, advisory plans, linked with architects by some other professionals and some active laymen.

. . . The social ideology that has emerged is essentially this: the best community life is to be provided in small, reasonably low-density communities. Building upon the traditional form and social organization of the village, an image of desirable community life is held up as an ideal. This does not insist that communities be only villages. It accepts the existence and continuing importance of large cities, but seeks to introduce into their further growth or their rebuilding a local-community social and physical environment as a town planning goal. For further growth the answer is new towns or the deliberate and controlled expansion of certain already existing small towns. For rebuilding within the larger city, neighbourhood units and communities (each embracing several nighbourhood units) are to be worked toward.

This social ideology also places great stress on providing every family with immediate access to their own garden. This is a very deep-seated and emotion-laden conviction. Without doubt it reflects values that are very much a distinctive part of British culture. For what proportion of British families it would seem to be so important a value that even some other values, such as accessibility to work or to the central urban areas, would be sacrificed in its favour it is more difficult to know. . . .

It is fascinating to conjecture just how many different images of town planning the evolving activity of town planning has needed to take into account and to seek to assimilate. Clearly, town planning in its formative period could not afford to hew too narrowly to any preconceived, rigid line. In order to get political support, to attract capable professionals, and to live up to the idea of comprehensive planning, it gathered in a welter of programmes and ideas. In part, no doubt, this was strategically imperative. It was either gather in, or be gathered in by one or another of the ring of activities and professionals on every hand.

But in this process, town planning came to accept and gradually to build around certain basic ideological propositions that while not too openly in conflict were not completely congruent. It is characteristic of such a process, aided as it was by the political character of the determination of its major policies, that something of a web of propositions would come to be accepted without their internal inconsistencies or strains being highlighted or reduced. . . .

Education for Planning, Report of a Working Group
at the Centre for Environmental Studies (1973),
pp. 10, 53–4, 61–2, 71–2, 75–6

Planner

In a planning-managing system it is probably impossible, and at least unproductive, to distinguish an individual called a planner. All those engaged in the managing or governing process, if this process is a planning process, will require planning knowledge and planning capability and are, in a sense, planners.

We use the word 'planner' because it is convenient and short. But we mean by it a person contributing to urban governance through the planning process:

whatever his precise role in the managing system (he may be a politician, a director, a manager, an analyst, a model builder);
whether he is engaged within or without a statutory planning process (planners may be in community organisations for instance);
whether a member of a professional institution or not;
and regardless of the particular policy field with which he is concerned (it may be the physical environment, economic development, education, the local authority budget, or organisation itself – and so on).

We exclude, for purposes of this report, planners contributing to national, industrial or commercial governance, though we would imagine that there would be an overlap between these and urban and regional planners in terms of the planning knowledge and capability they need. . . .

The urban planning process of the future

Planning practice, as we have described it, has evolved to serve the needs of particular kinds of organisation at particular times. Opinions about it are therefore strongly coloured by its history. Town planning methods are associated with legislation on land use and the kinds of policies it has tended to produce. And so it has come to be identified with some 'good' values: the quality of the environment, protection of the public from unscrupulous property developers; and with some 'bad' values: the closing of options for the future, the limitation of personal choice. Corporate planning, as it is emerging from the administrative tradition in local government, is also coloured by the particular situation in which it obtains. To some people it represents the 'good' value of effective government of urban problems, and to others the 'bad' value of directive or centralised management. It is only when defined in very abstract terms that planning is value-free.

In looking ahead, therefore, to foresee the planning process that people are likely to demand for the specific purpose of community governance, we cannot hope to define it in any detail without embodying in it some values. As a working group we believe that the values that are inherent in the ensuing paragraphs are widely held at the present time. These characteristics of an ideal planning process are being canvassed in research, in practice, in education and in the journals. But we recognise that our selection of them, and the emphasis we give them, is the result of our own working group's priorities and preferences.

First, however, it is worth trying to dissociate planning from its institutional history and see it in simple and rather abstract terms, as it may apply to any kind of organisation. Perhaps all one can say of planning at this level is that it is steersmanship or *governance* in organisation. Any organisation, if it is to have purpose, must plan. In a planning process, what is planned is choice or decision. The kinds of choice with which planning is concerned are broadly:

> choice as to goals and objectives: where we want to go and when we want to be there;
> choice as to policies and programmes that will get us there (and selection of information and methods of analysis to be used in generating policies);
> choice as to means: raising and allocating resources to implement the policies and programmes;
> and finally, choice about organisation itself, the nature of its management structure and planning processes.

Finally, the more sets of decisions to be taken now and over time depend upon each other, the more forethought and analysis are needed. It is complexity and uncertainty in decision situations that have stimulated the development of a planning process, planning knowledge and planning capability.

Planning is clearly a continual process, with no logical end point or conclusion. The stages in a planning cycle are frequently spelled out by planning theorists. It is interesting to see that they are usually closely similar to the stages of the managing cycle spelled out by management theorists. The relationship between managing and planning is difficult to define – and our working group disagreed on this for some time. Some of us felt that planning was a distinct element in a managing process. Others of us felt, and this eventually became the dominant feeling in the group, that planning was more or less co-extensive with management and was best described as *a principle or style informing the managing process*. We recognise, however, that this depends on a certain use of the term 'management' – which emphasises 'steersmanship' more than the administering of activities according to predetermined policy. Beyond that, however, we have to determine with what characteristics this planning principle will endow the governing process, and our reading of current opinion and our own views led us to the following formulation. We believe that the community is likely to seek a planning process whereby urban governance will become: (1) anticipatory, (2) analytical, (3) objective-oriented, (4) evaluative, (5) innovatory, (6) apparent, (7) responsive, (8) connective, (9) effective and (10) adaptive. . . .

Community governance, as we have tried to identify it in preceding chapters, seems to need knowledge that can be categorised as three kinds.

A Community and environment knowledge	B Organisation knowledge	C Operations knowledge
E.g.	E.g.	E.g.
people	government	information systems
work	community	numerical description
income	organisation	multivariate analysis
spending	behaviour	matrix algebra
residence	structure	model-building
opportunity	purpose	computation
movement	values	design
building	politics	system theory
place	power	simulation
nature	decision	programming
food	intervention	network analysis
farming	control	planning procedures
industry	responsibility	PPBS
leisure	accountability	etc.
shopping	audit	
learning	etc.	
health		
markets		
finance		
etc.		

. . . In Chapter 4 we described the planning process as being more or less co-terminous with the managing or governing process itself. We defined it as a principle or style in governance, that gives the process certain characteristics. And we defined the planner as anybody needing planning knowledge and capability in order to contribute to this process. As a consequence, we have to distinguish between some of the different roles in a governing system, and foresee differences that should perhaps arise in courses of education designed to serve them. At a very simple level it is possible to differentiate four roles: the *technical planner*; the *manager-planner*; the *decision-'taker'*; and the *public*.

In most kinds of planning organisation there will be people who contribute what might be termed the *technical input* to the planning process: seeking, organising and analysing data, modelling the planned and planning systems; refining the field of choice in the service of those who are finally responsible for decision. The rapidly increasing amount and the improving quality of data about city and community, and greater analytical capacity due to the computer, make educational courses serving this technical component of planning a serious need now.

A course designed to prepare a student for the technical planner role would clearly need to draw heavily on the substantive material of planning sciences ('operations knowledge' C). But it might also require a focus on some particular element of community knowledge (A). A technical transport planner will need understanding of people's income and spending patterns, car ownership, employment, and housing, for instance. He will also need a certain amount of organisation knowledge (B), since one of the roles of the technical planner is to extend the range of usefulness of scientific methods within the managing system.

Second, there will be planners who are more in the nature of managers, as this term is commonly used. They initiate the work of technical analysis and take up where it leaves off. They use the planning scientist's decision models but make the return to the world of action, depending heavily on judgement and problem-solving ability. A course to serve such *manager-planners* would clearly need to pursue a learning method designed to increase cognitive power, and would need to give relatively heavy weighting to organisation knowledge (B), since organisation is the manager's main means of creating and pursuing policy. Operational planning-managing courses, with strong problem-focus and student-centred learning methods, are badly needed at present on almost every topic of community governance, including health, education, housing, recreation, social care and physical development.

Third, we should think of the educational needs of those who take decisions between the alternative possibilities revealed by the planning process. An example of special significance in the urban administration is the *elected member* of a local authority. It is unlikely that a councillor would have the time to learn the technical skills of the planner or even to develop his planning capability. He might feel the need, however, for a course that would give him a wide-ranging view of the many aspects of city and community (A). And he might benefit from an overview of organisation of the working of local government in the community (B). We urge the development of formal educational opportunities of the kind that are useful and practicable, i.e. brief in duration, accommodating in attendance requirements, and appropriately located, for councillors or people wishing to seek election to local councils or service on statutory boards. . . .

The need for a common awareness

We have made the case for, and foreseen the development of, a varied provision of urban and regional planning education. In a situation in which so many different fields of higher education, and so many types of planning course, are contributing to urban and regional governance, it is clearly important that all those engaged in planning processes in the city, with their many different kinds of background, role and institutional interest, should be helped by their various educators to share a language and recognise a common purpose in the community. The problem can be illustrated by considering town planning. As the substantive material that has to be comprised in spatial and physical planning knowledge has grown more and more extensive, and as it has become evident that a single kind of environmental planning course can no longer be expected to encompass it all, the question has arisen of how planners educated in different ways and for different roles may be enabled to work together as one team.

What is the nature of the connecting awareness that is needed by those who play complementary parts in urban governance, and how can it be achieved? Each planner, with his particular standpoint in the urban system and detailed knowledge relevant to one type of problem, needs a consciousness of the whole city and its life, of the relationship between its parts, and, especially, between the policies designed to influence them. And he needs, with others, a common consciousness of purpose: the activity of governance itself. But, since his main concern is operations within his own field, his main need is for awareness of the interaction of his aspect of the city with the whole, his policy field with the rest.

We have described a field of planning education that is a kind of inter-meshing pattern. Perhaps in some areas of the field there will be an actual substantive overlap: elements of knowledge that may be appropriate in identical form for students of different kinds of planning course. More commonly, however, we believe that courses with different foci will logically call for different knowledge. It seems likely, therefore, that if planning education is to be as varied as we believe it must be, it is not possible to rely on shared knowledge to achieve a common awareness. Rather it must be sought through a shared conception of what planning is, of what planning knowledge and capability are, and of their use: urban governance.

It is for this reason, that we believe it is important that planning educators should themselves share some unifying concept of urban governance, planning knowledge and planning capability, such as that tentatively put forward in this paper, and should engage in a policy discussion about education for urban governance that can ensure that this concept is continually revised and refined.

A cynic might be tempted to say that the less successful the planners have been in the past the more grandiose are their claims for their future role. Planning as a once-for-all exercise has failed to cope with urban change; rather than ceasing, however, it must now become a continuous process and planners, drawn from all disciplines, must, on the basis of their own integrated learning, have a finger in every pie. Is it possible that the planners have overstated their own case? We may accept the argument that there is a need for planners to have new skills with which to attempt to deal with old and new problems; we may applaud them for asking questions of themselves which few other professions (especially lawyers) do, but we should be prepared to consider the possibility that the new skills may be no more successful than the old in solving problems, and that what might be needed is less, not more, planning; simpler, not more sophisticated, techniques.

These and other questions are increasingly being asked by a range of people of different disciplines, ideologies and backgrounds. For want of a better term I have called this the anti-planning view, but this may be over-simple. What people as diverse as Betjeman and Simmie have in common is not a desire to let the property developer rip, but a concern that planners lack vision, sensitivity and imagination, believing that science is an adequate substitute for them, lack an understanding of the social processes and effects of planning, and believe that technical judgements do not involve value judgements. What is wanted therefore is an aesthetically and socially more sensitive type of planning; and more consideration of the issue of who gains and who loses by planning. How likely is this to come about? How desirable would it be? How apt are the proposals of the Centre for Environmental Studies working group for bringing it about?

J. Betjeman,[20] 'The Town Clerk's View',
Collected Poems (John Murray, 1958), pp. 166–9

... I cannot say how shock'd I am to see
The *variations* in our scenery.
Just take for instance, at a casual glance,
Our muddled coastline opposite to France:
Dickensian houses by the Channel tides
With old hipp'd roofs and weather-boarded sides.
I blush to think one corner of our isle
Lacks concrete villas in the modern style.
Straight lines of hops in pale brown earth of Kent,
Yeomen's square houses once, no doubt, content
With willow-bordered horse-pond, oast-house, shed,
Wide orchard, garden walls of browny-red—
All useless now, but what fine sites they'ld be
For workers' flats and some light industry.
Those lumpy church towers, unadorned with spires,
And wavy roofs that burn like smouldering fires
In sharp spring sunlight over ashen flint
Are out of date as some old aquatint.
Then glance below the line of Sussex downs
To stucco terraces of seaside towns
Turn'd into flats and residential clubs
Above the wind-slashed Corporation shrubs.
Such Georgian relics should by now, I feel,

Be all rebuilt in glass and polished steel.
Bournemouth is looking up. I'm glad to say
That modernistic there has come to stay.
I walk the asphalt paths of Branksome Chine
In resin-scented air like strong Greek wine
And dream of cliffs of flats along those heights,
Floodlit at night with green electric lights.
But as for Dorset's flint and Purbeck stone,
Its old thatched farms in dips of down alone—
It should be merged with Hants and made to be
A self-contained and plann'd community.
Like Flint and Rutland, it is much too small
And has no reason to exist at all.
Of Devon one can hardly say the same,
But "South-West Area One" 's a better name
For those red sandstone cliffs that stain the sea
By mid-Victoria's Italy—Torquay.
And "South-West Area Two" could well include
The whole of Cornwall from Land's End to Bude. . . .
Hamlets which fail to pass the planners' test
Will be demolished. We'll rebuild the rest
To look like Welwyn mixed with Middle West.
All fields we'll turn to sports grounds, lit at night
From concrete standards by fluorescent light:
And over all the land, instead of trees,
Clean poles and wire will whisper in the breeze.
We'll keep one ancient village just to show
What England once was when the times were slow—
Broadway for me. But here I know I must
Ask the opinion of our National Trust. . . .
So don't encourage tourists. Stay your hand
Until we've really got the country plann'd.

J. F. Simmie,[21] 'Physical planning and social policy',[22]
(1971) *Journal of the Royal Town Planning Institute*,
450–53

Failures of physical planning
There can be no doubt that physical planning has played a part in the
inadequate efforts of central and local government to create equal life
chances, combat poverty, provide adequate housing for those who are
relatively deprived and to prevent unemployment. This is a particularly
severe indictment of physical planning because aspects of these four
problems are central to its *raison d'être*. Three of the reasons why it has not
contributed more to the solutions of these problems are:

(i) its narrow outlook
(ii) lack of competence
(iii) its predominantly upper class and paternalistic ideology.

In many ways physical planning has a narrow professional outlook reminiscent of a medieval guild. In 1904 Geddes was recommending wide-ranging surveys of the social origins and conditions of towns as a basis for planning, but his proposals were considered too drastic for those times. When the Town Planning Institute was founded in 1914 by members of the existing architects', engineers' and surveyors' institutes there was, not surprisingly, some ignorance of all but the most superficial social aspects of the growth of cities. Unfortunately this led to a narrowing of the focus of physical planning from its social *raison d'être* and the broad conception of Geddes, to a small sector of town planning concerned with the physical manifestations of town life and confined within a very limited and restricted legalistic framework. Consequently, few plans have matched or seriously considered the diversity and complexity of the issues with which they are dealing. Nevertheless, a common defence of plans is that they must be confined within the range of current powers. But, as Westergaard points out in his comments on the Greater London Development Plan, 'If such powers are inadequate, it is an essential function of planning to say so; to set out the alternatives; and thus, to demonstrate the consequences if new powers are not made available.'

Not only is physical planning confined within a legalistic strait-jacket, but its focus is often further narrowed by planning for trends. Trend planning usually starts with projections of current situations into the future and the plan consists in harmonizing public and private development with these trends. Thus, if poverty, bad housing and unemployment exist when the plan is formulated it is likely that these features will be unconsciously projected into the future and not greatly ameliorated as the plan is implemented. Such planning, as Westergaard again points out, assumes that many factors are fixed 'and not ranges of alternative figures within which the choice of particular value is, in part or whole, a matter of policy judgement'.

Very often plans purport to be normative in so far as they start with goals and then define the means for achieving these goals. On closer examination, however, it is usually found that these goals are not seriously referred to throughout the plan and that there is a continual tendency to revert to trend planning. . . .

A second reason for the relative failure of physical planning in social terms has been the lack of competence of many of its practitioners. This may be seen primarily as the result of planning methodology generated from an unspecified belief in physical determinism and over-simplifications of the problems to be dealt with. This has resulted in the failure to produce plans adequate to urban social problems. Among the instances of this process at work was the uncritical adoption, by planners devoted to change in the physical environment, of the neighbourhood concept. Thus, while housing shortages are concentrated in the inner areas of the conurbations and manifested most acutely in obsolete housing and shortages of small self-contained accommodation, physical planners have been busily planning outer ring or, further out, new towns with neighbourhoods full of accommodation unrelated to the demographic structure of the population or the location of the most poorly paid employment. Such planning effectively imposes a tax on the poor by requiring them either to move into a decreasing supply of therefore increasingly expensive inner residential areas or incurring increased and unnecessary journey-to-work and housing costs.

Another example of the problems that planning has failed to deal with is the speed and magnitude of urban change. Thus, while statutory planning was approached gradually, some of the conurbations and other large towns grew rapidly. . . .

. . . It was left, however, to transportation planners to unravel the resulting urban congestion and change, formulating new kinds of master plan, and introducing electronic data processing to physical planners. Despite the introduction of this new tool many planners have been content to take replacement decisions in a data vacuum. In Dennis's case study of planning in Sunderland, some planners even saw no need for data and were content to condemn whole areas on the basis of a cursory visit from a moving car.

Another characteristic of physical planning which has contributed to its failure to support radical social reform is its political neutrality. Unlike the other local government functions of education and housing, the two main political parties have no distinguishable differences in planning policy.

This may be partly the result of planners' efforts to invest their activities with the cloak of science. This has involved developing unnecessary and meaningless jargon to baffle politicians and public alike, and the resistance to public participation in planning in the shape of community fora suggested by the Skeffington Committee. Participation in general has been handled in a paternalistic, public-relations way with no opportunity to debate the goals and priorities of plans or, as in one case, reweighting the goals defined by the public to give them priorities defined by the planners. So far, nobody has taken a radical political view of physical planning. This is critical if an effective attack is to be made on urban poverty, bad housing, unemployment, pollution and congestion.

Such a political impetus is also needed in physical planning if the third reason for its relative failure is to be combated. Since its inception, it has developed an essentially upper class ideology. The results have been that planning costs have fallen more heavily on the poor and its benefits accrued more directly to those who can already compete in a market economy. Secondly, although planning demands interference with the market in favour of changing market distribution of the social product and establishing alternative goals, physical planning has conspicuously failed to do this, and private interests and private appropriation of community increased land values have continued to flourish. Thirdly, physical planning has in no way shared its power with its clients as behoves any institution in a democratic society.

Upper class ideology in planning is exemplified by the garden city, garden suburb, new town thinking of the twentieth century. The fundamental social problems of poverty and bad housing have been largely evaded by these movements. The belief that the best aspects of town and country could be combined in the garden city represented an erroneous and idealized notion of country social life and increased the costs of housing and journey to work for those who could least afford to bear them.

Not only have costs been increased for the poor but also the paternalistic and vague concept of balanced communities has, in practice, increased the social and physical segregation of the population. . . .

Conflict between the goals of planners and their clients is greatest in inner residential areas. There, housing conditions are worst, incomes are largely the lowest and alternative accommodation is often more expensive. Nevertheless, planners are decreasing the choices open to such groups by demolition and thereby forcing them either into adjacent slums or into distant estates. Either way costs are increased. Whatever else planners do, they should rehouse the residents of slums without increasing costs of accommodation or journey-to-work. This is not likely to be achieved by current policies of rehabilitation relying on filtering to provide vacated properties for the poor.

A second aspect of upper class ideology in physical planning is the failure to recognize that to be in favour of planning is to be in favour of either ensuring that market forces produce a specified set of results or of interfering with those forces so that those goals are obtained. This, physical planning has conspicuously failed to do. There are three examples of this failure:

(i) over-reliance on the private sector in housing
(ii) insufficient resistance to development lobbies
(iii) the failure to appropriate communally increased land values. . . .

(b) Developers

To write about developers is as difficult as it is to write about planners, but for very different reasons. Planners have a lot to say for themselves and the problem is to pick out the wheat from the chaff. Developers on the other hand do not write about what they are doing and the writings by others that do exist are rarely the sober assessments that might be looked for in a book such as this. There is thus a special need for a preliminary introduction to developers.

The first point to make about developers is that unlike planners or lawyers they are not a recognised profession, with a professional organisation and journal. The leaders of the planning profession – Burns, Amos, Bor – whose views appear in this book can in some sense be regarded as representative of the profession; the judgements of the Divisional Court and beyond also give, in an authoritative manner, the views of lawyers on planning. It is doubtful whether one could assemble an authoritative collection of statements by developers on planning.

Primarily this is because the word 'developers' covers such a wide body of persons, and institutions. Well-known names such as Harry Hyams,[23] the Levy Brothers[24] and Lord Samuel[25] are developers; so too are companies such as British Land, Metropolitan Estates Property Co. and Ravenseft Properties. While the names of those companies might suggest that they have connections with the world of property development, there are many organisations which have connections which are not so apparent. The Proprietors of Hays Wharf, the Church Commissioners for England, and Stock Conversion are three examples from a very great number which includes many insurance companies. Local authorities are also regarded as 'developers', whether they are in formal partnership with a property company, whether they have merely given permission to such a company to develop, or whether they are actually going to develop themselves. Finally planners and architects are regarded by many people as 'developers'; community action groups in Westminster for instance would regard the chief planning officer of Westminster to be as much a developer as Richard Seifert, who has been described as running 'the archetype of an architect's practice for developers',[26] and who is responsible for such buildings as Centre Point, Drapers' Gardens[27] and the Royal Garden Hotel in Kensington.

Can such a wide category of persons and institutions be lumped together in one mould because they are known by the same name? The case for the answer 'yes' is quite simply that they all have in common one major aim: to demolish existing buildings and replace them with new and more profitable buildings. A typical 'lumping together' statement, which is also anti-planning and development (as most such statements are; why?) was contained in a *Sunday Times* colour supplement in April 1973:

We are faced in fact with the prospect of a London almost entirely drained of its individual character (except in certain expensive carefully preserved little islands). . . .

This is the price that has to be paid for our shining new 20th century city with its concrete subways and multi-storey car parks and steel pedestrian barriers. There was a time when we might have been brainwashed into accepting it by the architects' drawings and planners' brochures, with their cloudless skies and trees and pram-pushing mums. But the great difference now is that, in the past few years, we have actually seen something of this future – enough at any rate to realise that planners' dreams are one of the Big Lies of the age. The real tragedy of London in the past 15 years is that, on a scale unequalled in any other old city in Europe, we have allowed massive-scale development to become a kind of mania – the answer to every problem. This is not just the fault of the private developers, although it is usually they who collect most of the brick bats. Public institutions are just as much to blame – whether they be office-hungry government departments, London University (responsible for a remarkable amount of architectural damage) or simply the planners themselves, whose schemes become increasingly grandiose and inhuman.

On this analysis the crucial issues in planning can be seen always in terms of the people versus the planners/developers.

The alternative answer would suggest that 'developers' have multiple aims and cannot therefore be lumped together. A common aim may be to put up a development which does not make a loss, but thereafter aims might diverge; civic pride and a desire to present a new image to the world as in Newcastle's city centre redevelopment; aesthetic and cultural satisfaction as in the public development on the South Bank in London; capital gains and thus the wherewithal for more development as with all property companies; reduced rates and/or more money for socially beneficial uses as with many local authorities and the Church Commissioners, or a safe investment as with insurance companies and the managers of property bond funds. How can these developers be criticised or, less frequently, praised on the same basis when their functions are so clearly very different?

Whether it was logically correct or politically fair to do so, the climate of opinion in the early 1970s permitted all developers to be seen as one, and that one to be no better than a speculator and beyond redemption. Just how far and how fast the climate of opinion has moved can be gauged by contrasting a statement by Mr Macmillan when Minister of Housing and Local Government in 1952 with a White Paper produced by his Conservative successor Mr Rippon in 1973. In 1952, in introducing the Town and Country Planning Bill which abolished the development charge of the 1947 Act, Mr Macmillan said: 'The people whom the Government must help are those who do things: the developers, the people who create wealth whether they are humble or exalted.'[28] The White Paper proposed measures 'to remedy the shortage of building land and so remove the occasion for windfall profits based on scarcity values'[29] and further legislation (the land hoarding charge) to prevent the first legislation being frustrated by land speculators who 'can with impunity continue to hoard land with planning permission'.[30]

What has caused this turn-about in official and unofficial attitudes towards developers? Five possibilities may be advanced:

(a) In the boom years for development – the 1950s and 60s – developers were too blatant, and made too great a profit on their development. Cotton's garish model of Piccadilly redevelopment in 1959,[31] Hyams's Centre Point, unlet since 1964 while its value continues to rise, are two conspicuous examples of this possibility which began to alert journalists, amenity groups etc., to developers' activities.

(b) What was put up tended to be aesthetically nondescript at best, appalling at worst. Developers in a sense are being made into scapegoats for the failure of planners (who are for this purpose being distinguished from developers) to insist on a better design or a better blending into the urban environment. The windy, soulless shopping centres, the claustrophobic office blocks, the high-rise flats far out from the centre of town may have been put up by developers but they were sanctioned by planners. A question to ponder here is: why does there appear to be a greater official disenchantment with developers than with planners?

(c) In a sense, following on from (a) and (b), development in the sense of the replacement of old by new buildings has become more and more conspicuous so that more and more people notice and are uneasy about what they notice. This is the thrust of the *Sunday Times* piece on London quoted above and it is a theme which is repeated up and down the country in centres of national importance such as Bath, of more local concern such as Kendal or Leamington Spa. What distinguishes this point from the previous two is that however worthy the motives behind development, however low-key the presentation of plans, however pleasing the architecture, there comes a point when the sheer volume of new development creates concern within the community where it is taking place. That point has now been reached in many areas, hastened no doubt by the considerations referred to in points (a) and (b).

(d) The existence of a bipartisan belief in government regulation and control of the economy on an ever-increasing scale. Until the Control of Office and Industrial Development Act 1965, developers were largely unregulated except by the Town and Country Planning

Acts which did not appear to be too great an obstacle to their plans. Thereafter planning controls have increased, particularly in the areas of the conservation of old buildings and the publicity attendant on new development, as well as general controls over the economy (apart from a temporary hiccup in 1970–1). An illustration of the effect of the latter on property development is the Bank of England letter to the clearing banks in 1972 to limit their lending for purposes of property development in order that more of it could be channelled into lending for productive purposes. When controls seemed not to be working in this area there has once again been a resort to the scapegoat of the developer: it is the developer rather than the system of planning as such who is at fault and if only the controls are tightened up all will be well. Again the question arises: why does this analysis find such a ready and widespread acceptance?

(e) A fifth possibility is the connection between property development and corruption in local government. Until very recently, this was not a subject which attracted much attention, so that its influence on attitudes towards developers may be marginal. It should not however be overlooked. The publicity surrounding the Poulson corruption cases, the Battersea corruption case and the peculiar circumstances of the ministerially revoked planning permission for a new hotel in the Avon Gorge at Bristol have all highlighted this issue. Lord Henley, the Chairman of the Council for the Preservation of Rural England has referred to it as 'the whiff of systematic corruption by organisations devised for that purpose, of people who can influence decisions on development in favour of those who bribe them . . .'[32] Even where no corruption in a legal sense of the term has taken place, there is sufficient evidence of deals between developers and local authorities which, though lawful, give rise to the kind of concern which manifests itself in hostility towards developers.

Should we now take the final step and transfer all powers of development into the public domain? Would that lessen corruption and increase social awareness? Should we try to ensure that private developers become more socially aware of the possible effects of their developments?

(c) Lawyers[33]

The third of the trio of groups whose interaction shapes the day-to-day workings of the planning system is the lawyers and their field of expertise, the law. In some respects the most baffling questions in this section arise here. The law provides the constitution of the planning system: law and lawyers are intimately involved in the administration of planning, yet in some way, lawyers have always stood aloof from planning, and a mutual suspicion exists between planners and lawyers.

Is there then some fundamental conflict between planning and law? Or is it that it is lack of understanding of the roles, differences and possible similarities of each that has led to the present antipathy? Has there always been conflict between law and the notion of control of land use or is it a product of legal concern about the administration of land-use control rather than its existence *per se*? What are the implications of this antipathy for the planning system? As with other questions in this chapter, possible answers may emerge in the course of this book.

Since the rest of the book assumes the co-existence of planning and law, however uneasy that co-existence may be, the one extract in this section is a classic statement of the impossibility of that co-existence. Should we treat it seriously or regard it as naïve and impractical?

F. H. Hayek,[34] *The Road to Serfdom* (1944),
Chapter VI: Planning and the Rule of Law

Nothing distinguishes more clearly conditions in a free country from those in a country under arbitrary government than the observance in the former of the great principles known as the Rule of Law. Stripped of all technicalities this means that government in all its actions is bound by rules fixed and announced beforehand – rules which make it possible to foresee with fair certainty how the authority will use its coercive powers in given circumstances, and to plan one's individual affairs on the basis of this knowledge. Though this ideal can never be perfectly achieved, since legislators as well as those to whom the administration of the law is entrusted are fallible men, the essential point, that the discretion left to the executive organs wielding coercive power should be reduced as much as possible, is clear enough. While every law restricts individual freedom to some extent by altering the means which people may use in the pursuit of their aims, under the Rule of Law the government is prevented from stultifying individual efforts by *ad hoc* action. Within the known rules of the game the individual is free to pursue his personal ends and desires, certain that the powers of government will not be used deliberately to frustrate his efforts. . . .

. . . as planning becomes more and more extensive, it becomes regularly necessary to qualify legal provisions increasingly by reference to what is 'fair' or 'reasonable'; this means that it becomes necessary to leave the decision of the concrete case more and more to the discretion of the judge or authority in question. One could write a history of the decline of the Rule of Law, the disappearance of the *Rechtsstaat*, in terms of the progressive introduction of these vague formulae into legislation and jurisdiction, and of the increasing arbitrariness and uncertainty of, and the consequent disrespect for, the law and the judicature, which in these circumstances could not but become an instrument of policy. It is important to point out once more in this connection that this process of the decline of the Rule of Law had been going on steadily in Germany for some time before Hitler came into power, and that a policy well advanced towards totalitarian planning had already done a great deal of the work which Hitler completed.

There can be no doubt that planning necessarily involves deliberate discrimination between particular needs of different people, and allowing one man to do what another must be prevented from doing. It must lay down by a legal rule how well off particular people shall be and what different people are to be allowed to have and do. It means in effect a return to the rule of status, a reversal of the 'movement of progressive societies' which, in the famous phrase of Sir Henry Maine, 'has hitherto been a movement from status to contract'. Indeed, the Rule of Law, more than the rule of contract, should probably be regarded as the true opposite of the rule of status. It is the Rule of Law, in the sense of the rule of formal law, the absence of legal privileges of particular people designated by authority, which safeguards that equality before the law which is the opposite of arbitrary government.

A necessary, and only apparently paradoxical, result of this is that formal equality before the law is in conflict, and in fact incompatible, with any activity of the government deliberately aiming at material or substantive equality of different people, and that any policy aiming at a substantive ideal of distributive justice must lead to the destruction of the Rule of Law. To produce the same result for different people it is necessary to treat them differently. To give different people the same objective opportunities is not to give them the same subjective chance. It cannot be denied that the Rule of Law produces economic inequality – all that can be claimed for it is that this inequality is not designed to affect particular people in a particular way.

The unpredictability of the particular effects, which is the distinguishing characteristic of the formal laws of a liberal system, is also important because it helps us to clear up another confusion about the nature of this system: the belief that its characteristic attitude is inaction of the state. The question whether the state should or should not 'act' or 'interfere' poses an altogether false alternative, and the term *laissez-faire* is a highly ambiguous and misleading description of the principles on which a liberal policy is based. Of course, every state must act and every action of the state interferes with something or other. But that is not the point. The important question is whether the individual can foresee the action of the state and make use of this knowledge as a datum in forming his own plans, with the result that the state cannot control the use made of its machinery, and that the individual knows precisely how far he will be protected against interference from others, or whether the state is in a position to frustrate individual efforts. The state controlling weights and measures (or preventing fraud and deception in any other way) is certainly acting, while the state permitting the use of violence, for example, by strike pickets, is inactive. Yet it is in the first case that the state observes liberal principles and in the second that it does not. Similarly with respect to most of the general and permanent rules which the state may establish with regard to production, such as building regulations or factory laws: these may be wise or unwise in the particular instance, but they do not conflict with liberal principles so long as they are intended to be permanent and are not used to favour or harm particular people.

To say that in a planned society the Rule of Law cannot hold is, therefore, not to say that the actions of the government will not be legal or that such a society will necessarily be lawless. It means only that the use of the government's coercive powers will no longer be limited and determined by pre-established rules. The law can, and to make a central direction of economic activity possible must, legalise what to all intents and purposes remains arbitrary action. If the law says that such a Board or Authority may do what it pleases, anything that Board or Authority does is legal – but its actions are certainly not subject to the Rule of Law.

If, however, the law is to enable authorities to direct economic life, it must give them powers to make and enforce decisions in circumstances which cannot be foreseen and on principles which cannot be stated in generic form. The consequence is that as planning extends, the delegation of legislative powers to divers Boards and Authorities becomes increasingly common.

The Rule of Law thus implies limits to the scope of legislation: it restricts it to the kind of general rules known as formal law, and excludes legislation either directly aimed at particular people, or at enabling anybody to use the coercive power of the state for the purpose of such discrimination. It means, not that everything is regulated by law, but, on the contrary, that the coercive power of the state can be used only in cases defined in advance by the law and in such a way that it can be foreseen how it will be used.

4. The continuity of laws

(a) Introduction

Our system of public regulation of the use of land is widely regarded as one of the most comprehensive in the non-Communist industrialised world. It also has a very long history, stretching back far beyond the Housing, Town Planning, etc. Act 1909, which is the starting point of most legal discussions.[35] This point is worth stressing, since, just as many of the problems regarded as being of fundamental concern today are only modern variants of long-standing problems, so, many of the legal procedures and solutions suggested for dealing with them can either be paralleled in former statutes, or can be seen as almost logical extensions of powers or procedures first enacted in the last century or earlier. In addition, reference to the existence of early laws is further indication of the long-standing nature of many current problems. This section then is concerned with giving an indication both of the long legislative history of land-use planning in England and of the various continuities and themes of the law over the last 130 years.

(b) Pre-Industrial Revolution legislation

An Act for the Punishment of them which cause corruption
near a city or great town to corrupt the air, 1388[36]

Item, for that so much dung and filth of the garbage and entrails as of beasts killed, as of other corruptions, be cast and put in ditches, rivers and over waters, and also within many other places within, about and nigh unto divers cities, boroughs and towns of the Realm, and the suburbs of them, that the air there is greatly corrupt and infect, and many maladies and other intolerable diseases do daily happen, as well to the inhabitants, and those that are conversant in the said cities, boroughs, towns and suburbs, as to other repairing and travelling thither, to the great annoyance, damage, and peril of the inhabitants, dwellers, repairers, and travellers aforesaid:

(2) It is accorded and assented, that proclamation be made as well in the City of London, as in other cities, boroughs and towns, through the realm of England, where it shall be needful, as well within franchises as without, that all they which do cast and lay all such annoyances, dung, garbages, entrails and other ordure in ditches, rivers, waters and other places aforesaid, shall cause them utterly to be removed, avoided and carried away betwixt this and the feast of St. Michael next ensuing after the end of this present parliament, every one upon pain to lose and to forfeit to our lord the King.

(3) And that the mayors and bailiffs of every such city, borough or town, and also the bailiffs of franchises, shall compel the same to be done upon like pain.

(4) And if any feel himself grieved, that it be not done in the manner aforesaid and will thereupon complain him to the chancellor after the said feast of St. Michael, he shall have a writ to make him of whom he will to complain to come into the Chancery, there to shew why the said penalty should not be levied of him.

((5) (6) omitted)

An Act against the erecting and maintaining of cottages, 1589[37]

For the avoiding of the great inconveniences which are found by experience to grow by the erecting and building of great numbers of cottages which are daily more and more increased in many part of this realm;

(2) ... That after the end of this session of parliament, no person shall within this realm of England make, build or erect, or cause to be made, convert or ordain any building or housing made or hereafter to be made, to be used as a cottage for habitation or dwelling, unless the same person do assign and lay to the same cottage or building four acres of ground at the least. ...

(3) Upon pain that every such offender shall forfeit to our sovereign lady the Queen's majesty, her heirs and successors, ten pounds of lawful money of England, for every such offence.

(II. omitted)

III. And be it further enacted by the authority aforesaid: That all justices of assizes and justices of peace in their open sessions and every lord within the precinct of his leet and none others shall have full power and authority within their several limits and jurisdictions to enquire of, hear and determine all offences contrary to this present act. ...

((2) omitted)

IV. Provided always: That this statute, or anything therein contained shall not in any wise be extended to any cottage which shall be ordained or erected to or for habitation or dwelling in any city, town corporate or ancient borough or market-town within this realm,

(2) nor to any cottages or buildings which shall be erected ordained or converted to and for the necessary and convenient habitation or dwelling of any workmen or labourers in any mineral works, coal mines, quarries or delfs of stone or slate or in or about the making of brick, tile, lime or coal within this realm; so as the same cottages or buildings be not above one mile distant from the place of the same mineral or other works and shall be used only for the habitation and dwelling of the said workmen;

((3) omitted)

(V. omitted)

VI. Provided also, and be it enacted; That from and after the feast of All-Saints next coming there shall not be any inmate or more families or households than one, dwelling or inhabiting in any one cottage, made or to be made or erected;

((2) omitted)

An Act for Rebuilding the City of London, 1667[38]

(I, II omitted)

III. ... That no building or house for habitation whatsoever, be hereafter erected within the limits of the said city and liberties thereof, but such as shall be pursuant to such rules and orders of building and with such materials as are herein after particularly appointed. ...

(2) and if any person or persons shall presume to build contrary thereunto, and be convicted of the same. ... That then and in such case, the said house so irregularly built as aforesaid, shall be deemed as a common nuisance.

(3) and the builder and levier thereof shall enter into a recognizance

... for abatement and demolishing the same in convenient time, or otherwise to amend the same according to such rules and orders as aforesaid. ...

IV. And that the said irregular buildings may be the better prevented, or more effectually discovered.

(2) be it further enacted by the authority aforesaid; That the lord mayor, aldermen and common council of the said city shall and may at their will and pleasure elect, nominate and appoint one or more discreet and intelligent person or persons in the art of building to be the surveyor or supervisors to see the said rules and scantlings well and truly observed. ...

((3) omitted)

V. And to the end that all builders may the better know how to provide and fit their materials for their several buildings;

(2) be it enacted, That there shall be only four sorts of buildings and no more; and that all manner of houses so to be erected, shall be of one of these four sorts of buildings, and no other; (that is to say) the first and least sort of houses fronting by-lanes; the second sort of houses fronting streets and lanes of note; the third sort of houses fronting high and principal streets; the fourth and largest sort, of mansion-houses for citizens or other persons of extraordinary quality, not fronting either of the three former ways: and the roofs of each of the said first three sorts of houses respectively, shall be uniform.

VI. (The mayor, aldermen and common council to say which are to be by-lanes, streets or lanes of note and high and principal streets)

(VII. omitted)

It is not suggested that these statutes, dealing as they do with what are now referred to as pollution control, urban sprawl, overcrowding and urban renewal are the direct ancestors of the modern legislation on these topics, but some of their features are paralleled in the modern law. The peremptory command to remove garbage by the feast of St Michael on pain of certain forfeitures was echoed in the Deposit of Poisonous Wastes Act 1972 which applied, *inter alia*, stiff criminal penalties to fly tippers. The appeal to the Chancellor is paralleled in a multitude of modern statutes by the appeal to the Minister; were the courts of law looked upon with disfavour even in the fourteenth century as an appellate tribunal from the administration? The attempt to prevent urban sprawl and limit country cottages to workers only is an early precedent for *Fawcett Properties Ltd* v. *Bucks. County Council*;[39] was it any easier of enforcement? The heaping of powers onto the justices to police this early example of development control was paralleled by the system which prevailed under the 1947 Act until 1959. Finally, the early examples of a local building inspectorate, the planning of urban development by a local authority, and the power to enforce planning control by demolition of offending buildings all illustrate continuity of approach to a continuity of problems. Is there then any part of our much-vaunted planning system which is truly original? The extent to which there is may be better judged when we have examined the themes and continuities within the development of the post-Industrial Revolution legislation.

(c) Post Industrial Revolution legislation

It was the enclosure movement and the Industrial Revolution which between them produced the major urban centres of England and Wales in the nineteenth century. The problems which these threw up produced, although more slowly, the realisation that the defects of urban growth could not be cured by criminal legislation on the pre-Industrial Revolution pattern but required a more comprehensive approach, combining more effective units of local and central government with a wider range of powers given to each. A full study of the evolution of a comprehensive approach to urban problems would be out of place in this context; what will be looked at here is the more modest issue of the evolution of certain types of powers of land-use control and development since the beginning of 'modern' legislation on this subject in the 1840s.

The evolution of the law can be seen in terms of three principal themes, all of which are still in issue in the 1970s. They are as follows:

(a) The steady growth of public power expanding ever outwards from its initial concern with nuisance in an individual house, to embrace all aspects of development within a region.

(b) A constantly shifting balance between public and private power over land use and development, with public power usually gaining over private.

(c) A continuity of legal techniques and procedures to regulate land use.

These will now be considered *seriatim*.

(a) The Removal of Nuisances Act 1846 was concerned with nuisances in individual houses and empowered public officials to remove them. The Public Health Act of 1848 extended the range of powers available to officials, but still basically kept to the individual house as its frame of reference. The Local Boards of Health, which could be established under the Act after petition by the inhabitants of towns and cities and a public inquiry, would have powers vested in them and were empowered to put drains into a house whose owner refused to do so, to pull down a house whose owner had commenced laying out the foundations without obtaining permission from the Board, and to register, make bye-laws for and inspect common lodging houses.

It was not until 1875 that the next major step forward occurred. By the Artizans' and Labourers' Dwellings Improvement Act local authorities were first given power to demolish areas of housing in a town on grounds and according to procedures which have scarcely changed since. Indeed this Act may be taken to be the model on which much future legislation in this field was based.

All the (by now) standard features of slum clearance administration were present: the report to the local authority by a medical officer of health that an area was unfit for human habitation; the resolution of the local authority to proceed to a clearance scheme; the approval of the scheme by the Local Government Board after a public local inquiry. Only in respect of the final stage was the legislation of 100 years ago different: the Board's approval took the form of a provisional order which needed to be confirmed by Act of Parliament.

In terms of the extension of powers, the next step forward or more pertinently outwards, was taken by the Housing for the Working Classes Act 1890, which empowered local authorities to build houses for the working classes both on land cleared under improvement area procedures and on undeveloped lands. This Act may be regarded as the first to confer positive construction powers on public authorities as opposed to the more negative regulatory powers hitherto only available.

Arguably most of the Acts of the nineteenth century were to some extent reactions, after the event, to bad housing conditions which had been exposed by private pamphleteering and public committee reports. The 1890 Act, however, was an attempt to use public power to get ahead of the problems and was therefore a very clear forerunner of the 1909 Housing, Town Planning, etc. Act. This Act, by introducing the possibility of planning development in advance of its happening, 'was acknowledged at the time to represent the acceptance of something new in the control of the further development of towns'.[40] It 'permitted local authorities, if they were so disposed, and if they obtained the consent of the Local Government Board to prepare town-planning schemes, but only for land about to be developed'.[41] Among the matters these schemes covered were streets, structures and buildings, open spaces, preservation, sewerage, lighting and water supply. Ashworth comments on its scope as follows:

The administrative detail which did much to determine the scope of town planning in practice was settled in 1910 and embodied in regulations made by the Local Government Board under the provisions of the Act. The nature of the regulations appeared to be influenced mainly by a determination to make plain that everyone who might conceivably be affected, however minutely, by a town-planning scheme should have the fullest time and opportunity to make his view known about it. . . . Altogether statutory town planning was marked by the most drastic limitations. Its application was an option exercisable only in the face of deterrents; it applied in any case only to a small proportion of land and a narrow range of conditions; and it was concerned only with the physical layout of land and buildings; the social considerations which might guide that layout were left either to be disregarded or to be sought empirically for every separate scheme.[41]

It may be suggested that if the Act had not been seen as introducing potentially large powers, their exercise would not have been so hedged about with restrictions.

Although town planning had been introduced, it was as an optional power – and remained so – for local authorities to use or not as they saw fit even after the 1932 Town and Country Planning Act which extended the scope of the powers from land about to be developed to include any land. This did in fact increase the amount of land brought under town-planning schemes, but it took the exigencies of war to bring about the next extension of power: first by the Town and Country Planning (Interim Development) Act 1943, which extended the powers of the 1932 Act to all areas of the country irrespective of whether a local authority had adopted a resolution to prepare a town-planning scheme; and then in the immediate aftermath of war, the New Towns Act 1946 and the Town and Country Planning Act 1947.

Between them these two Acts represented the most significant extension of power over land use since the Acts of 1875. They imposed mandatory duties of preparing development plans and controlling development – which was defined in the widest possible fashion[42] – on local authorities. They conferred wide powers on

central government to co-ordinate and approve plans, to act positively to bring about dramatic land-use changes, i.e. creation of new
towns, and, via the financial provisions, made it clear that the right
to use and gain financial benefit from the development of one's
land had been converted into a privilege (exercisable at the discretion of the public authorities) to develop one's land and a no-right
to gain financial benefit from doing so. Though the financial
provisions of the Act lasted only a short time, the right to develop
one's land has been permanently lost; and alterations to the law
since then have on the whole increased rather than decreased the
amount of control over land use.

The 1947 Act conferred planning powers on counties and county
boroughs and this then was the geographical scope of statutory
planning. The next step was to go from county-wide to regional
planning. Regional planning had existed from the 1940s[43] and
several regional plans were produced from that date on, but it was
not until 1968, by the Town and Country Planning Act of that year,
that regional planning considerations were formally incorporated
into the law. From the mid-1960s onwards, an increasing number of
government-sponsored regional and sub-regional surveys were
produced, all designed to provide a broader framework within which
land-use control could operate.

But it was not only the geographical scope of planning that was
extended by the 1968 Act; the range of matters that had to be taken
into account in drawing up a plan was also greatly extended, so that
the physical use of land became only one matter to be considered
alongside population growth projections, transport policies, financial considerations and social implications of planning – to name
only four other matters that had to be dealt with in the new development plans. As we saw in the preceding section, the planners themselves see planning as the key discipline in the integrated science
of urban governance so that the law, which now gives them a very
wide scope, is still a little way behind their idea for which they
are still pressing. It would therefore be unwise to assume that
the extensions of power brought about by the 1968 Act are the
last.

The public health aspects of bad housing prompted the first
legislation in the 1840s, while a concern to get on top of all conceivable urban problems now motivates the planning and allied
legislation. Are those problems any nearer solution now with the

panoply of legislation at the planners' command than they were in 1848 after the enactment of the Public Health Act?

(b) Alongside the continuous expansion in the scope of land-use planning has come a continuous increase in public power, which has shifted more and more decision making from local to central government, and from the private to the public sector. The first point may be illustrated by the numerous occasions on which powers have first been given to local authorities, to be exercised or not by them as they thought fit; later these were replaced by duties which local authorities were required to perform, but still retaining some discretion as to the manner of performance; while later still they were replaced either by central government direction or central government exercise. A small example is the Building Regulations: starting their life as so many local bye-laws; they then became fairly standardised through model bye-laws produced by the Ministry of Housing (as it then was); after a 1961 amendment of the Public Health Act 1936, they became regulations produced by the Department, administered locally but with an appeal to the Minister in certain circumstances.

Planning and housing are two further matters where this same process can be seen at work. Planning was at first discretionary; later it became mandatory, and the thrust of its administration from 1947 has been in the direction of increasing central government involvement via more and more planning manuals, regional and sub-regional studies sponsored in whole or in part by the Department, and circulars advising on one matter, requesting information on another and directing action on a third. Even the Local Government Act 1972, allegedly designed to boost local government by creating fewer and stronger units, has at the same time placed the Department in the key role of umpire and final court of appeal on the question of the division of powers and responsibilities relating to planning between the county and the district authorities.[44] On housing (out of many examples over the years) the latest can be mentioned as being the most contentious – the fixing of rents for local authority housing. For years local authorities were limited only by the concept of reasonableness – a concept given a broad interpretation by the courts.[45] Then in swift succession came central government encouragement to introduce rent rebate schemes,[46] followed by central government control of rent increases on a temporary basis to help the fight against inflation,[47] followed finally by the Housing Finance Act 1972 which took away virtually all local authority discretion in the matter of fixing rents and turned them into agents of the central government, enforcing its policies.[48]

Against this almost continuous one-way traffic, there is very little going the other way – very little devolution from central to local government. Where there is, e.g. in the making of local plans under the Town and Country Planning Act 1971, this is not so much devolution of the power to plan as the splitting of it into two, and the conferring of the lesser part of it on the local authorities, while retaining control over the greater part of it – structure planning – within the Department. Planning and housing powers which are, at the moment, in the exclusive control of local authorities – e.g. the power to declare conservation areas and improvement areas – are recent additions to the land-use armoury and in common with other and earlier beginnings have started their life as discretionary powers; how long are they likely to remain with that status?

The second point – the shift from private to public decision making – may seem rather obvious; what is not quite so obvious is the speed with which it came about. We may distinguish four situations in the urban environment:

(i) Private enterprise is left virtually free and untroubled, to do what it likes subject only to the common law remedies of nuisance and trespass. To all intents and purposes this era ended in 1846.

(ii) Private enterprise is left to develop land but is subject to certain conditions imposed and regulated by public power. The tentative beginnings of this approach may be traced to the two Acts of 1846 and 1848 discussed above. Most private development is still subject to this approach, the difference between 1846–8 and 1974 being the increase in the controls over private development.

(iii) Statute provides for a partnership between public and private enterprise in urban development. There was a glimmering of this in the 1848 Public Health Act, which gave Local Boards of Health power to purchase land so as to lay out streets and open spaces, but purchase was to be by agreement only. The use of compulsory purchase powers as a meaningful public contribution to development can be dated from the Artizans' and Labourers' Dwellings Improvement Act 1875, where public power could purchase and clear land while private enterprise was to redevelop it. This approach continues today.

(iv) Public power develops the land and private enterprise is cut out. There had been previous abortive attempts to confer powers of development on local authorities prior to the Housing for the Working Classes Act 1890 from which may be dated the commencement of the fourth stage. The first was the Labouring Classes Lodging Houses Act 1851. The Act of 1875 conferred powers on local authorities to build after demolition, but only with the express approval of the Local Government Board. These Acts had not been successful – indeed the Royal Commission on Housing for the Working Classes 1884–5 had referred to them as dead letters[49] – and the same Commission had highlighted the failure of private enterprise to provide sufficient low-cost housing. The result was the 1890 Act and the beginning of the council estate. This approach too is still in evidence today.

Thus, in the space of just forty-four years, policy and legislation had run the full range of options open to a society that was not going to take the final step of abolishing private enterprise and private land ownership completely. Indeed, since 1890 the only genuine innovations, arguably an attempted fifth stage, have been in the area of whole or partial land or development value nationalisation – attempted twice (in 1947 and 1967) but by no means finally dismissed as a possible solution to urban problems. The main debate since 1890 has been over approaches (iii) and (iv) and the mix that there should be between them, the Labour Party on the whole favouring approach (iv) the Conservatives approach (iii). The overwhelming part of approach (ii) is accepted on a bipartisan basis, while approach (i) has long since ceased to be in existence.

What has changed since 1890, and this is of great importance, is the general socio-economic climate within which land-use planning operates. Governments nowadays accept a far greater responsibility for managing the economy and providing for the social welfare of the people, so that the total involvement of public power in land-use planning decisions is much greater than in 1890. Partnership between public and private enterprise (and the senior partner in terms of totality of power and finance is often public enterprise[50]) exists now as it has done for 100 years, but it extends or could extend over a very wide area; not just slum clearance, but new towns, industrial estates and major recreational facilities. Public enterprise on its own involves not just houses for the working classes on a modest scale, but vast new housing estates on the outskirts of London, Birmingham, Manchester and other large cities, major new communication networks such as motorways, airports and underground railways, new sources of power and industrial development. Together, all these specific developments have permanently altered the balance between public and private decision making in land-use planning; none of them however represents a further advance beyond the fourth approach adopted in the nineteenth century.

(c) The continuity of legal techniques and procedures is a similar story to that outlined in (b) above; procedures and techniques were evolved in the nineteenth century; since then there has been expansion, refinement, much discussion and many decisions of the courts concerning them, but no real innovation – unless the public examination introduced by the Town and Country Planning (Amendment) Act 1972 be regarded as such.

Four techniques of the exercise of power may briefly be mentioned as illustrations of this theme. First, the public local inquiry held by an inspector whose report is considered and acted upon by departmental officials. It was the technique to be used in the Public Health Act 1848 to determine whether that Act should apply to any locality; and in the Public Health Act of 1875 as an aid to the Local Government Board in deciding whether to approve a clearance scheme; it featured too in the first town-planning legislation in 1909. More discussed, criticised and praised than virtually any other administrative device and undergoing constant re-evaluation, it appears to be totally indestructible in the land-use planning world.

The second technique is the inspection: involving notice of intention to enter premises or land, entry, inspection, report to an authority (local or central); followed by one of a variety of actions: summons to court, draft clearance order, action by a minister. The inspection was a feature of the Act for rebuilding the city of London 1667, it featured in the Removal Nuisances Act of 1846 and the Public Health Inspectorate now is the cornerstone of the administration of public health, housing and pollution control legislation at the local level. The Alkali Inspectorate likewise has been a major national pollution control agency for well over 100 years.[51] Unlike the public local inquiry, public health, etc., inspectorates in land-use planning have been very little discussed or written about notwithstanding that their powers are in effect much greater than the 'hearing' inspectorate. This may be because they exercise their powers out of the limelight of a public hearing and in respect of people who may be less vocal than those refused planning permission or opposing a new public development.[52]

The third technique is the permission, the licence or the register – basically a way of public vetting of private action. Examples are numerous: in 1848 Local Boards of Health were empowered to register and inspect common lodging houses for the working classes;[53] in 1969 local authorities were empowered to register and supervise houses in multi-occupancy;[54] in 1848 certain offensive trades (now for the most part to be found in Class IX of the Town and Country Planning (Use Classes) Order 1972)[55] could not be newly established without the consent of the Local Board of Health.[53] The necessity in most cases to obtain planning permission before development is, and always has been, a key feature of the post Second World War planning legislation. The technique is used quite frequently in pollution control legislation to authorise exemptions from control. Throughout this whole period, these approvals have been issuable subject to such conditions as the relevant authorities have thought fit, thus creating a controlling device of exceptional flexibility. Its use in the planning field is considered in more detail in Chapter 5.

Finally, mention may be made of the procedures associated with compulsory purchase and compensation. Although these generally involve both a public inquiry and entry onto the land, the point to be made here is that although there have been several Acts dealing with both the procedure of acquisition and the assessment of compensation over the years, the basic framework of both goes back to the Land Clauses Consolidation Act 1845.

What are the reasons for this basic continuity and does it give strength or the reverse to the planning system? The first question may be discussed here; the second may be left for consideration throughout the book. Two factors may contribute to the continuity; the existence of a system of private property in land and the presence of courts concerned to uphold that system by insisting on procedural due process before private property is 'interfered with' in any way. Reference has already been made to the general relationship between lawyers' attitudes towards planning and their stress on private property, and this can be seen as yet another aspect of that relationship, in that all these procedures do assume that while public control and regulation of land use is necessary, it must operate within the framework of private property and not so as to undermine it. Those occasions when procedure (and substance) appeared to or were thought to be doing so have provided some of the major flash-points of controversy in the land-use field.

The theme of judicial protection of private property through procedural due process is one which should emerge through a study of the planning cases gathered together in this book. This is not the place to write an essay surveying all the relevant cases but rather to introduce the theme via *Cooper* v. *Wandsworth Board of Works*, generally regarded as being the beginning of the long line of cases in which the courts have insisted that, irrespective of the terms of the legislation (unless it contains a direct prohibition against a hearing), before a person's property is interfered with by the public authorities he must be given an opportunity to be heard first. *Cooper* was not in fact the first case in which this principle was enunciated, but it was the first reported case in which the issue so clearly involved the 'modern' land-use control legislation and as such had an importance far beyond the particular facts. Byles J's statement that 'the justice of the common law will supply the omission of the legislature' summed up the general legal attitude to this legislation and helped fix the approach of the courts thereafter. How far this approach is desirable; how far it is, can be or should be maintained in the changed circumstances of the modern indus-trial state are matters which should be considered both here and throughout the book.

Cooper v. *Wandsworth Board of Works* (1863)
143 E.R. 414

ERLE CJ. . . . This was an action of trespass by the plaintiff against the Wandsworth district board, for pulling down and demolishing his house; and the ground of defence that has been put forward by the defendants has been under the 76th section of the Metropolis Local Management Act, 18 & 19 Vict. c. 120. By the part of that section which applies to this case, it is enacted that, before any person shall begin to build a new house, he shall give seven days' notice to the district board of his intention to build; and it provides at the end that, in default of such notice it shall be lawful for the district board to demolish the house. The district board here say that no notice was given by the plaintiff of his intention to build the house in question, wherefore they demolished it. The contention on the part of the plaintiff has been that, although the words of the statute, taken in their literal sense, without any qualification at all, would create a justification for the act which the district board has done, the powers granted by that statute are subject to a qualification which has been repeatedly recognized, that no man is to be deprived of his property without his having an opportunity of being heard. The evidence here shews that the plaintiff and the district board had not been quite on amicable terms. Be that as it may, the district board say that no notice was given, and that consequently they had a right to proceed to demolish the house without delay, and without notice to the party whose house was to be pulled down, and without giving him an opportunity of shewing any reason why the board should delay. I think that the power which is granted by the 76th section is subject to the qualification suggested. It is a power carrying with it enormous consequences. The house in question was built only to a certain extent. But the power claimed would apply to a complete house. It would apply to a house of any value, and completed to any extent; and it seems to me to be a power which may be exercised most perniciously, and that the limitation which we are going to put upon it is one which ought, according to the decided cases, to be put upon it, and one which is required by a due consideration for the public interest. I think the board ought to have given notice to the plaintiff, and to have allowed him to be heard. The default in sending notice to the board of the intention to build, is a default which may be explained. There may be a great many excuses for the apparent default. The party may have intended to conform to the law. He may have actually conformed to all the regulations which they would wish to impose, though by accident his notice may have miscarried; and, under those circumstances, if he explained how it stood, the proceeding to demolish, merely because they had ill-will against the party, is a power that the legislature never intended to confer. I cannot conceive any harm that could happen to the district board from hearing the party before they subjected him to a loss so serious as the demolition of his house; but I can conceive a great many advantages which might arise in the way of public order, in the way of doing substantial justice, and in the way of fulfilling the purposes of the statute, by the restriction which we put upon them, that they should hear the party before they inflict upon him such a heavy loss. I fully agree that the legislature intended to give the district board very large powers indeed: but the qualification I speak of is one which has been recognised to the full extent. It has been said that the principle that no man shall be deprived of his property without an opportunity of being heard, is limited to a judicial proceeding, and that a district board ordering a house to be pulled down cannot be said to be doing a judicial act. I do not quite agree with that; neither do I undertake to rest my judgment solely upon the ground that the district board is a court exercising judicial discretion upon the point: but the law, I think, has been applied to many exercises of power which in common understanding would not be at all more a judicial proceeding than would be the act of the district board in ordering a house to be pulled down. . . .

BYLES J: I am of the same opinion. This is a case in which the Wandsworth district board have taken upon themselves to pull down a house, and to saddle the owner with the expenses of demolition, without notice of any sort. There are two sorts of notice which may possibly be required, and neither of them has been given: one, a notice of a hearing, that the party may be heard if he has anything to say against the demolition; the other is a notice of the order, that he may consider whether he can mitigate the wrath of the board, or in any way modify the execution of the order. Here they have given him neither opportunity. It seems to me that the board are wrong whether they acted judicially or ministerially. I conceive they acted judicially, because they had to determine the offence, and they had to apportion the punishment as well as the remedy. That being so, a long course of decisions, beginning with *Dr. Bentley's case*[56], and ending with some very recent cases, establish that, although there are no positive words in a statute requiring that the party shall be heard, yet the justice of the common law will supply the omission of the legislature. . . .

5. Judicial regulation of land use via nuisance

(a) The concept at work

No discussion of the evolution of planning would be complete without a consideration of the common law of land-use control, those attempts by the judges to fashion a set of principles for dealing with anti-social or conflicting land uses known as nuisance, and *Rylands* v. *Fletcher*.[57] These principles are still with us and nuisance at least still plays a significant if diminishing part in the law of land-use control.

The common law of land-use control operates at two levels: it has a direct role in determining the pattern of permissible land uses between neighbours, and it has had and has an indirect effect on some of the law and administration of planning. First, an activity may be held by the courts to be an actionable nuisance, notwithstanding that its perpetrator has obtained planning permission to carry it on. It is no defence to say that since a public body has authorised the activity it cannot be a nuisance, because the public body in acting as it does is not purporting to decide on the legal claims of neighbours *inter se*. Its function is to decide whether, from a public point of view, the activity or development is objectionable on some 'public' ground; quite often a ground for objection is that the activity would be an example of 'bad neighbour' development, but even then a determination that the development is not unneighbourly is not conclusive since the neighbours are not by right afforded an opportunity to state their case, and the public body does not consider the matter in terms of the law of nuisance. Two questions arise here: first, should there be some way of resolving claims under the law of nuisance at the same time as an application for a major development is made? Secondly, to what extent do the courts pay and to what extent should they pay some attention to the fact that the activity complained of has been permitted by the local planning authority? These questions raise in turn further and more fundamental issues: first, the place of the individual owner of property in the planning process, and the extent to which he should be enabled to have recourse outside the planning process for the resolution of these disputes. Second, the merits of courts for the resolution of these disputes as opposed to more specialist bodies.

The indirect effect of the common law principles of nuisance on planning law can best be seen in relation to some of the rules dealing with applications to develop.[58] Some applications must be publicly advertised by means of a notice on the land in question and time must be provided for the receipt of objections before the local planning authority decides on them. The list of such applications contains many examples of development which might well be regarded as actionable nuisances if they started up in a residential area. The Use Classes Order classifies certain uses of land into different groups and allows development without permission where the development consists only of a change of use within a group but not where development consists of a change from one group to another. This order is also framed with reference to notions of good neighbourliness; some changes of use, e.g. from a bookshop to a greengrocer, are innocuous if regrettable; some, e.g. from a greengrocer to a tripe shop, are unneighbourly even if benefiting the public at large. The former change could only with great difficulty be conceived of as an actionable nuisance; the latter might well be thought to be, and not only by those who dislike tripe.

Three further linkages may be noted. The concept of 'amenity' is an important tool in the development controller's armoury;[59] its meaning is not altogether clear[60] but it is possible that it owes something to the head of nuisance which allows a claim to succeed where there has been a substantial interference with the plaintiff's enjoyment of his land. A loss of amenity which may be a ground for refusing planning permission might amount to a substantial interference with enjoyment of land. Secondly, the continued existence of the law of nuisance has been used as an argument against the conferring of statutory rights on third parties – parties other than the applicant and the local planning authority – to appear at public inquiries into refusals of planning permissions.[61] Such persons have a right of action in nuisance only if they are neighbours to the proposed development and if the development is a nuisance;

planning law was not designed to confer additional rights on them. The extent to which this is a valid argument should be considered when some of the defects of the law of nuisance are examined.

The third linkage is more distant and tentative. Nuisance law attempts to allocate costs for particular activities to particular parties; sometimes a commercial concern has to bear a cost over and above that which, if left to itself, it would have been prepared to bear: *St Helen's Smelting Co* v. *Tipping*[62] and *Halsey* v. *Esso Petroleum*[63] are good examples of this. At other times, an individual landowner has to bear the costs of an activity which lowers the value of his land, or reduces the quality of his environment in his own estimation as in *Moy* v. *Stoop*[64] where the plaintiff failed in an action for nuisance in respect of children crying in a day nursery. Many of the difficulties of nuisance are in fact the inevitable result of the judges attempting to allocate the costs and benefits of many different conflicting activities in many different situations and areas. The courts here are engaged in a form of crude cost-benefit analysis, a more sophisticated version of which has now become fashionable in solving major planning decisions. In trying to put a price on peace and quiet as was attempted in *Hampstead and Suburban Properties Ltd* v. *Diomedous*[65] the courts are not doing anything intrinsically different from the Roskill Commission on the Third London Airport which used cost-benefit analysis to help them select a site on, *inter alia*, noise considerations,[66] or Warwickshire's Structure Plan which puts forward a policy of prohibiting 'further residential development within [an] area affected by excessive noise and [restricting] other forms of development if necessary'.[67]

Taken in isolation there may be a tendency to decry the efforts of judges at zoning, when they can be explained only in terms of what is reasonable or more crudely, 'What would be a nuisance in Belgrave Square would not necessarily be so in Bermondsey';[68] but set against the value judgements of many development plans, are they so different? Stripped of the pseudo-scientific jargon in which many plans are now written, are they based on anything else than that which the planners and their political masters consider reasonable? In this connection, and in reading the cases below, consider the following questions posed by Haar:

How does a court evaluate the pertinent factors in land-use disputes? How does it ascertain the value placed by the community on a particular land use, in comparison with other uses? Are these factors largely extraneous to legal syntax? Is there a generally accepted scale of social values relating to land uses to which courts can refer? Can some land-use activities be said to produce a direct public benefit, others to be carried on primarily for the benefit of the individual? Does judicial resolution of conflicts here reflect, in its results, the social economic, and political connections of the dominant class?[69]

St Helen's Smelting Co. v. *Tipping* (1865) 11 H.L.C. 642,
pp. 650–653

LORD WESTBURY LC: My Lords, in matters of this description it appears to me that it is a very desirable thing to mark the difference between an action brought for a nuisance upon the ground that the alleged nuisance produces material injury to the property, and an action brought for a nuisance on the ground that the thing alleged to be a nuisance is productive of sensible personal discomfort. With regard to the latter, namely, the personal inconvenience and interference with one's enjoyment, one's quiet, one's personal freedom, anything that discomposes or injuriously affects the senses or the nerves, whether that may or may not be denominated a nuisance, must undoubtedly depend greatly on the circumstances of the place where the thing complained of actually occurs. If a man lives in a town, it is necessary that he should subject himself to the consequences of those operations of trade which may be carried on in his immediate locality, which are actually necessary for trade and commerce, and also for the enjoyment of property, and for the benefit of the inhabitants of the town and of the public at large. If a man lives in a street where there are numerous shops, and a shop is opened next door to him, which is carried on in a fair and reasonable way, he has no ground for complaint, because to himself individually there may arise much discomfort from the trade carried on in that shop. But when an occupation is carried on by one person in the neighbourhood of another, and the result of that trade, or occupation, or business, is a material injury to property, then there unquestionably arises a very different consideration. I think, my Lords, that in a case of that description, the submission which is required from persons living in society to that amount of discomfort which may be necessary for the legitimate and free exercise of the trade of their neighbours, would not apply to circumstances the immediate result of which is sensible injury to the value of the property.

Now, in the present case, it appears that the Plaintiff purchased a very valuable estate, which lies within a mile and a half from certain large smelting works. What the occupation of these copper smelting premises was anterior to the year 1860 does not clearly appear. The Plaintiff became the proprietor of an estate of great value in the month of June 1860. In the month of September 1860 very extensive smelting operations began on the property of the present Appellants, in their works at St. Helen's. Of the effect of the vapours exhaling from those works upon the Plaintiff's property, and the injury done to his trees and shrubs, there is abundance of evidence in the case.

My Lords, the action has been brought upon that, and the jurors have found the existence of the injury; and the only ground upon which your Lordships are asked to set aside that verdict, and to direct a new trial, is this, that the whole neighbourhood where these copper smelting works were carried on, is a neighbourhood more or less devoted to manufacturing purposes of a similar kind, and therefore it is said, that inasmuch as this copper smelting is carried on in what the Appellant contends is a fit place, it may be carried on with impunity, although the result may be the utter destruction, or the very considerable diminution, of the value of the Plaintiff's property. My Lords, I apprehend that that is not the meaning of the word 'suitable', or the meaning of the word 'convenient', which has been used as applicable to the subject. The word 'suitable' unquestionably cannot carry with it this consequence, that a trade may be carried on in a particular locality, the consequence of which trade may be injury and destruction to the neighbouring property. Of course, my Lords, I except cases where any prescriptive right has been acquired by a lengthened user of the place.

On these grounds, therefore, shortly, without dilating farther upon them (and they are sufficiently unfolded by the judgment of the learned judges in the Court below), I advise your Lordships to affirm the decision of the Court below, and to refuse the new trial, and to dismiss the appeal with costs.

LORD CRANWORTH: My Lords, I entirely concur in opinion with my noble and learned friend on the Woolsack, and also in the opinion expressed by the learned judges, that this has been considered to be the proper mode of directing a jury, as Mr. Baron Martin said, for at least twenty years; I believe I should have carried it back rather farther. In stating what I always understood the proper question to be, I cannot do better than adopt the language of Mr Justice Mellor. He says, 'It must be plain, that persons using a limekiln, or other works which emit noxious vapours, may not do an actionable injury to another, and that any place where such an operation is carried on so that it does occasion an actionable injury to another, is not, in the meaning of the law, a convenient place.' I always understood that to be so; but in truth, as was observed in one of the cases by the learned judges, it is extremely difficult to lay down any actual definition of what constitutes an injury, because it is always a question of compound facts, which must be looked to to see whether or not the mode of carrying on a business did or did not occasion so serious an injury as to interfere with the comfort of life and enjoyment of property.

I perfectly well remember, when I had the honour of being one of the Barons of the Court of Exchequer, trying a case in the county of Durham, where there was an action for injury arising from smoke, in the town of Shields. It was proved incontestably that smoke did come and in some degree interfere with a certain person; but I said, 'You must look at it not with a view to the question whether, abstractedly, that quantity of smoke was a nuisance, but whether it was a nuisance to a person living in the town of Sheilds;' because, if it only added in an infinitesimal degree to the quantity of smoke, I held that the state of the town rendered it altogether impossible to call that an actionable nuisance.

Halsey v. *Esso Petroleum Co. Ltd* [1961] 2 All E.R. 145, pp. 148–161

The defendants had occupied an oil depot since 1896. Up to 1939, the depot stocked and distributed all kinds of oil, petrol and kerosene, as well as stoves and heaters. From 1936 to 1939 there was a night shift at the depot but only six road tankers were then used on the shift. In 1956 a night shift from 10 p.m. to 6 a.m. was commenced and the scale of this shift was much greater than in the years 1936 to 1939. After 1957 or 1958 the depot dealt solely with the three grades of fuel oil, namely, light, medium and heavy grades. Between 1953 and 1967 the through-put of oil on the depot had risen from 30,414,000 to 56,607,000 gallons and was continually increasing, the oil being pumped from river tankers into oil storage tanks at the depot and from the depot into road tankers. It was desirable to pre-heat all fuel oil before pumping it, and it was necessary to heat the medium grade oil to 120 degrees Fahrenheit and the heavy grade oil to 140 degrees Fahrenheit. These two grades were kept hot throughout transportation including the time while they were in the depot. There were two boilers at the depot; one, installed in 1921, had a metal chimney stack thirty feet high, the top of which was forty feet above the ground and the other, installed in 1949, had a metal stack fifty-two feet high. There were also a number of tanks and pumps. The pumps were originally steam driven but most of them had now been, or were being, changed over to electricity. The defendants had attempted to reduce the noise from the pumps but were only partly successful in so doing. In about 1958 complaints began about smuts from the chimneys. At that time the manager of the depot was aware that the effluent from the chimneys at times stained the pavement on both sides of Rainville Road. There followed a long history of complaints by local residents and in November, 1958, the residents, including the plaintiff, presented a petition to the manager of the depot complaining among other things of contaminated atmosphere. In response to a letter of complaint dated Dec. 31, 1959, from the medical officer of health the defendants had lagged the chimneys. They did nothing about the height of the chimneys which might have been a cause of the smuts.

VEALE J read the following judgment: The plaintiff in this action lives at 28, Rainville Road, a small terrace house in Fulham. The defendants are a very large and well-known company with many activities relating to oil. They operate an oil distributing depot at Fulham. The plaintiff alleges that the defendants are guilty of nuisance in law in relation to their operations at that depot.

The claim is broadly put on two bases: pollution of the atmosphere and noise; but that is perhaps an over-simplification. The alleged pollution takes the form of smells (which do not cause any real injury to health unless one is allergic to such smells) and also to deposits consisting of acid smuts and oily drops which fall on washing put out to dry, on fabrics inside the house such as curtains and on paintwork, including the paintwork of a motor car. The alleged noise comprises noise from boilers, pumps and vehicles, the latter category embracing not only the noise of the vehicle itself in motion but noises caused by the driver and workmen such as shouting, slamming doors and banging pipes.

It is important that the nature of the district should be borne in mind. I have seen a map of the district and also certain photographs. These are helpful but not as helpful as an actual view. There is an undoubted strip of industrial development on the river bank. This strip is zoned for industrial purposes. There are various kinds of industrial activity carried on, and the defendants' premises are not the only place where oil is dealt with. On the other hand the houses in Rainville Road and in the streets adjacent to Rainville Road are in a residential area. They are not affected by traffic in Fulham Palace Road. They are what might be described as nice small terrace houses. This area is zoned for residential purposes. In assessing the character of the neighbourhood, I have been assisted by what I have seen myself. . . . I have been referred to a very large number of authorities, but it seems to me that, save on one point to which I will refer later, there can be little dispute as to the law which has to be applied to the facts. . . .

So far as the present case is concerned, liability for nuisance by harmful deposits could be established by proving damage by the deposits to the property in question, provided, of course, that the injury was not merely trivial. Negligence is not an ingredient of the cause of action, and the character of the neighbourhood is not a matter to be taken into consideration. On the other hand nuisance by smell or noise is something to which no absolute standard can be applied. It is always a question of degree whether the interference with comfort or convenience is sufficiently serious to constitute a nuisance. The character of the neighbourhood is very relevant and all the relevant circumstances have to be taken into account. What might be a nuisance in one area is by no means necessarily so in another. In an urban area, everyone must put up with a certain amount of discomfort and annoyance from the activities of neighbours, and the law must strike a fair and reasonable balance between the right of the plaintiff on the one hand to the undisturbed enjoyment of his property, and the right of the defendant on the other hand to use his property for his own lawful enjoyment. That is how I approach this case.

It may be possible in some cases to prove that noise or smell have in fact diminished the value of the plaintiff's property in the market. That consideration does not arise in this case, and no evidence has been called in regard to it. The standard in respect of discomfort and inconvenience from noise and smell that I have to apply is that of the ordinary reasonable and responsible person who lives in this particular area of Fulham. This is not necessarily the same as the standard which the plaintiff chooses to set up for himself. It is the standard of the ordinary man, and the ordinary man, who may well like peace and quiet, will not complain for instance of the noise of traffic if he chooses to live on a main street in an urban centre, nor of the reasonable noises of industry, if he chooses to live alongside a factory.

[His LORDSHIP, having stated the introductory facts, went on to deal with the specific complaints. As to acid smuts, the evidence established that laundry hung out to dry in the immediate vicinity of the defendants' chimneys had been damaged by smuts causing holes in the laundry after it had been washed to remove the stains from the smuts. Black smuts up to the size of a sixpence were seen coming from the chimneys and falling in front of the plaintiff's house. The smuts when analysed showed a strong positive reaction for iron (the defendants' chimneys were iron) and for sulphuric acid, and in His LORDSHIP's opinion this was strong evidence of pollution of the atmosphere by a harmful substance. Further tests on smuts collected from Rainville Road indicated that the pollution consisted of sulphate. His LORDSHIP continued:] I have no doubt at all that the defendants had been the cause of the emission into the atmosphere of noxious smuts which had caused damage to the plaintiff's washing and to his motor car. The smuts are noxious acid smuts, and it does not matter whether they contain sulphate or sulphuric acid. For this damage the defendants in my judgment are liable, both as for a nuisance and under *Rylands* v. *Fletcher*.[70] It is not necessary for the plaintiff to prove or for me to decide precisely why this has happened. It is necessary for the plaintiff to prove the fact of it happening, and this I am satisfied that he has done.

. . . This nuisance to the plaintiff may, partly at all events, be due to the shortcomings of one of the chimney stacks. I do not know and I do not have to decide. The fact is that noxious smuts have come from the defendants' depot and have done damage.

I am not impressed by any argument based on the fact that noxious smuts are to be found elsewhere and on many urban buildings. In the vast majority of such places, although they may be unsightly, they do no damage or no appreciable damage, and their origin cannot be traced. In the present case, acid smuts have done damage and their origin has been traced. There is not and cannot be any doubt that the emission of acid smuts is a well-known problem. As is stated at p. 23 of the thirty-first report of the Department of Scientific and Industrial Research on the Investigation of Atmospheric Pollution, this is – and I quote – 'a form of pollution which is particularly troublesome in its effect'. One of the defendants' witnesses regarded it as being a particularly well-known trouble in the case of metal chimneys. Wherever fuel, whether coal or oil, is burnt, sulphur dioxide is discharged into the air. This does not depend on the efficiency of the combustion. The amount of sulphur dioxide so discharged depends on the amount of sulphur in the fuel. Although fuel oil frequently contains between three per cent. and four per cent. of sulphur, the manager of the defendants' depot told me on the fourth occasion that he gave evidence, that ninety per cent. of the oil burnt by the defendants comes from Thames Haven as opposed to ten per cent. from Purfleet. The sulphur content of Thames Haven oil is 2·2 per cent. on the average, which is low. But this case is not a complaint of damage by sulphur dioxide; it is a complaint of damage by H_2SO_4. What may happen is that the sulphur dioxide discharged up the chimney may combine with water vapour, as may very small quantities of sulphur trioxide, and it is then that sulphate or SO_4 is formed. This condenses and when in contact with particles of carbon, acid smuts may also be formed, and it is for this reason that lagging of the chimney may be important, since thereby this process is stayed and the chimney temperature is higher and above what has been called the acid dew-point.

The defendants' chimneys were lagged approximately two months after the complaint in December, 1959, by the medical officer of health, that is in approximately March, 1960. I have no details of what was done. It has certainly not stopped the emission of acid smuts, though it may have made them less frequent. [After referring to expert evidence, HIS LORDSHIP continued:] I find as a fact that lagging has not cured the emission of acid smuts, though they may now be less frequent. There is no defence to this action so far as noxious smuts are concerned.

I find the question of oily droplets more difficult to decide – not unnaturally, because they are not visible to the naked eye and the plaintiff cannot say that he has seen them fall. No claim for damage to his curtains is included in the statement of claim. On balance, after some considerable hesitation, I do not think that I can say that the plaintiff's laundry is in real and constant danger from oily droplets as opposed to acid smuts emitted from the defendants' depot. I have no doubt that there are occasions when these oily droplets do not disperse into the atmosphere as completely as they are said to do, and I am not prepared to dismiss, as I am asked to do, the tests carried out for the plaintiff. Nevertheless, I find myself in doubt on this one point as to the frequency and extent of any oily droplets as opposed to acid smuts, and I limit my finding that the defendants are guilty of nuisance causing damage to the plaintiff to the emission of acid smuts.

I turn now to the question of smell. At the time of my official view of the locality yesterday, on Feb. 22, there was no appreciable smell at all, either inside or outside the defendants' depot. But a large body of witnesses have given evidence of smell, and I have no doubt but that smells escape from the defendants' depot. That is not surprising of itself, because the depot is after all an oil depot. The defendants contend first that there is no smell escaping; alternatively that if any smell escapes, it does not amount to a nuisance; alternatively that if there is any smell, there is a prescriptive right to cause it.

Over a period of much more than twenty years, the defendants have dealt with different kinds of oil at the depot. I think from time to time, over the years, smells of oil have escaped. No doubt the frequency and intensity of these smells has varied, but more than one witness has told me that there has always been some sort of smell. What I might call the general background of occasional oily smells, is something in respect of which, in my judgment, the plaintiff is not entitled to complain. It is not, however, of this type of smell that the plaintiff does complain in this action. 'On occasions,' he says, 'the smell is much worse. You have to be there to realise it', he said, 'it really makes you feel sick'. The further and better particulars to para. 8 of the statement of claim refer to the smell which arises from heating oil and also use the words, 'a pungent rather nauseating smell of an oily character'. It is of this that the plaintiff complains in this action.

It is often very difficult to put into words the nature of a smell. I have had varous descriptions given to me. The plaintiff ascribed it to hot oil. His wife said it was an awful smell of burning oil, a sickly smell which made her feel sick in the stomach. 'Absolutely horrible', 'absolutely shocking', 'nauseating', 'definitely vile', are only some of the epithets which have been used by the witnesses. 'Nauseating' was a word used by Dr Barton-Wright among others. I have carefully considered the evidence of the different witnesses on this point. I find as a fact that over and above the occasional smell of oil which has been present from time to time for many years, during recent years and growing over the years in frequency and intensity, there has been emitted from the defendants' depot a particularly pungent smell, which goes far, beyond any triviality, far beyond any background smell of oil, and it is a serious nuisance to local residents, including the plaintiff. I have no doubt whatever but that this smell comes from the defendants' depot. This smell is not only strictly local to the defendants' depot but I accept the evidence which tracks it down to the depot. It is not necessary for the plaintiff to prove or for me to decide how and why it is caused; but it is significant that the defendants have in recent years turned over their total through-put to fuel oil. Fuel oil in its medium and heavy grades is heated, and the more you heat such oil the more it smells. I bear in mind that those working in the depot itself say they are not conscious of any smell except when, for instance, a cover on a tank is lifted. It is said that if an extremely sensitive person stood at the side of an oil tanker, he might smell something. It may be that those who work at the depot or for the defendants' company are used to oily smells and do not notice anything. The plaintiff does not work in the depot, and I am quite satisfied that there is on occasion a smell escaping from the depot, which is far more than what would affect a sensitive person. . . . and this is so frequent as to be an actionable nuisance.

It is true that neither the plaintiff nor his wife before the action made a specific complaint of smell; but they have in my judgment many matters of which they were entitled to complain. It is sufficient for me to say that I accept their evidence. The plaintiff did in fact sign the petition which complained of contaminated atmosphere. Whether or not this smell amounts to a nuisance depends of course on the whole of the circumstances, including the character of the neighbourhood and the nature, intensity and frequency of the smell. I hold that this smell, of which the witnesses have given evidence, and which may or may not be due to heated oil, does amount to a nuisance and further, that any defence of prescription in respect of it fails because the frequency and intensity of it which constitute the nuisance have not continued for anything approaching twenty years.

I approach this question with caution, as counsel for the defendants asked me to do, since there has been no injury to health, but injury to health is not a necessary ingredient in the cause of action for nuisance by smell, and authority for that proposition is to be found in the judgment of LORD ROMILLY, M.R., in *Crump* v. *Lambert*.[71]

I turn now to the question of nuisance by noise. This question relates to two distinct matters: the noise of the plant and the noise of the vehicles, the latter complaint including the noise of the vehicles themselves and the attendant noises made by drivers shouting and slamming doors and banging pipes. It is in connexion with noise that, in my judgment, the operations of the defendants at night are particularly important. After all, one of the main objects of living in a house or flat is to have a room with a bed in it where one can sleep at night. Night is the time when the ordinary man takes his rest. No real complaint is made by the plaintiff as far as the daytime is concerned; but he complains bitterly of the noise at night.

In dealing with the question of noise, I disregard entirely complaints of noise on new installations, such as pile driving. Although no doubt they are annoying to local residents, such noise is of a temporary character.

So far as the plant is concerned, there are really two distinct noises; that from the boilerhouse and that from the pumps. The latter are being changed from steam to electricity, and I think it is the fact that there are two noises, which has made the descriptions given by the witnesses vary. It is the noise from the boilerhouse which is of main importance to the plaintiff, because he lives opposite to it. The plaintiff says it goes on through the night, at some times being heavier than others, but when it comes to its peak his windows and doors vibrate terrifically. He cannot sleep through it. Mrs. Edy of 29, Rainville Road, puts a mattress against her door to stop the vibration. The defendants have very recently done something to make things better by soundproofing the walls of the boiler-house; but it nevertheless remains. Mrs. Carter at 19, Rainville Road, says she gets accustomed to it when it is quiet, but when it is noisy, it wakes her up.

I accept the evidence of the plaintiff as to noise and I hold it is a serious nuisance, going far beyond a triviality, and one in respect of which the plaintiff is entitled to complain. Because of the noise made by the boilers, I think that the plaintiff is not so much, certainly since the throbbing of the steam pumps ceased, troubled by the noise of the electric pumps. But that is because the noise of the pumps is largely drowned by the noise of the boilers and even if the noise of the boilers stopped, it might be that the plaintiff could justifiably complain of the noise of the pumps.

I have been assisted on this aspect of the case by the evidence of Mr. Glover. Scientific evidence is helpful in that it may tend to confirm or disprove the evidence of other witnesses. The scale of decibels from nought to 120 can be divided into colloquial descriptions of noise by the use of words: faint, moderate, loud, and so on. Between 40 and 60 decibels the noise is moderate, and between 60 and 80 it is loud. Between 80 and 100 it is very loud, and from 100 to 120 it is deafening. On Nov. 29, 1960, Mr. Glover took readings on a dawmeter outside the plaintiff's house. Six tests between nine and eleven o'clock in the evening showed readings of 64 to 68 decibels, all rising to about 68 as a peak. There was, therefore, a constant loud noise outside the plaintiff's house. When a tanker passed the reading was 83 decibels, though at the moment I am concerned with the plant and in particular the boilers. On Jan. 25, 1961, between six and eight o'clock in the evening inside the house, with the window open three inches, further tests showed that the noise inside the house was substantially above the maximum permissible intrusive noise, which is the level at which a noise would interfere with ordinary conversation. The noise outside the house was again found to be 68 decibels. This is something which happened, no doubt with variations in intensity, not just now and again, but every night and all night, and I have no doubt at all but that it is an actionable nuisance. I think that it would disturb an ordinary man.

It is contended for the defendants that the tests they made showed 59 decibels with the plant in operation, and 53 with the plant shut down, an increase of only six decibels. I find that the noise of the boilers is not the same at all times. I accept Mr. Glover's figure of 68. I think that this accords more with the plaintiff's description of the roar which I also accept. [His Lordship, after further referring to the scientific evidence, continued:] I bear in mind the observations of Lord Selborne LC in *Gaunt* v. *Fynney*,[72] where he deals with the difficulty of proof of nuisance by noise. Bearing in mind, I hope, all the relevant considerations, in my judgment the defendants are liable in nuisance for the noise of their plant, though only at night. Applying and adapting the well-known words of Knight Bruce V-C in *Walter* v. *Selfe*,[73] this inconvenience is, as I find to be the fact, more than fanciful, more than one of mere delicacy or fastidiousness. It is an inconvenience materially interfering with the ordinary comfort physically of human existence, not merely according to the elegant or dainty modes of living, but according to plain and sober and simple notions among ordinary people living in this part of Fulham.

The question of noise does not stop there. At intervals through the night tankers leave and come to the defendants' depot. It has been urged on me that the public highway is for the use of all, and that is true. But it must be borne in mind that these tankers are not ordinary motor cars; they are not ordinary lorries which make more noise than a motor car; they are enormous vehicles, some when laden weighing twenty-four tons, which, apart from the loud noise of the engine, may rattle as they go, particularly when empty and especially if they hit something in the road like a grating. They all enter the depot almost opposite the plaintiff's house, which involves a sharp turn in order to do so, often changing down into low gear at the same time. They leave by the exit gate which is also close to the plaintiff's house. Mr. Glover found that the noise of a tanker was 83 decibels – in the very loud category. So did Mr. Murphy. The plaintiff complains of this noise, especially when three or four vehicles arrive or leave at a time. This, again, is not something which happens at odd times. It now happens every night, though not always in convoy, and has happened since the night shift was introduced in November, 1956.

... The fact is that the defendants concentrate at their premises a number of particular heavy and noisy vehicles. They send them out at night, making a very loud noise as they go, and they direct them to return, and the vehicles make a further very loud noise as they come back.

The noise outside and inside the plaintiff's house is, in my judgment, attributable to the defendants' mode of operation of their depot, and the principles of law to be applied seem to me to be the same as those in respect of alleged nuisance by noise of the plant itself. Applying those principles which involve consideration of the whole of the relevant circumstances, I hold that the defendants are also guilty of nuisance in this respect, but only during the night shift. I do not think that any proper comparison can be made with noisy undertakings like railways, which are carried on under statutory authority, nor, in my judgment, can Rainville Road, Fulham, properly be compared with the Great North Road. ...

In my judgment, therefore, the defendants are liable to the plaintiff in respect of pollution, that is both smuts as well as smell, and also in respect of noise, that is both from the plant and from the tankers. I do not think that the senior executives of the defendants can have realised how serious an interference since 1956 their activities have been to the plaintiff's enjoyment of his property. Mr Knight, one of the depot's supervisers, would not live in the plaintiff's house if he were paid, though he may have been expressing that view solely because of the smuts. ...

So far as the future is concerned, I have considered the authorities to which I have been referred by both parties. I will not burden this judgment by reciting them. An injunction is a discretionary remedy, but the discretion should be exercised in accordance with accepted principles. One, but only one, of those principles is that the court is not a tribunal for legalising wrongful acts by an award of damages. I am fully conscious of the importance of the defendants' business. The question of remedy by injunction must be considered separately in respect of noise, smell, and smuts.

As to noise, I bear in mind the effect on the defendants of closing the night shift. Indeed, the evidence quantified the possible and probable loss of profit. I am asked to bear in mind the effect on the customers of the defendants, but the figures of estimated loss of profit are on the basis of the defendants making alternative arrangements to keep their customers supplied. I bear in mind that the defendants have in some respects done what they can to minimise the noise. Nevertheless, the plaintiff is entitled, in my judgment, to an injunction to limit it to the hours of the present night shift, namely, ten o'clock at night to six o'clock in the morning. There will be an injunction restraining the defendants by themselves, their servants or agents from so operating their plant at the depot, and from so driving their vehicles as, by reason of noise, to cause a nuisance to the plaintiff between the hours of 10 p.m. and 6 a.m. I am prepared to suspend the operation of this order for a reasonable time so that the defendants may make appropriate arrangements.

As to smell, again I think that the plaintiff is entitled to an injunction. I have felt some difficulty on this aspect of the case because I do not think that the occasional slight smell of oil per se is a matter which can be complained about as opposed to what is described as the pungent, rather nauseating smell. It is difficult to find precise words which will cover my findings on the facts, but I propose to grant an injunction in general terms restraining the defendants by themselves, their servants or agents from so conducting their operations at the depot as, by reason of smell, to cause a nuisance to the plaintiff. In this case there is no limitation as to the time of day or night, but again, I am prepared to suspend the operation of my order for a reasonable time if the defendants desire to make alterations or adjustments.

As to smuts, despite the argument of counsel for the plaintiff based on *Wood* v. *Conway Corpn.*[74] I do not propose either to grant an injunction or to award damages for the future. If future damage is caused by the defendants to the plaintiff, he will be able to bring a fresh action. I take this course primarily because the whole boilerhouse and the offending chimneys are to be pulled down. A new boilerhouse in a different position will be erected, and the chimney will be of brick and sixty-five feet high. It is to be hoped that the construction and operation of the new boiler-house will be such that this particular nuisance will be remedied. If it is not, and this nuisance continues as it was, I have little doubt at all that an injunction could be obtained to restrain it. ... I desire to make it clear only that I take this course because of the evidence given by the defendants that the new boilerhouse will be in operation by June, 1961. I require an undertaking from the defendants that that will be so by June 30, 1961. They will have liberty to apply to cover the case of un-foreseen circumstances arising; but I do not think in this repsect they have hitherto shown any real sense of urgency. Such sense of urgency they must now show.

Hampstead and Suburban Properties v. *Diomedous* [1968]
3 All E.R. 545, 546–551

MEGARRY J: On Nov. 28, 1958, the plaintiffs granted a lease of a shop at 122A, Finchley Road, Hampstead, for twenty-one years from Nov. 11, 1957, at a rent of £1,000 a year. By cl. 2 (17) of the lease, the tenants covenanted

> to use and occupy the demised premises throughout the tenancy as a shop in connection with the retail business of a fruiterer, a greengrocer and for the retail sale of flowers, seeds, bulbs, tinned goods, poultry, eggs and honey, butcher and seller of cooked meats, delicatessen and light refreshments, groceries and provisions, bread, cake and confection-ery and for no other purpose whatsoever.

By cl. 2 (18), the tenants covenanted

> not to use or suffer the demised premises or any part thereof to be

used for any sale by auction or for any offensive or noisy trade, business, manufactory or occupation or for any illegal or immoral purpose or for the sale of wine, beer, spirits or as a dwelling-house or club or so as to cause, in the opinion of the landlord, any nuisance, damage or annoyance (particularly by wireless or television apparatus or any musical instrument).

By cl. 2 (23), there was a covenant against assignment without the landlords' consent, such consent not to be unreasonably withheld.

In June this year the lease was vested in a company known as Haverstock Developments, Ltd. On June 24, a licence under seal was entered into between the plaintiffs, Haverstock Developments, Ltd. and the defendant. This licence was expressed to be supplemental to the lease. Put shortly, the licence granted to Haverstock Developments, Ltd. licence to assign the lease to the defendant. Secondly, it altered the user clause in the lease, providing that the lease should be read and construed as if, for the use specified in the lease as a use or purpose for which the premises should be used or occupied, there were substituted use as a licensed restaurant; there was also a proviso which I need not read. Thirdly, the licence modified the clause in the lease dealing with the sale of wine, beer and spirits so as to permit the sale of wine, beer and spirits to persons taking table meals in the premises demised by the lease, and for consumption by such persons as ancillary to their meals. In return, the defendant entered into certain covenants and obligations, including a covenant to pay the plaintiffs an additional rent of £450 a year.

The licence also provided that:

Without prejudice to the provisions of cl. 2 (18) of the lease, the assignee will not play music or musical instruments or permit music or musical instruments to be played within the premises in such a manner as to be audible to the extent of causing a nuisance or annoyance to the occupiers of any adjoining or neighbouring premises (including the flats situated above the premises) and in the event of any complaints being received by the landlords from the owner or occupier of any adjoining or neighbouring premises, the assignee will, at the request of the landlords (such request to be made only if, in the opinion of the landlords, the said complaint was reasonable) forthwith discontinue the playing of music or musical instruments within the premises until such time as effective soundproofing works to the premises (to be carried out in accordance with plans to be approved by the landlords and subject to such reasonable conditions as the landlords may impose) have been completed.

The lease was duly assigned to the defendant pursuant to this licence, and he now carries on a restaurant on these premises. Almost at once music began to be played in the restaurant and the plaintiffs began to receive complaints from tenants of theirs occupying flats above the restaurant. . . .

In these circumstances, it is hardly surprising that there was correspondence between solicitors for the plaintiffs and solicitors for the defendant. On July 17 the defendant's solicitors wrote this: 'We understand that your clients and our client's son had another meeting today, following which our clients have undertaken to suspend the playing of music after Saturday next, July 20, until soundproofing has been satisfactorily completed.'

By common consent, the soundproofing referred to in that letter has not been completed. Yet despite the undertaking, given to avert an application for an injunction, the music has continued unabated.

On Aug. 2 the plaintiffs issued a writ claiming three injunctions. Put briefly, the first seeks to restrain the use of the restaurant in such a way as to cause nuisance, damage or annoyance generally. The second is to a similar effect, save that it specifically refers to the playing of music and musical instruments in such a way as to cause a nuisance or annoyance to neighbours. The third seeks a total prohibition of the playing of music or musical instruments until such time as effective soundproofing has been carried out. . . .

It is plain from what I have said that there is a case for the defendant to answer. What, then, does he say? In brief, it is this. He files no evidence, and so controverts none of the facts alleged against him; it is accordingly plain that he has acted in prompt and flagrant breach of his covenants and undertaking. Instead, counsel on his behalf submits that this is a case which is totally unsuitable for an injunction; and he has urged five points in support of this contention.

First, he says that the covenants are too uncertain for an injunction. What, asks counsel for the defendant, is the standard of audibility 'to the extent of causing a nuisance or annoyance' to neighbours, and what is 'effective' soundproofing? Damages, he says, are the proper remedy, not an injunction. . . . The court is always slow to repose on the easy pillow of uncertainty; and there have been many instances of the grant of interlocutory injunctions to restrain the commission of nuisances, despite the difficulty that there often is in defining precisely what degree of smell or noise or vibration amounts to a nuisance. In the celebrated phrase of KNIGHT BRUCE V-C in *Walter* v. *Selfe*,[75] which I put to counsel for the defendant in argument, 'nuisance' is a term which must be construed according to 'plain and sober and simple notions among the English people'; and the courts are not unaccustomed to this standard.

The fact that a defendant enjoined from committing a nuisance may have some difficulty in going as close as he can to the dividing line without crossing it is, in my judgment, no reason for not enjoining him in a case where it is plain that wherever the line ought to be drawn he is overstepping it by a wide margin. I have no doubt that what is a nuisance or annoyance will continue to be determined by the courts according to robust and common-sense standards. Nor have I any hesitation in assuming that where there has been a breach of an injunction because of a genuine and understandable uncertainty about what is or what is not licit, the court will continue to exercise a proper discretion in dealing with the breach. Similar considerations apply to the argument on effective soundproofing. In the context I feel little doubt that 'effective sound-proofing' is soundproofing which is effective in preventing a nuisance or annoyance to neighbours. In my judgment, there is nothing in the point on uncertainty. In this I am comforted by the decision of the Court of Appeal in *Tod-Heatly* v. *Benham*,[76] which shows the court enforcing a covenant where the phrase in question was 'annoyance, nuisance, grievance or damage of the lessor', and so on.

Finally, there is the balance of convenience. To say that the inconvenience to the plaintiffs is 'nil', and that to them the case is 'essentially trivial', seems to me as much an exaggeration as to say that the loss to the defendant will be 'incalculable'. I have already dealt with the injury to the plaintiffs, and I need say no more about it. The defendant's claim is, in essence, that he will suffer an 'incalculable loss' if he is not permitted to continue his plain breach of the obligations which he so recently entered into and voluntarily undertook when he became an assignee of the lease. Stripped of the persuasions of counsel for the defendant's advocacy, the proposition is: 'I am making handsome profits by doing what I covenanted and undertook not to do: therefore it would be wrong for the court to stop me.' I can conceive of few propositions calculated to appeal less to equity.

In this connexion I must mention the emphasis of counsel for the defendant on the fact that this was an action brought not by the tenants but by the landlords, and his contention that I ought to disregard any injury or damage to those who are not parties to these proceedings. The case, he urged, was one between the plaintiffs and the defendant, and I must consider the hardship to the defendant, and disregard any hardship to other tenants of the plaintiffs. I do not consider this to be a correct analysis of the position.

The plaintiffs are making money by letting their property to tenants. The defendant is making money by providing a restaurant to which customers come for food, drink and music. The plaintiffs' tenants object to the music when played as loudly as it is; the defendant's customers like the music (or so I assume) when played at that volume. The case for each party is based in large degree not on any direct personal benefit or injury, but on the benefit or injury to that party's tenants or customers (as the case may be), and so to that party. In these circumstances, it seems to me that I am entitled to pay some regard to the social values involved. The point has not been argued, and I do not rest my decision on it. But it seems to me that it is of some relevance to consider whether it is more important for the plaintiffs' tenants to have the relative peace and quiet in their homes to which they have been accustomed, or for the defendant's customers to have the pleasure of music while they eat, played at high volume. When this comparison is made, it seems to me that it is the home rather than the meal table which must prevail. A home in which sleep is possible is a necessity, whereas loud music as an accompaniment to an evening meal is, for those who enjoy it, relatively a luxury. If, of course, the two can peacefully co-exist, so much the better; but if there is irreconcilable conflict, as there is at present in this case, I think it is the home that should be preferred.

This is a clear case. Without even an attempt at justification or excuse, the defendant claims the right on technical grounds to be left undisturbed in his breach of obligation until the trial of the action. In my judgment the technical grounds are wholly untenable, and accordingly I hold that the two injunctions sought by the notice of motion should be granted, to be effective until judgment in the action or further order.

(b) Does nuisance go too far or not far enough?

(i) Nuisance and pollution

It would be misleading to suggest that all recent nuisance cases can be seen as examples of attempts to control pollution. It would not, however, be misleading to state that the action for nuisance is seen by both amenity and industrial organisations as a powerful weapon in the fight over pollution control. *Halsey* v. *Esso Petroleum*[77] is one example of its use to control industrial pollution; the *Pride of Derby* case is another, and provides also a lead into one of the crucial debates in this area, namely the extent to which actions for nuisance should lie at the suit of private individuals or organisations against polluters who are in fact complying with standards laid down by river authorities or, in doing what they are doing, can point to statutory authorisation. Extracts from the continuing debate between the two points of view appear below. With which point of view do you agree and why?

In *Pride of Derby etc.* v. *British Celanese etc.*[78] an angling association which owned a fishery on the rivers Trent and Derwent brought an action against British Celanese Ltd, Derby Corporation, and the British Electricity Authority, claiming injunctions restraining each of the defendants from causing or permitting any effluent to flow or pass from their premises into the river Derwent or river Trent so as to pollute them. The plaintiff also claimed damages in trespass and nuisance against all defendants. The first defendant admitted that their activities polluted the rivers to the detriment of the plaintiffs and submitted to an injunction before the action; the second and third defendants denied liability. Derby Corporation, in addition, claimed that, even if a nuisance did arise from their sewage works, the effluent of which was the subject of the action, they were absolved from liability as they were under a statutory duty to do the things which created the nuisance. The plaintiffs won their case against all three defendants at first instance. On appeal, the British Electricity Authority obtained a variation in the order for an injunction, but Derby Corporation's appeal wholly failed. In dealing with its appeal, Denning LJ (as he then was) had this to say of an injunction to restrain a nuisance (p. 204):

The remaining question is whether an injunction should be issued against them. Counsel for the corporation argued that an injunction should not issue. The corporation, he said, could not dam back the sewage because that 'would cause a most frightful nuisance' to the inhabitants of Derby, and they could not extend their sewage disposal works because they were prohibited under the Defence (General) Regulations, 1939, reg. 56A, from doing so without the consent of the Minister of Works. These are strong reasons for suspending the injunction, but are no reasons for not granting it. The power of the courts to issue an injunction for nuisance has proved itself to be the best method so far devised of securing the cleanliness of our rivers, and in this connection it is significant that the law relating to nuisance has been expressly preserved by s.11(6) of the Rivers (Prevention of Pollution) Act, 1951. The issue of an injunction does not interfere with the power of the Minister to determine the proper order of priority of public works, but it does mean that, if these works are to be deferred, the court will want to know the reason why. Only an overriding public interest will suffice.

One organisation that would certainly agree with Lord Denning's sturdy defence of the action for nuisance is the Anglers' Co-operative Association, which was much helped also by *Martell* v. *Consett Iron Co.*[79] In that case the Court of Appeal held that the Association was not guilty of maintenance in financing an action in nuisance by one of its members, a riparian owner, against the Consett Iron Co. Since that case, the ACA has been a major thorn in the side of industry, which finds that compliance with bye-laws promulgated by water authorities is not a defence against actions for nuisance on the lines of the *Pride of Derby* case.

Final Report of the Trade Effluents Sub-Committee of the Central Water Advisory Committee (The Armer Committee) (MHLG 1960), chapter 5: Review of the Common Law, pp. 37–42

151. We have received evidence about the operation of the common law from a number of bodies. The *British Iron and Steel Federation* referred to court of law rulings that appeared to establish that a riparian owner had a right to receive the water to which he was entitled in its natural state, and that any form of pollution causing a sensible alteration in the character or quality of that water so as to render it less fit for any purposes for which in its natural state it was capable of being used was a violation of that right. Pollution, it was said, was thus actionable without proof of damage, and industrial concerns often found it extremely difficult to determine whether or not the discharge of an effluent into a river was a

violation of the proprietary rights of neighbouring riparian and fishery owners.

152. As they understood the position, the riparian owner who in a court of law had proved the violation of his right was in general entitled to an injunction to prevent the recurrence of the wrong as well as pecuniary damages, and although the remedy of injunction was discretionary, the courts during the last hundred years had regarded themselves as bound to grant a perpetual injunction to a riparian owner whose right had been violated and might continue to be violated, without having any regard to the inconvenience thereby caused to the defendant, which might be grossly disproportionate to the injury caused to the plaintiff by the continuance of the pollution. With some industrial effluents it might be physically impossible to avoid causing some pollution, and in such cases the only means of complying with an injunction would be to close down the works.

153. The Federation said they were much concerned about the increasing number of applications for injunctions. In recent years the courts had granted perpetual injunctions against industrial concerns and local authorities in the widest possible terms. If any local authority or industrial concern was forced to cause pollution in any degree it must seek the protection of legislation; the most that the courts could do was to suspend the operation of the injunction for a period to give the defendant a chance to find means to comply with it. An industrial firm that was unable to comply with a perpetual injunction would be left under a permanent threat of the sequestration and closing of its works and the imprisonment of its directors.

154. They stressed that the disposal of liquid effluents was an important problem for the iron and steel industry, for in the manufacture of iron and steel these effluents were produced in such large quantities that they could seldom be discharged into public sewers. It was the policy of the industry to continue to make every reasonable effort to find the technical means of disposing of its effluents without causing appreciable harm to private rights or to public amenities. In the production of iron and steel the industry was, however, handicapped by the absence of any standard by which it could be ascertained with reasonable certainty whether a river could be used for the disposal of effluent without the threat of an injunction.

155. In the River Boards Act, 1948, and the Rivers (Prevention of Pollution) Act, 1951, the Federation submitted, a system of public control of river pollution had been established under which standards of pollution could be prescribed in bye-laws made by the river boards for any stream or part of a stream in their areas. In exercising their powers to make bye-laws a river board had to have regard to the character and flow of the stream and the extent to which it was or might in the future be used for industrial and other purposes. Such standards would enable industrial concerns to determine with reasonable certainty whether they were complying with the Acts, but they would be of limited value to industry so long as injunctions were granted by the civil courts as at

present. Moreover, there might well be delay in prescribing such standards; river boards were not compelled to prescribe them, and the task of doing so was known to be difficult.

156. Accordingly the Federation proposed that legislation should be introduced to the following effect:

(1) (a) That (subject to sub-paragraph (2) below) a court should not grant an injunction which had the effect of prohibiting the discharge of liquid trade effluent into a stream if the defendant established:

(i) that it was not reasonably practicable within a reasonable cost to dispose of the effluent otherwise than by discharging it (directly or indirectly) into that or some other stream, and

(ii) that all reasonably practicable steps within a reasonable cost were being taken to prevent the effluent being unnecessarily poisonous, noxious or polluting.

(b) That the power of a court to grant an injunction to restrain the pollution of a stream should be limited to requiring the defendant to do or to refrain from doing what it was reasonably practicable within a reasonable cost to do or to refrain from doing, as the case might be.

(c) That in determining what was reasonably practicable the court should have regard to all relevant circumstances, including the character and flow of the stream, the extent to which it was and might in the future be used for industrial purposes and for other purposes, and the current state of technical knowledge, and generally to the national and public interest.

(2) That in so far as standards were prescribed in bye-laws made by river boards under the Act of 1951, the power of a court to grant an injunction to restrain the pollution of a stream should be limited to restraining non-compliance or ordering compliance with such standards. . . .

157. The *Federation of British Industries*, who also submitted evidence to us, said that there was a difference of opinion among their members as to whether any change in the existing common law was necessary or desirable; this was attributable to the fact that certain branches of industry were primarily concerned about water supplies from rivers and others were more concerned about the disposal of effluents. The latter considered that some modification of the existing law was a matter of urgent importance. On their behalf reference was made to the fact that a riparian owner in the event of continued pollution could generally obtain an injunction regardless of the inconvenience or expense involved in complying with it, and it was said that actions at common law had, as a result of publicity, become much more frequent in recent years than hitherto. It was also pointed out that industrial concerns were often indirectly affected by actions brought by riparian owners against local authorities accepting their effluents; such actions might result in the

concerns having to undertake additional treatment of their effluents or to contribute towards the cost of new works carried out by the local authority to enable it to comply with an injunction. They thought, moreover, that local authorities were often unwilling, because of the risk of common law action, to agree to the discharge of industrial effluents into their sewers.

158. The members of the Federation who thought that changes in the law were called for did not propose that common law rights should be abrogated to such an extent as to deprive a riparian owner of the remedy of an injunction to put a stop to unreasonable pollution of the water in which he had an interest; they did, however, recommend that legislation should be introduced whereby, in a case where the plaintiff was entitled to an injunction under the existing law, the Court, if satisfied by the defendant:

(a) that it was not reasonably practicable to dispose of the effluent otherwise than by discharging it into the stream in question; and
(b) that all reasonably practicable steps were being taken to prevent the effluent being unnecessarily injurious;

should have a discretion whether or not to grant an injunction, and in exercising this discretion should have regard to the whole of the relevant circumstances, including the extent of the pollution, the character and flow of the stream concerned, and the type of use to which the stream as a whole is put.

159. In their evidence to us the *British Coking Industry Association,* the *Gas Council* and the *National Coal Board* expressed concern because in their view the operation of the common law could result in the granting of injunctions without proof of damage and without regard to the cost of abating the nuisance. The view was expressed by the *Institution of Public Health Engineers* that a strict application of the common law standard, as set out in the judgment of Lord Macnaghten[80] ... would make it impossible for a local authority or industrial concern to discharge any effluent, however well purified, into a river. ...

161. The *Anglers' Co-operative Association* is a body that exists to provide expert advice and financial and technical assistance or indemnity to all who need it either to stop existing pollution or to prevent fresh pollution. In evidence to us the Association said that in their opinion the present state of the common law was satisfactory and that it was unnecessary to make any change in it. The common law on river pollution was part of the body of law that protected persons in the enjoyment of their property. Interference with proprietary rights in any water flowing in a natural watercourse constituted a tort, for which the normal common law remedy was an award of damages. The award of an injunction as well as damages, it was submitted, was never automatic; an injunction was granted to the plaintiff only if he could show that the defendant was likely to continue his wrongful conduct; moreover, the Court at the request of the defendant would generally suspend the operation of the injunction for an appropriate period to enable him to deal with the matter. In no case

within the experience of the Association had it been necessary for a polluter to close down his undertaking, and in many cases the cost of bringing the pollution to an end had proved to be surprisingly small.

162. As regards the suggestion that compliance with the bye-laws of a river board, or with the conditions attached to a river board's consent to a new discharge, should be a protection against proceedings under the common law, the Association pointed out that any such change in the law would be an expropriation of private rights – an expropriation which, since it would, in many cases, be for the benefit not of the public but of persons working for private profit, would go far beyond any existing provisions about compulsory acquisition. In the opinion of the Association there was no justification for singling out riparian rights for such treatment, which would be almost as objectionable if compensation were granted as if it were not.

163. The suggestion that provisions should be enacted which would enable the defendant in a common law action to avoid an injunction if he could prove that it was not reasonably practicable to dispose of the effluent otherwise than by discharging it into the stream in question or some other stream, and that all reasonably practicable steps were being taken to prevent the effluent being unnecessarily poisonous, noxious or polluting, were opposed by the Association on the additional ground that the phrases 'reasonably practicable' and 'unnecessarily poisonous' would make such provisions extremely difficult to interpret and enforce, particularly since what is not reasonably practicable one day may, in this age of rapid technical advance, become reasonably practicable soon after.

164. The Association at our request provided us with an interesting analysis of the cases, numbering 400, they had dealt with. This showed that, of an average of some ten cases a year which had been either settled out of court or in which writs had been issued during the last ten years, about one-third were cases of single or non-recurring pollution. Of the other two-thirds the vast majority were cases of long-standing pollution. Writs were issued in 32 cases of this category, and in all of them an injunction was obtained. The Association stated that usually the defendants submitted to an injunction on the advice of counsel, and in only 3 cases did it come to trial of the action. We were informed that in no case in which a polluter had asked for time to set his house in order had his request been refused.

165. As to damages, we were told that in one case £14,000 was paid (to six plaintiffs, to cover nine years' damage, including the maximum allowable under the Limitation Act of six years before the issue of a writ) and that the only other large sum was about £10,000 which had to be divided between 50 claimants.

166. On behalf of the *Salmon and Trout Association* it was submitted that it was a well established rule of the law of England that every person should conduct his affairs in such a way as not to damage any other person; thus the cost of effluent disposal was primarily a matter for the body discharging the effluent. If any national interest were involved, as might conceivably be argued if the cost of effluent disposal rendered an

industrial product uncompetitive in the export market, the proper remedy, it was suggested, would be an Exchequer contribution towards the cost, rather than tolerance of continuing river pollution.

171. In their approach to this matter we feel that it has not, perhaps, been sufficiently appreciated by those advocating a change in the common law that the statute law and the common law deal with two different aspects of the question of river pollution. The Rivers (Prevention of Pollution) Act, 1951, as this implied in its preamble, is concerned with the maintenance and restoration of the wholesomeness of rivers and other inland or coastal waters; the common law is concerned with the maintenance and protection of the proprietary rights of riparian owners. Having regard to their differing aims there would seem no necessary reason why the statute law and the common law should be expected to apply the same standards, nor does it necessarily follow that they cannot operate without incompatible or inequitable results.

173. Having carefully weighed the evidence before us, we do not think that it has been shown that the common law is operating in an inequitable way, or that there are convincing grounds for recommending a restriction of the right to apply for an injunction, especially as such a restriction would be, in effect, a compulsory acquisition of private rights for the benefit, in many cases, of other private persons. For these reasons we have come to the conclusion that no alteration is called for in the common law relating to river pollution.[81]

(ii) Nuisance and amenity

If industry's view is that the action for nuisance is too effective, there are also criticisms that it is not effective enough: that is, that it does not sufficiently prevent anti-social conduct or rather, to put it in Mishan's economic terms, that it does not operate to transfer the cost of sufficient anti-social conduct onto the person responsible for that conduct. Mishan's remedy is the creation by statute of a right of amenity, enforced by the courts.

E. J. Mishan,[82] 'The Rape of our Environment',
The Spectator, 14 July 1967

How, then, can the law be altered so as to remove existing inequities and, at the same time, to recognize the simple economic fact that privacy and quiet and clean air are scarce goods – far scarcer than they were before the war – and sure to become scarcer in the foreseeable future? . . . One has but to imagine a country in which men were invested by law with property rights in privacy, quiet and clean air – simple things, but for many indispensable to the enjoyment of life – to recognize that the extent of the compensatory payments that would perforce accompany the operation of industries, motorized traffic and airlines would constrain many of them to close down or to operate at levels far below those which would prevail in the absence of such a law, at least until industry and transport discovered economical ways of controlling their own noxious by-products.

The consequence of recognizing such rights in one form or another, let us call them amenity rights, would be far-reaching.

... So humble an invention as the petrol-powered lawn-mower, and other petrol-driven garden implements, would come also into conflict with such rights. The din produced by any one man is invariably heard by dozens of families – who, of course, may be enthusiastic gardeners also; if they are all satisfied with the current situation or could come to agreement with one another, well and good. But once amenity rights were legally enacted, at least no man could be forced against his will to absorb these noxious by-products of the activity of others.

Admittedly, there are difficulties whenever actual compensation payments have to be made, say, to thousands of families disturbed by aircraft noise. Yet once the principle of amenity rights is recognized in law, a rough estimate of the magnitude of compensation payments necessary to maintain the welfare of the number of families affected would be entered as a matter of course into the social cost calculus. And unless these compensatory payments could also be somehow covered by the proceeds of the air service, there would be no *prima facie* case for maintaining the air service. If, on the other hand, compensatory payments could be made (and their payment costs the company less than any technical device that would effectively eliminate the noise) some method of compensation must be devised.

It is true that the courts, from time to time, have enunciated the doctrine that in the ordinary pursuit of industry a reasonable amount of inconvenience must be borne with. The recognition of amenity rights, however, does no more than impose an economic interpretation on the word 'reasonable', and therefore also on the word 'unreasonable', by transferring the cost of the inconvenience on to the shoulders of those who cause it. If by actually compensating the victims – or by paying to eliminate the disamenity by the cheapest technical method available – an existing service cannot be continued (because the market is unwilling to pay the increased cost) then the inconvenience that is currently being borne with is to be deemed unreasonable. And since those who cause the inconvenience are now compelled to shoulder the increased costs, there should be no trouble in convincing them that the inconvenience is unreasonable nor, therefore, in withdrawing the service in question.

A law recognizing this principle would have drastic effects on industry and commerce, which for too long have neglected the damage inflicted on society at large in producing their wares. For many decades now firms have, without giving it a thought, polluted the air we breathe, poisoned lakes and rivers with their effluence, and produced gadgets that have destroyed the quiet of millions of families, gadgets that range from motorized lawn-mowers and motorcycles to transistors and private planes. What is being proposed therefore may be regarded as *an alteration of the legal framework within which private firms operate in order to direct their enterprise towards ends that accord more closely with the interests of society.* More specifically, it would provide industry with the incentive necessary to undertake prolonged research into methods of removing the potential amenity-destroying features of so many of today's existing products and services.

The social advantage of enacting legislation embodying amenity rights is further reinforced by a consideration of the regressive nature of many of these external diseconomies. The rich have legal protection of their property and have less need, at present, of protection from the disamenity created by others. The richer a man is, the wider his choice of neighbourhood. If the area he happened to choose appears to be sinking in the scale of amenity, he can move, if at some inconvenience, to a quieter area. He can select a suitable town house, secluded perhaps, or made soundproof throughout, and spend his leisure in the country or abroad at times of his own choosing. *Per contra*, the poorer the family the less opportunity there is for moving from its present locality. To all intents it is stuck in the area and must put up with whatever disamenity is inflicted upon it.

And, generalizing from the experience of the last ten years or so, one may depend upon it that it will be the neighbourhoods of the working and lower middle classes that will suffer most from the increased construction of fly-overs and fly-unders and road-widening schemes intended to speed up the accumulating road traffic that all but poisons the air. Thus the recognition of amenity rights has favourable distributive effects also. It would promote not only a rise in the standards of environment generally: it would raise them most for the lower-income groups that have suffered more than any other group from unchecked 'development' and the growth of motorized traffic since the war.

Is it that the courts have been unable or unwilling to adopt the standards suggested by Mishan, and if the latter, why? What is the difference between the standards proposed by Mishan and that proposed by Knight-Bruce V-C in *Waller* v. *Selfe*.[83] Is the interference a material one 'not merely according to elegant or dainty modes and habits of living, but according to plain and sober and simple notions among the English people'? Would Mishan's new right meet one criticism of nuisance law that in the final analysis it is the judges who determine what the average person has to put up with and is allowed to do in respect of his ownership of property and that it is their approach to the law in the past which has resulted, in Mishan's own words in 'the regressive nature of many of these [current] external diseconomies. . . . The richer a man is, the wider his choice of neighbourhood. . . . *Per contra*, the poorer the family the less opportunity there is for moving from its present locality.'?

(c) **Nuisance and public development: the defence of legislative authority**

Marriage v. *East Norfolk Rivers Catchment Board* [1949]
2 All E.R. 1021, pp. 1032–6

The defendant board, acting under powers contained in the Land Drainage Act 1930, dredged a river near the plaintiff's land. The board deposited the spoil on the south bank of the river, thus raising the height of that bank above that of the north bank. The river flooded; the flood waters, unable to escape into flood channels on the south side, spilled over on the north side, and caused the collapse of a bridge belonging to the plaintiff. The plaintiff brought an action in nuisance against the board, and lost at first instance. He appealed.

JENKINS LJ: The grounding of the plaintiff's case on nuisance or negligence (as opposed to trespass to the plaintiff's rights in respect of the flood channel as a riparian owner) is, in effect, an invocation of the general principle that Acts of Parliament by which statutory powers are conferred should not be construed as absolving those invested with them from liability, enforceable by action in the courts, in respect of any avoidable injury to others occasioned by the exercise of the powers.

We were referred to a number of well-known authorities in which this principle has been enunciated and illustrated. . . .

The general principle is thus well settled, but its application in any particular case must depend on the object and terms of the statute conferring the powers in question (including the presence or absence of a clause providing for compensation and the scope of any such clause), the nature of the act giving rise to the injury complained of, and the nature of the resulting injury. I venture to think that the questions which arise in any given case of this kind are substantially these. (i) Was the act which occasioned the injury complained of authorised by the statute? (ii) Did the statute contemplate that the exercise of the powers conferred would or might cause injury to others? (iii) If so, was the injury complained of an injury of a kind contemplated by the statute? (iv) Did the statute provide for compensation in respect of any injury of the kind complained of which was sustained through the exercise of the powers conferred? If the answers to all these questions are in the affirmative, then I think it must follow that the party injured is deprived of his right of action and is left to his remedy in the form of compensation under the statute.

To deal with the questions, in the above order, in relation to the present case. (i) The board clearly had power to dredge the river and deposit the spoil on the south bank under s. 6 (1), s. 34 (1) and s. 38 (1) of the Act. (ii) I think it is manifest that the Act did contemplate that the exercise of the powers conferred on the board would or might cause injury to others.

... (iii) I think that the injury complained of by the plaintiff was clearly of a kind contemplated by the Act. ...

There is, I think, an important distinction for this purpose between statutory powers to execute some particular work or carry on some particular undertaking (e.g., the construction and operation of the reservoir, in *Geddis* v. *Bann Reservoir Proprietors*[84], the provision of hospitals, in *Metropolitan Asylum District* v. *Hill*[85], and the construction and operation of the generating station, in *Manchester Corporation* v. *Farnworth*[86], and statutory powers to execute a variety of works of specified descriptions in a given area (the works in question being of such a kind as necessarily to involve some degree of interference with the rights of others) as and when the body invested with the powers deems it necessary or expedient to do so in furtherance of a general duty imposed on it by the Act (e.g., the powers conferred on the board in the present case by s. 6 (1), s. 34 (1) and s. 38 (1) of the Land Drainage Act, 1930, to execute works of the various descriptions therein mentioned in furtherance of the general duty, imposed on it by the Act (as appears by necessary implication from s. 12). of maintaining the main river in a due state of efficiency). In cases of the former class, the powers are, in the absence of clear provision to the contrary in the Act, limited to the doing of the particular things authorised without infringement of the rights of others, except in so far as any such infringement may be a demonstrably necessary consequence of doing what is authorised to be done. ... In cases of the latter class, such as the present case, it is obvious that, if the powers are subject to an implied limitation to the effect that they are to be exercised so as to not cause any avoidable infringement of the rights of others, the powers will in great measure be nullified and the manifest object of the Act will be largely frustrated. Thus, if the board in the present case could be sued in the courts, every time they dredged a reach of the river and deposited the spoil on one or other of the banks, by any riparian owner who could show that the effect of what had been done was to obstruct a flood channel and thereby increase the risk of damage to his premises by flood water, on the footing that this was an actionable wrong, notwithstanding the statute, the board could in every such case be restrained by injunction from carrying out the work. The injury or apprehended injury, would, moreover, always be avoidable by abandonment of the particular project, however beneficial that project might be to riparian owners other than the complainant, and the board would, therefore, never be able to defeat the complainant on the ground that the injury or apprehended injury was an unavoidable consequence of the exercise of its statutory powers.

In the absence of any provision in the Act for compensating persons injured by the exercise of the board's powers, difficult questions might arise as to the extent (if any) to which the Act should be regarded as depriving a person thus injured of his ordinary remedy in the courts, inasmuch as he would, if so deprived, be wholly without remedy, but the Act including, as it does, a provision for compensation in the shape of s. 34 (3), the considerations stated above seem to me to lead irresistibly to the conclusion that the intention of the Act was to make the board, acting in good faith and within their powers, the sole judge of what was necessary or proper to be done in the way of drainage operations for the benefit of their catchment area as a whole, and, within limits . . . to deprive persons injured by any exercise of the board's powers of their ordinary remedy by way of action and substitute the remedy by way of compensation prescribed by s. 34 (3). . . . In the present case the injury sustained by the plaintiff was sustained by reason of a normal drainage operation carried out in the usual way, *i.e.*, the operation of dredging and depositing the spoil along the bank. The injury might have been avoided if the spoil had been differently disposed. The effect of depositing the spoil on the south bank was to make that bank a foot or two higher than the north bank, instead of a foot or two lower as formerly, with the obvious consequence of increasing the liability of the north bank to flooding. . . . I cannot regard the facts as bringing home to the board anything worse than an error of judgment in under-estimating the effect which the heightening of the south bank at this particular point on the river might have in times of severe flood, and, in my view, an error of judgment of that order falls very short of the degree of negligence or reckless conduct on the part of the board which is required to remove the injury sustained from the category of injuries covered by the compensation provision.

(iv) It follows from what I have said above in dealing with the other three questions that, in my view, the provision for compensation which the Land Drainage Act, 1930, contains in the shape of s. 34 (3) does provide for compensation in respect of an injury of the kind complained of by the plaintiff in this case.

Having thus arrived at affirmative answers to the four test questions stated above, I am of opinion that the learned judge was right in his conclusion to the effect that the action was not maintainable, and that the plaintiff's proper and only remedy for the injury of which he complained was to claim compensation under s. 34 (3) of the Act.

Appeal dismissed

2

Decision Makers, Decision Making and Public Participation

1. Introduction

In the preceding chapter we looked at some of the problems of planning and its legislative and judicial antecedents. In this chapter we shall look at two essential matters that are at the heart both of the governmental process and of discussions on the process of planning: decision making and public participation. Just as some general understanding of the problems and legal procedures of planning must precede a detailed discussion of them, so a general understanding of who are the decision makers, how decisions are made, and what is meant by public participation is an essential prelude to examining how decisions are or appear to be made in relation to making plans, controlling development and developing; how in practice public participation is affecting or failing to affect customary practices and why, and what the effect is on any particular kind of legal framework for planning.

2. The decision makers

(a) Central government: structure

Since the advent of a comprehensive system of planning in 1947, one continuing problem for central government has been how to co-ordinate the various issues and concerns relating to planning and the environment. There have been many attempts to solve this problem,[1] and the latest is the Department of the Environment, which came into being on 12 November 1970. 'For the first time in

England it concentrated under one Minister as well as in one ministry all the statutory powers, patronage, budgetary control, and political decision making which had previously belonged to three separate and influential ministers and ministries, Transport, Public Building and Works, and Housing and Local Government.'[2] As with most governmental reorganisations, this one had been preceded by a growing realisation, both within and without Whitehall, that the tripartite division of responsibilities for planning, transport and government development was increasingly inapposite for dealing with the major problems of urban planning. Dame Evelyn Sharp, Permanent Secretary to the Ministry of Housing and Local Government for eleven years, had commented on the problem as follows.

> E. Sharp, *The Ministry of Housing and Local Government*, (1969), pp. 21–2

It is in the planning field that overlap with other departments is most in evidence. . . . Today . . . it is the relationship between the Ministry and the various economic departments (including with these the Ministry of Transport) that creates the main tensions. . . . The Ministry of Transport is responsible for roads and traffic, and it is quite impossible to deal with town planning in isolation from transport planning. The result of all this is that the planning staff of the Ministry spend an enormous amount of time in inter-departmental consultation; and it is sometimes suggested that it would all be easier if departmental functions were somehow re-arranged perhaps by the creation of an all-embracing Ministry of Planning whose Minister would be able to settle the clashes of interest and to integrate economic planning with land planning, road planning with urban planning. . . . Few among those involved in land planning are now content with the present distribution of responsibilities in this field.

It is true that Dame Evelyn Sharp went on to say 'it may be that, despite the discontents, the functions of the Ministry are about right as they are',[3] but it seems that she changed her views, for Aldous reports that the functions of the Department and in particular the decision to include road planning and construction within it was taken by the Conservative Government as a result of 'advice . . . tendered by a high-powered working party of ex-Whitehall knights and dames, among them Sir Eric Roll and Dame Evelyn Sharp. . . .'[4]

The basic reason for change was given by Mr Walker, the first Secretary of State for the Environment, in an open lecture at

Cambridge three months after the creation of the new department; before the DoE's advent 'the administrative machinery for dealing with our environmental problems was fragmented and due to that fragmentation was far less effective than was necessary. There were then three separate government departments where now there is one. The Ministry of Transport was frequently in conflict with the Ministry of Housing and Local Government and the Ministry of Public Building and Works had a certain contempt for both.'[5] The object of the change, part of a general reorganisation of central government was to 'match the field of responsibility of government departments to coherent fields of policy and administration',[6] with the DoE being responsible for 'the whole range of functions which affect people's living environment'.[7] Writing four years after the merger of the ministries, it might be thought that some tentative conclusions as to success or failure could be drawn, but this is doubtful.

According to Alvin Toffler, internal reorganisations of the bureaucracy are never likely to result in final solutions, but will merely be one of a series of reorganisations which take place in a desperate attempt to keep up with an ever-changing society and its problems.[8] Thus we would wait in vain for a stable Department to assess. But there is another major reason for not essaying even an interim assessment and that is the reorganisation of local government. A reorganised Department and a reorganised local government are both part of the same drive to equip the country with governmental institutions capable of getting to grips with urban problems; it would not therefore be a very useful exercise to try to judge the effectiveness of one reorganisation before the other has begun to bite. In the context of the planning process, it will be the late 1970s before we can begin to assess the merits or otherwise of reorganisation and all that will have flowed from it. The one comment that can be made already is that the good sense of the basic governmental reorganisation is admitted on all sides. One major stumbling block remains: the tensions and conflicts that exist between the Department of the Environment and the Departments for Trade and Industry, which are responsible for industrial location and regional development policies both of which are at the heart of planning.[9] Dame Evelyn Sharp referred to the tensions between the old Ministry of Housing and Local Government and the old Board of Trade;[10] the fact that both ministries are now parts of larger empires may well increase rather than reduce tensions. Is the answer to this problem more reorganisation, more inter-departmental committees, the devolution of power to provincial or regional administrations, or the acceptance of the likelihood of the disputes and their resolution by the Cabinet? A second question to consider here concerns the reorganisation that has taken place: the case against small, conflicting ministries is assumed to be conclusive; are there any dangers or defects in very large departments?

(b) Central government: functions[11]

Sharp, *The Ministry of Housing and Local Government*,
p. 144

An effective system of land planning must contain three elements. There must be a development plan, published as well as formulated, partly for the authority itself to work to, partly so that property owners and developers can know what the authority's intentions are. There must be machinery for controlling development to ensure that it takes place in conformity with the plan. And there must, even if only in the last resort, be machinery by which public authorities can ensure that essential development is carried out if private agencies are not prepared to do it.

The Department has responsibilities in all these areas, which may be classified as follows:

(i) *Policy formulation.* Policies may be laid down by means of laws: either a statute, e.g. the Town and Country Planning (Amendment) Act 1972 which introduced a new method of dealing with objections to and comments on structure plans; or regulations made under the authority of a statute, e.g. the Town and Country Planning (Structure and Local Plans) Regulations 1974[12] which indicate the kinds of matters which local planning authorities may, if they so choose, deal with in preparing these structure and local plans, and the manner in which they may deal with them. Policies are also formulated and 'offered' to local authorities and other bodies by means of ministerial circulars, reports, studies, bulletins, manuals, examples of all of which appear in later chapters. They are mentioned here because the total impact of the Department on planning cannot be measured solely in terms of laws or decisions on appeal or review from the activities of local planning authorities, and because it is important to realise that the totality of a department's power is much greater than the sum of the laws that it administers. This is well illustrated by the following extract:

Sharp, *The Ministry of Housing and Local Government,*
pp. 176–7

Equally important are the initiatives taken by the technical planning
staff in the development of policies. These can be summed up under two
heads. First, planning techniques which the planning staff of the Ministry
have done a great deal to develop. These include the techniques of survey
and of plan-drawing; working out standards of daylighting, space between
buildings, open space and so forth; methods of tackling the redevelopment
of central areas; ways of controlling the distribution and bulk of new
buildings while allowing flexibility to the developer; ideas for the layout
of residential areas; studies of the possibilities of area improvement; how
best to route overhead lines; the contribution that can be made by landscaping; and so on. Increasingly of recent years the planning staff have
engaged in practical exercises to test out theories, and in demonstrations;
usually in association with local authorities or new town corporations.
One example of these was the Deeplish study, published in September
1966[13]; a study of the possibilities of area improvement in a part of
Rochdale, which was followed by a pilot scheme of improvement conducted jointly by the Ministry and the Rochdale County Borough Council.
This contributed to the new approach to the improvement of old houses
which emerged in April 1968 as the White Paper 'Old Houses into New
Homes'.[14]

The second major contribution made by the planning staff towards the
development of policies lies in the field of research. The Ministry relies on
them for information about population forecasts; movements of people
and traffic; employment levels and prospects; the characteristics of land;
the whereabouts of mineral reserves; and so on.

(ii) *Supervisory and default powers.* These powers too stem both from
the law and the practice of the Department. The Town and Country
Planning Act 1971 as amended by the Local Government Act 1972
provides examples of both supervisory powers in relation to development planning by local authorities[15] and default powers – that is,
power to act where a local authority fails to – in relation to development control.[16] But it is not just in relation to local authorities that
the Department exercises a supervisory role in planning. The
Countryside Commission, New Town Development Corporations,
town development schemes are all supervised by the Department
by both formal (legal and administrative) and informal means.
Supervision must however be distinguished from enforcement;
what the Department is concerned with is not so much compelling
other bodies to pursue a particular course of conduct as trying to
ensure that a degree of consistency and realism informs the policies
and actions of these bodies. A circular suggesting a particular course

of action, or asking for information about the operation of a policy is as likely to achieve that end as is a decision that such and such *must* take place, although supervision may in the last resort include the latter.[17]

(iii) *Hearing and deciding powers.* The Department exercises these powers in a great many areas in the planning process, and indeed, for many lawyers this is all that planning means: the making of decisions, after a hearing, in respect of applications or objections to applications to do something to land. These are important powers, they occupy a great deal of time and many persons within the Department, but they do not by themselves add up to the planning process. All these powers are derived from the law and, as we will see,[18] must be exercised in accordance with certain rules and principles; they cover both original and appellate functions. The Department exercises an original judging function when the minister decides, after a hearing, whether to confirm a proposal of his own to, for example, designate a site for a new town or a line of a new road or build an office block for a government department, or approve/reject an application for development by a statutory authority, or where an application has been referred direct to him. Appellate judging functions are exercised when the minister decides, after a hearing, to confirm or reverse a decision by a local planning authority on a planning application, or the proposals put forward in a structure plan.

(iv) *Development powers.* The Department of the Environment is very much a development ministry. Unlike the old Ministry of Housing and Local Government, which had only reserve development powers itself and had to work through agencies such as New Town Development Corporations, the Department develops roads, offices, service establishments (which might be a mini new town) and has a close link with other major public developers and public development. The procedure for the exercise of its powers in this area is one of the most contentious subjects of planning and is referred to further in Chapter 5.

(c) Local authorities: structure

The other major decision makers in the planning process are the local authorities. The Local Government Act 1972 established a two-tier structure of local government (with the first tier called the county and the second tier the district) and divided these tiers into metropolitan and non-metropolitan areas, corresponding broadly to areas of continuous and large-scale urbanisation and areas where town and country appeared to be a natural unit of government. The Act created six metropolitan counties: the West Midlands, centred on Birmingham; Greater Manchester, centred on Manchester; Merseyside, centred on Liverpool; South Yorkshire, centred on Sheffield; West Yorkshire, centred on Leeds; and Tyne and Wear, centred on Newcastle and Sunderland. The obvious omission, London, has its own system of local government, established by the London Government Act 1963, upon which, in broad outline, the metropolitan structure was based. Beneath these metropolitan counties there are metropolitan districts, some of them former county boroughs, single-tier authorities, now reduced in status and power. To take the West Midlands as an example, there are seven metropolitan districts,[19] which either consist entirely of, or are based on, the following former county boroughs: Wolverhampton, Walsall, Dudley, Warley, West Bromwich, Birmingham, Solihull and Coventry. All these are substantial towns or cities in their own right.

The position of metropolitan areas may be contrasted with non-metropolitan areas. The Act creates thirty-nine non-metropolitan counties, whose only common characteristic is that they have all for various reasons been deemed not to be metropolitan counties. They range from Cornwall, which retains the exact boundaries of the pre-reorganisation Cornwall, to Hampshire, which includes both Portsmouth and Southampton (two towns which several commentators considered ought to have been the nucleus of an additional metropolitan county.[20] They include Avon made up of Bath, Bristol, and parts of old Somerset and old Gloucestershire; Cleveland, made up of Hartlepool and Teeside (an 'old' county borough which came into existence as a result of a previous local government reorganisation in 1967), and parts of the old counties of Durham and Yorkshire (the latter now no longer exists as one administrative unit); and the Isle of Wight, which now replaces Rutland (absorbed into the new Leicestershire) as the smallest and arguably the least defensible of the new counties.

Below all these counties are districts made up of amalgamations of a host of smaller authorities which used to rejoice in such titles as borough councils, urban district councils and rural district councils. To take Warwickshire (which retains most of its former area) as an example: fifteen former councils, five of them boroughs, eight of them rural districts and two of them urban districts were amalgamated to form five districts, each of them with one council. The Warwick District Council for instance is made up of Leamington Spa, Warwick town (both former boroughs), Kenilworth (formerly an urban district) and Warwick (formerly a rural district).

Finally, parish councils may continue in being, with certain administrative and boundary changes. Some former urban districts and boroughs which lost their councils on being amalgamated into second-tier districts were empowered, prior to their final dissolution, to resolve to resurrect themselves as parish councils from 1 April 1974. Many duly did so, among them Warwick Borough Council, now Warwick Town Council. These parish councils are empowered in turn to resolve that the parish shall have the status of a town and the council thereupon 'shall bear the name of the council of the town'.[21]

(d) Local authorities: functions

'Allocation of Functions in England',
DoE Circular No. 121/72

COUNTY COUNCILS (OUTSIDE METROPOLITAN AREAS) AND METROPOLITAN DISTRICT COUNCILS
Education
Youth employment
Personal social services
Libraries

ALL COUNTY COUNCILS	ALL DISTRICT COUNCILS
Museums and art galleries (a)	*Museums and art galleries (a)*
Housing	*Housing*
Certain reserve powers	Provision
	Management
	Slum clearance
	House and area improvement
Town Development (a)	*Town Development (a)*
Planning	*Planning*
Structure plans	Local plans (c)
Development plan schemes (b)	
Development Control (d)	Development Control (d)
	Advertisement control
Derelict land (a)	Derelict land (a)

National parks
Country parks (a)
Conservation areas (a)
Building preservation notices (a)

Tree preservation (a)
Acquisition and disposal of land
for planning purposes, development or redevelopment (a)

Country parks (a)
Conservation areas (a)
Building preservation notices (a)
Listed building control
Tree preservation (a)
Acquisition and disposal of land
for planning purposes, develop-
ment or redevelopment (a)

Footpaths and Bridleways
Surveys
Creation, diversion and
extinguishment
Orders (a)
Maintenance (e)
Protection (a)
Signposting

Footpaths and Bridleways

Creation, diversion and
extinguishment
Orders (a)

Protection (a)

Transportation
Transport planning
Highways (e)
Traffic
All parking
Public transport (g)
Road safety
Highway lighting
Footway lighting (a)

Transportation

Off-street parking (f)
Public Transport Undertakings
(h)

Footway lighting (a)

Environmental Health
Animal diseases

Environmental Health
Food and safety and hygiene
Communicable disease
Slaughterhouses
Offices, shops and railway
premises (j)
Factories
Home safety
Water and Sewerage (k)

Refuse disposal
Consumer protection (*e.g.* weights
and measures, trade descriptions,
explosives, food and drugs).

Refuse collection
Clean air
Building regulations
Coast protection
Cemeteries and crematoria

Police
Fire

Markets and fairs
Byelaws

Swimming baths (a)
Physical training and

Swimming Baths (a)
Physical training and

recreation (a)
Parks and open spaces (a)
Smallholdings

Airports (a)

recreation (a)
Parks and open spaces (a)
Allotments
Local licensing
Airports (a)

PARISH COUNCILS

Parish councils will, broadly speaking, retain their present functional responsibilities. In relation to the functions listed above they will have powers in connection with:—

Footpaths and Bridleways—
    Maintenance
    Signposting
Transportation—
    Off-street parking (f)
    Footway lighting
Cemeteries and crematoria
Swimming baths
Physical training and recreation
Parks and open spaces
Allotments.

The Act provides parish councils with a right to be consulted about planning applications affecting land in their areas.

NOTES

(a) Concurrent powers exercisable by county and district councils.

(b) In consultation with district councils.

(c) Except in national parks where counties would be responsible. Responsibility for local plans subject to development plan schemes or structure plan.

(d) Primarily a district council function except in the case of a national park or of "county matters" as defined in Schedule 16 to the Act.

(e) District councils may claim maintenance powers for footpaths, bridleways, and urban roads which are neither trunk roads nor classified roads.

(f) In accordance with the county transportation plan.

(g) Metropolitan counties will be Passenger Transport Authorities, non-metropolitan counties have co-ordination functions.

(h) Some non-metropolitan districts under local act powers.

(j) Fire precautions under the Offices, Shops and Railway Premises Act will be a county council responsibility.

(k) Subject to water reorganisation.

(l) Subject to amalgamation schemes.

The allocation of functions, taken in conjunction with the structure of local government, poses obvious questions. Is it really the case that Coventry District and Warwick District both have local plan-making powers? Coventry is formed from an old county borough that used to be empowered to exercise all planning powers without reference to other local authorities. It had a fine reputation as a planning authority, and in fact produced a structure plan before reorganisation took effect. Warwick District on the other hand is an amalgam of local authorities so small that none of them had even delegated development control powers by right, though all of them had some powers of control delegated to them by Warwickshire County Council. The answer lies in the development plan scheme, prepared by the county council in consultation with the district council, and the structure plan, both of which set out who does what in local planning. The details of this will be taken up in Chapter 3; here it is important to realise that, although neither the Local Government Act nor Circular 121/72 specifically say so, function in practice is related to size, capacity and former status, and there are differences between large metropolitan districts and small non-metropolitan ones. Why did the Act not spell these differences out instead of leaving them to be resolved by negotiations between the two tiers – with an ultimate reference to, and decision by, the Secretary of State?

The same comment may be made of development control (the granting or refusal of planning permission) and conservation powers; the latter is a concurrent power, the former is *primarily* a district council power, except where an application relates to a 'county matter' the description of which is, in parts, opaque, as we shall see in Chapter 5. These matters have to be 'arranged' by negotiations between local authorities in accordance with section 101 of the Local Government Act and taking account of ministerial views contained in circulars.[22] Thus here too, there is no common pattern and the exact details of any arrangement depend on a variety of factors: assessment of planning skills, size of second-tier authority, who is in political control of the various authorities, personal contacts and relationships all being relevant.

3. Interrelations between central and local government

Planning does not operate in two watertight compartments whose only link is the formal one of appeal or review by the public local inquiry. That much should have become obvious from the preceding part of this chapter, but since a great deal of the planning process is affected by the relationship between the Department of the Environment and the local authorities, it is necessary to consider this matter as a separate head of concern, and try to raise the issues and spell out the problems inherent in the relationship. A general overview of the relationship is contained in the following extract:

Sharp, *The Ministry of Housing and Local Government*,
pp. 25–33

The Ministry of Housing and Local Government has traditionally left the authorities to take the initiative in public health, housing, planning – though this is now changing; has no inspection system – though sometimes it will look back wistfully to the inspectors of the poor law; and would reject the idea that it should supervise what local authorities are doing. Here it should be noted that the Ministry has to deal with over 1,200 authorities (not counting parish councils) hundreds of them very small, since public health and housing are, in the counties, district council responsibilities. This is a very different matter from dealing mainly with county and county borough councils as other departments do. But primarily the reason for the Ministry's belief that authorities should, largely, be allowed to go their own way has been that the services for which it is responsible have been seen as essentially local services.

While the Ministry ordinarily leaves the initiative to the individual authorities, it frequently exhorts authorities at large to particular policies by manual or circular; and sometimes urges individual authorities to particular action, e.g. to push up their house-building programmes. But the main work of the Ministry, outside the field of local government organization and finance, consists in approving, modifying or disapproving proposals made by authorities; and in a continuous stream of legislation, most of which alters or extends the powers of authorities, or puts new obligations on them. As remarked above, the departmental philosophy is – or at any rate has been – that the services with which it is concerned are local services; that the Ministry should see that authorities have the necessary tools and should help them with advice, often derived from initiatives taken by individual authorities; but that beyond this its main responsibility is to see that authorities keep within the law and do not overstretch either their own or the national economy, and that the objections of rate-payers or others to what an authority proposes are given a fair hearing. This philosophy is, however, changing; and as it has become increasingly apparent that the old local government system is not able to do all that is now needed, so the Ministry has become increasingly interventionist. Intervention because of political disagreement is also becoming more common. . . . Formally speaking, for each local government service the functions of the responsible Minister on the one hand and of the local authorities on the other, and consequently to a large extent the relations between them, are regulated by Acts of Parliament. These functions and relations differ for different services, often for no more than historical reasons; there are, for example, striking differences in these respects between the Housing Acts and the Town and Country Planning Acts. Modern legislation tends increasingly to charge the Minister concerned with the duty to formulate and promote a national policy for the service; to enable him to give directions to the local authorities about their general administration of the service; to require his approval for all courses of action of any consequence which the local authority wishes to promote.

In practice statutory provisions of this kind are less important than they seem. Whatever may be inscribed on the legislative tablets, it is the tradition of British local authorities by and large to do what the Government of the day ask them to do, though they will do it at their own pace and in their own way. Head-on clashes do occur, but have been rare; though recently they have tended to increase. The personal prestige and influence of a Minister in his relations with local authorities is very great – even with authorities controlled by a party of a different political persuasion. For the Ministry, therefore, the theoretical nature of the Minister's powers is much less important than the practical state of its working relations with the authorities. The working relations are, nevertheless, shaped by the various provisions which require authorities to obtain certain consents from the Minister, or give aggrieved individuals a right to bring their objections or appeals to him. . . .

The most powerful weapon in the Ministry's armoury of controls is, nowadays, the loan sanction. No local authority can borrow money without the sanction of the Ministry except by an Act of Parliament. . . . The authorities are not free to decide their own priorities in capital expenditure. . . .

. . . Within these formal relationships are the personal relationships between the Ministry and the authorities. These are, in general, close and friendly. Officers of the Ministry know their opposite numbers in local government and are known to them. Many local government officers make it their business to know their way round the Ministry, whom to go to in order to find out how such and such a proposal is likely to fare, or why something seems to have stuck. Some will just drop in to find out what is cooking. Equally officers of the Ministry can turn to the officers of many local authorities for information, for help, for advice. Many members of local authorities also are well known inside the Ministry and never hesitate to go to the officer concerned with a particular question in order to push a point of view, to demand a quick decision, to talk over a problem. Departmental officers visit local authorities as much as they can, and though inevitably this is done most easily by the regional officers, some headquarters officers manage to make a point of regular visiting. Those who do manage it know that it is invaluable; for they get the feel of local government on its home ground as they never will from a series of deputations to Whitehall. . . .

Local authorities – and their officers – are oddly different in their relationship with the Ministry. Some believe only in going to the top. Some believe in going to the officer whom they know to be handling a particular subject, whatever his or her rank. This is undoubtedly the technique likely to bring the quickest results. After all, one can always go higher if the particular officer cannot – or will not – help; but as most civil servants, like other people, prefer to settle things themselves whenever they can – and usually resent the approach to higher authority until they have been given a chance – this is, in most cases, the way to start. . . . Although they often harry the Ministry through their Member of Parliament and occasionally write most acrimonious letters, face to face authorities almost never fail in friendliness to officers of the Ministry, and are always lavish in their hospitality. However tough the argument, however complete the disagreement, however much in private the authority curses the Ministry or the Ministry deplores the wrong-headedness of the authority, the sense of partnership for better or for worse usually holds firm. It is this which finally governs the relationship between the Ministry and local authorities.

Politics, personalities, pride and prejudice enter into the relationship as much as does law and finance (or lack of it). They must be borne in mind as we turn now to consider what Griffith has called the 'formal means of departmental influence',[23] for they provide the context within which the formal means operate as much as does the law, the most important aspect of which is that local authorities derive their powers from Acts of Parliament and not via delegation from the Department.

There are five means of influence, but concentration will be directed only to three as the other two – hearing and deciding powers and default powers – have been mentioned previously in relation to the functions of central government.

(a) Circulars

J. A. G. Griffith, *Central Departments and Local Authorities* (1966), pp. 54–5

All the departments dealing with local authorities issue annually a considerable number of circulars. These are formal documents normally signed by an Assistant Secretary or an Under-Secretary, and given a reference number. They fulfil however a large number of purposes.

Some circulars are designed simply to obtain information, normally of a statistical nature. Such circulars are invariably accompanied by a form which the local authority are asked to complete and return. An example of this type of circular is Ministry of Housing and Local Government circular 2/60 which sought information from local authorities on the progress of their slum-clearance.

Other circulars explain new Acts or Statutory Instruments. A series of Home Office circulars for instance explained the provisions of the Police Act 1964. Ministry of Education circular 6/62 explained the Standards for Schools Premises Regulations 1959.

Other circulars again introduce departmental publications – pamphlets, bulletins, handbooks, etc. Thus, for instance, Ministry of Housing and Local Government circular 56/64 introduced Planning Bulletin No. 6.

Some circulars are purely informative; an example of this type is Ministry of Housing and Local Government circular 62/64 which gave information about the establishment of a North-West Regional Office.

Finally and most importantly, some circulars give policy or technical guidance to local authorities. The guidance given in such circulars varies from the most vague to the most precise. Such variation occurs not only between the circulars of different departments but also between different circulars of the same department. Thus circular 25/58 of the Ministry of Housing and Local Government gave local authorities clear and detailed guidance on the treatment of planning applications in respect of petrol-filling stations. Yet circular 37/60 of the same Department on the review of development plans gave only broad, generalised advice about allocating more land for development and making more intensive use of existing urban land.

Even where fairly clear policy proposals are set forth the tone of circulars may vary considerably.

Stated thus, circulars seem a useful tool of administration and as the extract indicates they are met with frequently in planning. But what is their precise status in the hierarchy of formal relationships – less than an Act or Regulation but more than a speech? How much more? Consider the following comment by Griffith and contrast it with the extract from the 'JUSTICE' *Report on Compensation for Compulsory Acquisition and Planning Blight*:[24]

[Griffith; p. 55:]

In general so far as local authorities are concerned, guidance contained in circulars is generally followed. It is rare for a local authority to reject a departmental policy, clearly set forth in a circular.

[JUSTICE Report:]

127. Since our Report the Ministry of Housing and Local Government issued Circular 46/70, which listed a further seven descriptions of land in respect of which a blight notice could be served, all of them being land affected by the earlier stages of planning proposals, such as the submission of plans or a compulsory purchase order to the Minister for approval. We welcome this non-statutory extension of the blight notice procedure, particularly as it does succeed in defining the earlier point in time for service of a notice which we found difficult.

128. Two points, however, arise for comment. The first is that the Circular only recommends local authorities to accept blight notices in the non-statutory cases, and in the experience of our members not all local authorities are willing to use their discretionary powers in these cases. The second is that in the experience of our members, government departments are not as ready and willing to sanction loans and make grants in the non-statutory cases of blight notices as they are in the statutory cases, notwithstanding the assurance in Circular 46/70, and in the Department

of the Environment Circular Roads 8/72, that loan sanction and grants would be forthcoming in the non-statutory cases.

129. This to our mind makes it vital that the categories of blight notice in Circular 46/70 should be enacted in legislation as soon as possible. It is not satisfactory to leave them merely as recommendations to local authorities.

What is there to prevent a department from putting a policy into statutory form? Why might a department prefer a circular to legislation? To what extent is a circular legislation?

Shortly after the Second World War, the nature of circulars was considered in several cases arising out of the wartime powers of government to requisition houses to house the homeless or licence certain forms of activity,[25] where, largely because they purported to delegate central government powers to local authorities – subject to certain conditions – they were taken to be a species of delegated legislation (they altered existing law and made new law); but circulars no longer do that. Does this mean that they are no longer to be classified as legislation? Is it a satisfactory answer to the criticism of some lawyers to say that, whatever might have been the rights and wrongs of the administration of house requisitioning, the administration of planning needs a large element of flexibility and guidance from the centre and this can be achieved only by means of the circular and similar non-statutory publications?

It may finally be mentioned that even though circulars on planning have not been classified as delegated legislation it appears that some could be classified as custom and thus eventually 'ripen' into law as the following extract from Lord Wilberforce's speech, in *Coleshill and District Investment Co.* v. *Minister of Housing and Local Government* [1969] 2 All E.R. 525 at p. 538, suggests:

... they (the appellants) derive important support for [their] argument from the Minister's circular No. 67 of 15 February 1949 in which he stated that he was –

> advised that the demolition of a building does not of itself involve development, although of course, it may form part of a building operation or lead to the making of a material change in the use of the land upon which it stood.

The advice referred to may not have been quite correct (I return to this point) but in giving this information to planning authorities, the Minister was undoubtedly reflecting a common-sense and accepted opinion as to the general nature of development. I accept, of course, that, as an interpretation of the Act of 1947 under which it was issued, the circular has no legal status, but it acquired vitality and strength when, through the years, it passed, as it certainly did, into planning practice and textbooks, was acted on, as it certainly was, in planning decisions, and when the Act of 1962 (and I may add the Town and Country Planning Act 1968) maintained the same definition of 'development' under which it was issued.

Is Circular 67/49 as amended by Lord Wilberforce now law? If yes, in what way has its effect on planning practice changed; if no, how can it become law?

(b) Consultation

Consultation is implicit in much of what has been said in this chapter, both in terms of formal and informal relationships, but it must be stressed here for two reasons. First, there are, in some places, statutory requirements that before exercising certain powers, the Minister must consult with local authorities or some other planning body. Thus, before exercising his default powers under the Town and Country Planning Act, he must consult with the local planning authority concerned,[26] as likewise must he before he gives a direction to the authority to serve a listed building enforcement notice.[27] Secondly, as Wade has said, 'Consultation before rule-making, though not usually required by law is one of the major industries of government.'[28] To which might be added: before many other aspects of government as well. Thus it is not just regulations about structure planning on which consultation takes place but circulars too are sometimes sent round in draft; for instance, before Circular 52/72 on Publicity and Public Participation in Development Planning was issued, it was sent round a variety of organisations for their comments some nine months before it was officially published. So strong was the reaction of some organisations to the draft, that, contrary to custom, they published extracts from and commented on it 'in the hope that informed opinion can be rallied in sufficient strength to make the government think again'.[29] Griffith reports that in respect of the promotion of local Bills by local authorities (many of which seek, *inter alia*, to increase local authorities' planning or development powers), 'the officials of the Ministry of Housing and Local Government are in frequent communication with the promoters of Bills, and the influence which they exercise, says Erskine May, both by such consultation and by reports to Parliament serves to ensure protection of Crown or public rights and the observance of Public Acts governing any matter to which a Bill relates.'[30]

In addition to the consultation that takes place as a prelude to a specific set of regulations or a specific circular, in which the draft regulation or circular would be sent round, there is also the practice of sending round consultation papers on various projected legislative reforms; for instance, prior to the publication of the Water Re-organisation Bill in early 1973, local authorities were inundated with consultation papers on the subject. Consultation, in short, has become much more than an informal way of getting together 'to find out what is cooking';[31] it is, on both legal[32] and constitutional conventional grounds, a formal means of departmental influence, but unlike other formal means, and herein lies its importance, it generates a two-way flow of influence from the department to the local authority and vice versa. Of all the formal channels of influence and communication that exist, this is the one most susceptible to alteration and possibly expansion by new modes of public participation, for it is already the administration's bow in that direction.

(c) Adjudicatory functions between local authorities

This has not hitherto been a major means of influence in the planning process. Although the Department might find itself having to decide, on a planning appeal or in respect of a development plan, between the views of two authorities, this is part of its general deciding powers and not a special power conferred upon it to sort out the rival claims of two authorities to do or not to do a particular thing. However, the Local Government Act 1972 has conferred adjudicatory functions on the Department in respect of the production of development plan schemes,[33] which is perhaps sufficient commentary on the difficult and delicate task which such a scheme is designed to achieve, *viz.* the allocation by a county council of local plan-making functions between it and the various district councils beneath it. Here too, as in the hearing and deciding function, the presence of a formal power gives considerable informal leverage to the Department. This is exercised both by circular and through informal meetings.

4. Decision making: an introduction

It is easy to underestimate the complexity of the process of decision making. For lawyers the typical decision-making process is the judicial decision, publicly made after carefully phrased oral and written submissions, and based on a finding of the 'facts' of the case, followed by the application of law to those facts. We may be aware that beneath the surface, things are not quite what they seem, but apart from discussions of the finer points of precedent, we rarely explore beneath the surface. Yet we must try to do so in this book, because the typical decision-making process in planning takes place not in a court, but in a local authority committee or a department, and involves the interaction of experts with experts, experts with amateurs, amateurs with amateurs, and the bringing to bear of a host of considerations, both relevant and irrelevant, all of which we must try to take account of in assessing the efficacy of the planning process. The comments which follow are no more than the barest introduction to administrative decision making, designed to highlight the following points:

(a) Making a decision is not something which takes place in a short space of time, in an afternoon committee meeting for instance. Much evidence shows that the typical decision is made by a gradual process of whittling down alternatives, of perceiving issues with greater clarity, of taking up positions from a variety of motives, not all of them rational, or possibly respectable, and of responding to outside pressures over a period of time. Thus the people who appear to the public as being those who have 'taken the decision' are almost always at the end of a chain of lesser decisions which have crucially shaped the final decision. Decisions, in other words, are not and cannot be taken in isolation from what has gone before, or what is likely to transpire, from the values of the decision makers, and from what Simon has called organisational loyalties,[34] that is the values of the group or organisation to which the decision makers belong. Indeed as Brown emphasises, 'Decisions in large organisations belong to the organisation as a whole and are not attributable to any one individual. . . . The negotiations between individuals, the communication system, the formal rules – these and other factors interact to produce the decisions of the organisation.'[35]

(b) Both civil servants in a department and officers in a local authority are engaged in a process in which clear lines between policy and administration, and between policy making and fact finding are not easy to perceive. Nor are rules about the responsibility of ministers or local councillors for decisions they have taken clear to perceive, let alone base controlling devices or reforms of organisational structures on. The literature on decision making stresses the difficulty of pin-pointing who makes decisions, yet the theory of control over the administration is that some*one* can and must be held responsible for decisions that are taken, otherwise people at large will cease to have any say in their daily lives or any influence over the decisions that affect them. Part of the drive behind public participation in planning and in other fields is precisely because there is a general *feeling* that traditional methods of control of administrative decision making are less effective than of old at a time when more and more vital decisions are being taken which will affect our future. Is the problem that the controlling devices have failed to increase in scope and sophistication as fast as decision-making processes, or that potential controllers, and the public at large, are too easily mesmerised by the jargon of decision makers into believing that decisions are in some way inevitable and therefore uncontrollable?

(c) Taking this last point further, what is the role of the Minister and local councillor in the typical administrative decision-making process? How realistic is it to talk of ministerial responsibility for planning decisions when the minor decisions never reach the Minister, and the Minister can never hope to see more than a part of the information on the major ones before he announces 'his' decision? If anything, it is more difficult to see the role of the local councillor in decision making. Friend and Jessop's study of decision making in Coventry[36] provides one of the clearest and most sympathetic accounts of local authority decision making that has been produced for some time, and that certainly makes a case out for the influence of councillors on decisions and the manner in which they are reached, but the general conclusions of the Maud Report on the Management of Local Government are less sanguine.[37] My own view, based admittedly on very little experience[38], is that one can exaggerate the helplessness of the average councillor.[39] However, there is no substitute for local councillors (and ministers for that matter) becoming familiar with a particular field, and then being prepared to spend a great deal of time on the major issues and problems in that field, and their effect on the councillors' locality so that they can hold their own with the officers. This is a counsel of perfection – it may even be thought rather naïve – and unlikely to be realised except in a very small number of cases, but at least it will serve as an antidote to the 'Bains' philosophy which is sweeping local government:[40] that a reorganisation of the management structure of local authorities to take account of the corporate approach to their activities is the key to more effective and accountable local government. Arguably, the corporate management approach to government was behind the reforms that led to the DoE; while that might result in a more co-ordinated approach by the administration to the problem of the cities, will it lead to more accountability to Parliament and the electorate at large?

(d) The last point to bear in mind arises not so much from the readings that follow as from what has gone before. We must add to our awareness of the general complexities of decision making our awareness that in planning, as in other spheres of government, particular legal constraints and constitutional conventions and practices exist and have to be followed; some reforms might not be possible because they conflict with the law or the conventions, neither of which can, as a matter of practical politics, be altered; some reforms might be introduced which are thought to be necessary politically, but do not always make sense from the point of view of the student of decision making. Law and politics in short affect the procedures of planning as much as they do the substance; an obvious point, but one that is sometimes overlooked by lawyers and planners alike.

5. Public participation

(a) What and why?

A preliminary problem of public participation is that the phrase is misleading in so far as it suggests that all that has to be done is to inject into the decision-making process an element of general citizen involvement. The injection of a new element into the decision-making process is likely to be successful only if it is realised that the whole process will change, whether it is planned to change or not. The cause of public participation has suffered from the fact that this point has either not been seen or has been seen, only too clearly by administrators, politicians and planners. In the first case, enthusiastic acceptance of public participation runs the risk of turning sour as the total process threatens to change out of recognition or get out of hand. In the second, there is great reluctance to concede the case for public participation because of the changes it is feared it will bring about; alternatively, some arrangement or scheme called public participation is offered to the public who discover, too late, that the scheme has been devised to leave the total decision- and plan-making process virtually unaltered (here it is the public who turn sour on public participation). The main aim of this section is to explore the concept of public participation to see what it can involve, what it is thought to involve and what its implications and drawbacks are.

Public participation in planning is part of a much wider phenomenon covering regional devolution, industrial relations, management, local government in general, university government, arguably even the women's liberation movement; in all these contexts, people have been seeking a greater say and greater control over decisions that affect their immediate environment. If debate has appeared in the past few years to centre round participation in planning, this is in part because the effects of decisions about the physical environment are much more obvious to everybody and therefore more likely to stimulate an urge to object. It may also be in part because the terminology of participation has not hitherto been applied to such matters as trade unionists' desires to share in management, council tenants' associations' desire to share in housing management, or the Scottish Nationalists' desire for a measure of home rule for Scotland. They are however all born of the same feeling that as management or administration covers a wider and wider field and becomes more and more complex, as the bureaucracy grows, so the traditional means of making one's views felt – periodic elections, works or liaison committees, informal contacts between 'us' and 'them' (MPs, local councillors, public officials, management, professors) – are increasingly inadequate and need to be supplemented or replaced by new ideas and new structures, which will bring about more direct links or confrontations between governed and governors, planned and planners.

The materials which follow discuss these issues from widely differing angles. They illustrate the intensity of the debate on the subject (there is in fact no issue in planning which has generated such feeling both among planners and among commentators). The only way the merit of differing viewpoints can be adequately assessed is by considering examples of public participation in planning, and these appear throughout the book. In considering both the general discussions and the specific examples, certain problems and questions about public participation need to be borne in mind.

1. First and foremost, since public participation is directed mainly at the local level of decision making, the relationship between it and local authorities, and specifically local councillors' reactions to it, must be discussed. The Skeffington Report saw this as one of the

most important issues to be faced in public participation; Heap, since he first spoke out against public participation,[41] has consistently argued that it is incompatible with traditional local democracy. There is no doubt that a substantial measure of opposition to public participation comes from local councillors; at the conference at which Heap first spoke out there was substantial support for the Chairman of the Sheffield Planning Committee when he said that participation would provide a platform for congenital objectors, that people wanted to know what was happening but they did not wish to participate.[42] At a private meeting I attended to discuss the state of public participation in relation to one local authority's structure plan, it was said by an official that it was the councillors who had cut down the original scheme for public participation as being too long drawn out.

A different, more sophisticated and more constructive, analysis of the role of the local authority in an age of public participation is suggested by W. Hampton:[43]

'Little Men in Big Societies', (1971) *J.R.T.P.I.*,
168–170

The growth in scale of the functions provided locally is bringing difficulties for traditional administrative methods and hesitations about the workings of local democracy. Local authorities have ceased to be a method, indeed they have become part of the problem, of finding 'democratic ways of living for little men in big societies. . . .'

Participatory institutions cannot be developed unless all sides recognise that conflicts of interest may legitimately arise . . . planners must accept suggestions that upset the aesthetic simplicity of their drawings; and councillors must accept that not everyone who is not for them is necessarily against them. Conflict must be understood more frequently as Hegelian dialetic leading to better forms of the truth rather than a contest which only one side can win. . . .

Council members find it difficult to accept conflicts of this kind even though the issues are seldom related to party politics. . . .

If councillors and people are to come together in developing forms of democratic involvement, then representation and participation must cease to be mutually exclusive; the process might be considered in three stages. First, in the planning and development of policy, people must be encouraged to participate with their elected representatives in open and continuous discussion. The secrecy and mystique surrounding public decision-making, both at local and national level, is frequently a convenience rather than a necessity. Secondly, there comes a time when choices have to be made. These are properly the concern of the elected representatives; only the ballot box can confer the authority to make judgements on behalf of others. Councillors need, however, to distinguish between decisions involving choices which only they should make, and decisions which can be left to the people concerned. Judgements should not be made on behalf of others unless good reason exists. This brings us to the third stage. The *implementation* of policy may involve public participation. Once the representative body has allocated resources to particular needs, such as the provision of adult education in a given area or the improvement of a neighbourhood environment, then local people may participate in the using of these resources. . . . There is no need for council members to impose their view of the best way to proceed in matters only affecting a group capable of acting for themselves. The representative body could act much more frequently through voluntary organisations or neighbourhood committees. . . .

An increase in the opportunities for local participation will undoubtedly place an unaccustomed burden upon local authority officials thus increasing costs as more staff are employed. Such additional costs should be viewed against both the total sums spent by local authorities and the likely beneficial consequences. Democratic institutions are presumably concerned to implement policies acceptable to the people they serve: expense incurred in discovering the general consensus is surely worthwhile. . . .

The question that immediately arises is whether the reorganised local government structure and more particularly a 'Bains'[44] type management structure is apt to meet the problems as outlined above. Reorganisation has meant bigger units. As a consequence, the Bains Report recommends that more decision making be devolved onto officers, that there be fewer small sub-committees of councillors and less constant reporting back by officers to committees. How is public participation to be reconciled with that? The problem that emerges is that the bigger the unit of management or government, the more the need to supplement the role and work of the councillor, yet the less effective will any such supplementation be, unless it works in close co-operation with councillors. The challenge then is for those outside and those inside the local authority to realise that they are on the same side – that of democratic accountability for decisions – and for those inside the local authority – the councillors – to realise that traditional methods of accountability, such as elections, have not been and are not sufficient either to satisfy many people or to stop grave abuse of power.

2. Public participation is a blanket phrase applied to decisions of many different types. To take an obvious example: what is involved in public participation in relation to the siting of the third London airport is very different from what is involved in public participa-

tion in relation to the siting of an adult male probation hostel in Leamington Spa.[45] In each case the aim is to influence the decision makers, but the different scale of the two decisions and the level at which they are taken inevitably mean that different methods of public participation are needed. Some discussions of public participation have tended to overlook this fact.

Part of the reason for this may be the difficulty of constructing some kind of classification of decisions beyond the statutory classification of development plans and planning applications, which latter could be further sub-divided into 'ordinary' planning applications and those by government departments and statutory undertakers. This is at least a start in so far as it indicates that the scale of the decision is different in the three cases, but what is needed is a more sophisticated breakdown of decisions, which indicate where the crucial points are in the decision-making process in respect of a range of different decisions, for public participation to be effective, and the kinds of considerations that should be taken into account by those wishing to engage in public participation.

To illustrate this point, we can contrast three different decisions: to build a third London airport; to approve the Warwickshire Structure Plan, and to construct a series of roads in and around York. In each case the decision is one for a Minister; and in each case it would be widely acknowledged that to confine one's participation efforts to lobbying the Minister would be misguided, more so in the last two than in the first. But where should one direct one's efforts if not at the Minister? And what kind of efforts should they be? In the case of the third London airport, many pressure groups clearly thought that a maximum effort was needed at the Roskill Inquiry;[46] were they right? Once the government had taken the decision to site the airport at Maplin Sands and to introduce a Bill to provide for that into Parliament, the scene of action obviously shifted to Parliament. But what sort of action, and directed to whom? Was it a sound tactical move to petition against the Bill in the House of Commons,[47] so obtaining a reference to a select committee? Was the object to kill, to delay or to kill by delay?

Clearly, none of these tactics is relevant in the other two decisions. In the case of the Warwickshire Structure Plan, one might argue that there are two crucial points in the decision-making process:[48] the opportunity to comment on the draft structure plan, before the county council finally approve it; and the opportunity to comment on the final plan in order to lay a claim to participate in the public examination of the plan before a panel appointed by the DoE. But should one use both opportunities? To have had points considered and rejected by the county council might weaken their merit before the panel; yet one has no right to appear before the panel, so that a decision not to argue one's case at the draft plan stage might mean that it is never fully presented. What other factors should be taken into account? Should one have regard to the power of the DoE to insist on changes if it is convinced of a participator's case, or to the fact that the county planners might well be much more vehement in the defence of their plan at a public examination before outsiders, and less willing to make concessions, than might be the case at a more informal meeting at the draft plan stage?

In the case of the York roads controversy, a crucial difference from the preceding case is that the issue was much more specific and was debated in the more legalistic forum of a public inquiry. What difference in practice should that have made to the process of participation and objection? Should objectors have become more or less obdurate, have concentrated all their efforts on getting up a first-class case for the public inquiry or divided them between that and attempting to win over more local support? In other words, how much time, money and effort should be spent on quality and how much on quantity of objection?

These questions are not exhaustive but they and the issues raised by the materials are aimed at making the point that a commitment to public participation, a belief in its desirability, is not enough on its own to bring about effective public participation. Just as the decision-making process is complex, largely because the substantive matter that has to be decided is only one of the matters to which the decision maker has to have regard, so the public participation process is immensely complex because of the wide variety of matters that has to be taken into account by the participators.

3. As Hampton stresses, public participation involves conflicts of interest about the allocation of scarce resources. This is a point which tends to get glossed over in official publications about participation and is easy to lose sight of when one is immersed in the details of development plans and planning applications. It is however crucial in any discussion of the scope, efficacy and future of participation as Damer and Hague[49] emphasise. The way in which

decisions are made and the extent to which different interest groups are allowed to participate in and influence them have as much effect on the ultimate decision as any set of value judgements or political principles which are usually thought of as being decisive. In setting up a system of public participation, therefore, it is as well to be aware that one might also be ensuring that decisions about the allocation of resources go in one rather than another direction. Even something as apparently straightforward as where to hold a public meeting to discuss a draft structure plan or a major planning application can determine the sort of people who will come to the meeting and thus the reaction to the plan or application. It is perfectly natural for there to be political differences about public participation, once it is seen as being part of the wider issue of the allocation of resources; and here, as in other areas of planning, alleged 'technical considerations'[50] put forward to influence the amount or nature of public participation should be treated with considerable reserve. Indeed, one may go further and ask: to what extent does the increasing interest shown by planners in mathematical modelling, systems analysis, cost-benefit analysis and the like, all of which contribute to complicated-looking plans, serve an additional function of playing down the possible role of public participation (and of councillors) in planning?

4. A major criticism of public participation is that it leads to delay: delay in approving plans leads to their becoming out of date before they are approved; delay in approving a planning application increases the costs of development; both matters contribute to the bad reputation of the planning process. This is a beguiling rather than a conclusive criticism: for every developer who can be found complaining about delay, there is a secretary or member of an amenity group to be found complaining about attempts to push developments through without adequate time being given for consultation. No research has been done to find out which minority position more nearly accords with any general view on the planning process, assuming such a general view to exist. Short of ministerial approval of a plan coming the day after a local authority approves it, and that approval coming the day after the planners 'finish' it, any plan when finally approved runs the risk of being out of date to some extent.

More important however is the fact that the criticism assumes that the two questions – 'How can maximum acceptance be gained for the plan?' and 'How can the plan be put through the machine quickly?' – are opposed to each other. Are they? Can they not be both subsumed under the more general question: 'How can we, the planners, ensure that a plan is forthcoming which, because it respects people's ideas, values and views, gains wide and ready acceptance and does not have to be fought through a succession of committees, public examinations and ministerial conferences?'? Finally, on delay and the costs thereof, we must keep a sense of perspective: a plan, and even more directly a major development, represents a commitment of resources and a decision to alter the physical environment, probably permanently; delay means, as often as not, more information and a better opportunity to consider what decision to take. Is it not possible that even if delay does put up the cost of some development, it will also contribute to stopping other costly and mistaken development, and that in any event the cost of delay is only a very small part of the total cost of a development, as likewise is the cost of public participation in relation to the total cost of preparing a development plan?

People and Planning, The Skeffington[51] Report, (MHLG 1969: HMSO)

10 The advantages that flow from involvement of the public have been recognised by several local planning authorities whose work has, to some extent, anticipated the requirements of the Town and Country Planning Act 1968. That being so, it may be asked why there has been so little to show from past efforts and why, generally, the public has made so little impact on the content of plans. The reasons vary from place to place; but two general points emerge. They are:

(i) First, most authorities have been far more successful in informing the public than in involving them. Publicity – the first step – is comparatively easy. To secure effective participation is much more difficult.

(ii) Secondly, some of the authorities who have made intensive efforts to publicise their proposals have done so when those proposals were almost cut and dried. At that stage, those who have prepared the plan are deeply committed to it. There is a strong disinclination to alter proposals which have been taken so far; but from the public's point of view the opportunity to comment has come so late that it can only be an opportunity to object. The authority are then regarded more as an antagonist than as the representative of the community and what was started in good will has ended in acrimony.

11 Where information comes too late and without preliminary public discussion there is the likelihood of frustration and hostility. It may be that the plan produced is the one best suited to the needs of the community

but the reasons for decisions do not emerge, nor are people told why superficially attractive alternatives have been put aside. This failure to communicate has meant that the preparation of a plan, instead of being a bridge between the authority and the public, has become a barrier, reinforcing the separation that springs up so easily between the 'them' of authority and the 'us' of the public.

12 Often, too, organisations and individuals have made things worse when a plan has appeared because their approach has been too narrow and indiscriminately hostile. Problems affecting the whole of their community, and even extending beyond it, have been regarded in the light of sectional and local interests. Change has been regarded as desirable only if it occurs elsewhere or if it is of direct benefit to the interests they represent. . . .

18 The question of the cost in time and money which our proposals will involve has always been to the forefront in our discussions. We have never forgotten that planning is a means and not an end; and that its purpose is to set the framework within which houses, roads and community services can be provided at the right time and in the right place. Planning is not just a theoretical exercise that can proceed regardless of time; and greater public involvement will make demands on money and staff. But these are costs which must be accepted if the citizen is to be fully involved in democratic planning.

19 The objective is clear – to establish and maintain a better understanding between the public and the planning authority which will be of benefit to both. But the problem is how, in some areas, to strengthen, and, in others, to promote the new attitudes, the new ways of thinking, the new outlook upon which that understanding is founded. . . .

24 We have referred to some of the difficulties attendant upon public participation, but the expenditure of time and effort will be justified if it produces an understanding, co-operative public and planning better geared to public opinion. If objections can be anticipated or eliminated the formal stage of public inquiry will be smoother, less contentious and speedier.

25 Finally, we would emphasize that public involvement at the formative stage in the making of a plan in no way diminishes the responsibility of the elected representatives to make the final decision about the content of a plan. They, too, must be given the responsibility for deciding the best methods and timing of participation activities in their area. It is for this reason that we suggest a wide variety of methods on which we hope authorities will draw when undertaking this vital work. . . .

32 Public participation – the matter we are concerned with in our report – is the process that is to take place when plans are being prepared. It is something *additional* to the formal consultations that the planning authority undertake with other bodies directly concerned (for example, with district councils); and it is *additional* to the statutory rights of objection to a plan that has been prepared and placed on deposit. . . .

41 Planning is only one of the services that a local authority provide and it would be unreasonable to expect the public to see it as an entity in itself.

Services like education, social welfare, housing and refuse collection may have to be administered separately but they operate in an environment which people perceive as a whole. Participation, when plans are being prepared, has to be seen in this wider context; it will necessarily involve consideration of the quality of the whole environment and of any planned changes in it. Indeed public participation would be little more than an artificial abstraction if it became identified solely with planning procedures rather than with the broadest interests of people. The corollary of this is that all members of the local planning authority are involved and that the planning department must have the support of other departments in their participation activities. The experience of Coventry, to mention just one authority, was that the whole range of community interests was discussed when public meetings about their development plan proposals were held. All comments were noted and sent to the relevant department for action. This comprehensive involvement of the authority, which recognises that development plans affect the whole life of the area, is the only basis on which participation can sensibly proceed. . . .

43 The success of participation depends largely upon the local authority member. New responsibilities and opportunities will be thrust upon him. He may need to be supported by officers with planning, sociological, administrative and publicity expertise but he is the man at the heart of the activity. Participation adds to the importance of the office he holds and to the value of time and effort spent in holding it.

44 It would be easy to underestimate the pressures on the local authority member which pull him away from his constituency. He is elected to represent a comparatively small number of people, but as soon as he becomes a member of a council he has to think in terms of the council and its activities as a whole as well as being the representative of those who have elected him. . . .

45 . . . Yet despite those pressures the elected member should remain the link between the authority and the people he represents. . . .

46 Officers of the planning authority – mainly those of the planning department but supported by the others involved – will have a formidable task in carrying out the programme of public meetings and discussions with groups that will promote public participation. This must, however, be regarded as part of the job of any planning officer and not as an unwelcome accretion. We are concerned that these new responsibilities, which will often mean evening work additional to that which many officers already accept so willingly, should not become a grinding burden. This work should, therefore, be taken into account in assessing the weight of the officer's job.

47 We do not consider that a special branch should be set up within the planning department to deal solely with participation. Most of the work on participation will be borne by senior staff but it will permeate everyone's work. . . .

54 It may be argued that the public as a whole will never be sufficiently interested in planning to justify the effort required to involve them. One answer to this is the general point that educating people to participate in

the making of development plans is part of the wider problem of educating them to participate in local government affairs as a whole. It is a point of entry to civic matters as a whole. But, quite apart from this argument, there is clear evidence that many people feel dissatisfied because they have been unable to influence the work of their local planning authority. There is an active and willing audience waiting for authorities who encourage participation, and a particularly vigorous response may be expected when local plans are being prepared. . . .

57 People should not regard their role as a passive one in which they merely receive proposals and comment on them. They should be ready to give practical assistance in the creation of opportunities to participate, bringing to people's attention the proposals that will condition a town's future, and in helping others to give expression to their views when policies are being formulated. . . .

91 It was suggested to us frequently that the process of participation would be improved if special statutory rights of consultation were given to certain kinds of voluntary organisations. . . .

92 The arguments for giving special rights to bodies whose interest is specially concerned with the environment and physical planning are, at first sight, attractive. Certainly, many have shown themselves vigorous, well organised and possessing considerable expertise – and the increase in numbers throughout the country has been quite remarkable. Much as we admire the work of such groups, we think that it would be wrong to give statutory recognition to any organisation which represents only one of the multiplicity of interests affected by a plan. That does not mean that they will not be informed; they should be as soon as possible. There is, of course, the obligation upon the authority to provide adequate publicity and consider representations as laid down in the Act, but no one group should be in a privileged position. . . .

101 It would be unreasonable to expect members and officers of local planning authorities to acquire highly specialised skills in techniques of communication, but some knowledge and understanding of them is desirable. The best results from efforts to publicise planning proposals will be obtained where the member and officer can draw on the support and expertise of an information officer or, on occasions, on the advice of a consultant. . . . Their function will be to see that information is pub-licised in a way that is intelligible and stimulates comment. . . .

205 Two conflicting factors stand out in the consideration of the amount of time to be spent on participation activities; they are the need for organisa-tions to be given adequate time to consider material and the need to ensure that endless discussion does not frustrate action.

206 It is easy to underestimate the time that may be needed for a local organisation to consider planning proposals. The officers of most societies cannot work full-time on voluntary activities. Adequate notice has to be given to convene a meeting and time allowed for marshalling a corporate view before transmitting it to the authority. For some bodies even longer may be necessary, especially if a consensus of opinion cannot be obtained by way of a general meeting; for example, those organisations interested

in social welfare may be able to sound out views only by means of individual interviews. Local planning authorities should therefore allow as much time as possible when public comment is invited.

207 There is, however, another side to the coin. Any development plan is a sterile document until action is taken to implement its proposals. The public should be ready to recognise the need for steady progress when plans are being prepared, bearing in mind that there will be opportunities for formal objection when the final version of the plan is deposited and before it is finally approved by the Minister or adopted by the planning authority. . . .

210 When a plan shows that land or property is likely to be needed for future use by a public authority possessing powers of compulsory purchase, its value may be greatly affected. In extreme cases, it may be rendered unsaleable, and hardship may be caused to those who need to sell for personal or other reasons. . . . The danger we have to face is that widespread publicity for proposals at this stage may have a serious blighting effect on property. . . .

212 There is thus a conflict between, on the one hand, the desirability of giving full publicity at an early stage to proposals the planning authority are considering, so as to stimulate informed public discussion and, on the other hand, the need to avoid causing hardship to individuals by the casting of blight over land or property that may not be acquired for many years or, indeed, at all.

Sir Desmond Heap,[52] 'Ambience and environment –
the shape of things to be' (1973) *J.P.L.*, 201–15,
pp. 209–13

. . . so far as *the law* goes the only need and requirement for citizen participation is that set out in Part II of the 1971 Act. That Part applies only to the making and bringing into operation of development plans. In other words, *so far as the law is concerned* citizen participation has nothing whatever to do with the day-to-day control of development by the granting or the withholding of planning permissions. . . .

I myself have always had doubts about this business of citizen participation in the sophisticated world of town planning control. In saying this I am well aware that I am in danger of advocating town planning *by experts*. Well, if I am, I make bold to ask; and what is wrong with that? The training of a town planner takes years and years like the training of any other professional person and it must come as a bit of a bore to him now to learn that he must, at all times and in all places, when seeking to exercise his expertise, be constantly asking John Citizen about what he, the planner, ought to be adoing of.

One reason why I have always had my doubts about the principle of citizen participation is that it seems to me to strike at the very roots of elective democracy. If we do need to have this new idea, then surely this must indicate a breakdown in the customary system of democratic government by elected representatives.

If this system has any value at all, then the elected representatives having been elected, should, in my view, be allowed to get on with the job. Citizen participation substitutes, or tends to substitute, for the decision of the elected representative the decisions of the man in the street – the woman on the Clapham bus – and all this leads *not* to government by elected representatives but to government by plebiscite.

Another argument against citizen participation is the fact that it is nearly always negative in effect. At any Town Planning Inquiry which I myself have attended (and I must have attended at least three or four by now), I have never yet found any citizen or citizen group that ever came forward to advance the case of the local authority. Whenever these high-minded, talkative groups of citizens do turn up at an Inquiry, it is usually to criticise, in a completely negative fashion, whatever it is the planning authority seeks to do. On the law of averages the planning authority can't be wrong every time.

Another reason I doubt the validity of citizen participation is that it leads increasingly to what I would call 'town planning control by the angry neighbour'. I think it better that town planning control should be left in the hands of what can rightly be described as a relatively impartial body, namely, the planning committee of the local government authority charged by statute with the duty of exercising planning control.

One of the worst things about citizen participation is that the people participating are frequently ill informed about what is going on; they are actuated by a desire to see to it that whilst we have town planning control it must never be town planning control for them but always for somebody else. In the outcome, they frequently fail to get what they are advocating. In other words, town planning control, notwithstanding the efforts of citizen participation does often come out properly and fittingly on top. This having occurred, participating citizens are left with a sense, and sometimes a bitter sense, of frustration and the feeling that they have not had a fair deal. All this; and this is the worst of it, tends to lead to a division, which gets deeper and deeper, between the private citizen on the one hand and his representative on the elected local council on the other hand. . . .

I hope that when John Citizen comes forward to 'put in his oar' in the early formative stages of the new development plans (that is to say, at the time when the local planning authority's views have not finally frozen into position), John Citizen will come forward not to hinder that planning process but *to ease it on its way*, not only in his own particular, personal interest, but in the interest of all those other John Citizens around him. It is significant that the new town planning procedures provide an opportunity for John Citizen to make what are called *'representations'* (*i.e.* things which are very different from *'objections'*) about proposals which a local planning authority has it in mind to insert in its new structure plan or new local plan. John Citizen can thus come along to support the plan and not merely to object to it. . . .

If the elected representative is to be constantly consulting his electors to see what they would like him to do – this can only be regarded as the

break-down of elective democracy. After all the elected representative
has (or should have) many things to weigh in the balance – the sectional
interest of those who elected him is only one.

Seán Damer[53] and Cliff Hague,[54] 'Public
participation in planning: a review'[55] (1971)
42 *T.P.R.*, 212-32

It is our contention that the growth of the idea of public participation
in planning in this country can be explained with reference to five inter-
related factors. These are: (i) the example of American planning experience; (ii) the social ethic of planning; (iii) a general growth of interest in
participatory rather than representative democracy; (iv) a history of
bottle-necks and hold-ups in the administrative processing of plans;
(v) a growth of public interest in the urban environment. . . .

PARTICIPATION AS EDUCATION

The implications behind much of the Report[56] are that planning is an
apolitical activity operating in a culturally and politically homogeneous
society. Perhaps the most revealing comment in the whole Report is one
which deals not with participation as such, but with planning:

We have never forgotten that planning is a means and not an end;
and that its purpose is to set the framework within which houses, roads,
and community services can be provided at the right time and in the
right place.

Now as the planners are trying to provide the various facilities 'at the
right time and in the right place', it seems difficult for them to comprehend why there should be any conflict between themselves and the
public or between different sectors of the public. After all, nobody could
seriously argue that these facilities should be provided in 'the wrong
place at the wrong time'. Thus the only credible source of conflict
between planners and the public must lie in the latter's ignorance of
planning matters, and it is the fervent hope of Skeffington that such
ignorance can be eradicated by the education of the public through
participation and a sympathetic mass-media. Two themes which emerge
strongly from Skeffington are this need to educate the public, and
secondly an optimistic assessment of the likely pay-off from the practice
of participation. . . . It would be apposite at this juncture to recall a
comment of Herbert Gans: 'When people reject a planner's idea, it is
rarely because they are stupid or evil but because they have different
life-styles and goals'. . . . The Report is adamant that '. . . the responsibility for preparing a plan is, and must remain, the responsibility of the
local planning authority'. (para. 56). What the game is all about is
public relations – public relations for the planning profession. The purpose of public participation in planning is to make life easier for the
planners.

It is significant that the type of planning being taught in contemporary departments of town planning does not now correspond with the simpliste model offered by Skeffington. In modern departments, planning is generally perceived as a decision-making process, in which values play a crucial part. . . .

The Political Context of Planning
The fact that planning operates in a political context was raised by Skeffington, if not discussed; paragraph 45 (ii) states, realistically enough: 'It would be naïve to expect planning issues to be decided outside the political arena'. True, and while inexcusable that this obvious truth was not pursued further, there is something about the political nature of planning which is of much greater importance. Much of planning activity has to do with the distribution of scarce urban resources and facilities – albeit houses, open space, or whatever. In this context, planning is involved in a power struggle; this power is not just to do with the zoning of land, it has also to do with the fact that certain uses of land can enhance or constrain people's life-chances. As Ray Pahl has put it, 'planners are important gatekeepers in the urban system; their professional ideology has a great deal of influence in shaping the availability of resources in the city – resources which are frequently in short supply and over which there is a considerable amount of public conflict between the "have's" and the "have-nots", resources which can add a spatial dimension to the misery of those already deprived socially'. In such a situation it is positively obscurantist to talk about facilities being provided 'in the right place at the right time', or of educating the public to appreciate that the ideals of planners should really be its ideals also.

This very British view that the values subsumed in any plan must be public interest values, of which the planners are special guardians, has been widely criticised in the last decade, particularly by such writers as Webber and Davidoff. But the traditional notion is still esconced in British local authority planning, probably because of the well-established 'responsibility' ethic which is attached to local government in this country. Those who adhere to this stance fail to realize the realpolitik of the pluralistic society in which we live – that is, a society comprising a multitude of social groups having different, competing, and not infrequently conflicting sets of values. This view of society is neither cynical nor pessimistic; it clearly has some empirical reference, and it also allows for a comprehension of social change. . . . our argument has been that participation in planning is seen as a means to facilitate the goal of the speedy implementation of plans. Its proposals are, then, undemocratic in our understanding of that term. . . .

The Parameters of Participation
Even given this analysis, several problems remain. The first is this: Skeffington deals with local and city plans rather than regional or even national plans. Apart from the massive potential difference in physical scale between even a local and a city plan, there can also be great differences in the time-scale involved. Now in terms of planning matters alone, there is just no evidence to suggest which, if any, of these scales of plans

is tangible and comprehensible to the citizen. Commonsense would indicate that the smaller-scale local plans – because they are highly visible and often immediate in terms of time – offer the only real chance of public participation. But, ironically, this is perhaps the level where the potential to effect radical change is smallest; participation in local planning is unlikely to transcend purely cosmetic activity. While this cosmetic activity may be of huge importance to the local citizen – for example, in deciding between redevelopment or rehabilitation – it is miniscule compared with the urban system at large.

The second problem is that this is hardly 'participation' – especially not in the sense proposed by the Minister of Housing. The reason for this failure to address the real problems of participation is, we suggest, that a consideration of participation in planning *alone*, especially as conceived by Skeffington, misses the point. Planning does not exist in an administrative vacuum, it is firmly enmeshed in the organizational framework of local government. There is no reason why citizens should be especially motivated to participate in planning as opposed to other local government matters – except when their own immediate interests are directly threatened, as by compulsory purchase orders. Citizens will have to be motivated to participate *generally* in local political life before they can be expected to participate in decisions affecting solely matters to do with the physical environment. ... Much as one may wish it were otherwise, people's participation in local affairs only appears to 'take-off' when, first, there is an immediate, local *threat* and, secondly, when there is a real, tangible chance of such participation being *successful* in removing the threat. In fact, this kind of activity hardly justifies the name of 'participation' at all.

There are two other pessimistic probable outcomes of this official type of participation. First, it is not unreasonable to predict an early amelioration of relations between planners and middle class pressure groups of the civic and amenity variety; the whole tenor of Skeffington Report is that it is permeable to 'constructive' criticism, besides which some of these groups are genuinely able to offer expert help to local authorities on matters where the latter may neither have the time nor the expertise to effect thorough-going investigations. However, there is likely to be conflict if an authority, after consultation, takes a decision which contradicts the wishes of the pressure group. This kind of conflict is inevitable in that participation is being marketed as a commodity which will benefit *everybody*, and it is for this reason that disillusion is likely to set in when the goods do not come up to expectations.

The second probable outcome of the practice of this version of participation is still trouble, for despite the presence of a 'Community Development Officer', the Skeffington Report proposals will clearly tend to benefit the educated, articulate (middle class) sections of society at the expense of poorer, less articulate groups – the working class. ... On the one hand, then, if the poorer and less articulate are not to be adequately represented in the planning process, as we suspect will be the case, and if what are essentially political decisions about resource allocation are allowed to masquerade as value-free professional judgments, as they are and will probably continue to be, then the loser in the participation game will be precisely those sections of society least equipped to express and defend their needs – sections which also happen to be the losers in other 'games' – education, housing, occupational skill, etc. On the other hand, even if the poor do get a chance to express their opinions through the Community Development Officer, the planners should not be surprised if they are told that the people want more money, not more exhibitions. . . .

Proposals for more effective participation in planning are in a way out of place here, as the core of our argument is that without more participation in political life, and a consequent redistribution of power, participation in planning alone is meaningless. . . .

. . . More and more previously 'inarticulate' and 'apathetic' people are aware of the validity of a comment by Sherry Arnstein, an American planner:

> . . . participation without redistribution of power is an empty and frustrating process for the powerless. It allows the power holders to claim that all sides were considered, but makes it possible for only some of these to benefit. It maintains the status quo. . . .

(b) Two vehicles for public participation

(i) *The public local inquiry: two problems*

For the lawyer, the public local inquiry is the central institution of the planning process; amid the strange and murky world of maps, plans, flow charts, computer print-outs and planning jargon the inquiry is the light that shines out and gives off a familiar glow. It is around this beacon that the lawyer has organised his attack on the planning process in order to judicialise it, to make it appear as a process leading to a decision based on evidence given at a hearing which has been subject to the cut and thrust of cross-examination. The planner too has seen the inquiry either as a prize to be captured, or an obstacle to be circumvented. His strategy has been both to put forward alternatives to the traditional inquiry which might weaken its influence, and to favour a conception of planning as a continuous process which might render the clash of arms at the inquiry of less importance.

These two groups have now been joined by the environmental pressure groups or amenity groups which have increasingly come to perceive that the public inquiry, with all its drawbacks and faults, is incomparably the best platform they have for putting before the planners, the decision makers and the public at large their view of what sort of planning the country should have. Increasingly, then, for all three groups the public inquiry and its ramifications have become a touchstone of the kind of planning system that there should be.

We cannot explore all aspects of the public inquiry here[57] but two general problems – third parties and costs – will be considered as they bear on the effectiveness of inquiries from a public participation angle. 'Third parties' is the term used to refer to persons or organisations who intervene in a planning inquiry held to consider an appeal by an applicant – the first party – against a refusal of permission by a local planning authority – the second party. The intervention might be to support either side: indeed there may be several third parties, some of whom support the applicant, some of whom support the local planning authority's refusal, and some of whom adopt a totally independent line on the application. Amenity groups are almost invariably third parties. The problem of third parties is quite simply: what role ought they to have in the planning process? The movement over the years since 1958 has been in the direction of giving them a greater role in practice yet constantly denying them legal rights. The tension that this has generated is very obvious in relation to public inquiries.

The administrative practice sanctioned by the Department is that inspectors in general recognise third parties and allow them both to cross-examine the applicant and his witnesses, the local planning authority and its witnesses and to put a case via witnesses if need be. The inspector will then summarise the third-party case in his report, if necessary comment on it, and give his recommendation from which it may be seen whether the third parties were influential or not. *Prima facie* this appears to be a reasonable compromise; what is the problem?

First, because third parties have no legal right to appear and be heard at a planning appeal, they do not have to be informed that one is pending, or of its subject matter. They have to rely on the goodwill of the local planning authority,[58] on the press,[59] on the applicant if they are supporting him, or on the general public awareness of the application if it is a contentious one. They may accordingly miss an appeal or have too little time to prepare an adequate case. Secondly, they can never be entirely sure how far the inspector will allow them to go in their submissions at the inquiry; at what point he will rule that their submissions are irrelevant and cannot be taken into account. They are also in a weak position to challenge either the applicant, the local planning authority or, where they are appearing, a representative from a department, for not producing enough information if the first and second parties to the appeal are satisfied with the amount of information forthcoming from each other (as they may well be if they want the inquiry to be fairly narrowly confined, as opposed to third parties who might want the inquiry to range fairly broadly into the implication of the proposed development).

Thirdly, and most importantly, absence of legal rights for third parties severely limits their powers to object to the ultimate decision of the Minister, or to his conduct between the receipt of the report and his decision. The status of third parties is by no means clear in the eyes of the law and, as the cases in Chapter 6 show, they may have no legal redress against the Minister if they consider that he has in some way exceeded his power. Their main recourses are administrative or political: in the first case, the Council on Tribunals or the Parliamentary Commissioner for Administration; and in the second, a sympathetic MP or group of MPs and the press. Materials on the first case are contained in Chapter 6 but it is no secret that the two major clashes on inquiries between the Council on Tribunals and the government of the day concerned the rights of third parties and the activities of the Minister and his department after the inspector's report was submitted; on each occasion, the Council on Tribunals and the third parties came off second best.[60]

Should third parties be given legal rights to appear and be heard at public inquiries? To do so would run counter to the trend typified by the substitution of the public examination for the public inquiry into structure plans, for where a development plan is being considered, it is very difficult to tell who is a third party and who is a person directly affected; and in any case after a certain period when everybody has had a right to appear, the law now denies everybody the right to appear. But the trend itself may be in the wrong direction, so the question remains worth considering, particularly as it raises fundamental issues about the nature and purpose of planning and the people who should be involved in it.

There is clearly a link between the grant of legal rights to third parties and the question of the award of costs to successful objectors at inquiries. On this matter successive governments have refused to award costs to successful appellants at planning inquiries other than those listed below in Circular 73/65. It has indeed only been since 1965 that costs have been awarded to successful objectors to compulsory purchase orders on any scale on the basis of Ministry Circular 73/65. This circular followed, though it did not wholly accept, a report from the Council on Tribunals on the award of costs at statutory inquiries. The Franks Committee had recommended that the successful appellant/owner in planning appeals should be awarded his costs, but 'the Council was persuaded by the evidence before it that the proposal would have a harmful effect on planning administration'.[61] What are these harmful effects, and what is the distinction between a successful appellant in a planning appeal and a successful objector at a compulsory purchase inquiry? Why should not all objector/owners at a compulsory purchase inquiry be awarded their costs and/or be given legal aid as of right?

> MHLG Circular No. 73/65: 'The award of costs
> at statutory inquiries'

2. The Government has decided to accept the main recommendation in the report to the effect that costs should normally be awarded to successful objectors to compulsory purchase and analogous orders. Accordingly owners, lessees or occupiers of land on whom statutory notice of a compulsory purchase order has to be served will in appropriate circumstances qualify for such an award; in the analogous cases those who attend a local inquiry to defend their property may similarly, if successful, rank as qualified objectors.

AWARD OF COSTS TO QUALIFIED OBJECTORS

5. The new practice with relation to the award of costs to successful objectors will be applied to inquiries held after the date of this circular on behalf of the Minister of Housing and Local Government, into the following types of orders or proposals submitted to him for confirmation or approval:

(i) Compulsory acquisition of land;
(ii) Clearance Orders (Housing Act 1957, Part III);
(iii) Unfitness Orders (Land Compensation Act 1961, Second Schedule);
(iv) Proposals under section 4 (3) of the Town and Country Planning Act 1962 to designate land as subject to compulsory acquisition;
(v) Orders under section 27 of the Town and Country Planning Act 1962, revoking or modifying a planning permission;
(vi) Orders under section 28 of the Town and Country Planning Act 1962, requiring discontinuance of use, or alteration or removal of buildings or works.

Continued consideration will be given to the extension of this list to inquiries into further kinds of submissions that are of relatively infrequent occurrence, but may be considered as analogous in character, and further particulars may be issued by the Departments concerned, if necessary.

6. The Minister will normally make a favourable award of costs on application by a qualified objector who duly objected to an order or proposal concerning his property and who following a local inquiry had his objection sustained by the Minister's refusal to confirm the order or approve the proposal, or to do so in respect of the whole or part of the objector's property which was in question at the inquiry. The award will be made against the authority who made the order or proposal.

7. The Minister will consider making an *ex gratia* payment of costs to successful qualified objectors, following inquiries into similar orders or proposals initiated by himself (for example a revocation, modification or discontinuance order made by him in the exercise of his powers under section 207 of the Town and Country Planning Act 1962) and also following inquiries into orders under section 1 of the New Towns Act 1965, designating an area as the site of a proposed new town.

AWARD OF COSTS IN OTHER CASES
(a) Unsuccessful objectors
8. The council recommend that costs should not normally be awarded to unsuccessful objectors in compulsory purchase and analogous cases; but they qualified this by recommending that, when there was little or no merit in one objection over another and policy or chance was the determining factor as between one objector and another, the unsuccessful objector who had not behaved unreasonably, vexatiously or frivolously should be awarded his costs. In view of the impracticability of discriminating with obvious fairness between objectors in the manner proposed it has been decided not to make an award in cases of this kind.
(b) Unreasonable behaviour
9. In any case where it is alleged that a party has acted unreasonably, the Minister will in future have regard to the considerations set out in paragraphs 23–29 of the council's report before deciding whether to make an award of costs. This will apply to planning appeals and other types of proposals, many of which are not initiated by the authority concerned, as well as to cases of the kinds mentioned in paragraph 5 above. Awards of costs on grounds of unreasonable behaviour will, of course, arise only in very exceptional circumstances.

Extracts from *The Report of the Council on Tribunals on the Award of Costs at Statutory Inquiries*, Cmnd. 2471

AWARD OF COSTS IN CASES OF UNREASONABLE CONDUCT
23. We recommend as a rule of general application that costs should normally be awarded against a party who behaves unreasonably, vexatiously or frivolously in favour of a party who, being legally entitled to appear at the inquiry, has duly appeared thereat and has not so behaved. Although "unreasonably" is a word wide enough to cover "vexatiously" or "frivolously", in stating this rule we have chosen to adopt the words "unreasonably, vexatiously or frivolously" because they are of familiar

use in almost every branch of the law and have been judicially interpreted. This rule is intentionally worded in such a way that under it an award of costs could be made against a successful party, but we recognise that the circumstances in which such an order would be made will be rare. It is also intentionally confined to persons who are legally entitled to appear at the inquiry: we deal with the position of third parties in paragraphs 46 and 47.

24. The Ministry of Housing and Local Government have suggested that, in the field of planning appeals, the following general principles would seem to apply in considering whether an award of costs might be made on the ground of unreasonable behaviour:

(i) The main criterion is whether one party has been put to unnecessary and unreasonable expense (a) because the matter should never have come to inquiry or (b) because, although the appeal and inquiry could not reasonably have been avoided, the other party conducted their side of the procedure in such a way as to cause unnecessary trouble and expense.

(ii) It is reasonable to expect a higher standard of behaviour from planning authorities than from appellants, because the former ought to know more about the procedure and the strength of the arguments on both sides of a particular appeal.

Furthermore the Ministry take the view that these principles could be applied to other procedures subject to this important qualification that where a local authority initiated the proposal (for example, the compulsory acquisition of land by a local authority) it would generally be very difficult to make an award against an objector who was trying to retain his land or some right attaching to it.

25. We accept the principles put forward by the Ministry in the context of inquiries into planning appeals and recommend that they should be applied to all inquiries, subject to the qualification that it should be regarded as very exceptional to award costs against the citizen where a local authority or statutory undertaker initiated the proposal.

27. The Ministry have suggested that cases coming within the category where an inquiry might have been avoided but for the unreasonable behaviour of one of the parties are as follows:

(i) Where a previous decision of the Minister has made it quite clear what his decision will be.

For example:

(a) where there has been a recent appeal in respect of the same site and the same or very similar development, and the Minister has made it plain that this development should not be allowed, conditions have not materially changed, but the appellant, despite warnings about the previous decision, has persisted in pressing his case to inquiry;

(b) where the Minister has dismissed a previous appeal, but indicated that he would see no objection to an application in a different form, such an appliction has been made, but the authority have persisted in refusing permission.

(ii) Where the planning authority have been unable to support their decision (or their failure to give one) by any substantial evidence.

(iii) Where the appeal could have been avoided if the parties had got together to discuss it, or more information had been provided, and either (a) one party had refused to discuss it, though asked to do so, or (b) one party had refused to provide information which they could reasonably be expected to provide.

(iv) Where the appeal or the authority decision was obviously prompted by considerations which had little or nothing to do with planning – for example, if an application were made as part of a publicity campaign or a campaign against a neighbour or council, or if permission were refused primarily because of prejudice.

(v) Where it must have been obvious from previous decisions well publicised in official documents, or from official statements of law or policy in circulars, handbooks or memoranda, that an appeal was certain to be decided in a particular way.

One fundamental rule of decision making in planning, insisted upon by the courts, is that each planning application is considered on its merits, and not pre-determined in advance by a general policy. In view of this, how can it be 'obvious' from 'policy in circulars' 'that an appeal was certain to be decided in a particular way' and how can a party be regarded as behaving unreasonably if it appeals against the decision of a local planning authority precisely because it did purport to apply the policy to reach the obvious result?

We may return now to the position of third parties, armed with some knowledge as to the narrow ambit for the award of costs to successful appellants at a planning inquiry. Clearly any encouragement of third parties is going to increase the cost of inquiries, not just for the public authorities but for the appellant as well who may be a developer of small means. Would it be possible to devise rules to give the right of appearance to some third parties in respect of some types of applications only, e.g. those of a magnitude to require a ministerial as opposed to an inspectorial decision? Which third parties should have a right of appearance – contiguous neighbours, local amenity groups or national amenity groups? If a proposal to demolish and redevelop a row of Georgian houses is in issue, should the Georgian Society alone have a right of appearance, or might the Victorian Society be given rights as well?

Taking into account the issue of the overall cost of inquiries, we should also be asking what benefits are to be gained by society at large to offset against the increased costs which increased third-party – particularly amenity-group – participation will involve? The role which amenity groups now play in inquiries into major public developments, particularly road proposals, has already transformed those public inquiries from inquiries into applications to develop a particular line of road into inquiries about the necessity and desirability of a new road at all, and into several different possible alignments.[62] Equally, by adopting a liberal policy on third-party appearances at run-of-the-mill planning inquiries, governments have contributed to a blurring in the minds of the public of the difference between a third party and a statutory objector so that these public inquiries are now seen as much as arenas for public debate about a particular development as places where an owner of property can obtain permission to develop it. Is there any point then in continuing to keep separate the law and the practice? What altering the law would involve would be overt, public and official recognition that the public at large has a right to be consulted and put a point of view (which must be given equal weight to that of the public authorities and the applicant) on proposals for development. If governments are serious about providing increased opportunities for public participation, how can they do otherwise than confer such rights on the public?

One inhibiting factor on third parties is that they must bear their own costs (the Government did not accept the very modest proposal of the Council on Tribunals that in exceptional circumstances they may be awarded costs). Amenity groups operate on a basis of voluntary subscriptions and contributions and a major inquiry can quickly exhaust them financially, unless they are able to persuade expert witnesses, counsel and other professional people to give their services free or at a reduced cost. It has several times been suggested that amenity groups should receive their costs at inquiries since their contribution is basically to ensure that a good decision is reached on the basis of the fullest possible information; a matter which it is in the public interest to foster. The extracts from the House of Commons Select Committee on Scottish Affairs provide one of the fullest discussions of the issue in general terms, and the various letters to *The Times* are eloquent testimony to grass-root feelings on this issue. No favourable response by governments has yet been made to these suggestions. Why not? Do amenity groups overstate their own case; is there a distinction to be drawn between national groups – e.g. the Council for the Protection of Rural England – which are, almost by definition, disinterested in their opposition to any particular development and local groups which have mixed motives – both interested and disinterested – in opposing local developments?

The Award of Costs at Statutory Inquiries, Cmnd. 2471

The position of third parties

47. At first sight it would seem right that there should be no award of costs against third parties since a third party has no legal right to be heard at the inquiry and is heard only at the discretion of the person holding the inquiry who may stop him if he considers that he is behaving unreasonably. In practice, however, it may often be difficult to know, until he has presented his case, whether a third party has behaved unreasonably or not. There may also be cases where the local planning authority take a neutral line and the real contest lies between the appellant and a third party. In such circumstances, should not the third party be eligible to receive and liable to be condemned in costs? We are aware of the danger of inhibiting persons who wish to put forward *bona fide* objections by being condemned in costs, and we are not in favour of the view, save in exceptional circumstances, that a third party should be liable to pay costs because he has put forward objections without reasonable cause or because he takes an unreasonable time to present his case. We consider that it is a logical consequence that save in exceptional circumstances third parties should not be eligible to receive costs even where another party has behaved unreasonably. An illustration of an exceptional case would be the case of an adjournment of the inquiry caused by the fault or default of one of the parties which we deal with in paragraph 44: in such cases a special award might be made in favour of or against a third party, as the case may be.

Minutes of Evidence Taken Before the Select Committee on Scottish Affairs (Sub-Committee B), Session 1971–2, vol. 4, pp. 132–4, 179, 278–9, 281

Mr A. T. McIndoe, Planning Consultant; and Mr G. Gavin, Deputy Director of Planning, Glasgow Corporation:

B570. Could we go on now to a quite different problem which we have talked about with several other bodies, that is, that it has been suggested that appeals against Development Plans take too long to finalise, and that often taking part in appeals against Development Plans is beyond the means of individuals? And is there anything that you can suggest that could be done to improve this situation?—(Mr. *McIndoe*.) I would be quite happy to start on this, perhaps on the individuals' side, and to say that this is a very real source of grievance to people, especially those dealing with particularly major problems. I do not think there is anything confidential in the figure that I am quite pleased to give you, but I have made inquiries, because I was representing all the owners involved in the Hunterston Inquiry, which was the longest planning inquiry we have ever had. The owners' costs were just over £60,000. Can I stress the importance of this, because all these owners, if they had kept quiet and allowed this to go through – and it would have gone through automatically, I think, if they had kept quiet – stood to make a very considerable amount of money just by keeping quiet. I think there is something quite serious about a group of owners who will spend £60,000 out of their own pocket when, by keeping quiet, they could have made many, many times £60,000 just by selling the land for the purpose to which it was zoned. So, there is a very important public feeling about this, whatever a lot of people might say. A lot of people say that people like that are selfish. Well, it is not a question of selfishness at all, because, as I say, they would be much better off if they kept quiet. I think it is quite proper for me to say that why the Hunterston Inquiry is such a good example is that this was the longest inquiry we have had and, therefore, about the most costly. The Secretary of State informed the County Council, when they were promoting this proposal, that he would pay part of their costs. Now, in all seriousness, it seems to me a terrible thing that the Secretary of State would say to the County Council; "Well, don't be worried too much about the cost of this, because I will pay part of your costs", but the owners will have to pay £60,000. The reporter referred to costs, and the Secretary of State did nothing at all about it. Do let me make this clear: there were two sides, two legs, to the Hunterston Inquiry, the one was the zoning and the other was compulsory purchase; it was zoned and then there was a compulsory purchase order for implementing the zoning, for requiring the land. Now, under our Statutes, when you are successful in opposing a compulsory purchase order you, in nearly all cases, get your costs. But, when you oppose a Development Plan, to my personal knowledge in only one case in Scotland have costs ever been awarded – and that was a very minor thing. I think that is a source of great ill-feeling amongst people. Taking it further again on Hunterston, a tremendous amount of high-grade, technical information was put before the reporter, and therefore the Secretary of State, about Hunterston, by the objectors. I do not want to say too much, but a lot of people think it was more and of better quality than that which was put to him from other sources. In other words, the Secretary of State – whatever decision he made; I am not talking about decisions for the moment – was able to make a decision, and the reporter was able to make a decision because of the objectors' spending £60,000, that he would not otherwise have had information on these things. So, that is quite an important thing. The other thing is that – I, again, do not want to be too personal – I have appeared in many hundreds of inquiries in Britain into planning matters, and very, very rarely indeed, in my experience, has anybody who has come to me not proceeded with an objection, a technical objection, to a Development Plan, because of the cost of it.

Mr W. L. Taylor, BL, DL, JP, Hon Fellow RTPI, Chairman of Livingstone Development Corporation:

B708. I wonder if I might just challenge the assumption which seems to lie behind some of your remarks, that there is a great flood of potential litigants waiting to burst upon the scene if financial assistance is made available. The same sort of argument, I think, was used prior to the introduction of legal aid in civil and criminal causes. Would it not be feasible to tackle the problem in something like the same way as we tackle the problem of legal aid in that situation, and have a kind of steering committee which had to examine an objection to see if it had *prima facie* validity before assistance was given? Would that not weed out most of the frivolous or spurious cases and appeals which were concerned with compensation and matters like that? – It may be of interest that one of the Committees to which I gave evidence a long time ago was the Rushcliffe Committee, which gave rise to legal aid. I still think that there is still a tendency in planning appeals for a number of people to come forward in defence of the *status quo*, almost irrespective of what happens to be the *status quo*. I think there is a strong argument that present participation is inclined to protect the middle income, middle class, middle aged section of the community because they are the more articulate. I want to try to avoid this. I want to make sure that major issues are raised, not just those that concern individuals. The difficulty about trying to apply the present test which is applied in legal aid, is that at the moment you have got to go to a committee of lawyers and satisfy them that you have a *prima facie* case before you can get a certificate. I think that the planning processes are already beginning to stretch out in the sense of time, that the introduction of this additional element would begin to make the time element almost unacceptable.

Mr. A. B. Hume, Secretary; Mr. J. B. Beaumont, Under-Secretary; Mr. W. D. C. Lyddon, Chief Planning Officer, Scottish Development Department:

Mr. *Smith*.

B1144. The Committee has been concerned with the problem of public inquiries into planning matters. Arising out of increasing public concern with the environment, there has been a tendency recently for individual citizens, or groups of citizens, to wish to be represented at public inquiries. There has therefore arisen the problem of financing their representation at inquiries and the financing of expert witnesses and of other means whereby they could present their case adequately and properly. I am thinking particularly of the case where it is not an individual applicant for planning permission but a citizen, or groups of citizens, who are reacting to a proposal put forward affecting their area. Assuming that in principle the Government of the day decided that there was a case for assisting these objectors out of public funds, could that be worked out in some practical and satisfactory way, do you think? – I would see very great difficulty about that. This is a possibility that has been explored repeatedly. I think, if I may draw on your past evidence, which, of course, we have had the opportunity to read, the suggestion has been made that something like the legal aid system could be adopted. Clearly there must be some sieve or filter to avoid the sort of frivolous objections which the Franks Committee in 1957 feared if expenses were paid. I think it would be very difficult to establish *probabilis causa*, if that is the phrase, in a planning operation of this kind. The courts have their precedents. The lawyers who practise in them can judge whether a possible litigant is reasonably pursuing his aims in the courts. There are not precedents of that kind established in many planning fields, particularly of the sort which I think you had in mind where large new issues are arising, and the judgment of anybody whom one might ask to do this would have to be much more subjective than the more objective decision of your legal aid assessors, if that is the correct description. So that it seems to me that the sieve or the filter is difficult to devise.

B1145. If I might move on to these difficulties, would you accept that it is difficult for groups of citizens, or individual citizens, to mount an effective case at public inquiries and to be properly represented and to have proper expert witnesses without a considerable amount of money? – Yes, but if I may I would like to suggest that what is wrong is not the lack of funds but the procedures. The present inquiry procedures are of fairly long standing and were originally devised to examine a case in which public interest conflicted with private property or private interest. For that purpose fairly rigid legal procedures were introduced and increasingly as members of the Bar took these inquiries there were established procedures involving a need for counsel to protect the objector and to present his case. It seems to me that in recent years and months the nature of these public inquiries has changed. What happens now is that one gets public interest and public policy argued from two sides. You have mentioned the environmentalist. Perhaps they are on one side; perhaps the economic developers are on the other. I myself, and my colleagues would agree, question the wisdom of persisting with tight legal procedures in inquiries, treated as if they were held by courts of law, in this sort of case.

B1151. Just before we leave this point, may I test again this question of the practicability of it? Would it not be the experience of the Development Department, when they look at planning appeals or planning applications and objections, that they are able, on a fairly rough basis, to decide those that are going to be serious objections and have to be treated seriously, and those that are frivolous and obviously of very little importance? – May I suggest that even if we could do this, that is not the complete answer, because these tribunals, if set up, would have to be prepared to defend themselves against irate frivolous objectors whose applications for aid have been turned down? It is one thing to decide in our wisdom that something is frivolous; it is another to make a public defence of it.

The Times, 13 and 18 August 1973

THE COST OF PROTEST

From Mr Malcolm MacEwen

Sir, Having spent three days last week, unpaid, representing the Exmoor Society in a planning appeal inquiry, the difficulties faced by unofficial bodies or individuals at these inquiries has been brought forcefully home to me.

The substance of the matter (an appeal by Williton Rural District Council against the rejection by Somerset County Council of a proposal to build a car park in the heart of the medieval village of Dunster) is irrelevant to this issue. Our problem was that we could only afford to spend £200 on an inquiry which, we had originally thought, would only last one day. For this sum we were able to produce one expert witness in person, and another who submitted a written statement.

The rural district council, however, spent money like water. Its estimate, which was certainly exceeded, was £6,000 for a two-day inquiry, excluding the time of its own officials which must have run into a tidy sum. It employed at the inquiry a barrister, a solicitor, a solicitor's clerk, the District Surveyor (with his principal assistant to help him), a landscape architect (with his assistant), a planner and an engineer. The county council had a staff solicitor, three staff professional witnesses and an assistant. Had all these resources been applied to the solution of the problem (as the Exmoor Society had suggested before the inquiry took place) rather than to the defence of entrenched positions, the public might have got some value for its money.

In the event, largely because so much time was spent on the leisurely examination of these witnesses, and of the mountains of paper and photographs produced by the RDC's witnesses, the inquiry lasted three days. The public authorities can, by proliferating witnesses and paper, run up the costs and drive the amenity or other societies from the field.

Our budget only allowed for our witness to be present on one day. In the event, it was only possible to squeeze him in on the second day because the county council helpfully gave us precedence – and because I was prepared, on the spot, personally to guarantee the extra costs of a second day.

To add insult to injury, whereas we (who were, in my view, defending the public interest) will be unable to recover VAT on professional fees, the RDC will be able to recover it. Thus the scales are tilted even more against the citizen group. Has not the time come for such groups, provided that they have made a useful contribution at an inquiry, to be awarded costs?

Yours faithfully,

MALCOLM MacEWAN,

Manor House, Wootton Courtenay, Minehead, Somerset.

From Mrs. Barbara Maude

Sir, Mr. MacEwen (August 13) is lucky only to have had three days' inquiry to contend with! Here in the Midlands, which are threatened with some 200 miles of new motorways, the inquiries already held have run into many months; that at Bromsgrove, into a short stretch of the M42, has now been adjourned after seven weeks to make way for the next one; and at least six more are pending.

Not only are objectors having, willy nilly, financed as taxpayers and ratepayers the promotion of schemes to which they object, and the retention of QC and junior by the Minister, then having to find the money out of their own taxed incomes to achieve legal representation; but the system of holding separate inquiries into each section of motorway, and deciding their fate before the adjoining section is inquired into, hopelessly prejudices the possibility of any success there. Thus, the private citizen's resources are being wasted and his time and money taken, in what must appear to be an increasingly futile exercise.

Nor is this situation confined to the Midlands. The Transport Reform Group, which is the only national society prepared to help local people fight local battles, has been discussing the problems of objectors' costs with Mr Speed for the past year; for many of its member societies are small groups, for whom the cost of legal representation is quite beyond their resources; and no legal aid is available to individuals threatened with loss of home or livelihood, however straitened their means. Mr Speed points out that the Council on Tribunals decided against costs for objectors in 1965; and that he cannot work out how one would assess the amount even if this decision were now reversed. TRG has told him that most objectors would be perfectly happy to share among them the total spent at any one inquiry by the Department of the Environment or other promoting authority, but has so far failed to receive any comment on this suggestion from the Minister.

TRG is now collecting from its member societies details of the expenses incurred by them in fighting road proposals during the past two years; the total, which will be impressive, will, it is felt, provide a formidable basis for a fresh approach to the Council on Tribunals.

It is strange that this country lags so far behind the United States in this respect; there, not only are objectors reimbursed as of right, but their expenses are calculated as part of the normal engineering costs of any highway scheme.

Yours faithfully,
BARBARA MAUDE,
Chairman, Midland Motorways Action Committee,
5 Newington House, Banbury, Oxfordshire.

(ii) *Amenity groups*

Any consideration of the scope and ramification of public participation in planning must take into account the existence and role of amenity groups. Notwithstanding the fact that they have no place in the official legal framework of planning, our understanding of planning would be the less for excluding them.

The growth of amenity groups and the environmental movement in general in Britain may for our purposes be dated from 1957 – the year of the formation of the Civic Trust, a national body which stimulates voluntary action to improve the environment and gives support and advice to local amenity societies which may affiliate to it. At that time there were some 250 local amenity societies and groups in England; by mid-1973 there were over 1,000 and that number was increasing by about 200 a year. Over 900 societies were affiliated to the Civic Trust by 1972 and it must be remembered that that body does not generally allow more than one society per town to affiliate to it. Most towns and country areas threatened by major developments, roads, the demolition of historic buildings, or reservoirs now have an amenity group. In addition, *ad hoc* groups and committees are constantly being formed to fight specific developments, and on top of all these are the major national bodies such as the Civic Trust, the Council for the Protection of Rural England (CPRE) and the more recent Friends of the Earth.

So vast is the number and so disparate the organisation and aims of all these groups that some attempt at classification is necessary. Political scientists classify pressure groups into two categories.

There are those which are the spokesmen for particular sections of the community: trade associations, professional bodies, trade unions, church bodies, ex-servicemen's groups and the like. Then there are those which either advocate policies more or less beneficial to particular sections of the community or in other ways organise people with common attitudes: the Economic League and the Research Defence Society (against anti-vivisectionist pressures) on the one hand, temperance-reformers' and animal-lovers' societies on the other.[63]

In our particular field the Royal Town Planning Institute (RTPI) would be an example of the former type of group, the CPRE an example of the latter.

There is an important difference between those groups which speak for a recognisable section or interest in a society . . . and those which exist to promote a particular ideal or 'cause'. Membership of the former derive largely from those in a particular, relatively clearly definable, location within the social or economic structure, in virtue of which they are likely to be similarly affected by events (including government action or inaction). In principle, moreover, the total number of people in that location is discoverable, so that it is not obviously nonsensical for a group to say that it represents a certain percentage of those for whom it claims to speak. By contrast there is no comparable clientele (other than the whole body of citizens) for promotional groups which must attract members because of a consensus of opinion on a specific issue (such as the location of a new London airport) or because they share a more general disposition (such as the complex of anxieties about 'population, pollution and ecological balance which has brought people into the Conservation Society)' and not primarily, if at all, on the basis of their sharing other socially identifiable characteristics. This distinction can be important in terms of the methods, objectives and relationships with governments likely to be sustained by the two types of group.

At the same time as recognising the existence of the distinction it is also important to be aware that, in the planning field at least, there is a considerable overlap of aims and objectives between the two groups. Many professional organisations – the RTPI, the Royal Institute of British Architects, the Royal Institute of Chartered Surveyors, to name the three best known – are increasingly becoming concerned with general environmental goals, and thus on occasions take on the hue of promotional or attitude groups. Equally 'pro-development' trade associations and groups, such as the Road Haulage Association and the British Roads Federation, are being compelled by the climate of opinion to become concerned with these same general goals. The activities of these professional and trade associations cannot be ignored in any assessment of the total influence of pressure groups on the planning process – the existence and activity of the RTPI has already been alluded to – and if they are not further discussed here, and they are not, this is solely because the line has to be drawn somewhere.

The groups with which we are concerned are the 'pure' promotional or attitude ones. At the top of the hierarchy come the prestigious national bodies such as the Civic Trust with one archbishop, six peers and six knights on its board of trustees, the CPRE, and the Society for the Protection of Ancient Buildings, all with relatively easy access to government departments. Next come the conservation societies with a local base or interest but a national constituency, i.e. their local concern is regarded as of national importance: the Bath Preservation Trust is one of the best-known examples of these. Finally, there are the local societies which see themselves as having only a local constituency; one such is the Leamington Society, whose objects are worth quoting as being a good standard example of the genre. The Society was formed in 1956

> ... to encourage and promote the study of townscape in all aspects
> to stimulate public consciousness and appreciation of the beauty, character and history of the town and its surroundings and
> to encourage the preservation, development and improvement of the buildings, streets and other features which go to make the town a satisfactory place in which to live, work and enjoy leisure:
> to pursue these ends by such means as meetings, lectures, study groups and exhibitions.

Finally, it bears repeating that at any time there is a host of *ad hoc* groups formed to fight particular developments, such as the Stop The Inner Relief Road group at Warwick, the Tapster Valley Preservation Society to fight the route of the M40 and Clapham Action St Paul's Area in Lambeth to fight a compulsory purchase order.[64]

These groups operate in a variety of ways. The large ones may be consulted by government departments on proposed legislative or policy changes; they may offer their unsolicited advice to them and are usually quick to give evidence to committees and commissions set up to investigate planning and allied matters; e.g. evidence was given by many national groups to the Skeffington Committee, and has been given to the Royal Commission on Environmental Pollution. As an illustration, Bracey's description of some of the activities of the CPRE may be given:

> In its lifetime the C.P.R.E. has engaged in three major battles to obtain legislation with regard to: (i) advertisement control of roadside hoardings which threatened to deface so much of the countryside in the 1920s and 1930s; (ii) the Town and Country Planning Act which the C.P.R.E. campaigned for immediately the Council was formed; (iii) the National Parks and Access to the Countryside Acts. ...
> The C.P.R.E. has had its finger in many other legislative pies and has contributed towards the effectiveness of other bills ... and towards the preservation clauses in other pieces of legislation. M.P.s find themselves lobbied and briefed regularly and insistently when the occasion is held to demand such actions.
> ... The C.P.R.E. enjoys close relationships with most county planning departments and their committees, both directly from London and through its county branches. Matters taken up by the C.P.R.E. are frequently brought to its notice by county planning officers and its prestige is such that a county council welcomes its support and fears, or

at least does not care much for, its opposition at a planning appeal; the C.P.R.E. is frequently invited by a county council to examine proposals for development in association with, say, the Nature Conservancy or the National Parks Commission. The C.P.R.E. acts as an information centre on countryside matters for those seeking advice, either giving the answers itself or putting questioners in touch with organisations and individuals particularly qualified to deal with them. Lectures are given and exhibitions are held throughout the country; books and pamphlets are prepared and distributed[65].

Local groups perform much the same kind of role at a local level, though where relevant they do not neglect the national level. Thus both Bath amenity societies are energetic letter-writers to *The Times*; the Leamington Society and 176 other local societies gave evidence to the Skeffington Committee and STIRR of Warwick took part in a Warwick delegation to the Department of the Environment to protest about the inner relief road.

At the local level, the Leamington Society may be taken as a fairly typical example. It tried to ensure that a committee member checked the register of plans before each meeting of the Council's Plans Sub-Committee and if it considered that an application involved a threat to the Conservation Area or otherwise gave cause for concern, a letter was dispatched to the borough engineer and chief planner and sympathetic councillors forewarned. In addition, it submitted lists of buildings which it considered should be listed under the Town and Country Planning Act, and memoranda on other matters of concern. For instance, in 1972–3 the Borough Council was in dispute with the Warwickshire County Council on the question of what sort of street lighting should replace the then out of date and deficient lighting. The County, which had to pay, wanted as little high-pressure sodium (the softest and most expensive of the three possibilities, but the one that was best for the townscape) as possible; the Borough wanted the whole of the fairly extensive Conservation Area to be lit by high-pressure sodium. The Leamington Society was at one with the Borough Council on this; it fed it memoranda and letters and took up the cudgels with the County Council. Its activities helped stiffen the resolve of the Borough Council, which, aided also by the support of the Royal Fine Arts Commission, ultimately won considerable concessions from the County. Finally, the Society has also held public meetings on matters of concern to the town; in 1972 it was associated with a well-attended meeting to discuss the closure to traffic (other than buses) of the main shopping street of the town.

No doubt there are variations in the details of activities and in the success rates of different local groups, but taken overall it would be fair comment to say that they have a noticeable impact on planning at the local level. It is for this reason that national environmental organisations encourage the growth of local groups, for the stimulation of participation and awareness at the local level is an essential precondition of effective national action.

Is then all this enthusiasm and activity at local and national level the answer to the demand for more public participation? Several reasons may be advanced why it might not be.

(i) Local councils are very ambivalent in their attitudes towards local amenity groups. The more vigorous the group and the more willing it is to challenge received ideas and to propose its own, the more suspicious the local authority is inclined to become of it. There was clearly a wide gulf between the local council and its advisers and the amenity groups in Bath until the DoE brought them together in a study group. The following letters about Bath illustrate this tension.

The Times, 26 April 1972

From Sir Hugh Casson, RA

Sir, Nobody expects a lover to be fair, and there will be much sympathy for the passionate indignation of Mr Lees-Milne (article, *The Times* Saturday Review, April 22) against what he believes to be the gradual destruction of the city of Bath.

Nevertheless he will get nowhere – like most lovers – by merely wringing hands. Likewise your correspondent who implies that the corporation is a bunch of power-manic barbarians. This is baby talk, as unhelpful and misleading as to compare pictorially Royal Crescent with a 1972 building site.

Of course there have been terrible mistakes, and no doubt there will be more in the future. Of course experts don't always know best . . . or even better. Agreed much new building is second rate. (To "insist" upon better architecture is like "insisting" upon better poetry and better weather.) Agreed there should be more rehabilitation and less demolition. Agreed Bath should be better armed against the examples of public meanness and private greed that dominate our environment. But when all is said (so much) and done (so little) we return to the fact that the problems of Bath are not so much architectural as economic, social, moral and political.

What, for instance, do you say to a key employer who wishes to expand his premises in a vulnerable area? Tell him to go somewhere else and take his jobs with him? Advertise a riverside site as suitable for a restaurant, but what if the only offers are from industry? Let it lie idle indefinitely?

Agreed a jumble of little shops is charming, but how do you persuade somebody to take one on – or persuade a housewife to change her patronage from the supermarket? And why should she? All multi-storey car parks are bulky, noisy and inelegant, but where else can you put the cars, except in those elegant streets?

These are complex questions not made easier by over-simplification or name-calling. Is it not fair to say that part of our troubles stem from the fact that the clerics are traitorous, and until they leave the side lines and join in the arena, decisions are unlikely to become wiser?

Perhaps, perhaps not. Maybe they are better where they are, needling and questioning and complaining, valuable gadflies on the twitching hides of politicians and planners. I hope only they will occasionally remember that cities are people as well as buildings.

I remain &c,

HUGH CASSON,

35 Victoria Road, W8.

The Times, 29 April 1972

From Mr Arnold Haskell

Sir, Sir Hugh Casson (April 26) is a member of the Fine Arts Commission and the consultant architect to the Bath council. It would be interesting to know in which capacity he wrote his letter to *The Times*.

Yours, etc,

ARNOLD HASKELL,

Beechwood House, Widcombe Hill, Bath, Somerset.

The Times, 5 May 1972

From Mr. C. A. Comyns Carr

Sir, The damage being inflicted on Bath is being justified on the grounds of meeting the material needs of its citizens. But it is precisely because, as Sir Hugh Casson says (April 26), "cities are for people" that the present car-dominated plan for Bath is wrong. The public has been conditioned by the traffic forecasts into accepting urban road building as the only salvation for the future. Yet the real issues of internal transportation in this city are not being faced.

The array of ugly multi-storey car parks around the central area, which Sir Hugh views as essential repositories, would benefit only a minority of Bath's community. The Bath Traffic and Transport Plan offers nothing for those without the personal use of a car, still a majority even in the foreseeable future. Planning for public transport is virtually non-existent. It is interesting, therefore, to read in your issue of April 24 that only 12 per cent of shopping trips are at present made by car and that this figure will still only be 25 per cent in 1980. So much for the lip service paid to the needs of the housewife.

It is already well known that inadequate transport facilities for those without the use of a car contribute largely to social inequalities, restricted opportunities and social decay in our cities. Planning and financial support for public transport, here or nationally, bears no relationship to the scale of the need.

The same planning philosophy for Bath which has produced such disastrous results in relation to development will be equally disastrous when applied to transport.

Yours faithfully,
C. A. COMYNS CARR,
Committee, Bath Environment Campaign,
10 Lansdown Crescent, Bath, Somerset.

The Times, 26 June 1972
From the Chairman and Deputy Chairman of Bath Development Committee
Sir, The letter in your issue of June 22 over a number of distinguished signatures, rightly draws attention to the need for greatly increased national help to preserve Bath. But only in the last paragraph is there a mention of the all-important matter of money, and the general implication seems to be that Bath City Council has lamentably failed in its responsibilities. Looking at the past (of which, with much respect to your correspondents, we have more knowledge than they) we cannot entirely accept that view.

Bath's real trouble has always been that in an age of over-population, and that population a mobile one, there is no ideal solution to its modern difficulties. Since the war it has had to try to find a way between preservation of an incredible number of old buildings and countryside running right into the city, an up-to-date traffic plan, reasonable living accommodation for its inhabitants, and some industry by which these may earn a living. In 1964 it gave up the unequal struggle and (exactly as proposed by your correspondents) asked for help from the highest known quarter – Professor Sir Colin Buchanan. It not only commissioned a traffic and transport plan from him, but later on a plan for the city's conservation areas. All this was done in consultation with the appropriate ministerial departments of the last Government, and with their considered final approval. Also (be it noted) with that of the then trustees of the Bath Preservation Trust.

As one of the pilot towns for conservation schemes, and with plans made out, Bath hoped for Government money to help it on its way. All that it has ever had are the 50 per cent grants from the Historic Buildings Council towards such schemes as The Circus and Pulteney Street restorations, and a few other buildings lucky enough to be included when there was cash to spare. The City Council's allocation for this year for conservation projects is £39,500. This may seem small, but Bath is not a rich city, and it has many other responsibilities towards its citizens.

The council also felt itself inadequate, even with its own Planning Department, to arbitrate on new buildings in Bath. Partly because of this, partly because the Preservation Trust was also urging such a move, it appointed Sir Hugh Casson as architectural adviser. The trust itself has only twice in the past 10 years produced or modified designs for new buildings. When the Pulteney Bridge flood relief work was done by the River Board, the Council appointed Mr Neville Conder as landscape consultant. For not one of these appointments did the council receive any financial help from the Government. The work done by the Preservation Trust in the two instances in which it has itself been able to do restoration, was only made possible by philanthropy and legacies.

One of the chief and very proper concerns of your correspondents has been the preservation of the smaller houses on the outskirts of the city. Here it is proper for us to make several points.

(i) With the amount of money available any restoration work possible had to be concentrated on the central squares and terraces, many of which were in bad repair after the war.

(ii) Some of these little houses lack the space and light ever to make them acceptable by reasonable living standards, and the Government's rule book is strict on these points.

(iii) The Public Health Inspectors who propose closing orders on unfit houses have frequently been the means of bringing pressure onto owners to improve their houses.

(iv) Only recently has the Government given powers (if necessary compulsory) to buy listed buildings in bad order – but no money with which to do this; and only recently has there been a governmental move towards grants for restoration and improvement rather than slum clearance. And by slums we mean slums. How many of your correspondents have ever seen some of the conditions in the older Bath houses in the past – classified by one shocked visitor as worse than Glasgow? And even today we could still show some. How many people realize that a great part of Bath's attraction today is due to the continual process of general improvement over the past 10 years – slow to begin with, speeded up considerably by now? The Minister's recent proposals on two groups of houses scheduled as unfit – that owners, city council and preservation trust should together work out schemes for their restoration, have encouraged many of us who feel that this is the right path. But such work cannot be done for nothing, and often owners cannot or will not afford it.

Other times, other manners. Preservation is now *the* word, and fortunately so. Fortunate also that so many preservationists have recently come to live in Bath and its environs. We welcome them, we welcome every contribution that they can make in ideas, in improvements, in the responsible places that some of them fill in the city, and for any pressure that they can bring to bear on the Government to help.

But we should like them to accept that some of us, as City Councillors, also have a feeling for our city; that we are not all the lineal descendants of Attila the Hun; and that in the difficult past we have tried, within the many limitations of Government and local authority structures, to do our best for the city and the people that we represent. We have even tried at times to take a long-term view – and who, looking at Bath comprehensively, would like to say that they have the crystal ball for a reply

to such questions? No point of view is ever the whole picture; no solution is the perfect one; even beauty is relative.
Yours faithfully,
G. D. COMER, Chairman.
CICELY M. EDMUNDS, Deputy Chairman,
Bath Development Committee,
75 Lyncombe Hill, Bath, Somerset.

(ii) Amenity groups are self-selected and to rely solely on them for public participation runs the risk of getting a very lop-sided picture of what a community wants. Both the Skeffington Report and its main critics, Damer and Hague, recognise this. They are only following the findings of other sociologists that voluntary associations of all kinds tend to be the preserve of the middle class. The middle class has a different set of values and thus desires a different allocation of resources from the working class, or, at least, often desires an allocation of similar resources to its area of the town, which the working-class area might desire but cannot articulate, thus resulting in the preservation of one area of a town or a county at the expense of another. This point is highlighted by another letter from Bath which puts a point of view about that city not often heard in the national debate about its conservation.

The Guardian, 1973

Sir, – One welcomes the interest in Bath taken by the Architectural Review, the serious national press and in particular by your correspondent Judy Hillman.

If outrage from outside Bath can help to persuade the forthcoming Ministry Inquiry to reject Buchanan's East-West relief road plans, then so much the better. If preservationists throughout the country can influence the Government to provide necessary grants for the introduction of efficient public transport in the City, then so much the better. If popular demands from a nation determined to prevent the destruction of Bath's unique architectural heritage can make the Minister of the Environment provide the extra cash necessary for the modernisation and preservation of Bath's less acclaimed terraces and rows so that the indigenous people of Bath are not priced out of their city, then so much the better.

But if preservationists only want to save Bath as a museum piece for visitors and tourists, if they only want to maintain the Georgian façades in order to make Bath the snob centre of wealthy retirement at the expense of the local working population; if they are not prepared to give both money and consideration to improving the lot of the 1,000 priority cases on Bath's housing waiting list; if they are not prepared to provide light industrial and office employment for the people who live in the city and if they are not prepared to allow for educational expansion then the preservationists must be opposed.

Those of us who really want to save Bath realise that sacrifices must be made by *all* sections of the community.

The complete solution lies in the provision of adequate national grants to Bath Council in order that Bath can achieve the twin objectives of preserving the Georgian architecture *and* solving the social problems of providing homes, health, education, transport and employment. I suspect and regret that many preservationists are concerned only with the solution of the first of these objectives.

Mike Pepper.
(Labour Councillor).
Bath, Somerset, BA1 3BG.

(iii) Practically all amenity groups are under-funded and do not necessarily have a complete array of talent at their disposal. To put the whole or the main burden of public participation on them would be the equivalent of putting the whole burden of the social services on local voluntary welfare organisations. Just as they fill a useful, often a vital, supplementary role to the statutory services, so amenity groups should be seen as having a vital supplementary role to play to and within a statutory system that provides for public participation. Such participation should not be phrased in terms of un-enforceable discretions vested in local authorities, or non-statutory concessions to appear, be heard at and spend a great deal of money on a public inquiry, but as a required part of the planning process. In modern jargon, it should be seen as one of the costs of planning, the benefit of which is greater acceptance of or greater legitimacy for planning. To leave the main burden and cost of participation on amenity groups is to indicate that it does not have a high priority in official eyes, and to run the risk of its continuing to be a hap-hazard exercise. If public participation is regarded as valuable and worthwhile, as many official statements imply, then public funds need to be spent on it.

(c) New institutions of and approaches to participation

Two questions may be asked: to what extent does the new shape of local government and the new shape of the Department of the Environment render less necessary the need for new forms of public participation? To what extent do existing institutions of public participation need supplementing or replacing, and what might supplement and replace them?

(i) New structures of local and central government
There is nothing in the new shape of local government that leads one to suppose that new forms of public participation are not still needed. The main governing units are larger than before, and while this may be necessary for the efficient management of resources and services, it does nothing to ease the problems of alienation of people from their local authorities and from the planning process. It is true that parish councils remain in existence or have been sanctioned for some towns and rural areas, and that they have to be consulted about planning applications affecting land within their areas, but they have not hitherto been the basis of effective public participation, and in any event a large majority of the urban areas in the country are without parish councils. The Bains Report (which has been the basis of most of the management structures of the new local authorities) was hostile to the notion of area committees, which might have taken the place of parish councils in many towns and cities, and few local authorities have set them up. But a case can be made for them and at least one Metropolitan District Council – Stockport – has established them.

J. D. Stewart,[66] 'Area Committees – a new dimension',
L.G.C., p. 651, 22 June 1973

The area committee is a simple enough concept. It is a committee of a local authority concerned with a locality within the authority. All that is surprising about it is that it has to date been little adopted. . . . The point of the area committee concerned with all activities is that it brings in a new dimension: it brings a concern for the locality, a concern that goes beyond a particular service and centres more on general needs. . . . The interest of the member in the area for which he is elected is a strength the organisation can use and build upon both in its own right as a source of knowledge and information and as a basic building block in stimulating a corporate approach.

Many fear just a development [*sic*] as leading not to a corporate approach but to a new separation. . . . They fear parochialism. It is strange that at a time when we seek community involvement and dream of new institutions we condemn as over-narrow the interest of a councillor in his local community. . . . This leaves the way clear to consider one possible form an area committee might take. . . .
(2) The committees would meet monthly. Their meetings would be open to the public and they would meet in the locality for which they are responsible.
(4) The committees would discuss major problems facing their wards. They would invite representatives from community groups to assist in identifying and understanding problems.

(5) The committees would consider any major projects or developments in a service involving their areas prior to a decision by other committees, and would have the right to comment on them. . . .

Cities and counties have many levels, and we too often assume that a uniformity of approach at the centre is all that is required. . . . A sensitivity to the needs of locality within the authority is required as well as an awareness of general problems.

To what extent could area committees meet the criticism of local authorities by Hampton that 'local authorities have ceased to be a method, indeed they have become part of the problem of finding "democratic ways of living for little men in big societies"'?

(ii) *Community development*

Although existing institutions of participation have many unsatisfactory features, it is unrealistic to propose or assume a sweeping-away of them. What is needed is both reform of existing institutions and new institutions, and approaches to provide more opportunities for and a greater diversity of public participation. New ideas and approaches are being tried out and one of the most interesting and significant is the official and unofficial move towards advocacy or community planning and its corollary, community development. This move is very much a part of the wider issue of grappling with urban poverty, which is not examined here. All that the following purports to do is to provide some background information to the growth of community planning and to ask some questions about it.

Attention has already been drawn to the difference of involvement in participation between the articulate middle class and the (in respect of planning) less articulate working class. The Skeffington Report divided the population into the active minority and the passive majority, 'who although deeply affected by decisions do not make their voices heard because of diffidence, apathy or ignorance of what is going on'.[67] For this majority, the Report proposed that in connection with the making of the development plan, local authorities should be prepared to appoint community development officers whose role would be 'to provide a catalyst for local opinion'.

Skeffington, op. cit.

82 . . . we think it fair to say that the idea of the community development officer was criticised by a number of the organisations with whom we discussed it. . . .

84 The work of the community development officer would depend upon an identification of groups within the community, whether based on

neighbourhoods, industries or other interests. The community development officer should be able to advise the authority on such matters. His work with people would be primarily concerned with those who might not otherwise hear of proposals and take a part in influencing them, even if indirectly. It would be quite wrong for us to try to say how he should work. Communities vary greatly and he should have freedom to adapt his methods to local circumstances. The officer's work with people would have three main facets; to give information, to receive and transmit reactions, and to be a link with existing groups or to promote new local ones which would eventually stand on their feet as independent bodies for participation.

85 Clearly, the community development officer would work hand in hand with the planning officer and the information officer in establishing and maintaining communications with people. His work would ... involve giving simple explanations and sounding out opinions, to be followed up later by the planning officer. The views expressed to him would then be taken into account in the formulation of plans and other work of the authority.

This proposal did not find favour with the government which commented in Circular 52/72 'that the appointment of Community Development Officers is unlikely to be necessary solely in the specific context of development plans'.[68] However, by that date, the idea of community development officers had been developed independently of Skeffington and was seen as part of the attack on urban poverty.

The starting point for this development may be seen as the Home Office's Community Development Project which commenced in 1969. Its stated objectives are to study the needs and aspirations of people suffering social deprivation, to help people exercise increased control over their lives – enlarging their opportunities in directions which they themselves see as desirable – to increase the capacity of the relevant services to respond to both needs and aspirations more effectively and to develop hypotheses about the causes of and solutions to social deprivation, and through further testing of these hypotheses to develop criteria for allocating resources to meet such needs. The project involves both study and action and fourteen areas – mainly urban of a ward size – had Community Development Project teams at work in them by mid-1973.

One of these teams is in Coventry, located in Hillfields, an area of the city that is a mixture of high-rise council flats and clearance areas. The team has not concerned itself solely with physical planning, although inevitably with clearance taking place in the area, this has been a matter of concern for residents. A community association has been encouraged into being, an information centre opened and a range of individual welfare and other problems taken up. Over and above this, the team is concerned to build up more effective lines of communication between the people and their elected representatives in the belief that that is one way local government can develop a more responsive and effective policy-making and planning capability. Thus the rather general ideas of Skeffington have re-emerged – refined and sophisticated – after two years' work in the field, in Coventry. The CDP team has in effect decided that whatever the specific social problems of disadvantaged persons, part of the general solution must lie in increased participation and if necessary organisational and operational change at local and central government level. At the same time the work of the Coventry team has shown that neither increased participation nor more sophisticated management by themselves are likely to make a significant impact on urban poverty, and this must be borne in mind in any assessment of the usefulness of public participation.

Even where these project teams have not been established, local authorities are now appointing community or social development officers who have both a case-work and a community-development role, so that the idea that there is or may be a connection between social deprivation and lack of community participation in government may be said to be becoming generally officially accepted.

Mention may also be made of the community or neighbourhood councils, which though initially and still in some places a totally unofficial growth, are slowly being adapted by some local authorities and made use of for participation purposes.[69] These councils are different from amenity groups in that they are concerned with all issues in a locality and are elected on a one-man, one-vote basis. They are not confined to socially deprived areas – Lambeth and Stockport Councils for instance are both committed to a network of community councils throughout their areas. Being non-statutory, there is no common pattern of relationships between them and the local authority; for instance in Liverpool the councils are linked through a Neighbourhood Organisation Committee, a sub-committee of the Liverpool Council of Social Service, with no formal links with the city and only the beginnings of informal contact and consultations. In nearby Stockport the initiative for the establishment of councils came from the local authority, which has appointed community development officers to foster their growth. The councils seek out opinion on a continuing basis, conducting questionnaire surveys of local opinion on Stockport's services. As with official statutory local authorities, one of their problems is that of overcoming local apathy; another is being able to show that they can achieve results and this in turn means having good communications with the local authority, councillors and especially officials.

Once again, at the local level, we come back to the issue raised by Skeffington and the Coventry Community Development Project: effective participation depends upon a local authority being organised and structured in such a way that a continuous two-way flow of information from and to local communities about their needs and aspirations is possible and takes place. Would this be facilitated or hindered if community councils were made statutory and an obligatory part of all local authority structures?[70]

Alongside these official efforts must be noted the decision of the Town and Country Planning Association to establish a Planning Aid Service to provide 'on-the-spot advice on planning matters to groups and organisations involved in a planning débâcles'[71] and the growth of a multitude of self-styled, radical, community action groups or projects designed to challenge official action in respect of clearance areas or twilight areas. The Covent Garden Community Association is one such group; it has been particularly active in opposing the GLC's plans for that area.[72]

At a level below the official and statutory planning process, and often not concerned solely with land-use planning, there is thus a ferment of official and unofficial ideas and approaches to participation based on the community. Is this then the answer to the cry for genuine or meaningful participation? What are the drawbacks, if any, of relying on community action or participation for reactions to planning proposals? If community participation is the key, should it be made part of the statutory planning system, given rights and duties, and made subject to all the usual legal and administrative controls over its operation? If a developer – public or private – has complied with the law in respect of an application to develop, why should he pay any attention to the views of a non-statutory community council? Should not planners act like lawyers and keep separate their political and professional roles rather than confusing them as advocacy planning or community action does?

3

Creating the Plan

1. Introduction

The two preceding chapters have been concerned to set out something of the broader governmental background to planning, dealing with the questions of how decisions about planning are made and how one can influence the decision makers. In this chapter we turn more directly to the process of planning by considering the constitution of the process – the development plan to which all development is meant to relate. One overriding question about planning is whether this ideal is or should be attainable, but while this question may be asked here, we cannot hope for an answer until we have looked at both the development plan and development control, which latter is considered in later chapters. The questions with which this chapter is to deal are how and why the present system of development planning evolved, what problems it is designed to deal with and what problems are emerging or are likely to emerge in its operation. Have we now, with the reforms of 1968, arrived at the acme of perfection in relation to planning or are we still travelling hopefully?

2. Genesis of structure and local planning

Structure and local plans – the current type of development plan – were born of a desire to escape from what was seen as the rigidity of the 1947-style development plans, and move towards a concept of flexible or continuous planning. This concept of planning has two strands to it – spatial continuity and temporal continuity – the former of which raises the issue of regional planning, the latter the issue of the defects of the 1947 Act. Important though regional planning is, no more than an outline of the topic will be given here, sufficient to say what planners think it is, how they see its relationship to statutory structure planning, and how it is evolving in one region – the West Midlands.

(a) Regional planning

There have been few more seminal influences on the present system of town and country planning than the problem of regional imbalance and few more seminal reports than the Report of the Royal Commission on the Distribution of the Industrial Population. The problem of regional imbalance has been officially with us since 1928;[1] the solutions seem as far off as ever and depend only partly on the planning system in that the advancing of money under the Industry Act 1972 and its predecessors could quite easily be carried on without the existence of any law of town and country planning. However, regional planning is – both as a matter of law and of practice – related to statutory development planning, and the usefulness or otherwise of such relationship must therefore be considered.

Royal Commission on the Distribution of the Industrial Population, Cmd. 6153[2] (HMSO, 1940)

Terms of reference

... to inquire into the causes which have influenced the present geographical distribution of the industrial population of Great Britain and the probable direction of any change in that distribution in the future; to consider what social, economic or strategical disadvantages arise from the concentration of industries or of the industrial population in large towns or in particular areas of the country; and to report what remedial measures if any should be taken in the national interest. ...

G. McCrone,[3] *Regional Policy in Britain* (1969), pp. 104-5

When the Report of the Royal Commission appeared the War was in progress, attention was diverted to more urgent matters and the problem of the Special Areas had in any case, for the time being, disappeared. The Report did, however, form the background to the Distribution of Industry Act 1945 which incorporated some of its recommendations.

In many respects, the Barlow Report was a landmark in the development of thought on the regional problem in Britain. At the time of writing it still provides the most comprehensive review yet to be undertaken in Britain of the case for a regional policy. In several respects it was ahead of its time and many of the innovations which have been introduced into British regional policy in the 1960s were given clear expression in this report some twenty years earlier. Thus the report laid emphasis on the economic case for regional development. It regarded the congestion problems of some cities and the unemployment of the depressed areas as different aspects of the same problem; yet in the 1950s the Board of Trade regarded their regional development activities mainly as a social service for the peripheral areas. It was not until the 1960s, with the publication of the South-East Study, that the economic interconnection between congestion and the problems of the depressed regions was again brought into perspective.

Since the Barlow Commission were convinced of the economic case for regional development, they emphasized the need for research to promote sound economic development and to identify the problems of regions in advance of a critical situation arising so that appropriate redevelopment could be undertaken. Yet only in recent years has there been any major research activity by Government on the regional problem and much remains to be done.

Likewise, the Report emphasized the role of planning and the relationship of regional economic planning to physical planning. It stressed the importance of using new towns and public investment in infrastructure to spearhead regional economic development. The concept of growth areas is alluded to when it is suggested that some depressed areas may be incapable of development and the resources may have to be regrouped in those locations within the region which offer an environment suitable for development. These ideas were never properly developed in post-war legislation. Regional planning after the physical plans of the 1940s was abandoned until 1963; new towns were developed more as an instrument of urban and social policy than regional or economic, and, though some references were made to growth areas in post-war legislation, subsequent changes tied regional policy more closely to the criterion of unemployment with little regard for development potential. Yet in the 1960s these ideas were to reappear and form the basis of many of the changes in regional policy.[4]

From the mid 1960s onwards, regional planning, at least as regards the creation of institutions and the production of reports, has proceeded by leaps and bounds. In 1965 eight economic planning regions were established in England, with Wales and Scotland being constituted as separate planning regions in their entirety. The Regions were provided with Planning Councils and Boards. The Councils consist of members appointed as individuals having a wide range of knowledge and experience of their regions, and their main functions are to study and advise on the needs and potentialities of their regions, and to advise central government on aspects of national policy which have a bearing on regional development. The Boards consist of senior civil servants from the main government departments concerned with regional planning and their functions are to co-ordinate the regional economic planning work of Departments and to co-operate with the Economic Planning Councils in developing the long-term planning strategies for the regions.

If advise had been regionalised, decision-making remained at the centre, but in 1971, following the creation of the Department of the Environment, its regional offices were reorganised so that housing, planning and transport matters at the regional level could be dealt with in a comprehensive and integrated way.[5] Mention was made of the intention to decentralise the administration of work on local planning matters to the regional offices outside London to enable those offices to deal comprehensively with environmental questions affecting their Regions. During 1972 'most of the administrative casework involved in carrying out the Secretary of State's functions under the Town and Country Planning Acts and related legislation'[6] was transferred to the Regional Offices. 'In particular the regional offices will handle work in connection with development plans and the new structure and local plans, [and] many statutory appeals to the Secretary of State. . . .'[6]

In pursuance of their power to advise, the Regional Councils have sponsored or undertaken regional studies. The West Midlands may be taken as an example of their activities and the general progress of regional planning. In 1965 the West Midlands Council had referred to it by the government, *The West Midlands: A Regional Study*,[7] a report undertaken by a group of officials from Government Departments concerned with regional planning. . . . It drew together information about the region's economic, social and demographic structure and in analysing this material identified a number of problems. Of these, the most important were posed by the expected increase in the region's demand for houses. . . .'[8] The Council found the study a 'most valuable piece of work', and while differing from it on some matters were 'in general agreement with both its factual analysis and its suggestions'. It formed 'the starting point for much of the Council's work'[9] on its own first report which was published in March 1967. The introduction to that report – *The West Midlands: A Pattern of Growth* – indicates how the Council saw its function:

7. The detailed pattern of distribution of people and industry and the provision of services are based now, and must continue to be based, upon free decisions taken from day to day by very many private

persons and public and private bodies. But there is, as yet, no overall regional framework within which these decisions can helpfully be made. What is needed is general agreement on broad and flexible outline plans for the development of the region so that the individual day to day decisions will be given more purpose and coherence. Decisions that are piecemeal and unrelated will waste both public and private resources and produce an economic physical and social pattern less satisfactory than if there had been an agreed framework.

8. The Council's aim therefore has been to provide a draft framework from the discussion of which it is hoped that an agreed pattern of regional development will emerge.

10. The Council's first report . . . has deliberately sought to recommend measures which can reasonably be expected to be within the financial and other resources likely to be available. At every point the test of credibility has been applied.

11. The Council have been established to advise. They have no power and no executive authority. They have however formed views and recommended measures with an informed picture of the region as a whole before them. They therefore hope that what is offered by this report will form a credible basis on which executive decisions can be made by those who have the power and authority.

12. As a body concerned with regional matters the Council do not think questions of local planning and development appropriate for them unless these also have more than local implications. . . .

Despite the stress on credibility the Council's main conclusion – that it was desirable on social and economic grounds to contain the Birmingham conurbation within approximately its existing limits and in order to accomplish that over half a million people would need to be accommodated and found employment outside the conurbation by 1981 – was rejected by the central government in fairly forthright terms:

> The Government have been unable wholly to accept the overspill proposals . . . we have grave doubts about the viability of an overspill programme of the order of magnitude envisaged by the Council within the context of our policy for the distribution of industry. Many more people will almost certainly have to be accommodated within commuting distance from their work in the conurbation and further study of urban development along these lines is required.[10]

The Council has remained in being and produced another report in 1971 – *The West Midlands: An Economic Appraisal* – which, perhaps wisely, steered clear of arguments or proposals which would involve major new land uses. The 'further study' to which the government referred was prepared by another West Midlands regional body – the West Midlands Planning Authorities' Conference. The Conference consists of representatives of all the planning authorities in the West Midlands and its purpose is to study the problems and needs of the region and in particular of the conurbation and associated areas and to suggest proposals for their solutions. It is primarily a land-use planning body and the team it established to undertake the study was led by town planners and consisted largely of town planners drawn from constituent local authorities and the central government. Both because of this background to the study, and because constituent local authorities were, at the time the study was being made (and later considered after publication), beginning to prepare their own statutory structure plans, the report of the study – *A Developing Strategy for the West Midlands* – has been more influential on planning than previous regional reports. Since this has important implications for structure planning in the West Midlands, which will be looked at later in this chapter, some consideration of the procedures of the Report is necessary.

Terms of Reference of the West Midlands Regional Study
(approved by the Conference):

(1) To examine the problems of overspill and make proposals for their solution.

(2) For this purpose to make the necessary study of the immediate and long-term needs of the West Midlands Conurbation and associated areas, and to suggest both the broad strategy on such matters as land use, population, integration of communications and transport, employment and major planning issues of common interest and to make positive recommendations; and

(3) To draw into consultation for specific purposes officers of such other planning authorities, Government departments and new towns as may be necessary as occasions may arise to enable the Panel to carry out the tasks remitted to it.

The Report of the Study: A Developing Strategy
for the West Midlands, 1971[11]

307. The Preferred Strategy that has emerged from the process of testing and evaluation provides a policy concept, the validity of which must be assessed in terms of its practicability. We have to ask questions like "whether the Strategy is practicable in terms of the deployment of resources that it would entail and viable in terms of local government finance" or "whether any new legislation will be required to carry through its recommendations?"

308. At the outset of the Report, we made two points which are of critical importance to these questions. First, we stressed that the Strategy was to be a developing one, which would evolve over time in pace with the pattern of growth and opportunities in the Region. Secondly, we

made it clear that it was the firm aim of the Strategy both to deal with immediate problems and to face issues that would require clear cut decisions over the long term.

329. We see the role of Conference as a positive one, guiding the process of realisation through its successive stages. One way in which so diverse and far reaching a strategy might be implemented would be for Conference to adopt its realisation by presenting corporate views, while it would invite the appropriate authorities to use their powers to secure administrative action working within the Regional Strategy. In the main, the role of Conference in this context would be to ensure that in collaboration with others the overall supply met the overall need in housing and other fields.

330. Conference would be concerned, therefore, not with details. It would be necessary, however for Conference:–

(i) To ensure that the objectives of the Strategy are achieved in accordance with an appropriate programme, which would allow any degree of variation in time or scale that may be found necessary;

(ii) To make sure that the structure plans of local authorities are consistent with the adopted Regional Strategy; and

(iii) To achieve liaison between the different levels of government that would have a part to play in the implementation of the Strategy.

Report of the West Midlands Planning Authorities Conference, October 1972

E. THE REPORT ON OBSERVATIONS RECEIVED ON THE WEST MIDLAND REGIONAL STUDY

10. The observations indicate widely differing levels of understanding and equally divergent views on the implications of the Strategy. It is a fair comment to report that relatively few appear to have looked at the document in a regional sense. . . .

A considerable number of observations by their nature, relate more specifically to Structure Plans and can best be referred to Local Planning Authorities for consideration as their Structure Plans are drawn up.

We must also consider a parallel development in the land-use planning field – sub-regional planning. It was recognised in 1947 that a desirable planning unit might not always coincide with a local government boundary. The 1947 Act therefore empowered the Minister to set up joint planning boards for combined areas (either with the agreement of the local planning authorities concerned or, following a local inquiry, without their agreement) and joint advisory committees.[12] The former power was never used, and in so far as there was co-ordination of development plans on a regional basis it took place within the Ministry at the approval stage of the process.

But side by side with the growth of regional planning via *ad hoc* councils, boards and committees in the 1960s, the Ministry of Housing and Local Government began to promote the idea of sub-regional planning, in order to get co-ordination out of the Ministry and into the sphere of responsibility of local planning authorities. In the words of the Leicester and Leicestershire Sub-Regional Planning Study, the Minister, Mr Crossman, 'believed that in advance of, and without prejudice to any subsequent reform of local government functions and boundaries, co-operative planning ventures could begin between the towns and their surrounding countryside. His initial aim was to persuade the authorities in a small number of selected areas to come together and set up *ad hoc* teams to prepare long-term, 'broad-brush' plans for land uses and transportation. These were to be called 'sub-regional planning studies'.' Among those planning authorities so persuaded were Coventry City Council, Solihull County Borough Council and Warwickshire County Council who together in 1968 commissioned an independent study team to prepare a Coventry–Solihull–Warwickshire Sub-Regional Planning Study. The team which was led by and consisted overwhelmingly of town planners was finally assembled in early 1969 and its report was published in May 1971. This too has had an important influence on structure planning in the sub-region and so requires some indication of its terms of reference and processes.

> *Coventry-Solihull – Warwickshire Sub-Regional Study:*
> *A Strategy for the Sub-Region,* 1971

13.1 **Object.** The object of the study is to prepare proposals for the major land uses in the sub-region, having regard particularly to the development of population, employment, recreation and shopping in relation to each other and to transport. The purpose of the study is to serve as a bridge between regional considerations and the development plans of local planning authorities and to provide the authorities concerned with a common framework within which they can co-ordinate their plans and programmes. . . .

13.4 **Period.** The study generally should look forward towards the end of the century, although some elements may not be predictable with reasonable certainty for more than twenty years.

13.5 **General Content.** It will be necessary to examine the relationship of the study area to adjoining areas, to assess the development potential of the various parts of the study area and to consider for what form of development, if any, they may be suited. Account must be taken of the function, structure, requirements and potential of existing communities. Information will be sought from the Ministry of Housing and Local Government, any other Government Department and the West Midlands Economic Planning Council as to national and regional policies relating to the main components of the study. The study must take a realistic view of the resources likely to be available nationally for capital investment.

2.2 The writing of the Terms of Reference and the preliminary moves to establish the Study preceded the setting up of the West Midland Regional Study by the Planning Authorities' Conference although the Regional Study had been in progress for some nine months before the Sub-Regional Study Team was appointed and began technical work. Although not specifically covered by our Terms of Reference, the conjunction of the two Studies was an exceptional opportunity to work at the distinctly different level of sub-regional planning within a much fuller regional context than has been available to any previous sub-regional study. There is no precedent in Britain for such an opportune relationship, and we accordingly set out in a memorandum some aspects of our work on which we hoped for advice from the Regional Study and others in which our findings appeared likely to be significant to the development of the regional strategy. This memorandum was sent to the Regional Study, and was subsequently applied by us in relating sub-regional to regional factors in any specific aspect of the Study.

2.3 The publication of the Manual on Form and Content of Development Plans[13] late in the Study has made it possible to interpret the nature of this report and of the Study in relation to the Structure Plans discussed in the Manual.

2.4 The Manual describes (para. 4.6) a sub-regional framework for individual authorities' Structure Plans composed of decisions taken by the authorities jointly. It has been the purpose of the Study to crystallise these decisions, and thereby enable each authority to include in its Structure Plan a statement of its relationship to adjoining authorities within one or several sub-regional spheres of influence (para. 4.9).

2.5 The objectives penetrating throughout the Study will form part of the framework of aims which authorities will state (para. 4.11) regarding national, regional and sub-regional policies for the area of their Structure Plan, and the Study's essential contribution will be to the strategy part of the Structure Plans (para. 4.12). The approach of the Study has been to consider alternative strategies for the sub-region (para. 4.13), describing how far each measures up to the aims for strategic planning.

Deriving the Objectives

3.1 Our Terms of Reference suggested the broad scope of the Study, and from this starting point the goals and objectives were initially developed with help from the following sources:

    (i) The local knowledge of policy issues already in the minds of the Members of the three authorities, including the issues which led to the establishment of the Study in the first place.

(ii) Scrutiny of the Council minutes of the three authorities, particularly of the policy-planning committees and of their revenue and capital expenditure budgets.

(iii) Discussions with officers of the authorities, and reference to the Development Plans and reports of the authorities.

(iv) The items of local news and the editorial opinions of the newspapers circulating locally in different parts of the sub-region.

(v) A professional consensus as to what the Study should be planning for and of the economic, social and physical environment which the sub-regional strategy should seek to encourage.

3.2 We saw the purpose of the strategy as being to help the sub-region towards certain goals which were seen as the ultimate achievements of a social, economic and physical environment.

It is then the land-use rather than the economic aspects of regional planning that are specifically designed to influence structure planning. It is important to note therefore the relative importance of the contributions made by professional planners, elected councillors and the general public – either individually or via their organisations – to the regional and sub-regional planning process. Both reports were prepared by teams of professional planners assisted by outside consultants and supervised by planning officers from the constituent authorities. While many planning authorities had the opportunity to comment on both reports, it may be doubted whether many councillors read through them both, as opposed to relying on summaries prepared by their officers. Each report was accompanied by several volumes of technical appendices – how many of these would be read by councillors? To what extent is it likely that the Warwickshire county councillors who approved the recommended strategy of the Sub-Regional Study were aware of the implications, advantages and drawbacks of both the preferred strategies and their possible alternatives when they did so? How aware would they be that the decisions they were taking were political decisions about the allocation of scarce resources rather than technical decisions about different kinds of planning?

But although councillors at least had the opportunity to have their say on both regional and sub-regional studies, the general public were not so fortunate. In spite of the fact that the local press gave coverage to the Regional Study when it was published, there was little concerted effort to stimulate comment or generate public discussion on it. Only nine amenity groups commented on the report. The Sub-Regional Study was however presented to the public via a series of public meetings throughout the sub-region, some three and four months after its publication. The meetings took the form of a presentation, with slides, of the report by the leader or deputy leader of the study, followed by questions and discussion.

I attended a meeting at Warwick where, excluding council officials and councillors of the Borough Council, there were not more than thirty members of the public present. After the presentation of the report, which was both intelligible and reasonably neutral, discussion started. Most of the discussion was on the effect of the preferred strategy on Warwick, and in particular on the necessity for new roads – the Stop the Inner Relief Road Campaign was then into its stride. A very small number of people attempted to question some of the assumptions and concealed value judgements in the report; and while the team leader and his officials were prepared to discuss these matters, some of the other members of the public, and in particular the Warwick borough councillors, resented this line of questioning and accused those questioners of wasting time when the meeting was for the benefit of the people of Warwick.[14]

Who, if anybody, was 'to blame' for what happened at the public meeting? If no one, how could this exercise in public participation have been structured differently? If planners use sophisticated techniques to arrive at conclusions, should they not spell out how those techniques are used? How can people unfamiliar with the planning process, except at a very simple level, be brought to realise that the best, indeed the only way, to mount an effective challenge to the practical on-the-ground implications of a plan is to challenge the plan's assumptions and philosophy? Given that neither regional nor sub-regional planning have any statutory base, or statutory mechanism for the consideration of objections, how could a member of the public or an amenity group ensure that their objections were considered? Finally, as a lead into our consideration of structure planning, what are the implications of regional and sub-regional planning as discussed in the following extracts for the production and consideration of structure and local plans?

DoE Circular No. 44/71

Regional planning: structure plans
44. In recent years, increasing importance has been attached to the need for planning development and other use of land, including transportation, over a wider area than the area of existing individual authori-

ties and to the growing physical relationship between neighbouring areas: and to relating physical, economic and social planning. There has been growing recognition of the need for regional planning and for it to be both more closely related to development planning and taken more into account in the preparation by local authorities of their statutory development plans. This approach is reflected in a number of the provisions of Part 1 – in, for example, the references to neighbouring areas: and, above all, in the requirement that local planning authorities, in formulating their policy and general proposals for their structure plan in respect of the development and other use of land, shall have regard to the economic planning and development of the region as a whole. It is reflected, also, in the fact that groups of authorities have been invited to collaborate in the preparation of structure plans and in the extent to which the areas covered by these groups have been or are the subject of work at regional or sub-regional level. This approach will need to underlie the various stages of structure planning.

45. Considerable experience has been gained over recent years, notably over the last few, of regional – including regional economic – planning; of the nature and scope of the further work that needs to be done; and of the need to develop further co-operation and effective working relationships between the Regional Economic Planning Councils and Boards, and the Standing Conferences or other groupings of local authorities for planning purposes. The Government have announced in the White Paper on Local Government in England (Cmnd. 4584) that they will continue to pursue the preparation of regional strategies by the creation of teams comprising the Standing Conferences, the Regional Economic Planning Councils and central Government. Material on regional or sub-regional matters is already or will increasingly become available. The current validity and depth of this material, and the circumstances of the different regions, vary considerably. But in all cases it contributes to the regional background essential to the preparation of plans under the new development plan system. In formulating their structure plans, authorities should frame them in the light of the studies, reports and strategy documents prepared or published by Government Departments, Regional Economic Planning Councils and Boards, and local planning authorities acting jointly or within a Standing Conference, read together with the published Government replies to them. ... The regulations (Schedule 1, Part II), (vi) provide for the written statement of a structure plan to include such indications as the local planning authority think appropriate of the account they have taken of these matters.

W. Burns,[15] 'National and regional planning policies
– England', (1971) *J.R.T.P.I.*, 308

... The third issue that needs to be clarified is the relationship between Structure Plans and Regional Strategic Plans. The terms of reference for the South-East Joint Planning Team were to provide a regional framework:

(1) for the local planning authorities to carry out their planning responsibilities including the preparation of structure plans; and,

(2) for Government decisions on investment, and economic and social policies relating to the region's future development.

It seems to me that a regional strategic plan must give a sufficiently clear brief to structure plan authorities to enable them to prepare their plans:

(1) around a realistic population figure;

(2) with a role that is clearly seen in relation to other areas; and

(3) against a general background of availability of resources, constraints and opportunities that only a regional plan can indicate.

On the other hand, it is crucial that the regional plan should not try to solve local problems, but should leave scope for local initiative to take into account the special local conditions, problems and possibilities. Everyone will accept, I hope, that regional strategic plans and structure plans must be prepared in an iterative way, i.e., that the broad regional plan should be seen as variable if structure plans indicate either that other possibilities can with real advantage be exploited or, alternatively, that undue sacrifices are needed in local terms to achieve the objectives set out in the first round of the regional work. But let me not overstress this aspect. Clearly a regional strategic plan must be seen as of critical importance to structure planning and variations from it will need very clear and positive substantiation.

In the South-East Strategic Plan we tried to indicate the relationship and linkages between the various growth areas and to set down for structure plan guidance the possibilities that needed to be explored and the constraints that appeared to be important from a regional point of view. ... I feel reasonably satisfied, myself, that the framework is adequate for the next round of planning, i.e., the preparation of the structure plans which, in turn, will indicate whether or to what extent the regional strategic plan should be varied in the future.

(b) The defects of the 1947-style development plan

Two distinct strands of criticism were levelled at planning as it operated under the 1947 Act: the first concerned the nature of the development plan as it evolved in practice; the second the nature of the local government system. An attempt to meet the first criticism was made by the Town and Country Planning Act 1968; the second by the Local Government Act 1972. Both criticisms must be examined before the solutions are considered.

(i) The rigid plan

The criticisms on this score are conveniently summarised in the Report of the Planning Advisory Group – *The Future of Development Plans* – as seminal a report on the pre-1968 reforms system in the planning world as the Franks Report[16] has been in the administrative world. The group was appointed in May 1964 to assist the relevant government departments in a general review of the planning system. Their report gave no indication that outside evidence had been asked for or received. The composition of the committee (five local authority planners, eight central government officials, three town or county clerks, three city or county treasurers, one chartered surveyor/estate agent in private practice and one planning consultant) must be borne in mind when the problems of the structure planning they recommended are considered.

The Future of Development Plans (HMSO 1965)

The Merits and Defects of the present Development Plans

1:20. The main merits of the present development plans have lain in the basis they have provided for the exercise of development control, and for projecting probable land uses and values, particularly in urban areas. They gave public confidence to the exercise by local government of the novel planning controls and provided machinery for public objection to specific proposals.

1:21. This stemmed from the definition of 'development plan' in the 1947 Act as a plan 'indicating the manner in which the local planning authority propose that land in their area should be used'. They were in fact to serve essentially as land-use allocation maps providing the basis for development control. The original intention was that the allocations should be drawn in with a 'broad brush' and that the rigidity of detailed zonings (on the pattern of the 1932 Act system) should be avoided. But the statutory definition and the notational techniques adopted have resulted in a constant tendency towards greater detail and precision. The plans have thus acquired the appearance of certainty and stability which is misleading since the primary use zonings may themselves permit a wide variety of use within a particular allocation, and it is impossible to forecast every land requirement over many years ahead. In practice the plans are most precise when they reflect the pattern of existing use and far less clear in depicting future changes.

1:22. It is interesting to compare the 1947 Act definition of a development plan with the wording in the first draft of the Bill where it was defined as 'A plan indicating the general principles upon which development in [the] area will be promoted and controlled'. Here the emphasis is on general principles, and on the positive aspect of promotion as well as on the negative aspects of control. This is very much the kind of emphasis which we would like to see re-introduced into the planning system. The main defects of the present system flow from the abandonment of this concept.

1:23. The initial development plans produced in the early years following the 1947 Planning Act meant that for the first time the whole country was covered by relatively detailed plans setting out the planning policies for each area. But it has proved extremely difficult to keep these plans not only up to date but forward looking and responsive to the demands of change. The result has been that they have tended to become out of date – in terms of technique in that they deal inadequately with transport and the inter-relationship of traffic and land use; in factual terms in that they fail to take account quickly enough of changes in population forecasts, traffic growth and other economic and social trends; and in terms of policy in that they do not reflect more recent developments in the field of regional and urban planning. . . .

1:28. On the other hand, the development plans have not provided an adequate instrument for detailed planning at the local level. While the town maps may present a reasonably clear picture of land use, they do not convey any impression of how the land will in fact be developed or redeveloped, or what other action may be taken in the area to change its character or to improve the environment. They give little guidance to developers beyond the primary use zoning. They make no contribution to the quality of urban design or the quality of the environment. . . .

1:29. Finally, the attempt to process all these detailed plans through a centralised procedure, including provision for objections (of which there may be hundreds or even thousands on a single plan) and public local inquiry, has inevitably led to very serious delays which tend to undermine public confidence in the system. . . .

(ii) The inappropriate structure of local government

The Report of the Royal Commission on Local Government,[17]
Cmnd. 4040

87. The fragmentation of England into 79 county boroughs and 45 counties, each with its own independent authority concerned with its own interests, has made the proper planning of development and transportation impossible. It is obvious that town and country must be planned together, as the evidence given to us recognised. There being no provision for this under the present structure, central government has tried to fill the gap: by producing regional plans itself, by the appointment of regional economic planning councils, by persuading local authorities to work together on land-use and transportation surveys and on sub-regional plans, by taking power to establish passenger transport authorities. But none of these devices is satisfactory, since none puts responsibility squarely on local government or provides for continuous and comprehensive planning allied with power to implement the plans.

88. The division between county boroughs and counties meanwhile builds into the system a division of interest where, in fact, there is a common interest. The county councils are concerned, naturally, to defend their territory against the encroachment of the towns; the county borough councils, which must encroach, are concerned, equally naturally, to do it in the way easiest for themselves. Boundary ambitions and fears have dominated the work of local government for many years past. The

needs of the population must be defined, and plans made to meet them, over the areas in which the needs have got to be satisfied; and the authorities which make the plans must be in a position to see that they are carried out. As we said above when discussing the planning functions, no local government area, however big, can ever finally be self-contained for planning purposes. But areas must be big enough to enable responsible authorities to meet most of their needs. Further, there must be arrangements, rooted in local government, for planning the broad use of land over areas wider than those of the operating authorities, so that needs which have to be met beyond their boundaries can be provided for. Nothing has been worse for local government than the fights between authorities over land.

89. Within the counties, the division of responsibility between county and district councils is a great weakness. The present district pattern is, as we have shown, irrational. But even if that were cured by the creation of larger districts, the weakness due to the division of responsibilities would remain. One of the major difficulties in the present structure is that the county councils have no general development powers, and in particular no general house-building powers. This partly explains the negative attitude some of them have taken towards the needs of the municipalities; their powers are largely negative. The county councils which have tried to help the hard pressed towns have had enormous difficulties, since for many purposes they must work through the district councils. They can plan the use of the land; they cannot see that their plans are implemented. They cannot do business with their powerful municipal neighbours on equal terms. . . .

92. It is not only the physical manifestations of divided responsibility that are wrong under the present system in the counties. It is also the attitudes which the division necessarily engenders. No single authority is responsible for thinking about the totality of related services and their adequacy for local needs; no single authority is responsible for considering the community as a whole. So county and district councils are, inevitably, providers of services rather than proper units of self-government.

The evolution and criticisms of the pre-reform period thus presented the reformers with a difficult challenge: on the one hand, lawyers' pressure for formality and certainty in planning had pushed the development plan towards greater detail and precision than planners thought desirable;[18] on the other, the necessity to increase the scope of planning so as to comprehend the interrelatedness of virtually all local government services and neighbouring local authority areas required plans that were not certain and precise but flexible enough to allow for change. How, if at all, could these conflicting pressures be reconciled and the way opened to 'better plans and better results'?[19]

3. The reforms of 1968 and 1972: towards a solution?

The PAG Report on development plans and the Royal Commission's Report on local government both sparked wide-ranging debates on their respective subject matters, neither of which have been stilled by the enactment of legislation designed to give effect to all (in the case of the PAG Report) or some (in the case of the Royal Commission's Report) of their recommendations. Legislation however inevitably changed the nature of the debate; whereas it had previously been about whether the proposals were feasible or desirable, after legislation it tended to concentrate on the challenges and problems involved in operating the new system; though, because of the difference in time between legislation reforming the planning system and the local government system, part of the debate on local government reform hinged on the difficulties or benefits this would create for the new style of development plans. Effectively, however, the reformed planning system is being operated by the reformed local government system and the rest of this chapter is constructed accordingly.

In reading the following sections, consider these questions: how realistic were the proposals; how sensible were their critics, how accommodating or convincing were the respective governments to their critics; what changes were there between initial and final legislative proposals; what were the common themes that seemed to run through the debates and discussions; what conclusions might be drawn about the efficacy of the legislative process or the understanding of MPs and Ministers of the planning process? How far have the ideals of the PAG survived their translation into law and its explanation in ministerial circulars and manuals? How far is all the departmental advice compatible with the flexibility and devolution of powers which the new system is meant to herald? Have the reforms dealt with the problems as seen by the critics of the old systems?

(a) Proposed reforms in the planning system and the debate thereon

Objectives   *Report of the Planning Advisory Group*, op. cit.

1:1. We have approached this review of the planning system with the following as our main objectives:

(1) to ensure that the planning system serves its purpose satisfactorily both as an instrument of planning policy and as a means of public participation in the planning process;

(2) to improve the technical quality of development plans and to strengthen their policy content, so that they provide an adequate framework for future development and redevelopment, and a sound basis for development control;

(3) to get the level of responsibility right, so that only matters of general policy and major objectives are submitted for Ministerial approval, and matters of local land use are settled locally in the light of these considerations;

(4) to simplify planning administration.

1 :2. Planning is not simply a matter of allocating land for various kinds of development. It is also concerned with the form of development and redevelopment, and with the quality of the physical environment that is produced. In the end what matters is not simply where development takes place: its form is equally important and the planning system will be judged by the quality of the results it produces.

1 :3. The interest of central government in physical planning is concerned less with the detail of land use than with the deployment of population and employment, the inter-relationship of traffic and land use in terms of urban structure and urban renewal, and with the quality of environment in town and country, in terms of development standards, recreational opportunities and community services.

1 :4. At the local level, however, these issues must be translated into terms of land allocation and development control, and the system must ensure that this can be done effectively. We have assumed that the planned allocation of land and development control will continue to be the basis of planning at the local level. We see no practical alternative to this as the means of ensuring efficient and economical development, and of settling specific disputes about the use of land in a particular locality.

1 :5. The planning system in fact has to serve an immense range of purposes. It cannot be a simple process. The problems of physical development and redevelopment with which it has to deal are often highly complex, involve investment decisions of great magnitude and extend across many related fields of policy. Many different agencies, public and private, are involved and many different interests are affected.

Needs of the future

1 :33. We have tried to forecast the main requirements of policy and general needs that development plans should serve in the years ahead and what are likely to be the forces operating on the system. We must expect fast growing population, with higher expectations demanding higher standards, more mobile both in daily life and recreation. This will mean a surge of physical development on a scale that this country has not previously seen and this will occur, overwhelmingly, in and around the towns. We therefore need a development plan system which will

(1) guide the urban development and renewal which is certain to take place;
(2) promote efficiency and quality in the replanning of towns;
(3) encourage better organisation and co-ordination of professional skills so that town and country are planned as a whole;
(4) stimulate more purposeful planning of rural and recreational areas.[20]

A new planning framework

1:35. We see no way of improving the planning system without radically changing the form and content of development plans. To achieve this it is in our view essential to recognise and promote two levels of responsibility in plan making – the central responsibility of the Minister for policy and general standards, and the local responsibility for detailed land use allocation and environmental planning. The Minister must retain effective supervision of the policy or structural elements, and the local planning authorities must assume full responsibility for matters of local detail and local interest.

1:36. What we now propose is that each local planning authority should still be required to submit development plans for Ministerial approval. The content of these plans, however, will be limited to the major issues of policy affecting the area concerned and those matters in which the Minister has an interest. They will be primarily statements of policy illustrated where necessary with sketch maps and diagrams and accompanied by a diagrammatic or 'structure' map designed to clarify the basic physical structure of the area and its transport system.

1:37. Thus for the county boroughs and other urban areas over 50,000 population we propose a new type of *urban plan* which concentrates on the broad pattern of future development and redevelopment and deals with the land use/transport relationships in an integrated way, but which excludes the detailed land use allocations of the present town maps.

1:38. Similarly, for the counties we propose a new form of *county plan* which deals with the distribution of population and employment, the major communications network, the main policies for creation and conservation, green belts, and the general development policy for towns and villages. The county plan will include urban plans for towns over 50,000 population and other areas of special importance – notably those planned for major expansion.

1:39. Both the urban plans and the county plans will be required to identify the *action areas*, which are the areas that require comprehensive planning (for development, redevelopment or improvement) and on which action is to be concentrated over the next ten years or so. These are wider in scope than the present C.D.A.'s, and replace them as the means of comprehensive redevelopment.

1:40. The urban plans and county plans will be submitted to the Minister for approval. They should provide a coherent framework of planning policy. But within this broad policy framework there will need to be more detailed plans of a local character, filling in the detail and implementing the intentions of the policy plans.

1:41. We therefore propose that local planning authorities should have power to prepare *local plans* which will serve as a guide to development control and a basis for the more positive aspects of environmental planning. These local plans will not be submitted for Ministerial approval but must conform with the policies laid down in the urban plan or county plan, and will be subject to a procedure leading to formal adoption by the planning authority.

1:42. Local plans will be varied in character and there may be plans for small towns, for villages, for town centres or for districts within an urban plan. But the most significant of these local plans will be those for the action areas.

1:43. The type of plans which we recommend cannot be produced by planning authorities acting in isolation. They require to form part of a regional pattern and also of what may be called a sub-regional pattern.

1:44. The regional context will be set out in plans prepared by the Economic Planning Boards and Councils. These are likely to be primarily concerned with creating the conditions for economic growth in some regions and controlling the pace of growth in others, within the framework of national economic planning. As a part of this process they will have to be concerned with physical planning issues which are of regional significance, with the overall distribution of population and employment, green belt policy and any other limitations on growth in the conurbations. They must also encompass other physical factors of regional significance such as communications, water resources and major industrial projects; the economic implications of major development projects (motorways, docks, airports); and the impact of economic decisions on physical planning. It will consequently be necessary to associate local planning authorities with the regional planning process and to ensure that their development plans give effect to the intentions of the regional plan.

1:45. The new urban plans and county plans will form the main link between regional plans and local land-use planning. But regional policies will not always be sufficiently detailed to secure consistency in the urban and county plans. There are areas – particularly conurbation and other areas of complex urban growth – where certain problems, such as population deployment, communications pattern, the siting of industrial and commercial centres, have to be solved over a wider area than that of a single local planning authority. The identification of problems and areas requiring a 'sub-regional' approach and the preparation of unified plans covering them, have to be recognised as essential planning tasks.

1:47. In drawing up these new proposals, we have paid particular attention to the position and rights of the individual under the planning system. We hope that the emphasis we lay upon the preparation and adoption by the local planning authority of local plans will mean that the individual is better informed and more consulted on planning matters. There is, however, an important change in the nature of the individual's rights of objection. At present, because development plans show detailed land allocations, detailed objections to their provisions can be and frequently are made, and are decided by the Minister on the basis of an inspector's report. We do not envisage that this will be possible under the new form of submitted plan, because it will not go into such detail. At the stage of the urban plan or county plan submission, the Minister will be considering issues of general policy and principle, and objections or representations will be addressed to these issues rather than to detailed proposals. But at the stage when the local planning authority publish a draft local plan showing their proposals for the area in detail, the authority will be required to afford an opportunity for detailed comments, representations or objections to be made; and they must take these views into account in deciding whether to amend the plan before formally adopting it. The Minister will have reserve powers to call in a local plan and deal with it himself, where exceptional circumstances warrant this.

Urban planning

2:1. The dominant task of urban planning over the next twenty years will be the physical reshaping of the large towns and cities, the modernisation of their road and transport systems, the redevelopment of town centres and the wholesale renewal, whether by comprehensive improvement or redevelopment, of obsolescent housing. This process will call for a radical re-appraisal of the town's functions and of the distribution of activities within the town. The attempt to establish a reasonable balance between accessibility and environmental standards will be a major pre-occupation. . . .

Scope

2:8. Urban plans must be designed primarily to deal with urban problems. They are not the vehicle for deciding regional policies, though they must give effect to decisions reached in the context of the regional plan. . . .

2:37. The ultimate aim is to get the plan established as the long-term policy objective for the town and this necessarily involves a long and complex process of preparation, negotiation and consultation – both before and after the Minister has given his approval to the plan. The stage of statutory submission of formal plans is only one element in the planning process and it is not necessarily the most important. What matters most is to produce a soundly based, forward looking plan, and to secure public support for its implementation. . . .

County planning

3:3. For the future, we consider it most important that county planning authorities should develop their planning policies on a county-wide basis, rather than concentrate the greater part of their attention on particular town map areas. This is important for two reasons. Firstly, the county plan is a crucial link between regional planning and local land-use planning. It should be one of the main instruments for working out the detailed distribution of population and employment within the general framework of the regional plan. Secondly, there is no doubt that the explosive growth of population and car ownership, increased personal incomes and greater leisure will have a tremendous impact on country and coastal areas. . . .

Local planning

5:4. We recommend that the need for planning in detail at the local level should be recognised as an integral part of the new system. Specific provision should be made for local plans to be prepared by the local planning authority in accordance with the general policies set out in the plans submitted for Ministerial approval. The emphasis should be on the building up of planning at the local level, not only as a corollary to the reduction in the amount of detail contained in plans submitted for Ministerial approval, but also as an essential instrument of positive and comprehensive environmental planning.

5:7. Local planning authorities should not feel obliged to undertake the preparation of more local plans than they can reasonably cope with. It is essential that the new system should not become as overloaded at the local end as the present system has tended to overload the centralised procedure. But detailed planning at the local level is a vital component of the planning process. It is a job that needs to be done and our proposals provide a practical means of doing it.

Thomas Sharp,[21] 'Planning planning', (1966) *J.T.P.I.*, 209

. . . I want to say at the outset that, in my view, the PAG report is a hopelessly unbalanced and dangerous document. . . . their main aim seems to have been nothing more than to produce a system of planning that gives the least possible trouble to the planners. And of course to the Ministry concerned with planning. . . .

I don't want to go into all PAG's proposals for reforming the planning machinery. Their report is an extraordinarily muddled piece of presentation; and it would be too involved a business to try to sort it out here. I merely want to look at the proposals so far as they affect the public interest. It is, of course, obvious that these proposals *could* achieve what the Group mainly seem to want to achieve – to make planning easier for the planners. And that, no doubt, would be fine, if it were the consideration that mainly mattered, and if it didn't involve detriment to other interests. But it is far from being the main consideration, and the proposals that are made do involve detriment to other interests, including an interest of a very special kind, namely the public interest.

Their intention is clearly shown in two ways – in the kind of documents that are to be used, and in the kind of opportunities that are suggested for objection to the plans they are supposed to refer to.

I would like first to take a glance at their documents – particularly the documents relating to towns. *Documents* is the right word, for none of the general matter associated with the new procedures can be dignified by the name of *plans* in the sense that that term is generally understood, that is to say as plans showing with precision the present detailed form of a town and what is to be done with it. There seems to be one exception – the limited areas covered with what are called 'action area plans', plans for areas to be comprehensively redeveloped. The rest of the illustrative material is quite simply pictorial; picture documents, simple cartoons;

mere broad elementary illustrations; mere blobs of colours placed on sheets of paper completely innocent of all precise information as to the towns to which they refer. They are, of course, deliberately so. That is their intention. They are not intended to be *plans* at all in a properly drawn sense. They are to be merely graphically presented policy documents. The report makes this perfectly clear in several of its passages. I need only quote one of them. Referring to the Group's new form of 'urban plan' the report says that 'most, if not all, of the proposals which the plan should cover can best be set out in writing, supported by sketch plans or diagrams in the text'. The plain fact is that it is deliberately intended that the public should not be informed in any detail at all of proposals and controls which affect them as individuals or as members of individual groups. They are not to know the specific boundaries and identifiable localities of even the broadest proposals. They are to be denied any information on matters which they may be concerned with personally as landowners or householders as well as citizens – matters, for instance, such as land use zoning, the actual lines of road proposals, and so on.

Why is it to be like that? The report suggests that this kind of so-called planning 'provides the public with a clearer picture of what is proposed for the town as a whole' and gives 'a greater sense of local responsibility and greater scope for public participation in the planning process'. What absolute nonsense that is! What it amounts to broadly is one of two things. Either the public is too stupid to understand a properly detailed plan, and should therefore be treated as a collection of children to be fobbed off with pictures reduced to a level of elementary simplicity – either that, or it is too clever; too clever for the comfort of the people who have to prepare, defend and approve properly drawn plans. The Group do not indicate which opinion they incline to. Perhaps it is as well: for the first is too insulting a belief to be publicly declared. But the undeclared intention is perfectly clear. It is simply to save trouble – to save trouble to the primary planners in planning offices, but mainly trouble to their Ministerial counterparts in the Civil Service.

PAG's method of saving trouble is not merely to simplify statutory planning to mere policy statements, but even more blatantly to deny the public any real rights of proper appeal against such proposals as may be made. It is true that one isolated and unsupported passage in the report says that plans submitted for the Minister's approval (that is to say the county plan and the urban structure plan) 'would be subject to the normal procedure of advertisement, objections and public inquiry held by one of the Minister's inspectors'. But it is impossible to find any amplification, illustration or further reference to that. The report is silent to an ominous degree as to what is intended even here, on these two documents. We have only vague evasions – statements about a 'more flexible form of (Ministerial) approval . . . directed primarily at endorsing the plan in terms of policy . . . rather than at specific approval of particular objects'; and, as well as that, recommendations that 'Ministerial approval should not necessarily apply to all the aspects of the plan or to all aspects with the same degree of finality'. All the same, vague as they are, all references to this matter in the report indicate quite clearly that if there are indeed to be any rights of individual objection at any stage they are to be limited to the policy plans for the town as a whole and will not be permitted or accepted in relation to any particular considerations whatever. And if the report is unhelpfully reticent about it, the Chairman of the Group himself on one public occasion has let himself go and been definite enough – and remember that he is also the Under-Secretary concerned with planning at the Ministry. At a meeting at the RIBA he put it quite bluntly. 'Under the PAG proposals,' he said, 'the individual would not have the right of access to the Minister about any matter in a development plan.' And by development plan he meant all plans made under the Planning Acts and not merely the statutory documents.[22]

The trouble that PAG want to avoid is the troublesome business of having Public Inquiries into planning proposals. It is true that the public may be given the opportunity of making representations and objections to proposals at one late minor stage in the planning process. If and when the documents called 'local plans' are produced, then that dangerous animal, the public, *may* be unmuzzled and permitted a growl if it feels like it. But there is no certainty, no compulsory requirement, that it need ever be unmuzzled. The opportunity need never be given at all. Local plans need never be prepared. 'We do not suggest,' says the report, 'that it will be possible or even desirable to prepare detailed local plans for every town and village in a county or for every district of towns covered by an urban plan' (and you will remember what a local plan is to be: it is to be 'highly descriptive . . . in a lively and vivid style of presentation, much less formal than a statutory plan': in other words another pictorial cartoon again). The preparation of these permissive local plans 'will be undertaken in the light of local planning problems and priorities and will be governed very largely by the availability of professional staff and technical resources'. And 'planning authorities should not feel obliged to undertake the preparation of more local plans than they can reasonably cope with'. What generosity! What tenderness of consideration for demo-cratic principles and legal rights! But even this nugatory gesture is made derisory by the fact that such plans as may be made public out of the kindness of heart of the planning authority are to be 'a local responsi-bility and not submitted for Ministerial approval'. The public's 'views' on the plans are to be expressed 'in writing'. They will then be 'considered' by the people who made them. There will be no public arguments, no embarrassing confrontations, no hearing by any independent authority. All the troublesome public can do is to send a little letter to the planners. Who can simply reject it out-of-hand. And that will be the end of that.

The delays which will be saved are those which occur in the approval of the plans after hearing objections to them at the Public Inquiry – and even then only in one particular stage of that part of the process. The stage where the delays mainly occur, that is the stage within the Ministry is simply not mentioned at all in the report. One would have thought that it would not have taken miraculous powers of insight to realize that there is something odd about the fact that while it takes the Inspector who has held the Inquiry a matter of mere weeks to present his report and recommendations – while it takes only weeks for that, it can take administrative civil servants years to decide whether he had done his job properly. One would have thought that the PAG people would have seen some place there where they might save delays: that they might have seen that the proper way to deal with a blockage of circulation is to cure the cause rather than to kill the patient. But no: they have been so obsessed with the troublesome public's troublesome individual interests, as are their Ministerial begetters, that they have decided that it is the public that is to blame, not the public authorities; and that the way to avoid the difficulty is to deny the public, as individuals, any real rights at all in the plan-making process.

That is a pretty far step. Even PAG, however, have not dared to go so far as to deny the right of appeal where an individual is refused planning permission to do something with his own property. And it is surprising that they do not seem to have realized what effect the continuation of this right will have in circumstances where you have merely broad cartoons instead of real plans. And that applies particularly in the land-use zoning which attracts PAG's special condemnation. Numerous possible applicants must now be deterred from making submissions merely by seeing that what they would like to do on a particular site is at odds with the provisions of an official plan. And they are even more deterred from appealing against a refusal. But if there is no plan with specific provisions and the applicants have had a refusal on what they regard as a merely *ad hoc* decision, then the feeling that they should appeal will be very much stronger. So while objections to official plans may be ruled out, appeals on development applications will almost certainly increase. And since an application appeal is likely to be more time-consuming than an objection to a development plan, the trouble and the delay which it is the professed intention to avoid will almost certainly be increased.[23]

Indeed it seems to me almost certain that a very substantial number of present appeals arise from the vagueness of content of even the present development plans. Plans which contain no firm specified controls on matters like housing-density, site-coverage and so on, and which depend on phrases like the not uncommon one that 'each application will be judged on its merits' – plans like that simply invite objections against decisions made under them. Firm plans and planning provisions which have been approved by a higher authority after a Public Inquiry will be far more acceptable or at least will be regarded as far less open to challenge, and therefore be less productive of appeals, than *ad hoc* decisions made under vague controls that seem to have no reference to any firm plans. If it is essential somehow to reduce the burden of appeals – and indeed it is – one way to do it, it could be argued, would be to take the exactly opposite line to that suggested by PAG, and produce firmer not looser plans. . . .[24]

House of Commons Standing Committee G:
Committee Stage of the Town and Country Planning
Bill 1968; Session 1967–8, Vol. IX, cols 75–6, 81–2

The amendments discussed below related to the preparation of the structure plan. They were being proposed to what is now section 7(5)(6) and (7) of the Town and Country Planning Act 1971.

MR WELLBELOVED: I still make no apology for having tabled an Amendment which strikes at the base of the Bill, because the Bill starts with three principles with which I am not wholly in agreement and the Clause embodies them. The intention is to relieve the Minister and his Department of a considerable amount of work, to speed up the process of planning appeals and to confer power on local planning authorities. I do not necessarily agree that these three aims are desirable.

I think that the effect of the Amendment would be to put into the Bill an air of precision which would prevent hardship to the individual, which I believe to be the fundamental purpose of any planning Act. If we leave it at 'indicate', it will mean that when it comes to structure plans showing what an action area will be, nobody will know the limits of that action area. The structure plan will be published, and people in the locality will still have only a star or a diamond on the plan to tell them that their areas are to be subject to quite substantial improvement.

How long after the publication of the structure plan will the local plan be brought into being?

How will the Minister deal with local planning authorities which lag behind, which have areas shown on the structure plan as being necessary for prompt action but do not promptly prepare their local plans? What will he do to make certain that the time lag between the publication of the structure plan and the publication of local plans is as short as possible?

If, in the structure plan, it is necessary to have a circle which indicates an area which is crying out for urgent action, for rehabilitation or for comprehensive redevelopment, why is it not possible to put that in the structure plan on a clearly defined basis? The survey must have taken account of the area concerned. It must have taken account of all the factors which are necessary for the production of a local plan to deal with an action area. There is no point in putting a diamond on the structure plan if the area has not been surveyed. Or are we to assume that someone will look at an area on the structure plan, decide that it is pretty old, that the houses are 80 years old and then make it an action area? Surely, this is not necessary. There will have been a proper survey, and, that being so, it ought to be possible to designate the area which is to be an action area.

If the designation of an area is to be decided by a local planning authority, we will get back to the old cry that the local authority is judge and jury in all matters, because it will say not only what will take place in the action area, but how wide it should be. In my view this detail should be set out in the structure plan.

Amendment No. 136 provides that the diagrams, illustrations, and so on, should be on the basis of an Ordnance Survey map. I press the Minister to consider this. I do not think that it is vital in built-up areas, but it is important in areas of historical interest, in special areas and in green belt areas. It is indefensible that a structure plan should not show clearly all the areas of green belt and land which it is agreed should be preserved. This can only be shown if it is done on an Ordnance Survey map, as present development plans are shown.

MR MACDERMOT (Minister of State, Ministry of Housing and Local Government): Let me return to the main point, which is the amount of detail which should be given in the structure plan of what is envisaged by way of action in the action area and why we do not want that to be put on an Ordnance Survey map.

Having regard to some of the things that have been said about the action areas being indicated only in a diagrammatic way, I think that perhaps insufficient regard is being paid to the fact that the structure plan is primarily a written statement, and it will be to the written statement that people will look to find the indication of what is intended in the action area. The structure plan, in the written statement, will discuss and consider the problems which give rise to the need for action and assess the extent of that need and the nature of the development that will be required in order to deal with it. It will indicate the nature of the development, redevelopment or improvement and, as the Bill makes clear, may indicate whether that action should be partly by one method or partly by another and the nature of the treatment to be selected. It would indicate the extent of the effort which is anticipated and foreseen. It would involve assessment of the costs and a fairly detailed costing of the kind of action that is to take place. The Minister would, of course, be required to be satisfied – we have already discussed this point – that those costings were realistic and that early action on those matters was something that could be anticipated within the levels of anticipated future investment programmes. In this way, as far as the nature of the development is concerned, people will get a fairly good general indication from the written statement of the structure plan.

But why do we not want the areas defined? There are two reasons. First, if the boundaries of an action area are to be defined precisely in the structure plan and this requires approval by the Minister, it immediately means that the Minister and his staff will get involved again in the kind of detail which we are seeking to avoid. That is the first and basic reason. Secondly, it is, we think, likely, at least in many cases, to intensify rather than reduce the problem of planning blight and it may actually be misleading. It will not be until one gets down to actual detailed planning that one will be able to have any confidence in any boundaries that might have been drawn in the structure plan. If we sought to draw boundaries in the structure plan, it is almost certain that they would have to be amended at later stages of the formulation of those plans and that then people who had thought that they were caught, as it were, might find that they escaped; and people who thought that they would escape might find that they were brought within the area of the redevelopment.

It would again raise the problem to which I referred earlier. It would mean that people would start raising objection to structure plans not on the basis of the general nature of the proposals and their rightness, their wisdom and their practicality, but would be putting forward objections on the basis of individual property interests, which, again, is something we want to avoid if we are to achieve the division which is implicit in the separation of structure plans and of local plans. . . .

The following extracts are from a debate on amendments to what is now section 8 of the 1971 Act (cols 109–111, 117–19, 128, 165, 168–9).

MR MURTON: I beg to move Amendment No. 20, in page 4, line 7, leave out from beginning to end of line 9 and insert:

(1) The local planning authority, in preparing a structure plan, shall take such steps as will secure—.

. . . As drafted, the Clause does not give sufficient scope to local authorities to take full heed of public opinion before drawing up their plans.

. . . What we aim to do by this series of Amendments is to persuade the Government that something more positive should be written into the Clause to make it imperative in the minds of the local authority that there should be the fullest and widest possible consultation before any irrevocable decisions are taken.

MR MACDERMOT: . . .

One of the difficulties is that we do not want to set down a form of wording which would suggest that at every stage of the preparation of a plan the local authority has to publicise what it is doing. Obviously this would not be workable; one has to allow the planning authority, as I say, to assemble its ideas so that it can present them in a fairly complete and coherent form. . . .

I do not think that this is necessarily a matter to try to write into the legislation. . . .

There are difficulties about some of the Amendments. Amendment No. 20 omits the wording, as, I think, does Amendment No. 21, that the local authority shall take such steps as will 'in their opinion' secure adequate publicity, and so forth.

MR ROWLANDS: I wish that Amendment No. 21 did, but it did not.

MR MACDERMOT: My hon. Friend supported the point. The point is that the Committee should not misunderstand the effect or purpose of those words. The effect of the words in law is to exclude challenge in the courts of the adequacy of the publicity.[25] But the matter does not rest there; it does not mean that the local authorities will be judges in their own cause of the adequacy of their publicity. This is an administrative matter and a matter which is to be covered by suitable and proper administration. We in the Ministry will be exercising a supervisory role over that administration. One of the things that we have done is to write into the Bill subsection (3) of the Clause, which will require the planning authority to submit a report to the Minister of the steps which it has taken for publicity and consultation.[26]. . .

The principle of that Amendment is, I think, helpful. It suggests that at that stage, if the Minister feels, irrespective of the merits of the plan, that there has not been adequate publicity or consultation, he will be able to remit the matter to the planning authority in order that it shall carry out this stage properly.

That would be the right procedure for questioning and, if necessary, overriding the decision of the local authority about what constitutes adequate publicity. It is a matter that we want dealt with properly in the administrative procedures, and at a relatively early stage, rather than leaving it to be a point which could be challenged in the courts at a very late stage after a lot of work had been done which would have been abortive if it were shown that the publicity has not been adequate.

MR PAGE: . . .

May I give a warning from the other side of the fence? There is a great temptation to say, 'Individuals must be informed; we must give all the publicity; we must publish it all; we must let everybody come in and say what he wants to say about the structure plan.' But we must strike a balance between public participation and efficient procedure. Our present complaint is that development plans have taken too long, that the whole planning system is delayed. Do not let us be too pedantic. Let us make certain that the public will participate, but we shall have to lay down some strict timetables for this participation if it is not to be interminable, as it has been with present public inquiries. Periods of six weeks' publicity have been discussed. We need to talk about weeks, and not months. If the local authority is told to give publicity for a certain number of weeks, that will hasten the procedure, and we shall get the balance between public participation and efficient procedure.

MR MACDERMOT: . . .

I hope that the objections to the structure plan will be confined to the general policies and proposals for the development of the area as a whole, as set out in the written statement. I hope that there will not be so many individual objectors, and I expect that it will be the more organised bodies of opinion, in one form or another – industrial, commercial, trade or amenity – which will put forward objections.

I do not think that we can avoid the right to an inquiry. In important matters we must leave the legal right to individuals as well as to organised bodies to pursue their objection to an inquiry.

Certainly I expect every structure plan will be likely to lead to a public inquiry. It will be such an important document, affecting so many people and affecting the future of the area for such a long period ahead, that it will be very surprising if everyone is happy about it. People will not feel that the matter has been properly considered unless they are able to pursue their objection to the point of a public inquiry,[27] to have it reported upon, and to be sure that the Minister is fully seized of their objections before he arrives at a decision. I hope that it will prove to be a more streamlined procedure and will concentrate attention more specifically upon the matters with which structure plans will deal.

(b) Proposed reforms in the local government system and the debate thereon

House of Commons Standing Committee D,
session 1971–2: Committee Stage of the Local
Government Bill 1972, cols 1878–84, 1886, 1900–03,
1923

The Bill before the Committee proposed to vest structure plan-making powers in the new county planning authorities and local plan-making powers in the new district planning authorities. A development plan scheme prepared by the county would guide the making of local plans. The following debate was on an amendment which would have had the effect of vesting local plan-making powers in the county planning authorities while still requiring them to make a development plan scheme which could permit some districts to make local plans.

MR ROPER: With the Amendment we come to one of the most difficult parts of the Bill, in the sense that . . . we are trying to find a technical solution for planning in a very difficult situation. . . .

In trying to find the best solution to this difficult problem we are working in a far from ideal situation. Like the Minister, we are trying to make the best of a bad job. The bad job is the decision made by the Government to throw out the unitary system of the Redcliffe-Maud report and replace it by the two-sphere or two-tier system of the county or district. All the difficulties that we shall have on the Clause and on the Schedule will be the direct result of the Government's decision to choose the dual system.

On planning, one would imagine that the recent history of the difficulties of developing satisfactory planning arrangements in Greater London, when one has a dual system, would have taught the Minister not to fall into this trap again.

On planning, we must remember that one of the strongest arguments for reorganisation of local government was to have large organisations that could plan a whole area at one time. The Royal Commission met this problem by accepting the system of unitary authorities.

The Government came out initially with the two-sphere system. It is worth reminding ourselves of the words of Government's White Paper of February, 1971, paragraph 21 of which states that

Planning control, however, raises issues of close local interest. All planning applications should be made to the district councils, both within and outside the metropolitan counties. The district councils should, as of right, take by far the greater number of planning control decisions, provided that the professional advice comes from officers who are part of a unified staff structure, serving both counties and districts, so that local needs are reflected in the detailed implementation of development plans.

Then follows this sentence, which is the key:

Responsibility for broad planning policies and for the development of both structure and local plans must, however, rest with the county councils.

The Government have changed their mind about joint planning teams because of the hostility shown in many quarters. We have seen the difficulty of having bicephalous bodies. Bodies which are responsible both to county and district might have the same difficulty as the Government have in this Committee where they have Ministers with responsibility to the Department of the Environment and to Wales. One can see the very considerable difficulties which bicephalous bodies in any context can create.

The way in which the Clause is drafted apparently gives power to make local plans not to the county, as was suggested in the White Paper, but to the district councils. The first objection to this is the fact that at the moment there is a shortage of adequate planners to undertake such work. The Royal Town Planning Institute, in a survey of 1,250 non-county boroughs, urban and rural districts, could find no more than 90 chartered town planners. Therefore, with the exception of a few of the larger towns such as Bristol, Plymouth or Coventry, which have well developed professional plan resources, much of the professional planning expertise of the country is concentrated in the counties. The vast majority of districts, especially those below a population of 60,000, will not have anything like the resources that will be needed for proper plan making.

This lack of satisfactory professional resources is the main reason why the bulk of professional bodies in this field – bodies such as the Royal Institute of British Architects, the Royal Town Planning Institute, the Royal Institute of Chartered Surveyors and the Town and Country Planning Association – have come out in opposition to the way in which the Government have organised this Clause. I am particularly interested this morning to see that the Royal Town Planning Institute supports the Amendment. We cannot suggest that these professional bodies are acting in a partisan way. They are not speaking up for the counties against the districts – for one party *versus* another; they are trying to find, in a difficult situation, a better method of organising planning. . . .

MR BLENKINSOP: . . . Like the Minister, I was on the Committee that considered the Town and Country Planning Act, 1968, later consolidated into the 1971 Act, and I entirely agree with my hon. Friend the Member for Farnworth (Mr. Roper) when he suggested that provisions in that Act might very well have been different if we had conceived the number of planning authorities proposed now under the Bill.

I can testify that this was a matter which we discussed a great deal at that time and there were a number of anxieties about the whole question of allowing a local authority to be judge and jury in its own cause. One of the points constantly made was that we were talking about a new period in which we would have a great diminution in the number of planning authorities, and this relatively small number would clearly have the qualified staff and everything else needed for this purpose.

Therefore, I seriously suggest that we are in danger of going back from what was agreed under the 1968 procedures which had all party agreement at that time. I regard this as a very serious matter, and those who will have the thankless task of carrying out the work, as planning officers and as elected representatives on local authorities, will have to face the arguments and all the difficulties which I believe the Bill will inevitably present them with.

MR PAGE [Minister for Local Government and Development]: It might be convenient if I intervene here, because a number of questions have arisen which I may be able to answer. . . .

The plan-making function as drafted in the Bill is divided between the counties – to prepare the structure plan, which is the statement of planning policy over the county area – and the districts – to prepare the local plans, which are the details that affect the public. The drawing of the lines on the Ordnance Survey map allows the ordinary member of the public to see how the planning will affect his town, his street, his plot, and so on.

There is no difficulty in that division of function, provided that one can set a beginning and an end to it, and provided that there is full consultation between the two authorities undertaking the two different parts of that function – the structure plan and the district plan. . . .

In the Bill we are building, I hope strong district authorities which, although strong and comparatively large, will still be in close contact with the people. One could not deprive an authority of that sort of the right to prepare its own local plan, if it chose to do so and was able to do so. It is impossible to talk about the powers of district authorities, what we want them to do for their areas, without giving them the right, as the whole basis of that, to plan for how the area will develop in its residences, commercial offices, factories and the whole character of its set-up.

In the two-tier system of the Bill, we are substituting our ideas of counties and districts for numerous kinds of authority which exist today – the counties, the county districts, and the county boroughs. Amongst those – and we are talking about the planning function – the counties and the county boroughs are the local planning authorities, carrying out the whole plan-making function. In future, what will be involved will be drawing the structure plan and the local plan and, as the hon. Member for Farnworth (Mr. Roper) has mentioned, such plans as subject plans, which may not be local but may cover a wide area dealing with a particular subject.

These are the main local planning authorities that will be replaced. In replacing them, we are depriving the 80 county boroughs, which are local planning authorities at present, of a substantial part of their planning function. We are depriving them of the right to prepare their structure plans. Can we really go to the extent of depriving them of the right to prepare – if they have the team to do it and the desire to do it – their district plans?

. . . If we are to succeed, we must put a beginning and an end to it, as I said, and between those two extremes there must be consultation all the way through. To make the beginning to this process, we must put it firmly in the hands of one or other authority to initiate it. This is what we have done in the development plan scheme.

In the Amendments to which we shall come later we have given the counties the responsibility of preparing that scheme, in short, saying who does what. In studying what shall go into that development plan scheme, obviously the county will look at the planning staffs of districts within the county, the areas covered by the districts, the sorts of problem arising in those districts – and, indeed, those problems will vary as much as the staffs in the district will vary from one to the other – and will propose to those districts, in consultation, perhaps that X district and Y district take over the local plan-making entirely, and that Z district does not have at this stage the team to do the work and therefore the county will undertake it. In many cases, it may not be necessary to have a local plan in that area. I am sure that in some of the districts, which are mainly county districts, one can delay a local plan for some considerable time.

Passing from that to the stage where the development plan scheme is prepared, if there is then some friction between the county and one of the districts within that county, the county having denied the district its right to prepare the district plan, there can be a reference to the Secretary of State. I am not anxious that my Department should go over these claims in detail, or even the dispute in detail, but I am sure that we can settle disputes of this sort fairly rapidly on general principle rather than look at the matters in great detail. Later on in this Clause the power is reserved to the Secretary of State to amend and give directions about a planning scheme.

4. The problems of the solutions

Structure and local planning became part of the law in October 1968, but it was made clear that the preparation of structure plans would commence only in areas so designated by the Minister from time to time and that this would turn in part on whether the local planning authority had the staff to handle the new system. In the event, it was almost three years before the first orders were made which empowered specified local authorities to proceed to make a structure plan,[28] and the same length of time elapsed before the

Ministry promulgated the Town and Country Planning (Structure and Local Plans) Regulations.[29] However, some time before statutory authority to plan was given, the Minister had invited some planning authorities to proceed with structure planning. The terms of one such invitation, which was published in the minutes of the Town and Country Planning Committee of the Warwickshire County Council, are given below. Consider carefully their implications for the relationship between structure and regional planning and public participation in structure planning. Consider also the meaning and implication of the following statement recorded in the minutes of that Committee for the April 1971 meeting of the Council:

Authority to prepare these new plans is contained in Part I of the Act which may in fact be brought into force by the Secretary of State for the Environment by means of Commencement Orders on different days in different areas. No Orders have however yet been made for any part of the country *and until this is done it will not be possible to carry out any of the statutory procedures laid down in the Act, although the County Planning Officer has been authorised to undertake the necessary preliminary work.*[30]

> Warwickshire County Council Town and Country
> Planning Committee; Minutes of the October 1970
> meeting

In July last representatives of the West Midlands Local Planning Authorities met Mr. R. GRAHAM PAGE, the Minister of State at the Ministry of Housing and Local Government to discuss the desirability of allowing all the West Midland Authorities to commence the preparation of the new type Structure Plans. The County Council were represented at this meeting by our Deputy Chairman who, following the meeting, received a letter from Mr. PAGE which we feel will be of interest to members of the Council and which we accordingly set out below.

At our meeting last Friday I promised to write to the West Midland local planning authorities who had not yet been invited to do so, to start now on the necessary preparatory works towards the formulation of structure plans within their areas.

It is not our intention to make formal commencement orders at the present moment. The absence of an order in no way inhibits an authority from carrying out plan work on the basis of the new Act, including the necessary preparation of a survey, and those planning authorities who have already embarked on structure plans have encountered no problems in operating on this informal basis. When the regulations have been made setting out the relevant procedural steps in the plan process it will probably be appropriate for us to consider what commencement orders should be made.

I know from our discussion that all authorities are fully alive to the need to ensure that structure plans are prepared within the framework of an agreed regional strategy and that the contents of the plan accord with that strategy. Until the strategy is available therefore and the Government's views on it have been published, authorities will no doubt wish to concentrate on the preliminary plan work and avoid committing themselves to strategic assumptions which might not be endorsed in the strategy.

I was also impressed by the importance which all authorities appeared to attach to the need to liaise closely with their neighbours in the preparation of structure plans. I accepted the force of the argument that at the present time there was no need to contemplate the creation of any more formal grouping arrangements, but it might be useful if we planned to re-assess the position when the regional strategy is available. Once the priorities in the region have been identified it may well prove mutually convenient for some authorities to consider what arrangements for collaborative working in key areas would be helpful. I understood that, in any case, you and the authorities associated in the sub-Regional Study would use the machinery which is already in operation on the Study work as a basis for continued joint cooperation in the preparation of structure plans for the areas affected by the Study. I hope therefore your authority will now regard this as a formal invitation to proceed with structure planning for your area and I would be glad to have your response in due course. I am asking the officers in the Department's Regional Office to keep in close touch with the work you are now undertaking, as well as with the progress of the regional study. Copies of the Department's new Development Plan Manual will be sent to your officers shortly.

Despite the slow start to structure planning, by the end of 1974, over three years after the first commencement orders had been made, there was a wide range of authorities (for whom commencement orders had been made) preparing structure plans. Already, too, certain problems or challenges to the system were in existence, and the ones discussed below embrace the main areas of concern about it. The overriding questions with which these problems must be approached are: has the reformed system any better chance than the old of getting on top of the problems to which planning is thought to have something to offer, or is it doomed to impotence in the not-so-long run? And if the latter, is it because crude party politics prevent rational planning decisions being made? Is it because planners fail to communicate with the public, so that plans are misunderstood and ignored? Is it because too much attention continues to be focused on the 'how' of decision making and too little on the 'what' and the 'why'? Is it because the reformed system is too ambitious or not ambitious enough? In looking at these questions, we shall consider the progress of structure planning both in general and in particular, by looking at Warwickshire's structure plan as one of the earliest to be considered at a public examination and raising in an acute form some of the problems to be discussed.

(a) Local government reorganisation

If it is possible to sum up the aims of local government reorganisation, it may be said that they were to create a more rational set of local government areas and a more rational structure, both of which would contribute to a more democratic and a more efficient system of local government. But, like planning itself, the reorganisation of local government is a political and not merely a technical matter. Political considerations inevitably influenced the eventual outcome both of boundaries and structure, the latter by the basic decision to have a two-tier rather than a one-tier system, the former by particular boundary decisions all over the country, many of them fought long and hard in both Houses of Parliament, during the Bill's 355-day passage through Parliament. One such boundary problem was connected with Coventry. The dispute here was not between rival political parties but between the political parties and the planners and administrators; the former wanted Coventry to be part of the West Midland Metropolitan County for political reasons,[31] the latter considered it should be the focal point of a Coventry city region, which would in fact be called Warwickshire. In the House of Lords debate on the White Paper on local government reorganisation[32] Lady Sharp was very critical of the Coventry decision; and the attitude of Warwickshire to its neighbour as set out in its structure plan testifies to the essentially political decision that was taken and is a salutary reminder that that is what planning is.

Many other boundary disputes were pressed to the vote – some repeatedly – during the passage of the Bill and no purpose would be served by detailing any one of them. In general, however, many of them arose out of efforts to exclude from urban areas (be they metropolitan counties like Greater Manchester, or districts like Sheffield, or non-metropolitan districts like Bristol and Plymouth) areas of low-density high-class residences, villages or open spaces, where inhabitants feared that incorporation into an urban district would mean higher rates, higher residential densities and, from their perspective, a worse environment. Not all the special pleadings were successful but where they were, the effect has been to put tight boundaries around the most urbanised parts of the country, a policy which some critics argued was evident in the government's plans for reorganisation from the beginning.[33]

Will not the effect of 'tight' boundaries allied to the lack of 'enforceable' regional planning be to recreate the kind of major planning and development confrontations that plagued relations between Birmingham and its two bordering counties – Warwickshire and Worcestershire – from the mid-1950s onwards?[34] And if this is so, what will local government reorganisation have achieved other than put new names to the local authorities conducting the same old disputes? If this is thought to be too extreme, it is worth asking why the fixing of boundaries occupied so much time and energy of parliamentarians during the passage of the Local Government Bill; was it just because some people preferred to be under an authority named Y rather than one named X, or was it because they suspected that urban counties and districts would have different policies on planning, housing and the environment from more rural counties and districts? A further general question may be posed: is it not a chimera to seek after a local government system that will enable more effective plans to be made?

Further problems will emerge at the stage when local plans begin to be prepared by planning authorities different from those that prepared structure plans, and/or when county planning authorities make development plan schemes which do not give district planning authorities the local plan-making powers to which they consider they are entitled. Sections 10C and 14 of the Town and Country Planning Act 1971[35] are crucial and must be carefully considered here:

10C.—(1) The functions of a local planning authority of preparing local plans under section 11 of this Act shall, subject to the following provisions of this section, be exercisable by the district planning authority.

(2) Subject to regulations under this section, it shall be the duty of the county planning authority in consultation with the district planning authorities to make, and thereafter to keep under review and amend, if they think fit, a scheme (to be known as a development plan scheme) for the preparation of local plans for those areas in the county in which sections 11 to 15 of this Act are in force, except any part of the county included in a National Park, and—

(a) the scheme shall designate the local planning authority or authorities (whether county or district) by whom local plans are to be prepared for any such area and provide for the exercise of all functions of a local planning authority under those sections in relation to any such plan exclusively by the authority designated in relation to that plan; and

(b) references in those sections to a local planning authority shall be construed accordingly.

(3) A development plan scheme may include such incidental, consequential, transitional or supplementary provision as may appear to the county planning authority to be necessary or proper for the purposes or in consequence of the provisions of the scheme and for giving full effect thereto, and, without prejudice to the foregoing provision, shall—

(a) specify the title and nature of each local plan for the area in question and the part or parts of the area to which it is to apply and give an indication of its scope;

(b) set out a programme for the preparation of the several local plans for that area; and

(c) where appropriate indicate the relationship between the several local plans for that area, specifying those which should be prepared concurrently with the structure plan for that area.

(4) As soon as practicable after making or amending a development plan scheme the county planning authority shall send a copy of the scheme or the scheme as amended, as the case may be, to the Secretary of State.

(5) A structure plan prepared by a county planning authority may provide, to the extent that provision to the contrary is not made by a development plan scheme, for the preparation of local plans exclusively by the county planning authority and, where it so provides, shall also provide for the exercise exclusively by that authority of all other functions of a local planning authority under sections 11 to 15 of this Act, and any provision included in a structure plan by virtue of this subsection shall be treated for the purposes of the other provisions of this section as if it were contained in a development plan scheme.

(6) The Secretary of State may direct a county planning authority after consultation with the district planning authorities—

(a) to prepare a development plan scheme before a date specified in the direction; and

(b) where it appears to the Secretary of State that any such scheme should be amended, to amend it in terms so specified before a date so specified.

(7) Where a district planning authority make representations to the Secretary of State that they are dissatisfied with the proposals of the county planning authority for a development plan scheme, or a county planning authority fail to comply with a direction under subsection (6) of this section to make or amend such a scheme, the Secretary of State may himself make or, as the case may be, amend the scheme; and any

scheme or amendment so made shall have effect as if made by the county planning authority.

(8) The Secretary of State may make regulations—

(a) providing for the content of such schemes;

(b) requiring or authorising county planning authorities to take prescribed procedural steps in connection with the preparation of such schemes.'

14.—(1) After the expiry of the period afforded for making objections to a local plan or, if such objections have been duly made during that period, after considering the objections so made, the local planning authority may, subject to section 12 of this Act and subsections (2) and (3) of this section, by resolution adopt the plan either as originally prepared or as modified so as to take account of any such objections or of any matters arising out of such objections.

(2) The local planning authority shall not adopt a local plan unless it conforms and, in the case of a local plan prepared by a district planning authority, a certificate is issued under subsection (5) or (7) of this section that it conforms generally to the structure plan as approved by the Secretary of State. . . .

'(5) Where a district planning authority have prepared a local plan for any part of their area the structure plan for which has been approved by the Secretary of State, they shall request the county planning authority to certify that the local plan conforms generally to the structure plan and, subject to subsection (6) below, the county planning authority shall, within the period of one month from their receipt of the request or such longer period as may be agreed between them and the district planning authority, consider the matter and, if satisfied that the local plan does so conform, issue a certificate to that effect; and if it appears to the county planning authority that the local plan does not so conform in any respect, they shall, during or as soon as practicable after the end of that period, refer the question whether it so conforms in that respect to the Secretary of State to be determined by him.

(6) The Secretary of State may in any case by direction to a county planning authority reserve for his own determination the question whether a local plan conforms generally to a structure plan.

(7) Where on determining a question referred to or reserved for him under subsection (5) or (6) of this section the Secretary of State is of the opinion that a local plan conforms generally to the relevant structure plan in the relevant respect or, as the case may be, all respects he may issue, or direct the county planning authority to issue, a certificate to that effect, and where he is of the contrary opinion, he may direct the district planning authority to revise the local plan in such respects as he thinks appropriate so as to secure that it will so conform and thereupon those subsections and the preceding provisions of this subsection shall apply to the revised plan.'

DoE Circular No. 74/73: *Local Government Act 1972. Town and Country Planning: Co-operation Between Authorities*

3. The essential feature of this allocation of functions is that the new county planning authorities will have the statutory responsibility for establishing and maintaining the general strategic policies within their areas; while the new district planning authorities will bear the main general responsibility for the character of development within their individual areas. Both have thus the opportunity to play a part in the development and implementation of planning policies consistent with the overall strategic requirements of their areas. But although planning responsibilities are broadly distributed in this way planning is an inter-related process and this will need to be reflected in the arrangements made between authorities. The test of the effectiveness of the arrangements will be the extent to which the public will receive the planning service it is entitled to expect.

7. The main objectives are to secure a constructive relationship—
  (i) between county and district planning authorities (and, where applicable, between county and county and district and district);
 (ii) between development plan and development control work;
(iii) between 'planning' and transportation together with the other services and functions directly linked to them.

8. The main requirements are—
  (i) to ensure a full understanding at member level of the respective planning policies of the authorities concerned and the co-ordination of their policies;
 (ii) to maintain momentum in policy and plan making; to secure continuity and avoid delay – particularly in handling planning applications not decided on April 1, 1974; and to carry through schemes already initiated;
(iii) to decide on those arrangements which enable staff (particularly qualified and experienced staff) to be used to the best advantage (whichever authority employs that staff);
 (iv) to make clear arrangements for the collection, use and exchange of information;
  (v) to define and co-ordinate procedures so that duplication is reduced to a minimum and unnecessary misunderstanding or conflict at the formal stages is avoided.

11. The aim should be for elected bodies to lay down for the guidance of officers the clearest possible instructions as to what matters need to be referred for discussion (and where necessary decision) of committees and joint committees, so that formal reference to these bodies is reduced to a minimum. . . .

ANNEX I
Development Plans

1. Even more than in the past, when the county was the one formal plan-making authority in their area, there will need to be, in readiness for

the changeover at April and thereafter, close co-operation between county and districts.

2. District councils must be even more closely involved in structure plan work, and committed to following it through in their local plan and development control work. The relationship between counties and districts must recognise the continuing structural role of counties as well as the important new role which districts will have as of right in local planning: and thus enable both authorities to make their contribution to plan-making.

3. It is not just a question of considering whether and, if so, what adaptations of existing machinery might suffice. Nor is it enough to rely simply on the formal consultation, important though this is, required by statute or regulations.

5. The Act contains two specific pieces of machinery designed to promote effective co-operation in the planning field and to minimise delay, dispute and duplication.

(i) *The development plan scheme.* This is the document in which the county, following consultation with districts, will set out the allocation of responsibility for preparing local plans and the programme for them; and indicate their scope and, as appropriate, the relationship between them. It will need to be based on the arrangements, including those relating to the use of staff, agreed between the authorities. It may, in suitable cases, need to refer to these arrangements; but setting them out in the formal scheme, certainly in any detail, would make it less useful as the tool it is meant to be, as well as too elaborate and detailed. The setting out of these arrangements should be in a separate document from the development plan scheme; both can, of course, be readily revised as circumstances change.

(ii) *Certification.* The requirement for a certificate is designed to establish that any local plan which has been prepared is in general conformity with the structure plan. By co-operation and close working between them, authorities can secure that the request for a formal certificate results in its issue without delay.

The Secretaries of State have formal powers to settle disputes on a development plan scheme, or to determine questions about conformity referred to them. They wish to use these powers only as a last resort: whether or not they have to exercise them will depend primarily on authorities.

DoE Circular No. 58/74: *Structure Plans*

Certification

11. The requirement for conformity is not new, nor is the concept of consultation and close cooperation between county and district planning authorities throughout the plan-making process. The need to obtain a certificate is therefore not an onerous addition to the process but simply a safeguard. By that stage any doubts about conformity should already

have been fully discussed in the course of consultations and have been resolved, so that the certificate can be granted well within the time limit of a month: it is only to allow for unforseen difficulties that the period may be extended. If however the county planning authority are unable to give a certificate and the district planning authority cannot agree to change the local plan, the matter is referred to the Secretary of State for determination. Such references should be made only as a last resort; it is hoped that authorities which seem unlikely to be able to resolve for themselves a particular disagreement will seek the Department's informal advice before embarking on a formal application to the Secretary of State. This is indeed a normal practice. Informal discussion is more likely to achieve speedier results, and is particularly important where, as in this case, the procedures are new.

Planning Brief
12. County planning authorities are required to consult district planning authorities during the preparation of structure plans, and they have been strongly recommended to maintain continuing close contacts throughout the preparation period. Even so, it will be helpful to district councils in their preparation of local plans for a planning brief to be prepared by the county council in association with district councils, supplementing the published material of the structure plan by setting out the thinking behind the plan and relating its aims, objectives and policies to the more detailed treatment appropriate to the local plan. This brief, which is not subject to approval by the Secretary of State, is not part of the statutory process and does not have to be formally submitted to the Secretary of State; it is intended to be a helpful means of coordinating the approach to the problems of the area in the two different levels of plans. In some areas there may be advantages in the county issuing an interim planning brief, in advance of the structure plan being approved, to help with informal local plans.

In what kinds of circumstances might a county planning authority be disinclined to allow a district planning authority to make all or any local plans? If the burden of a county planning authority's case is that it has greater expertise in the subject matter of a local plan – e.g. conservation or transport – is the Secretary of State likely to find in favour of a dissatisfied district planning authority which makes representations to him under sub-section (7)? What help, if any, could either tier of authority derive from the following statement of the Minister, Mr Page?

One could not deprive an authority of that sort (the strong district authorities the Bill is building) of the right to prepare its own local plan if it chose to do so and was able to do so. It is impossible to talk about the powers of district authorities, what we want them to do for their areas, without giving them the right as the whole basis of that to plan for how the area will develop in its residences, commercial offices, factories and the whole character of its set-up.[36]

Is the county planning authority ever likely to put forward a different case? Why is the county planning authority given the option by sub-section (5) of either preparing a development plan scheme which empowers it to make the local plans or providing by a structure plan that it shall make the local plans? What limitations are there on the power of the Secretary of State to make or amend a development plan scheme? To what extent does the introduction of a development plan scheme with the possibility of the Secretary of State having to intervene and adjudicate between disputing local planning authorities detract from the aim of the reformed planning system? What did the Minister, Mr Page, mean when he said of disputes between local planning authorities over the development plan scheme: 'I am not anxious that my Department should go over these claims in detail, or even the dispute in detail but I am sure that we can settle disputes of this sort fairly rapidly on general principles rather than look at the matters in great detail'?[37] What remedy would a district planning authority have if it was informed by the Minister that its case had been decided according to 'general principles' without the matter being looked at in great detail? Upon which authority is there a duty to make a local plan?

(b) The scope and form of structure planning

The Department of the Environment has issued a plethora of rules and advice on how to structure plan, but it is the local planning authorities which have to produce the structure plans, and a variety of commentators are at hand to admonish or help. At the same time, local authorities are being urged to adopt new forms of management and internal organisation. What are local authorities doing in this matter? What effect, if any, has structure planning had on corporate planning and vice versa? Can structure plans and local plans be kept in distinct boxes as the law and the advice assume?

Town and Country Planning Act, 1971

DEVELOPMENT PLANS
Survey and structure plan
6.—(1) It shall be the duty of the local planning authority to institute a survey of their area, in so far as they have not already done so, examin-

ing the matters which may be expected to affect the development of that area or the planning of its development and in any event to keep all such matters under review.

(2) Notwithstanding that the local planning authority have carried out their duty under subsection (1) of this section, the authority may, if they think fit, and shall, if directed to do so by the Secretary of State, institute a fresh survey of their area examining the matters mentioned in that subsection.

(3) Without prejudice to the generality of the preceding provisions of this section, the matters to be examined and kept under review thereunder shall include the following, that is to say—

(a) the principal physical and economic characteristics of the area of the authority (including the principal purposes for which land is used) and, so far as they may be expected to affect that area, of any neighbouring areas;

(b) the size, composition and distribution of the population of that area (whether resident or otherwise);

(c) without prejudice to paragraph (a) of this subsection, the communications, transport system and traffic of that area and, so far as they may be expected to affect that area, of any neighbouring areas;

(d) any considerations not mentioned in any of the preceding paragraphs which may be expected to affect any matters so mentioned;

(e) such other matters as may be prescribed or as the Secretary of State may in a particular case direct;

(f) any changes already projected in any of the matters mentioned in any of the preceding paragraphs and the effect which those changes are likely to have on the development of that area or the planning of such development.

7.—(1) The local planning authority shall, within such period from the commencement of this section within their area as the Secretary of State may direct, prepare and send the Secretary of State a report of their survey under section 6 of this Act and at the same time prepare and submit to him for his approval a structure plan for their area complying with the provisions of subsection (3) of this section.

(2) The said report shall include an estimate of any changes likely to occur during such period as the Secretary of State may direct in the matters mentioned in section 6(3) of this Act; and different periods may be specified by any such direction in relation to different matters.

(3) The structure plan for any area shall be a written statement—

(a) formulating the local planning authority's policy and general proposals in respect of the development and other use of land in that area (including measures for the improvement of the physical environment and the management of traffic);

(b) stating the relationship of those proposals to general proposals for the development and other use of land in neighbouring areas which may be expected to affect that area; and (*c*) containing such other matters as may be prescribed or as the Secretary of State may in any particular case direct.

(4) In formulating their policy and general proposals under subsection (3)(*a*) of this section, the local planning authority shall secure that the policy and proposals are justified by the results of their survey under section 6 of this Act and by any other information which they may obtain and shall have regard—

(*a*) to current policies with respect to the economic planning and development of the region as a whole;

(*b*) to the resources likely to be available for the carrying out of the proposals of the structure plan; and

(*c*) to such other matters as the Secretary of State may direct them to take into account.

(5) A local planning authority's general proposals under this section with respect to land in their area shall indicate any part of that area (in this Act referred to as an 'action area') which they have selected for the commencement during a prescribed period of comprehensive treatment, in accordance with a local plan prepared for the selected area as a whole, by development, redevelopment or improvement of the whole or part of the area selected, or partly by one and partly by another method, and the nature of the treatment selected.

(6) A structure plan for any area shall contain or be accompanied by such diagrams, illustrations and descriptive matter as the local planning authority think appropriate for the purpose of explaining or illustrating the proposals in the plan, or as may be prescribed, or as may in any particular case be specified in directions given by the Secretary of State; and any such diagrams, illustrations and descriptive matter shall be treated as forming part of the plan.

(7) At any time before the Secretary of State has under section 9 of this Act approved a structure plan with respect to the whole of the area of a local planning authority, the authority may with his consent, and shall, if so directed by him, prepare and submit to him for his approval a structure plan relating to part of that area; and where the Secretary of State has given a consent or direction for the preparation of a structure plan for part of such an area, references in this Part of this Act to such an area shall, in relation to a structure plan, be construed as including references to part of that area.

10B[38].—(1) A structure plan submitted to the Secretary of State for his approval may be withdrawn by the local planning authority, or the local planning authorities or any of them, submitting it by a notice in that behalf given to the Secretary of State at any time before he has approved it, and shall in that event be treated as never having been submitted. . . .

11[39] (1) Where a county planning authority are in course of preparing a structure plan for their area, or have prepared for their area a structure plan which has not been approved or rejected by the Secretary of State, the local planning authority to whom it falls to prepare a local plan for any part of that area may, if they think it desirable, prepare a local plan for all or any of that part of the area.

(2) Where a structure plan for the area of a county planning authority has been approved by the Secretary of State, the local planning authority to whom it falls to prepare a local plan for any part of that area shall as soon as practicable consider, and thereafter keep under review, the desirability of preparing and, if they consider it desirable and they have not already done so, shall prepare one or more local plans for all or any of that part of the area.

(3) A local plan shall consist of a map and a written statement and shall—

(a) formulate in such detail as the local planning authority think appropriate the authority's proposals for the development and other use of land in that part of their area or for any description of development or other use of such land (including in either case such measures as the authority think fit for the improvement of the physical environment and the management of traffic); and

(b) contain such matters as may be prescribed or as the Secretary of State may in any particular case direct.

(4) Different local plans may be prepared for different purposes for the same part of any area. . . .

(6) Where an area is indicated as an action area in a structure plan which has been approved by the Secretary of State, the local planning authority shall (if they have not already done so), as soon as practicable after the approval of the plan, prepare a local plan for that area.

(7) Without prejudice to the preceding provisions of this section, the local planning authority shall, if the Secretary of State gives them a direction in that behalf with respect to a part of an area for which a structure plan has been, or is in course of being, prepared, as soon as practicable prepare for that part a local plan of such nature as may be specified in the direction.

(8) Directions under subsection (7) of this section may be given by the Secretary of State either before or after he approves the structure plan; but no such directions shall require a local planning authority to take any steps to comply therewith until the structure plan has been approved by him.

(9) In formulating their proposals in a local plan the local planning authority shall secure that the proposals conform generally to the structure plan as it stands for the time being (whether or not it has been approved by the Secretary of State) and shall have regard to any information and any other considerations which appear to them to be relevant, or which may be prescribed, or which the Secretary of State may in any particular case direct them to take into account.

(9A) For the purpose of discharging their functions under this section a district planning authority may, in so far as it appears to them necessary to do so having regard to the survey made by the county planning authority under section 6 of this Act, examine the matters mentioned in subsections (1) and (3) of that section so far as relevant to their area.

Town and Country Planning (Structure and Local Plans)
Regulations S.I. 1974 No. 1486

9.—(1) The policy formulated in a structure plan written statement shall relate to such of the matters specified in Part I of Schedule 1 as the local planning authority may think appropriate.

(2) The policy and general proposals formulated in a structure plan written statement shall be set out so as to be readily distinguishable from the other contents thereof.

(3) A structure plan written statement shall include a reasoned justification of the policy and general proposals formulated therein.

Matters to be contained in written statement

10. In addition to the other matters required to be contained therein by the Act and by these regulations, a structure plan written statement shall contain the following matters, namely, such indications as the local planning authority may think appropriate of the items set out in Part II of Schedule 1.

Reconciliation of contradictions in structure plans

46.—(1) In the case of any contradiction in a structure plan between a separate part prepared under regulation 8 and the rest of the plan, the provisions of the separate part shall prevail.

(2) Subject to paragraph (1) above, in the case of any contradiction in a structure plan between the written statement and any other document forming part of the plan, the provisions of the written statement shall prevail.

Reconciliation of contradictions in local plans

47. In the case of any contradiction between the written statement and any other document forming part of a local plan, the provisions of the written statement shall prevail.

Reconciliation of contradictions between local plans

48. In the case of any contradiction between local plans for the same part of any area, the provisions which are more recently adopted, approved or made shall prevail.

SCHEDULE 1
STRUCTURE PLANS

PART I
MATTERS TO WHICH POLICY IS REQUIRED TO RELATE
BY REGULATION 9(1)

The matters to which the policy formulated in a structure plan written statement is required to relate by regulation 9 (1) are such of the following matters as the county planning authority may think appropriate:

   (i) Distribution of population and employment.

  (ii) Housing.

 (iii) Industry and commerce.

 (iv) Transportation.

  (v) Shopping.

 (vi) Education.

 (vii) Other social and community services.

(viii) Recreation and leisure.

 (ix) Conservation, townscape and landscape.

  (x) Utility services.

 (xi) Any other relevant matters.

PART II
MATTERS REQUIRED BY REGULATION 10 TO BE CONTAINED IN WRITTEN STATEMENT

The matters required by regulation 10 to be contained in a structure plan written statement are such indications as the county planning authority may think appropriate of the following:

   (i) The existing structure of the area to which the plan relates and the present needs and opportunities for change.

  (ii) Any changes already projected, or likely to occur, which may materially affect matters dealt with in the plan, and the effect those changes are likely to have.

 (iii) The effect (if any) on the area of the plan of any proposal to make an order under section 1 of the New Towns Act 1965 (designation of sites of new towns) or of any order made or having effect as if made under section 1 of the New Towns Act 1965 or of any known intentions of a development corporation established in pursuance of such an order.

 (iv) The extent (if any) to which town development within the meaning of the Town Development Act 1952 is being, or is to be, carried out in the area to which the plan relates.

  (v) The existing size, composition and distribution of population and state of employment in the area to which the plan relates, and estimates of these matters at such future times as the county planning authority think relevant in formulating the policies of the plan, together with the assumptions on which the estimates are based.

 (vi) The regard the county planning authority have had to the current policies with respect to the economic planning and development of the region as a whole.

 (vii) The regard the county planning authority have had to social policies and considerations.

(viii) The regard the county planning authority have had to the resources likely to be available for carrying out the policy and general proposals formulated in the plan.

(ix) The broad criteria to be applied as respects the control of development in the area, or any part of the area, to which the plan relates.

(x) The extent and nature of the relationship between the policies formulated in the plan.

(xi) The considerations underlying any major items of policy formulated in the plan as respects matters of common interest to the county planning authority by whom the plan is prepared and the county planning authorities for neighbouring areas, and the extent to which those major items have been agreed by the authorities concerned.

(xii) Any other relevant matters.

DoE Circular 44/71: *Town and Country Planning Act 1968—Part I: The Town and Country Planning (Structure and Local Plans) Regulations 1971: and Memorandum*

1. We are directed by the Secretary of State for the Environment and the Secretary of State for Wales to draw to your attention the Town and Country Planning (Structure and Local Plans) Regulations 1971 (of which a copy is enclosed) and the memorandum annexed to this circular. . .

The memorandum is designed to make available in a common form for all authorities basic information about the new system and advice on it: it should be regarded as the principal document for this purpose, though it will need to be read in conjunction with the Development Plans Manual and with the further advice the Departments will be issuing. . . .

The Memorandum

14. The terms 'county structure plan' and 'urban structure plan' have come into common usage, but a distinction between them is not to be found in the Act or the regulations. The range of matters which ought to be considered for possible inclusion in a structure plan (as outlined in the manual) will be the same for every structure plan, whatever the area to which it relates: the actual selection of contents in any case, and the depth in which they are treated, is to some extent bound to depend on the characteristics and needs of the particular area to be covered by the plan. Nor is there a distinction of authorship as between county and county borough councils; both will have occasion to prepare structure plans dealing with urban areas.

15. A county council in the structure plan for their area (or in appropriate cases, part of it) will deal with the strategic issues and put forward their policy and general proposals on them for the whole of the area to which the plan relates. In this they will cover, amongst other things, the urban areas – other than county boroughs – within it and their relationship with other areas. The White Paper 'Town and Country Planning'

and the debates on the Bill indicated that, within an administrative county, there may be major planning issues and problems for an urban area – particularly as regards its internal structure – which need to be treated and brought before the Secretary of State for approval in a more closely argued and self-contained form than would be possible if they figured only as items in a plan relating to the whole of a county.

16. Regulation 8 provides that, for any part of the area to which a structure plan (other than that for a county borough) relates, which is or which it is proposed should become urban or predominantly urban, a county council may, with the consent of the Secretary of State, and shall if he so directs, formulate in addition policy and general proposals specifically for that part in a separate part of the plan. This separate part is to be prepared as if it were a structure plan. . . .

33. The manual deals at some length with the possible content of the written statement, in so far as it is feasible to do so in general terms. It should be read together with the regulations and this memorandum. The regulations and memorandum cover also the form of the written statement and the scope it provides for presenting issues in a way which brings out that it is the central feature of the new plans. But much will depend on the particular area being dealt with, which will have its own distinctive character and problems. Local planning authorities will therefore need a large measure of freedom in deciding on the precise way in which to treat the written statement, and the Secretaries of State ask them to treat these statements in the way the authority consider most appropriate to cover the matters with which the plan for their area deals. This applies particularly to such matters as overall length, depth of argument and style of presentation. The Act and regulations specify a number of features, mostly of a major kind, to secure a basic consistency in the form and content of written statements. They do so by reference to the matters to which policy and proposals in written statements are to relate; to the matters which are to be contained in them; and to the matters to which local planning authorities are to have regard in formulating their policy and proposals. . . .

41. The written statement is to include a reasoned justification of the policy and general proposals in the case of a structure plan (proposals in the case of local plans). A mere statement of policy or proposals by itself will not be sufficient. Authorities will often have considered other policies and proposals and they will be able to refer to these, to the appropriate extent, when they set out the grounds on which they have selected the policy and proposals formulated in the plan.

Relationships

42. An important feature in a structure plan will be the extent to which the policies formulated in it are related and the nature of this relationship: and the regulations accordingly provide for this to be brought out in the written statement. Similarly, the regulations require an indication of the extent and nature of the relationship between the proposals formulated in a local plan.

The Development Plans Manual (HMSO 1971)
3.10 The structure plan performs the seven closely related functions set out below. . . .

1 Interpreting national and regional policies
Structure plans must be prepared within the framework set by national and regional policies. They interpret these policies in terms appropriate to the area in question.

2 Establishing aims, policies and general proposals
The structure plan should contain a statement of the planning authority's aims for the area, and the strategy, policies and general proposals which are designed to achieve these aims.

3 Providing framework for local plans
Just as structure plans are prepared within the context of national and regional policies, so they set the context within which local plans must be prepared. Thus the broad policies and proposals in the structure plans form a framework for the more detailed policies and proposals in local plans.

4 Indicating action areas
In particular, the structure plan should indicate the action areas and the nature of their treatment. These are the priority areas for intensive action. Like other local plans, action area plans cannot be put on deposit or adopted, though they can be prepared, before the Minister has approved the structure plan. But the procedure differs from that for other local plans in that the authority's general proposals for comprehensive treatment must have been included in the approved structure plan, or in an approved amendment to it; the preparation of the action area plan is then obligatory.

5 Providing guidance for development control
Local plans provide detailed guidance on development control. But a universal coverage of local plans is likely to take many years to achieve and may even be unnecessary. In these parts of the area not covered, or not yet covered, by a local plan, the structure plan will provide the basis for development control. . . .

6 Providing basis for co-ordinating decisions
The preparatory stages of the plan will provide a forum for discussion between the various committees of the planning authority and district councils who deal with, for example, housing, roads and open spaces; they will also offer an opportunity to bring together, through consultation and negotiation, other public bodies such as statutory undertakers, river authorities and regional hospital boards, who are likely to be concerned with important aspects of the plan. Later, the structure plan itself will provide a co-ordinated basis upon which these various interests can develop the individual programmes of work for which they have executive responsibility.

7 Bringing main planning issues and decisions before Minister and public
The structure plan will be the means of bringing the authority's intentions, and the reasoning behind those intentions to the attention of the Minister and the public.

3.12 Not only will the plan contain decisions, it should also explain to the Minister and the public how these decisions were arrived at.

4.11 The authority will state, explain and give the reasoning behind the specific intentions underlying the plan, i.e. the aims, as derived from a study of the national, regional and sub-regional policies for the area and from an examination of the existing structure as revealed by the results of survey. Among the aims of a structure plan might be one to protect the historic centre of a town from the adverse effect of traffic, to steer new urban development in certain general directions or to ensure that new industry should have the benefit of deep water access from the sea; these would derive from the authority's general intentions to create an efficient physical structure and a good environment. Efficiency and environment run like threads, often crossing each other, right through the process as the plan is refined from broad intentions, through aims, to the strategy and detailed changes, and it is really a matter of judgment how best to give scope for the creation of both. Thus the aims for efficiency and environment may be in conflict, even mutually exclusive; for example easy assess by motor car to the town centre may be incompatible with the conservation of its architectural quality. There may be conflict even between aims of similar general purpose, e.g. between one whose object is to make the most use of fixed capital in the central area (shops, offices, etc.) and another whose object is to ensure that investment in shops and offices should be channelled to those parts of the town most readily accessible by road. Where conflicts of this nature occur the statement should explain how the aims have been ranked in importance, or at least where and why one has been given dominance over others. Although aims should be sufficiently precise to guide the plan in a specific direction, they should offer room for the examination of alternative strategies that might, to a greater or lesser extent, achieve them. A statement of aims will be valuable as a broad indication of what the plan is trying to do and the direction which should be taken by the changes it proposes; it will serve to secure the co-ordination of the policies and proposals in the plan. Without this statement the authority, the public and the Minister will have difficulty in judging the value of individual decisions that make up the strategy.

4.13 Where compatible with the aims, a choice of alternative strategies may need to be examined. Perhaps these will to some extent employ different assumptions. The statement should set out the assumptions behind these alternative overall strategies, and explain how far each measures up to the aims of the plan. It should show where, in the course of comparing alternatives, an element of one strategy has been combined with those of another in reaching the strategy that has been chosen. This process of choice and decision will have to rely upon subjective assessments where a full comparison of alternative strategies is beyond the scope of present quantitative methods. But the statement should set out the reasons for the selection of the chosen strategy and show how the individual policies and proposals are relevant to the achievement of the stated aims.

4.17 The strategy should also highlight any unresolved planning issues. ... Where proposals are provisional, having had to be made upon incomplete evidence, this should be made clear. ...

7.4 Four closely related functions are common to most local plans. ... They should be compared with the functions of structure plans (3.10) to certain of which they are complementary.

1 Applying strategy of structure plan
Local plans must conform generally to the approved structure plan; they will develop the policies and proposals in it, showing as precisely as possible the changes proposed in the development and other uses of land.

2 Providing detailed basis for development control
The broad guidance on development control in the structure plan will be refined where local plans have been prepared. These will give more precise information to developers by allocating sites for particular purposes, by defining the areas to which particular development control policies will apply, and by explaining those policies in terms of standards and other criteria.

3 Providing basis for co-ordinating development
The planning policies and proposals in local plans will be used as a basis for co-ordinating public and private development and expenditure over the areas covered by them.

4 Bringing local and detailed planning issues before public
While the structure plan is intended to bring before the public matters which affect the structure area as a whole, a local plan will be concerned to draw their attention to more detailed planning issues in parts of that area; it will do so in terms that will inform property owners and developers how their interests will be affected and where the opportunities lie.

DoE Circular 98/74: *Structure Plans*

2. The increased activity of the last two years has ... revealed that some clarification and updating of past advice to authorities on the functions and scope of structure plans is now required, so that authorities may avoid unnecessary expense and time in the preparation of their plans. This Circular therefore sets out advice to authorities about what they should concentrate on when preparing their structure plans, so that effort may be concentrated on what is essential and not dispersed on inessentials, whilst, at the same time, the quality of structure plans (which are becoming of ever-increasing importance with the progressive obsolescence of the old development plans) should thereby be improved.

6. The plan-making authority, after appropriate consultations (including consultation with districts and public participation ...) must finally

decide which are the key structural issues for its area. These will vary from area to area, but for most authorities the key issues will include:

 a. The location and scale of employment
 b. The location and scale of housing (including new development, redevelopment and rehabilitation) and
 c. The transportation system.

7. Some other issues which may be of particular importance are:
 d. The extent of conservation of the character of the area (whether urban or rural)
 e. The extent of provision for recreation and tourism
 f. The location and scale of shopping centres and
 g. The location and scale of land reclamation.

27. Planning, in short, is a continuous process which is not completed when a plan is produced. The plan is necessary as a statement of the authority's intentions at a particular time for the initiation, encouragement and control of development, but the assumptions on which these intentions are based must be regularly monitored and the plan must be amended if and when necessary (probably about every 3–5 years).

CONCLUSIONS

32. To sum up, in preparing structure plans authorities should:
 a. make explicit the assumptions (and the reasons for those assumptions) on which the structure plan is based
 b. concentrate on essentials, i.e. their key issues
 c. deal with those issues in whatever depth is necessary to provide reasoned justification for the chosen policies, and
 d. in general, plan for about 15 years ahead.

Authorities should then also:

 e. monitor their assumptions regularly so that the plans can be adjusted or amended and brought up-to-date whenever any divergence between reality and assumption is great enough to make this necessary.
 f. roll the plan forward approximately every five years to cover a further five years (unless the rolling forward has already been done as a result of an earlier review) so that the plan again covers in general about 15 years.

33. It is hoped that this guidance, by clarifying the task of authorities, will help to expedite the preparations of structure plans, which are now so urgently needed as a guide to development and development control.

STRUCTURE PLANS
QUESTIONS IN WHICH THE SECRETARY OF STATE
IS INTERESTED

1. *National policies*
Does the plan correctly interpret national policies (as evidenced by White Papers, Departmental Circulars etc)?

2. Regional policies
Is the plan compatible with the guidelines of accepted regional strategies and policies?

3. Policies of neighbouring planning authorities
Is the plan compatible with adjoining structure plans or, where appropriate, with the master plans of New Town Development Corporations?

4. Internal coherence of the plan
Do the policies chosen constitute decisions on the issues selected as being of key structural importance?
Does the plan show the reasoning and justification for policies and proposals?
Are the policies put forward in the plan consistent with, and related to, each other?

5. Practicality
Are the demands on financial resources controlled by Government Departments in scale with what available advice indicates is likely to be forthcoming?
Are the demands on other resources realistic?
Is the plan likely to be useful as a basis for local plans and as a general guide to development and development control?

6. Unresolved controversy
How well does the plan deal with points which have aroused substantial public controversy?

7. Monitoring
Is the plan in a form likely to facilitate monitoring and review?

(i) County structure plans, urban structure plans and local plans
The PAG Report drew a clear distinction between county and urban structure plans.[40] It further recommended that urban plans be prepared for towns of over 50,000 population as part of the county plan. The Act provides for the possibility of structure plans being made for part of an area – for the whole of which a structure plan has already been prepared – but neither the circulars nor the development plans manual give clear advice on the relationship between county structure plans and county urban plans, or between county urban plans and local plans for urban areas within counties. According to the PAG Report these local plans should be of two kinds – district plans and action area plans – and the Regulations provide for this accordingly. Thus no less than four types of plans were recommended for county urban areas, and there is nothing in the Act or regulations to prevent these four types of plans from being produced. The fact that the relationship between the plans was

imprecise did not matter while one authority had to produce them all; now that plan making is divided between county and district planning authorities, the relationship between the plans assumes great importance. Warwickshire may be looked at as an example of such relationships.

The County Structure Plan was submitted to the Minister in March 1973. It stated that:

Because of their complexity, closer examination in structure plan terms is being given to the five growth areas. . . . Accordingly separate Structure Plans will subsequently be prepared for the following six urban areas (referred to as Urban Structure Plans – USP): USP 1 Warwick, Leamington and Kenilworth. . . . The Structure Plans for these areas will accord with the overall context set by this County Structure Plan. Although specific proposals in respect of them will be contained in the respective Structure Plans for those areas the following paragraphs outline certain problems and proposals which are of County significance. . . . An investigation of the capacity and detailed planning of central Leamington will be carried out in this separate Structure Plan. . . .[41]

The USPs were to be produced after the County Structure Plan, and indeed the public examination of the latter was timed by the Department of the Environment to take place before any USP had been produced. The following extract from the public examination into the County Structure Plan raises the issue of the relationships between the various types or levels of structure plan.

Public Examination into the Coventry, Solihull and Warwickshire structure plans, 16 November 1973, Transcript,[42] pp. 10, 24–5, 27, 29

MR HEATON:[43] . . . At the moment I want to concentrate on the question of the amount of growth in Bedworth/Nuneaton, and I understood Leamington wanted to say something on that point. If they do, would they take that opportunity now, please, before we get on to . . . .

PROF. MCAUSLAN:[44] . . . I am a little concerned that this fundamental point about the relationship between the county structure plan and the urban structure plan cannot be discussed before we get involved in discussions on particular urban structure plans, as we almost inevitably are beginning to do. It does seem to me that the prior question as to what is the relationship between the two, and can we indeed discuss them when half the Warwickshire plan is not here, must be sorted out before we begin to discuss the Bedworth/Nuneaton urban structure plan, or the Warwick, Kenilworth, Leamington . . . .

MR HEATON: I do not think it is any good in pursuing that line too far, because you can make your point, and I have some sympathy with it, but I mean, the panel have to deal with the papers which have been referred to them by the Secretary of State. Here is the Warwickshire, and Worcestershire,[45] and other structure plans, not as yet accompanied by urban structure plans, but that is the manner in which it has been put before the panel. . . .

PROF. MCAUSLAN: . . . perhaps I could go on and develop the points that I tried to develop about an hour ago on the relationship between urban structure plans and the county structure plan[46] . . . . There is one entity called the structure plan, and this entity is dealing broadly with policies concerning the allocation of resources primarily within, but not exclusively within, the area of the local planning authority. That one entity may be in parts. Whether the parts are bound up or whether they are produced separately is neither here nor there, but the fact that they can be in parts and the fact that the Secretary of State may approve a structure plan in part only does not mean that there are two distinct entities – namely, a county structure plan at the top tier and an urban structure plan as the bottom tier – and it does not mean that the bottom tier is to be based on the top tier, and it is this that Warwickshire at the moment are doing. This is their approach – that there is a two-tier structure plan: a county structure plan and, based on the county structure plan, an urban structure plan.

Personally, I think that what they are doing infringes both the Act and the Regulations.[47] I am not going to make too much of that, because the Act is general and it confers so much power on the Secretary of State that it seems to me that he could wind up this proceeding tomorrow and he would not be acting outside his powers.[48]

What is more important is the way in which Warwickshire approach the question of this structure plan. It infringes, I think, the spirit of the Act and the philosophy of structure planning. The structure planning in a county involves a consideration of conflicting policies concerning rural and urban expansion, conflicting policies of urban conservation and urban development between traffic and transport considerations and the like.

We believe that there cannot be any meaningful discussion of these in any forum if all that we have in front of us is half a plan, if the urban dimension is being kept back until the rural dimension is settled. We believe that it is precisely this inter-relationship between town and country which the philosophy of a structure plan is designed to overcome, and indeed this tripartite debate about the Coventry, Solihull and Warwickshire structure plan is designed to overcome the boundaries between town and country.

It seems to us that we are really in an extraordinary position, that while there can be a sort of discussion between the urban parts of the sub-region (namely, Coventry, Solihull) and the rural parts of the sub-region (namely, rural Warwickshire), there cannot be the same kind of discussion on the interrelationship between rural and urban Warwickshire because there is no urban Warwickshire plan.[49]

MR HEATON: I think that DoE may wish to make some comments on the procedural points that have been made.

MR SAUNDERS (DoE): A question has been raised on the technicalities of whether it would be possible, in effect, to defer decisions on the Warwickshire county structure plan until urban structure plans were available or to reopen in the discussion of urban structure plans the county structure plan.

I think that on a question of sheer technicality the latter cannot be done. There is a county structure plan before the Secretary of State at the moment and the panel's report will contribute to the decisions by the Secretary of State on that county structure plan.

PROF. MCAUSLAN: I wonder if, at the risk of being told it is a procedural point, I would just ask the representative from the DoE what precisely is the technical reason (I think the word was 'technical') why the county structure plan will have to be considered and approved, if necessary, before the urban structure plans are publicly examined? I do not quite understand how this can be a technical matter. Could he elaborate on this a little bit?

MR SAUNDERS: The point I was trying to make that there is a submitted structure plan which the Secretary of State has accepted as a submitted structure plan. Whether other people feel he was right in accepting it – that is a matter of opinion[50] – but this plan has been accepted as a structure plan submission, and therefore the processes are being followed through which will lead to decisions on that structure plan, but as I made clear earlier, we have not yet seen any decision letters on a structure plan, and therefore it is not clear to what extent decisions on an individual structure plan will express reservations about the content of that plan. But, the procedure once set in motion will obviously follow through logically to a decision on the structure plan which is now being discussed at this examination.

Can the Minister approve a county structure plan before he approves an urban structure plan for part of the county? Would it be (a) lawful, (b) sensible from a planning point of view to produce and examine at separate times the six USPs for Warwickshire?

Relationships between different sorts of structure plans primarily affect only the county planning authorities, and in the case of Warwickshire could be explained away as a case of an understaffed planning office trying to make sure that some sort of structure plan, even if not a complete one, was available for the new local authorities to base policies on from 1 April 1974. But no such explanation would be sufficient to show the relationship between the USP for, e.g. Leamington, Warwick and Kenilworth, and the local plans for those areas. If an USP for Leamington is to carry out 'an investigation of the capacity and detailed planning of central Leamington',[51] how is that different from the district local plan proposed by PAG in the following terms:

The urban plan will show the basic structure of the town, and the action area plans provide the means for working up proposals in detail. But the need for detailed local planning in these large urban areas is not limited to the action areas. There must be a link between the broad strategy of the urban plan and the specific action area proposals. . . . Local plans of this character will provide a more detailed basis for development control than the urban plan itself. . . .[52]

and described in the Regulations as a local plan which is based on a comprehensive consideration of matters affecting the development and other use of land in the area to which it relates?[53]

What would be left for a district planning authority covering the areas of Leamington, Warwick and Kenilworth to put into a district local plan? What advice would you give to a district planning authority which considered that a county planning authority had covered local plan matters in a structure plan and wished to challenge the structure plan accordingly? What advice would you give to a county planning authority that, fearful lest it trespass upon the preserves of a district planning authority, asked for clarification of the difference between

the existing structure of the area to which the plan relates and the present needs and opportunities for change[54]

being a matter which a *county* planning authority may if it thinks it appropriate include indications of in its written statement accompanying a *structure* plan, and

the character, pattern and function of the existing development and other use of land in the area to which the plan relates and the present needs and opportunities for change[55]

being a matter which a *district* planning authority may if it thinks it appropriate include indications of in its written statement accompanying a *local* plan?

Is it feasible to assume that a structure plan can be made without, at the same time, a great number of embryo local plans beginning to take shape? And if that occurs what will be the reality of local plan making by district planning authorities?

(*ii*) *The effect of the Act, Regulations and Manual on structure and local planning*

(a) The *Guardian* of 11 December 1970 reported that the then Ministry of Housing and Local Government's Development Plans Manual had been criticised by planners in some areas which are doing pilot work on the new system [who] say the manual calls for too much detailed information to be given in the structure plans and that it harks back to the 1947 Planning Act which the new system will replace. An academic critic calls it 'sadly out of date'. . . . The new plans are meant to be more flexible and more positive than the old ones and in that respect the manual is criticised. One of the planners doing pilot work, Mr Francis Amos of Liverpool, says it offers the unadventurous planner the opportunity to do an old style plan. A member of the team which is producing structure plans for Greater Leicester and Leicestershire said that too much detail was required particularly for the rural areas.

(b) *The Times*, 3 September 1971

The law and lawyers were laying a dead hand on reformed town planning procedures intended to be flexible and speedy, Mr Francis Amos, president of the Royal Town Planning Institute complained today.

Speaking at the town and country planning summer school at Southampton University, Mr Amos, planning officer for Liverpool, recalled that the system of 'structure plans' provided for by Parliament in 1968 had been intended to avoid the delays of the old system, to be highly flexible and to be under continuous review. Unfortunately, regulations made so far under the Town and Country Planning Act promised to destroy these qualities.

The outline that was fairly flexible in the Planning Advisory Group report has been turned into a terribly cumbersome process, which will employ lots of lawyers and misemploy lots of planners. It is not sensitive to change, and not flexible.

It also cut across the need in modern management methods for regular reviews and updating. They wanted to see management systems that tested aims and means aiding structure planning, not structure plans cramping local government.

It is not often that one finds the long-standing tension between lawyers and planners brought to the surface quite so sharply. But are the complaints justified? Consider first the Structure and Local Plan Regulations. What are the most important duties imposed on an authority preparing a structure plan? They are contained in Part III (Consultation) and Parts IV and V (Form and Content of Structure and Form and Content of Local Plans). As regards consultation, the authority *shall* consult certain public authorities, *shall* give them adequate opportunity to express views and *shall* consider such views before finally determining the plan. Is it this that is 'a terribly cumbersome process'? What are the arguments for conferring only a power to consult as opposed to a duty?

It is possible, however, that it is the Regulations dealing with form and content that have aroused the planners' concern. How does the following Regulation destroy the qualities of flexibility and sensitivity to change?

9(1) The policy formulated in a structure plan written statement *shall* relate to such of the matters specified in Part I of Schedule 1 *as the local planning authority may think appropriate.*

(2) The policy and general proposals formulated in a structure plan written statement *shall* be set out so as to be readily distinguishable from the other contents thereof.

(3) A structure plan written statement *shall* include a reasoned justification of the policy and general proposals formulated therein.[56]

How many lawyers or amenity groups would regard Regulation 9(1) as pinning a local planning authority down to do anything at all, let alone preventing it from adopting modern management methods? What does it require the local planning authority to do?

The remainder of the Regulations cover the procedure for the adoption, abandonment, approval or rejection of structure and local plans, and their availability to the public. The procedures for adoption, etc. require the local planning authority and the Minister to use certain forms, prepare and advertise certain information, consider objections, if any, and wait for certain periods before taking decisions. There is no doubt that these procedures will prevent a district planning authority rushing through an important amendment to its local plan with inadequate publicity, consultation and consideration of objections. It may also be suggested that in view of some lawyers' concern about the implications of the local planning authority's power to approve its own local plan, these Regulations are quite deliberately designed to prevent such a possibility. If it is this which Mr Amos is complaining about, then the lawyers' worst fears about planners will be confirmed. Is there a basic incompatibility between flexibility as understood by planners and procedures which require recommendations and decisions to be taken in a certain way following a certain time-scale as urged by lawyers?[57]

What might the Secretary of State do if a plan was submitted to him which complied with the Act and the Regulations but was at variance with the guidance contained in the Manual?[58]

(iii) Structure planning and corporate planning

The modern management methods to which Mr Amos referred in

his criticism of the influence of law on structure planning were corporate planning – a method of local government management which is now widespread, in theory, if not in practice, with the adoption of the Bains Report[59] by most of the reformed local authorities. Mr Amos appears to believe that there is a close link between structure and corporate planning.[60] In his comments on the survey of structure planning carried out in 1972[61], Mr Smart, the County Planning Officer of Hampshire, stated that 'there is also ample evidence to suggest that structure planning is taking place to the detriment of the introduction of corporate planning'.[62]

While then there may be some agreement that the two types of planning are related, there is less agreement on how they are related. Take for example the statement that appears in Warwickshire's Structure Plan: 'The Structure Plan concentrates on essentials but at the same time is in sufficient detail to provide a sound base for corporate planning during the transitional period and earlier years of the new authorities.'[63] This does little to improve our understanding of the relationship beyond confirming that there is thought to be one. The extract from Stewart and Eddison that follows sets out to explain what each type of planning involves and what the possible relationships between them could be. Note particularly their references to structure planning as being felt to be 'too restrictive', and as having 'a more rigid procedure' than corporate planning. What do they mean by these comments? Is this the same point as Amos was making? From the points of view of (a) a member of the public and (b) a local councillor, should structure planning be made more 'flexible' or corporate planning more 'rigid'? How do you see the interrelationships developing?

> J. D. Stewart[64] and Tony Eddison,[65] 'Structure Planning and Corporate Planning', (1972), *J.R.T.P.I.*, 367

There are two main lines of development in planning in local government. The first is the development of structure planning under the 1968 Planning Act. The second is the development of corporate planning in local government – the development of local authority policy planning. . . .

It would be difficult to define precisely the area of concern of structure planning but in many ways the point of emphasis remains land-use planning extended to a general concern with the physical environment and to a lesser extent with the social and economic environment. It may have grown out of its origin in land-use planning, but remains physical planning.

In practice a variety of approaches is being adopted towards structure planning and indeed, structure plans themselves appear to be taking differing forms. The West Midlands Conurbation authorities with the Department of the Environment, see structure plans as having the following qualities :-

(a) they should attempt to meet social and economic objectives.
(b) they are part of a continuous planning process, which informs about the consequences of decisions.
(c) they should represent the authority's intentions for an area, in the way in which the authority intends to use its powers or influence to affect the future of that area.
(d) they should be as realistic as possible in relation to the available resources.

Two additional points can perhaps be added. The first is that early attempts at structure plans, such as this one, will be exploratory. Rather than being viewed as definitive, they should be seen as an initial basis on which to build a continuing and improving planning process. The second is that if plans are to be used with confidence in decision-making, it is important that they should not be firmer than the ability to forecast the future. If they are, then they may well commit resources in directions which will be regretted in the future.

A structure plan is a new form of development plan. It is no longer restricted mainly to the arrangement of land uses. It is concerned with the overall management of investment and land within an authority. This calls for a change in approach to the preparation of development plans. Previously, the approach was directly through survey and analysis to a plan which was a statement of a desirable end-state. A structure plan appears to demand an approach which produces a statement of intended direction, derived from an examination of the various alternative directions an authority could take. (West Midlands Conurbation Authorities Project Report).

. . . Corporate planning could be defined as being concerned with the 'social, economic and physical systems of an area so far as they are affected or can be affected by the activities of the authority'. This is wider in scope than the definition of structure planning.

Some have argued that corporate planning is necessarily narrower in scope than structure planning since the former is concerned with the activities of the authority, whereas the latter is concerned with a much wider range of activities – activities which affect land-use whether they are carried out by the authority or not. But this ignores the wide-ranging impact and concern of the local authorities' activities. These activities are not undertaken for their own sake but for their impact on the environment. The activities of education departments, social services departments, health departments, engineering departments, affect between them virtually all the activities that are affected or are likely to be affected by structure planning – and many more besides. . . .

Apart from the area of scope of corporate planning as defined here, implicit in the concept is the requirement that the approach to it should be a corporate one, that is to say that rather than conceiving, in isolation, a series of separate service plans the policies of the local authority should be derived from an integrated approach, should recognize in the planning process itself the inter-related nature of the problems which a local authority seeks to solve.

There is perhaps another conception that underlies the aspirations given expression in corporate planning and also in structure planning. It is the concept of community planning which would be wider in scope than structure planning, but also wider in scope than corporate planning.

This would be concerned not with planning merely the activities of local authorities or of planning land-use, but of planning the activities of other organizations. It would, in a very real sense, be planning for the community. It would secure, in so far as it was possible to secure, that the various organizations which affect the life of the community would plan their activities together. . . . There are some critical differences between structure planning and corporate planning that must be borne in mind:

1 Structure planning has a legislative base. Corporate planning has none.
2 Structure planning has a direct relationship to the stated requirements of central government. These requirements are reflected in the Development Plan Manual to the exclusion of other important related requirements, for instance capital budgets are treated, revenue is not. Corporate planning is not related to any direct requirements of central government.
3 Structure planning is therefore a more rigid procedure. Corporate planning is a more flexible movement but probably more difficult to define.
4 Structure planning is conditioned by its origin in land-use planning. Corporate planning is sometimes, although not necessarily, by an origin in financial planning.

It is, however, important to note that there are inevitably many common or related elements in both structure planning and corporate planning.

1 *Understanding the environment*
Both structure planning and corporate planning require a background understanding of the social, physical and economic environment in which the authority is set.

2 *Interpreting national and regional policies*
A local authority is set in a wider context; the impact of that wider context must be understood. At times that wider context is expressed as constraints, in other instances as influences upon the authority.

3 *Problems present and foreseen*
Planning requires problem identifications. Plans are not made in the abstract. Objectives are not set without regard to problems.

4 *Setting Objectives*
The local authority cannot be pursuing different objectives in structure planning from the objectives it pursues in corporate planning.

5 *Considering alternative ways of achieving the objectives*
Alternative solutions cannot be considered merely in terms of structure planning. We are concerned with solutions to problems in the community, some of which will lie in structure planning or in land-use, many more will not, but all solutions are probably related and must be seen against a set of common objectives.

6 *Monitoring*
The continual monitoring of the environment by the authority, that is part of any planning process, must feed both into structure planning and corporate planning. ... Authorities that are seeking to develop both structure planning and corporate planning must determine what is to be the relationship between them.
  ... Three main possibilities exist:

1. That the structure plan should be developed, adapted and extended so that it could also be the corporate plan. The difficulties about this proposal are, first that the structure plan raises special problems of central control, legislative procedures, appeals. Those developing corporate planning may feel the structure plan to be too restrictive a framework; and, secondly, that the origin of the structure plan in land-use planning may be felt to provide too restrictive a framework by, for example, the social planners.
2 That structure planning and corporate planning be recognized as separate procedures, but that the elements in each one be identified and where common or related elements are found, clear relationships are established. The problem here is to secure that what is wanted is actually achieved. The pattern of inter-relationships could be so complex as to be virtually unworkable.
3 There should be a central planning procedure within the authority from which a variety of planning procedures within the authority would be derived and to which they would contribute. ...
  This third solution is the only solution that will achieve real integration of planning within the authority and will adequately use its skills and experience. ...

DoE Circular No. 98/74: Relationship Between
Structure Plans and Corporate Plans

31. It is important to distinguish between structure plans and corporate plans (or the Community plan, such as is suggested in the Urban Guidelines Studies (DoE Circular 136/73)). Structure plans cover a longer period than corporate plans, are statutory, and must of necessity take into account policies and investment of both the public and private sector in the area. The corporate plan is an optional, domestic tool of management. There will often be common elements in structure and corporate plans, and clearly, therefore, there should be no conflict between them: the various policies should be integrated. The two types of plan as at present developed, however, serve different purposes, though

each forms part of a greater whole and much of the continuing process of monitoring and policy making will be common to both.

(iv) Structure planning and social planning[66]

One of the stimuli behind the evolution of structure planning was the regional problem in Britain and the belief that economic planning, particularly regional economic planning, was a key to the solution of that problem. Structure plans were seen as the main link between regional plans – primarily economic – and local land-use planning. Since the mid to late 1960s there has come to the fore another development in planning – social planning – which while not superseding regional planning as a matter of concern for planners, has quickly come to equal it in importance. It does involve looking at urban problems from a different perspective and it must be asked whether structure planning is an appropriate vehicle for the incorporation of social planning into the planning process.

Like regional planning, social planning has been in existence and written about before it made its current impact on the planning process. The Central Housing Advisory Committee Report; *The Needs of New Communities*[67], recommended that each new community should have a social development plan as well as a physical development plan, the former of which would be concerned 'not only with the provision of physical amenities but also with the staffing of services at both county and district level and with all those functions which are the responsibility in the new towns of a Social Relations Officer and his staff. It would show how the social services and community facilities were to be provided, by whom and when.'[68] Social development was defined as 'policies and programmes directed towards meeting social needs', and the main function of the plan was seen as ensuring that there was adequate co-ordination between the different authorities providing statutory services such as education, health and social welfare programmes.

At about the same time as that report was published, the Plowden and Seebohm Committees reported on primary education[69] and the provision of local authority and allied personal social services[70] respectively. Both these reports were influential in stressing that policies other than those of purely physical renewal were vital if any impact was to be made on urban areas of acute social need. Both recommended that priority be given to areas of special need by way of the allocation of 'extra resources comprehensively planned in co-operation with services both central and local, concerned with health, education, housing and other social needs'.[71] Again, the impact of black people on social relations in the inner city contributed to new thinking on urban problems. Though often represented in emotional terms as a 'threat' to 'normal' urban life, the generation of the emotion, however unjustified, was in itself a factor in pushing official thinking in new directions.

The reports and problems had an effect on legislation; in particular the Local Government Grants (Social Needs) Act 1969 established the urban aid programme 'designed to raise the level of social services in areas of acute social need and thus help to provide an equal opportunity for all citizens'[72]. Cullingworth[73] comments on the evolving programme and its implications as follows:

Problems of an Urban Society, Vol. 2, pp. 141–3, 149

The identification of areas of special social need and the devising of appropriate programmes is still at a primitive stage and it is not at all clear on what issues policies should be concentrated. An experimental Community Development Project is under way aimed at finding 'ways of meeting more effectively the needs of individuals, families and communities, whether native or immigrant, suffering from many forms of social deprivation'.[74]

... it is clear that policy is shifting markedly from capital projects to community action, what remains unclear is how community action is to be organised, by whom and with what objectives. ...

Much work remains to be done in this field not only in relation to the assessment of deprivation, but also in relation to the means by which social improvement can be achieved. This involves a development of local community programmes of a character which is relatively new to Britain – with a high degree of local direction and control within a supportive statutory framework of social service education, training and income-maintenance .... A major element in social planning is to determine the areas of competence for social action by statutory services, voluntary bodies and local community groups. Each of these has a different role to play: and only the first can be 'planned' in the usual sense of the term. The others can be assisted – though only if it is accepted that they may have objectives which differ from those of governmental bodies or may wish to achieve shared objectives by 'unconventional' means.

Social planning is an *aspect* of planning. It is concerned with social goals and the ways in which programmes and plans can be elaborated in an attempt to meet these goals. As such it is an approach, a way of thinking which should permeate all planning. It should not be separated from 'physical' planning or any other type of planning since these are all aspects of a total activity. Further it is more than assessing the social implications of a physical planning operation. It is concerned with the explicit formulation of the goals which these operations are to be instrumental in achieving, and the means by which they are to be achieved.

Can this approach be incorporated into structure planning? The Act does not specifically require planning authorities to have regard to social planning as it does to 'economic planning and the development of the region as a whole',[75] but the Regulations do encourage both county and district planning authorities to indicate in their written statement the regard they have had to social policies and considerations, a clear invitation to incorporate social planning into their sphere of action. There is however little evidence that this has been done. Official advice from the Department has been virtually non-existent. In contrast to three long paragraphs on regional planning and structure plans in Circular 44/71 the paragraph on social considerations, after referring to the Regulation mentioned above has only this to say: 'This is intended to enable them, in the depth they consider appropriate to the matters and area their plans cover to relate their policy and proposals for the development and other use of land to social needs, problems and opportunities.'[76] The survey on structure planning referred to above had nothing to report on social planning (though corporate planning and different planning techniques featured a good deal) and the following comment by McLoughlin is negative evidence that there is nothing in fact happening in this area:

The preceding paragraphs demonstrate one sort of evidence of a certain uniformity, or lack of experimentation, in the face of a new and challenging form of public policy-making and expression. Another kind is provided by the evidence of how structure planning at the moment is dominated by the planning departments and the professional town planners. It may be wrong to conclude that other skills and agencies are being excluded from structure planning but it certainly appears as if this involvement is being very powerfully controlled by the town planners. We must doubt whether the original aim of the Planning Advisory Group to make the development plan system much more widely based and more fully cognisant of the social and economic interrelationships of environmental and other policy fields can fully be realized under these circumstances.[77]

There were in the comments on the survey differences of opinion as to whether planners or other officers were responsible for the failure to forge links with other departments. Mention must also be

made of the possibility that deliberate decisions were taken, as was
the case with the Warwickshire County Structure Plan, to exclude
considerations of social planning on grounds of lack of time, and
that not everything could be dealt with, however desirable in
theory it was that it should be.[78]

In so far as social planning involves a wider perspective to planning, is it desirable that planners incorporate it into structure
planning? Specifically, do you consider that planning should
involve itself in determining 'the areas of competence for social
action by statutory services, voluntary bodies and local community
groups'[79] as Cullingworth sees social planning doing, or as Stewart
and Eddison say of community planning – an equivalent concept –
it 'would be concerned not with planning merely the activities of
local authorities or of planning land use, but of planning the
activities of other organisations . . .'?[80]

To what extent would the communities concerned benefit if the
CDPs and the community action groups discussed in Chapter 2
were incorporated into the planning process in the way Cullingworth suggests? Does the absence of a specific statutory duty to have
regard to social planning indicate that the statutory provisions
relating to structure and local plans are too flexible or not flexible
enough? What advice would you give to a community action group
which wished to make representations (a) that social planning
should be included within a structure plan which had not included
it; (b) that social planning should not be included within a structure
plan which had included it? Is there a basic incompatibility between
on the one hand, structure and local planning that is grounded in a
land-use planning origin and sees an alteration of the physical
environment as the key to social improvement, and, on the other,
social planning that has evolved from a realisation that it may be
the human community that needs altering and uplifting alongside
or even instead of the physical environment?

(c) Are there enough planners to go round?
There are two aspects to this question – quantity and quality – both
recognised by the PAG

Clearly the new system . . . will require more and better trained planning
staff. . . . It will also call for more and better training facilities for planners. . . . What we are proposing is undoubtedly a highly sophisticated
planning system. If it is to be fully developed and effectively utilised

there will need to be a much better understanding of the determinants of urban development, urban form, and the functions of the countryside, and much greater knowledge of the social needs and aspirations of the community.[81]

(i) Quantity

No doubt because it is invidious to do otherwise, most public discussion has centred on the question of quantity, referring to the question of quality rather coyly in terms of the possible lack of qualified planners. A memorandum of the RTPI put the case of lack of quantity for planning in the reformed local government system, and members from both sides of the House showed themselves to be aware of the problem during the committee stage of the Local Government Bill.[82] McLoughlin's survey seems to confirm some of the fears expressed in the memorandum and the debate. He reports that 'in terms also of staff numbers and skills, structure planning seems to be working on a shoe-string. . . . Many authorities report the strain that structure planning is placing on them. . . .'[83] The structure plans he was surveying were being produced by the unreformed planning authorities; Ashworth's letter highlights the problems that local government reform is producing.

The Times, 13 December 1973: *From the President of the Royal Town Planning Institute*

Sir, . . . Confusion is the apt word to describe the present local government reorganization game; and the impact on the planning process is likely to be dramatic if not traumatic.

There is an absolute shortage of planners which will, of course, only be rectified by long-term training and a decision about this should be taken now. Most planning schools could expand their courses now if the Government would sanction an increase in the numbers of grants available to students to fill the places thus made available.

That is for the long term: meanwhile there are certain steps that could be taken to alleviate the problem:

1. Government finances could be made available for an expansion of the courses conducted earlier this year at which people already engaged in the planning field are able to further equip themselves. This could enable people with training and experience in disciplines closely allied to planning to play a vital role in the planning process until a sufficient body of fully trained planners is built up.

2. The active consideration of allowing people from other spheres such as Central Government, new towns, etc., to be considered for local authority posts. The dangers of denuding those other spheres, particularly in the education field, would have to be seriously noted, but the barriers cannot be maintained indefinitely.

3. A speedy appraisal of the total planning staff needs of the new councils and intervention by Central Government to ensure that where sufficient new staff to cope have already been appointed, no further appointments be made *pro tem*.

4. Directives to ensure that neighbouring authorities make the best use of all staff available in the area (say the county) irrespective of which authority is employing them on April 1.

These last two steps would encourage the districts and counties alike to take the only sensible attitude, namely that planning must be regarded as a whole and who does what is irrelevant. They might even go so far as to unify planning staffs until the total shortage referred to above is overcome.

Of course, the staff shortage is only one aspect of the problem. The confusion that arises from the strange allocation of planning functions and the apparent ignorance of the relationship between planning and transportation are two more issues that will give rise to frustration, delay and, most important of all, disillusion with the planning function of local government.

Is it too much to hope that even at this late stage the Government could be persuaded to believe that the situation is *really* serious and recognize that, however much it might want to devolve responsibility to local government eventually, there is meanwhile a supervisory and directing role that only it can perform?

Yours faithfully,

GRAHAM ASHWORTH.

(ii) Quality

The problem of quantity may be thought to be essentially a short-term one, though it is worth stressing that it is in the short term that structure and local plans are being made. The problem of quality is a more long-term one and therefore more serious. I believe that structure planning, as envisaged by the PAG, by the leaders of the RTPI, by the CES and possibly by some planners within the Department of the Environment, is too sophisticated and complicated a method of planning for a large number of planners in local planning authorities fully to comprehend or operate. The system was devised by a group which consisted of the very best of planners, administrators and treasurers from local authorities; but it was devised for the very best, working in ideal conditions, and not for the average over-worked planner working in cramped conditions with inadequate facilities at his disposal. Even if there are planning departments that are or think they are firmly in command of the techniques and theories of structure planning, it may be doubted whether all of their councillors are, so that the closer the structure plan is to the ideal of the PAG, the further removed it may become from lay comprehension.

McLoughlin provides some support for these views, as does the extract from the Layfield Report on the GLDP. McLoughlin reports that many of the structure plans are staying close to the official advice of the Department, and both he and some of his commentators – naturally, leaders in the planning world – appear to regret this and speak of 'lost opportunities'.[84] I think many planners might see the Department's advice and particularly its manual as a life-line without which they would be lost. Far from opportunities being lost, chaos has been averted.

Mr Amos is reported in the *Guardian* of 11 December 1970 as saying that the Manual offers the unadventurous planners the opportunity to do an old-style plan. But how many adventurous planners are there and what does being an adventurous planner mean? If it is true that the old-style development plan made 'no contribution to the quality of urban design or the quality of the environment' – an assertion as easy to make as it is impossible to prove – is it not possible that this was due as much to the faults of the planners as of the law? It is far easier to change the law than the planners and this seems to have been forgotten or conveniently ignored by governments and planners alike. Structure planning is seen as giving a new lease of life to a profession which has been heavily criticised for planning and development mistakes. As the Greater London Development Plan put it, while 'the Planner was once a maker of physical designs which the builder had to translate into a series of structures, in the society of the present time and the future the Planner is much more than that . . . he is equally deeply involved with the efficient functioning of the economy, the growth of communities. . . .'[85] But the evidence that the average planner is capable, ready or willing to shoulder these extra burdens is slender.

In the era of old-style plans, there were good, bad and indifferent development plans and so it will be again in the era of structure planning. The indifferent and bad plans, though made with the aid of sophisticated techniques, will not be of much greater help to developers than the old-style plans because they will have been made by people who for all their willingness – and some are at least as sceptical as they are willing – do not understand 'the determinants of urban development, urban form, and the functions of the countryside' and do not have the required 'much greater knowledge of the social needs and aspirations of the community'.[86] Who does have this understanding and knowledge to such an extent as would justify them producing structure plans in which 'the emphasis is on the dynamics of urban growth and renewal, on the relationship between land uses and the interrelationship of land use and transport' and where the principal aim 'is to provide a basic planning document which is capable of expressing in a clear and integrated way the policies and objectives that are to shape the town's future'?[87]

McLoughlin may be right in suggesting that the practice of structure planning is probably not in keeping with the original aim of the PAG 'to make the development plan system much more widely based and more fully cognisant of the social and economic inter-relationships of environmental and other policy fields'. He is wrong in suggesting that this would make structure planning 'impotent' and 'irrelevant' and that it should be making 'a major contribution to the wider policy-making process' by, *inter alia*, involving 'wide sectors of local government'.[88] With very few exceptions, planners have neither the necessary skill nor knowledge to make major contributions to the wider policy-making process and a structure plan will be a more useful document to the extent that it explicitly recognises that. The danger facing structure planning in short is not that it will be too unadventurous and narrow in outlook, but that too many planners will be seduced by the visions of the PAG and the CES into believing that they and their work are the sun around which all local government revolves and produce as a consequence wordy and woolly structure plans 'full of sound and fury but signifying nothing'.

Report of the Committee of Inquiry into the GLDP, 1973

2.9. . . . We were . . . impressed by the very high calibre of the staff needed to do some of the work. Whether authorities themselves will have staff of the requisite calibre to prepare plans of a suitable quality is a matter which gives rise to great concern. It is clear that there cannot be many technical officers available to authorities in this country who have the great ability and command of the material that was shown by many of the GLC and Borough Council witnesses at this Inquiry.

2.13. . . . We should not like it to be thought . . . that some of the requirements in the Development Plan Manual, which are not met by the GLDP, are not very valuable, and that the GLDP, in not meeting them, is not a great deal poorer because of their absence. We particularly have in mind the requirement that alternative strategies should be examined and that the reasoning behind the authority's intentions should be fully explained. This comparison makes clear not only the lack of specific policies and information in the GLDP, but also demonstrates how far the GLDP differs from proposed structure plans. It also throws doubts, perhaps, on the practicability of preparing structure plans which conform with Appendix A of the Development Plan Manual. Although the planning of London presents problems of the greatest difficulty because of the form of local government and the continual interest of the national Government, the planning resources of the metropolis, in terms of manpower and skill available to the GLC are, perhaps, proportionally greater in relation to other parts of the country and other authorities, than are the problems of London in relation to theirs. If the GLC could only, with the greatest difficulty, and after extensions of time, produce a plan containing relatively limited information, diffuse aims and vague policies, the chances of success for those structure plans presented by local authorities lacking the resources and skilled manpower of the GLC must be open to doubt. We are certain that unless local authorities obtain, and make use of, technical expertise in the fields[89] which are for the first time given emphasis in the Development Plan Manual, then the aims of the new system will not be realised.

2.17. It will be apparent from our findings that we consider the GLDP has the gravest defects. In spite of the great and inevitable difference that will exist between the GLDP and other structure plans, it seems to us that some of these defects are likely to be present in other structure plans unless action is taken to ensure that they are not. These are:

(a) Over ambition.

. . . It seems to us that local planning authorities must accept that structure plans are, above all, documents which bring together what is known to be happening and which contain the most accurate forecasts, without their being distorted by hopeful projections of the results of untried policies. . . .

(b) Inconsistent treatment of the substance.

(c) Failure to relate information to policies. One of the most notable features of the GLDP is the independence of the policies in the Plan from the facts gathered in the Report of Studies and other documents. In many cases we had the greatest difficulty in seeing why the facts led to the solution set forth in the Plan; in some cases, e.g. the population targets, we never found out at all. Much of this difficulty came about because the GLC, when faced with a variety of solutions to a problem, chose one on political grounds and then presented it as inevitable. We think it right that political considerations should form part of the planning process and that, when an authority decides on a plan it should do so in accordance with political principles. What we do not accept, however, is that the choice should be presented as inevitable. In our view it should be presented as a choice preferred for political reasons amongst alternatives, and not represented as the only logical consequence of technical information. Unless it is made clear to authorities preparing structure plans that this is how political considerations should be taken into account, and it may be that not all authorities will understand the important advice about 'reasoned justification' given in para 41 of the memorandum accompanying Circular 44/71 in this light, we fear that other structure plans may suffer from the same defects in this respect as the GLDP.

(d) Failure to relate policies to aims.

(e) Failure to present aims in meaningful terms. The GLDP Written Statement is full of statements of aims which do not mean anything[90] because they can mean anything to anyone. It is not perhaps being too cynical to believe, indeed, that such aims were inserted because they could mean anything to anyone. The temptation for authors of such plans as the GLDP, who have to try to please many different groups, authorities and interests, is to choose such wording in order not to offend anyone too deeply.

(d) Public participation

We have considered public participation in general terms in Chapter 2; we must now consider its operation specifically in the areas of structure and local plans. Is public participation feasible here? What is the law on the matter and how is it administered in practice? What are the apparent snags? It is clear from the parliamentary debates on the Town and Country Planning Bill in 1968 that while everyone was very enthusiastic about the need for more public participation in plan making, they were equally concerned to speed up the plan-making process, and the attempted resolution of the dilemma between more speed and more participation provides the key to the evolving practice and law here. The discussion will consider four major areas: pre-submission public particiation; the public examination into the structure plan; regional and sub-regional planning; and public local inquiries into local plans.

(i) Pre-submission public participation

Town and Country Planning Act 1971

8.—(1) When preparing a structure plan for their area and before finally determining its content for submission to the Secretary of State, the local planning authority shall take such steps as will in their opinion secure—

> (a) that adequate publicity is given in their area to the report of the survey under section 6 of this Act and to the matters which they propose to include in the plan;
>
> (b) that persons who may be expected to desire an opportunity of making representations to the authority with respect to those

matters are made aware that they are entitled to an opportunity of doing so; and

(c) that such persons are given an adequate opportunity of making such representations;

and the authority shall consider any representations made to them within the prescribed period.

(2) Not later than the submission of a structure plan to the Secretary of State, the local planning authority shall make copies of the plan as submitted to the Secretary of State available for inspection at their office and at such other places as may be prescribed; and each copy shall be accompanied by a statement of the time within which objections to the plan may be made to the Secretary of State.

(3) A structure plan submitted by the local planning authority to the Secretary of State for his approval shall be accompanied by a statement containing such particulars, if any, as may be prescribed—

(a) of the steps which the authority have taken to comply with subsection (1) of this section; and

(b) of the authority's consultations with, and consideration of the views of, other persons with respect to those matters.

(4) If after considering the statement submitted with, and the matters included in, the structure plan and any other information provided by the local planning authority, the Secretary of State is satisfied that the purposes of paragraphs (a) to (c) of subsection (1) of this section have been adequately achieved by the steps taken by the authority in compliance with that subsection, he shall proceed to consider whether to approve the structure plan; and if he is not so satisfied, he shall return the plan to the authority and direct them—

(a) to take such further action as he may specify in order better to achieve those purposes; and

(b) after doing so, to resubmit the plan with such modifications, if any, as they then consider appropriate and, if so required by the direction, to do so within a specified period.

(5) Where the Secretary of State returns the structure plan to the local planning authority under subsection (4) of this section, he shall inform the authority of his reasons for doing so and, if any person has made to him an objection to the plan, shall also inform that person that he has returned the plan.

(6) A local planning authority who are given directions by the Secretary of State under subsection (4) of this section shall forthwith withdraw the copies of the plan made available for inspection as required by subsection (2) of this section.

(7) Subsections (2) to (6) of this section shall apply, with the necessary modifications, in relation to a structure plan resubmitted to the Secretary of State in accordance with directions given by him under subsection (4) as they apply in relation to the plan as originally submitted.

Town and Country Planning (Structure and Local
Plans) Regulations, 1974. No. 1486

Prescribed period for making representations

5. The prescribed period for the purposes of section 8 (1) or 12 (1) of
the Act shall be such period (not being less than six weeks) as shall be
specified by an authority when giving publicity thereunder to the matters
proposed to be included in a structure local plan.

PART III CONSULTATION

Consultation

6.—(1) Before finally determining the content of a structure plan the
county planning authority shall—

    (*a*) consult all district planning authorities whose areas or any part
        thereof are comprised in the area to which the plan relates with
        respect to the content of the plan;

    (*b*) afford the latter a reasonable opportunity to express their views;
        and

    (*c*) take those views into consideration.

    (2) A county planning authority preparing a structure plan or a county
or district planning authority to whom it falls to prepare a local plan
shall—

    (*a*) consult the following—
        (i) where the area of land to which the plan relates includes
           land within the area of a new town, the new town develop-
           ment corporation;
        (ii) such other authorities or bodies as the local planning auth-
           ority preparing the plan think appropriate or the Secretary
           of State may direct;

    (*b*) afford the new town development corporation and the other
        authorities or bodies consulted under (*a*) above a reasonable
        opportunity to express their views; and

    (*c*) take those views into consideration.

DoE Circular 52/72: *Town and Country Planning Act 1971:
Part II Development Plan Proposals: Publicity and
Public Participation*

7. With regard to the structure plan, the Government have proposed a
new form of inquiry – an examination in public of the policies and strategies embodied in the plan. For the examination in public it will be
important to ensure that the public has had full opportunity of participating in the formative stage of the structure plan and that, as a result,
the important issues will have emerged in public debate – whether
through the press, television and radio for the locality, public meetings,

conferences and correspondence with elected members and officials and so on. The selection of issues and participants for that public examination will be closely linked with the thoroughness of the prior public participation. The Secretaries of State will be concerned with the effectiveness of public participation in this context when considering whether they are satisfied as to the adequacy of the steps taken by authorities on publicity and public participation. Of course, until the experience of the earliest groups of authorities preparing plans is available it is impracticable to form final views on how best to achieve appropriate publicity and public participation, but the following points will provide some present guidance for authorities.

8. Authorities should focus their attention on the ways in which they can best discharge the statutory duties placed on them in respect of publicity and public participation. In carrying out these duties it is for the local planning authorities to decide which of the suggestions and recommendations in the Report can usefully be adopted. The views which the Secretaries of State have formed at this stage on the Skeffington Committee's main recommendations are set out in the annexe to this circular. The Secretaries of State wish to emphasise that the aim should be compliance in depth with the terms of the Act's provisions on public participation and the production of effective plans within a timescale which is acceptable overall.

13. Regulation 5 prescribes a minimum period of six weeks which an authority must allow for representations to be made about the matters which the authority proposes to include in its plans. Authorities have discretion to choose a longer period than six weeks if they consider this appropriate. In reaching a decision they will doubtless consider such factors as the extent to which publicity has already been given to the proposals; the methods of publicity they intend to use; the extent to which they are going to give publicity concurrently in the areas to which the plan relates to all the matters they propose to include; the extent of the area to which the plan relates; and the complexity of its proposals. What is absolutely essential is that three things should be made known from the outset, (1) that the authority is encouraging comments, (2) the way in which such representations are to be submitted and (3) what timetable the authority has laid down for receiving representations.

ANNEX

Recommendation III

'Representations should be considered continuously as they are made while plans are being prepared: but in addition, there should be set pauses to give a positive opportunity for public reaction and participation. Local planning authorities should concentrate their efforts to secure participation at two stages. These stages apply to both structure and local plans and are (a) the presentation following surveys of the choices which are open to the authority in deciding the main planning issues for the area in question and (b) the presentation of a statement of proposals for the area in question. Where alternative courses are available, the authority should put them to the public and say which it prefers and why.'

5. Public participation at the stage when real choices are available is likely to be well worthwhile; it could prove valuable to authorities in assisting them finally to select the appropriate strategy on which to base their plan and it may also help to reduce the amount of representations at the statutory participation stage. If, and at whatever stage, authorities decide to present alternatives, however, they should do so in a way which will cause the least possible danger of blight. It may be that in some cases the authority will reach the conclusion that blight is being increased by rumours in the absence of publicity upon feasible options. The danger can never be entirely eliminated whatever publicity course is adopted since it is inseparable from forward planning, publicity and public participation; it is one of the prices to be paid for them; but it should be minimised. Only realistic alternatives should be published and where the local planning authority have a clear preference they should indicate this. So far as possible alternatives should be described only in generalised terms, so that they cannot be related to precise areas of land. Once alternatives have been made public, any blight effect should be removed as quickly as practicable; first by the speedy submission of the structure plan containing the chosen strategy and secondly, once the structure plan has been approved, by publishing the local plan, which will define proposals with more precision . . . .

Recommendations IV–VI

'Local planning authorities should consider convening meetings in their area for the purpose of setting up community forums. These forums would provide local organisations with the opportunity to discuss collectively planning and other issues of importance to the area. Community forums might also have administrative functions, such as receiving and distributing information on planning matters and promoting the formation of neighbouring groups.

Local planning authorities should seek to publicise proposals in a way that informs people living in the area to which the plan relates. These efforts should be directed to organisations and individuals. Publicity should be sufficient to enable those wishing to participate in depth to do so.

Community development officers should be appointed to secure the involvement of those people who do not join organisations. Their job would be to work with people, to stimulate discussion, to inform people and give people's views to the authority.'

6. The Secretaries of State are of the opinion that it will often be advantageous if groups representing different interests could meet together to discuss their different views: but whether this is practical and how it should be done is essentially a local matter. There are a number of existing organisations which will be concerned with structure and local plans; and authorities will wish to enable them to play a constructive part in public participation. The form which any new organisations set up in

response to major or local issues which emerge is bound to depend in large measure on these issues.

7. Local authorities themselves will be able to consider what methods, including publicity, are available to them to encourage those described in the Report as 'non-joiners' to interest themselves in the preparation of plans which are likely to affect them or the area in which they live. Much could usefully be achieved by ensuring that local councillors are kept fully informed about plans, contents and the steps for publicising the proposals concerning them. Where a significant or potentially contentious proposal arising from the needs of a Government Department, statutory undertakers or other public authority is to be included in a plan, the local planning authority should discuss with them the best ways of publicising the proposal and seek their co-operation in discussions with the public. The Secretaries of State are, however, of the opinion that the appointment of Community Development Officers is unlikely to be necessary solely in the specific context of development plans.

16. *Cost.* It is recognised that local planning authorities will be particularly concerned about the extra demands that public participation will make both in terms of staff time and resources and of the time taken to put the plan forward. It has already been indicated in this circular that the Secretaries of State attach great importance to the fact that the Act refers to the steps which will in the opinion of the authority secure adequate publicity and participation. Cost, of itself, should not be regarded necessarily as a decisive factor in reaching this judgment; expenditure incurred would rank as relevant for the purposes of rate support grant.

Who is responsible for establishing and operating the procedures for public participation? Whose opinion has to be satisfied that these procedures have ensured adequate public participation? Is the person who has to be satisfied as to the adequacy of public participation required to consider any particular information in arriving at his opinion on this matter; if so, what information and who provides it? Consider the following problem. A structure planning authority has failed specifically to inform the officers of a council tenants' association of their opportunity to make representations on the matters which it is proposed to include in a structure plan on the grounds (a) that the tenants' association does not consist of persons who in the opinion of the planning authority are expected to desire an opportunity to make representations and (b) by publishing an advertisement in a local newspaper that copies of the draft plan are available for inspection during office hours in various council offices, the authority has in their opinion given adequate publicity to the matters which they propose to include in the plan. What advice would you give to the association which wished to know what action it could take against the planning authority?

The Act is deliberately general in its terms so that public participation should not become 'a formalised or rigid process but should be flexible enough to meet all types of local need'. In so far as any generalisations about public participation may be made, McLoughlin's survey reports as follows:

The new development plan system with its emphasis on explicit aims and objectives and on the importance of publicity, consultation and participation, calls for greater involvement of the public at large, identifiable groups within the community and local authority members. This does in fact seem to be happening but with what success it is far too early to say. Certainly there is a high proportion of exercises which either have a formal steering committee of members or who keep in close touch with councillors (or both). Councillors are being involved not only in rubber-stamping progress reports but, almost everywhere, they are involved in debating policy issues thrown up by structure plan work and putting forward ideas for their officers to consider and advise on in the context of making a structure plan. Contacts with the public at large, whether via the media of mass communication or via social surveys, is obviously proving more uncertain and difficult. Not only are most authorities lacking in any relevant experience but also considerable expense is involved for which no special help seems to be forthcoming.

As we have noted above, in 26 of these exercises the planners intended to have discussions about the objectives of structure planning 'a number of times' with councillors and the public. This may indicate an awareness of the need to regard public policy-making as a learning process heavily dependent on feedback. . . .[91]

A better approach to the possible ways of public participation is to look at an example and consider what conclusions may be drawn from it. Warwickshire's performance – as befits one of the first structure plans to be submitted to the Minister and publicly examined – may be considered. The conflict between participation and speed, already noted, was made more acute in Warwickshire's case by the decision of the County Council in 1971 to submit a structure plan to the Secretary of State before the changes in local government boundaries and organisations took place. (Submission in fact took place in early 1973, before the newly elected embryo local authorities had begun to function in any meaningful way.) That decision in itself inevitably raised a question mark over the commitment to public participation, and was the crucial factor in determining the whole timetable and nature of the participation exercise. In June 1971 when the Council had before it a report from its Planning Committee on the preparation of a project report[92] as an aid to the preparation of a structure plan, the Committee spoke of 'allowing a period of up to twelve months for consultation and public participation prior to submission' with the structure plan being prepared in draft form by mid-1972. In August 1972, when the draft structure plan and report of survey were published, the timetable for participation had been drastically truncated. All comments on the draft plan had to be in by 1 November, and the County Council aimed to give formal approval to the structure plan in February 1973. No reason was given at the time or later for the change of timetable, but the following report of the Town and Country Planning Committee, prepared for the September 1972 meeting of the County Council, may be thought to provide some explanation for the change:

The Government have also issued a circular on publicity and public participation which stresses the importance, in embarking on the new structure plan system, of giving the public the opportunity to participate in the formative stage. It mentions that public participation does not need to be unlimited and stresses the necessity to keep the period for preparing and approving the plan within an acceptable timetable.

The Town and Country Planning Act, 1971, requires that local planning authorities shall give adequate publicity in their area to the report of the survey and to the matters they propose to include in the plan and lays down a minimum period of six weeks as the time in which people who may be expected to want an opportunity of making representations may do so. In accordance with these requirements, copies of the draft County Structure Plan have been placed on sale, exhibitions have been mounted, mainly at public libraries, public meetings have been arranged throughout the County and a leaflet and poster drawing the public's attention to the arrangements have been widely distributed. Six meetings have been held to date and, despite this publicity, the attendance of members of the public at these meetings has, to say the least, been very disappointing. The period within which the public have been given an opportunity to submit their views is three months, ending on the 1st November. Some comment has been received that this is not long enough but we feel that the time allowed is adequate in view of the need to complete the submission of the plan by next Spring.

Turning now to the nature of the participation exercise, it was, as the above extract shows, based on the format of the public meeting and the public exhibition of maps and diagrams from the draft plan. It is important to stress that this was all the public participation there was for the draft county structure plan. There was no survey of people's attitudes, ideas and desires for the future development of Warwickshire, no meetings with local councillors before, or local amenity groups at any time before or after the publication of the draft plan, and no attempt made to use the local press, before or after the initial conference on the publication of the plan in August 1972.[93]

The sufficiency of this amount of public participation may be judged by comparing Warwickshire's practice with the Department's *Management Network for Structure Planning, a suggested approach only.* This breaks the production of the plan down into 107 steps and indicates 5 steps where public participation could take place – the first being step 18, the last, step 97. Warwickshire's public participation exercise started at step 97, long after major policy decisions had been taken. The choice, at that stage, of a programme of some fifteen public meetings throughout the county confirmed the general impression of lack of enthusiasm for participation. The format of the public meeting where the planners on the platform present the plan to the public and then answer or avoid answering questions is better suited to an attempt to sell the plan to the public than to stimulate a reasoned debate on alternatives, and so it proved. Some adjustments were made to the plan before it was approved by the County Council and submitted to the Secretary of State, but the main policies and philosophies remained, because they had not been (indeed could not have been in the time and format available) challenged. The Planning Committee's views on the exercise implied that the public was at fault in not taking more interest. Do you agree?

This exercise in public participation was regarded by the Secretary of State as adequately achieving the purposes of paragraphs (a) to (c) of sub-section (1) of section 8 of the Town and Country Planning Act 1971. Did it? What recourse would a member of the public have who disagreed with the Secretary of State's conclusion? Would the position be improved if the Act contained a legal definition of public participation, and/or the Regulations were more detailed and explicit on what was required to discharge the duties of consultation, of giving adequate publicity to proposals, and of considering views and representations made on those proposals?

Despite the Planning Committee's defence of its participation exercise, it adopted a markedly different approach in respect of the production of urban structure plans. A questionnaire posing possible alternative areas of growth for the Leamington–Warwick–

Kenilworth urban area and listing alternative policies on such matters as transport, housing and the environment for grading in order of preference was sent out to the accompaniment of some publicity.[94] Meetings with local councillors were held to try and explain the thinking behind the alternatives. Whether this was a better attempt at participation turns on three things. First on the adequacy of the questionnaire.[95] Did it ask the right questions? Why were some possibilities, e.g. no growth for the area, not posed? How could one indicate that some of the alternatives posed were false or clashed, etc? Secondly, on the precise relationship between the county and the urban structure plan: to what extent did the questionnaire assume that the county structure plan was unalterable? Thirdly, on whether the private meetings with local councillors were designed for an exchange of views on matters not yet finalised or to sell a policy already decided upon. On all these matters views inevitably differed and suspicions existed, engendered partly by the earlier experiences of participation.[96]

It might be argued that the example of Warwickshire is a loaded one, designed to show public participation at its worst, and that an example drawn from a more enlightened authority – e.g. Coventry – would be fairer. To the outsider, Coventry *is* more enlightened. It was singled out for commendation by the Skeffington Committee for its participation procedures.[97] Certainly the amount of information made available to the public about the plan and the survey far exceeded that of Warwickshire. But even in Coventry there was criticism from amenity and community groups on the speed at which the plan was being produced, and this criticism was repeated at the public examination into the plan. However, such criticism of the choice of example is misplaced. In considering the practice of pre-submission public participation from a problem-orientated point of view, the question is not: 'how do the more enlightened planning authorities behave?', but 'how do the less enlightened planning authorities behave and still keep within the law, and what can be done to make them behave in a more enlightened manner?'

(ii) The public examination

The public examination introduced into the planning process by the Town and Country Planning (Amendment) Act 1972 has replaced the public local inquiry as the vehicle for the consideration of a structure plan in public. Its place in the evolution of the public inquiry cannot be dealt with here; rather we shall consider its genesis and attributes as part of the structure planning process by looking at the terms of the Act, at the DoE document: *Structure Plans: The Examination in Public,* and finally, at the first such examination into the structure plans of Warwickshire, Coventry and Solihull.

In reading these materials, consider the following issues. Was the scale of the public inquiry into the GLDP a decisive factor in influencing the government to adopt the public examination for future structure plans?[98] If not, what was it about that inquiry that caused the government to turn away from such a well-tried administrative device? Are you satisfied that fundamental objections to future structure plans will be forthcoming and pressed as vigorously under the public examination procedure as they were under the public inquiry procedure used to examine the GLDP? Should lawyers be banned from representing parties at a public examination? How would you reconcile the following statements of the Layfield Commission:

We owe much to the careful and lucid explanation of the many complex technical issues which were given us by Counsel and the other representatives of the parties. . . . We found . . . throughout the Inquiry that our understanding of the issues was advanced by the manner in which the cases of Objectors were presented.[99]

The G.L.C. have in some respects shown a commendable willingness to accept criticism . . . but . . . throughout the Inquiry they were hampered by the procedure of cross-examination and reply which inevitably encourages defensive attitudes and puts a higher premium on answering back than on self-analysis.[100]

What is it about the format of the public examination that will encourage 'self-analysis' by planning authorities in the face of critical comment by objectors rather than 'defensive attitudes'? Who is better served – the planning authority or the public – by pre-submission public participation followed by a public examination as opposed to a public local inquiry? What redress has (a) an objector who considers that he should have been invited to participate in the public examination, (b) an objector who participated but is dissatisfied with the procedures that were followed?

Town and Country Planning Act 1971

9.—(1) The Secretary of State may, after considering a structure plan submitted (or resubmitted) to him, either approve it (in whole or in part and with or without modifications or reservations) or reject it.

(2) In considering any such plan the Secretary of State may take into account any matters which he thinks are relevant, whether or not they were taken into account in the plan as submitted to him.

(3) Where on taking any such plan into consideration the Secretary of State does not determine then to reject it, he shall, before determining whether or not to approve it—

> (a) consider any objections to the plan, so far as they are made in accordance with regulations under this Part of this Act, and
>
> (b) cause a person or persons appointed by him for the purpose to hold an examination in public of such matters affecting his consideration of the plan as he considers ought to be so examined.

(4) The Secretary of State may after consultation with the Lord Chancellor make regulations with respect to the procedure to be followed at any examination under subsection (3) of this section.

(5) The Secretary of State shall not be required to secure to any local planning authority or other person a right to be heard at any examination under the said subsection (3), and the bodies and persons who may take part therein shall be such only as he may, whether before or during the course of the examination, in his discretion invite to do so:

Provided that the person or persons holding the examination shall have power, exercisable either before or during the course of the examination, to invite additional bodies or persons to take part therein if it appears to him or them desirable to do so.

(6) An examination under subsection (3)(b) of this section shall constitute a statutory inquiry for the purposes of section 1(1)(c) of the Tribunals and Inquiries Act 1971, but shall not constitute such an inquiry for any other purpose of that Act.

(7) On considering a structure plan the Secretary of State may consult with, or consider the views of, any local planning authority or other person, but shall not be under any obligation to do so.

(8) On exercising his powers under subsection (1) of this section in relation to any structure plan, the Secretary of State shall give such statement as he considers appropriate of the reasons governing his decision.

Structure Plans: The Examination in Public (HMSO 1973)

The Code of Practice

2.10 ... The traditional form of inquiry, which has come to involve many formalities of a kind apt for dealing with detailed property matters, has only rarely proved suitable for exploring also the policy issues inherent in major development plan submissions. Such an inquiry, specifically related to objections, would be unlikely to bring out, in such a way as to inform the Secretary of State effectively about them, those matters – including alternatives – with which he should be concerned at structure plan level.

2.11 Moreover, retaining the traditional form of inquiry would mean the duplication of proceedings at structure plan and local plan level. A great deal of time would inevitably be taken up with detailed objections to both types of plan, particularly if individual objectors felt they had to safeguard their interests by seeking a personal hearing on the structure plan as well as on local plans. It is therefore inappropriate to have, in sequence, the same kind of traditional inquiry into objections first to the structure plan and then to local plans.

2.12 It is now widely recognised that not enough importance has in the past been paid to the need for reasonable speed in considering and deciding development plans, or to the price paid for delay – which can include prolonged uncertainty and blight. In the new context of the structure and local plans system, the traditional inquiry procedure would become protracted to a totally unacceptable degree. It is therefore being replaced by an examination in public, relevant to the character of structure plans.

3.1 The primary purpose of the examination in public is to provide the Secretary of State with the information and arguments he needs, in addition to the material submitted with a structure plan and to the objections and representations made on it, to enable him to reach a decision on the plan. . . .

3.3 . . . The examination itself needs to be seen as forming only a part, though a very important part, in the process by which the Secretary of State considers and decides structure plans.

3.10 The Secretary of State's selection of matters will be based on the structure plan itself; on the local planning authority's statement about publicity and public participation, and consultation; and on objections and representations made on the plan as submitted. . . .

3.12 Not all key issues will throw up matters which need to be selected for reference to the examination in public. The treatment of many of them in the plan will have proved to be generally acceptable. The Secretary of State will be concerned to select only those matters arising on the plan on which he needs to be more fully informed by means of discussion at an examination, in order to reach his decision.

3.13 Matters which need to be examined are likely to arise, principally, from clashes between the plan and national or regional policies, or those of neighbouring planning authorities; from any conflicts between the various general proposals in the plan; or from issues involving substantial controversy which has not been resolved. These examples do not mean that there will be no other matters appropriate for examination; but an examination will not be concerned with every provision in a plan, any more than with pursuing all comments on it, whether objections or representations.

3.17 The selection of matters is closely linked with the effectiveness of public participation and consultation. The more constructively they are carried out, the more the matters which do need to be selected will stand out and the more effectively they can be examined. Public participation and consultation provide the most suitable opportunity for authorities to bring out the alternatives they have considered, with their grounds for preferring the one they are proposing to put forward; and for any other realistic alternatives there may be to emerge. These stages will show the extent to which alternatives are opposed or supported, and make it easier to bring out, in the description of a selected matter, any alternative which clearly needs to be examined.

3.18 *Objections*. The Secretary of State has a statutory duty to consider all objections to a structure plan.

3.22 Objections should be relevant to the plan, and have regard to the fact that a structure plan is essentially a written presentation of policy and general proposals. It will not be appropriate, or indeed possible, in the context of the examination, or even in the consideration of the structure plan, to deal with objections which are really directed to detail instead of to structural issues.

3.26 The Department will look at all objections to see whether they are related to the structural level and, if so, whether they give rise to matters which should be selected for the examination. If the Department are in doubt about the meaning of an objection, about the grounds for it or, above all, about its relevance to the structural level, they will ask the objector for clarification. This will secure that objections can be considered more effectively. This is important: the Secretary of State's selection of matters for the examination will not reflect all the objections made, but he will take all objections into account before reaching his decision on the plan as a whole.

3.28 The material described above as forming the basis for the Secretary of State's selection of matters for the examination will also help to point to those authorities, organisations and individuals whom he should consider inviting to take part in it. In selecting participants, the basic criterion will be the effectiveness of the contribution which, from their knowledge or the views they have expressed, they can be expected to make to the discussion of the matters to be examined. The local planning authority responsible for the structure plan will always be invited.

3.29 As the examination is directed to discussion of the selected matters, and not to hearing objections, it is not intended that all those who have objected should be invited to the examination: the volume and content of objections as a whole will be known from written material. Where objections give rise to matters selected for the examination, not all those whose objections or representations relate to those matters will be invited to take part in the discussion. The aim will be to select participants who can, as part of their contribution to the discussion, reflect the objections which are significant to the structure plan level. Participants will not necessarily be restricted to those who have made objections or representations.

3.30 Individuals as well as organisations will be eligible for selection.

The nature of the examination

3.45 The essential feature will be that of a probing discussion, led by the Chairman and other members of the panel, with the local planning authority and the other participants. Throughout, the aim will be to secure a satisfactory examination of those matters which the Secretary of State has selected so that, by this means, he can obtain the further advice he needs before proceeding to his decision on the plan as a whole.

3.46 Particular attention will be paid to matters on which it seems likely that changes may need to be made at the decision stage, including those involving alternative proposals. To be constructively considered at the examination, alternatives will need to have been reasonably well developed in advance. They are likely to have been identified mainly from the earlier stage of public participation. They may also come from, for example, objections or representations: or these may give specific alternatives greater weight or precision.

3.47 A primary aim is to ensure that the examination investigates the selected matters in public and in such depth that there should be no need to re-open the examination later in order to pursue further argument relating to changes which the Secretary of State proposes to make as part of his decision. It is his aim that, where he needs to differ from the plan as submitted, he should do so as far as possible by expressing reservations in his reasoned decision letter (which forms part of the plan): and that modifications of any formal kind (which entail altering the plan itself) should not be proposed unless essential on major issues.

3.48 The Chairman and other members of the panel will take an active part in the examination. An important feature of their role will be to ensure that relevant points of view can be explored.

3.50 The arrangements at the examination, and the conduct of it, will be designed to create the right atmosphere for intensive discussion but to get away from the formalities of the traditional public local inquiry. . . .

3.52 . . . It is important that participants should not feel that unless they are professionally represented they will necessarily be at a disadvantage or their contribution not effectively made. The active part which the panel will be taking means that if they consider that participants (whether a group or an individual) have a relevant point or argument worth pursuing but which the participants cannot themselves develop sufficiently, it will be for the Chairman and panel to take it up and pursue it.

4.5 Some objections may straddle the structure and local plan levels. An objection apparently related only to detail may in fact be relevant, at least by implication, to the structure plan. For example, the reference to a proposal in a structure plan may indicate its location only approximately. Existing development and the topography of the area may virtually dictate the precise position of the proposed development when it is worked out and comes to be considered at the local planning stage. People or groups who were concerned about the effect of the proposal on their property, might take the view that an objection belonged more appropriately to the local planning stage, only to find that, by that stage and because the structure plan had been approved, it was then too late to argue effectively that the proposal, because of its detailed impact on properties in the area, should not be carried out at all. Thus an objection apparently concerned only with detail might in fact have an important structure plan component.

4.6 ... Safeguards to prevent such prejudice are incorporated in the new arrangements.

4.9 A further safeguard is that, as the Secretary of State's decision letter on a structure plan will point out, approval of a structure plan cannot be taken to imply that the Secretary of State has thereby approved subsequent detailed proposals, regardless of their precise local effect. This will apply particularly to proposals to which there had been objections on which he had formed no view because they were matters more appropriately considered at the local plan stage with the help of the public local inquiry into a local plan. . . .

Does 4.9 mean that in some circumstances a local plan need not 'conform generally' to the 'structure plan as it stands for the time being'? If not, what does it mean?

The first public examination took place during November and December 1973. It examined jointly the Coventry, Solihull and Warwickshire structure plans. As the Code of Practice had foreshadowed, the issues which were discussed at the examination had been carefully chosen by the regional office of the DoE and appeared designed to highlight the various conflicts between the three planning authorities. They also allowed conflicts within the various plans to be debated. Those private objectors who were invited to participate had their objections and representations and their potential contribution fitted into an overall DoE-planned framework. The impression that was given by the programme for discussion was that the public examination was seen by the DoE as very much a part of the administrative machinery for deciding between conflicting policies of local authorities to which outsiders were to be admitted, to the extent that it was felt that their contributions might support preliminary positions adopted by the DoE on those conflicts. In practical terms therefore, by dispensing with the formalities of the public inquiry, including procedural rules, the DoE has been able to turn the clock back and ensure that its version of the public inquiry, urged on but not accepted by the Franks Committee is, in its guise of a public examination, reinstated in the planning process. The institution exists primarily as an aid to the Minister; only very secondarily as a vehicle for public participation. The administration has control over the institution, and not the public and the lawyers, as is increasingly the case with the public inquiry.

The course of the discussions at the examination confirmed the impression of administrative control of the institution. They also belied the Code's statement that 'the essential feature will be that of a probing discussion led by the Chairman and other members of the panel. . . .' On some issues, the panel was prepared to probe, to ask local planning authorities awkward questions and expose inconsistencies. On others, it was prepared to allow private participants to probe in the same manner. But there were issues of great importance that were left hanging in the air:[101] assertion by one local planning authority would be met by assertion by another and no follow-up by panel or participants would occur; planning officers from different planning authorities were reluctant to engage in open and probing combat with each other, and the panel was disinclined to push them. This suggests that it is not so much the presence or absence of lawyers, procedural rules and cross-examination that deters or encourages local authority planners to be frank, as the presence or absence of a public forum. Planners are appointed officials and not elected politicians. Neither their professional standing nor their career prospects are likely to be enhanced by what might be represented as public wrangling with colleagues, particularly when they are colleagues with whom one has to co-operate in the future. As at public inquiries, it was the unofficial private objectors who injected a combative spirit to the proceedings.

Notable absentees from the examination were local elected politicians, appearing either to defend their plans or attack those of a neighbouring authority. This lent an air of slight unreality to the proceedings and may have further inhibited the planning officers, who were reluctant to exceed their briefs as agreed upon by their respective planning committees and councils. The plans rarely came alive as political documents full of policies about the allocation of scarce resources. Instead, because too much of the discussion was conducted with low-key exchanges between officials careful not to over-commit themselves, they appeared as technical documents, devoid of current importance or future implications.

From an administrative point of view, the examination may be counted as a success: the three plans were examined within the six-week timetable allowed; virtually no issues outside those programmed were discussed; few lawyers appeared for objectors or those making representations;[102] the examining panel was clearly in control of the proceedings, and would no doubt argue that the examination was probing enough for their purposes even if it did not satisfy all the objectors. This is not to mean that no improvements will be made to the process. It was acknowledged that the first examination was bound to be experimental to some extent and the Department was keen to obtain the views of its participants.[103] But changes, if they are made, will be within the parameters described above. The public examination is and will remain more of an administrative than a participative institution.

(iii) Regional and sub-regional planning
It may be thought strange that these topics surface again under the heading of aspects of public participation. But the issue is quite straightforward. Increasingly, structure plans are based on regional and sub-regional surveys. These surveys are not subject to any statutory public consideration, yet once approved by the Secretary of State they provide the policy foundations for the structure plans. This means therefore that however enlightened a planning authority is prepared to be in respect of structure plan public participation, the policy choices open both to the authority and to the participators will have been circumscribed long before structure planning or participation gets under way.

An illustration of this comes from the West Midlands and Warwickshire and may help explain the paucity of public participation in relation to Warwickshire's structure plan. Warwickshire's planners had before them both the West Midland Regional Survey and the Coventry–Solihull–Warwickshire Sub-Regional Study.[104] Neither had been formally approved by the Secretary of State but both had been accepted, subject to some slight differences of emphasis, by, *inter alia*, the Warwickshire County Council. The structure plan makes specific reference to and draws on the work done for the Sub-Regional Study[105] which, it will be recalled, had been explained to the public at a series of public meetings. Both that and the Regional Survey provided the parameters for the structure plan and made it less relevant or possible to respond to the views of the public on fundamental policies; hence the public were never invited to offer such views.

Does not the growth of non-statutory regional and sub-regional planning undermine public participation in structure planning or at the very least render it less useful and effective? Should regional and sub-regional planning be put on a statutory basis, at least to the extent that the plans are subject to a public examination before they are approved by either the Secretary of State or the relevant local authorities?

Consider in this respect the decision of the DoE to hold a joint public examination of the Coventry, Solihull and Warwickshire structure plans despite a decision by the Warwickshire County Council that 'no action should be taken to initiate joint working or submission of joint structure plans as permitted by the Town and Country Planning (Amendment) Act 1972'[106] following a request by the Secretary of State in Circular No. 72/72 to consider such joint working and submission. What is the legal authority for this decision by the DoE? How could a participant in the public examination ensure that the policies of the Sub-Regional Study were as open to question and discussion as those of the three structure plans? What advice would you give to a person who had made no objection to the Warwickshire structure plan within the statutory period and informs you that had he known, during that statutory period, that the Warwickshire plan was to be considered jointly with the Coventry and Solihull plans, he would have made objections on grounds that embraced all three plans? Has such a person any remedy? Consider also the implications for the making and public examination of structure plans of the statement by the chairman of the panel examining the plans that the panel was not in session to examine the Coventry–Solihull–Warwickshire Sub-Regional Study.

(iv) Public participation into local plans

1. PRE-SUBMISSION PARTICIPATION

We have hitherto concentrated on public participation in structure planning, but it is a requirement also in local planning. As we have seen in section 4(a) of this chapter, local planning has been complicated by the provisions of the Local Government Act 1972, so that it is not possible to state with any degree of confidence which tier of which local authority will make which local plans. Whichever authority makes them however, section 12 of the 1971 Act sets out in the same terms as does section 8 (for structure plans) the obligations, such as they are, for pre-submission participation and consultation, and the DoE's circular on public participation does not significantly distinguish between section 8 and section 12 participation. No useful purpose would therefore be served by reproducing those sections of the Act and the Regulations dealing with local plan pre-submission participation.[107]

This is not to say however that no problems exist. Two situations may be considered here.

(a) Where both the county and the district planning authorities are preparing local plans: the county on e.g. transport and roads, the district on e.g. housing and conservation. How is a disagreement between the two authorities on the adequacy or otherwise of the report of survey and its consequent publicity to be resolved? The county might wish to rely on paragraph 12 of Circular 52/72 which sanctions reliance on previous publicity and participation in respect of a structure plan survey; the district might have been dissatisfied with the structure plan participation and want to try its own hand at participation. There appears to be nothing to stop the two authorities going their own way on local plan pre-submission participation. Is this desirable? What advice would you give an amenity society that wished to object to the adequacy of local plan participation by the county – e.g. public meetings on the proposed plan only – by reference to the amount and type of local plan participation provided by the district – e.g. surveys, meetings with different groups, alternative draft plans, etc?

(b) Where the district planning authority is the sole local plan-making authority. Section 11(9A) states:

For the purpose of discharging their functions under this section (preparation of local plans) a district planning authority may in so far as it appears to them necessary to do so having regard to the survey made by the county planning authority under section 6 of this Act examine the matters mentioned in sub-sections (1) and (3) of that section so far as relevant to their area.

This section was added by the Local Government Act 1972, being thought essential in view of the two-tier plan-making system brought into being by that Act. But does this sub-section authorise a district planning authority to make a survey of the matters contained in section 6(1) and (3)? What is the difference between empowering an authority 'to institute a survey . . . examining the matters which might be expected to affect the development of the area'[108] and empowering an authority 'to examine' those same matters? Is a district planning authority confined to re-examining the same facts contained in the survey instituted by the county planning authority or may it attempt to find fresh facts? A possible case in point could arise out of the increasing interest being shown in social planning. Where a structure plan and its survey make no reference to social planning – as is the case with Warwickshire – could a district planning authority examine the matters which might be expected to affect the development of its area from a social planning perspective even if this meant carrying out or instituting fresh surveys? Would a local plan containing an explicit social planning element conform generally to a structure plan that did not?[109]

The possibility of further surveys by the district planning authority, and of local plans being made on the basis of two different surveys, further complicates the pre-submission public participation procedures. Two different surveys might necessitate two different exercises in public participation to add to the differences which might arise from two different authorities making local plans. There is, no doubt, much to be said both for flexibility in public participation procedures and for acknowledging that different local plans may by virtue of their subject matter require different types of participation, but one is bound to query the present open-endedness of the law and administration on pre-submission local plan participation. What advantages are gained by whom from the present lack of clarity? Is it a sufficient answer to criticism to say that problems will not arise because common sense and a spirit of compromise will prevail among planning authorities?

2. THE PUBLIC LOCAL INQUIRY

Section 13 of the 1971 Act states:

13.—(1) For the purpose of considering objections made to a local plan the local planning authority may, and shall in the case of objections so made in accordance with regulations under this Part of this Act, cause a local inquiry or other hearing to be held by a person appointed by the Secretary of State or, in such cases as may be prescribed by regulations under this Part of this Act, by the authority themselves, and . . . .

(b) the Tribunals and Inquiries Act 1971 shall apply to a local inquiry or other hearing held under this section as it applies to a statutory inquiry held by the Secretary of State, but as if in section 12(1) of that Act (statement of reasons for decisions) the reference to any decision taken by the Secretary of State were a reference to a decision taken by a local authority.

(2) Regulations made for the purposes of sub-section (1) of this section may—

(a) make provision with respect to the appointment and qualifications for appointment of persons to hold a local inquiry or other hearing under that subsection, including provision enabling the Secretary of State to direct a local planning authority to appoint a particular person, or one of a specified list or class of persons;

The Regulations referred to in sub-section (2) above had not been made by the end of 1974 but the Town and Country Planning (Structure and Local Plans) Regulations[110] contain further directions about the public local inquiry into the local plan.

33.—(1) Where, for the purpose of considering objections made to a local plan, a local inquiry or other hearing is held, the local planning authority who prepared the plan shall, as part of the consideration of those objections, consider the report of the person appointed to hold the inquiry or other hearing and decide whether or not to take any action as respects the plan in the light of the report and each recommendation, if any, contained therein; and the authority shall prepare a statement of their decisions, giving their reasons therefor.

(2) The authority shall make certified copies of the report, and of the statement prepared under paragraph (1) above, available for inspection not later than the date on which notice is first given under regulation 35.

35.—(1) Where a local planning authority decide to adopt a local plan, they shall, before adopting the plan, give notice by advertisement in the appropriate form (Form 12) specified in Schedule 3, or a form substantially to the like effect, and shall serve a notice in the same terms on any person whose objections to the plan have been duly made and are not withdrawn, and on such other persons as they think fit.

(2) After complying with paragraph (1) above, the authority shall send the Secretary of State by recorded delivery service a certificate that they have complied therewith; and, subject as mentioned in section 14(3) of the Act, the authority shall not adopt the plan until the expiration of twenty-eight days from the date on which the certificate is sent:

Provided that, if before the plan is adopted, the Secretary of State directs the authority not to adopt the plan until he notifies them that he has decided not to give a direction under section 14(3) of the Act, the authority shall not adopt the plan until they receive such notification.

No part of the reformed planning machinery has been subjected to such strong criticism as this. Even the taking away of a right of appearance at a public inquiry and the substitution for it of a privilege of appearance at a public examination at the structure plan level, which could be said to infringe the principle of *audi alteram partem*, has not roused the same criticism as these provisions which are regarded as infringing the principle of *nemo iudex in sua causa*. The extracts which follow set out a possible 'safeguard' power contained in section 14 of the 1971 Act to prevent abuse of the power conferred on the local plan-making authority and a ministerial explanation of how the provisions might operate. In reading these materials, take into account that the number of potential local plan-making authorities has been increased by the Local Government Act 1972 from 127 to 420, and consider what differences, if any, this fact makes to the explanations of the provisions.

Town and Country Planning Act 1971

14.—(3) After copies of a local plan have been sent to the Secretary of State and before the plan has been adopted by the local planning authority, the Secretary of State may direct that the plan shall not have effect unless approved by him.

'(4) Where the Secretary of State gives a direction under subsection (3) of this section, the local planning authority shall submit the plan accordingly to him for his approval, and

(*a*) the Secretary of State may, after considering the plan, either approve it (in whole or in part and with or without modifications or reservations) or reject it;

(*b*) in considering the plan, the Secretary of State may take into account any matters which he thinks are relevant, whether or not they were taken into account in the plan as submitted to him;

(*c*) subject to paragraph (*d*) of this subsection, where on taking the plan into consideration the Secretary of State does not determine then to reject it, he shall, before determining whether or not to approve it—

   (i) consider any objections to the plan, so far as they are made in accordance with regulations under this Part of this Act;

   (ii) afford to any persons whose objections so made are not withdrawn an opportunity of appearing before, and being heard by, a person appointed by him for the purpose; and

   (iii) if a local inquiry or other hearing is held, also afford the like opportunity to the authority and such other persons as he thinks fit:

(*d*) before deciding whether or not to approve the plan the Secretary of State shall not be obliged to consider any objections thereto if objections thereto have been considered by the authority, or to cause an inquiry or other hearing to be held into the plan if any such inquiry or hearing has already been held at the instance of the authority;

(*e*) without prejudice to paragraph (*c*) of this subsection, on considering the plan the Secretary of State may consult with, or consider the views of, any local planning authority or other

persons, but shall not be under an obligation to consult with, or
consider the views of, any other authority or persons or, except as provided by that paragraph, to afford an opportunity
for the making of any objections or other representations, or to
cause any local inquiry or other hearing to be held;
and

(f) after the giving of the direction the authority shall have no
further power or duty to hold a local inquiry or other hearing
under section 13 of this Act in connection with the plan.'

House of Commons Standing Committee G,
7 March 1968: Committee stage of the Town and
Country Planning Bill 1968, cols 299–301

The speech which follows was made by the Minister of State,
Ministry of Housing and Local Government, Mr MacDermot, on
an amendment that sought to provide that where the local planning
authority resolved against the recommendation of the inspector
relating to objections made to the local plan, those objections might
be referred to the Minister at the request of any person or persons
who objected.

A difficult position could arise if, even after an inquiry, even after a
recommendation by the inspector, the local authority still says, that the
matter raises what is, for them, [*sic*] and that they, the locally elected
planning authority, are the people to decide policy for this area, within
the overall policy of the approved structure plan, and that their decision
is so-and-so.

The Ministry could not consider the issue in isolation. It would have
to consider it in relation to the whole of that local plan, considering all
the policy underlying it in relation to the rest of the detail of that local
plan; that would require very detailed consideration by the Ministry.
We shall have our power of 'call in' and there will be cases where we
think it right to use it. An issue of this kind might be a case in which
the power would be used. And we still have the power of 'call in' even
after the provisional resolution by the local authority rejecting a recommendation of the inspector has been made. But the discretion whether
the issue should be decided at Ministry level ought to rest with the
Minister, not with the objector. To give the objector the right to impose
upon the Ministry the duty of going into all that detail is too heavy.
The Minister should be left to decide. There will be time, even after a
local authority has rejected the inspector's recommendation and given
its reasons for doing so, for the Minister to decide whether to call it in if
he is asked to do so at that stage.

It has been suggested that I might argue that there is always the
remedy of the courts. I have never suggested that remedy. I do not recall
using that argument on this kind of issue. It was certainly a slip if I did,
because this kind of issue could not go to the courts. The appeal to the

courts is on whether the proper procedure has been followed. But on the matter of substance, which would be an issue of policy, there would be no appeal to the courts.

It is easy to say with horror in one's voice that a local authority is not bound to accept and can even reject the recommendation of the inspector. We all have the greatest respect for inspectors, but they are not democratically elected planning authorities. They are a very good vehicle for ensuring that objections are properly heard, that an independent, qualified and expert mind is brought to bear and to express an opinion, but when that has been done the decision should rest with the democratically elected authority which may be either the Minister or the local authority.

Essentially, what we are considering here are local issues and local policies. If a matter raises more than local policy, it is an issue which will come up in the structure plans and will, therefore, be decided by the Minister, but what we are dealing with here is, *ex hypothesi*, a local matter raising a local question of policy. It is said – and again I quote one of my hon. Friend's phrases – that the local authority may be hell-bent to get its plans through. It may be hell-bent, but it will be subjected to some rigorous procedures as the Bill stands. I do not want to go over them again – hon. Members will remember the provisions for publicity and consultation in the formative stages and so on. What a local authority does and its reasons for doing so at every stage will be exposed to publicity – and local publicity – and it will have to answer for its actions at the end of the day.

The amendment raises the basic issue of whether we want to delegate to local planning authorities the power to determine local plans, subject to the supervision and the power of 'call in' of the Minister. If the attitude of mind about which hon. Members are worried really exists, that fact will become patent if, unreasonably and through sheer obstinacy and with no valid policy, a local authority rejects substantial objections and recommendations of the inspector, without giving convincing reasons for doing so. That is the kind of case in which the Minister would exercise his power of 'call in'. But the decision on that must rest with the Minister and not with the objector, and it would not be right, therefore, to give the objector the right of appeal which the Amendment suggests.

Which one of the following two (hypothetical) local plan-making authorities would be more likely to refuse to accept a recommendation of the inspector: Newtown District Council, a small newly created district council with a small planning staff which has never prepared a development plan before, but has been allowed, with some misgivings by the county, to prepare one now and has relied exclusively on the report of survey prepared for the county's structure plan for its facts and analysis; or Oldtown District Council, a former county borough with a large, enthusiastic and well-qualified planning department having a great deal of experience in preparing development plans, which has examined afresh many of the matters covered in the metropolitan county's report of survey and applying all the latest techniques of planning and participation has come up with what it calls 'a bold and imaginative plan to take the district into the twenty-first century'? Why?

Is it a sufficient answer to the criticisms to say that the local plan-making authority 'will have to answer for its actions at the end of the day'? What does this mean? Should the inspector have the power to make binding recommendations? Is there any way in which the decisions of the local plan-making authority on the local plan can be brought before the Secretary of State other than through the exercise of his call-in powers? How accurate is it to say: 'This kind of issue could not go to the courts. The appeal to the courts is on whether the proper procedure has been followed. But on the matter of substance, which would be an issue of policy, there would be no appeal to the courts.'?[111]

(e) Is structure planning obsolescent?

In his comments on McLoughlin's survey Amos wrote:

The first round of structure plans are bound to be experimental and are bound to have imperfections. They may also have to change their priorities to reflect changing political circumstances; it would therefore be prudent to pay more attention to developing reviewing techniques so that improvements and revisions can be effected with minimum disturbance to current activities. This means the development of cyclical structure planning processes, regular dialogues with elected representatives, sensitive monitoring systems and extensive information services.[112]

He envisaged therefore that while structure planning would continue, its nature would change. Instead of the plan, which has to be revised by cumbersome procedures once every so many years, there would be a rolling plan, never complete yet always up to date. An alternative possibility is that the first generation of structure plans will also be the last. Both possibilities may briefly be considered.

The first possibility is based on two grounds: (i) the increasing sophistication of techniques of planning which will enable planners to monitor and control development much more closely than has been the case in the past,[113] and (ii) the assumption that ideas derived from structure planning will spread throughout the management of local government, and together with corporate planning cause all local government to become more plan-oriented. Put in professional terms, the planning department will become the key department of the new local authorities and the structure plan will become the authorities' key policy document covering all aspects of their work.

This vision of what structure planning should become is not Amos's alone but his comment has been taken as representative of the approach and as providing an insight into his criticisms, discussed earlier, of the legal strait-jacket into which structure planning is being put. There can be no doubt that given the framework of the Act and the Regulations, and the advice contained in the Manual, structure planning could not develop along the lines suggested by Amos. Should the legal framework be changed? What advantages would there be and for whom if structure planning assumed a greater role in local government than it has at present? On the evidence of this chapter, are you satisfied that the present scope of structure planning is sufficiently well understood and practised for progress to a higher plane of planning to be feasible? To what extent can broadening the scope of structure planning be seen to be in line with the historical tradition of planning of constantly seeking just a little more power, to be able to do the job properly? Will this extra power be given to planners if, in ten to fifteen years' time, we discover that all the problems of urban planning are still with us? Is there not a possibility that in striving to plan everything, the planner will finish up by planning nothing as structure planning becomes a matter of 'developing reviewing techniques so that improvements and revisions can be effected with minimum disturbance to current activities'?[114]

The alternative possibility may also be introduced by a planning officer's comment on McLoughlin's survey. Evans, then Nottingham's City Planning Officer asked: 'Can we be sure that sufficient professional planners will find adequate job satisfaction in the structure planning field as compared with the more direct involvement to be found in local plan production and implementation?'[115]

That is one approach and an important one to the fundamental issue here of the balance between the structure and the local plans. Clearly, if the professionals involved forsake structure for local planning, the former will atrophy and it may be that the first possibility discussed above is being held out to planners as a bait to keep them involved in an exercise which they would otherwise quickly tire of. But the other approach which I find to be more likely is that governmental and public pressures will cause structure planning to be slowly abandoned for local planning.

One example of this has already occurred in London. Owing to the length of time the inquiry into the GLDP took, the requirement that London boroughs produce structure plans was removed by statute[116] and they were encouraged to proceed direct to local planning. Given constraints of time in other words, local plans were seen as more important than structure plans. We have seen, in the section on public participation, the stress that is constantly being laid on the necessity for speeding up the plan-making process. Given this approach, is there not a possibility that the London example might be repeated elsewhere in the future? Are the new metropolitan counties going to devote their energies to producing structure plans for areas that are already covered by regional and/or sub-regional studies, and in some cases partly covered by structure plans, or are they going to negotiate a development plan scheme with their districts dividing up the making of local plans and then start making them? Even if a metropolitan county was minded to produce a structure plan, would it be allowed to by the DoE?

Other aspects of local plans may be mentioned. There is no end to the possible number or types of local plan. The local authorities have much more control over the total process than they do over the structure plan process. The majority of local planning authorities are empowered only to make local plans. The majority of planners will be on much more familiar ground with local planning than with structure planning; the latter 'can so easily become somewhat ethereal',[117] whereas the former is concerned much more with the physical aspects of planning – drawing lines on maps. The general public and particularly those parts of it concerned professionally or as pressure groups with land use – builders, chartered surveyors, conservationists – will be much more concerned with what local plans have to say than with what structure plans have to say, however mistaken that attitude may be (in that it means one might seek to influence policy after it has been decided by the structure plan). Lawyers will concentrate on the local plans; they will feel more at home at the local inquiry into it, both because the procedures will be familiar and because the subject matter of the inquiry – the effect of planning proposals on people's use of land – is easier to grapple with. All these factors will operate as pressures to produce local plans, at first under the aegis of the structure plans but later instead of and as a substitute for revised structure plans.

Consider the following as a possible evolution on these lines: local plans will come to have the status of the old-style development plans while structure plans will be slowly relegated to the background. Broad policies will be introduced via local plans so that those likely to be affected by them can see their implications on the ground, and so that local authorities can retain more control over what planning policies they adopt. To counter this trend, the Secretary of State will either have to 'call in' local plans or legislate to prevent local plans from dealing with broad policies. Which would he do?

Is there anything about the system of structure and local planning to suggest that it will last longer than previous planning systems or that there will be successive generations of structure plans?

4

Development and its Control: Private Law

1. Introduction

We have hitherto been concerned with what might be called macro-planning law, culminating in a detailed examination of the development plan. For many people, however, these aspects appear somewhat peripheral to their concerns for they wish to know what they can do to their land tomorrow and how they can do it, or alternatively how they can stop their neighbour doing something to his land, particularly where the 'neighbour' is a public authority intent on some major development. These matters may for convenience be subsumed under the heading of micro-planning law, and focus on development and its control.

Development control, as set out in the Town and Country Planning Acts is concerned primarily with the public control of land use by private owners and developers, but there exist also some important antecedents of public planning law, particularly the restrictive covenant and the lease, which are to be considered in this chapter. Both development and its control are relevant here for, as will be seen, these techniques have been and are still being used both to develop land in a particular way and to control its future use once developed. One of the general issues which should be borne in mind in reading this and the next chapter is the relationship between restrictive covenants and the public planning process; is there still a place for covenants in the law of land-use planning and if so, what is it? Why have the many reports and recommendations on the alleged deficiencies in this branch of the law over the last few years not yet been implemented, apart from a reform aimed at increasing public control over restrictive covenants? Why are covenants still so important a branch of land law?

An attempt may be made to give a preliminary answer to this last question, as it will help set the scene for the topics to be discussed in this chapter. A restrictive covenant is described by the Law Commission[1] as follows:

7. In the context of this Report the term 'restrictive covenant' describes an agreement made between neighbouring landowners which enables one of them to impose a specific restriction on the use of the other's land and is intended to remain in force between subsequent owners of the relevant land after the parties to the agreement have ceased to own their respective interests in it. For example, a person who owns five acres of land may sell three of those acres to a builder subject to a covenant that he will not permit the land to be used otherwise than for residential purposes and that no more than a specified number of dwellinghouses will be built on it. The vendor may accept a similar restriction on the use of the land which he retains.

The main appeal of restrictive covenants is that they afford a private developer and/or landowner power over the use of land after he has ceased to own it, and a public authority developer a technique of exercising power over land which is freer of administrative and legal constraints than are the techniques available under the planning Acts. Such exercises of power are not necessarily bad, but, being exercises of power over other people's land use, they should be judged, as are other such exercises of power, by their effectiveness in achieving socially beneficial uses of land. We must also consider the ways in which it is possible both to circumvent their technical defects, so that their underlying purposes may be carried out, and to alter or remove them when they are no longer achieving those purposes.

This whole area of law has been described by Beuscher as a bewildering conceptualist jungle full of semantic swamps.[2] He was describing American law but the description is equally apt for English law. We shall not try and traverse the whole jungle but one area we must plunge into after an initial introduction to the subject is that of the difference between annexation and assignment of restrictive covenants. Is there any meaningful distinction between them?

2. Restrictive covenants running at equity

The refusal of the common law to countenance the enforcement of the burden of a covenant against any person other than the original covenantor was circumvented by a line of authority starting with *Tulk* v. *Moxhay*[3] in 1848. As a result of this decision it was established that the courts of equity would enable a restrictive or negative covenant to be enforced against a person into whose hands the restricted land has passed, unless he had purchased the land for value, without notice of the covenant.

Tulk v. *Moxhay* (1848) 2 Ph. 774, 41 E.R. 1143

In the year 1808 the Plaintiff, being then the owner in fee of the vacant piece of ground in Leicester Square, as well as of several of the houses forming the Square, sold the piece of ground by the description of 'Leicester Square garden or pleasure ground, with the equestrian statue then standing in the centre thereof, and the iron railing and stone work round the same,' to one Elms in fee: and the deed of conveyance contained a covenant by Elms, for himself, his heirs, and assigns, with the Plaintiff, his heirs, executors, and administrators, 'that Elms, his heirs, and assigns should, and would from time to time, and at all times thereafter at his and their own costs and charges, keep and maintain the said piece of ground and square garden, and the iron railing round the same in its then form, and in sufficient and proper repair as a square garden and pleasure ground, in an open state, uncovered with any buildings, in neat and ornamental order; and that it should be lawful for the inhabitants of Leicester Square, tenants of the Plaintiff, on payment of a reasonable rent for the same, to have keys at their own expense and the privilege of admission therewith at any time or times into the said square garden and pleasure ground.'

The piece of land so conveyed passed by divers mesne conveyances into the hands of the Defendant, whose purchase deed contained no similar covenant with his vendor: but he admitted that he had purchased with notice of the covenant in the deed of 1808.

The Defendant having manifested an intention to alter the character of the square garden, and asserted a right, if he thought fit, to build upon it, the Plaintiff, who still remained owner of several houses in the square, filed this bill for an injunction; and an injunction was granted by the Master of the Rolls to restrain the Defendant from converting or using the piece of ground and square garden, and the iron railing round the same, to or for any other purpose than as a square garden and pleasure ground in an open state, and uncovered with buildings.

THE LORD CHANCELLOR [Cottenham], (without calling upon the other side). That this Court has jurisdiction to enforce a contract between the owner of land and his neighbour purchasing a part of it, that the latter shall either use or abstain from using the land purchased in a particular way, is what I never knew disputed. Here there is no question about the contract: the owner of certain houses in the square sells the land adjoining, with a covenant from the purchaser not to use it for any other purpose than as a square garden. And it is now contended, not that the vendee could violate that contract, but that he might sell the piece of land, and that the purchaser from him may violate it without this Court having any power to interfere. If that were so, it would be impossible for an owner of land to sell part of it without incurring the risk of rendering what he retains worthless. It is said that, the covenant being one which does not run with the land, this Court cannot enforce it; but the question is, not whether the covenant runs with the land, but whether a party shall be permitted to use the land in a manner inconsistent with the contract entered into by his vendor, and with notice of which he purchased. Of course, the price would be affected by the covenant, and nothing could be more inequitable than that the original purchaser should be able to sell the property the next day for a greater price in consideration of the assignee being allowed to escape from the liability which he had himself undertaken.

That the question does not depend upon whether the covenant runs with the land is evident from this, that if there was a mere agreement and no covenant, this Court would enforce it against a party purchasing with notice of it; for if an equity is attached to the property by the owner, no one purchasing with notice of that equity can stand in a different situation from the party from whom he purchased. There are not only cases before the Vice-Chancellor of England, in which he considered that doctrine as not in dispute; but looking at the ground on which Lord Eldon disposed of the case of *The Duke of Bedford* v. *The Trustees of the British Museum*[4], it is impossible to suppose that he entertained any doubt of it. In the case of *Mann* v. *Stephens*[4a] before me, I never intended to make the injunction depend upon the result of the action: nor does the order imply it. The motion was, to discharge an order for the commitment of the Defendant for an alleged breach of the injunction, and also to dissolve the injunction. I upheld the injunction, but discharged the order of commitment, on the ground that it was not clearly proved that any breach had been committed; but there being a doubt whether part of the premises on which the Defendant was proceeding to build was locally situated within what was called the Dell, on which alone he had under the covenant a right to build at all, and the Plaintiff insisting that it was not, I thought the pendency of the suit ought not to prejudice the Plaintiff in his right to bring an action if he thought he had such right, and, therefore, I give him liberty to do so.

With respect to the observations of Lord Brougham in *Keppell* v. *Bailey*,[5] he never could have meant to lay down that this Court would not enforce an equity attached to land by the owner, unless under such circumstances as would maintain an action at law. If that be the result of his observations, I can only say that I cannot coincide with it.

I think the cases cited before the Vice-Chancellor and this decision of the Master of the Rolls perfectly right, and, therefore, that this motion must be refused, with costs.

(a) Evolution and nature

Before turning to consider the current rules governing the creation and enforcement of restrictive covenants, two important matters arising out of this case may be touched on. First, the case and its subsequent evolution applies only to restrictive or negative covenants. The problem connected with the enforcement of positive covenants and the distinction between the two will be dealt with later. Secondly,

12. Although the original basis of the *Tulk* v. *Moxhay* rule was that anyone who purchased with notice of a restrictive covenant would be restrained from breaking it, later decisions have established that this applies only where the covenant is imposed for the benefit of other specific land so that an equitable obligation is imposed on one piece of land for the benefit of another. Restrictive covenants, therefore, have become closely analogous to easements and profits-a-prendre, being obligations imposed on a servient tenement for the benefit of a dominant tenement.[6]

The particular kind of easement to which restrictive covenants are thought to be most closely anologous is the equitable negative easement.[7] Examples of negative easements are the right to light and the right to support, both of which involve the owner of the servient tenement being under an obligation not to do something in the first case, not to obstruct the light of the owner of the dominant tenement; in the second, not to withdraw support from the dominant owner's land or building. Negative easements were known to the law before *Tulk* v. *Moxhay* and *a fortiori* before *London and South Western Railway* v. *Gomm*[8], the case which first clearly held that a restrictive covenant created an interest in land analogous to a negative easement. Why did the law develop thus? Why could not negative easements have fulfilled the role of restrictive covenants, and why did restrictive covenants, after starting off on a different line of approach, come so soon after their creation to be regarded and decided upon on the basis that they were like negative easements?

The reason for this evolution of the law lay in the constant conflict between two opposing principles of law, conflict which still exists today and still contributes to the confused development of this branch of the law though in a different aspect from the one under discussion. The opposing principles were, and are, keeping the land as free as possible from clogs and fetters which hinder its commercial use, and keeping men to their bargains and commitments they have freely entered into. The application of the first principle led to a disinclination on the part of the courts to expand the category of property interests that clogged the use of the land, and among these, negative easements ranked high. A good statement of this attitude to negative easements is contained in the speech of Lord Blackburn in *Dalton* v. *Angus*[9], a case on the easement of support. After discussing some sixteenth-century cases on the easement of light, he goes on to discuss their rationale as follows:[10]

The distinction between a right to light and a right of prospect, on the ground that one is matter of necessity and the other of delight, is to my mind more quaint than satisfactory. A much better reason is given by Lord Hardwicke in *Attorney-General* v. *Doughty*[11], where he observes that if that was the case there could be no great towns. I think this decision, that a right of prospect is not acquired by prescription, shews that, whilst on the balance of convenience and inconvenience, it was held expedient that the right to light, which could only impose a burthen upon land very near the house, should be protected when it had been long enjoyed, on the same ground it was held expedient that the right of prospect, which would impose a burthen on a very large and indefinite area, should not be allowed to be created, except by actual agreement. And this seems to me the real ground on which *Webb* v. *Bird*[12] and *Chasemore* v. *Richards*[13] are to be supported. The rights there claimed were analogous to prospect in this, that they were vague and undefined, and very extensive. Whether that is or is not the reason for the distinction the law has always, since *Bland* v. *Moseley*,[14] been that there is a distinction; that the right of a window to have light and air is acquired by prescription, and that a right to have a prospect can only be acquired by actual agreement.

This attitude found a modern echo in Lord Denning's judgement in *Phipps* v. *Pears*[15] where it was argued that a right to make use of a neighbour's house as protection from the weather could exist as an easement.

. . . a right to protection from the weather (if it exists) is entirely negative. It is a right to stop your neighbour pulling down his own house. Seeing that it is a negative easement, it must be looked at with caution. Because the law has been very chary of creating any new negative easements. [He gave an instance of the law's refusal to recognise a right to a view]. The reason underlying these instances is that if such an easement were to be permitted it would unduly restrict your neighbour in his enjoyment of his land. It would hamper legitimate development. . . . Likewise here, if we were to stop a man pulling down his house, we would put a brake on desirable improvement.[16]

However, if urban development was thought to involve a restriction on the growth of negative easements, it also, as the facts of *Tulk* v. *Moxhay* themselves indicated, showed up the desire on the part of some landowners to create restrictions on the future use of land in the interests of that same urban development, and the unfortunate results that might flow from a refusal on the part of courts to enforce such restrictions. At common law, a contractual, as opposed to a property, basis to enforce restrictions was thwarted by the doctrine of privity of contract, but the courts of equity were able to outflank such a doctrine by applying their own equitable doctrine of notice. The application of such a doctrine was in order to allow enforcement of restrictions to be on a contractual basis, as was made clear in *Tulk* v. *Moxhay*, when the Lord Chancellor said: '... but the question is, not whether the covenant runs with the land, but whether a party shall be permitted to use the land in a manner inconsistent with the contract entered into by his vendor, and with notice of which he purchased.'[17]

But to base these restrictions on the use of land on contract and notice was to open the flood-gates to all sorts of clogs on commercial dealings with land, clogs moreover, which a plaintiff could enforce though he had no interest in the land which required protection. This appeared the more likely after Knight Bruce LJ had stated the principle involved as follows in *De Mattos* v. *Gibson*:[18]

Reason and justice seem to prescribe that, at least as a general rule, where a man, by gift or purchase, acquires property from another, with knowledge of a previous contract, lawfully and for valuable consideration made by him with a third person, to use and employ the property for a particular purpose in a specified manner, the acquirer shall not, to the material damage of the third person, in opposition to the contract and inconsistently with it, use and employ the property in a manner not allowable to the giver or seller.

Stated thus widely, the principle was applied in two brewery cases – *Catt* v. *Tourle*[19] in 1869 and *Luker* v. *Dennis*[20] in 1877 – where brewers were held entitled to enforce covenants on publicans who had bought public houses with knowledge of the covenants preventing the sale of beer on the premises other than that produced by the brewer enforcing the covenant. In neither case did the brewer own land which could be benefited from the covenant.

At this point the first principle – that of limiting clogs on land – was brought to bear on restrictive covenants in order to limit their applicability. In *London and South Western Railway* v. *Gomm*[21], a case involving a positive covenant and therefore unenforceable, Jessel M R took the opportunity to restate the principle of *Tulk* v. *Moxhay* and place it firmly on a property basis in a judgement which was later described as 'contrary to the previous authorities'.[22]

The doctrine of that case, rightly considered, appears to me to be either an extension in equity of the doctrine of Spencer's Case to another line of cases, or else an extension in equity of the doctrine of negative easements; such, for instance, as a right to the access of light, which prevents the owner of the servient tenement from building so as to obstruct the light. The covenant in *Tulk* v. *Moxhay* was affirmative in its terms, but was held by the Court to imply a negative. Where there is a negative covenant expressed or implied, as, for instance, not to build so as to obstruct a view, or not to use a piece of land otherwise than as a garden, the Court interferes on one or other of the above grounds. This is an equitable doctrine, establishing an exception to the rules of common law which did not treat such a covenant as running with the land, and it does not matter whether it proceeds on analogy to a covenant running with the land or on analogy to an easement. The purchaser took the estate subject to the equitable burden, with the qualification that if he acquired the legal estate for value without notice he was freed from the burden. That qualification, however, did not affect the nature of the burden; the notice was required merely to avoid the effect of the legal estate, and did not create the right, and if the purchaser took only an equitable estate he took subject to the burden, whether he had notice or not.

As might be expected, the contract and property principle were both used for some time thereafter to support restrictive covenants, but the property principle increasingly gained favour, and by the beginning of the twentieth century was recognised as the basis of the enforcement of restrictive covenants. In *London County Council* v. *Allen*[23], the question was posed whether the LCC could enforce a covenant not to build on certain land wanted for the development of roads with notice of which Allen had obtained the land and built on it, notwithstanding that the LCC owned no land that could be benefited from the covenant. In the Court of Appeal, Scrutton J, after surveying the history of the principle, summed up the position as follows:

I think the result of this long chain of authorities is that, whereas in my view, at the time of *Tulk* v. *Moxhay* and for at least twenty years afterwards, the plaintiffs in this case would have succeeded against an assign on the ground that the assign had notice of the covenant, since *Formby* v. *Barker*[24], *in re. Nisbet and Potts' Contract*[25], and *Millbourn* v. *Lyons*[26], three decisions of the Court of Appeal, the plaintiffs must fail on the ground that they have never had any land for the benefit of which this 'equitable interest analogous to a negative easement' could be created, and therefore cannot sue a person who bought the land with knowledge that there was a restrictive covenant as to its use, which he proceeds to disregard, because he is not privy to the contract. I think the learned editors of *Dart on Vendors and Purchasers*, 7th ed., vol. ii, p. 769, are justified by the present state of the authorities in saying that 'the question of notice to the purchaser has nothing whatever to do with the question whether the covenant binds him, except in so far as the absence of notice may enable him to raise the plea of purchaser for valuable consideration without notice.' If the covenant does not run with the land in law, its benefit can only be asserted against an assign of the land burdened, if the covenant was made for the benefit of certain land, all or some of which remains in the possession of the covenantee or his assign, suing to enforce the covenant.

Almost sixty years later, a modern commentator could state confidently:

A restrictive covenant, meeting the appropriate requirements, is an interest in property as it is enforceable against persons with whom there is neither privity of contract nor privity of estate. The original covenantee can enforce it against successors in title to the original covenantor's land as can successors in title to the original covenantee's land where the benefit of the covenant has passed to them by virtue of the doctrine of annexation or of assignment or of development schemes. Moreover it can pass by conveyance or by demise or by descent. However, since it was the courts of equity that took the step of converting a restrictive covenant from a personal into a property interest a restrictive covenant is an equitable interest in land.[27]

Although the nature of a restrictive covenant can now be regarded as settled, the conflict of principle between the contract and property bases of enforcement, between in effect different judicial notions of what best contributes to urban development has continued. However, it has been transformed, within the ambit of property, into the highly technical problems of how to create and who can enforce restrictive covenants, the matters of annexation and assignment referred to in the quotation above. The problem may be stated thus: once a restrictive covenant was regarded as having a property basis, it was necessary to point to a connection between the covenant and the land; the covenant has to 'touch and concern' the land, or it has to have 'the capacity to benefit' the land or it must 'accommodate the dominant tenement'. Failure to show this results in inability to enforce a covenant – *London County Council* v. *Allen* where there was no land which the covenant could benefit. The test of 'accommodation' then cuts down the occasions on which a covenant can be enforced.

In order to cut down the occasions still further, the courts have insisted that clear words of annexation are needed to link a covenant to a plot of land when that land is sold or otherwise transferred. Failure to show clear words of annexation might again result in inability to enforce a covenant. This is the property, or 'no clogs' principle at work. The contract or 'liberal' principle has in effect been used by the courts to outflank the doctrine of annexation by opposing to it the doctrine of assignment, whereby the benefit of a covenant can be assigned to a covenantee, using appropriate language, without the necessity for words of annexation. Assignment in theory represents a liberalisation of annexation; in practice this does not always appear so, since adherents of the property principle might deny that a form of words has had the effect of assigning a set of covenants to a covenantee by adopting a narrow or strict approach to the law, while adherents of the liberal approach might find annexation to have taken place on slender evidence. Hence the law has become confused and technical as different points of view about the merits of restrictive covenants masquerade as disputes about the technicalities of annexation and assignment. Unfortunately it is still necessary to know something of these technicalities and the difference between annexation and assignment, but we shall try not to lose sight of the purpose and function of restrictive covenants as we do so.

(b) Annexation

D. J. Hayton[28], 'Restrictive Covenants as Property Interests', (1971) 87 *LQR*, 539 at pp. 551–3

For a person, other than the original covenantee, to have the benefit of a restrictive covenant as the owner of land to which the covenant is annexed, the following requirements must be satisfied.

(1) Intention to benefit the land (and the landowners merely by virtue of their ownership). To show that the covenant is intended to pass with the land automatically and be enforceable by the landowner for the time being it is normally necessary that the intent be manifested by some appropriate words of annexation. The covenant may either (i) be expressed to be for the benefit of certain land or (ii) be made with the covenantee as owner for the time being of such land and others claiming such land under him.

(2) Ascertainment of benefited land. It is necessary that the precise land intended to be benefited is either (i) expressly identified in the deed or (ii) capable of ascertainment from the terms of the deed through the

admission of extrinsic evidence for the purpose of elucidating the terms of the deed.

(3) Intention to benefit either (i) the land as a whole or (ii) the whole and each and every part of the land. A person owning the whole land needs only show annexation to the whole land, whilst a person owning part of the land needs show annexation to his part. A covenant annexed only to land as a whole can only be enforced by the owner of the whole, except that a person with substantially the whole can enforce it where it is clear that the covenant was intended to be enforceable so long as a substantial part of the whole remained.

(4) The covenant must be capable of benefiting the ascertained land *qua* land. As established by decisions of the Court of Appeal at the turn of the century the basis of the doctrine of restrictive covenants depends upon the covenantee having some dominant land that is capable of being benefited by the covenant given by the owner of the servient land. The requirement is often expressed by stating that the covenant must touch and concern the land but, as submitted earlier, is better expressed by stating that the covenant must accommodate the dominant tenement.

If the covenant is annexed only to the land as a whole it must benefit the land as a whole if it is to be enforceable. If the covenant is annexed to each and every part then it is enforceable by a person who has a part which is benefited, in fact, even though there may be some parts which are not benefited.

These requirements seem reasonable enough, and indeed they are reasonable, as they should give effect to the intentions of the covenanting parties. The consequences flowing from a holding that a covenant is annexed to land as a whole are completely reasonable if, on a proper construction of the covenant it is quite clear that the parties intended the covenant only to be enforceable by the owner for the time being of the whole and not by an owner for the time being of any part.

However, in recent years, an arbitrary presumption of construction seems to have crept in presuming covenants to be taken for the benefit of land as a whole and so denying the claims of owners of part only of the land. To give effect to their claims the doctrine of assignment has sometimes been invoked as in *Russell* v. *Archdale*,[29] *Re Jeffs Transfer (No. 2)*[30] and *Stilwell* v. *Blackman*[31]. In all these cases a covenant, though annexed to land as a whole, was held to be enforceable by owners of part only of the land, to whom there had been an express assignment of the benefit of the covenant. But, as Sholl J. pointed out in *Re Arcade Hotel Pty Ltd.*,[32] there is surely a logical contradiction involved in saying that one can assign to the purchaser of part of the benefited land 'the benefit of a covenant which ex hypothesi is so expressed as to confine that benefit to the land while it is enjoyed by one owner and as a whole and no longer, nor otherwise.'

Rogers v. *Hosegood,* [1900] 2 Ch.388

In 1869 Rogers and others, who carried on the business of builders in partnership under the name of Cubitt & Co, were the owners in fee (subject to a mortgage) of some land at Palace Gate, Kensington, which they had laid out in plots suitable for the building of large private dwelling houses. One of the plots was conveyed by the partners to William, Duke of Bedford, subject to covenants which might as far as possible bind the premises thereby conveyed and every part thereof and enure to the benefit of the partners and their successors that not more than one dwelling house should stand on the plot and that that house should be used as a private residence only. The covenant was entered into with the four partners only and not with the mortgagees. In the same year, the Duke purchased another plot adjoining the first one, subject to the same covenants.

In 1872 Sir John Millais purchased a plot from the partners, separated from the Duke's two plots by an intervening plot. Millais's deed did not recite the covenants but the plot was conveyed in 1873 together with 'all the rights, easements or appurtenances belonging or reputed to belong thereto'. At the time of the conveyance Millais knew nothing of the covenants contained in the Duke's deeds nor did the conveyance to him contain any express assignments of those covenants to him. In 1876 the partners, so far as they lawfully could, released Francis, Duke of Bedford (who had succeeded William), and his two plots from the covenant restricting the number of houses that could be built on the plots. Subsequently Rogers became the sole owner in fee of two plots of land near the Bedford and the Millais plots.

The defendant had purchased the two plots from persons claiming through the devisees of William, Duke of Bedford, with notice of the restrictive covenants to which they were subject. He proposed to erect on those two plots (and an adjoining one which he had similarly acquired) a block of flats. Rogers and the devisees of Millais brought an action for a declaration that the use of the two plots for that purpose would be an infringement of the covenants contained in the two deeds of 1869.

COLLINS LJ read the judgment of the Court (LORD ALVERSTONE MR, and RIGBY and COLLINS LJJ) as follows: ... No difficulty arises in this case as to the burden of the covenants. The defendant is the assignee of the covenantor in respect of the two plots of land comprised in the conveyances of May 31 and July 31, 1869, and he took with notice of the covenants now sought to be enforced. Nor have we any hesitation in accepting the conclusion of FARWELL J that the buildings which the defendant proposes to erect will involve a breach of those covenants. The

real and only difficulty arises on the question – whether the benefit of
the covenants has passed to the assigns of Sir John Millais as owners of the
plot purchased by him on March 25, 1873, there being no evidence that
he knew of these covenants when he bought. Here, again, the difficulty is
narrowed, because by express declaration on the face of the conveyances
of 1869 the benefit of the two covenants in question was intended for all
or any of the vendor's lands near to or adjoining the plot sold, and therefore for (among others) the plot of land acquired by Sir John Millais, and
that they 'touched and concerned' that land within the meaning of those
words so as to run with the land at law we do not doubt. Therefore, but
for a technical difficulty which was not raised before FARWELL J, we
should agree with him that the benefit of the covenants in question was
annexed to and passed to Sir John Millais by the conveyance of the land
which he bought in 1873. A difficulty, however, in giving effect to this
view arises from the fact that the covenants in question in the deeds of
May and July, 1869, were made with the mortgagors only, and therefore
in contemplation of law were made with strangers to the land: *Webb* v.
Russell[33], to which, therefore, the benefit did not become annexed. That
a court of equity, however, would not regard such an objection as de-
feating the intention of the parties to the covenant is clear; and, therefore
when the covenant was clearly made for the benefit of certain land with
a person who in the contemplation of such a court was the true owner of
it, it would be regarded as annexed to and running with that land, just
as it would have been at law but for the technical difficulty.

We think this is the plain result of the observations of HALL VC in the
well-known passage in *Renals* v. *Cowlishaw*[34], of JESSEL MR in *London and
South Western Ry. Co.* v. *Gomm*[35], and of WOOD VC in *Child* v. *Douglas*[36] . . .
in equity, just as at law, the first point to be determined is whether the
covenant or contract in its inception binds the land. If it does, it is then
capable of passing with the land to subsequent assignees; if it does not, it
is incapable of passing by mere assignment of the land. The benefit may
be annexed to one plot and the burden to another, and when this has
been once clearly done the benefit and the burden pass to the respective
assignees, subject, in the case of the burden, to proof that the legal estate,
if acquired, has been acquired with notice of the covenant. The passage
inclosed in a parenthesis in the report of the judgment of HALL VC in
Renals v. *Cowlishaw* supports the same view, nor are the general observations or the decision of the case itself inconsistent with it. . . . These
authorities establish the proposition that, when the benefit has been once
clearly annexed to one piece of land, it passes by assignment of that land,
and may be said to run with it, in contemplation as well of equity as of
law, without proof of special bargain or representation on the assignment.
In such a case it runs, not because the conscience of either party is
affected, but because the purchaser has bought something which inhered
in or was annexed to the land bought. This is the reason why, in dealing
with the burden, the purchaser's conscience is not affected by notice of
covenants which were part of the original bargain on the first sale, but
were merely personal and collateral, while it is affected by notice of those

which touch and concern the land. The covenant must be one that is capable of running with the land before the question of the purchaser's conscience and the equity affecting it can come into discussion. When, as in *Renals* v. *Cowlishaw*, there is no indication in the original conveyance, or in the circumstances attending it, that the burden of the restrictive covenant is imposed for the benefit of the land reserved, or any particular part of it, then it becomes necessary to examine the circumstances under which any part of the land reserved is sold, in order to see whether a benefit, not originally annexed to it, has become annexed to it on the sale, so that the purchaser is deemed to have bought it with the land, and this can hardly be the case when the purchaser did not know of the existence of the restrictive covenant. But when, as here, it has been once annexed to the land reserved, then it is not necessary to spell an intention out of surrounding facts, such as the existence of a building scheme, statements at auctions, and such like circumstances, and the presumption must be that it passes on a sale of that land, unless there is something to rebut it, and the purchaser's ignorance of the existence of the covenant does not defeat the presumption. We can find nothing in the conveyance to Sir John Millais in any degree inconsistent with the intention to pass to him the benefit already annexed to the land sold to him. We are of opinion therefore, that Sir John Millais's assigns are entitled to enforce the restrictive covenant against the defendant, and that his appeal must be dismissed. . . .

(c) Assignment

D. J. Hayton, 'Restrictive Covenants as Property Interests', op. cit., pp. 554-5

For a person to have the benefit of a restrictive covenant as the assignee of the benefit of the covenant the following requirements must be satisfied according to the currently accepted view.

(1) Intention to benefit the covenantee (and his assigns) by giving the covenantee an assignable covenant that benefits his land and is intended to burden land nearby. There must thus be an intention to benefit land: otherwise the covenant would be a personal covenant in gross and unenforceable except as between the parties to the covenant. If it is not expressly stated that the covenant is made with the covenantee and his assigns (so as to be assignable) then it is implied by section 78 (1) of the Law of Property Act 1925 if the covenant is one 'relating to any land of the covenantee.' However, for a covenant to relate to land it must be a covenant that is intended to benefit land *qua* land. Section 78 thus does not do away with the need to show an intention to benefit land as, indeed, the latter part of section 78 (1) recognises: 'For the purposes of this subsection in connection with covenants restrictive of user of land "successors in title" shall be deemed to include the owners and occupiers for the time being of *the land of the covenantee intended to be benefited*.' Assignable covenants thus only differ from annexed covenants in that there are no appropriate words of annexation annexing the covenants to land so the covenantee is

free to give or to refuse the benefit of the covenants to a purchaser of his land.

(2) *Ascertainability of benefited land.* It is necessary that the benefited land be indicated in the conveyance or be otherwise shown with reasonable certainty, even by parol evidence alone.

(3) The covenant must be capable of benefiting the ascertainable land. This is the same requirement as for annexation.

(4) There must have been no separation between the title to the land and the covenant but equitable entitlement to the covenant under a settlement or a contract or a will or an intestacy will suffice. The doctrine exists not just to enable the covenantee to protect his property but to enable the covenantee, if he wishes, to assign the benefit of the covenant on sale so as to sell his land to his best advantage. If the benefit is not assigned on such a sale then the covenant has not been needed to sell the covenantee's property to his best advantage and the covenant as a property interest is *functus officio.* Thus a subsequent assignment of it to a purchaser is of no avail: there is no property interest to be assigned.

These four requirements have so far been treated as completely comprehensive so that it might appear that any assignees of the covenant together with the land are able to enforce it so long as they have an interest in any part of the ascertainable land benefited by the covenant.

However, it is submitted that on principle and on authority there is a fifth implicit requirement for otherwise logical contradictions arise as will shortly be shown.

(5) The covenant must have been taken to enable the covenantee the better either (i) to dispose of his land as a whole or (ii) to dispose of the whole and each and every part of his land. A person, owning the whole of the land, to whom there has been an assignment of the benefit of the covenant, needs only show that the covenant was taken to enable disposal of the whole to the best advantage. A person, owning part of the land, to whom there has been an assignment of the benefit of the covenant, needs show that the covenant was taken to enable disposal of the parts to the best advantage. A covenant taken only for the disposal of land as a whole can only be enforced by the owner of the whole, except that a person with substantially the whole can enforce it where it is clear that the covenant was intended to be enforceable so long as assigned with a substantial part of the whole.

If the covenant were taken for the better disposal of the land as a whole it must benefit the land as a whole if it is to be enforceable. If the covenant were taken for the disposal of each and every part then it is enforceable by a person who has a part which, in fact, is benefited, even though there may be some parts which are not benefited. . . .

Marten v. *Flight Refuelling Ltd* [1961] 2 All E.R. 696

May 4. WILBERFORCE J read the following judgment: The plaintiffs in this case seek to establish the enforceability of, and, so far as possible, to enforce, a restrictive covenant said to affect certain land in the parish of Tarrant Rushton in the county of Dorset now owned by the Air Ministry (the second defendant) on behalf of the Crown and occupied by Flight Refuelling, Ltd., the first defendant (referred to hereinafter as 'the defendant company'). . . .

I begin by stating the conveyancing facts relevant to the creation of the covenant. The Crichel Estate is a large agricultural estate in Dorset of about seven thousand five hundred acres which has for many years been in the ownership of the family of the first plaintiff, Mrs. Marten. On the western side of it and forming part of it was a farm of some 562 acres known as Crook Farm, which since 1920 has been farmed by a Mr. Harding under a tenancy agreement. Some two hundred acres of this farm had been requisitioned in July, 1942, by the Air Ministry for use as an aerodrome, and by March, 1943, some steps to establish the aerodrome had been taken. In 1943 the legal estate in the property was vested in the second plaintiffs, Hoare Trustees, as special executors of Lord Alington, the former tenant for life of the estate, who had died in 1940. Under the trusts of a settlement made in 1928, the equitable owner was the first plaintiff, who is Lord Alington's daughter, she having an interest in tail male. She was at this time an infant, having been born in 1929. On Mar 25, 1943, the second plaintiffs conveyed the whole of Crook Farm by way of sale to Mr. Harding, and it is under that conveyance that the restrictive covenant arises. I must refer in detail to certain provisions of this document. . . .

Clause 2 was, so far as material, as follows:

> The purchaser hereby covenants with the vendor and its successors in title (1) That no part of the land hereby conveyed nor any building or erection thereon shall at any time hereafter be used for any purpose other than agricultural purposes without the previous written consent of the vendor or its agent Provided always that if the vendor should sell all or any part of its land immediately adjoining or adjacent to the land hereby conveyed either free from any restriction as to user or on terms permitting the same to be used for any purpose other than agricultural purposes or if the vendor should agree with the town or country planning authorities that all or any part of the land immediately adjoining the land hereby conveyed may be used for purposes other than agricultural purposes the purchaser shall be at liberty to use or sell all or any part of the land hereby conveyed either free from any restriction as to user or subject to the same conditions as to user as those imposed by the vendor on such sale or agreed with the town or country planning authorities as the case may be . . .'

That is all that I think I need read of the conveyance.

The first plaintiff, having attained her majority on Sept. 12, 1950, disentailed the property and became its absolute owner. On Sept. 18, 1950, the second plaintiffs assented to the vesting in her of the Crichel Estate in fee simple, but the assent contained no reference to the covenant. Meanwhile, the Air Ministry, still in possession of the requisitioned land (which I shall refer to as 'the blue land'), in 1947 permitted the defendant company to occupy the aerodrome, and the company entered into occupation as licensee. I shall refer to the terms of its occupation. In or about 1954 the Air Ministry decided to purchase the blue land, and in April, 1955, the ministry served on Mr. Harding's executors a notice to treat in respect of the greater part of it. On July 1, 1958, this portion of the blue land was conveyed by Mr. Harding's executors to the Air Ministry, the conveyance being expressed to be subject to the restrictive covenant so far as the same was valid, subsisting and capable of being enforced. This left a small parcel of the blue land (which has been referred to as 'the communal site') still under requisition, and it remained under requisition until after the issue of the writ and until after the joinder of the Air Ministry as a defendant. It has since been conveyed to the Air Ministry, but it is conceded that in this action no relief can be granted in respect of the user of it.

The points which arise for decision are the following: (i) Are the plaintiffs, or is one of them, entitled to the benefit of the restrictive covenant? (ii) Is the blue land subject to the burden of the restrictive covenant? (iii) Can the covenant be enforced to any and what extent against either of the defendants? (iv) What relief (if any) in equity should be granted to the plaintiffs? First, are the plaintiffs, or is one of them, entitled to the benefit of the restrictive covenant? This involves several subsidiary questions, namely (a) whether the covenant was entered into for the benefit of any land of the covenantee; (b) whether that land is sufficiently defined or ascertainable by permissible inference or evidence; (c) whether that land is, or was, capable of being benefited by the covenant; (d) whether, since the first plaintiff is not the express assignee of the covenant, the action can be brought by the second plaintiffs or by the first and second plaintiffs jointly.

Question (a): This would appear to be a simple point. The covenant is of the type considered in the leading case, *Tulk* v. *Moxhay*, that is to say, a covenant imposed on land sold by a vendor and restricting its user – precisely the same kind of case to which the doctrine of restrictive covenants binding in equity has been developed. As to these, LORD COTTENHAM LC said:

> That this court has jurisdiction to enforce a contract between the owner of land and his neighbour purchasing a part of it, that the latter shall either use or abstain from using the land purchased in a particular way, is what I never knew disputed.

He held that such a covenant would be enforced in equity, regardless of whether it ran with the land at law, against any purchaser with notice. However, an elaborate argument was addressed to me by the defendants to support a contention [Question (b) above] that the benefit of the covenant was not available to the plaintiffs. The conveyance, it was said, does not 'annex' the benefit of the covenant to any land so that it would pass automatically on a conveyance of the land to a purchaser. Further, it does not indicate that it was made for the benefit of any land, and, even supposing that it was so made, it does not identify, or provide any material on which to identify, what that land is.

It is, however, well established by the authorities that the benefit of restrictive covenants can pass to persons other than the original covenantee, even in the absence of annexation, provided that certain conditions are fulfilled. There is, however, dispute as to the nature of these conditions. The defendants' contentions are, first, that there must appear from the terms of the deed itself an intention to benefit some land, and, secondly, that the precise land to be benefited must also be stated in the deed, or at least must be capable of ascertainment from the terms of the deed by evidence which is admissible in accordance with the normal rules of interpretation of documents. They rely principally on the decision in *Re Union of London & Smith's Bank, Ltd.'s Conveyance, Miles* v. *Easter*[37] and submit that the decision of UPJOHN J in *Newton Abbot Co-operative Society, Ltd.* v. *Williamson & Treadgold, Ltd.*[38] which appears to admit parol evidence for the purpose of identifying the land to be benefited, goes too far.

I proceed, therefore, first to examine *Miles* v. *Easter*. The facts in the case were, briefly, that the defendant Easter, who was one of the persons seeking to enforce the covenant, was the owner of the greater part of certain land coloured green which had previously been owned by the Shoreham Company. That company was possessed of certain lands of considerable but undefined extent, including some foreshore land and some land coloured yellow. The conveyance of 1908, by which the covenant was imposed, contained other covenants expressed to be made '. . . with the purchasers their heirs and assigns or other the owners or owner for the time being of the land coloured pink or any part or parts thereof . . .' i.e. in language adapted and intended to annex the benefit of these other covenants to particular land. The covenant which the defendant was trying to enforce was not in this form at all; it used no language of annexation. In these circumstances the Court of Appeal, affirming the decision of BENNETT, J., held that it had not been shown that the covenant was taken for the benefit of the green land, and, in doing so, they relied particularly on the existence of the other land, which might, for all that appeared from the document, have been intended to benefit from the restriction, and on the contrast in the conveyancing language used. In the judgment of the Court of Appeal, read by ROMER LJ, the following passage occurs:

> In the first place the 'other land' must be land that is capable of being benefited by the covenant – otherwise it would be impossible to infer that the object of the covenant was to enable the vendor to dispose of his land to greater advantage. In the next place this land must be 'ascertainable' or 'certain' to use the words of ROMER LJ, and SCRUTTON LJ, respectively. For, although the court will readily infer the intention to benefit the other land of the vendor where the existence and situation of such land are indicated in the conveyance or have been otherwise shown with reasonable certainty, it is impossible to do so from vague references in the conveyance or in other documents laid

before the court as to the existence of other lands of the vendor, the extent and situation of which are undefined.

This passage is clearly and carefully expressed, and I resist the invitation of the Attorney-General to interpret it in the light of certain expressions (to my mind less clear) in the judgment of BENNETT, J at first instance. It shows that the court's opinion was that the existence and situation of the land to be benefited need not be indicated in the conveyance, provided that it could be otherwise shown with reasonable certainty, and the natural interpretation to place on these latter words is, first, that they may be shown by evidence dehors the deed, and, secondly, that a broad and reasonable view may be taken as to the proof of the identity of the lands. This general approach would, I think, be consistent with the equitable origin and character of the enforcement of restrictive covenants, which should not, I think, be constricted by technicalities derived from the common law of landlord and tenant.

Against this approach, the Attorney-General relied strongly on a passage of the same judgment, where ROMER LJ said this: '. . . the first question that has to be considered is whether or no an intention is shown in the deed of Oct. 23, 1908, that the restrictive covenants should enure for the benefit of any particular land of the covenantees. The Attorney-General argued that this showed that the court considered that only the deed of conveyance could be looked at. With all respect, I do not think that this consequence follows.

In that particular case, reliance was placed on the deed, and on the deed alone: the fact that the court confined its consideration to the terms of the deed does not, in the circumstances, carry any implication that no other evidence than the deed itself could be considered.

Before passing to *Newton Abbot Co-operative Society, Ltd.* v. *Williamson & Treadgold, Ltd.*, I should add that the rule as stated by the Court of Appeal in *Miles* v. *Easter* seems to me to be clearly in line with other statements of principle made by the courts. . . .

I pass now to the *Newton Abbot* case. The facts were that the original covenantee was the owner of a property called Devonia, in Fore Street, Bovey Tracey, on which she carried on business as an ironmonger. The original covenantors were the purchasers from her of other properties in Fore Street opposite Devonia, and the covenant was (briefly) against carrying on the business of an ironmonger. There was no reference in the conveyance by which the covenant was imposed to any land for whose benefit it was made, the only mention of Devonia being that the vendor was described as 'of Devonia'. The action was between assigns of the covenantee's son, who inherited her estate, and assigns of the covenantors. UPJOHN J held that the benefit of the covenant was not annexed to Devonia, but held that, looking at the attendant circumstances, the land to be benefited was shown with reasonable certainty and that the land in question was Devonia.

That decision was attacked by the Attorney-General in a lively argument, and I was invited not to follow it. Of course, it relates to its own special facts, and, no doubt, I could leave it on one side. But I see nothing in it contrary to the principles which appear to be securely laid down. Here were two shops in common ownership facing each other in the same street, one of them, Devonia, an ironmonger's shop. The shops opposite are sold with a covenant against carrying on an ironmonger's business. What could be more obvious than that the covenant was intended for the protection or benefit of the vendor's property Devonia? To have rejected such a conclusion would, I venture to think, have involved not only an injustice but a departure from common sense. So far from declining the authority of that case, I welcome it as a useful guide. But it is only a guide, and I must ultimately reach my conclusion on the facts of the present case. These I now consider. They are not in dispute. I have the fact that the Crichel Estate is, and for many years has been, not merely a conglomeration of separate farms and cottages, but a recognizable and recognized agricultural unit. Its identity in 1943 has been established by an agreed map: it has, in fact, hardly changed since 1928, the date of the vesting deed mentioned in the conveyance, or up to the present time. It has been managed as one for a number of years – thus, no doubt, acquiring its own character – is surrounded by its own ring fence, has its mansion house, secondary residence, home farm, farm cottages, woodlands, ornamental water, all the indicia of an extremely valuable unit. Its character was entirely agricultural, with the single exception of the paper mill at Witchhampton, and it is surrounded by other similar, or at least comparable, estates in a district which is entirely agricultural – in the words of one witness, 'a rather unique area'. The property sold in 1943, Crook Farm, was before the sale a part of the estate, the purchaser, Mr. Harding, being, as was his father before him, tenant of the farm from the estate: it was also a wholly agricultural property. The vendors of the farm were the second plaintiffs, selling in the character of fiduciary owners of the Crichel Estate as a whole: in taking any restrictive covenant, they had, of course, no individual or personal interest or any interest other than as owners of the estate as a whole.

On these facts I consider that I should come to the conclusion that the covenant was taken for the benefit of land of the vendors, that land being the Crichel Estate. In doing so, I do not, so it seems to me, go outside such surrounding or attendant circumstances as, in accordance with the authorities, it is legitimate for the court to take into account. A decision based on the mere wording of cl. 2 of the conveyance would, in my judgment, be unduly narrow and, indeed, technical and would go far to undermine the usefulness of the rule which equity courts have evolved that the benefit of restrictive covenants may be capable of passing to assigns of the 'dominant' land or of the covenant in cases other than those of annexation. I would add two observations. First, the rules in *Miles* v. *Easter* properly relate to cases where the covenant is sought to be enforced by an assign from the original covenantee. In this case, however, the second plaintiffs are the original covenantees and the first plaintiff is the person for whose benefit in equity the covenant was taken. To that important extent the plaintiff's case is stronger than that of the defendant in

Miles v. *Easter*. Secondly, in holding that the covenant was for the benefit of the Crichel Estate, I mean the Crichel Estate as a whole – as a single agricultural estate which it was and is, and I express no opinion whether it enures for the benefit of each and every part, for example, if parts are separately sold off. That is not a question which arises in this case. . . .

Question (c): Was the land capable of being benefited by the covenant? On this point, as on those last dealt with, the answer would appear to be simple. If an owner of land, on selling part of it, thinks fit to impose a restriction on user, and the restriction was imposed for the purpose of benefiting the land retained, the court would normally assume that it is capable of doing so. There might, of course, be exceptional cases where the covenant was, on the face of it, taken capriciously or not bona fide, but a covenant taken by the owner of an agricultural estate not to use a sold-off portion for other than agricultural purposes could hardly fall within either of these categories. As SARGANT J said in *Lord Northbourne* v. *Johnston & Son*[39]: 'Benefit or detriment is often a question of opinion on which there may be the greatest divergence of view, and the greatest difficulty in arriving at a clear conclusion.'

Why, indeed, should the court seek to substitute its own standard for those of the parties – and on what basis can it do so? However, much argument was devoted to this point, and evidence was called as to it. These I must consider.

First, it was said that a mere examination of the figures showed that the covenant could not benefit the estate: the Crichel Estate extends to some seven thousand five hundred acres, and it was asked how such covenant could benefit the estate as a whole. In my view, there is no such manifest impossibility about this. I have already referred to the character of the estate, and I can well imagine that for the owner of it, whether he wished to retain it in his family or to sell it as a whole, it might be of very real benefit to be able to preserve a former outlying portion from development. This seems to me to be a question of fact to be determined on the evidence: and I note that, when a similar argument was placed before the court in *Re Ballard's Conveyance*[40], CLAUSON J while accepting it in the absence of evidence, showed it to be his opinion that evidence could have been called.

Then it was said that, as the blue land was already an aerodrome when the covenant was imposed, the covenant could be of no benefit, at least as regards that land. I reject this argument. The vendors may well have had to accept the prospect of user as an aerodrome, so long as the necessity continued, but to prevent the land thereafter being turned to other non-agricultural purposes may well have been a valued objective. I think that it was in this case. Next it is said that the covenant was useless because in any event there was plenty of other land in the same area in the vicinity of the estate which was free from restrictions. I have no difficulty in rejecting this argument. Why should not a vendor protect what he can, and is such protection useless because other land (at the relevant date itself all solidly agricultural) might be desecrated? Is a covenant against using premises for a certain trade useless because adjoining premises may be so used? (Compare the *Newton Abbot* case.) This contention, in my judgment, fails.

Lastly, an argument was based on the first proviso to the covenant. This was, in effect, that, if the vendors should sell any adjoining or adjacent portion of the estate retained by them free from any obligation to use for agricultural purposes, the purchaser was likewise to be liberated from the covenant. This, it was suggested, showed that the purchaser's covenant could not be for the benefit of the retained land. The reason, so the argument ran, was that the obvious benefit, and possibly the sole benefit, of the covenant was to reserve any development value which land in the vicinity might have for the vendors: but the existence of the proviso – which enabled the purchaser to develop if the vendors did so – prevented this benefit from arising, and ergo there was no benefit in the covenant. I find this argument altogether too subtle. The purpose of the proviso seems to me to be a much simpler one, and to have been simply to anticipate the natural grievance which the purchaser might have if his land was confined for ever to agriculture while the vendors were free profitably to develop the immediately adjoining land. As such, it is completely consistent with the vendors' overriding desire to preserve the agricultural character of their own estate and of the land sold off. There is another defence based on the proviso with which I will deal later, but this particular argument I reject.

I now examine the evidence as to the capability of the covenant to benefit the vendors' land. . . . Taken as a whole, the evidence comes to this: a restriction of this character, in relation to such an estate as the Crichel Estate was at the relevant date and is at the present time, is of value in that it preserves a measure of control over adjoining land. In relation to that part of the adjoining land which, in 1943, was already being used as an aerodrome, so far from the covenant being useless, it was of positive value, because the departure from agricultural use which had already taken place inevitably gave rise to uncertainty as to the future of the land and opened the door to possible further development: the covenant prevented the door from being opened further. . . . It is on this general approach that, in my view, the benefit of the covenant is to be assessed, rather than in relation to particular effects which the breach of it might produce. Indeed, much of the evidence, particularly as to noise and effect on amenity, seemed to me to be more relevant to an action for nuisance, which this is not, than to the action as it is. . . . But in so far as it is relevant to take particular matters into account, I am prepared generally to accept Commander Marten's evidence that the installation of a substantial industrial undertaking on the edge of the estate might well have concrete detrimental effects on the management of the estate, making it more difficult to provide housing for estate employees and to get or retain labour, and causing the installation of increased services in the way of roads, electrical cables, etc., which would change the character of the place. . . . Lastly, I should add that I reject a line of argument to the effect that development of the restricted land, by bringing with it development, or the possibility of development, of the Crichel Estate, would actually raise land values rather than diminish them. The owners of the Crichel Estate are surely entitled to set other values above those of this character of enrichment.

Question (d): Can the action be brought by the first plaintiff or by the two plaintiffs jointly? I can deal with this point quite shortly. The second plaintiffs are the original covenantees, and the first plaintiff is the person for whose benefit in equity the covenant was made. Taken together, the plaintiffs represent the whole legal and equitable interest in the covenant. The matter appears, therefore, to be completely covered by the judgment of SARGANT J in *Lord Northbourne* v. *Johnston & Son*, the reasoning of which I adopt. So much was not really contested by the Attorney-General, who, however, reserved the right to challenge that judgment should this case go to a higher court. This brings me to a conclusion on the first main point, and I accordingly hold that the plaintiffs are entitled to the benefit of the restrictive covenant.

The second main question is whether the blue land is subject to the burden of the restrictive covenant. Now the covenant was duly (in April, 1943) registered against the land under the provisions of the Land Charges Act, 1925, s. 10 (1), as a land charge Class D (ii), and purchasers of the land, therefore, take with notice of it: Law of Property Act, 1925, s. 198 (1). The Air Ministry, having purchased the land in 1958, is not in the position of a purchaser for value without notice, nor is the defendant company, which has no legal estate at all. It is not said that the covenant has been taken over or extinguished by any statutory procedure – as can be done under the Lands Clauses Acts. The covenant, therefore, binds the land in its present hands. This does not, of course, mean that it can necessarily be enforced at the present time against either defendant – that I shall consider shortly – but, conversely, even if it is not enforceable against either defendant, because of some statutory right which they, or one of them, may have to use the land for other than agricultural purposes, that does not prevent the covenant from continuing to bind the land. I refer to *Manchester, Sheffield & Lincolnshire Ry. Co.* v. *Anderson*[41]. . . . I proceed now to the issues of enforcement and remedy, to my mind the most difficult part of the case. First, I must endeavour to state the legal position of the Air Ministry and of the defendant company under the legislation by which the ministry acquired the land, and, secondly, I must find what activities precisely are now being carried on by the defendant company on the land, and endeavour to relate those activities to the statutory purposes for which the land was acquired. . . .

The position may be summed up by saying that the defendant company was given rights over the airfield in the nature of a tenancy, paying a very substantial rent: that the company was left free to carry on its own business: that it undertook the maintenance of the airfield, and that the Air Ministry was empowered to resume occupation in an emergency. The company was in a position to, and, no doubt, it expected to, carry out work, for reward, for the Air Ministry and other government departments while it was there, but the carrying out of this work, other than the maintenance of the airfield, was not part of the terms of occupation; nor was it something which the company was bound to do.

What, in fact, did the company's activities consist of? Broadly they fell, at all material times, under four headings: (i) maintaining the airfield and its facilities; (ii) design and development of flight-refuelling equipment and the fitting of this equipment to Royal Air Force aircraft; (iii) work on 'Meteor drones'; and (iv) miscellaneous.

. . . On these facts I have now to consider the position of the defendant company in relation to the restrictive covenant. The activities of the company taken as a whole, are quite clearly industrial activities and are admitted to be such in the company's defence. They are undertaken by the company in the normal course of carrying out the purposes for which it exists. They are equally clearly activities in breach of the restrictive covenant. . . . I cannot accept the general argument that it is enough to show that the defendant company's presence on the airfield is in the national interest. That may be so, but it does not follow that the company's activities should not be circumscribed, even if to do so might involve, for the company or even for the Air Ministry, a less economical method of operation. I see no legal basis on which a mere plea of national interest can be an answer to a claim to enforce a restrictive covenant. Nor do I accept the company's argument that, once it is shown that the bulk of its work is within the statutory authority, I should take no notice of other activities which are outside it. Both of these arguments, in my judgment, seek to extend the statutory protection too far.

On the other hand, I think that the plaintiffs go too far the other way when they invite me to deal with the case as if the company were merely occupying the site under a lease and carrying out contracts for a government department. That seems to me to overlook the point that the airfield has been acquired under statutory powers and must be taken to have been so acquired to enable certain statutory purposes to be fulfilled. In the ultimate analysis, the question for the court appears to me to be this: How much of the company's activity should be treated as done for the purposes for which the airfield may be considered to have been acquired? And in answering this question the court must, as was said in *Hawley* v. *Steele*[42], adopt a broad approach and must take great care not to embark on inquiries or to make distinctions in a matter which is essentially for the administrative discretion of the government.

Applying these tests, and accepting, as I think that I must accept, the evidence of the ministry's witnesses as to the needs of the service and the requirements of defence, I have already said that the company's work in maintaining the airfield and keeping it ready for operational use is clearly and immediately within the statutory purposes. The work on flight refuelling of service aircraft and on 'Meteor drones' appears on balance to me to be equally so. No doubt, this work could be done elsewhere: possibly the work on the 'Meteor drones' could be done by other firms (though, in fact, none does it); but, given the fact, which again I accept, that an airfield on the spot is necessary to enable each of these categories of work to be done, the Secretary of State would have been justified in acquiring under the Defence Acts an airfield to enable them to be done, and he must equally, in my judgment, be entitled, having acquired an airfield, to authorise them to be done on the airfield so acquired. It cannot, in my view, make any difference that, instead of doing this type of work himself, he commits it to an individual or a company, nor that, having chosen his instrument, he uses the latter as an independent contractor rather than as an agent, nor that, to enable the contractor to do the job, he grants him a lease or a licence. In all cases the land is being used for the statutory purposes for which it is acquired and such user is protected from attack.

The protection of the statute, therefore, in my judgment extends to the company's work on flight refuelling for the Royal Air Force and to the work on 'Meteor drones'. Moreover, I think that, in so far as the company manufactures and sells flight refuelling equipment for other users, it should not be deprived of the protection so long as this activity represents but a reasonable concomitant of its work for the services. It would be unreasonable, in my judgment, and not in accordance with the principles stated so clearly in *Hawley* v. *Steele* to permit the company to store any products made surplus to the requirements of the services while forbidding it to sell them to other consumers. It is a question of degree, no doubt, at what point the company's production assumes the dimensions of a separate activity, but I am content to hold that on its present scale that portion of the flight refuelling activity which is beyond what is needed for service purposes ought not to be prohibited.

That leaves the nuclear work and that done for the Belgian Air Force. Neither of these, in my judgment, falls within the statutory protection, even when extended as generously as I have thought right to extend it: the first obviously not, the second because there is not a sufficient connexion, on the evidence, between it and the purposes for which the airfield was acquired: it is simply a case of the company, by its independent initiative, going out and securing a contract which it is profitable to acquire. As to these two activities, therefore, I have seriously to consider whether the plaintiffs should be granted an injunction to restrain them. Before I do so, I must consider what are the company's intentions with regard to the future. Is there a real and substantial threat to extend the company's industrial activities, or, as was submitted to me by the defendants, is there no real risk of that? The answer to this question may well have an effect on the action which the court may take with regard to the company's present work . . . . There exists, therefore, in my judgment, a perfectly definite threat that what I may call 'non-statutory activities' at Tarrant Rushton will be extended and greatly extended. I think that the plaintiffs are entitled to be protected against this threat, and, indeed, that it is for the sake of this protection that this action has mainly been brought.

That brings me to the question of relief which I now have to consider in relation (a) to the existing non-statutory activities and (b) to the future. Unfortunately, there are issues left even at this stage. . . . The plaintiffs, it is said – and Commander Marten admitted as much – never drew the attention of the company to the existence of the restrictive covenant and the first the company knew about it was on the issue of the writ. It was, of course, on the land charges register, and s. 198 of the Law of Property Act, 1925, provides that entry on the register is to be notice to all the world: nevertheless, I think that I must take the plaintiff's silence into account. It cannot be said that this silence amounts to acquiescence, because the plaintiffs were consistently opposing the continuance of the airfield and of the company's industrial activities, though this opposition was not based on the covenant; but it is claimed that, had the covenant been mentioned, the company's action might have taken a different course at some points. . . . I think that there is substance in this contention, but limited substance. The two non-statutory activities which may have been affected are the nuclear work, the main part of which is on the blue land in hut No. 1000, and the work for the Belgian Air Force which is done in hangar No. 4, also on blue land. The hangar could not be moved, but the work could have been transferred, and still can be, no doubt with some dislocation. Hut No. 1000 could be moved or its installations transferred, probably with more dislocation. In respect of both of these activities I am reluctant, in the circumstances, to grant an injunction which would compel their immediate removal. I go further, and say that I am not willing, on the basis of the use to which these buildings are being put at the present time, to order their removal at all. The only effect of such an order would be to cause another hangar or hut, as the case may be, to be used on unrestricted land, and nothing whatever would be gained from the plaintiffs' point of view by so doing. The weapon of an injunction should not be used where no practical purpose would be served. On the other hand, I think that the plaintiffs are entitled to be protected against any extension of these uses and against any further development of purely industrial activities on the restricted land. . . .

Marten's case points to the fact that a distinction has to be drawn between covenants taken for the benefit of the land as a whole, which can be enforced only by a successor in title to the original covenantee who has obtained all the land, and covenants taken for each and every part of the land which may be enforced by successors in title to the original covenantee who have obtained only part of the land, provided that they can show that their part can be benefited by the covenant, and that the covenant is in terms either assigned to them or annexed to each and every part of the land. This distinction is clearly a matter of great importance.

In the past large estates may have had covenants annexed to them on their sale and, when in more recent times, these estates are divided up and sold off in individual lots, the purchasers may find that they cannot enforce the covenants because the wrong formula was used in the original annexation or assignment. They may therefore be unable to prevent development which they regard as undesirable and thought they could protect themselves against. A good example of this is *Re Jeffs' Transfer*[43], the facts and issues of which were as follows:

STAMP J: The plaintiff, a Mr. Frank Rogers, owns a piece of land at Chorleywood, known as 'Greensleeves'. It is situate on land formerly known as the Chorleywood Estate (Loudwater), and subsequently as the Loudwater (Troutstream) Estate, and I will refer to it as 'the estate'. It was originally, before the sale had taken place, an estate of about 135 acres in extent. The plaintiff, being minded to erect a cottage on part of his land, which would contravene the terms of covenants entered into by a predecessor in title of his, applied to the Lands Tribunal under s.84 of the Law of Property Act, 1925. A considerable number of persons objected and the application to the Lands Tribunal was stood over pending the decision of this court whether any and, if any, which of these persons is or are entitled to enforce the covenants in question. Some of the objectors have fallen out, and it is common ground that one of them, Loudwater (Troutstream) Estate, Ltd., who is an express assignee of the benefit of the covenants, is entitled either for that or some other reason to enforce the covenants. The objectors with whom I am concerned are persons who derive title from the original covenantees, without having an express assignment of the benefit of the covenants.

It is common ground that there is no building scheme enabling the owners of the several plots on the estate to enforce the covenants imposed on them, one against the other, and, put shortly, the question which I have to determine is this – whether the benefit of the covenants was annexed to each and every part of the estate so as to pass without any express assignment to the purchasers of parts of it.

(The covenant in issue was in the following terms):

... and the purchaser for himself and his assigns and to the intent that the covenants may bind the land into whosesoever hands the same may come but so that the purchaser shall not be liable in damages for any breach thereof which may occur in respect of any part of the said land after he has ceased to be seised thereof covenants with the vendor ... (and here come the vital words) ... for the benefit of the remainder of the Chorleywood Estate (Loudwater) belonging to the vendor to observe and perform the restrictive conditions and stipulations specified ...

Schedule 2 of the covenant contains a long list of stipulations which are set out in numbered paragraphs. The stipulation on which the objectors rely is this:

One private dwellinghouse only with stabling or garage and outbuildings to be used in connexion therewith shall be erected on the whole of the land hereby agreed to be sold and the adjoining land of the purchaser ... and no building of any nature shall be erected on any part of the land ... without the consent of the vendor in writing ....

After discussing which of two arguments *ad absurdum* on the extent of the enforceability of the covenant would have produced the more 'Gilbertian' situation, the judge decided that the defendants/objectors arguments were the more absurd and they could not accordingly object to the breach of or enforce the covenant. In the event, since it was conceded that Loudwater (Troutstream) Estate Ltd could enforce the covenant, the issue of the breach or modification could be ventilated either in court or in the Lands Tribunal, but the drafting 'failure' prevented those immediate neighbours most interested in enforcement from appearing in either forum. What benefits are gained by such decisions?

Once again it seems as if this distinction is part of the continuing clash of principle between property and contract in this area of law, for both in the case discussed and in the other similar ones, the doctrine of assignment has been used by the courts to allow enforcement of a covenant by an owner of part of the land where the doctrine of annexation would have prevented it. It may be doubted whether such refinements add to the usefulness of the law, and it is probably such situations that have resulted in some recent cases adopting a liberal approach to the enforcement of covenants to give effect 'to common intentions notwithstanding any technical difficulties involved'.[44] The Law Commission too has attempted to grapple with the problems thrown up by this distinction.

(d) The development scheme

In dealing with problems of annexation and assignment we have inevitably concentrated on technicalities. It is important to realise then that once a set of restrictive covenants is firmly attached (to use a neutral word) to the land, it affects the way the land is used, often over a very long period of time. This functional approach to restrictive covenants is emphasised by a consideration of the development scheme: from one approach just another way to create a set of covenants, but from our perspective, the best example of the use of covenants as a conscious planning tool. As such, the following considerations and questions should be borne in mind as the cases are read.

There has been an evolution in the cases from strict insistence on certain attributes of a development or building scheme to a more liberal approach to those same attributes. To what factors would you attribute this evolution? Would you agree with Hayton that paying less regard to technical requirements detracts from 'the vital characteristic of all property interests, viz. definability, ascertainability and stability, and in particular, because the uncertainty thereby created casts doubt on many titles, . . . [inhibits] the marketability and the development of land?'[45] A development scheme places a great deal of power in a landowner/developer. What restrictions are there on the exercise of this power? Should there be any restrictions or controls other than the original granting of planning permission and the market; i.e. potential purchasers not buying into the scheme because they do not like the covenants imposed by the developer? What is and what should be the relationship between a development scheme and statutory planning control?

Baxter v. *Four Oaks Properties* [1965] 1 All E.R. 906

CROSS J: The plaintiffs in this action are the owners of four houses in Lichfield Road, Four Oaks, Sutton Coldfield, Warwickshire – the first plaintiff Hilda Baxter of No. 145, the second plaintiff Madge Esme Finnemore of No. 147, the third plaintiff Joseph Allsop of No. 139, and the fourth and fifth plaintiffs Robert Anthony Ryder and Anne Veronica Ryder of No. 135.

The defendants, Four Oaks Properties, Ltd., purchased No. 143, Lichfield Road, which adjoined the property of the first plaintiff, on Oct. 10, 1963. They at once proceeded to pull down the house and to put up on the site a three-storey building, consisting of nine self-contained flats approached by a common staircase, and at the back of the site nine garages for use by the tenants of the flats. The plaintiffs contend that the erection of this building, or, alternatively, the user of it as flats, constitutes, or will constitute a breach of certain restrictive covenants which they are entitled to enforce against the defendants. The facts are as follows:

In 1891 Lord Clanrikarde owned an estate of some 288 acres at Sutton Coldfield known as the 'Four Oaks Estate', the eastern boundary of which was formed by a public road called at the south end the Lichfield Road, and further north the Four Oaks Road. By various conveyances executed over a period of some ten years he sold the whole of the estate for building development in plots of various sizes. It was his intention that the whole estate should be residential but that the cost of the houses to be erected should not be uniform throughout. To effect the purpose which he had in mind, the whole estate was divided into several parts, the part with which this action is concerned being that abutting on the Lichfield and Four Oaks Road.

The first purchaser of a plot on this part was one Samuel Hope. On Apr. 27, 1891, an indenture (which I will call the 'Lichfield Road deed of covenant') was expressed to be made between Lord Clanrikarde of the one part and Samuel Hope and all other persons whose names are or might thereafter be entered in the second column of Sch. 2 thereto, being purchasers of lands forming parts of the Four Oaks Estate as delineated on the plan thereto annexed of the other part. The recital and operative part of this Indenture were as follows:

WHEREAS by an Indenture of Conveyance bearing even date with these presents and made between the said Marquess of Clanrikarde of the one part and the said Samuel Hope of the other part for the consideration therein mentioned the said Marquess of Clanrikarde hath conveyed to the said Samuel Hope his heirs and assigns a certain piece or parcel of land being part of the Four Oaks Estate and fronting on a road shown on the said plan and leading from Sutton Coldfield to Lichfield and Little Aston being the piece or parcel of land coloured blue on the said plan and identified by the name 'Hope' written upon it TO HOLD the same unto and to the use of the said Samuel Hope his heirs and assigns AND in the said Indenture of Conveyance is contained a covenant by the said Samuel Hope with the said Marquess of Clanrikarde that he the said Samuel Hope his heirs and assigns and all persons claiming under him will at all times hereafter perform and observe certain covenants and conditions as to building on the said piece or parcel of land and as to the user of the said piece or parcel of land therein specified AND WHEREAS it is intended that all other persons who may be or become purchasers of any lands forming part of the said Four Oaks Estate and fronting on the said road shall enter into covenants as to building on such lands as to the user thereof similar to the covenant in that behalf contained in the hereinbefore recited Indenture of Conveyance to the said Samuel Hope NOW THIS INDENTURE WITNESSETH that for giving effect to such covenants respectively IT IS HEREBY AGREED AND DECLARED that the said Samuel Hope and every other person who shall be or become a purchaser of any land forming part of the said Four Oaks Estate and fronting on the said road and their respective heirs and assigns and all persons claiming under them respectively shall whether they shall or shall not have respectively executed these presents perform and observe the covenants and conditions contained in Sch. 1 hereunder written so far as such covenants and conditions respectively may relate to the lands purchased by them respectively AND IT IS HEREBY FURTHER AGREED AND DECLARED that in the event of any breach by the said Samuel Hope or any such person as aforesaid or by their respective heirs or assigns or by any person or persons claiming under them respectively of the said covenants and conditions respectively or any of them it shall be lawful for any other person for the time being entitled to any land being part of the said Four Oaks Estate and fronting on the said road or having any estate or interest in such land without any further consent or concurrence of the said Marquess of Clanrikarde his heirs or assigns to bring such action or take such steps as may be necessary or proper or restrain such breach PROVIDED ALWAYS that the covenant and conditions contained in Sch. 1 hereunder written shall not apply to or affect any lands forming part of the Four Oaks Estate other than such lands as front on the said road.

The covenants and conditions in Sch. 1 were as follows:

1. No dwellinghouse or other building (other than the existing cottage adjoining Doe Bank House or other than a building used for the purposes of and as appurtenant to a dwellinghouse) of a less cost for materials and labour of construction than £750 or in the case of a pair of semi-detached houses than £1,200 shall be erected or built or suffered to remain upon any part of the lands above mentioned between Hartopp Road and Bracebridge Road or of a less cost than £1,000 in the case of a single house or £1,500 in the case of a pair of semi-detached houses upon any part of the lands above mentioned between Bracebridge Road and Blackroot Road. 2. No dwellinghouse or other building other than a porch or oriel or bow window or balcony shall be erected or built or suffered to remain upon any part of the lands above mentioned so as to project beyond the building line shown on the plan hereto annexed. 3. No dwellinghouse or other building on any part of the lands above mentioned shall be used for the sale or supply of wine beers or spirits or for the sale or supply of victuals or as an hotel or inn or for any trade or business whatever or otherwise than as a private residence or for any purpose which may be or grow to the annoyance damage or disturbance of any person who may be or become the owner or occupier or any other part of the lands above mentioned.

Schedule 2 was in six columns; the first containing numbers, the second the names of purchasers, the third the description of the plots bought by them by reference to the plan, the fourth the date of the conveyance to the purchasers, the fifth the signatures and seals of the purchasers, and the sixth the signatures of witnesses to the purchasers' signatures. Mr. Hope headed the list, having presumably signed the indenture on Apr. 27, 1891. Besides the conveyance to him, seventeen other conveyances are referred to in this schedule – the last in date being on July 22, 1899. Some signatures appear twice, since the same purchasers bought different plots at different dates. The plan shows a number of plots fronting on Lichfield Road and Four Oaks Road coloured in different colours and marked with the names of the respective purchasers. The plots are of varying sizes. There is no evidence that Lord Clanrikarde laid out the part of his estate fronting on Lichfield and Four Oaks Road in plots before beginning to sell it off. He appears to have sold plots, of the size which purchasers wished to take, to purchasers as they came along. . . .

. . . By their writ, which was issued on Mar. 4, 1964, the plaintiffs claim against the defendants declarations: (i) that they are entitled to enforce against the defendants the covenant contained in the Lichfield Road deed of covenant and the conveyance to Edward Rawlins, and (ii) that the erection of this block of flats, or alternatively its user as flats constitutes, or will constitute, a breach of the covenants, and consequential relief by way of injunction or, alternatively, damages.

The defendants had the clearest possible notice of the existence of the covenants in question when they purchased No. 143, Lichfield Road, and there can be no doubt that they are bound by them. They further concede that the benefit of Mr. Rawlins' covenants with Lord Clanrikarde contained in the conveyance of Dec. 14, 1894, and the Lichfield Road deed of covenant were annexed to any part of the estate fronting on Lichfield Road or Four Oaks Road, which was still owned by Lord Clanrikarde at that date, and that accordingly the third plaintiff and the fourth and fifth plaintiffs, who derive title to 139 and 135, Lichfield Road respectively from persons who bought plots from Lord Clanrikarde after Dec. 13, 1894, and were entitled to enforce the covenants against the defendants. The defendants contend, however, that the first and second plaintiffs who derive title to 145 and 147, Lichfield Road from persons to whom Lord Clanrikardo had sold their plots before Dec. 14, 1894, are not entitled to the benefit of the covenants entered into by Mr. Rawlins on that date.

It is, of course, clear that a vendor who sells a piece of land to 'A' and subsequently sells another piece of land to 'B' cannot, as part of the later transaction, annex to 'A's' land the benefit of a restrictive covenant entered into by 'B' if it was not part of his bargain with 'A' at the time of the sale to him that 'A' should have the benefit of it. On the other hand, for well over one hundred years past where the owner of land deals with it on the footing of imposing restrictive obligations on the use of various parts of it as and when he sells them off for the common benefit of himself (in so far as he retains any land) and of the various purchasers inter se a court of equity has been prepared to give effect to this common intention notwithstanding any technical difficulties involved. In the early days it was not unusual for the common vendor to have prepared a deed of mutual covenant to be executed by each purchaser. If the various sales all took place at the same time – as they would, for instance, if all the land in question was put up for sale by auction in lots – then the various purchasers would, no doubt, be brought into direct contractual relations with one another on signing the deed; but if the common vendor sold off different lots of land at intervals, it might well happen that by the time a later purchaser executed the deed, one of the earlier purchasers was dead. In such a case it would be difficult to found the right of the successors in title of the deceased earlier purchaser to enforce the covenants against the later purchaser or his successors in title on any contract between the two original purchasers, even though each signed the deed.

The view taken by the courts has been rather that the common vendor imposed a common law on a defined area of land and that whenever he sold a piece of it to a purchaser who knew of the common law, that piece of land automatically became entitled to the benefit of, and subject to the burden of, the common law. With the passage in time it became apparent that there was no particular virtue in the execution of a deed of mutual covenant – save as evidence of the intention of the parties – and what came to be called 'building schemes' were enforced by the courts if satisfied that it was the intention of the parties that the various purchasers should have rights inter se, even though no attempt was made to bring them into direct contractual relations. A statement of the law on this point which is often quoted is contained in PARKER J's judgment in *Elliston* v. *Reacher*[46]: . . . .

In my judgment, in order to bring the principles of *Renals* v. *Cowlishaw*[47] and *Spicer* v. *Martin*[48] into operation it must be proved (i) that both the plaintiffs and defendants derive title under a common vendor; (ii) that previously to selling the lands to which the plaintiffs and defendants are respectively entitled the vendor laid out his estate, or a defined portion thereof (including the lands purchased by the plaintiffs and defendants respectively), for sale in lots subject to restrictions intended to be imposed on all the lots, and which, though varying in details as to particular lots, are consistent and consistent only with some general scheme of development; (iii) that these restrictions were intended by the common vendor to be and were for the benefit of all the lots intended to be sold, whether or not they were also intended to be and were for the benefit of other land retained by the vendor; and (iv) that both the plaintiffs and the defendants, or their predecessors in title, purchased their lots from the common vendor upon the footing that the restrictions subject to which the purchases were made were to enure for the benefit of the other lots included in the general scheme whether or not they were also to enure for the benefit of other lands retained by the vendors. If these four points be established, I think that the plaintiffs would in equity be entitled to enforce the restrictive covenants entered into by the defendants or their predecessors with the common vendor irrespective of the dates of the respective purchases. I may observe, with reference to the third point, that the vendor's object in imposing the restrictions must in general be gathered from all the circumstances of the case, including in particular the nature of the restrictions. If a general observance of the restrictions is in fact calculated to enhance the values of the several lots offered for sale, it is an easy inference that the vendor intended the restrictions to be for the benefit of all the lots, even though he might retain other land the value of which might be similarly enhanced, for a vendor may naturally be expected to aim at obtaining the highest possible price for his land. Further, if the first three points be established, the fourth point may readily be inferred, provided the purchasers have notice of the facts involved in the three first points; but if the purchaser purchases in ignorance of any material part of those facts, it would be difficult, if not impossible, to establish the fourth point. It is also observable that the equity arising out of the establishment of the four points I have mentioned has been sometimes explained by the implication of mutual contracts between the various purchasers, and sometimes by the implication of a contract between each purchaser and the common vendor, that each purchaser is to have the benefit of all the covenants by the other purchasers, so that each purchase[r] is in equity an assign of the benefit of these covenants. In my opinion the implication of mutual contract is not always a perfectly satisfactory explanation. It may be satisfactory where all the lots are sold by auction at the same time, but when, as in cases such as *Spicer* v. *Martin*, there is no sale by auction, but all the various sales are by private treaty, and at various intervals of time, the circumstances may, at the date of one or more of the sales, be such as to preclude the possibility of any actual contract. For example, a prior purchaser may be dead or incapable of contracting at the time of a subsequent purchase, and in any event it is unlikely that the prior and subsequent purchasers are ever brought into personal relationship, and yet the equity may exist between them. It is, I think, enough to say, using LORD MACNAGHTEN's words in *Spicer* v. *Martin*, that where the four points I have mentioned are established, the community of interest imports in equity the reciprocity of obligation which is in fact contemplated by each at the time of his own purchase.

The defendants naturally rely on PARKER J's second requirement and argue that, as Lord Clanrikarde did not lay out the part of his estate which faced Lichfield Road in lots before he began to sell it off, there could be no enforceable building scheme here, even though Lord Clanrikarde and the purchasers from him may have thought that there was.

It is, however, to be observed that *Elliston* v. *Reacher* was not a case in which there was direct evidence, afforded by the execution of the deed of mutual covenant, that the parties in fact intended a building scheme. The question was whether one could properly infer that intention in all the circumstances. In such a case, no doubt the fact that the common vendor did not divide his estate into lots before beginning to sell it is an argument against there having been an intention on his part and on the part of the various purchasers that there should be a building scheme, since it is, perhaps, prima facie unlikely that a purchaser of a plot intends to enter into obligations to an unknown number of subsequent purchasers. I cannot believe, however, that PARKER J was intending to lay it down that the fact that the common vendor did not bind himself to sell off the defined area to which the common law was to apply in lots of any particular size but proposed to sell off parcels of various sizes according to the requirements of the various purchasers must, as a matter of law, preclude the court from giving effect to clearly proved intention that the purchasers were to have rights inter se to enforce the provisions of the common law.

I find support for this view in the judgment of SIMONDS J in *Lawrence* v. *South County Freeholds, Ltd.*[49]. In my judgment, therefore, not only the third, fourth and fifth plaintiffs but also the first and second plaintiffs can enforce their covenants against the defendants. . . .

I will therefore make a declaration that the plaintiffs are entitled to enforce the covenants against the defendants, and that the use of the building in question as flats will be a breach of the relevant covenant. . . .

The writ was issued on Mar. 4. After some delay the plaintiffs served notice of motion for an interlocutory injunction, which came before BUCKLEY J on Apr. 17. By that time work had progressed above the first floor. The judge made no order on the motion, and the building was completed in the autumn. It is no higher than the house which used to stand on the site, and the front portion containing six flats, two on each floor, covers approximately the same area; but there is a spur, containing three flats, which projects westwards from the main block and covers part of what had been the garden of the old house. The chief objection to the flats from the point of view of the first plaintiff's house (No. 145) is that the projection overshadows the west side of, and destroys the privacy of, her garden. Further objections are the noise that will be created by the use of the nine garages and the unattractive appearance of the building. The same objections no doubt apply with equal force to No. 141, the house immediately adjoining No. 143 to the south, but the owner of that house is not objecting since he himself hopes to build flats on the site of his house and has obtained planning permission for that purpose. The chief object of the second, third, and fourth and fifth plaintiffs in suing is to establish that the covenants are enforceable and prevent user as flats, though the second and third plaintiffs also contend that the erection and user of these particular flats will in fact injure them. On Nov. 2, 1964, the first plaintiff entered into a contract to sell her house to a Mr. Chapman, completion being fixed for January, 1965. She was still living in the house when the action was tried on Dec. 15 to 18.

As I have pointed out, there is no covenant against erecting a block of flats. The plaintiffs cannot, and do not, ask for an order that the defendants pull down the building which they have put up; they ask only for an order that the defendants do not use the building as flats. The effect of granting such an order would, of course, be to put the plaintiffs in a very strong bargaining position, for, unless the defendants were prepared to leave the building unused, they would be forced to buy a release of the injunction. Nevertheless, what the plaintiffs would get in the end would only be damages – though, no doubt, more damages than they would get if no injunction were granted. A further objection to the granting of an injunction is the sale of No. 145 by the first plaintiff. I do not see how I could grant an injunction to her. On the other hand, the other plaintiffs are far less affected by the erection and user of the flats than she was. Finally, it is to be borne in mind that the defendants did not deliberately act in a way which they knew would involve a breach of covenant. They thought – wrongly, as I have held – that the covenant did not extend to flats. All these considerations lead me to think that this is a case where I ought not to grant an injunction but should award damages instead.

Finally, I come to the question of the amount of damages to be awarded. Counsel on both sides proceeded on the footing that the proper measure to apply in the circumstances was what the various plaintiffs had suffered, and would suffer, as owners of their several properties, by reason not only of the prospective user of the building as flats but also of its erection and existence as a building. I propose, therefore, to deal with the problem on that footing.

Mr. Ryder, the fourth plaintiff, said very frankly on behalf of himself and his wife that the defendants' flats were too far away from the house to inflict any measureable damage on them. Their concern was to establish the legal position, since their neighbours to the immediate south had obtained planning permission for flats. The position of the fourth and fifth plaintiffs is, therefore, adequately safeguarded by the declaration which I have made.

The first plaintiff, as I have said, has sold her house, but it was not suggested that the erection of the flats was the cause of her selling. Evidence was given as to the effect which the existence and prospective user of these flats had on the amount of the purchase price. I do not propose to review it in detail, but I have considered it and in the light of it I propose to award her £500 damages.

The second and third plaintiffs are appreciably less affected than the first plaintiff, since the flats can only be seen, and seen at some distance, from their gardens. On the other hand, they are still living in their houses, and as they can remember the old state of affairs, and contrast it with the invasion of privacy constituted by the flats, they are probably more affected than a purchaser of their houses. Again, I do not propose to review the evidence in detail. I will award £100 to the second plaintiff, Mrs. Finnemore, and £150 to the third plaintiff, Mr. Allsop.

Re Dolphin's Conveyance [1970] 2 All E.R. 66

By an originating summons dated 22nd July 1968 the plaintiffs, the Birmingham Corporation, sought a declaration that the freehold land comprised in two conveyances, dated respectively 27th February 1871 and 26th March 1877 were no longer subject to restrictive covenants contained in the conveyances on the part of E. M. Coleman, or alternatively for a declaration whether any or all of the restrictive covenants were now enforceable and if so by whom. The defendants, Frank Herbert Boden, Kenneth Eaton Bradley, Ronald Duncan Thomson Cape, and Edwin Douglas Ramsay Shearman, were representative owners of other lands within the Selly Hill Estate who sought to enforce the covenants.

STAMP J: This originating summons is concerned with some land forming part of an estate known, or formerly known, as the Selly Hill Estate. The estate is now within the area of the city of Birmingham. The plaintiffs' predecessor in title, one Coleman, bought the land nearly 100 years ago subject to certain restrictions which Coleman covenanted to observe. That the plaintiffs bought their land with notice of these covenants, is not in question.

There are numerous persons who, being owners of other parts of the Selly Hill Estate, claim to be entitled to enforce the covenants against the plaintiffs. The plaintiffs, by this summons, to which four representatives of the numerous persons have been made defendants, ask, in effect, for a declaration that no person is entitled to enforce them. They wish, as part of their housing programme, to redevelop their land in a way inconsistent with the restrictions which, on one view, are designed to secure the preservation of the Selly Hill Estate as an exclusively residential estate, to use modern parlance, of low density, and to that end provide that no building other than a detached dwelling-house shall be built on the estate, such detached dwelling-house having not less than one-quarter acre of land including the site of the dwelling house.

One Robert Dolphin, who died on 19th December 1870, was a solicitor in Birmingham. He had had an estate of over 200 acres near Birmingham which included what came to be known as the Selly Hill Estate. Some years before his death Robert Dolphin had sold off all or the greater part of this estate under that name. The Selly Hall Estate, or part of it, subsequently became the subject of proceedings in this Division before SWINFEN EADY J and I have before me a transcript of his judgment. The relevance of the Selly Hall Estate to the present proceedings is that I have before me a conveyance dated 2nd September 1861, on which there is a plan on which is shown, as is indicated in the body of that conveyance, the whole of the estate called the Selly Hall Estate and 'certain lands adjoining thereto all belonging to the said Robert Dolphin'. The lands adjoining the Selly Hall Estate are clearly delineated on the plan. A part of them lay to the east and part to the west of the Selly Hall Estate. The part to the west was of an area of some 30 acres. . . . The town clerk of the plaintiffs produces a plan in which is delineated the land to the west of the Selly Hall Estate to which I have referred and he says of it, in his affidavit, that that is the extent of Robert Dolphin's Selly Hill Estate. . . His conclusion to the effect that the Selly Hill Estate was identical with the parcel of land to the west of the Selly Hall Estate, shown on the plan on the conveyance of 2nd September 1861, to which I have referred, is in my judgment, inescapable. . . .

I find that all the conveyances of the several portions of the Selly Hill Estate by the Dolphin family, except the last, were, so far as material, in identical form. I will read the earliest of them, which was made on 27th February 1871, between Ann Dolphin and Mary Dolphin of the one part, and Edward Mountford Coleman of the other part, and was, in fact, not only the earliest of the known conveyances but one of those under which the plaintiffs derive their title. I will, for convenience, refer to it as 'Coleman's Conveyance'. . . . It contained a covenant by the purchaser, Coleman, in the following terms:

> AND the said Purchaser doth hereby for himself his heirs and assigns covenant with the said Vendors their heirs executors administrators and assigns as follows. . . .
> FIFTHLY AND that every Dwellinghouse which shall be erected upon the said piece of land hereby conveyed as aforesaid shall cost at least the sum of Four hundred pounds sterling and shall not adjoin any other Dwellinghouse but shall be built detached from any other
> SIXTHLY AND that every Dwellinghouse shall have attached to it at least one quarter of an acre of ground including the site of such Dwellinghouse
> SEVENTHLY AND FURTHER . . . .
> the Vendors for themselves their heirs and assigns Covenant with the said Purchaser his heirs and assigns that on Sale or Lease of any other part of Selly Hill Estate it shall be sold or leased subject to the stipulations above mentioned numbered 1, 2, 3, 4, 5, 6, 7 and that the Vendors their heirs or assigns will procure a covenant from each

Purchaser or Lessee upon Selly Hill Estate to the effect of those Seven stipulations.

. . . In view of these covenants by the vendor in the several conveyances, I cannot do otherwise than find that the covenants were imposed, not only for the benefit of the vendors or of the unsold part of their estate, but as well for the benefit of the several purchasers. As a matter of construction of the conveyances, I find that what was intended, as well by the vendors as the several purchasers, was to lay down what has been referred to as a local law for the estate for the common benefit of all the several purchasers of it. The purpose of the covenant by the vendors was to enable each purchaser to have, as against the other purchasers, in one way or another, the benefit of the restrictions to which he had made himself subject.

Holding, as I do, that these covenants were imposed for the common benefit of the vendors and the several purchasers, and that they had a common interest in their enforcement, I must, in a moment, turn to consider what is, in my judgment, the separate and distinct question whether there is an equity in the owner of each parcel to enforce the covenants against the owners of the other parcels. But, before considering that question, I must advert to an argument advanced by counsel for the plaintiffs on the effect of the covenants themselves. He points out that the covenants by the purchasers are not expressed – as they would have been in a deed of mutual covenant – to be with the other purchasers, and that there is no covenant by the vendor to enforce the covenants which he has agreed to extract from the other purchasers. No doubt this is so; but, in my judgment, it does not lead to a result which assists the plaintiffs. Had the vendors covenanted to the effect that they would enforce the restrictions, it would, no doubt, have emphasised the intention that all the purchasers should benefit, but would also have shown, on the authority of *White* v. *Bijou Mansions Ltd.*[50] that the covenants were not intended to be enforceable by direct action by one purchaser against another. Counsel also urges that each purchaser was content to leave it to the vendors whether or not to enforce the obligations which they covenanted to impose on the other purchasers. I cannot accept this submission. If the vendors were to have no obligation to bring actions to enforce the restrictions – and I accept counsel's submission that they had not – the covenant by the vendors to impose the conditions on the other purchasers was nothing more nor less than useless unless the purchaser himself was to have the right to do so. The absence of a covenant by the vendor to enforce the restrictions against the other purchasers leads to, and not away from the conclusion that each purchaser was to have reciprocal rights and obligations vis-á-vis the others. How otherwise could effect be given to the intentions?

As CROSS J pointed out in the course of the judgment[51] to which I have already referred, the intention that the several purchasers from a common vendor shall have the benefit of the restrictive covenants imposed on each of them, may be evidenced by the existence of a deed of mutual covenant to which all the several purchasers are to be parties. That common intention may also be evidenced by, or inferred from, the circumstances attending the sales; the existence of what has often been referred to in the authorities as a building scheme. . . .

In *Elliston* v. *Reacher* PARKER J laid down the necessary concomitants of such a scheme. What has been argued before me is that here there is neither a deed of mutual covenant nor a building scheme. . . .

In my judgment, these submissions are not well founded. To hold that only where one finds the necessary concomitants of a building scheme or a deed of mutual covenant can one give effect to the common intention found in the conveyances themselves, would, in my judgment, be to ignore the wider principle on which the building scheme cases are found and to fly in the face of other authority of which the clearest and most recent is *Baxter* v. *Four Oaks Properties Ltd*. The building scheme cases stem, as I understand the law, from the wider rule that if there be found the common intention and the common interest referred to by CROSS J the court will give effect to it and are but an extension and example of that rule. . . .

There is not, therefore, in my judgment, a dichotomy between the cases where effect has been given to the common intention inferred from the existence of the concomitants of a building scheme and those where effect has been given to the intention evidenced by the existence of a deed of covenant. Each class of case, in my judgment, depends on a wider principle. Here the equity, in my judgment, arises not by the effect of an implication derived from the existence of the four points specified by PARKER J, or by the implication derived from the existence of a deed of mutual covenant, but by the existence of the common interest and the common intention actually expressed in the conveyances themselves. . . .

I can approach the matter in another way. The conveyances of the several parts of the estate taking the form they do and evidencing the same intention as is found in a deed of mutual covenant, I equate those conveyances with the deed of mutual covenant considered by CROSS J in *Baxter* v. *Four Oaks Properties Ltd*; the deed which he did not treat for the purposes of his judgment as itself bringing all the successive purchasers and persons claiming through them into contractual relations one with the other, but as showing the common intention. So equating them, I follow what I conceive to be the ratio decidendi of *Baxter* v. *Four Oaks Properties Ltd* and give effect to that intention by holding that the restrictive covenants are enforceable by the successors in title of each of the original covenantors against any of them who purchased with notice of those restrictions.

3. Use by public authorities

It was indicated at the beginning of the chapter that public authorities, no less than private developers, make use of restrictive covenants. After *LCC* v. *Allen*[52] it was possible for them to enforce covenants, in the absence of amending legislation, only where they retained land that could be benefited or accommodated by the covenant. This was not always possible to arrange, particularly in an *LCC* v. *Allen* situation, and in that case Scrutton J expressed himself forcibly on the position where no land was retained:

> I regard it as very regrettable that a public body should be prevented from enforcing a restriction on the use of property imposed for the public benefit against persons who bought the property knowing of the restriction, by the apparently immaterial circumstance that the public body does not own any land in the immediate neighbourhood. But, after a careful consideration of the authorities, I am forced to the view that the later decisions of this Court compel me so to hold.

It was not however until 1936 that the Housing Act of that year reversed the decision in that case insofar as it affected local housing authorities.[53] The section was repeated in the 1957 Housing Act and is reprinted below. It is important to note that the power it confers on local authorities is only for the purposes of that Act.

151. Where—
    (a) a local authority have sold or exchanged land acquired by them under this Act and the purchaser of the land or the person taking the land in exchange has entered into a covenant with the local authority concerning the land; or
    (b) an owner of any land has entered into a covenant with the local authority concerning the land for the purposes of any of the provisions of this Act:

the authority shall have power to enforce the covenant against the persons deriving title under the covenantor, notwithstanding that the authority are not in possession of or interested in any land for the benefit of which the covenant was entered into, in like manner and to the like extent as if they had been possessed of or interested in such land.

Similar powers have been available to local planning authorities since the Town and Country Planning Act 1932.[54] The current powers are contained in the Town and Country Planning Act 1971 as follows:

52. (1) A local planning authority may enter into an agreement with any person interested in land in their area for the purpose of restricting or regulating the development or use of the land, either permanently or during such period as may be prescribed by the agreement; and any such agreement may contain such incidental and consequential provisions (including provisions of a financial character) as appear to the local planning authority to be necessary or expedient for the purposes of the agreement.

(2) An agreement made under this section with any person interested in land may be enforced by the local planning authority against persons deriving title under that person in respect of that land, as if the local planning authority were possessed of adjacent land and as if the agreement had been expressed to be made for the benefit of such land.

Notwithstanding these two provisions, which it might be thought give ample covenanting power to local authorities, many of them seek further powers via local Acts. Typical of these is the Leicester Corporation Act 1956, which provides as follows:

6 – (1) Every undertaking given by or to the Corporation to or by the owner of any legal estate in land and every agreement made between the Corporation and any such owner being an undertaking or agreement —
   (a) given or made under seal on the passing of plans or otherwise in connection with the land; and
   (b) expressed to be given or made in pursuance of this section;
shall be binding not only upon the Corporation and any owner joining in the undertaking or agreement but also upon the successors in title of any owner so joining and any person claiming through or under them.

What are the justifications for conferring or allowing local authorities to acquire these powers? They are in addition to powers to restrict development contained in the Town and Country Planning Act and e.g. the Highways Acts 1959–71. What controls exist over their exercise? The words 'with the approval of the Minister' were contained in section 37(1) of the Town and Country Planning Act 1962; they have been removed from the successor section – 52(1). Why? Is this a cause for concern? What is the significance of the reference to 'regulating' the development or use of land as opposed to 'restricting' it in section 52? In the notes to this section in the *Encyclopedia of Planning Law and Practice*, it is said that 'It is not possible under this section to impose an obligation to do a positive act which will bind the land. A covenant to pay or expend money fails to bind the land. . . .'[55] Given that the last sentence is a correct statement of the general law, do you agree with that analysis of the section?

Consider the following problem: The Oldtown District Council concludes an agreement under section 52 with the Oldtown Property Co Ltd that the company will use only Portland stone in the building of an office block in a conservation area and will pay the Council an annual sum of money thereafter as a contribution towards the costs of keeping the building and its surrounds clean. The company is taken over by the Mammoth Development Co Ltd when the office block is half built. This company declines to continue to use Portland stone on grounds of the expense and states that it will not pay the Council any money under the agreement. Advise the Council.

It is not only local authorities that have obtained powers to enforce covenants in gross. Another public authority that has this power is the National Trust, a body whose primary function is to protect areas of natural beauty from development or its effects. Such a power is therefore vital to its effective operation. However, certain problems exist in relation to the enforcement by the National Trust of restrictive covenants; the question of the width of a covenant and the question of whether the covenantee should have the last word on its enforcement.

The first of these questions is potentially more serious for the National Trust. The first case below may be compared with *Marten* and two questions should be considered: would the decision be the same today, given the current approach of giving effect 'to common intentions notwithstanding any technical difficulties involved'?[56] In any event should the same approach to enforcement be adopted in relation to the National Trust with its public duties as is taken in relation to private developers?

National Trust v. Midlands Electricity Board [1952]
1 All E.R. 298

VAISEY J: These proceedings relate to a place both of interest and also, more particularly, of natural beauty, namely, the Malvern Hills. They consist, as is well known, of a short and narrow range with about twenty summits varying in height from nine hundred to fourteen hundred feet and forming the watershed between the Severn and the Wye. One of these heights, known as Midsummer Hill, is and has at all material times been owned and occupied by the National Trust, and it has been declared inalienable under certain provisions of the National Trust Act, 1907. At the date of the deed next to be mentioned the Ecclesiastical Commissioners for England were the owners of certain lands in the neighbourhood of Midsummer Hill known as Castlemorton Common, Shady Bank Common, and Holly Bed Common, to which I will refer as 'the common lands.' By that deed, which is dated Apr. 28, 1936, and made between the said Ecclesiastical Commissioners, of the one part, and the National Trust, of the other part, after recitals which *inter alia* state that the Ecclesiastical Commissioners had agreed to impose on the common lands the restrictive covenants thereinafter contained for the benefit of Midsummer Hill and for the purpose of preserving the amenities of the Malvern Hills, it is witnessed that in pursuance of that agreement the Ecclesiastical Commissioners 'with intent and so as to bind as far as practicable [the common lands] into whatsoever hands the same may come and to benefit and protect Midsummer Hill aforesaid' covenanted with the National Trust at all times thereafter to observe the stipulations and restrictions contained in the schedule thereto. I turn to the schedule, and read the first two of the four paragraphs of which it consists:

> (1) No act or thing shall be done or placed or permitted to remain upon the land which shall injure prejudice affect or destroy the natural aspect and condition of the land except as hereinafter provided. (2) No building shall at any time hereafter be erected upon any part of the land by or with the consent of the covenantors [the Ecclesiastical Commissioners].

On May 1, 1936, the said restrictions were duly registered under the Land Charges Act, 1925, s. 10 (1), as a land charge affecting the common lands. By virtue of the Church Commissioners Measure, 1947, the functions and property of the Ecclesiastical Commissioners were vested in the second defendants, the Church Commissioners for England, who thereupon became, and still are, the owners of the common lands.

The first defendants to this action, the Midlands Electricity Board, are one of the area boards constituted by or under the Electricity Act, 1947, s. 1, s. 2 and s. 3, and the area which they are concerned to administer consists of the counties of Hereford and Worcester and parts of Gloucestershire, Oxfordshire, Shropshire, Staffordshire and Warwickshire (including Birmingham). Shortly before the commencement of this action, the board entered on a small part of the common lands and erected or began to erect some poles to carry an overhead electricity supply line across part of the common lands. These poles are wooden poles in pairs connected by cross-struts, and are about forty-two feet in height. Lines of cable are carried across the top of the poles and link them together in a continuous line. The National Trust alleges that the erection, existence and maintenance of these poles and this electric supply line constitute a breach of the restrictive covenants. They plead that they have thereby suffered damage, that their enjoyment of Midsummer Hill has been seriously disturbed, and, in particular, that the view from Midsummer Hill over the common lands is prejudicially affected. They claim a declaration that they are entitled to enforce the restrictive covenants against both the defendants, and are entitled to an injunction to restrain the erection or maintenance of certain of the poles and the suspended supply line. They claim also a mandatory order to pull down and remove some of the said poles.

The first and fundamental point to be considered is the meaning and effect of the restrictive conditions. . . .

The matter . . . in my view, rests on the first of the restrictions, which it will be remembered is to this effect: 'No act or thing shall be done or placed or permitted to remain upon the land which shall injure prejudice affect or destroy the natural aspect and condition of the land except as hereinafter provided.' The exceptions do not throw any light on the point which has arisen here. In my judgment, the wording of this restriction is extremely inapt and ill-considered. It may, perhaps, be paraphrased thus: 'No act shall be done and no thing shall be placed or permitted to remain on the land which shall injure prejudice affect or destroy the natural aspect and condition of the land.' It would be difficult to find wider, vaguer and more indeterminate words than those. 'Affect' following the word 'prejudice' cannot, I think, mean 'prejudicially affect' and must, therefore, mean 'affect whether prejudicially or otherwise,' that is to say, change or alter. Who is to say and what is to be the criterion of such qualification as might have been introduced by such words as 'in the opinion of the National Trust' after the words 'which shall,' a qualification which would appear to have been accepted as sufficient in *Marquess of Zetland* v. *Driver*[57] where the words were 'no act or thing shall be done or permitted [on certain lands] which in the opinion of the vendor may be [*inter alia*] prejudicial or detrimental to the vendor and the owners or occupiers of any adjoining property or to the neighbourhood.' It is, no doubt, easy to suggest some acts and things which would come within the prohibition – if, for example, the land were ploughed up or turned into a car-park or building estate. The difficulty here is to ascertain the limits of the prohibited acts. The burning of bracken, for instance, would, I should have thought, obviously affect the aspect and condition of the land. During the hearing counsel for the National Trust was driven to admit that the placing of a basket for litter on a short pole or a seat or a bench would amount to a breach of the condition. It is to be noted that it is both the aspect and the condition of the land which must be injured, prejudiced, affected, or destroyed. What does 'aspect' mean? Presumably the appearance, but viewed from what point? If a man chooses to stand with his eye against one of these poles, obviously he would be able to see nothing of the land, but that cannot be what is meant. What does 'condition' mean? I construe that as referring to the presence or absence of cultivation. How do these poles affect the condition of the land? It remains just the same as before. My garden remains a garden even though the post office erect a telegraph pole on it. In my judgment, the omission of any criterion by which these vague and uncertain words can be brought under some control is fatal to the validity of the restriction. I think it is void for uncertainty. It is so vague that it is really impossible of apprehension or construction, and, in my judgment, it is wholly unenforceable, but, whether it be wholly unenforceable or not, in my view, the erection of these poles does not come within the prohibition at all. They do, it is true, 'affect' to some extent the 'aspect' of the land, but how and to what extent they affect the 'condition' of the land I fail to see. The land remains in the same condition now that it was before the poles were erected except possibly in regard to the few square inches on which the poles stand. The land remains open country, heath or scrub exactly as it was before the poles were put on it. This extraordinary combination of 'aspect' and 'condition' seems to me to involve an interference with the land both in its appearance and in its condition which what has been done and what it is proposed to do do not come anywhere near satisfying.

If, however, I am wrong both as to the unenforceability of the condition and as to the absence of any relevance in its terms to what has actually happened, there is the further difficulty how any restriction so worded can be said to benefit or protect Midsummer Hill. The nearest of these poles to Midsummer Hill is at least eleven hundred yards distant from it. No doubt, the poles are visible from Midsummer Hill on a reasonably clear day, but the effect of their presence or absence from the landscape must be quite infinitesimal. I may here observe that the National Trust has now obtained statutory powers to impose and enforce restrictions in gross, but the present case is not within those powers. I have here to deal with the ordinary case of protected and restricted land, assuming, contrary to my view, that the common lands have been validly restricted by the deed of Apr. 28, 1936. I think that Midsummer Hill has not been validly protected in the circumstances and it is only as the owners of Midsummer Hill that the National Trust can have any right of action in respect of these covenants.

If I am wrong on all these points, the further question arises whether the first defendants, the electricity board, have acted within and are proposing to act within their statutory powers and thereby are relieved from any obligation to observe the restrictions and excused for any breach of them which the erection of these poles would otherwise entail. In my judgment, this question must be answered in the affirmative. . . .

Gee v. The National Trust [1966] 17 P. & C.R.7

LORD DENNING M R: In Cornwall there is a lovely inlet of the sea called the Helford River. In 1938 Mrs. Hext owned a large house towards the head of the river, two or three farms and other buildings. Altogether some 300 acres. She was minded to do what she could to see that the beauty and character of her land should not be impaired. So she made a covenant with the National Trust. It is important to notice that she did not convey a single acre or a single square yard of her land to the National Trust. She took advantage of an Act which enabled the National Trust to accept covenants from an owner of land, even though the National Trust had no land there themselves. Mrs. Hext on December 14, 1938, made a covenant with the National Trust. She covenanted that after her death the land should be subject to restrictions. The particular restriction which she imposed upon it was: 'No building shall at any time be erected upon any part of the land except such farmhouses, cottages, outbuildings, greenhouses and other buildings as shall reasonably be required for proper farming, cultivation, management or enjoyment or to increase the amenities of the estate, including the mansion house and gardens.' In short, after her death, no buildings (other than those mentioned) were to be erected on any part of these 300 acres.

Mrs. Hext died in September 1940. The estate was carried on by her successors. They sold portions of it to purchasers who took with notice of the covenant. So the National Trust continued to have these restrictions upon it. But they did relax them from time to time. They permitted quite a number of buildings to be erected. The question is whether one more house should be allowed there or not.

At the old village of Helford the river is about 100 or 200 yards wide. Across the river there is a small group of houses, which form a hamlet called Helford Passage. A few years ago there was a little Watch House, an inn called 'The Ferry Boat Inn' and a few cottages. In 1959 the National Trust granted permission for an extension of the buildings there. They allowed 'The Ferry Boat Inn' to be extended by a new wing. They agreed to a modern house called 'Demelza' to be built there. They gave approval for several holiday flats to be built on a slight rise. Nineteen flats have already been built in this small hamlet of Helford Passage.

About three years ago Mr. Gee bought the little Watch House, which stood in about ¾ acre of land. He had notice of the covenant with the National Trust. He extended the Watch House and made it into a very nice house, together with a swimming pool. Now he wants to put another house on that three-quarters of an acre. The proposed house is to cost £15,000 to £16,000, and is designed by a well-qualified and distinguished architect. Mr. Gee has already been to the local planning authority. At first they refused permission but he appealed to the Minister. An inquiry was held by the Minister's Inspector. He recommended that planning permission should be given to Mr. Gee for this extra house. He explained his reasons in a very clear report. He said that this site was one 'which offers great scope and challenge for an interesting architectural scheme.' He also said that a dwelling would be comparatively unobtrusive on the landscape. There would be no detriment to the visual amenities of the area if the proposal was carried out. The site was fairly well screened with trees and the proposal would have a natural setting. It would integrate into the general grouping of the riverside development. He added that it 'would not create a precedent for further development along the banks of the Helford River . . . as the contours of the land preclude any further development in that direction.' Upon that report the Minister was satisfied that this proposed house would cause no damage or injury to the amenities of the area. It would fit into this secluded valley without injuring anyone. So he granted planning permission.

But the National Trust had the benefit of the restrictive covenant: and they objected to the house. In view of their objection, Mr. Gee applied under section 84 of the Law of Property Act 1925 for the restriction to be removed or modified. The Lands Tribunal, having viewed the site and considered the evidence, took the view that the proposed new house would not impair the visual amenities of the adjacent land. The Lands Tribunal also thought that, if you considerd the National Trust as the deemed owner of land adjacent to the site, they would not be damaged by this proposed house. Nevertheless, the Lands Tribunal exercised their discretion against Mr. Gee. They held that his application to modify should be rejected. From that there is an appeal to this Court.

The application is made under section 84 (1) (c) of the Law of Property Act 1925, as amended. It gives the Lands Tribunal power to modify a restriction on being satisfied that the proposed discharge or modification will not injure the persons entitled to the benefit of the restriction. The persons entitled to the benefit of the restriction here are the National Trust. But the National Trust have no land of their own adjacent to this site. So under the ordinary law they would not have any claim to intervene at all – see *London County Council* v. *Allen*. But, by section 8 of the National Trust Act 1937, Parliament gave power to the National Trust to accept covenants restricting planning development or use. Parliament also went on to say that the National Trust 'shall have power to enforce such agreement or covenant against persons deriving title under the grantor in the like manner and to the like extent as if the National Trust were possessed of or entitled to or interested in adjacent land and as if the agreement or covenant had been and had been expressed to be entered into for the benefit of that adjacent land.' The Lands Tribunal held that the National Trust must be *deemed* to be the owner of adjacent land. But there is a difficulty about this. There is no land specified. We do not know the area or extent of that adjacent land, nor where it would be situated. In these circumstances I am inclined to think that we do not have to deem any particular land to be in the ownership of the National Trust. Section 8 is simply machinery to give the National Trust a standing to enforce the restriction where they would have no standing at common law. I am prepared to accept the view that the National Trust, when a covenant of this kind is made, is entitled to enforce it so as to protect the interests of which they are the custodians in this country. They are, under the statute, the custodians of the natural beauty of our land, the cliffs and downs, fields and woods, rivers and shores; and of the stately homes, historic buildings, cottages, and barns. In respect of any injury to their interest as custodians of our natural beauty, I think they would be qualified to insist on these covenants.

But even so, the question is: As such custodians, would the proposed discharge or modification injure them? The Lands Tribunal have found it would not injure them as deemed owners of any of the adjacent land. Equally it seems to me it would not injure them in their capacity as custodians of the natural beauty of our land. The evidence is indeed all one way. It was accepted by the Minister's Planning Inspector and the Lands Tribunal. This one single house will fit snugly into this small wooded valley. It should architecturally be a pleasing feature. It will not do any damage to the amenities or beauty of the district. Therefore, sub-section (c) is satisfied.

Now, there is the remaining question: ought the Lands Tribunal in its discretion to modify the covenant or not? It has been held by this Court in the case of *Driscoll* v. *Church Commissioners for England*[58] that it is a matter for the discretion of the Tribunal. The Tribunal have refused to exercise their discretion, and they put it on two grounds: First, they seem to have thought that, if a modification were to be permitted here, landowners would be less inclined to enter into covenants in the future.

Secondly, it might prejudice the appeal which the National Trust are making for money called Enterprise Neptune. Those two reasons do not appeal to me in the least. The National Trust themselves have granted permission for a considerable development, just across the road, in the shape of this big house, these holiday flats, and so on. If that does not prejudice the willingness of people to enter into covenants, or respond to an appeal, nor should the fact of giving permission in this case, especially when the Minister and the Lands Tribunal think it will not injure anyone.

The truth is that the National Trust in this case wish to have the last word on whether this house should be built, no matter what the Tribunal or anyone may say. But Parliament has not given them the last word. Section 84 of the Law of Property Act applies to these covenants with the National Trust. That is shown by the National Trust Act 1939, section 5, which expressly says, in another connection, that section 84 should not apply to restrictions imposed by certain leases. It can be inferred that Parliament intended that section 84 should apply to such covenants as we have got in this case.

It seems from the evidence of the National Trust representatives that they feared this would 'create a precedent' and would be 'the thin end of the wedge.' I see no basis for this fear. The Inspector said the contours of the land would preclude any further development. This one house will not be driving in the thin end of the wedge.[59]

Appeal allowed.

4. Positive covenants

We next consider the problems posed for urban development by the non-enforceability of positive covenants and the methods used to circumvent this rule of law.

*Report of the Committee on Positive Covenants Affecting
Land*[60] Cmnd. 2719/1965

The General Problem
Difficulties of Enforcement of Positive Covenants

2. ... The burden of a positive covenant cannot under the existing law be made to run with the servient land. Our main task therefore has been to examine to what extent difficulties are caused by the fact that a positive covenant cannot be enforced against the owners or occupiers for the time being of the servient land or building once the original covenantor has parted with his interest, and to put forward solutions to these difficulties.

3. The difficulties arise, and we have so considered them, in two contexts: first in the normal traditional context of covenants between neighbours as to such matters as fencing, boundary walls and the repair of roads; and secondly in relation to modern developments in building and construction, particularly the provision of flats, by conversion or new

erection, and the planned laying out of housing estates with common facilities and amenities. The evidence we have received leaves us in no doubt that the present position in both contexts mentioned above is unsatisfactory. . . .

It is true that the purchaser from the original covenantor will usually have given an indemnity covenant to the covenantor and similar covenants may have been passed down through the chain of successive owners of the land, but such a chain of covenants will ensure that the present owner of the land repairs the wall or fence only if the person seeking to enforce the covenant can trace the first covenantor and if there has been no break in the chain of indemnities. . . .

5. The inconveniences of the present law are accentuated in the case of divided buildings and blocks of flats because of the large extent to which each owner of a flat depends for the comfort and enjoyment of his home on the maintenance and repair of the rest of the building, the continuance of any services provided for his flat and the upkeep of any amenities included in the development. It is of the greatest importance to the owner of each unit that the common parts of the building, entrances, passages, stairs, attics, etc. should be properly repaired and maintained, that amenities like gardens, access roads and private drives should be kept in good condition and repair, and that parts of the building which, although in the occupation of one owner, may provide support or shelter for the property of others should not be allowed to deteriorate. Any failure to repair and maintain the common parts, or to afford the necessary shelter or support, may seriously affect not only the comfort of the flat dwellers, but also the value of any unit in the building. The evidence before us shows that, because under the present law it is not always possible to impose effective obligations to do these things, freehold flats are not generally considered to be a satisfactory security for a mortgage. Building Societies and other potential mortgagees, are reluctant to make any advances on such properties; or, if they do, they will advance only a substantially smaller proportion of the total value than they would advance on other comparable properties. The practice of local authorities is not uniform. Some will make full advances on freehold flats, while others will not; and we had evidence of one which is normally prepared to advance up to 100 per cent of its property manager's valuation on the security of dwelling houses, but limits advances for freehold flats to three-quarters of that valuation if the flats are purpose-built, and to two-thirds of the valuation if they are the result of conversion. Many building societies, we understand, will not make loans on the security of freehold flats at all.

6. The lack of adequate powers to enforce obligations against the owners for the time being of land or buildings also affects the public interest, as it may lead to the neglect of those parts of private buildings or estates which are held in common. Modern high density private development tends to leave a large part of the developed area in common ownership. Some decades ago such land would usually be split into houses and gardens in individual occupation, but now up to 70 per cent of the area

may consist of drives, paths, grass verges, communal gardens and play-grounds. It is socially desirable that such common property should be properly maintained.

7. Local authorities have a particular interest in the enforcement of positive obligations as property owners and as planning authorities. They frequently sell land for a purpose which is of importance to the community, like the erection of a church or factory, or the construction of dwelling houses to particular specifications, and take appropriate covenants from the purchasers. Sometimes, as in the case of large industrial development areas, the building programme covers a long period of years and the land may pass through a number of hands before the last buildings are due to be constructed. Local Authorities also frequently wish to impose positive obligations on landowners as part of their general planning functions. Some powers to enforce such obligations are conferred on planning authorities by statutes to which we refer later in this Report, and some local authorities have acquired additional powers by local Acts, but the lack of a general power to enforce covenants is causing them difficulty. We have been given a number of examples where a local authority, having been given an undertaking by covenant for the execution of works, like the erection of roadside fencing or the construction of specified dwelling-houses, were later unable to enforce the covenant because the ownership of the land was no longer in the covenantor.

The Committee's recommendations, which have not yet been implemented, fall into two categories: Covenants between Neighbours, and Special Problems of Blocks of Flats and other Multiple Units.

Report, op. cit.

10. We recommend, first, that the assignability and enforcement of positive covenants should, as far as possible, be assimilated to that of negative covenants. Broadly speaking, . . . in the case of positive covenants as in that of negative covenants the burden should run with the land encumbered, and the benefit should run with the land advantaged.

SPECIAL PROBLEMS OF BLOCKS OF FLATS AND OTHER
MULTIPLE UNITS

36. The recommendations we have made so far would go some way towards meeting the special needs of owners of flats or other parts of divided buildings to which we referred at the beginning of this Report; but they would not provide a complete answer. In such multiple units every owner is dependent for shelter and support on the maintenance and repair of adjoining, superjacent and subjacent units; and the amenities and services available in each unit (water, gas, electricity, central heating, telephone, ventilation, drainage, refuse disposal, etc.) may depend for their continuance on access through, and maintenance of the means of access in, other units or common parts in the building. In order to afford the occupants the fullest enjoyment of their own units and to preserve the value and integrity of each unit, there must therefore be a far higher

degree of interdependence between adjoining properties than is normally the case between neighbouring land or buildings. Between flat owners compliance with mutual obligations is vital and consequently there is a special need for effective and rapid enforcement. To a lesser extent this is also true in regard to building estates consisting of individual houses where an area has been developed as one estate with substantial areas of land to be used in common by the owners of the individual properties. And even where the occupants are less interdependent the value of each property must to some degree be affected by the general state of repair of the remainder of the estate, the efficiency of the services provided and the maintenance of the common amenities.

37. The recommendations made in the earlier part of this Report would enable the owners of blocks of flats or building estates to impose and enforce positive obligations, and if the appropriate wording was used they would also enable the owners of individual units to enforce the obligations *inter se*. They would not, however, be sufficient to ensure that the obligations would in fact be imposed in all the appropriate cases, nor that, once imposed, they would be effectively complied with. . . . Particularly where the block of flats or the development area is a large one, the amount of time and energy required to see to these matters would call for volunteers of exceptional public spirit and, unless some management machinery is set up, there is a risk that some, if not all, of the obligations would be allowed to go by default. It is not only the proprietary interest and comfort of the owners that is at stake; there is also the public interest in the preservation of the nation's stock of housing and the proper maintenance of the common parts surrounding the buildings. Land devoted to common use, as we have mentioned earlier, nowadays often represents a large proportion of a developed estate.

38. In our opinion it is therefore important to ensure that at least the essential obligations will in future be imposed in every such development; and that facilities for imposing a more comprehensive scheme of mutual covenants and of management for the mutual benefit of the owners of units in multiple developments are so readily available that the developer will have every inducement to adopt it. But, if there are to be binding mutual obligations to repair and maintain divided buildings, it is also important to ensure that these mutual covenants will not have the effect of artificially prolonging the life of obsolete or decayed structures and so obstruct redevelopment. . . .

42. We have . . . studied the system recently introduced in New South Wales by the Conveyancing Strata Titles Act of 1961. Very broadly this system provides for the registration in the local equivalent of our Land Registry of a detailed plan showing the exact boundaries of the building and of the various units in it (the 'Strata Plan'). Certificates of title to a registered unit are issued upon registration, and each unit carries with it a share of the common parts. The proportion which the value of each unit bears to the total value of the building constitutes the basis for that unit's liability to contribute towards common expenditure and for its owner's share in the common parts and his voting rights in the management of

the building. Each unit owner holds shares in a body corporate which automatically comes into existence on registration of the Strata plan and he has powers and duties in relation to the management and upkeep of the building. Easements of support, shelter, and the passage of water, sewerage, drainage, gas, electricity and other services are implied in favour of and against each unit. The body corporate acts through a council elected by the unit owners. If a unit owner fails to comply with his obligations to maintain and repair his own unit, or to contribute towards the common expenditure, the body corporate is empowered to bring proceedings in the courts against him. In the event of serious damage being suffered by the building and in case of its complete destruction, powers are conferred on the court to decide on the application of any insurance money and on the disposal of the property and the distribution of the proceeds of any sale. An outline of the Strata Titles system appears in Appendix B.[61] It seems to us that the adoption of a system on these lines has considerable advantages for large developments. A Strata Titles system would in our opinion supply a ready-made and effective scheme for implying all necessary easements and covenants and for providing an effective machinery of management and enforcement. We recommend that it should be made available for optional adoption. If adopted, it should involve stated legal consequences as outlined above. A title to a flat comprised in the plan together with all the rights and obligations covered by the system would be transferable by simple registration; much trouble and expense in conveyancing would be saved.

44. We ... recommend as an alternative to the Strata Titles system the provision of a simple statutory model scheme which should be available for adoption, in the same way as the Companies Act 1948 provides model articles for a limited company. It should be capable of variation by agreement between the parties and should be suited to a house converted into a small number of flats or a small block of flats. It is important that it should be adequate to deal with the services most commonly found in such developments, like refuse disposal and the maintenance of common gardens. By way of example we set out in Appendix C[61] a statutory model scheme of a kind which we would expect to be suitable for adoption in many cases, although some adaptations would frequently be required to fit the particular circumstances. The scheme would provide a definition of the building and the common parts, the latter to include the roof and the foundations. There would be covenants by the owner of each unit to repair and maintain his unit, so as to preserve the support, shelter and protection enjoyed by the remaining parts of the building. The owner of each unit would covenant to contribute to a fund for the upkeep of the common parts. He would be given a right of access to any other unit to execute covenanted repairs which the owner of that unit has failed to carry out and a right to apply to the court for an order charging expenses incurred in doing such repairs on the unit of the defaulting owner. All questions relating to the management of the common parts, their upkeep and insurance, could be dealt with by the decision of an appropriate majority of unit owners (or their mortgagees).

45. We are conscious of the danger that such a system of obligations to repair and maintain the existing parts of a building could, if it were applied to old and decrepit structures, tend to keep buildings in existence beyond the end of their socially desirable life. There is also a serious risk that property speculators might take advantage of such a system to extract excessive contributions towards maintenance and repair from some unit-holders. However, a sufficient safeguard should be found in our recommendations on the powers which should be given to the court to deal with buildings whose effective life has come to an end.

46. If legislation were passed making a Strata Titles scheme and a simple model scheme available for adoption, we would hope that the overwhelming majority of future property developments would be made subject to one or other of them. However, no matter how flexible the schemes are made, in the infinite variety of possible forms of multiple units there will always be some for which they are inappropriate. Moreover, where the number of units is very small, there is little need for any form of management and even in medium size developments, if there are no services and the common parts are not extensive, the owners can sometimes be left to look after the enforcements of the covenants and the running and repair of the common parts themselves.

47. However, we do not consider that in future any horizontal division of buildings or the erection of any horizontally divided units should be permitted without the imposition of certain minimum obligations. If none are adopted by the developer, we recommend the statutory imposition of a few minimum obligations which are inseparable from the ordinary enjoyment of the units. There would be definitions, as in the Scottish practice and in the statutory model scheme suggested by us, of the rights of the individual owners to roofs, walls, floors, ceilings, eaves, etc. There would also be obligations to provide and maintain shelter and support and to allow free passage of water, gas, electricity, soil and other usual services existing in the building from the time of the creation of the units; there should be a right of access to any other part of the building to effect necessary repairs which the owner of that part had failed to execute, and a right to recover the expenses of such repairs. But the right of entry should, except in emergencies, be exercisable only after reasonable notice of intention to enter. We recommend that these minimum obligations should apply to all buildings with horizontally divided units which come into existence after the enactment of the appropriate legislation.

48. We do not recommend the statutory imposition of obligations automatically on any existing multiple units. . . .

An exception must, however, be made where it is necessary to impose obligations in the general interest of the owners or to take steps to prevent the decay of buildings or amenity land, which being a national asset should be entitled to special protection. Where such considerations apply, we do consider that the court or the Lands Tribunal should be given power to make such orders as may be just in all the circumstances for dealing with a particular problem concerning support, shelter or the passage of services which may have arisen. . . .

We also recommend that, in the general interest of the owners or to prevent the decay of buildings or amenity land, it should be open to the court to order, on an application by two or more owners of the units in an existing building or estate, that the Statutory Model Scheme or (exceptionally) the Strata Titles Scheme should henceforth apply with or without modifications, and subject to such conditions, as to payment of compensation or otherwise, as may be fair.

End of Effective Life of the Building

49. While we believe that our recommendations will further the national interest in the nation's stock of houses, we would not wish our proposals on the imposition and enforceability of covenants for the repair and maintenance of buildings to have the effect of prolonging the life of a house beyond what is socially desirable. . . .

We therefore recommend that the court should be given power on the application of one or more unit-holders to declare that the life of the building has come to an end and to make such order as it thinks fit for the sale of the land and the distribution of the proceeds among the unit-holders. The power of the court would be exercisable not only where the buildings had fallen into decay but also where some calamity had led to its destruction. . . .

50. . . . some provision for the ownership of the common parts will be required in those cases where the optional schemes are not adopted, and the developer does not wish to retain the common parts, or having retained them dies, becomes bankrupt, or disappears. A solution may lie in providing machinery for vesting the common parts in appropriate ownership and particularly for so vesting them in all the unit owners as tenants in common no matter how many there may be. The court should be given power on the application of the unit-holders to vest the common parts in a corporate body, a manager, or the unit-holders as tenants in common, as it thinks fit.

Many of these recommendations seem eminently sound, so that it may be thought strange that no official notice has been taken of them. There are two possible reasons for this. First, the Law Commission suggested that its recommendations on restrictive covenants could embrace positive covenants as well in the light of the Wilberforce Committee Report, but then went on to a further study of all appurtenant rights including easements and profits-à-prendre with a view to producing a code embracing the whole field of such rights and obligations. A final report of this study had not appeared by November 1974.[62] Secondly, many of the recommendations, particularly in the second category, could be acted on by developers of multi-unit developments without the necessity for legislation. As an illustration of what can be done under existing law, two techniques of control of a development and enforcement of covenants pioneered by Wates Ltd in some of their South London developments, will be discussed.[63]

Prior to the Leasehold Reform Act 1967[64] Wates built both free-hold and leasehold estates. Since that Act they have concentrated on freehold, but whether the estates are freehold or leasehold, they are based on a division of land into individual plots and communal or amenity land. It is in respect of this communal land and other common parts of the developments that two management schemes have been devised.

The first scheme is known as the Trust Instrument Scheme. The amenity land (which expression includes here other common parts) is conveyed in fee simple to a management company. The object of this company, which is incorporated as a private company under the Companies Act, is the management of the amenity lands including the enforcement of covenants relating to it. Its share capital is divided into 100 £1 shares, all of them held by the two directors, employees of Wates named in the Articles of Association. These two directors enter into a deed of declaration of trust in respect of the shares, and are constituted as trustees of the shares for the individual plot owners 'so as to procure that the management is conducted as far as possible in accordance with the wishes of the plot-owners, ascertained in accordance with the Rules' of the Trust Deed, and in proportion of one fraction for each plot held by the plot-owners. The trustees, who may number between two and five, are appointed and can be removed by the plot-owners at general meetings which must be held at least every third year to approve the budget of the company and appoint and remove trustees. The Trust Deed contains limitations on what the trustees may do: they may not alter the share capital of the management company nor sell or distribute the trust property. There is thus established a system of management in which some or quite possibly all of the trustees are representatives of the plot-owners acting in their interests. The two initial director trustees can be removed by a general meeting but it is assumed that they or persons nominated by them will constitute the effective managers.

The management company owns the amenity land, and the trustees use the company to manage the land on behalf of the plot-owners. The advantages claimed for this scheme are (i) the developer, Wates, can hand over the land of the estate yet still maintain some control of it through owning indirectly the shares in the management company and appointing the initial director/trustees; (ii) one entity – a company – owns the amenity land, rather than a multitude of individual owners each with cross-easements in respect of the land they do not own; (iii) the plot-owners can be involved in the control of the management of the amenity lands via their rights at general meetings, and can use all the amenity land by virtue of their status as beneficiaries enjoying trust property under a trust; (iv) professional managing agents can be the more easily employed and controlled as they can be made directors and trustees of the company and so closely associated with the plot-owners in management.

The major disadvantage is that in the event of a clash of opinion over policy or management between Wates and the plot-owners, the scheme does not appear to have a mechanism for resolving it; one or the other side has to back down. This is probably unavoidable and it might be argued that this disadvantage is slight compared to the possible alternatives: Wates – only management on leasehold; no formal scheme of management at all, and trust to luck that sufficient public-spirited plot-owners will keep the development in good shape; or finally a complicated system of cross-easements, positive and negative covenants and a reliance on the doctrine of *Halsall* v. *Brizell*[65] to see things through.

The second scheme is known as the Resident Type Scheme and is used where a mixed development of flats and houses is built. A management company is established with initially two employees of Wates as directors. Two types of shares are issued – 'A' and 'B'. In one development there were 132 'A' shares at £2 each and 528 'B' shares at 25p each. Each owner of a house or flat was required, as a term of the contract to purchase the same, to purchase one 'A' share in the company. Holders of 'A' shares were obliged to observe and perform all the covenants relating to the property of which they were owners. The 'B' shares, which carried limited voting rights, were taken up by a subsidiary of Wates. Wates lease the amenity lands and the main structures and common parts of the flats to the management company whose function is to manage the property and enforce the covenants when necessary. As with all companies, there is a board of directors and an annual general meeting, at which the share-holders in the company may vote for or against any director or set of directors. The plot-owners can thus have a board of directors consisting entirely of themselves, making the day-to-day decisions about management, including decisions as to whether to employ professional agents and whether to enforce both negative and positive covenants against plot-owners who may refuse to pay an annual service charge, or let the company (or its agents) into his house or flat to get at the common parts of the development.

The developer drops out of day-to-day management but remains associated with the development via his position as owner of the freehold of the amenity land, etc. and owner of the dominant share-holding in the management company. He can thus be brought into, or intervene in, management when necessary. If the greater disso-ciation of the developer from the development is one advantage of this scheme, two disadvantages are: first, that some parts of the development remain in leasehold tenure while the rest is in freehold; and secondly, the scheme costs more to set up and run because under the Companies Act any company with more than fifty share-holders must be a public company and comply with the rules thereof.

From the particular perspective of this section of this chapter then, these two methods provide for the enforcement of positive as well as restrictive covenants and indicate that for a developer willing to take the trouble, enforcement is not too much of a problem. If it is to work well, however, it requires some residents on the develop-ment to be forthcoming to act as trustees, directors, managers and all residents to accept the decisions of those few, at least most of the time. This might not always occur; either apathy or continued bick-ering might set in and in those circumstances some kind of fall-back arrangement is needed. Wates provided for this in their schemes by ensuring that they retained sufficient power to manage if necessary; the Committee on Positive Covenants, however, seem to have assumed that the owners of the individual units within a multiple development would always co-operate so that no fall-back position was needed. Was this a sound assumption? Would you think that owners of units coming to the development fifty years after it had started would be as willing to participate in self-government and to pay dues as owners of units coming to the development in its first five to ten years? If not, why not? If a fall-back manager was to be provided for by law, which of the following three possibilities would you think most desirable and why: the local housing authority after application to the court for a management order; a court-appointed manager after application by a percentage of unit owners, with the court having a discretion as to who is appointed; enforcement of statutory minimum obligations as proposed by the Committee at the suit of any unit owner?

From a wider perspective, it is interesting to note that schemes such as those developed by Wates fall into place as examples of participation in the control of one's own environment, examples which, as we shall see, have been repeated in the area of leasehold development. What these management schemes create are amenity pressure groups, operating to preserve a particular locality or development both from non-conformists inside – the non-gardeners, the-hanging-washing-up-outsiders, the noisy-party-givers – and from 'undesirable' developments outside – the council estate, the higher density private development, any new development which would increase traffic through the estate, new roads, etc. What should be our attitude towards such groups? Are they to be welcomed as re-inforcing town or county-wide amenity groups and as extra checks on local planning authorities, or are they to be treated with some reserve as the very worst example of middle-class pressure groups out to preserve their own small piece of the environment at the expense of the environment of a great many others?

5. Public control of covenants

This matter raises in turn an equally wide issue which transcends the difference between positive and negative covenants, though at the moment, for obvious reasons, it arises only in relation to restrictive covenants. Covenants may have been imposed many years ago, some indeed stretching back to the mid-nineteenth century. In the inter-vening period, countryside has become town, low-density suburb has become surrounded by high-density public and private develop-ment, and large old houses have begun to be converted into two, three, four or more flats. Interspersed among these developments may be isolated pockets of old development or quite large estates, both still protected by restrictive covenants. It might well be argued by developers, both public and private, or by the owners of some protected plots that the covenants are now obsolete, a hindrance to modern standards of density and a prime cause of what has now be-come virtually a non-conforming use in the neighbourhood. What mechanisms, if any, exist for such arguments and their inevitable counter-arguments to be put, assessed and acted upon? Is there any way in which what are basically two contrasting sets of arguments about what public policy demands can be weighed and acted upon? This section deals with the answers to these questions, with the circumstances under which restrictive covenants may be modified or discharged and the grounds for such an exercise of power.

Powers have been available since the Law of Property Act 1925. They have undergone two changes. First, in 1950 the Lands Tribunal (established by the Lands Tribunal Act 1949) took over the jurisdiction to modify restrictive covenants under section 84(1) of the Law of Property Act 1925, from a body of persons known as the Official Arbitrators, and has exercised the jurisdiction ever since. Second, a major extension and reorganisation of the powers of the Lands Tribunal was enacted by section 28 of the Law of Property Act 1969, which amended and expanded the scope of section 84 of the Law of Property Act 1925. The first part of this section concentrates on the reasons for the reforms of 1969, the parliamentary discussion of the reforms, and the exercise by the Lands Tribunal of its powers after the reforms. The second part examines other possible ways of modifying or discharging restrictive covenants with special reference to racial restrictive covenants.

(a) Section 84, Law of Property Acts 1925-69

G. H. Newsom, Preface to Preston & Newsom,
Restrictive Covenants Affecting Land, 4th edn (1967)

The fourth edition of this book goes to press just thirty years after Mr Preston and I began to consider writing the first. The atmosphere surrounding the law of restrictive covenants has altered radically in that time. . . .

. . . In 1950 the Lands Tribunal took over the jurisdiction of the Official Arbitrators under section 84 (1), and from the outset analysed the three paragraphs of section 84 (1) much more closely than the Official Arbitrators had done. This analysis showed very soon that no question of the Tribunal's discretion can arise unless the applicant establishes positively that his case falls within one or other of the paragraphs, that the requirements of the paragraphs are stringent, and that if they are satisfied there is practically never any room for the award of compensation. The result has been that the Tribunal, in contrast with the Official Arbitrators, has dismissed a high proportion of the applications made to it, and that it has seldom modified covenants except in plain and obvious cases. I have myself only once been in a case before the Tribunal in which the applicant has succeeded against active opposition maintained to the end of the hearing. Further, the Tribunal has in only two cases awarded compensation. Moreover, although the Tribunal was always much stricter than the

Official Arbitrators, it was held by the Court of Appeal in *Re Ghey &
Galton's Application*[66] not to have been strict enough. . . .

While it may, to a superficial view, seem paradoxical that restrictions
on the user of land should be upheld in the name of liberty, there is a
serious social question to be solved. In an increasingly crowded island,
how far can privately imposed restrictions be allowed to stand permanently
in the way of private development which the planning authorities think
desirable? Public development presents no problem, since the burdened
land is taken compulsorily and the aggrieved parties are left to their
remedy in compensation; and if private development is unduly hampered,
the tendency will be to encourage development under public authority.
It would surely be a pity if too severe a refusal to modify restrictive
covenants and too rigid an enforcement of them in their unmodified state
led to a sweeping increase in the use of statutory powers. The present
problem would be much less acute if the prospects were now as good as
they were thirty years ago, that any given set of restrictions would either
be held unenforceable or be altered under section 84 (1), the aggrieved
parties in the latter event being awarded compensation. The immediate
way forward thus appears to me to consist in the amendment of section
84 (1) so as to restore to the Lands Tribunal the powers, which the Official
Arbitrators believed thirty years ago that they had, of granting both
modifications and compensation fairly freely on a case being shown for
the proposition that a restriction is out of date or stands in the way of
reasonable development. It would be neither necessary nor desirable to
encourage very large awards of compensation: the model which I have
in mind is the scale of damages which the court considers appropriate to
award in lieu of an injunction under Lord Cairns' Act. If the modification would cause really substantial damage, it should not be granted.

House of Lords Debates, vol. 301, cols 582–4, 593–5,
597–8: Committee Stage of the Law of Property Bill 1969

THE LORD CHANCELLOR[67] moved Amendment No. 8: . . . It extends and
clarifies the jurisdiction of the Lands Tribunal under Section 84 of the
Law of Property Act 1925 to modify or discharge restrictive covenants and
makes consequential and other minor amendments to Section 84. . . .
The new clause implements, with modifications, the recommendations
on the powers of the Lands Tribunal contained in Propositions 9(*a*) and
11 of the Law Commission's Report on Restrictive Covenants (Law
Com. No. 11), enlarges the powers of the court to issue declaratory judgments in accordance with a recommendation in Proposition 10(*b*) of the
Report, and corrects certain anomalies and makes certain improvements
in provisions of Section 84 which are not referred to in the Report. . . .

. . . VISCOUNT COLVILLE OF CULROSS: . . . The second point which I
should like to raise comes under the new subsection (1B). As I have always
understood the situation in the past, one of the things that the Lands
Tribunal has made quite clear is that it does not very much matter what
the local planning authority has said about the use of the land in granting

planning permission: the Lands Tribunal is going to look at the question in the light of the situation arising under the covenant. You can go there and tell them to your heart's content that you have planning permission for a block of flats 563 feet high, but they will not modify a covenant which says that the land shall not be occupied by more than one house unless they do so within the terms of the covenant and in the context in which the covenant was imposed.

All that goes. The new subsection (1B) is a major change which allows them to take into account, for the first time, the development plan, and, indeed, a pattern of individual permissions that have been given. This is immensely important on questions like density – 'How many houses should there be on this site although there is a covenant which says that there shall only be two?', or 'How many flats?' and questions of that sort. I think there is a danger here – I may be wrong but I put this forward for consideration – that one is going a little too far. If the Lands Tribunal is allowed to say that the covenant can be discharged because it is contrary to the public interest, and it then looks at an actual planning permission that has been given for a site which is in conformity with a development plan which says that when the area is re-developed the density shall be 140 persons to the acre and sees that there has been one other planning permission for an individual curtilage to be re-developed in this way, it may well be that we shall swing too far the other way. We shall cease to take account at all of the character of the area which the covenant sought to set up.

People have bought their houses in this area – not only the people next door; it may be people from outside who are not enabled to benefit from the specific covenant. Perhaps their land was sold at slightly the wrong time before the covenant was first imposed. Nevertheless, they are, I think, sometimes entitled to a little of the consideration in the public interest as well. There are people who have gone there because it is an area of low density development – I am basing this to a certain extent on the sort of case that I have met, but it is applicable in other spheres as well – and it may well be that the Lands Tribunal, in view of the words of this Amendment, will start to think that it is no longer at all important to take into account the context of the covenant. The only thing it has to do instead is to see whether or not it approves of the view taken by the local planning authority. I should not think that this is what the noble and learned Lord and those who advised him really want.

Probably what is wanted is a mixture of the two concepts. Do not rule out the local planning authority's view – let us give that its proper role in the consideration – but, equally, do not let us go overboard on it. Let us also take account of what the covenant could have been intended to achieve in preventing re-development over a rather long period of time. . . .

LORD WILBERFORCE: . . . I would certainly give my recognition to the extent to which the noble and learned Lord has consulted expert opinion in Lincoln's Inn and elsewhere, and has, I think, obtained their substantial agreement to what is in this Amendment. So with some reluctance, which I would imagine is probably shared by those advising the noble and learned Lord, I would be prepared to accept the way in which this has been done; namely, by taking the structure of the existing section and doing the best one can with it.

More significant, perhaps, is to be sure that we understand the extent to which the Amendments to the second limb of (1)(a), together with the new subsection (1A), really go. The noble Viscount pointed out some of the changes, but they really are very radical. The existing power to modify restrictive covenants under the second limb was limited to the case where 'the reasonable user' of the land would be impeded without securing substantial benefit. That has been replaced by 'some reasonable user', any reasonable user, which is very much wider; and, as regards the benefit to the owner, it now has to be 'benefits of substantial value', which one gets from (1A)(a). In addition to that, as pointed out under the new subsection (1B), the Lands Tribunal is given very wide powers to take into account 'the development plan and any declared or ascertainable pattern for the grant or refusal of planning permissions. . . .'

I think one has to face the fact that this makes such a substantial inroad into existing restrictive covenants that the whole nature of them is really changed to the detriment of the persons now entitled to the benefit of them, and I do not think it is very easy to see that from the way in which this is presented. When one looks simply at Section 84(1)(a) or the first Amendment, it does not look as if very much amendment is being made, but when you add it all up one sees how very substantial the inroad into this particular kind of right is.

Law of Property Act 1925–69

84. – (1) The Lands Tribunal shall (without prejudice to any concurrent jurisdiction of the court) have power from time to time, on the application of any person interested in any freehold land affected by any restriction arising under covenant or otherwise as to the user thereof or the building thereon, by order wholly or partially to discharge or modify any such restriction on being satisfied –

(*a*) that by reason of changes in the character of the property or the neighbourhood or other circumstances of the case which the Lands Tribunal may deem material, the restriction ought to be deemed obsolete; or

(*aa*) that (in a case falling within subsection (1A) below) the continued existence thereof would impede some reasonable user of the land for public or private purposes or, as the case may be, would unless modified so impede such user; or

(*b*) that the persons of full age and capacity for the time being or from time to time entitled to the benefit of the restriction, whether in respect of estates in fee simple or any lesser estates or interests in the property to which the benefit of the restriction is annexed, have agreed, either expressly or by implication, by their acts or omissions, to the same being discharged or modified; or

(*c*) that the proposed discharge or modification will not injure the persons entitled to the benefit of the restriction;

and an order discharging or modifying a restriction under this subsection may direct the applicant to pay to any person entitled to the benefit of the restriction such sum by way of consideration as the Tribunal may think it just to award under one, but not both, of the following heads, that is to say, either—

(i) a sum to make up for any loss or disadvantage suffered by that person in consequence of the discharge or modification; or

(ii) a sum to make up for any effect which the restriction had, at the time when it was imposed, in reducing the consideration then received for the land affected by it.

(1A) Subsection (1)(aa) above authorises the discharge or modification of a restriction by reference to its impeding some reasonable user of land in any case in which the Lands Tribunal is satisfied that the restriction, in impeding that user, either—

(a) does not secure to persons entitled to the benefit of it any practical benefits of substantial value or advantage to them; or

(b) is contrary to the public interest;

and that money will be an adequate compensation for the loss or disadvantage (if any) which any such person will suffer from the discharge or modification.

(1B) In determining whether a case is one falling within subsection (1A) above, and in determining whether (in any such case or otherwise) a restriction ought to be discharged or modified, the Lands Tribunal shall take into account the development plan and any declared or ascertainable pattern for the grant or refusal of planning permissions in the relevant areas, as well as the period at which and context in which the restriction was created or imposed and any other material circumstances.

(1C) It is hereby declared that the power conferred by this section to modify a restriction includes power to add such further provisions restricting the user of or the building on the land affected as appear to the Lands Tribunal to be reasonable in view of the relaxation of the existing provisions, and as may be accepted by the applicant; and the Lands Tribunal may accordingly refuse to modify a restriction without some such addition.

(2) The court shall have power on the application of any person interested—

(a) to declare whether or not in any particular case any freehold land is, or would in any given event be, affected by a restriction imposed by any instrument; or

(b) to declare what, upon the true construction of any instrument purporting to impose a restriction, is the nature and extent of the restriction thereby imposed and whether the same is, or would in any given event be, enforceable and if so by whom.

Neither subsections (7) and (11) of this section nor, unless the contrary is expressed, any later enactment providing for this section not to apply to any restrictions shall affect the operation of this subsection or the operation for purposes of this subsection of any other provisions of this section.

(3) The Lands Tribunal shall, before making any order under this section, direct such enquiries, if any, to be made of any government department or local authority, and such notices, if any, whether by way of advertisement or otherwise, to be given to such of the persons who appear to be entitled to the benefit of the restriction intended to be discharged, modified, or dealt with as, having regard to any enquiries, notices or other proceedings previously made, given or taken, the Lands Tribunal may think fit.

(5) Any order made under this section shall be binding on all persons, whether ascertained or of full age or capacity or not, then entitled or thereafter capable of becoming entitled to the benefit of any restriction, which is thereby discharged, modified or dealt with, and whether such persons are parties to the proceedings or have been served with notice or not.

(7) This section applies to restrictions whether subsisting at the commencement of this Act or imposed thereafter, but this section does not apply where the restriction was imposed on the occasion of a disposition made gratuitously or for a nominal consideration for public purposes.

Re Mercian Housing Society Ltd's Application (1971)
23 P. & C. R. 116

Sir michael rowe qc: By this application dated October 14, 1970, and amended on March 2, 1971, The Mercian Housing Society Ltd – not a housing association – asked for the modification of certain restrictive covenants subject to which it had bought a freehold property known as 'The Uplands,' 63 Upland Road, Birmingham. 'The Uplands' is within the boundaries of an estate known as The Selly Hall Estate which was brought into being in the early 1860s by a Birmingham solicitor called Robert Dolphin. It is not, I think, necessary to go into any great detail about the conveyances which imposed the restrictions because it was common ground that these restrictions were common to the whole Estate and that all the owners in the Estate were entitled to the benefit of them.

Briefly the restrictions were:
(1) That no building other than dwelling-houses with suitable out-buildings and offices should be erected on any plot.
(2) That every dwelling-house whether detached or semi-detached should have attached to it at least one-quarter of an acre of land including the site of the dwelling-house.
(3) That every dwelling-house and building should be built not less than fifteen feet from the road adjoining the land on which the same is erected and that not more than two dwelling-houses attached together should be built on any part of the land.
(4) That not more than one house should be built on the land affected by this restriction.

No. (4) was contained in a later conveyance of a particular plot or plots.

The modification sought was to permit the erection of six blocks of flats of three storeys each, together containing fifty-one flats, and of fifty-one garages in accordance with a full planning permission granted by the council for the City of Birmingham on November 30, 1967. Certain conditions were imposed 'in order to safeguard the visual amenities of the area,' the most important of which was that 'a landscaping and tree planting scheme to be first approved by the local planning authority is to be carried out and completed on the site to the satisfaction of the local planning authority within a period of six months from the date of the cessation of building operations.'

In fact before the permission was granted Mr. P. G. Marks, F.R.I.B.A., the architect to the Society, had had prolonged negotiations with the City's planning officers much of which was concerned with the preservation of the trees and landscape of 'The Uplands.' The plan eventually agreed preserved over 99 per cent. of the trees and the most important part of the landscaping.

Upland Road is a busy one and 'The Uplands' stands close to its junction with Selly Park. Except for some stabling at its eastern end, now used as garages, which is at street level, the property of some 2·685 acres stands high above Upland Road protected by a retaining wall. The house which was built before 1914 is a large one and stands above and just to the east of the stabling. Though in the past a fine house it is now too large and uneconomic for single private occupation. The drawing room faces north-east and looks out on to a really charming 'glade'. This glade consists of quite a wide lawn gradually sloping down from the house to a pond which though part of 'The Uplands' is not included in the land the subject of this application. This lawn is flanked on either side by trees and shrubs: many of these trees are big and fine and a number of them are rare in this country. This glade, as I have called it, is undoubtedly a fine piece of landscaping which I should think is unique in Birmingham, and I am not surprised that on February 19, 1971, the city engineer and planning officer wrote to Mr. Marks informing him that on February 11 the Public Works Committee resolved to make a provisional tree preservation order under the provisions of the Civic Amenities Act 1967 for all the trees of whatever species within the site of 63 Upland Road, Selly Park, and that the town clerk was at present preparing this order. . . .

I have said that the Selly Hall Estate began in the 1860s. It is situated reasonably close to the city centre and close to the University and the Queen Elizabeth Medical Centre from both of which the Society would expect to get customers. Its history is sufficiently well illustrated by the key to a plan put in by Mr. H. A. Gould, one of the surveyors called for the objectors. This shows that of a total of 308 properties on the estate 210 are post-1918 private houses, sixty-four are pre-1918 private houses, ten are pre-1918 houses now used as apartments or hostels, fourteen are pre-1918 houses converted into flats, four are commercial premises, and six are in institutional use. Amongst the uses are a hostel for railwaymen, another for discharged prisoners, and the Methodist International Home which has a recently added hostel. It is pretty clear, even from this short description, that the Estate is still in large measure a good residential estate and that generally speaking the covenants have served and are serving a useful purpose in preserving its character and, from the number of objections received, it is also obvious that the residents through their Association attach importance to them. Indeed the Society abandoned at the hearing one of its original contentions namely that the restrictions were obsolete.

The Society's grounds for making this application as put forward at the hearing therefore were:

(1) that the continued existence of the covenants would impede the reasonable user of the land by the erection and use of the flats proposed;

(2) that the restrictions impeding such user do not secure to the persons entitled to the benefit of them any practical benefit of substantial value or advantage to them as the unmodified restrictions would permit the erection of buildings destroying the landscaping gardens and grounds which can be better preserved by the erection of flats and continued use of the ornamental grounds and gardens in connection with the occupation thereof;

(3) that the restrictions are contrary to the public interest because the objects of the applicants are to provide housing for the benefit of the public on a non-profit-making basis;

(4) no person entitled to the benefit of the restrictions will suffer loss or disadvantage from the modification.

I do not think the third ground is of any importance and it was not pressed. The real questions arise under (1) and (2) and (4) – would a flat development be a reasonable use of the site? Would such use involve the loss of any practical benefits of substantial value or advantage to the residents on the Estate generally and the adjoining owners in particular? And I think, as it was put in evidence and argument, ground (2) introduces the question whether it is not in the interests of the Estate and of the public generally that the trees and landscaping of 'The Uplands' should be preserved. . . .

The main points of the evidence on both sides can be summarised reasonably shortly but I hope fairly. For the Society it was said that the flats would help to satisfy a great demand by the young professional and executive classes and by retired people: whereas flats could be built retaining the glade and 99 per cent. of the other trees, this would not be possible if eight or nine separate houses were built – they must wreck the entity which would be a bad thing all round; the flats with their garages had been so sited that they would be invisible, or almost invisible, even to the nearest houses and would certainly be no worse than the alternative of eight or nine houses each probably with a height of twenty-eight feet; no-one would suffer any injury particularly as the Society would pay agreed substantial sums to Dr. Mathews, Mrs. Mathews and to Mrs. Faulks to enable them to carry out additional screening. It was inevitable that the pre-1918 houses would be converted to flats or put to institutional uses but few, if any, of them had potentialities for flat development – the only possible site being well to the south adjacent to a house called Highfields and even this might well pose constructional problems that would make flat development impracticable. The Society's experience in building flats in other quite good residential areas proved that flats and houses were not irreconcilable.

The evidence for the objectors fell into two parts. First there was the general case that the introduction of purpose-built flats into the Estate would mean a lowering of its residential standards and would be the thin end of the wedge. The change from eight to nine houses to fifty-one flats involved a major departure from the established density; it would mean many more people and more cars and therefore more noise. The whole Estate would go down and values would drop. Eight or nine houses could be built without destroying the trees. In a planning context the Society's lay-out might be good but it would mean an alien type of building.

The second part of the evidence related to the effect on individual objectors particularly Mrs. Faulks, Mrs. Matthews and Dr. Mathews. Each of the properties Nos. 70, 54 and 48, Selly Wick Road would be severely injured. The amounts of compensation claimed were £2,000 for No. 70, £4,000 for No. 54 and £1,250 (allowing £750 for one house in the garden) for No. 48. This depreciation would result from the loss of privacy and seclusion as well as from the general decline in value of the Estate. . . .

I come now to my conclusions, in formulating which I was greatly assisted by my view. I very soon came to the conclusion that Mr. Marks' Block No. 1, alongside No. 70 Selly Wick Road, ought not to be allowed. Its erection would have a devastating effect on the amenities and value of No. 70 and a serious effect on No. 54, the principal rooms and the best of the garden of which would face it and be overlooked from the flats. . . .

The remainder of the Society's scheme stands on a different footing. It would be a crying shame if the glade was destroyed and the Society's scheme avoids this and preserves many more trees elsewhere, whereas both schemes put forward by the objectors would inevitably fragment the glade and involve much more destruction of trees. But this consideration might have to be put on one side if the Society's scheme would be 'the thin edge of the wedge' and lead to a proliferation of flat schemes all over the Estate. My tour of the Estate convinced me that this would not be so. It would never be permitted in relation to the 210 post-1918 houses and the pre-1918 houses are much more likely to be the subject of conversions than of re-development. It is conceivable that a scheme for flats on the land near Highfields might be put forward and that would have to be judged on its merits: the problems there would I think be different in many ways from those I have to consider now.

Secondly, I do not think that low blocks of flats are necessarily incompatible with or detrimental to a good class residential estate. Sometimes they might be but in this case I am sure the great bulk of objectors would not be damnified at all if this scheme, apart from Block 1 and its garages, were permitted.

But there remains the more difficult question as to the effect on Nos. 54 and 48 Selly Wick Road both of which are very nice indeed. As to No. 54, its main outlook is to the west. It would have only oblique views of Blocks 3, 4 and 5 from the house though of course from the garden the view would be direct if the flats were not screened. There is to be a solid eight-foot fence along the north-western boundary and inside there is already a pretty effective screen of trees and shrubs as well as some more to the north of the road. Even as matters are, I think the loss of seclusion and privacy would be minimal. Part of the £500 which the Society agreed to pay for additional protection was clearly attributable to Block 1 which will not be erected and I think £250 would be enough. If this sum is wisely spent I am sure the loss will be non-existent. I can understand the fears of the owner but I believe that the facts will soon dispel them.

Fears were expressed as to noise. Inevitably the flat scheme would generate more noise from people and cars than a house scheme but I do not think it would be materially greater and it would be in large measure baffled by the fence and wall and trees. After a week or two I doubt whether those living in Nos. 48 and 54 would be conscious of it unless they deliberately let it prey on their nerves.

I have therefore come to the conclusion that the applicants have made out a case for a modification of the covenants so as to permit the greater part of their scheme, which is a reasonable use of the site and will not in my opinion injure the persons entitled to the benefit of the restrictions, provided £500 is paid to Mrs. Matthews and £250 to Dr. Mathews for additional protective work.

Re Wards Construction (Medway) Ltd's Application
(1973) 25 P. & C. R. 223

J. S. DANIEL QC: This is an application by Wards Construction (Medway) Limited under section 84 of the Law of Property Act 1925 as amended by the Law of Property Act 1969. It seeks a modification of a covenant restricting the building on the subject land except by detached or semi-detached houses.

The larger part of the land in question is a roughly triangular plot with a frontage of 75 feet on to the eastern side of Nelson Road, Gillingham. . . .

The restrictions were imposed by conveyances of November 28, 1881 (the larger part) and July 27, 1881 (the remainder).

The purpose of the application is to enable the erection on the application site of a block of twelve flats with twelve car spaces.

The grounds of the application were said to be those falling within section 84 (1) (a), (aa) and (c) of the Act. Briefly the applicants' case was that there had been changes in the neighbourhood so that many properties nearby had ceased to be used purely as private dwelling houses; that the proposed development was a reasonable user of the land and would be impeded by the covenant without securing practical benefits of substantial value to the persons entitled to the benefit of the covenant; nor would they be injured by the proposed modification.

This part of Gillingham lies north of the main road going from the Medway towns towards Sittingbourne. Canterbury Street comes in north west from the main road; Napier Road and Nelson Road (which I have already mentioned) debouch a little further north. The area seems to have been developed, mainly for residential use, at about the turn of the century. A fairly large area was lotted up, sold and developed and some of this was subjected to covenants similar to those in question; an exception was another triangular area called on the plans the 'Tavern Lot' and situated in the apex between Canterbury Road and Nelson Road. This is only a few yards across the road from the application site. The Tavern Lot was clearly intended for use as an inn originally, but it has now become the office, yard and store of Wards Holdings, a company of which the applicants are a subsidiary.

The application site remained vacant until 1939. During the war a large static water tank was constructed on it. The tank is now empty. In 1951 Ward Bros (Gillingham) Ltd. made an application asking for a modification to permit the erection and use of a warehouse and garage on most of the (present) application site. This earlier application was objected to and was refused. . . .

In considering whether the restriction secured practical benefits of substantial value, and whether any injury would result from the proposed flats, Mr. Wright suggested that building within the covenant might produce a result more harmful to the objectors than the flats; a pair of semi-detached houses might be sited in such a position that even more obstruction to sun and light would be caused, indeed the curved frontage made this positively probable; again, town-houses, now a fashionable method of development, might be built within the covenant having two or three storeys and no limit in height; the flats would be a great improvement on the empty tank and on other things which might happen if the applicants failed, such as an extension of the garage.

I have inspected the application site both from near by and obliquely from the gardens of the objectors' properties. I have also made a tour of the streets in the environs. It was accepted that, apart from the covenants, a block of twelve flats in this position was a reasonable user of the site for private purposes. It was also of course common ground that the restriction unless modified would impede this user.

I am not satisfied that any of the suggested changes are such that the restriction ought to be deemed obsolete. As regards the site itself this may be to some extent an eyesore and the objectors may have been somewhat supine in not objecting to it before. No doubt some suitable development would be a good thing, but I cannot see any reason for therefore saying that the restriction should go. As to the neighbourhood the suggested changes did not impress me. Wards' own site is not inhibited by this restriction. The hotel and garage are the sort of uses which tend to crop up in residential areas and there is no doubt at all that the area as a whole, as all the evidence showed, remains predominantly residential.

think that conversion of existing buildings to flats is, in an area of this kind, less important a change than the construction of new buildings of a different kind. Indeed it is arguable that conversion into flats scarcely bites on the particular restriction in this case. . . .

Then comes the question whether impeding the proposed user secures practical benefits of substantial value. This involves balancing various factors against each other. No doubt the land should be developed. There is a shortage of land and the town-planners would like to see the density increased. Planning permission has been granted for the twelve flats. On the other hand the objectors are entitled prima facie to veto anything but detached or semi-detached houses and they obviously do not like this particular proposal. It may be, as Mr. Wright suggests, that the present situation is unsatisfactory and that projects even less attractive than the twelve flats could within or even in breach of the restriction emerge. I think these arguments *in terrorem* need more certainty before they can carry much weight. On balance I take the view that these objectors do secure practical benefits of substantial value in impeding this proposal. Here is a group of people who with respect are typical of the kind of people who live in this kind of residential area. Some of them had special reasons for wanting a feeling of space and quiet; it is likely that such an area will attract a few such persons. But even ordinary people not infrequently value space and quiet and light. I think the present proposal would blot out the sky and some of the valuable sunlight. These are substantial benefits. I think even the existing state of affairs would be preferable to the objectors. I fully realise that there may be difficulties in building semi-detached houses economically though having regard to the 'historic site value' I do not feel very certain about this. Whether some other kind of residential development would meet the objectors is a matter of speculation. For the reasons I have already stated the question of compensation does not arise and the application cannot succeed under subsection (1) (*aa*).

To what extent do these decisions bear out Lord Wilberforce's view that the amendments make 'such a substantial inroad into existing covenants that the whole nature of them is really changed to the detriment of persons now entitled to the benefit of them . . .'?

The Law Commission considered that the Lands Tribunal 'should be directed to consider . . . the development policy for the area. So far as policy matters are concerned, however, the Tribunal being a judicial body, should have regard only to settled policy and should not be involved at all in the formulation of future policy.'[68] Is such a distinction possible? Does sub-section (1B), which invites the Tribunal to 'take into account the development plan' comply with such a distinction? If the development plan is fifteen years old, could the Tribunal take into account proposals contained in a new draft structure or local plan?

Writing about the new section 84 in (1972) *Journal of Planning Law*, 62, almost two years after it had come into force, Mr Newsom had this to say:

> ... I think that there must have been a considerable number of cases in which the new provisions have led to an agreed modification of restrictions in circumstances in which there would have been no modification at all under the old law. Thus, before the amendments, it was very difficult to obtain a modification, and the intending applicant was often advised not to start any proceedings. If he did start, it was a reasonable risk for any person in the neighbourhood to oppose him. There was a very good chance that an opponent might defeat the applicant, even if his own title was dubious, since an applicant was in effect required, in order to succeed, to show that the restriction was obsolete or that no one would be injured by the modification. Nor was there any adequate means, since *Re Purkiss' Application*[69] of challenging the title of an objector. The situation is very different now. First, the title of an objector can be challenged at a preliminary hearing under the new subsection (3A) and, as we shall see, the objectors have all been eliminated at this stage in several cases. Second, it is now possible to obtain a modification by showing broadly that one's project is a reasonable one, that it will not substantially injure anyone, and that if it will do any injury compensation would be an adequate remedy to the person injured. My impression is that there must have been a good many cases in which these rules have enabled an applicant to obtain by negotiation what he has wanted. In *Re Mercian Housing Society Limited's Application* Ref. LP/21/1970, it appears that before the hearing the applicants had made offers of sums of money to certain objectors, who in fact did not accept them. There may well have been a good many cases where such offers have been made and have been accepted. . . .
>
> My provisional conclusion is that, so far as cases have been dealt with by the Lands Tribunal, the new legislation is working satisfactorily. On the other hand it has probably affected development in a good many more cases than have in fact come to anything in the Tribunal. Evidently the loosening of the law has not produced an unmanageable body of litigation. I understand that the Registrar of the Lands Tribunal has developed a small team of specialists in his office to deal with these cases under section 84, so that there is no reason for any substantial interlocutory delays on the part of the Tribunal. . . .

(b) Other controls

Restrictive covenants may be compulsorily acquired by public authorities. They may also be overriden in accordance with section 127 of the Town and Country Planning Act 1971, by a local authority or a person deriving title under them for the purposes of 'the erection, construction or carrying out, or maintenance of any building or work on land which has been acquired or appropriated by a

local authority for planning purposes . . .' Many local authorities
have in addition taken power by local acts to suspend restrictive
covenants. A recent example is contained in the Coventry Corporation Act 1972:

4.—(1) If the Corporation—
(a) acquire land by agreement; or
(b) enter into an agreement to acquire land; or
(c) have acquired land by agreement before the passing of this Act; or
(d) appropriate (whether before or after the passing of this Act) land
which has been previously acquired by agreement;

for a purpose for which they are for the time being or could under any
enactment for the time being in force be authorised to acquire the land
compulsorily and the land is, before such acquisition or agreement to
acquire, affected by any restriction arising under covenant or otherwise
(other than a restriction imposed by any enactment) as to the user
thereof or the building thereon, the council may, subject to the provisions
of this section, by resolution suspend the operation of such restriction.

(4) Any person claiming to be entitled to the benefit of the restriction
may object to the suspension of the restriction by sending notice of his
objection and of the grounds thereof to the appropriate Minister. . . . and
by sending a copy thereof to the Corporation.

(5) If any objection is duly made as aforesaid and is not withdrawn,
the resolution shall be of no effect unless and until it is confirmed by the
appropriate Minister and, before confirming the resolution, the appropriate Minister shall cause a public local inquiry to be held into the proposed suspension of the restriction and, after considering the report of the
person who held the inquiry, may confirm the resolution.

(9) The Corporation shall pay compensation in accordance with the
provisions of section 10 of the Compulsory Purchase Act 1965 in respect
of any entitlement to the benefit of a restriction suspended under the
powers of this section and loss suffered in consequence thereof, and the
amount of such compensation shall be determined in case of dispute in
accordance with the Land Compensation Act 1961.

(10) Any restriction suspended under the powers of this section shall
be unenforceable so long as the Corporation are the owners of the land
to which the restriction relates. . . . and, if compensation is paid by the
Corporation under subsection (9) of this section in respect of the suspension of a restriction relating to the building upon or use of land, that
restriction shall remain unenforceable in respect of such building or use
notwithstanding any subsequent conveyance or disposition of the land to
any other person. . . .

It must however be noted that local authorities cannot claim some
kind of immunity from the effect of restrictive covenants on the
grounds that they are performing public duties or fulfilling public
needs. In *Earl of Leicester* v. *Wells-next-the-Sea UDC*[70], the local

authority had purchased 19 acres of the plaintiff's 32,000-acre Holkham Estate in 1948 for allotments, under the Small Holdings and Allotments Act 1926. They undertook, by restrictive covenant, 'not to use or permit the use of the property' for any other purpose than allotments. Demand for allotments having declined in the 1960s, the local authority decided that the land could be put to better use for housing development. They applied to the Minister of Agriculture for his consent to the appropriation of the land for housing purposes. Consent was given and the land was offered for sale, under section 105 of the Housing Act 1957, for development for privately owned dwellings. The Earl applied to court for an injunction to restrain any sale except on the terms of the sale by him to the local authority in 1948. Among the arguments advanced by counsel for the local authority as to why the injunction should not issue were the following (pp. 89–91):

PLOWMAN J: His fifth point is that the covenant was ultra vires the defendants and he cited authority which undoubtedly establishes that a corporation acts ultra vires if it fetters its right to use land for the purposes for which that land was acquired: see, for example, *Ayr Harbour Trustees* v. *Oswald*,[71] Re *South Eastern Railway Co. and Wiffin's Contract*[72], and Re *Heywood's Conveyance*[73]. But those cases are not, in my judgment, applicable in the present case because the restrictive covenant with which I am concerned, so far from fettering the defendants' use of the land for the purpose for which they bought it, in fact assisted that purpose.

Of more relevance to the present case is *Stourcliffe Estates Co. Ltd.* v. *Bournemouth Corpn.*[74], the headnote to which is as follows:

When a corporation purchases land by agreement for any of the purposes for which it is authorised to acquire land by the Public Health or other public Acts, or by its special local Acts, it is not ultra vires for the corporation to enter into covenants with the vendor restricting the erection of building upon the land purchased which it might erect under other powers given to it for the benefit of the public, provided that such restrictions do not prevent the user of the land for the particular purposes for which it was acquired.

COZENS-HARDY MR: Can it seriously be contended that the corporation cannot accept as a gift, or make a purchase of land for a park subject to any restrictions of any sort or kind, such as, to give one which is a very reasonable and very common one, that no intoxicating liquors shall be sold on part of it? Of course, if (counsel for the Corporation's) argument is right, such a condition would be impossible. But, further, if they have taken this conveyance of this land in terms subject to these restrictive covenants, can they hold it free from those restrictions? That again is a proposition which seems to me to be startling. If the deed is wholly ultra vires I can understand it, but to suppose that the corporation could be allowed to retain the land and to repudiate the consideration or part of the consideration for it is a proposition to which certainly I could not give my adhesion.

Those observations seem to me to be applicable to the present case and I therefore reject counsel for the defendants' fifth submission.

His sixth and last submission was that this is not a case in which the court in the exercise of its discretion should grant any injunction. He submitted that this was a conflict between private right and public need and that public need should prevail. In my judgment, however, the judicial discretion, which I accept that I have, ought to be exercised in favour of granting an injunction. I see no reason why the defendants should not be held to the bargain into which they freely entered, and I propose to grant an injunction accordingly.

The form of injunction will need care and must be framed in such a way as not to prevent the defendants from developing the land for housing pursuant to any other statutory powers which may be or become available to them. For example, the possibility of operating s.84 of the Law of Property Act 1925, or s.127 of the Town and Country Planning Act 1971 was referred to during the hearing.

Why did the local authority not proceed under either section 84 of the Law of Property Act 1925–69, or section 127 of the Town and Country Planning Act 1971 in the first place? The court accepted the argument of the plaintiff, supported by a wealth of detail in an affidavit from the estate's managing agent, that 'the covenant afforded and continues to afford great benefit and much needed protection to the Holkham Estate as a whole, as well as to the particular parts of that estate adjacent to the allotment land.' Do you find that credible?

Another general provision is contained in section 165 of the Housing Act 1957. The Law Commission[75] appeared to consider that this section was still relevant, as does Newsom.[76] In what circumstances might it be advantageous to use this section as opposed to section 84 of the Law of Property Act 1925–69?

Housing Act 1957

165. Where the local authority or any person interested in a house applies to the county court and—

(a) it is proved to the satisfaction of the court that, owing to changes in the character of the neighbourhood in which the house is situated, the house cannot readily be let as a single tenement but could readily be let for occupation if converted into two or more tenements; or

(b) planning permission has been granted under Part III of the Town and Country Planning Act, 1947, for the use of the house as converted into two or more separate dwelling-houses instead of as a single dwelling-house.

and it is proved to the satisfaction of the court that by reason of the provisions of the lease of or any restrictive covenant affecting the house, or otherwise, such conversion is prohibited or restricted, the court, after giving any person interested an opportunity of being heard, may vary the terms of the lease or other instrument imposing the prohibition or restriction so as to enable the house to be so converted subject to such conditions and upon such terms as the court may think just.

Alliance Economic Investment Co Ltd v. Berton (1923)
21 L.G.R. 403

The plaintiffs were the assignees of a lease of a house in College Road, Dulwich on the Dulwich College Estate. The lease contained a provision that the lessees should not without the lessor's prior consent use the house for any purpose other than that of 'a private dwelling house'. The defendant was one of the lessors.

The plaintiffs claimed that owing to changes in the neighbourhood, the house could not readily be let as a single tenement. They therefore applied to the county court pursuant to sec. 27 of the Housing, Town Planning etc. Act (the forerunner of sec. 165) for an order varying the terms of the lease.

BANKES LJ: ... The section makes two points clear. First, that the onus of proof is upon the applicant; secondly, that the difficulty in letting as a single tenement must be proved to be owing to changes in the character of the neighbourhood. It is in these last words that the difficulty lies. What constitutes a change of character, of what does a neighbourhood consist? It is easy to say, as was said, by Sir Arthur Wilson in *Mayor of Wellington* v. *Mayor of Lower Hutt*[77], that the question is entirely one of circumstances. That does not assist one in arriving at a conclusion as to what it is permissible to take into account in any particular case in arriving at what constitutes a change of character, or what area is comprised within a neighbourhood. It is easier to indicate what it is not permissible to take into account than to define the limits of what is permissible. For instance, changes in a neighbourhood must not be taken into account unless they are changes which have affected the character of the neighbourhood. Great changes may have taken place in the mode of life of all the inhabitants of a neighbourhood owing to heavy taxation and loss of income. Carriages and motor cars may have had to be given up, women servants substituted for men servants, all entertaining abolished, and though the inhabitants have entirely changed their mode of life, they continue to occupy the same houses, and I do not think that such a change as

I have indicated constitutes a change of character of the neighbourhood within the meaning of the section.

Again, I think that it is quite possible that in a neighbourhood consisting of large houses the bulk of the houses may be converted into high-class flats without altering the character of the neighbourhood. The class of people who occupy the flats may not differ sufficiently from the class who had previously occupied the houses as to justify any finding that the character of the neighbourhood had changed. I gather from the judgment of the learned County Court Judge that such an alteration as I have last suggested would not, in his opinion, affect the amenities of a neighbourhood.

I pass now to consider what is indicated by the expression 'neighbourhood'. In this connection it is impossible to lay down any general rule. In country districts people are said to be neighbours, that is, to live in the same neighbourhood, who live many miles apart. The same cannot be said of dwellers in a town where a single street or a single square may constitute a neighbourhood within the meaning of the section. Again, physical conditions may determine the boundary or boundaries of a neighbourhood, as, for instance, a range of hills, a river, a railway, or the line which separates a high-class residential district from a district consisting only of artisans' or workmens' dwellings. Again, I think that the physical conditions of some particular area may entitle it to be considered as a matter of law as a neighbourhood within the meaning of the section. The circumstances must be exceptional, but I think that they may exist. . . .

It appears to have been contended below that it was not open to the learned Judge to take into consideration any changes which may have occurred in the surrounding districts. I do not think that such a contention can possibly be supported. It seems obvious that changes occurring outside a neighbourhood may materially affect the character of the neighbourhood. For instance, a neighbourhood in a country district may become so surrounded by working-class dwellings, factories, tram lines or omnibus routes as to drive all the inhabitants out of the neighbourhood and to render it uninhabitable by the class of persons who formerly inhabited it. If this occurs, the area of the neighbourhood in question may not have been increased by an acre, but a great change may have taken place in the character of the neighbourhood owing to an outside cause or causes. On the other hand, if, in spite of all outside changes, the same people or the same class of people are prepared to occupy the houses in the neighbourhood because of its special physical conditions but are not prepared, because of the general fall in incomes, to pay the same rents for the houses as were formerly paid, I doubt whether it could be said that there had been any change in the character of the neighbourhood within the meaning of the section. . . .

SCRUTTON L J: . . . On the section itself, the word 'neighbourhood' is vague, probably intentionally so, but I agree with the view taken by SALTER J, that if the changes of character of one locality does in fact affect the letting qualities of houses in another and adjacent locality, both may be included in the term 'neighbourhood.' An attractive and secluded private estate may be deteriorated in letting value by a change of character of the surrounding country, which may be considered the 'neighbourhood', from fields to working-class dwellings, and it will be useless to urge that the private estate remains in itself, as it was, inhabited by the same class of people, if in fact the change in surrounding character has rendered it harder to let the estate houses as a whole than in flats.

A more difficult expression to construe is 'change of character.' For instance, does a locality 'change its character' because it is difficult to get servants all over England, and, therefore, people of the class inhabiting it desire to live in flats and small houses rather than large ones? This cause would, undoubtedly, render flats more lettable than whole houses. Does a locality change its character because all its inhabitants are poorer, and therefore, reduce their standard of living in housing accommodation, which again would affect the comparative letting value of whole houses and flats? Must the cause of the change of character be one peculiar to the locality; or will a general cause affecting all localities suffice? . . .

Whoever tries it* has to answer these questions:—

1. Is the house not readily lettable as a single tenement? If No,
2. Is it readily lettable converted into two or more tenements? If Yes,
3. Is the above result (1 and 2) due to changes in the character of the neighbourhood, finding what exactly is the neighbourhood he considers, and what are the changes in its character?

*A retrial was ordered.

Finally, the question of racial restrictive covenants may be raised, as an illustration both of the role of public policy and of attempts to deal with specific types of covenants by statute. The little known Kenyan case of *Commissioner for Local Government etc.* v. *Kaderbhai* may be thought somewhat dated but its presence reminds us that there is judicial precedent for such covenants and for deliberately ignoring their public policy implications. The Canadian case of *Noble and Wolf* v. *Alley* is an alternative and more recent Commonwealth precedent. Given the existence of section 5 of the Race Relations Act 1968, what must be considered here is which way would the English courts go if a racial restrictive covenant came before them, and why?

Commissioner for Local Government, Lands and Settlement
v. *Kaderbhai* [1931] A. C. 652 P.C.

LORD ATKIN: This is an appeal from an order of the Court of Appeal for Eastern Africa, varying an order of the Supreme Court of Kenya, which dismissed a motion by the applicant Abdulhusein Kaderbhai for a mandamus addressed to the appellant, the Commissioner for Local Government Lands and Settlement in Kenya.

The Commissioner had given notice of an auction sale of town plots at Mombasa at which Europeans only were to be allowed to bid and purchase. The notice contained the further special condition that during the term of the grant the grantee should not permit the dwelling-house or outbuildings which had to be erected upon it to be used as a place of residence for any Asiatic or African not a domestic servant employed by him. The applicant, who is an Indian subject of His Majesty resident in Mombasa, on August 10, 1928, by notice of motion dated August 9, moved the Court for a mandamus commanding the Commissioner to allow the applicant to bid for and purchase at the auction sale of the plots on Mombasa Island, notified to be held on August 11, and also commanding the respondent to cancel or annul the condition No. 5 of the special conditions, being the condition above referred to, restricting the use of the dwelling-house. . . .

The disposal of Crown lands in Kenya is regulated by the Crown Lands Ordinance, No. 12 of 1915. The case made by the applicant is that under the provisions of the ordinance the Commissioner is bound to permit all members of the public or, alternatively, all subjects of the Crown to bid and purchase at an auction of town plots, and is equally bound not to insert in the lease of any such plots restrictive conditions adversely affecting the Asiatic or African population of Kenya, at any rate, to such an extent as to make a purchase by them of no practical value. The case of the Commissioner is that the terms of the ordinance do not prevent him from imposing the restrictions of which complaint is made. It is desirable to point out that the Courts are concerned only with the bare question of law – namely, the powers of the Commissioner under the ordinance. Questions of policy, or, in other words, how the legal powers shall be exercised, are not matters for the legal tribunal, but have to be determined by the appropriate constitutional authority. Approaching thus the construction of the ordinance it is found that it is divided into twelve parts.

Part III. is headed Disposal of land within township (I.) offering of town plots:—

15. The Commissioner of Lands may cause any portion of a township which is not required for public purposes to be divided into plots suitable for the erection of buildings for business or residential purposes, and such plots may from time to time be disposed of in the manner hereinafter prescribed.

16. Leases of town plots may be granted for any term not exceeding ninety-nine years.

17. Before any town plot is disposed of under the next succeeding section the Commissioner of Lands shall determine: (a) The rent which shall be payable in respect of such plot; (b) the upset price at which the lease of such plot will be sold; (c) the building conditions to be inserted in the lease of the plot; and (d) the special covenants, if any, which shall be inserted in the lease.

18. Leases of town plots shall, unless the Governor shall otherwise order, in any particular case or cases, be sold by auction. . . .

The contention of the applicant which has found favour with the Court of Appeal is that the provision in s. 18 that leases of town plots shall be sold by auction involves that, in the absence of express and unequivocal words, the sale cannot be restricted to a particular section of the community. SHERIDAN A C J thought that the ordinance itself indicated that no restriction was to be placed on the bidding. He referred to the absence in s. 19 of any requirement that notice should be given of such a restriction as compared with s. 27 (c) relating to the notice in sales of agricultural land, and attached importance to the words of s. 20: 'all persons bidding at the sale.' GUTHRIE-SMITH ACJ thought that the Commissioner would be violating his duty as a trustee for the Government by restricting the class of purchasers. He thought that such a limitation tended to reduce the price, since it cut out a class of potential bidders. MUIR MACKENZIE J considered that on a comparison of the sections regulating the sale of town plots with the sections regulating the sales of agricultural land, as there was a mandatory provision in s. 27 (c), that the Commissioner should state whether persons other than Europeans will be allowed to bid and no such provision in s. 17, it must be taken that express power to restrict was given as to agricultural land and was not given as to town plots.

After careful consideration of the judgments in the Court of Appeal their Lordships find themselves unable to agree with the decision. Prima facie the Crown and the servants of the Crown, exercising the right of disposing of Crown property, have at least the rights of private owners of making the disposition in any way that appears to them to be best in the interests of the Crown. The servants of the Crown, if given disposing power by statute, must comply with the terms of the statute, but within those terms their duty is to act honestly in what they conceive to be the ultimate interests of the Crown or of the public. In such disposition, unless it is expressly given by statute, there does not exist, and never has existed, any legal right of any particular member of the public to take part. Sales or leases, if permitted to be by private treaty, are regulated by the duty which the servant of the Crown owes to his superior, but owes to no individual member of the public. If the statutory duty of the Crown servant is to sell by auction, that duty must, no doubt, be observed. Their Lordships would agree that such a duty imposed by statute would ordinarily involve a duty to sell by public auction; but if there is no further express provision there would seem to be no reason for further limiting the discretion of the officer as to the terms and conditions of the public auction which he shall decide to hold. If there can be restriction of user there seems no objection to limiting the bidders to those capable of the restricted user. If plots are reserved for dwellings for the industrial classes, it might well be expedient to restrict bidding to members of that class. In the very case in question bidding is to be limited, apparently without objection, to persons who have not already purchased a plot, and if to them why not, if thought desirable, to persons who had not already purchased a similar plot at a previous sale? Township plots include land for commercial purposes, and there would appear to be no reason why in appropriate cases the user should not be restricted to the building of wharves, warehouses or factories, or why the bidding should not reasonably be restricted to approved intending wharfingers, warehousemen or factory owners. If the words, 'sell by auction', therefore, stood alone, there seems to their Lordships no reason why there should not be imposed a restriction as to the bidders. If any restriction be allowed the question whether the restriction should be based on racial distinctions is obviously not one of law, but of policy. Their Lordships cannot entertain the view that to restrict bidding is necessarily to sell at a disadvantage. In respect of residential plots in particular the very opposite result may be attained.

But in the present case the words of the ordinance construed as a whole appear to indicate that the words 'sell by auction' in s. 18 are not confined to selling without restriction, but do involve the power to sell by restricted auction. Their Lordships' examination of the clause relating to the sale of agricultural land leads them to the opposite inference to that formed on the same clauses by the Court of Appeal. The only disposing power given under either part is by ss. 18 and 26. The leases are to be sold by auction. The empowering words are identical. Prima facie, they should convey the same power. But the nature of the power in respect of agricultural lands can be discovered from the provisions of s. 27 as to notice, and from s. 27 (c) it is obvious that the Legislature contemplated that in the sale of which notice must be given, there was to be a power of restriction. If therefore power to sell by auction in s. 26 gives a power of restricted auction what reason is there for assuming that the same words in s. 18 give a different power? With great respect to those who have expressed a contrary opinion, the fallacy is in assuming that a clause as to notice has anything to do with granting or limiting a power of disposition which has to be found independently. The value of the notice clause is to call attention to the powers which are assumed to be given, and which can only be given, in the identical terms of ss. 18 and 26. . . .

If, as their Lordships have indicated, the Commissioner had the power to impose the general restriction as to bidding, it was not contended by counsel for the applicant that objection could be made to the restrictive condition as to user. Their Lordships entertain no doubt that the objection on this head fails.

Noble & Wolf v. *Alley* [1951] 1 D.L.R. 321

Appeal from a judgement of the Ontario Court of Appeal affirming a High Court judgement on a vendor's and purchaser's motion that a certain racial restrictive covenant was valid and enforceable.

The judgment of KERWIN and TASCHEREAU JJ was delivered by KERWIN J: This land had been purchased in 1933 by Mrs. Noble from the Frank S. Salter Co. Ltd., and in the deed from it to her appeared the following covenant:

And the Grantee for himself, his heirs, executors, administrators and assigns, covenants and agrees with the Grantor that he will carry out, comply with and observe, with the intent that they shall run with the lands and shall be binding upon himself, his heirs, executors, administrators and assigns, and shall be for the benefit of and enforcible by the Grantor and/or any other person or persons seized or possessed of any part or parts of the lands included in Beach O'Pines Development, the restrictions herein following, which said restrictions shall remain in full force and effect until the first day of August, 1962, and the Grantee for himself, his heirs, executors, administrators and assigns further covenants and agrees with the Grantor that he will exact the same covenants with respect to the said restrictions from any and all persons to whom he may in any manner whatsoever dispose of the said lands. . . .

(f) The lands and premises herein described shall never be sold, assigned, transferred, leased, rented, or in any manner whatsoever alienated to, and shall never be occupied or used in any manner whatsoever by any person of the Jewish, Hebrew, Semitic, Negro or coloured race or blood, it being the intention and purpose of the Grantor, to restrict the ownership, use, occupation and enjoyment of the said recreational development, including the lands and premises herein described, to persons of the white or Caucasian race not excluded by this clause.

Although the deed was not signed by Mrs. Noble, I assume that she is bound to the same extent as if she had executed it.

Each conveyance by the company to a purchaser of land in the development contained a covenant in the same form. . . .

Whatever the precise delimitation in the rule in *Tulk* v. *Moxhay* may be, counsel were unable to refer us to any case where it was applied to a covenant restricting the alienation of land to persons other than those of a certain race. Mr. Denison did refer to three decisions in Ontario: *Essex Real Estate Co.* v. *Holmes*[78]; *Re Bryers & Morris*[79]; *Re McDougall & Waddell*[80], but he was quite correct in stating that they were of no assistance. The holding in the first was merely that the purchaser of the land there in question did not fall within a certain prohibition. In the second an inquiry was directed, without more. In the third, all that was decided was that the provisions of s. 1 of the *Racial Discrimination Act*, 1944 (Ont.), c. 51, would not be violated by a deed containing a covenant on the part of the purchaser that certain lands or any buildings erected thereon should not at any time be sold to, let to or occupied by any person or persons other than Gentiles (non-semitic (*sic*)) of European or British or Irish or Scottish racial origin.

It was a forward step that the rigour of the common law should be softened by the doctrine expounded in *Tulk* v. *Moxhay* but it would be an unwarrantable extension of that doctrine to hold, from anything that was said in that case or in subsequent cases, that the covenant here in question has any reference to the use, or abstension from use, of land. Even if decisions upon the common law could be prayed in aid, there are none that go to the extent claimed in the present case.

The appeal should be allowed. . . .

The judgment of RAND, KELLOCK and FAUTEUX JJ was delivered by RAND J: Covenants enforceable under the rule of *Tulk* v. *Moxhay* are properly conceived as running with the land in equity and, by reason of their enforceability, as constituting an equitable servitude or burden on the servient land. The essence of such an incident is that it should touch or concern the land as contradistinguished from a collateral effect. In that sense, it is a relation between parcels, annexed to them and, subject to the equitable rule of notice, passing with them both as to benefit and burden in transmissions by operation of law as well as by act of the parties.

But by its language, the covenant here is directed not to the land or to some mode of its use, but to transfer by act of the purchaser; its scope does not purport to extend to a transmission by law to a person within the banned class. If, for instance, the grantee married a member of that class, it is not suggested that the ordinary inheritance by a child of the union would be affected. Not only, then, is it not a covenant touching or concerning the land, but by its own terms it fails in annexation to the land. The respondent owners are, therefore, without any right against the proposed vendor.

On its true interpretation, the covenant is a restraint on alienation. . . .

The effect of the covenant, if enforceable, would be to annex a partial inalienability as an equitable incident of the ownership, to nullify an area of proprietary powers. . . .

I would, therefore, allow the appeal. . . .

Estey J delivered a separate concurring judgement. Locke J dissented on the ground that the point before the Supreme Court had not been considered by the lower courts and should not therefore be considered by the Supreme Court. *Appeal allowed.*

House of Commons Standing Committee B:
Debate on the Committee stage of the Race Relations
Bill 1965; session 1964–5; vol. 1, cols 389–92

New Clause 6. – (Discriminatory restrictions on the transfer of interests in land.)

For the avoidance of doubt, it is hereby declared and enacted that any covenant, agreement or stipulation in or collateral to or in contemplation of any conveyance, disposition or transfer of any interest in land (whether the same be effected before or after the passing of this Act) shall be void in so far as it purports to prohibit or restrict the conveyance, disposition, grant or transfer of any interest in land to any person or persons by reference to colour, race or ethnic or national origins. – [*Mr. Chapman.*]

Brought up, and read the First time

MR. CHAPMAN: I beg to move, That the Clause be read a Second time. I can be brief about this new Clause. It is worded in this way because there is a good deal of evidence that, although discriminatory restrictions on the transfer of interests in land are void under common law, the position is not clear. It hangs, partly on the vagueness of the restriction which a person tries to write into the documents concerned – conveyances, agreements, and so on. The new Clause is intended to avoid doubt. It has no effect other than declaring what a large part of the law is understood to be anyway. It merely tries to make it explicit.

The main reason for the new Clause is to parallel Clause 2 of the Bill which outlaws discrimination in the transfer of tenancies. The new Clause does much the same thing with regard to the transfer of freehold property. It makes unlawful any covenants, agreements or stipulations which try to practise discrimination in the transfer of freeholds. This is on the lines of emphasising and making declaratory which is largely understood to be the position under the common law. It has a wider effect which makes it absolutely clear that we are condemning this kind of thing as well as simply repeating what we understand the law mainly to be. I think that it has a propaganda effect which is useful in terms of this kind of Bill. This is fairly simple, and I hope that the Committee will feel that it is worth while to add this to the kind of discrimination which we want the Bill to outlaw.

SIR F. SOSKICE[81]: My hon. Friend the Member for Birmingham, Northfield (Mr. Chapman) has not responded to the hon. Member's appeal. I would agree with the hon. Member for Birmingham, Selly Oak (Mr. Gurden) that propaganda enactments are not a common feature of our Legislative system, and they are not altogether to be encouraged. I can see what my hon. Friend means, but I do not feel that I can advise the Committee to accept the new Clause. One has to consider how far it goes and what its implications are. As hon. Members know, covenants binding land either run with the land or do not. They either bind successive owners of the interest in the land or they do not. A covenant restraining a freeholder, a purchaser, from alienating his freehold in favour of a coloured person would undoubtedly not be a covenant which ran with the land. It would be a covenant which bound nobody except the purchaser. It would operate in law simply as a covenant between the vendor of the freehold interest in the land and the purchaser of that interest. It would have no binding effect on anybody to whom the purchaser sold the land.

Therefore, a covenant of this sort would have the most limited operation. Anybody could get out of it if they wanted to by selling the land to anybody else, who could then sell it to a coloured person. A covenant of that sort, even if enforceable in law as a covenant which does not offend against the principles of uncertainty or public policy, is one which can be only of the most limited application, because it would operate only as a contract between the vendor and the purchaser. I am very anxious, in those circumstances, to advise the Committee to see that the Bill – within what is sometimes called its limited scope – is at least effective within that scope. I cannot think that the sort of covenants which my hon. Friend has in mind – bearing in mind their limited application and

inherent limited enforceability – are a sufficient mischief to make it justifiable to insert into the Bill a special provision dealing with the disposal
of freehold interests in land.

As I have said before, basically the Bill deals with public order. . . .
The covenants binding freeholds in land, although no doubt they exist,
are of such limited application and are so easy to evade that I hope that
my hon. Friend will accept from me that if one is trying to define clearly
what the Bill does, it is not enough simply to put in another Clause
dealing with a comparatively minor mischief and leaving out a number of
areas where the mischief is far more serious and which we have also left
out for reasons which I hope have commended themselves to the Committee. For these reasons, I hope that he will not wish to press the new
Clause.

The clause was not put to the vote and no such provision was put
into the Race Relations Act 1965.

Race Relations Act 1968, s. 5

It shall be unlawful for any person having power to dispose, or being
otherwise concerned with the disposal, of housing accommodation, business premises or other land to discriminate,

(a) Against any person seeking to acquire any such accommodation,
premises or other land by refusing or deliberately omitting to dispose of it
to him. . . .

Would this section render racial restrictive covenants illegal? See
Garner (1972) 32 M.L.R. 478.

Property Law Act 1952 as amended by the
Property Law Amendment Act 1965 (N.Z.) s. 33A

(1) Any provision in or in connection with any disposition of property
(whether oral or in writing) made after the commencement of this section shall be void to the extent that its effect would be to prohibit or
restrict the transfer, assignment, letting, sub-letting, charging, or parting
with the possession of the property or any part thereof, by any party to
the disposition or his successor in title, to any person by reason only of
the colour, race or ethnic or national origins of that person or of any
member of his family.

(2) For the purposes of this section, the term 'disposition' means—
    (a)   A sale, lease or letting, sub-lease or sub-letting, or licence; or
    (b)   A mortgage; or
    (c)   An agreement for any such disposition as aforesaid.
(3) This section shall bind the Crown.

The Conveyancing and Law of Property Act RSO 1970,
c. 85 s. 22

Every covenant made after the 24th day of March 1950 that but for this
section would be annexed to and run with land and that restricts the

sale, ownership, occupation or use of land because of the race, creed, colour, nationality, ancestry or place of origin of any person is void and of no effect.

6. The long lease

(a) General

Long before restrictive covenants on the freehold made their appearance, long leases or building leases were a recognised private law technique for the control of land use. Leasehold tenure of large estates still exists at the present and many of the social and political issues surrounding this form of control came to a head in the debate on the Leasehold Reform Bill in 1967, which introduced far-reaching changes into the law and thus the management of the estates. It is these issues that are the subject of this section of the chapter, which opens with some background – factual and legal – material on the estates.

Some of the most desirable real estate in the country is held on long leases, the ground landlord being either a famous family, or a company owned by such a family, or trustees acting on behalf of such a family. A few examples may be given. In London much of Oxford Street and the property behind it, up to and including Grosvenor Square, much of Belgravia and Pimlico, is owned by the Duke of Westminster and administered on his behalf by the Trustees of the Grosvenor Estate. An extensive amount of Chelsea is held on long leases from the Cadogan Estate, administered by a company in which the Earl of Cadogan and his son, the Viscount Chelsea, have considerable interests. Parts of Hampstead are owned by Eton College, a charitable foundation. In Birmingham there are two major residential estates in what would generally be regarded as, or very near to, the centre of the city, both of them primarily of low density and regarded therefore as highly desirable: the Calthorpe Estate which owns the Edgbaston area, and the Bournville Village Trust, an offshoot of Cadbury's, which owns the Bournville Estate.

What follows is based principally on my investigation of these two latter estates.[82] The general issues apply, it is suggested, to all these leasehold estates. Three topics may be discussed (the last of which broadens out into a consideration of the Leasehold Reform Act): the amount and nature of day-to-day control of lessees by the ground landlord; development, redevelopment and relations with the local planning authorities; and finally reactions to, and developments after, the Leasehold Reform Act 1967.

(b) Control by the ground landlord

All the major estates are run by professional agents – usually chartered surveyors – and employ a wide variety of personnel. At
Bournville for instance – an estate containing 6,000 houses, on
approximately 1,000 acres of land, including open spaces, clinics,
schools, etc. – there is a staff of around fifty which includes an estate
architect and a building and maintenance department. The majority
of the houses at both Bournville and Edgbaston are leased on 99-
year leases, but a small number at the former estate are leased on
999-year leases or let on a weekly tenancy. The Bournville Trustees
have put forward their case for their control of the lessees as follows:

The Bournville Village Trust (Birmingham 1956), Chapter 12

... It has always been among the principal objects of the Trustees that
the Estate should be developed harmoniously, that due regard should be
paid to existing features, that there should be architectural good manners,
and that the effect should not be spoiled by untidy sheds, ugly extensions,
or strident advertisements. To some extent this control is now in the hands
of Local Authorities through the 1947 Town and Country Planning Act,
but it seems doubtful whether the busy Planning Officer has the time for
the detailed administration required.

In evidence before the Government's Leasehold Committee[83], which
published its Report in 1950, the Trustees stated:

The peculiar value of leasehold control is that it continues after development has taken place; it permits therefore, not only positive and
flexible planning control in new development but can, to a large extent, be
used to protect the developed area and its users from deteriorative tendencies and misuse. This protection is afforded to individual users of land
as well as to the community at large. The chief limiting factor appears
to be that of size. Unless the area controlled is large enough for deterioration in the property round it to have little effect on the major part of the
estate, it may be that the deterioration taking place in the district, as a
whole, will affect even a well-planned and carefully-managed leasehold
estate. It can be said that the present developed area of Bournville
(650 acres) appears to be amply large enough to afford this sort of
protection.

Practical experience indicates fairly clearly that there is no way of
securing the same ends by other methods. Covenants agreed at the transfer of freehold very rarely stand up against much subsequent pressure
from the occupant. At the other end of the scale, retention of all interest
in the property by the landlord such as occurs under the terms of rented
houses throws a heavy burden on the landlord; where estates such as
those now required by local authorities are concerned, it must make for

rigid, inflexible planning and estate development; the responsibility for maintaining the value and amenities of the estate, a responsibility by no means wholly limited to finance, is thrown upon the landlord. The value of the leasehold system appears to lie in the continuing relationship which it involves. The payment of ground rent provides a substantial basis for this continuing relationship. The financial interest of the ground landlord is, in the long run, clearly on the side of maintaining the estate in good condition. The right, for the duration of the lease, of entry and possession normally accorded to the lessor in the case of non-compliance with certain conditions of the lease is a particularly effective sanction. To a large extent, the ground landlord represents the interest and views of the body of lessees *vis-à-vis* the individual lessee. Under leasehold control of the sort exercised at Bournville, each household is assured not only of a fairly high standard of estate maintenance, but of a fairly high standard of maintenance in the houses and gardens of the neighbourhood. He is protected, for the duration of his lease, from undesirable development on neighbouring properties. Indeed, these considerations are the main strength of the Trust's case when, as ground landlord, it insists on the stricter observance of covenants by individual lessees.

It is important that the sort of control implied in the relation between ground landlord and lessees on a large estate should be recognised as being very different from the controls now enforceable by local planning authorities.

What are the covenants in the leases that 'protect the developed area and its users from deteriorative tendencies and misuse?' First of all, the negative or restrictive covenants. Lessees may not lop or fell trees on their land without previous written consent. They may not erect any building or other structure of a permanent or temporary nature on the land without the written permission of the landlord. This includes the erection of TV and radio aerials in respect of both of which permission is rarely given. There may not be placed on the land any caravan, boat, trailer, placard, notice, nor anything which may be regarded by the landlord as an eyesore or detrimental in any way to the amenities, aspect or outlook of the neighbourhood. No alterations may be made to the houses, in particular to their elevations. The houses are to be used only as single family dwellings, no multiple occupancy is allowed and no profession or business may be carried on from the premises.

Secondly, positive covenants. Lessees are under an obligation to repair, maintain and where necessary replace walls or fences along the boundaries of their property. They must keep the hedges in good trim, put and maintain the gardens and grounds of their property in good order and repair, and endeavour to preserve free from disease all timber trees and other trees on the property. They must paint, repair and keep in good tenantable order and repair both the exterior and the internal structural parts of the dwelling house, and inevitably they must let the landlord and his agents onto their property. These conditions and covenants are fairly typical of residential estates; the only significant difference in the Calthorpe Estate leases, for instance, being a reservation of full ownership of all trees on the estate in the landlord, with rights of entry on to the lessee's land to look after them. Another common difference is the reservation to the estate of the obligation to repair and paint the exterior of the houses.

These covenants add up to an extensive measure of control and it is of some importance therefore to examine how and to what extent they are enforced, and how breaches are discovered. First, as to discovery of breaches, these come to light, either through inspections by employees of the estates, or through complaints from individual residents or through complaints from residents' associations. Second, as to enforcement. Up to the time when I investigated the management of the Bournville Estate, it had never found it necessary to go to court to enforce a covenant since the creation of the estate in 1900. It estimated that it had between an 80–90 per cent success ratio in enforcement by the writing of letters to the lessee concerned and discussing the matter with him or her. It was admitted that there had been and were 'awkward customers' who were reluctant to comply with the covenants and that some lessees had sold up and left over the years because they did not like the paternalistic control that was exercised over them.

It was also admitted that some covenants were more rigidly enforced than others (trailers, boats and caravans were very severely discouraged as well as TV aerials). On the other hand, 'lessees are given freedom to paint their houses in odd colours', despite the covenant against doing anything detrimental to the amenities (local residents' associations are relied upon to moderate too idiosyncratic a colour scheme). Other estates too adopt a policy of selective enforcement of covenants – the Calthorpe Estate, for instance, vigorously enforces its zoning covenants.[84] One area of this estate has become a centre of professional offices and chambers; this is accepted and non-residential uses elsewhere are pressured into closing or moving to this professional area. The estate also enforces the covenant against the hanging-out of washing on Sundays.

The public inquiries into the management of the Bournville and Calthorpe Estates, which took place as a result of the Leasehold Reform Act, reported that the willingness to enforce the covenants in the leases and the kind of covenants there were had had a material effect on the maintenance of the estates as good-quality, low-density, garden-type suburbs. Whether this is regarded as a commendation for the estates rather depends on what the aims of the estates are, and what effect if any the maintenance of those aims has had on the surrounding urban areas. This in turn involves a consideration of relations between the estates and the local planning authorities.

(c) Development and planning of estates

The Bournville Village Trust is a charity founded in 1900 by Cadbury with the aim of showing that good housing conditions could be provided for members of the working classes on an economic basis. As such it may be regarded as part of the garden-city movement, for the Trustees were empowered also to provide sites for schools, churches and museums. These original aims have been slowly changed: 'Over a period of nearly 70 years since its foundation the aims of the Trustees have evolved so that they are now attempting to produce a balanced community containing a wide variety of different income groups and providing proper communal facilities.'[85] What this means in practice is that while some of the older residents and houses may be working class, and some again let on weekly tenancies at a low rent, the more modern houses and developments are clearly and deliberately designed for the professional middle classes. The local planning authority has raised no objection to this; indeed it is doubtful whether it could. What is to happen when the early leases begin to fall in, in about twenty years' time? Will the concept of a 'balanced community' survive or will the aims of the Trustees have evolved further to the position of the Calthorpe Estate, which is avowedly to create and maintain an area of low-density, high-quality housing to attract the upper income and social groups of Birmingham – the community leaders – to live in central Birmingham rather than commute from Four Oaks, Sutton Coldfield, Solihull or further afield?

These questions are raised, not so as to cast doubts on the *bona fides* of the Trustees and managers of the estates, but in order to bring out the fact that the policies of these large residential estates greatly affect the living conditions of people, both now and in the future, both on and off the estate, and the social conditions of the town or city. They are, in short, as influential as many local planning authorities are without being accountable to the electorate or a wider constituency than their own residents and consciences. In these circumstances, the role of the local planning authorities is crucial. How do they exert control over the estates?

On the basis of my investigations – and I must stress that they do not cover all the major estates – I would say that relations between them and the planning authorities were close and marked by a willingness on the part of the planning authorities to fit in with the plans of the estates. The story of the Calthorpe Estate Development Plan may be taken to illustrate this conclusion.[86] The Birmingham Development Plan of 1952 showed an inner density zone of between 90–144 habitable rooms per acre and an outer density zone of 60 habitable rooms per acre (a special exception was however made for the Calthorpe Estate, classified as an outer density zone by the city corporation: its density was to be 36 habitable rooms per acre). The estate then appointed an architect to draw up an Estate Develop- ment Plan working within the framework of the Birmingham De- velopment Plan. The plan produced an ingenious tripartite approach to the problem of density. The estate was divided into three zones: a thin, outer, high-density zone of up to 100 habitable rooms per acre to be developed in the form of high-rise blocks of council flats; a slightly thicker, medium-density zone of between 40–60 habitable rooms per acre to be developed principally as three- to six-storey blocks of private flats; and the largest zone of all, consisting of well over half the estate, low-density at between 18–20 habitable rooms per acre. The whole complied with the Birmingham require- ment of 36 habitable rooms per acre; the core of the estate was preserved, as it had always been; and the outer zone merged with the surrounding high-density council developments. The plan was accepted by Birmingham in 1958 and has been acted on since then.

What should one's attitude be to these facts? Should one commend the estate and the corporation for these subtle and far-sighted plans and decisions, which made a contribution to the city's need both for housing land and its need to retain good-quality housing and open space in the inner city? What other cities manage to achieve that? Or should one, on the other hand, criticise both parties for putting the interests of a small minority (to which both parties belonged)[87] before those of a much larger body of inner-city residents, both on and off the estate, who could have been accommodated at a lower density than 100-plus habitable rooms per acre but instead find themselves either in tower blocks in the inner city or in estates like Chelmsley Wood on its outskirts?

On a more fundamental issue, do these and other facts recounted here cause one to feel that the power of the estates and their managers over their lessees and beyond are too great, and cannot be justified in our modern society where political democracy goes hand in hand with great housing shortages? Should such detailed private planning and control over people's use of their land co-exist alongside public planning? If, as the Bournville Trustees have said, 'it seems doubtful whether the busy planning officer has the time for the detailed administration required' of an estate, might this not be an indication that, except in special circumstances – e.g. the conservation of historic areas and buildings – detailed administration of land use is neither necessary nor desirable? To put the other point of view, is it not accepted that the private ownership of land and houses is a sure way to maintain and preserve them? At a time when so much attention is being given to conservation and improvement as opposed to clearance and redevelopment, is it not sound policy to rely on and encourage the large, major landowners to exercise their powers to the full to maintain the quality of their estates? Public planning is designed to supplement and build on private planning, not to replace it.

Arguments such as these have long existed in relation to the major estates, but they came to a head in connection with the Leasehold Reform Act 1967 and the estates' reactions to it. It is to this matter therefore that we must now turn.

(d) The Leasehold Reform Act and its aftermath

At common law, when a 99-year lease came to an end the land and the building thereon reverted to the ground landlord, irrespective of whether he had put up the building in the first place. The landlord then had the option of renewing the lease – at a higher ground rent – or redeveloping the site. If, as was usually the case, several leases were timed to fall in together, the landlord would obtain a large area which he could redevelop as one, thus ensuring both orderly and comprehensive development and updating the land uses of his estate. The problem with this common law approach was the position of the lessee: whether he wanted to or not he had to leave his home if the landlord wanted it for redevelopment; and if the landlord did not, he might be faced with a much higher ground rent to pay, one which reflected current rather than ninety-plus-year-old property values.

Increasingly, the position of the tenant became the Achilles heel of the leasehold system. The more the concentration on tenants' rights in rent control legislation, the more anomalous became the position of the unprotected tenant under the long lease. Debate on whether lessees should be allowed compulsorily to buy out the land-lord – leasehold enfranchisement – had been part of the political agenda since the 1880s in Wales, and spasmodically in England during the twentieth century, becoming of more importance as the century wore on and the leases on central areas of towns – often occupied by working-class housing – began to fall in. Some ameliora-tive legislation was passed in 1954[88] as a result of the Report of the Committee on Leasehold Reform, but this did not go far enough for some people. The Labour Party committed itself to leasehold en-franchisement if it was returned to power, and duly introduced such a measure in 1967 – the Leasehold Reform Act. In essence this pro-vides that lessees coming within the terms of the Act have the alter-native, at the expiry of their lease, of either purchasing the freehold from the landlord (in effect this would be a compulsory purchase at the suit of the lessee) or obtaining a fifty-year extension of the lease (again if necessary compulsorily). In both cases, where agreement cannot be reached on the price to be paid for the freehold or the new ground rent to be charged for the renewed lease, resort may be had to the Lands Tribunal.

We are concerned here with the effect of such provisions on the large leasehold estates. From the outset of the Bill – indeed from the publication of the White Paper which preceded the Bill[89] – the major estates were united in their view that the proposed legislation would be a disaster for them as it would lead to the progressive break-up of the estates, uneven and incoherent future development, and a deterioration of the amenities looked after by the landlord in the interests of all. The estates were unconvinced that the planning authorities would be capable or sometimes willing to maintain them.[90] It was to meet these strongly voiced criticisms, while at the same time attempting to preserve the principle of leasehold enfranchisement, that the government introduced clause 19 of the Bill, later to become section 19 of the Act.

House of Lords Debates, vol. 285, cols 662–5

Report stage of the Leasehold Reform Bill. Debate on an amendment by Lord Brooke of Cumnor to clarify clause 19.

LORD KENNET[91]: My Lords, the noble Lord, Lord Brooke of Cumnor, said that he hoped the schemes under Clause 19 would cover use, appearance and redevelopment alike. I must apologise for not having been sufficiently comprehensive last time, but I would confirm what my right honourable friend said: I hope so, too. I imagine that the meaning of the words 'regulate the redevelopment' is intended to be to say (of course I must be careful here not to trespass on the functions of the courts, because the courts will be coming in all the time on the schemes) how new development is to be done; whether the new building is to be a 90-storey hotel, or a two-storey house like the ones beside it, or whether it is to have a flat roof or gables, and so on. To 'regulate the development' will be simply to say what the new development will be and what it will be like. What, of course, it does not mean is what this clause is not intended to do (and I think it would be most unlikely the Government could ever accept any Amendment which made it do so); that is, to enable a freeholder to withhold enfranchisement on the grounds of getting more watertight control over redevelopment. This would be going too far, in my judgment, and I hope that, having said that, I have, within the bounds of Parliamentary propriety, satisfied the noble Lord in his quest for definitions. . . .

Presumably the landlord and the former tenants, together in agreement, or, if not, then one party (or, since the recent Amendment, the other party) without the agreement of the other, having got the Minister's certificate, will go to the court and say, 'We want an agreement which will control the following sorts of things.' Among the sorts of things may or may not be the height of new development; the shape of the roof of new development; the colour of new development; the material of new development. It will be up to them to propose to the court, and up to the court, in the event of disagreement between the parties to the scheme, to adjudicate between them.

LORD BROOKE OF CUMNOR:[92] My Lords, I believe that as mover of the Amendment I have the right of reply. I am afraid that I am not at all satisfied with what the noble Lord has said. He suggested that the scheme would say how the new development is to be done. I can understand a scheme saying that certain things are not to be done, but unless there is some central control there will not be a comprehensive scheme of redevelopment. I have had some experience in the planning world—

LORD KENNET: My Lords, may I interrupt the noble Lord? I did not say that the scheme would settle how redevelopment was to be done. I should imagine that it would be more in the nature of defining what aspects of the new development would be subject to the scheme. I cannot imagine a scheme saying, if a new block was to be built there: 'The block shall look like this.' I can imagine a scheme which would say, 'The appearance of a new block, as defined in such and such a way, shall be subject to the scheme.'

LORD BROOKE OF CUMNOR: My Lords, I took down the noble Lord's words, and what I took down was that the scheme would say how new development is to be done. What is troubling me is this: that though you can, by a scheme, or by planning legislation, or otherwise, prevent various things from being done, you can secure that a comprehensive plan will be carried out only if somebody has some unified control over that. May I give an example from another field, with regard to the control of high buildings? You can, by planning control, ensure that high buildings will not be in certain positions and will not break the skyline at certain points. But you cannot, unless there is unified control, ensure that there will be a high building erected at point A or B or C. That will depend on the owner of that particular plot of land.

As I see it, what the Government are likely to achieve by this clause is that when a well-managed estate is broken up, a scheme may be agreed by the High Court to forbid certain types of redevelopment. But I cannot see how that scheme can ensure that simultaneous redevelopment of high quality is to take place, if the area in question is then owned by a number of different individuals, some of whom do not wish, or are not able, to redevelop when the rest of the redevelopment is going forward.

The noble Lord, Lord Kennet, is saying on behalf of the Government that this, the securing of far-sighted unified redevelopment, is less important than enabling the existing leaseholders to secure their capital gains on their houses. He is saying that what he cannot contemplate is any interference with enfranchisement, and on these well-managed estates enfranchisement means capital gains to the leaseholders. I am saying that before we legislate to provide for these untaxed capital gains to individuals who hold leases on these well-managed estates, we should consider carefully what we are sacrificing. It appears to me that we are sacrificing the ultimate opportunity of comprehensive, wise and far-sighted redevelopment of the quality which we had in the original development. This is why I have been pressing the Government. Certainly up till now I have not seen any way in which this redevelopment can be secured except on the lines of the earlier clause of the noble Lord, Lord Silsoe, which would stop enfranchisement in these areas.

Leasehold Reform Act 1967

19.—(1) Where, in the case of any area which is occupied directly or indirectly under tenancies held from one landlord (apart from property occupied by him or his licensees or for the time being unoccupied), the Minister on an application made within the two years beginning with the commencement of this Part of this Act grants a certificate that, in order to maintain adequate standards of appearance and amenity and regulate redevelopment in the area in the event of tenants acquiring the landlord's interest in their house and premises under this Part of this Act, it is in the Minister's opinion likely to be in the general interest that the landlord should retain powers of management in respect of the house and premises or have rights against the house and premises in respect of the benefits arising from the exercise elsewhere of his powers of management, then the High Court may, on an application made within one year of the giving of the certificate, approve a scheme giving the landlord such powers and rights as are contemplated by this subsection.

For purposes of this section 'the Minister' means as regards areas within Wales and Monmouthshire the Secretary of State, and as regards other areas the Minister of Housing and Local Government.

(2) The Minister shall not give a certificate under this section unless he is satisfied that the applicant has, by advertisement or otherwise as may be required by the Minister, given adequate notice to persons interested, informing them of the application for a certificate and its purpose and inviting them to make representations to the Minister for or against the application within a time which appears to the Minister to be reasonable; and before giving a certificate the Minister shall consider any representations so made within that time, and if from those representations it appears to him that there is among the persons making them substantial opposition to the application, he shall afford to those opposing the application, and on the same occasion to the applicant and such (if any) as the Minister thinks fit of those in favour of the application, an opportunity to appear and be heard by a person appointed by the Minister for the purpose, and shall consider the report of that person.

(3) The Minister in considering whether to grant a certificate authorising a scheme for any area, and the High Court in considering whether to approve a scheme shall have regard primarily to the benefit likely to result from the scheme to the area as a whole (including houses likely to be acquired from the landlord under this Part of this Act), and the extent to which it is reasonable to impose, for the benefit of the area, obligations on tenants so acquiring their freeholds; but regard may also be had to the past development and present character of the area and to architectural or historical considerations, to neighbouring areas and to the circumstances generally.

(4) If, having regard to the matters mentioned in subsection (3) above, to the provision which it is practicable to make by a scheme, and to any change of circumstances since the giving of the certificate under subsection (1), the High Court think it proper so to do, then the High Court may by order—

(a) exclude from the scheme any part of the area certified under that subsection; or

(b) declare that no scheme can be approved for the area;

and before submitting for approval a scheme for an area so certified a person may, if he sees fit, apply to the High Court for general directions as to the matters proper to be included, in the scheme and for a decision whether an order should be made under paragraph (*a*) or (*b*) above.

(5) Subject to subsections (3) and (4) above, on the submission of a scheme to the High Court, the High Court shall approve the scheme either as originally submitted or with any modifications proposed or agreed to by the applicant for the scheme, if the scheme (with those modifications, if any) appears to the court to be fair and practicable and not to give the landlord a degree of control out of proportion to that previously exercised by him or to that required for the purposes of the scheme; and the High Court shall not dismiss an application for the approval of a scheme, unless either—

(*a*) the Court makes an order under subsection (4)(*b*) above; or

(*b*) in the opinion of the Court the applicant is unwilling to agree to a suitable scheme or is not proceeding in the matter with due despatch.

(6) A scheme under this section may make different provision for different parts of the area, and shall include provision for terminating or varying all or any of the provisions of the scheme, or excluding part of the area, if a change of circumstances makes it appropriate, or for enabling it to be done by or with the approval of the High Court.

(7) Except as provided by the scheme, the operation of a scheme under this section shall not be affected by any disposition or devolution of the landlord's interest in the property within the area or parts of that property; but the scheme—

(*a*) shall include provision for identifying the person who is for the purposes of the scheme to be treated as the landlord for the time being; and

(*b*) may include provision for transferring, or allowing the landlord for the time being to transfer, all or any of the powers and rights conferred by the scheme on the landlord for the time being to a local authority or other body, including a body constituted for the purpose.

In the following provisions of this section references to the landlord for the time being shall have effect, in relation to powers and rights transferred to a local authority or other body as contemplated by paragraph (*b*) above, as references to that authority or body.

(8) Without prejudice to any other provision of this section, a scheme under it may provide for all or any of the following matters:—

(*a*) for regulating the redevelopment, use or appearance of property of which tenants have acquired the landlord's interest under this Part of this Act; and

(*b*) for empowering the landlord for the time being to carry out work for the maintenance or repair of any such property or carry out work to remedy a failure in respect of any such property to comply with the scheme, or for making the operation of any provisions of the scheme conditional on his doing so or on the provision or maintenance by him of services, facilities or amenities of any description; and

(c) for imposing on persons from time to time occupying or interested in any such property obligations in respect of maintenance or repair of the property or of property used or enjoyed by them in common with others, or in respect of cost incurred by the landlord for the time being on any matter referred to in this paragraph or in paragraph (b) above;

(d) for the inspection from time to time of any such property on behalf of the landlord for the time being, and for the recovery by him of sums due to him under the scheme in respect of any such property by means of a charge on the property;

and the landlord for the time being shall have, for the enforcement of any charge imposed under the scheme, the same powers and remedies under the Law of Property Act 1925 and otherwise as if he were a mortgagee by deed having powers of sale and leasing and of appointing a receiver.

(10) A certificate given or scheme approved under this section shall be registered under the Land Charges Act 1925 as a local land charge; and where a scheme is so registered—

(a) the provisions of the scheme relating to property of any description shall, so far as they respectively affect the persons from time to time occupying or interested in that property, be enforceable by the landlord for the time being against them, as if each of them had covenanted with the landlord for the time being to be bound by the scheme; and

(b) in relation to a house and premises in the area section 10 above shall have effect subject to the provisions of the scheme, and the price payable under section 9 shall be adjusted accordingly.

(13) Where it appears to the Minister—

(a) that a certificate could be given under this section for any area or areas on the application of the landlord or landlords; and

(b) that any body of persons is so constituted as to be capable of representing for purposes of this section the persons occupying or interested in property in the area or areas (other than the landlord or landlords), or such of them as are or may become entitled to acquire their landlord's interest under this Part of this Act, and is otherwise suitable;

then on an application made by that body either alone or jointly with the landlord or landlords, a certificate may be granted accordingly; and where a certificate is so granted, whether to a representative body alone or to a representative body jointly with the landlord or landlords,—

(i) an application for a scheme in pursuance of the certificate may be made by the representative body alone or by the landlord or landlords alone or by both jointly and, by leave of the High Court, may be proceeded with by the representative body or by the landlords though not the applicant or applicants; and

(ii) without prejudice to subsection (7)(*b*) above, the scheme may, with the consent of the landlord or landlords or on such terms as to compensation or otherwise as appear to the High Court to be just, confer on the representative body any such rights or powers under the scheme as might be conferred on the landlord or landlords for the time being, or enable the representative body to participate in the administration of the scheme or in the management by the landlord or landlords of his or their property in the area or areas.

It is interesting to note that whereas the debates on clause 19 concentrated on the problems of redevelopment if the estates were broken up, the case for a scheme of management had to put as much on the grounds of 'maintaining adequate standards of appearance and amenity' as of redevelopment. Do you think the case against enfranchisement on these estates was made out? Is the answer 'but freehold property is redeveloped under modern planning legislation every day', satisfactory; if not, why not? Do you agree with the following criticism by Mr Page of the section:

Clause 19 provides that the benefits to be afforded to a landlord who manages his estate well and comes up to the standards laid down in subsection (1) of the Clause shall be granted, as it were, by a certificate of the Minister – the Minister shall decide whether an estate comes up to the criteria set out in subsection (1). After that there can be an application to the High Court for a scheme to be approved by the court.

This would seem to me to be the wrong way round. I should have thought that the provision of a scheme was the sort of administrative matter which might be settled by the Minister, but that whether conditions are or are not satisfied, whether the estate is or is not well managed, was a matter for judicial decision and not for administrative decision by the Minister.[93]

Why do you think the section is in the form it is? Does sub-section (13) undermine the principles behind the rest of the section? What benefits will accrue to a lessee on an estate which has been granted a scheme of management who exercises his right to enfranchisement?

Leasehold Reform Act 1967, s. 19:
Calthorpe Estate, Edgbaston

Application by the Trustees of the Calthorpe Estate, Edgbaston, for the issue of a Certificate under the provisions of section 19(1) of the above Act. Report of the Inspector, J. G. Jefferson, PPTPI, FICE, FIMun.E, appointed to hold a hearing into the above application on 23 July 1969.

2. Up to the date of the hearing 128 individual representations had been received by the Ministry. In general 37 supported the application, 84 opposed it and the remaining 7 did not make their attitude clear. In addition 2 petitions had been received; one signed by 15 persons supported the application and the other signed by 27 persons opposed it.

3. At the opening of the hearing 5 people had expressed a wish to speak in support of the application and 12 in opposition.

5. The Estate lies on the west side of Birmingham and at its nearest point is some three-quarters of a mile from the centre of the City. It has an area of about 1,500 acres, or nearly 2½ sq. miles. It is some 14 miles round the perimeter and contains upwards of 30 miles of public highway. At the present time there are roughly 4,000 dwellings on the Estate and the population is about 15,000.

CONCLUSIONS

282. In considering the case put forward by the applicants and the representations of the opponents I have thought it right to consider, first of all, the suggestion that adequate powers of control exist under the Planning Acts, for if this were the case the need for a scheme under Section 19 could hardly be justified. This proposition was put forward by many of the speakers and by no less than 17 of those who made written representations.

283. In my opinion this matter needs to be viewed from three standpoints:

    (a) the control of alterations to property and the day-to-day control of minor development

    (b) control of the development of the unbuilt-up areas of the Estate, and

    (c) re-development.

284. As to (a) the evidence given at the hearing and my own experience lead me to the view that the control which a Local Planning Authority can exercise to prevent minor changes of use, alterations to the appearance of buildings, the erection of outbuildings, fences etc, or to secure the care and maintenance of trees and landscaping, is much less that most of the opponents would consider necessary on an Estate such as this.

285. As to (b) there was a good deal of criticism of the development which had been allowed in the northern part of the Beech Lanes Estate; but it should be remembered that this development had received the approval of the Local Planning Authority. Whether that Authority were in a position to require development of a higher standard of design, layout, or materials of construction may be a matter of opinion; but the fact remains that they had approved the application for planning permission and it appears to me to be highly unlikely that any higher standard would have been achieved if the Estate Company had not been in the picture at all.

286. As to (c.) it was generally agreed that most of the re-development which had taken place was of high quality. This was mainly due to the

fact that relatively large areas had been made available to the developers so that comprehensive schemes were made possible.

287. If, as a result of enfranchisement the potential re-development areas are split up into small plots of freehold property without any overall control of schemes of re-development, the appearance of such schemes is likely to be much less satisfactory than those which have recently been built.

288. I would draw attention to Plan C, the areas said to be 'ripe for re-development'. I am in no doubt whatever that when the time for re-development arrives these areas should be developed on a comprehensive basis and not piecemeal; but the administrative difficulties with which a Local Planning Authority are faced in securing comprehensive development are formidable. For these reasons I consider that the powers which the Local Planning Authority possess under the Planning Acts are insufficient by themselves to maintain the high environmental quality of the Calthorpe Estate.

289. Most of the speakers who addressed me at the Hearing were agreed that some form of management control would be necessary. Mr Stewart thought that there should be 'public participation'. Few other speakers had any suggestions as to how an alternative form of management control might be exercised.

290. I think this is a matter for the High Court to decide and I do not think that a certificate should be withheld because the applicants have not, at this stage, put forward positive proposals for some form of joint administration.

291. The main reason advanced for withholding a certificate was that the existing management service given by the Estate Company is unsatisfactory in a number of ways and that there has been a failure to enforce covenants. The applicants' answers to these criticisms are set out in paragraphs 233 to 242 of this Report.

292. After listening to the evidence and after inspection of the properties referred to, I am satisfied that it is unreasonable to expect a high standard of maintenance in those areas where the leases are about to fall in, and because of the age of the property the area is due for re-development.

293. I have some sympathy with the lessees who feel dissatisfied on this point; but I do not feel that it is sufficient reason for withholding a certificate. Over the area of the Calthorpe Estate *as a whole* I am satisfied that the standard of maintenance is high.

294. This may be due in no small measure to the fact that the Estate caters, in the main, for a wealthy section of the community, lessees who can afford to occupy relatively expensive living accommodation and to keep it well-maintained. But the evidence showed that the quality of the environment which exists today is largely due to the control which has been exercised in the past by the Trustees of the Estate and my own observation confirms this view. The cases which were drawn to my attention, where the quality of design, layout, construction and maintenance of property might be said to have fallen below the high standard prevalent on the estate were exceptions to the general rule.

295. As to the argument that freeholders are likely to maintain their property in a satisfactory and neighbourly way, without any need for a management scheme, I think this may be partially true; but I think that, without some form of management control, difficulties would arise in the case of those freeholders who were not prepared to be co-operative.

296. Again, this may be a matter for the High Court; and I do not think the argument justifies the withholding of a certificate – particularly having regard to the fact that nearly everyone who spoke at the Hearing was in favour of *some* sort of management control.

297. The fears expressed by some of the objectors that under a scheme of management freeholders might be called upon to pay for amenities not directly related to their own properties were to some extent dispelled by assurances given on behalf of the applicants. I do not think these fears are sufficient justification for withholding a certificate.

298. After hearing the evidence I do not think that the Trustees can be blamed for allowing development at densities higher than some of the objectors consider proper. This is a policy which has been forced upon the Trustees by the approved Development Plan, indeed the evidence was that they would have preferred to have developed at lower densities but were not permitted to do so.

299. I think that the case for excluding certain areas (e.g. some of the commercial areas, some of the open spaces, or some of the fringe areas) should be considered by the High Court. I do not think that a case was made for the exclusion of any of these areas at this stage.

300. There was evidently a strong feeling about the quality of the development in the northern part of the Beech Lanes Estate. The applicants admitted that some of the criticism was justified. It is clear that there has been a lack of supervision especially of some of the painting but I do not regard this particular lapse on the part of the Estate management as sufficient to justify withholding a certificate. If anything, it supports a case for increased management control rather than otherwise.

301. There were some complaints of a lack of good public relations between the lessees on the Estate and the Calthorpe Estate Staff. I was not in a position to judge how far these complaints were justified; but it is a matter which will no doubt receive consideration by those concerned.

302. There was undoubtedly an anxiety on the part of some of the opponents that the charges which would be levied by the Company under a scheme of management would be excessive. The applicants' assurances on this point are given in paragraph 270(e) of this Report. This is really a matter for the High Court.

303. To sum up I was impressed by the arguments in favour of retaining some degree of management control in this area, I am satisfied that this would be in the public interest, and I reached the conclusion, after listening to the evidence and after an inspection of the area, that the arguments of those who opposed the application were not sufficiently strong to justify withholding the grant of a certificate.

RECOMMENDATION

304. I recommend that the application by the Trustees of the Calthorpe
Edgbaston Estate for the issue of a certificate under Section 19(1) of the
Leasehold Reform Act 1967 in respect of the Calthorpe Estate Birming-
ham be granted.

The Minister granted a certificate by a letter dated 29 April 1970.

One of the major critics of the Trustees and their record of management was the Calthorpe Tenants' Association, whose secretary
was a Mr Grey. Among the suggestions put forward by the Association was that in the event of a certificate being granted under section
19, provision should be made for the residents of the estate to be associated with its management. The management of the estate was
opposed to this on the grounds that no useful, positive purpose
would be served by it. Furthermore, it felt that in fact it would
merely delay management decisions and exacerbate relations between management and tenants. The management was employed
by and answerable to the Trustees and not the tenants, and would
inevitably therefore, on occasions, have to run counter to wishes of
tenants.

This dispute between the Trustees, who supported the management, and the Calthorpe Tenants' Association went on after the
Minister's decision in favour of the Trustees and came to a head
over whether certain matters were fit to be included in a management scheme, prepared in pursuance of the Act. A summons was
taken out under section 19(4) by the Trustees of the estate to ask
the court to decide on certain issues of principle in relation to the
management scheme.

Re Calthorpe Estate, Edgbaston, Birmingham
Anstruther-Gough-Calthorpe and Others v. *Grey*[94] *and Others*
(1973) 25 P. & C. R. 120

FOSTER J: . . . Originally, there were nine matters in dispute, but both
before and during the hearing five of the points ceased to be matters of
dispute and only four remain for me to consider. . . .

Question C: Should an option to repurchase be included in the scheme?

For the purpose of this question I will assume in favour of the landlords the following facts:

1. There is an overall scheme for the redevelopment of the estate
which runs to the year 2000.

2. Many parts of the estate consist of leasehold properties, the leases of

which terminate about the same time, so that comprehensive redevelopment can take place in selected areas.

3. If in one of these areas a leaseholder had purchased the freehold and was not under any obligation to resell the property to the landlords, the redevelopment of that area will be seriously impeded.

On those assumptions the question of law arises, whether such an option can be included as part of a scheme under section 19.

The relevant subsections of section 19 are subsections (1), (3) and (8).

For the landlords, it was submitted (a) that it was the intention of Parliament in enacting section 19 to protect approved leasehold estates from the consequences of enfranchisement and to ensure the continuance of the beneficial aspects of such estates for the general benefit of the neighbourhood. (b) Paragraph 21 of the scheme granting the landlords an option to repurchase was consistent with that intention. The Calthorpe Estate was in the middle of a forty-year redevelopment plan approved by the Birmingham City Council. (c) The court should look at the words of section 19 and construe them to see if they are wide enough to include such an option. If there was any doubt as to the true construction, the court should so construe them as to produce a sensible or preferable result.

For the defendants it was submitted: (a) The proposed provisions of paragraph 21 of the scheme were nothing more or less than provisions investing the landlords with compulsory powers of acquisition; (b) The purpose of Parliament was contained in the preamble to the Act. The preamble is in these words: 'An Act to enable tenants of houses held on long leases at low rents to acquire the freehold or an extended lease'.

In *Re Sherwood Close (Barnes) Management Co. Ltd.*[95] GOULDING J said:

Part I of the Act of 1967 gives tenants of houses held on long tenancies at low rents, as defined by the Act, a right to acquire the freehold or an extended lease of their houses wherever the tenant has the residential qualification specified in the Act and the house is within certain limits of rateable value. This policy of leasehold enfranchisement was formerly the subject of political controversy, and its opponents were quick to point out that in many cases the removal of a common landlord's control would damage the amenities and depreciate the value of properties on well-managed estates. Some concession to that point of view is made by section 19 of the Act, which preserves a degree of control over enfranchised houses if a management scheme is authorised by the appropriate Minister and approved by the court. It is important, I think, in construing section 19 to remember that it is a limited concession to arguments whose general application was not accepted by Parliament. In other words, it is not legitimate for me to enlarge the natural meaning of provisions in section 19 merely because I may think it would be beneficial to all concerned to do so. A benevolent canon of construction of that kind is in my judgment excluded because Parliament has decided, generally speaking, that a resident long lessee has the right to become a freeholder if he wants to, even though the exercise of his rights may be to the material disadvantage of himself and his neighbours.

In *Re Abbots Park Estate*[96] PENNYCUICK VC considered the *Sherwood Close* case, but expressed no disagreement with the paragraph of GOULDING J's judgment which I have read, though it is fair to say that in both those cases there was no opposition to the application.

(c) The powers envisaged by section 19 are only powers of management to regulate development in the area concerned.

(d) It would be startling if when section 1 gives the tenant a right to acquire the freehold in certain circumstances, that right could be negatived by a provision of a scheme under section 19. The primary purpose of the Act would thus be frustrated.

(e) If Parliament had an intention to permit the landlords to repurchase, it is extraordinary that there are no provisions at all in regard to the right, the price, the obligation or the method. Particular reference was made to section 17, which gives in certain circumstances the landlord the qualified right to terminate extended leases for the purpose of redevelopment, and provisions as to compensation are to be found in section 17 (3).

Conclusion. In my judgment, the submissions made by the defendants are correct. Section 19 is only dealing with powers of management for the general benefit of the neighbourhood and it is not possible for the court to construe the words 'regulate redevelopment in the area' so as to negative the whole purpose of the Act.

Question A. Should provisions be made in the scheme for the participation of a tenants' association in the scheme?

The original suggestion made by the tenants' association was far too wide and unworkable in practice. Agreement has been reached as to the composition and powers which could be given to what has been called 'An Amenity Committee' if the court thinks such participation should be included in the scheme. The landlords have, however, strongly urged that the Calthorpe Tenants' Association has not the necessary backing from the tenants to be considered as representing the general body of tenants on the estate. It is said that if at a future date an association could claim to be representative, it could apply to the court for an alteration to the scheme, so as to include some such provisions. There are some 4,500 tenants on the Calthorpe Estate. The membership of the Calthorpe Tenants' Association is at present some 450 persons (or 10 per cent. of all tenants), and of Chad Hill Residents' Association some 160 persons. The former association has been in existence since 1967 and strong efforts have been made both by circulars and by canvassing to increase its membership, but these have been unsuccessful. It was contended for the association that what they lack in numbers they make up in the quality of the members. To some extent, that is true. But there are a great many tenants of considerable standing who are not members. I have come to the conclusion that no association at present has a sufficient membership to be representative of the estate tenants as a whole. On the other hand, I find that it would be a hardship and an unwarranted expense for an association which was representative to have to apply to the court for a variation of the scheme. I think that the best course (and I am not dealing with the legal consequences if this course is not accepted) would be to insert the proposed provisions in the scheme, naming no particular association, but subject to a condition precedent that the provisions would not become operative unless and until there is an association the membership of which equals or exceeds a stated percentage of the total number of estate tenants. What that percentage should be should, I think, be considered in chambers, when the scheme falls to be considered in detail.

5

Development and its Control: Public Law

1. Introduction

In this and the next chapter we come to what many people would regard as the heart of the planning process: that part of it that impinges most upon the ordinary citizen and upon which the most time and effort has to be spent each year – the day-to-day control which is exercised by local and central government planners over the use of land on the basis of decisions given in respect of planning applications. Although these chapters are concerned with individual cases, a fundamental issue runs through them both. What if any, is the connection between the development plan and development control? Is the planning process designed to emphasise and encourage such a connection or does it rely on serendipity? These are questions to which our attention should be constantly directed.

Development control is the major area for legal expertise in the planning process, involving as it does technical procedural rules, abstract concepts, and general legal principles, such as natural justice and abuse of powers, to a much greater extent than elsewhere in the process. It is, however, precisely because the role of law and lawyer is so important here that we must be on our guard against assuming that it is all important. The law may be said to be concerned with three things here: (i) it sets out a procedure to be followed for the seeking of, and the giving of, decisions on planning permissions; (ii) it sets out the limits within which planning controls operate and is therefore inevitably involved in making decisions on whether those limits have been overstepped, and (iii) it provides mechanisms and remedies for legal challenges to the process if people feel aggrieved with it. All these are important and an understanding of them is essential to our understanding of the planning process in action, but they are only a part of that process in action; we should be and shall be equally concerned with what happens within the legal framework: how do developers and planners use or bend or even ignore the system of legal rules to achieve their ends or frustrate each other's? How does development control work in practice? How are day-to-day decisions made and what kind of influences are or may be at work in their making? The answers to these questions may lie in an examination of legal rules and their interpretation by the courts, but they also lie elsewhere. We shall accordingly be looking closely at the role of the local planning authority, its officers and members, the informal negotiations that precede the formal application and often continue after it is before the local planning authority's committee; the place of the public local inquiry in this branch of the process, and the alternative mechanisms to the court which the aggrieved applicant can use to challenge the process, particularly the Parliamentary Commissioner for Administration. In addition, we must also attempt to understand how the planner looks at development control and what techniques and skills he brings to bear on its operation.'

What is required therefore is a framework which focuses our attention on the planning process in action, on the interrelationship between law and informal processes, and the interactions between the main actors – planners, developers, lawyers and councillors – and on the key problems these processes and people try to solve. The framework adopted is one which looks at the control of development in three stages: at the local authority level, at the central government level, and at the judicial level – which level also embraces the Parliamentary Commissioner for Administration and the Council on Tribunals and attempts to probe the interactions between actors and institutions at all these levels. As a preliminary, however, the legal justification for control – the constitutional framework – must be set out. Aspects of its interpretation will be considered throughout this and the next chapter.

Town and Country Planning Act 1971

22.—(1) In this Act, except where the context otherwise requires, 'development', subject to the following provisions of this section, means the carrying out of building, engineering, mining or other operations in, on, over or under land, or the making of any material change in the use of any buildings or other land.

(2) The following operations or uses of land shall not be taken for the purposes of this Act to involve development of the land, that is to say—

(*a*)   the carrying out of works for the maintenance, improvement or other alteration of any building, being works which affect only the interior of the building or which do not materially effect the external appearance of the building and (in either case) are not works for making good war damage or works begun after 5th December 1968 for the alteration of a building by providing additional space therein below ground;

(*b*)   the carrying out by a local highway authority of any works required for the maintenance or improvement of a road, being works carried out on land within the boundaries of the road;

(*c*)   the carrying out by a local authority or statutory undertakers of any works for the purpose of inspecting, repairing or renewing any sewers, mains, pipes, cables or other apparatus, including the breaking open of any street or other land for that purpose;

(*d*)   the use of any buildings or other land within the curtilage of a dwellinghouse for any purpose incidental to the enjoyment of the dwellinghouse as such;

(*f*)   in the case of buildings or other land which are used for a purpose of any class specified in an order made by the Secretary of State under this section, the use thereof for any other purpose of the same class.

(3) For the avoidance of doubt it is hereby declared that for the purposes of this section—

(*a*)   the use as two or more separate dwellinghouses of any building previously used as a single dwellinghouse involves a material change in the use of the building and of each part thereof which is so used;

(*b*)   the deposit of refuse or waste materials on land involves a material change in the use thereof, notwithstanding that the land is comprised in a site already used for that purpose, if either the superficial area of the deposit is thereby extended, or the height of the deposit is thereby extended and exceeds the level of the land adjoining the site.

(4) Without prejudice to any regulations made under the provisions of this Act relating to the control of advertisements, the use for the display of advertisements of any external part of a building which is not normally used for that purpose shall be treated for the purposes of this section as involving a material change in the use of that part of the building.

23.—(1) Subject to the provisions of this section, planning permission is required for the carrying out of any development of land.

(5) Where planning permission to develop land has been granted for a limited period, planning permission is not required for the resumption, at the end of that period, of the use of the land for the purpose for which it was normally used before the permission was granted.

(6) In determining, for the purposes of subsection (5) of this section, what were the purposes for which land was normally used before the grant of planning permission, no account shall be taken of any use of the land begun in contravention of the provisions of this Part of this Act or in contravention of previous planning control.

(8) Where by a development order planning permission to develop land has been granted subject to limitations, planning permission is not required for the use of that land which (apart from its use in accordance with that permission) is the normal use of that land, unless the last-mentioned use was begun in contravention of the provisions of this Part of this Act or in contravention of previous planning control.

(9) Where an enforcement notice has been served in respect of any development of land, planning permission is not required for the use of that land for the purpose for which (in accordance with the provisions of this Part of this Act) it could lawfully have been used if that development had not been carried out.

24.—(1) The Secretary of State shall by order (in this Act referred to as a 'development order') provide for the granting of planning permission.

(2) A development order may either—

(a) itself grant planning permission for development specified in the order, or for development of any class so specified; or

(b) in respect of redevelopment for which planning permission is not granted by the order itself, provide for the granting of planning permission by the local planning authority (or, in the cases herein-after provided, by the Secretary of State) on an application in that behalf made to the local planning authority in accordance with the provisions of the order.

(3) A development order may be made either as a general order applicable (subject to such exceptions as may be specified therein) to all land, or as a special order applicable only to such land as may be so specified.

(4) Planning permission granted by a development order may be granted either unconditionally or subject to such conditions or limitations as may be specified in the order.

(5) Without prejudice to the generality of subsection (4) of this section—

(a) where planning permission is granted by a development order for the erection, extension or alteration of any buildings, the order may require the approval of the local planning authority to be obtained with respect to the design or external appearance of the buildings;

(b) where planning permission is granted by a development order for development of a specified class, the order may enable the

Secretary of State or the local planning authority to direct that the permission shall not apply either in relation to development in a particular area or in relation to any particular development.

2. Control at the local planning authority level

(a) Extent of control

As the following table shows, control at the local planning authority level is of great importance quantitively. Since no appeal lies from an approval of a planning application, it is equally clear that qualitatively the influence of local planning authority decisions is very great. A major question to be considered here is whether the realities of decision making in the local authorities live up to the responsibilities which the planning process has put upon them.

Statistics for Town and Country Planning (HMSO 1974)

... The figures do *not* include:—

(i) applications 'called in' for decision by the Secretary of State for the Environment and the Secretary of State for Wales;
(ii) applications within New Town areas which had been referred to the Secretary of State for decision;
(iii) the Secretary of State's decisions on appeals.

The returns provided information about the number of applications which local planning authorities had to determine. Where there were successive applications for the development of the same site each was counted as a separate application. An outline application, and any subsequent requests for approval to detailed plans, were counted as separate applications although legally they constitute a single application. ...

Planning applications: England and Wales

	A. Building, engineering and other operations	B. Changes of use	All classes	Percentage of decisions which were refusals
Number of applications:				
1962	348,020	49,281	397,301	16·1
1963	364,437	47,126	411,563	16·0
1964	411,740	49,975	461,715	18·0
1965	394,036	49,351	443,387	17·7
1966	366,705	48,347	415,052	16·7
1967	370,431	52,122	422,553	15·2
1968	372,785	53,501	426,286	15·7
1969	353,008	49,706	402,714	14·9
1970	360,936	53,365	414,301	15·1
1971	404,455	58,846	463,301	16·7
1972	547,927	66,935	614,862	19·8
1973	553,243	69,409	622,652	21·1

				Percentage change in number of applications
Increase or decrease:				
1962–63	+ 16,417	−2,155	+ 14,262	+ 3·6
1963–64	+ 47,303	+2,849	+ 50,152	+12·2
1964–65	− 17,704	− 624	− 18,328	− 4·0
1965–66	− 27,331	−1,004	− 28,335	− 6·4
1966–67	+ 3,726	+3,775	+ 7,501	+ 1·8
1967–68	+ 2,345	+1,379	+ 3,733	+ 0·9
1968–69	− 19,777	−3,795	− 24,572	− 5·8
1969–70	+ 7,928	+3,659	+ 11,587	+ 2·8
1970–71	+ 43,519	+5,481	+ 49,000	+11·8
1971–72	+143,472	+8,089	+151,561	+32·7
1972–73	+ 5,316	+2,474	+ 7,790	+ 1·3

(b) **Who controls?**

(i) Which councils control?

The Local Government Act 1972 brought about changes as to which local authority was to exercise control of development similar in intention, and therefore possibly similar in potential confusion, to the arrangements for the making of local plans. The power to exercise control is vested in district councils, but on certain matters that power is shifted to county councils. The statutory provisions appear below, followed by a DoE circular suggesting ways in which the two levels might co-operate.

Local Government Act 1972, Schedule 16

15.—(1) The functions of a local planning authority of determining —

- (*a*) applications for planning permission under Part III;
- (*b*) applications for determining under section 53 whether an application for such permission is required;
- (*c*) applications for an established use certificate under section 94;

shall, subject to sub-paragraph (2) below be exercised by the district planning authority.

(2) The functions of a local planning authority of determining any such application as aforesaid which appears to the district planning authority to relate to a county matter shall be exercised by the county planning authority unless the application relates to a county matter mentioned in paragraph 32(*d*) below and the district planning authority propose—

- (*a*) to refuse planning permission;
- (*b*) to determine that an application for planning permission is required; or
- (*c*) to refuse an application for an established use certificate as respects the whole of the land to which the application relates.

(3) Every application mentioned in sub-paragraph (1) above shall be made to the district planning authority, and in the case of an application for planning permission that authority shall send a copy of the application as soon as may be after they have received it to the county planning authority and also to the local highway authority, if not a local planning authority, except in any case or class of case with respect to which the county planning authority or the local highway authority, as the case may be, otherwise direct.

(4) The foregoing provisions of this paragraph shall not apply to applications relating to land in a National Park. . . .

17. The Secretary of State shall include in a development order under section 24 provision enabling a local highway authority to impose restrictions on the grant by the local planning authority of planning per-

mission for the following descriptions of development relating to land in the area of the local highway authority, that is to say—

(b) any other operations or use of land which appear to the local highway authority to be likely to result in a material increase in the volume of traffic entering or leaving such a classified or proposed road, to prejudice the improvement or construction of such a road or to result in a material change in the character of traffic entering, leaving or using such a road.

18. The provisions which may be contained in any such order shall include provision—

(a) requiring a county planning authority who are determining any application mentioned in paragraph 15 above and relating to a county matter, or an application for approval of a matter reserved under an outline planning permission within the meaning of section 42 and so relating, to afford the district planning authority for the area in which the land to which the application relates is situated an opportunity to make recommendations to the county planning authority as to the manner in which the application shall be determined and to take into account any such recommendations;

(b) requiring a county or district planning authority who have received any application so mentioned or any application for such approval (including any such application relating to land in a National Park) to notify the district or county planning authority, as the case may be, of the terms of their decision, or, where the application is referred to the Secretary of State, the date when it was so referred and, when notified to them, the terms of his decision.

19. Except in the case of any description of operations or use of land specified in an order made by the Secretary of State, the county planning authority for any area may give directions to the district planning authority for any part of that area as to how the district planning authority are to determine any application under the Town and Country Planning Act 1971 in any case where it appears to the county planning authority that any proposals in the application would substantially and adversely affect their interests as local planning authority. . . .

24.—(1) The functions of a local planning authority of—

(a) making orders under section 45 revoking or modifying planning permission, or under section 51 requiring discontinuance of use, or imposing conditions on continuance of use, or requiring the alteration or removal of buildings or works, or

(b) serving enforcement notices under section 87 or stop notices under section 90,

shall, subject to sub-paragraph (2) below, be exercisable by the district planning authority.

(2) In a case where it appears to the district planning authority that the functions mentioned in sub-paragraph (1) above relate to county matters they shall not exercise those functions without first consulting the county planning authority.

(3) Those functions shall also be exercisable by a county planning authority in a case where it appears to that authority that they relate to a matter which should properly be considered a county matter.

32. In the foregoing provisions of this Schedule 'county matter' means in relation to any application, order or notice—[2]

(d) the carrying out of operations or a use of land which, in either case—
(i) would conflict with, or prejudice the implementation of, fundamental provisions of the structure plan for the area in question or fundamental proposals for such a plan or for alterations to such a plan to which publicity has been given in pursuance of section 8;
(ii) would conflict with, or prejudice the implementation of, fundamental provisions of a development plan approved under Part I of Schedule 5, or any enactments replaced by that Part, so far as in force in the area in question or with proposals submitted to the Secretary of State for alterations or additions to such a plan;
(iii) would be inconsistent in any respect with the provisions of a local plan for the area in question prepared by the county planning authority or proposals for such a plan or for alterations to such a plan to which publicity has been given in pursuance of section 12; or
(iv) would be inconsistent in any respect with any statement of planning policy adopted by the county planning authority or with any proposals of theirs for development which in either case have been notified by them to the district planning authority. . . .

DoE Circular No. 74/73

ANNEX 2: PLANNING CONTROL

1. In planning control it will be of paramount importance that there be no doubt or misunderstanding on the part either of the authorities or the public about where the responsibility for decision rests. Subordinate legislation will provide that applicants should be entitled to be informed when responsibility for handling of applications has been transferred from one authority to another. Normally, however, the point of contact between the public and planning authority will be at district level; and it is open to authorities to agree that consultations should be in general carried out by the district planning authority and decisions issued through the district even where 'county matters' are involved. There will of course always be some cases where the advantage will lie in handling by the county planning authority throughout, *e.g.* mineral applications. But it will normally be convenient for the public to be able to get the maximum information about matters affecting their application from the district planning authority where otherwise an inquiry to a distant county or area headquarters could be involved.

2. Because development control arrangements are essentially matters to be settled between county and district planning authorities no provision was made in the Local Government Act 1972 for statutory development control schemes under which disputes could have been referred to the Secretary of State for arbitration. It is nevertheless considered that informal development control schemes should in general be drawn up in each area. While these schemes are unlikely to be of interest to the great majority of applicants for planning permission they should nevertheless be public documents available to the press and the public who have a right to know what arrangements have been made for joint working between authorities. Development control schemes should show clearly the range of matters covered and the way in which they are dealt with. . . .

3. Close consultation between planning authorities on policy issues will be necessary if procedural arrangements on the above lines are to work smoothly. There will in some cases be existing policy statements and informal plans which will have to be taken into account until they have been reviewed by the new authorities. Development control policies should, as far as possible, be embodied in structure and local plans as appropriate. There will always, however, be policies which cannot be included in current development plans. It was to take account of this that the provision relation to 'any statement of planning policy adopted by the county planning authority' was introduced into paragraph 32 (*d*) (iv) of Schedule 16. Such statements of policy should, of course, be fully discussed with the district planning authorities concerned before adoption and should, in the view of the Secretaries of State, relate to matters which it would in due course be appropriate to embody in a structure plan. Arrangements for consultation on such policy statements should, it is suggested, be included in the development control scheme.

Why are development control arrangements *essentially*[3] matters to be settled between county and district planning authorities without recourse to the Secretary of State for arbitration?

Great stress is put on not laying down 'rigid rules and procedures' for schemes of co-operation, but at the same time ensuring that there is full understanding at the members' level 'of planning policies of different authorities and their co-ordination and that duplication is reduced to a minimum and unnecessary misunderstanding or conflict at the formal stages is avoided'.[4] Are these two aims compatible? Under the old local government system, counties were empowered, or in some cases required[5], to enter into formal delegation agreements with lower-tier planning authorities, setting out the respective powers of each to exercise development control and arrangements for resolving differences. In what ways will informal development control schemes be better than the old delegation agreements? In practice, will there be much difference apart from the name? Who might be the main beneficiaries from the stress on informality – councillors, planners or developers? Why?

(ii) The planners and control

Turning from the question of which authority has jurisdiction over development control, we must now consider those parts of the relevant authority which exercise or influence the exercising of the power of development control on its behalf. This involves an examination of the organisation and work of the planning department, some central government constraints on that work and the work and role of the committee that makes decisions or recommendations on applications on behalf of the authority.

A formal description of the planning department would state that unless power to decide had been specifically delegated to a named planning officer, the role of the planners was to advise 'their' committee on the decisions it should reach on the applications coming before it, and to be available to members of the public to assist them in their contact with the planning system. To concentrate on the first part of the role, an antidote to the formal description is contained in the following extract from the *Management Study on Development Control*[6]:

Our investigations have shown that approximately 70% of all planning applications are of a simple nature. In all the authorities visited, a large proportion of these applications are determined by a committee or by the council without presentation of details, without discussion and in accordance with the recommendations of the officers. In one authority about 65% of applications are not described to the committee. The date and recommendations are included in a supplementary schedule which is not circulated to members but which they can examine in a committee room if they wish. Normally the recommendations of the officers are adopted by a block vote.

From these observations it is our conclusion that between 60% and 70% of all development control applications are already effectively delegated to the staff for decision. . . .

My own, admittedly limited, experience suggests that these figures are an underestimate of the number of applications effectively left to officers to deal with. Whether that is so or not, it is clear that officers have more effective power than formal descriptions would allow. How do officers exercise this power and how do they see their role when exercising it? The following extract helps us towards answers to both these questions.

J. B. McLoughlin, *Control and Urban Planning*
(1973) pp. 92–101, 106–111

. . . It was found in the examination of the work of seventy caseworkers in the seventeen authorities tested earlier that there is a remarkable consistency in the sources and types of information which they seek in order to frame their recommendations. This consistency is with respect to the whole set of caseworkers. We could not find any significant differences between the seventeen authorities; minor differences in the pattern were between the caseworkers rather than reflecting on the problems or backgrounds of the planning authorities or their administrative areas. This may suggest two things: first the influence of statutory requirements which are universal; secondly, that caseworkers may share a common ideology or set of principles and attitudes to their job, irrespective of their employing authority. With obvious minor variations, the approach of caseworkers to their task seems broadly similar in areas as different as Ross and Cromarty, Manchester, Camden and Lincoln. . . .

. . . case files themselves contain a bare minimum of documentation which is of value. Typically they contain the application forms themselves, copies of essential consultation letters and memos. Very rarely do they contain the caseworker's notes on visits to the site. Hardly ever does the case file contain notes of meetings with the applicant, discussions with colleagues, telephone conversations and so forth. Yet, as we shall see, these are often some of the crucial sources of information for a recommendation. . . .

By far the most important documentary source of information was *other case files* and information about *precedents* generally – gathered for example by informal conversations with colleagues who had dealt with similar applications or cases in the vicinity. Next in importance come the various *maps associated with the statutory development plan* closely followed by the relevant *Acts, Statutory Instruments and Circulars*. Of somewhat less significance were *non-statutory plan maps*, that is the physical plans produced for various purposes but which for a variety of reasons have not been put into statutory form and thus are kept in a 'bottom-drawer' status[7]. Very often such schemes are prepared especially for the guidance of development control. . . . Also of moderate significance were committee resolutions and reports. Other sources of documentary information of moderate significance included office survey maps (e.g. of the age and condition of buildings) and statutory plan texts (e.g. the 'written statement' required by the 1962 Act). Of rather low significance were the texts accompanying non-statutory plans. . . .

Colleagues in other groups provided a great deal of information to help the caseworkers. The importance of contacts in the *planning department itself* and in the *engineer (or surveyor's) department* was overwhelming. The most frequent contacts in the planning department were with fellow caseworkers and officers in the 'design' section, i.e. those working in detailed physical planning; very little contact was maintained with 'plan' colleagues, i.e. those working on broader, strategic matters of policy for the area as a whole. . . . Of much less significance were contacts with the clerk's department (on legal matters) and the estate and valuer's department (typically on the extent of council property or interests in land). Contacts with the housing, welfare, education and other departments were minimal or non-existent. . . .

One of the most important sources of information for the caseworker is the *site visit or inspection* and ranks alongside the use of other case files and contacts with the applicant, planning and highways colleagues as a formative influence on the recommendation. . . . It gives him opportunities, whether deliberately sought after or not, to talk to people in the locality and gain impressions of their views about changes in the area and to hear something about their problems concerning the physical environment. This, of course, is especially true of urban areas. By far the most common reason for inspection of the site of applications was to judge or estimate 'the effect of the proposal on its surroundings', but gaining information about the site itself and gathering material which had been omitted from the application (e.g. the location of trees on the site; the height of adjoining buildings) was also significant. . . .

Consultation with the applicant is another very significant factor on framing a recommendation. Very rarely is this done merely in order to obtain complete factual details; these can be obtained by letter, telephone and the site visit. Usually a meeting with the applicant, with or without his architect, surveyor or other advisers, is in the nature of a *discussion and negotiation* about aspects of the application. . . .

Consultation and contact with the general public was of moderate importance to caseworkers. . . .

Caseworkers try to formalize the basis of their view to the greatest extent possible. In other words, they seek *decision rules* in the form, for example, of a development plan map, a precedent such as an appeal decision, a land requirement by another department, a proposed road alignment, a national or local standard applicable to the case in question, and so forth. . . . Beyond this, caseworkers were strongly inclined to look to their colleagues either directly and informally over a cup of tea, or more formally via a memorandum. . . .

There is a considerable detachment of caseworkers from 'plan' work and especially from its higher-level 'policy' and research manifestations. We interviewed some caseworkers who had not spoken to such colleagues inside six months or more. Often regret was expressed on both sides. People felt that there *should* be more interaction and were puzzled why this did not occur. . . . Many caseworkers could not find anything useful or relevant to their work in the generalized plans and policy studies produced by their colleagues in such sections. Mixed feelings ranging from animosity and perhaps jealousy to vague puzzlement and disconnection characterized the caseworkers' attitudes. They increasingly doubted the usefulness *for them* of generalized plans and policies; they wanted much more specific guidance and advice.

Attitudes to the general public were predominantly helpful and considerate. Caseworkers realize the trouble, expense and anxiety which applicants must bear and realize that (apart from architects, builders and so on) for most people a planning application is an unusual experience. They need help and guidance. . . . Many caseworkers felt that *even more* helpful contact would be necessary in future. A more articulate and less deferential general public would need more explanation and justification of planning attitudes and decisions. Development control could evolve into one important element of public participation and some officers positively relished the prospect. Others were doubtful, even cynical. Public participation would be another demand on already precious time and most members of the public: 'don't know what they want anyway. All they're interested in is their own house.' The officer quoted seemed unaware of the irony that it is the applicant's house which development control affects! A considerable number of caseworkers, not only the younger ones, believed that contact with applicants and the public could be very valuable in providing feedback in a system for monitoring the effectiveness, relevance and impact of policies.

Attitudes to councillors fell into two broad categories. On the one hand we see the 'technocrat' view which regards the advice and recommendations coming from the caseworker and others as 'value-free' and based on purely professional and technical considerations. This view, in its extreme form, resents the councillors' 'messing about' with recommendations and will not come to terms with the perfectly proper political roles of the councillor as representative and decision taker. Caseworkers who hold such views resent committee members coming into the office to ask questions about a case which is coming up and about which the councillor may have been approached by a constituent. They are even cynical when discussing the presence on the planning committee of local landowners and builders who 'upset' recommendations because of their vested interests. Councillors, in this view, are not fit to make decisions about land development because of their lack of professional understanding: 'Why, they even try to read the plans upside down!'

Such extreme views are rare and it is more common to find considerable respect for councillors for a number of reasons. Prominent among these is the recognition by the caseworker that the councillor too has an intimate knowledge and understanding of the 'grass-roots' in the area – especially his own ward – and his knowledge of people, problems, motives, opportunities and the 'art of the possible' complements that of the caseworker. In terms of subject matter and detail, they are often talking the same language though from different standpoints.

Caseworkers were generally sure of the value of development control. . . .

This description of the planning officer at work highlights the question of informality at the pre-application stage, and its effect on decision making. Informality can neither be wholly commended nor wholly condemned; it cannot be stopped, but ought it to be discouraged? What must be done is to try and separate out acceptable from unacceptable informality. Is one test to apply to ask whether a planning officer would be inhibited in the advice he gave to a committee because of the advice he gave to a developer whose application is before the committee? Would this then rule out expressions of opinion by officers to developers of likely reactions by committee members to applications? Should officers confine themselves to technical advice and eschew policy advice? Is it always possible to tell the difference between a question asking for technical advice and one asking for policy advice? Is the whole question one which can be dealt with only by 'feel' and 'instinct' or should codes of professional conduct, declarations of interest by officers as well as members of local authorities and statutory provisions, be used to spell out right conduct? In so far as the proposals of the *Management Study on Development Control* and the *Bains Report on The New Local Authorities: management and structure* come out strongly in favour of delegating decision making to officers, views which the Local Government Act 1972[8] makes possible to implement, is the problem of informality nearer or further away from solution?

Consider these questions and the general issue of informality in relation to the following case: R & Co Ltd applied for permission to construct and operate a rail-served, ready-mixed concrete plant in the railway yards at Leamington Spa. The application first came before the Plans Sub-Committee of the Borough Council on 16 July 1973, accompanied by a report from the Public Health Department dated 4 May 1973, describing a visit made by a member of that Department, and a planning officer, to another plant owned by R & Co Ltd. 'We were escorted by the Coventry area manager and a representative from the planning section of R & Co Ltd parent services group.' The report dealt exclusively with noise and dust pollution and contained recommendations to eliminate this if the permission were to be granted.

The sub-committee was prepared to recommend to Warwickshire County Council, the planning authority on this matter, that permission be granted. Subsequently, amenity groups expressed concern on the matter and one – SLAM – wrote a detailed letter to the committee outlining objections to the proposals on traffic movement and pollution grounds. This letter was sent to R & Co for its comments. Its reply dealt with the issues raised in SLAM's letter but in doing so seemed to indicate that discussions with the borough's officers had ranged over a variety of matters not mentioned in the report of 4 May, or any report thereafter. Thus on wrong deliveries

R & Co stated: 'The wash trough and settlement chamber system for dealing with any returned loads has already been explained to the satisfaction of your Council's officers.' On landscaping, R & Co stated: 'If it were felt however that additional screening would further reduce the usual aspect of our operations, we would repeat our offer to discuss and agree a suitable landscaping scheme with your Council.' On traffic movements: 'We have already produced a considerable amount of data of traffic generation from the depot and the technical aspects of the plant restricting production have been discussed in some depth with your Planning Officers'. On access: 'The details of the accesses themselves (on to a main road) have already been considered and are accepted in principle by your Highways Department. ... The question of peak time flows has already been discussed in some detail and agreed with yourselves.'

It is not necessary to suggest, and I do not in any way suggest, malfeasance or *mal fides* on the part of the relevent officers, but the fact is that none of the matters quoted above were put before the Sub-Committee at its July meeting when the application was on the agenda. Allowing for a certain amount of bluff on the part of R & Co on the depth of the discussions[9], it still appears that the informal process had gone a long way before the formal process began to operate. Had it gone too far? Were the matters discussed technical matters upon which councillors would not expect to be invited to offer an opinion? If officers cannot use their own judgement on what to discuss, what is the point of having officers at all? Why do you think pollution questions but not traffic questions were put before the Sub-Committee? If you do not think the procedure here was correct, what would you have (a) advised as an officer, (b) done as a committee member, and do you think any set of procedural rules would help to bring about a more satisfactory balance of responsibilities?

(iii) Central government constraints on local control

The mechanics of the control of development at the central government level will be looked at in some detail in the next part of this chapter, but the control itself must be mentioned here. One could divide the constraints from the DoE into two: specific and general. Specific constraints refer to decisions given by the Department on appeal from the decisions of particular local planning authorities; if they have any precedent value at all, it is usually only in relation to the particular planning authority from which the appeal came, and even then, if the decision is disliked, it might have very little effect. A good illustration comes from Leamington Spa in relation to its office development policy. This policy seeks to restrict office development to 20,000 square feet per year; in pursuance of the policy, applications to develop offices are refused from time to time and disappointed applicants occasionally appeal. The Department naturally does not regard itself as bound by the policy and accordingly allows some appeals. The attitude of the Leamington Spa Plans Sub-Committee and its officers to these decisions was that they were unfortunate aberrations brought about by inspectors' misunderstandings of the policy and its rationale, which are in no way invalidated by the decisions. Such specific pressure may therefore be minimal.

Much more important are the general constraints which come from circulars, manuals and other forms of advice. In the area of development control, the three most important sources of advice are circulars, development control policy notes, and planning bulletins.

The role of the circular has been outlined in Chapter 2; it is enough here to indicate the areas covered by them (and the quantity which planning officers are subject to) by giving the titles of a selection. By the end of 1974, the *Encyclopedia of Planning Law and Practice*, a standard work in virtually every planning office, contained over 750 pages of ministerial circulars and information dating back to 1949, the vast majority of which consisted of circulars setting out the Department's views on the procedures and policies of planning. Taking the period since the establishment of the Department in late 1970, the following is a selection of matters that have been covered by circulars:

56/71	Historic Towns and Roads
71/71	Development of Agricultural Land
72/71	Disused Railways in the Countryside
73/71	Publicity for Conservation
3/72	Sunlight and Daylight – Planning Criteria and Design of Buildings
52/72	Development Plan Proposals: Publicity and Public Participation
53/72	General Information System for Planning

102/72   Land Availability for Housing
10/73   Planning and Noise
71/73   Publicity for planning applications, appeals and other proposals for development

Development control policy notes were introduced in 1969 by MHLG Circular No. 23 of that year which set out their purpose as follows:

1. We are directed by the Minister of Housing and Local Government and the Secretary of State for Wales to say that they have decided to publish a series of notes on development control policy and a complete set of the first batch is enclosed. The policies outlined in the notes are not new; they are those on which the Departments are concurrently operating. In some instances they have already been published in such documents as the Bulletins of Selected Planning Appeals, which these notes supersede. The policies will be reviewed from time to time and revised notes on these subjects will be issued, as well as additional notes on subjects not covered by the present batch.

2. The Ministers believe that these notes will be helpful to all those concerned in the operation of planning control – in particular to local planning authorities and district councils exercising delegated powers, to appellants and their professional advisers, and to inspectors exercising functions transferred to them under Part III of the Town and Country Planning Act 1968. While the notes contain general guidance, the Ministers wish to emphasise that they should not be interpreted as set formulae for settling planning applications and appeals without regard to the circumstances of individual cases or to any special expression of policy for particular cases contained in the development plan.

3. The notes will be available from Her Majesty's Stationery Office either in batches or singly, and it is hoped that local authorities will draw the attention of applicants to them at an early stage where this would be helpful.[10]

Planning bulletins were introduced in 1962, as follows

MHLG Circular No. 38/62 on Planning Bulletin No. 1:
'Town Centres – Approach to Renewal'

2. This is the first of a series of planning bulletins designed to provide local authorities with information and advice on the problems of urban development and redevelopment. . . .

3. The scope and purpose of the bulletins will vary. Some will be largely technical in content, others will give guidance on current Ministerial policy: some will deal with both policy and technical matters.

6. This present bulletin does not aim to give comprehensive advice on town centre problems. A second bulletin is in preparation which will illustrate examples of successful town centre planning at home and

abroad; and a third will deal with the problems of car parking provision in central areas. Further bulletins will deal with various other aspects, including technical advice on the trends in town centre layout and design.

8. It is intended to develop the series as experience and knowledge of urban planning matters increase. The bulletins will be revised and re-issued as necessary. Suggestions from local authorities for improvements in later editions or for other bulletins in the series will be welcome.

It is difficult to say what effect these departmental publications have. Presumably, the Department think that they serve a useful purpose, otherwise they would not produce so many, but many questions remain to be answered about how local planning authorities make use of them.[11] Do they make them freely available to developers? Are all officers familiar with them or at least are those employed in development control familiar with the development control policy notes? Is there a danger that planning officers may be in receipt of too much information and advice, leading either to paralysis of decision making or to a too uncritical rejection (or acceptance) of most advice received? One of the few pieces of central government advice which we do know was acted upon is the town centre map, suggested in the first planning bulletin. Many towns now have these maps, which will ultimately be superseded by action area plans. These are non-statutory policy documents, but being suggested by the Ministry (as it then was), they are likely to have more regard paid to them by the Department on appeal than other local authority policies. They have, however, been criticised as being in effect attempts to alter statutory development plans without going through statutory procedures of publicity and inquiry.[12] Could this criticism be generalised? Could it be argued that departmental advice, if constantly acted upon, would operate to deprive local planning authorities of much of their discretion? If so, would this matter?

(v) The councillors

The role of councillors and their committees has been examined in Chapter 2 and is raised implicitly in the one case set out above. It is not proposed to examine them specifically further. By way of summary, it may be said that while some research has shown that councillors seem to have little influence on planning or other decisions – Buxton's impressionistic survey may be mentioned here[13] – other research seems to suggest that at least some councillors have a considerable influence on the evolution of planning policy and its implementation – Dennis's studies of Sunderland are one example.[14] Generalisations in this context are dangerous, even about the same local planning authority, which may change dramatically after an election or imperceptibly after the election of a new chairman of committee, the appointment of a new chief planning officer, or the establishment of a new amenity group in the area. All that can be said by way of generalisation is that as with the officers, so here; formal statements on the lines of 'committees consisting of councillors decide planning applications' are not merely unhelpful, but positively misleading in so far as they direct attention away from an awareness of the need to probe the problems of conflicts of interest and corruption and the relationships between councillors and officers, and between formal procedure at the committee and informal procedures outside it. The existence and importance of these problems and relationships should be borne in mind in the ensuing sections of this part of the chapter.

(c) How is control exercised?

There are two questions that must be asked by any potential applicant for permission to develop: 'Do I need permission?' And, if the answer to that question is 'yes', 'May I have permission to develop?' Logically, an applicant should clear up the first question before proceeding to the second and so, logically, it might be thought we should consider the first question before the second. But for three reasons the order of consideration is reversed. First, in terms of sheer quantity, applications for permission to develop and the problems to which they give rise far outweigh the problems of developing with a deemed permission. Secondly, the local authority has comparatively little role to play in dealing with the issues arising out of developing on the basis that one does not need permission. These are matters where the courts have played a significant role, and thus in terms of the framework of this chapter will be dealt with after the role of the local authority has been examined. Finally, as a matter of practice, many small-scale applicants apply for permission 'to be on the safe side', irrespective of whether as a matter of law it is necessary and these too may be classified as applications to develop.

So that the problems to be discussed may be seen within an overall framework, the 'pathway of a case file' is set out first.

J. B. McLoughlin, op. cit., pp. 88-9

Application filed
Decision and application dispatched to applicant — Observations receive
Decision notice checked   Consultation with D
Decision drafted

Approval
notice issued

PLANNING COMMITTEE   Historic buildings or

Agenda drafted
Final checking of amended draft
Conditions checked
Passed to Chief Executives Dept
Recommendation drafted
Planning Officer's recommendation
Recommendation formulated
Co-ordination of consultations

Development Plan Section ——————→ Observations
Representations   Assistant Planning Officer
resulting   Engineer
from advert.   Public Health
                         Divisional Road Engineer
                         Ministry of Agriculture
                         Adjoining authority
Building   Additional consultations
regulations   Forwarded to parties consulted
applications   Amended plans received
                         Additional information requested

Meeting with
applicant ←————— Preliminary consideration of application
                 Consultations determined
                 Site visit
Advert.in   Advert draft preparation
local paper   Application acknowledged
                 Plotted ——————————→ Coded
                 Entered in register
                 Completed application made into file
                 Application checked for correctness
                 Passed to development control section
                 Passed to Planning Officer for preliminary consideration

Entered in post book
Date-stamped
Application received in post

Let us then look at the problems of how to apply for permission. They may be broken down into three sub-divisions: the application for permission; the determination of the application, and the communication of that determination. All three stages pose problems which will now be examined.

(i) The application

Town and Country Planning (General Development) Orders
1973 to 1974

5 (1) . . . An application to a local planning authority for planning permission shall be made on a form issued by the local planning authority and obtainable from that authority . . . and shall include the particulars required by such form to be supplied and be accompanied by a plan sufficient to identify the land to which it relates and such other plans and drawings as are necessary to describe the development which is the subject of the application . . . and a local planning authority may by a direction in writing addressed to the applicant require such further information as may be specified in the direction to be given to them . . . to enable them to determine that application.

The above provision deals with the application as if it were solely a matter between the applicant and the local planning authority. This is not so, however, and the thrust of changes in the law and administration over the past decade has been in the direction of increasing opportunities for the public to be involved and consulted over planning applications at the local authority level.

(a) PUBLICITY[16]

Town and Country Planning Act 1971

26.—(1) Provision may be made by a development order for designating the classes of development to which this section applies, and this section shall apply accordingly to any class of development which is for the time being so designated.

(2) An application for planning permission for development of any class to which this section applies shall not be entertained by the local planning authority unless it is accompanied—

(a) by a copy of a notice of the application, in such form as may be prescribed by a development order, and by such evidence as may be so prescribed that the notice has been published in a local newspaper circulating in the locality in which the land to which the application relates is situated; and

(b) by one or other of the following certificates, signed by or on behalf of the applicant, that is to say—

(i) a certificate stating that he has complied with subsection (3) of this section and when he did so; or

(ii) a certificate stating that he has been unable to comply with it because he has not such rights of access or other rights in respect of the land as would enable him to do so, but that he has taken such reasonable steps as are open to him (specifying them) to acquire those rights and has been unable to acquire them.

(3) In order to comply with this subsection a person must—

(a) post on the land a notice, in such form as may be prescribed by a development order, stating that the application for planning permission is to be made; and

(b) leave the notice in position for not less than seven days in a period of not more than one month immediately preceding the making of the application to the local planning authority.

(4) The said notice must be posted by affixing it firmly to some object on the land, and must be sited and displayed in such a way as to be easily visible and legible by members of the public without going on the land.

(5) The applicant shall not be treated as unable to comply with subsection (3) of this section if the notice is, without any fault or intention of his, removed, obscured or defaced before the seven days referred to in subsection (3)(b) of this section have elapsed, so long as he has taken reasonable steps for its protection and, if need be, replacement; and, if he has cause to rely on this subsection, his certificate under subsection (2)(b) of this section shall state the relevant circumstances.

(6) The notice mentioned in subsection (2)(a) or required by subsection (3) of this section shall (in addition to any other matters required to be contained therein) name a place within the locality where a copy of the application for planning permission, and of all plans and other documents submitted with it, will be open to inspection by the public at all reasonable hours during such period as may be specified in the notice, not being a period of less than twenty-one days beginning with the date on which the notice is published or first posted, as the case may be.

(7) An application for planning permission for development of any class to which this section applies shall not be determined by the local planning authority before the end of the period of twenty-one days beginning with the date of the application.

Town and Country Planning General Development Orders
1973 to 1974

8.—(1) The following classes of development are designated for the purposes of section 26 of the Act:—

(a) construction of buildings for use as public conveniences;

(b) construction of buildings or other operations, or use of land, for the disposal of refuse or waste materials or as a scrap yard or coal yard or for the winning or working of minerals;

(c) construction of buildings or other operations (other than the laying of sewers, the construction of pumphouses in a line of sewers, the construction of septic tanks and cesspools serving single dwelling-houses or single buildings in which not more than ten people will normally reside, work or congregate, and works ancillary thereto) or use of land, for the purpose of the retention, treatment or disposal of sewage, trade waste or sludge;

(d) construction of buildings to a height exceeding 20 metres;

(e) construction of buildings or use of land for the purposes of a slaughterhouse or knacker's yard; or for killing or plucking poultry;

(f) construction of buildings and use of buildings for any of the following purposes, namely, as a casino, a funfair or a bingo hall, a theatre, a cinema, a music hall, a dance hall, a skating rink, a swimming bath or gymnasium (not forming part of a school, college or university), or a Turkish or other vapour or foam bath;

(g) construction of buildings and use of buildings or land as a zoo or for the business of boarding or breeding cats or dogs;

(h) construction of buildings and use of land for motor car or motorcycle racing;

(i) use of land as a cemetery.

DoE Circular No. 71/73: 'Publicity for Planning Applications, Appeals and Other Proposals for Development'

2. In the view of the Secretaries of State the basic principle should be that opinion should be enabled to declare itself before any approval is given to proposals of wide concern or substantial impact on the environment; and that this should be so whether the proposal is that of a Government Department, a local authority, statutory undertakers or a private developer. Local planning authorities will sometimes have to judge proposals by principles which may not reflect the views expressed by people in the immediate locality but it will nevertheless assist them not only in deciding those applications but also in their wider planning responsibilities to be aware of local feeling about significant proposals.

3. Planning is concerned to ensure that in the development of land the public interest is taken fully into account. Its objective is not the safeguarding of private property rights as such; nor, in particular, to protect the value of individual properties or the views to be had from them. Those who argue for a right for neighbours to be notified individually of *all* prospective development do not give sufficient weight to this. There are, however, occasions when the public interest may require that the interests of those immediately affected by even a comparatively minor proposal should be taken into account as a planning consideration.

4. It has been suggested that, as an alternative to notification of neighbours there should be a general requirement for the display of a site notice whenever an application for planning permission is made, so that those who might feel that the public interest might be involved could express a view. Such a requirement, it is argued, would overcome the objection of principle to universal notification and would be no more than a

projection of the planning register, which is already available for public inspection. The Secretaries of State have carefully considered this point but have come to the conclusion that the objections to such a move outweigh the advantages. The planning system is administered by democratically elected local councils and the Government would not wish to impose absolute duties across the whole field of that administration. Furthermore, from a practical point of view the desire for more publicity has to be weighed against the need not to overload the planning machine. There were in 1972 over 600,000 planning applications, the majority in respect of quite minor development. This represents a 40 per cent increase in two years. The display of site notices in every case would be bound to lead to a large volume of correspondence on matters which would not be a material consideration in reaching planning decisions and would give rise to misunderstanding as well as to unwarranted delay in the handling of applications.

7. The Secretaries of State take the view that the selective approach is the right one and that pending legislation local authorities should ask applicants to display a site notice where permission is sought for development which, in the authority's opinion, is likely to have a substantial impact on the neighbourhood. It is impossible to lay down precise rules and it must be for authorities to decide the circumstances in which the public interest is sufficiently involved to warrant publicity. But the Secretaries of State consider that it would normally be right for applicants to be asked to post site notices where development would, in the authority's opinion:

(a) introduce a significant change in a homogeneous area;

(b) affect residential property by causing, eg. smell, noise or vibration;

(c) bring crowds and or noise into a generally quiet area;

(d) cause activity and noise at late or early hours in areas where this is not usual;

(e) otherwise have an adverse effect on the general character of an area, eg. tall buildings which do not come within the requirement in Article 8 (1) (d) of the 1973 General Development Order but which would, nevertheless, have a substantial impact; or

(f) constitute a departure from the development plan which would not have to be advertised under the terms of the Town and Country Planning (Development Plans) Direction 1965 (or in London the 1966 Direction).

22. The arrangements set out above relate in general to planning applications formally made to local planning authorities. Where proposals for development are not the subject of a formal planning application – for example because the development is to be undertaken by a Government Department, or the local planning authority or is development carried out by statutory undertakers in circumstances where they do not need to apply for permission – the general principles underlying these arrangements should still be applied in deciding whether local publicity – including notification to parish councils and community councils – is necessary.

Agreement has been reached on this following discussions with the local authority associations and with Government Departments which themselves carry out development or have responsibility for statutory undertakers. . . .

23. The Secretaries of State consider that the public should have the same opportunity to express views on proposals for development by local planning authorities as they would if the development were to be carried out by a private developer. . . .

25. Where proposals for development by statutory undertakers are the subject of planning applications, arrangements for publicity will, of course, be those referred to earlier in this Circular. But there will also be a need to publicise some proposals for development covered by the permissions given to statutory undertakers in the General Development Order. The following paragraphs, which have already been promulgated in Circular 12/73 (GDO Circular), (Welsh Office Circular 23/73), amount to a code of practice which has been commended to the statutory undertakers by the appropriate Ministers.

27. Some statutory undertakers already make it a practice to let the local planning authority know of any substantial projects (and, in a number of cases, of comparatively minor ones). But the practice varies; and the Ministers concerned are asking statutory undertakers to ensure that both planning authorities and the public know of proposals for permitted development that are likely to affect them significantly before the proposals are finalised. . . .

DoE Circular No. 142/73: 'Streamlining the Planning Machine'

7 (viii) . . . Decisions on publicity should, save in exceptional cases, be taken by officers.

DoE Circular No. 80/71: 'Development by Government Department's

1. Development by the Crown does not require planning permission. But before proceeding with development Government Departments will consult local planning authorities when the proposed development is:

(a) One for which, if the Government Department were a private developer, local authority or statutory undertaker, specific planning permission would be required.

(b) A change of use not within any of the classes set out in the current Use Classes Order.

(c) A motorway service area or motorway maintenance compound, a lorry area, picnic site or lavatories, proposed in connection with a trunk road.

As regards (a) above, Departments will use the General Development Order, as operating in the area concerned at the time when a proposal is being considered, as a general guide to the kinds of development which they may carry out without consultation. The General Development Order does not deal with certain special forms of development undertaken by Government Departments; but in deciding whether consultation is appropriate Departments will apply the exemptions granted by the Order to private bodies, local authorities and statutory undertakers, *mutatis mutandis*, to their own development.

4. Even where consultation would not be required on the basis set out above Departments have agreed to notify the local planning authority of development proposals which are likely to be of special concern to the authority or to the public – for example where there could be a very substantial effect on the character of a conservation area, or where there could be a significant planning impact beyond the Department's own site, whether visually or otherwise (*e.g.* in the generation of traffic). In any notification case of this kind the local planning authority will be given an opportunity to decide whether, in their view, the proposal should be advertised so as to give the public a chance to comment and for discussion with the Department about ways in which the proposal might be amended to overcome any planning difficulty.

5. Departments have agreed also to bear in mind that in any event, whether consultation is required or not, an early preliminary approach to the planning authority will often be useful particularly in the case of development likely to be of special local concern to the public or to the local planning authority. Of course, neither such an approach nor any of the consultation procedures can fully apply to proposals involving national security.

While the law requires certain classes of development to be advertised (and a certificate to that effect to be provided by the applicant), publicity over and above that is to be left largely to the discretion of the local planning authorities and agreements between them and developers. Is this a satisfactory arrangement? Some local planning authorities are better at insisting on publicity than others; some have more active amenity groups than others, checking the planning registers, and then commenting on applications. If the collective view of the Secretaries of State is that 'the basic principle should be that opinion should be enabled to declare itself before any approval is given to proposals of wide concern or substantial impact on the environment . . .', why not give legislative expression to this view? Local authorities are being encouraged to engage in joint ventures with developers to redevelop city centres and develop housing and industrial estates;[17] will participating local authorities be more or less willing to ensure that the developers agree to adequate publicity for development proposals? Do you agree with the analysis of the system of planning contained in paragraphs 3 and 4 of Circular

No. 71/73? Do you think that a proper balance between speed of decision making and participation is struck by it? Site notices have a tendency to disappear or be (or become) illegible and the Act makes provision that these circumstances do not amount to non-compliance with the rules as to site notices. Does not this provision render them virtually useless as a means of informing the public of possible development?

Despite the methods of publicity suggested or required, an almost universal complaint is that people do not know what is being proposed either at all or until it is too late to comment on it. What is the remedy for this state of affairs? Does the fault, if fault there be, lie with the law, its administration by the local planning authorities, the press or the voluntary amenity groups? Or does the problem go deeper and really involve a clash of philosophies about planning; on the one hand, the philosophy set out in paragraphs 3 and 4 of the circular, and on the other, a philosophy that poses the people *against* the planners, puts the 'democratically elected local councils' in the same camp as the planners, and requires that the people be allowed to determine their own environment?

(b) CONSULTATION AND INFORMING

In addition to publicity, local planning authorities are also required to consult and inform certain other authorities in respect of certain types of planning applications as follows:

Town and Country Planning General Development Orders
1973 to 1974

13.—(1) Before permission is granted by a local planning authority for development in any of the following cases, whether unconditionally or subject to conditions, a local planning authority shall consult with the following authorities or persons, namely:—

(a) where it appears to the local planning authority that the development is likely to affect land in the area of any other local planning authority:—

(i) with the district planning authority in whose area the land affected is situate (except where that land is in a National Park);

(iii) where the land affected is in a National Park, with the county planning authority in whose area that land is situate;

(b) where it appears to the local planning authority that the development is likely to create or attract traffic which will result in a material increase in the volume of traffic entering or leaving a trunk road or using a level crossing over a railway, with the Secretary of State at such office or address as he may appoint;

(*f*) where the development consists of or includes:—

    (ii) the carrying out of building or other operations or use of land for the purpose of refining or storing mineral oils and their derivatives;

    (iii) the use of land for the deposit of any kind of refuse or waste; with the water authority. . . .

(*g*) where the development is of land in an area of special interest notified to the local planning authority by the Nature Conservancy Council in accordance with section 23 of the National Parks and Access to the Countryside Act 1949, with the Nature Conservancy Council; except where that Council dispense with this requirement.

(3) The Secretary of State may give directions to a local planning authority requiring that authority to consult with the authorities, persons or bodies named in such directions in any case or class of case which may be specified in such directions and, before granting permission in any such case or class of case, the local planning authority shall enter into consultation accordingly.

(4) Where under this article a local planning authority are required to consult with any authority, person or body as to any application, they shall give not less than 14 days' notice to such authority, person or body that such application is to be taken into consideration, shall not determine the application until after the expiration of the period of such notice, and shall, in determining the application, take into account any representations received from such authority, person or body'.

13A.—(1) A county planning authority, before determining any of the following matters relating to a county matter, namely:—

(*a*) an application for planning permission under Part III of the Act;

(*b*) an application for determining under section 53 of the Act whether an application for such permission is required;

(*c*) an application for an established use certificate under section 94 of the Act;

(*d*) an application for approval of reserved matters;

shall afford the district planning authority for the area in which the land to which the application relates is situated an opportunity to make recommendations to the county planning authority as to the manner in which the application shall be determined and shall take any such recommendations into account.

We have seen that consultation is a standard form of administrative practice by central government and that this practice is occasionally required by the law. In writing about statutory consultation in respect of subordinate legislation, Garner has noted that 'consultation is not, of course, a precise word, nor can the process of consultation be given any exact formality. . . . Where it is required by the statute, consultation must be genuine, and if it is not adequate, it seems that any delegated legislation subsequently made would be invalid as having been made in a manner contrary to that provided for in the enabling statute . . ..'[18] It is important to note that the provisions as to consultation between local or other authorities quoted above are much more detailed and precise than those that confer a duty on ministers to consult. Contrast the above provisions with section 1 of the New Towns Act 1965, which empowers the Minister to designate an area as the site of a new town 'if (he) is satisfied, after consultation with any local authorities who appear to him to be concerned, that it is expedient in the national interest . . ..' Why is this? If ministers 'would not wish to impose absolute duties' on local authorities in respect of publicity for applications, why have duties in such detailed form been imposed in respect of consultation?

A more important matter is: what happens if consultation does not take place in accordance with the order? In the 1940s the courts, in interpreting section 1(1) of the New Towns Act 1946 (similar to the section quoted above) did not seek to impose too onerous a duty on the Minister.[19] Would the same attitude prevail in the 1970s in respect of local planning authorities?[20]

So far as informing is concerned, consider the following:

Local Government Act 1972, Schedule 16

20.—(1) Where a district planning authority have been notified in writing by the council of a parish or community wholly or partly situated in the area of that authority that the council wish to be informed of every application for planning permission relating to land in the parish or community or of every application so relating for approval of a matter reserved under an outline planning permission within the meaning of section 42, or of any description of such applications, and receive any such application or, as the case may be, an application of any such description, they shall inform the council in writing of the application indicating the nature of the development to which the application relates and identifying the land to which it relates.

The Town and Country Planning General Development Orders
1973 to 1974

13B.—(1) A district planning authority, on receiving any application of which the Council of a parish or community are entitled to be informed, shall as soon as practicable notify that council of the application, and of the name of the local planning authority who will determine it and shall notify that authority, if not the district planning authority, of the date on which they give such notification.

(2) On being notified of any such application the council of the parish or community shall as soon as practicable notify the local planning authority by whom the application will be determined whether they propose to make any representations as to the manner in which the application should be determined, and shall deliver any such representations to that authority within 14 days of the notification to them of the application.

(3) The local planning authority shall not determine any such application before—

(i) notification by the Council of the parish or community that they do not propose to make any representations; or

(ii) receipt of representations from the council of the parish or community; or

(iii) the expiration of 14 days from the date when the council of the parish or community are notified,

whichever shall first occur, and in determining the application the local planning authority shall take into account any representations received from the council of the parish or community.

What is the difference between informing and consulting an outside body if in each case the planning authority is required to take into account any representations received from the outside body?

(c) OWNERSHIP CERTIFICATES

We may now consider the problems arising out of section 27 of the 1971 Act. The section itself may be thought straightforward and sensible; indeed, the wonder is not that it exists, but that it did not exist until the Town and Country Planning Act 1959 implemented a recommendation of the Franks Committee to that effect. The problems, which may have wider application than purely this section, arise from ministerial advice about and a judicial decision on it.

27.—(1) Without prejudice to section 26 of this Act, a local planning authority shall not entertain any application for planning permission unless it is accompanied by one or other of the following certificates signed by or on behalf of the applicant, that is to say—

(a) a certificate stating that, in respect of every part of the land to which the application relates, the applicant is either the estate owner in respect of the fee simple or is entitled to a tenancy thereof:

(b) a certificate stating that the applicant has given the requisite notice of the application to all the persons (other than the applicant) who, at the beginning of the period of twenty-one days ending with the date of the application, were owners of any of the land to which the application relates, and setting out the names of those persons, the addresses at which notice of the application was given to them respectively, and the date of service of each such notice;

(c) a certificate stating that the applicant is unable to issue a certificate in accordance with either of the preceding paragraphs, that he has given the requisite notice of the application to such one or more of the persons mentioned in the last preceding paragraph as are specified in the certificate (setting out their names, the addresses at which notice of the application was given to them respectively, and the date of the service of each such notice), that he has taken such steps as are reasonably open to him (specifying them) to ascertain the names and addresses of the remainder of those persons and that he has been unable to do so;

(d) a certificate stating that the applicant is unable to issue a certificate in accordance with paragraph (a) of this subsection, that he has taken such steps as are reasonably open to him (specifying them) to ascertain the names and addresses of the persons mentioned in paragraph (b) of this subsection and that he has been unable to do so.

(7) In this section 'owner', in relation to any land, means a person who is for the time being the estate owner in respect of the fee simple thereof or is entitled to a tenancy thereof granted or extended for a term of years certain of which not less than ten years remain unexpired, and 'agricultural holding' has the same meaning as in the Agricultural Holdings Act 1948.

MHLG Circular No. 48/59

47. Local planning authorities should see that a certificate in one or other of the prescribed forms, duly completed, is furnished by the applicant in each case. It is not their duty to check the accuracy of the statements made in the certificates but this does not preclude them from questioning the statements in a certificate if they see good reason to do so.

R v. *Bradford-upon-Avon UDC ex parte Boulton*
[1964] 2 All E.R. 492

This was a motion by the applicant, Raymond Percy Boulton, for an order of certiorari to bring up and quash a decision of the first respondents, Bradford-on-Avon Urban District Council, dated May 7, 1963, whereby, acting under delegated powers from the Wiltshire County Council, the local planning authority, they approved certain plans on behalf of Mr J. A. Francis relating to a house proposed to be built by him in Bradford-on-Avon. The second respondent to the motion was the clerk to the county council, the third, fourth and fifth respondents were Mr Francis, Mr Huggins and Mr Bowyer, who are subsequently mentioned in the course of summarising the facts.

In 1962, Mr Christopher Bowyer, a builder and chairman of the Bradford-on-Avon Urban District Council, who owned a piece of land in Bradford-on-Avon which was originally part of the curtilage of a dwelling-house, was minded to have it used for building development. Mr Francis, the assistant planning officer of the Wiltshire County Council, was interested in becoming the owner of the proposed new house on the land. He invited Mr Bowyer to apply for and see if he could obtain outline planning permission for the development of the land. On Sept. 7, 1962, Mr Bowyer made application to the council for outline planning permission. . . . Bowyer also submitted a certificate under s. 37 (1) (a) of the Town and Country Planning Act, 1959, stating that he was the owner of the site in fee simple. On Oct. 3, 1963, outline planning was granted by the council subject to certain conditions, one of which dealt with vehicular access to the site. Mr Francis then had detailed plans prepared by an architect, Mr Huggins, who submitted them on behalf of Mr Francis to the council for approval of the plans under art. 5 (3) of the Order of 1950. On one side of the proposed access to and from the land was a party wall and a party pillar. Drawing F. 11/3 of the detailed plans showed the party wall and party pillar set back to a distance needed to improve the line of sight of a driver of a vehicle leaving the proposed new development. The proposed alteration of the party wall and pillar necessitated obtaining the adjoining owner's consent, but the architect, on behalf of Mr Francis, did not get her consent, because he had acted for her previously and assumed that she would give her consent. The plans made no reference to the fact that the adjoining owner had an interest in the party wall and pillar. With the detailed plans was submitted a document in the form provided for an application for permission to develop land which showed for the first time that Mr Francis was the applicant, the previous application having been made by Mr Bowyer. . . . There was also submitted to the council a document purporting to be a certificate under s. 37 (1) (a) of the Act of 1959. This certificate, which was dated Mar. 15, 1963, was signed by a subordinate of the architect and was expressed to be signed on behalf of Mr Francis. It certified that Mr Francis was the owner in fee simple of the land; but in fact he was not, for he was still in the process of negotiating to acquire the land and Mr Bowyer was still the owner. The certificate also made no reference to the fact that the party wall and pillar were on part of the land in which the adjoining owner was interested; and the court intimated that the certificate was open to criticism on these grounds. In due course permission to develop the land in accordance with the detailed plans was granted. As a result of local objections, the council reconsidered the whole matter but decided not to revoke the permission.

WIDGERY J (after considering whether the applicant could bring an action for certiorari[21], continued): . . . It must, I think, be borne in mind that he is seeking to have quashed the decision of the first respondents, the council, of May 7, 1963, that is to say, the approval of the final details. The way in which it was put by counsel for the applicant in his opening of the case was under two heads; first of all, he submits that the council were induced to reach their decision on May 7 as a result of having been misled by false information supplied by Mr Francis. In opening the case, counsel I think, recognised that he had to go so far as to say that there had been a fraud on the part of Mr Francis, and that it was on that basis that he sought to say that certiorari should go. It will, I think, be apparent from what I have already said that the certificate which was submitted in support of the detailed plans was an inaccurate certificate, and it is said by counsel that the plans themselves were inaccurate and misleading. For my part, I do not think that the plans were misleading. The plans in themselves do not speak to title, and do not in fact indicate whether or not the applicant has put himself in a position to carry out the proposed development therein referred to. It is a commonplace that people often seek planning permission before they incur the expense of buying some of the land necessary, and merely to apply for permission for a particular development does not of itself warrant an ability to carry out that development at the time of the application.

So far as the certificate was concerned, however, it was clearly wrong for the reasons and to the extent to which I have referred. Whether the council were misled in a sense that, had they been in possession of a correct certificate and had they been in all respects in possession of the correct information, they would have come to a different conclusion, I for myself very much doubt. They were being asked to approve a perfectly sensible and proper proposal, and it seems to me very difficult to believe that they would have rejected that proposal merely because they had been told that Mr Francis might have some difficulty in regard to implementing it in detail. I think that the council would have been perfectly entitled to say that that was a matter for Mr Francis, that they would consent to the proposal if he could carry it out, and, if he could not carry it out, then no harm would be done. Accordingly, it seems to me that counsel for the applicant is in difficulty in saying that the council were misled in the sense of induced to take a different course by anything which happened. But, of course, the point at which this submission of his really meets its downfall is his complete failure to prove any kind of fraud on the part of Mr Bowyer, Mr Francis, Mr Huggins, or, indeed, any of the others concerned. I am entirely satisfied, and it must be said as firmly as possible, that there is no shred of evidence at all that any of those gentlemen did anything which was in any way improper, and certainly no shred of evidence of fraud. Accordingly, that approach of counsel for the applicant as I see it must fail.

His alternative approach is under s. 37 of the Town and Country Planning Act, 1959. He draws attention to the opening words of s. 37 (1), to the effect that a local planning authority shall not entertain any application for planning permission unless the appropriate certificate is submitted with the application. He says, and I think with force, that those words 'shall not entertain' are apt words to limit the jurisdiction of the planning authority in consideration of the application, and his submission is that if, as in this case, when the final details were submitted, the certificate submitted with them was a certificate which was false as to the facts contained in it, that that deprives the planning authority of jurisdiction and thus gives this court an opportunity to quash the authority's decision. For my part, I think that there are two answers to that submission, either of which is sufficient to defeat it. First of all, I do not think that a planning authority loses jurisdiction to deal with an application for planning permission if the application is accompanied by a genuine certificate signed by or on behalf of a genuine applicant merely because there is some factual error in the contents of the certificate. I think, as has been urged on us by counsel for the respondents, that to hold otherwise would give rise to very serious complications in the way of those who have to buy and sell property, because, amongst other things, it must be remembered that a purchaser buying land is often very much influenced by the presence or absence of a planning permission obtained by his seller. If purchasers have to investigate not only whether a certificate was submitted when the application for permission was made, but also whether the certificate was correct in its own factual averments, it seems to me that a very grave complication would be put in their way. I am content, however, to go to the actual words of s. 37 (1) (a) of the Act of 1959, and it seems to me that, on those plain words, jurisdiction is conferred on the authority if the application is accompanied by a genuine certificate in the approved terms, in the terms prescribed by the subsection, by the actual applicant, and I do not think that a factual error in the certificate deprives the authority of jurisdiction under the section.

The other ground on which, as I see it, this argument must fail is that, in my opinion, the application for planning approval of details made in this case was not an application for planning permission at all, and, therefore, did not attract the need for a certificate under s. 37. . . .[22] *Application dismissed.*

What is the purpose of requiring a section 27 certificate from an applicant? Is that purpose served if the certificate is regarded as valid, notwithstanding factual errors, so that a local planning authority does not lose its jurisdiction to consider an application accompanied by a genuine if erroneous certificate? What kind of error might turn a genuine but erroneous certificate into a non-genuine certificate?

If it is not the duty of the local planning authority to check the accuracy of statements made in a certificate, and if purchasers are not obliged to check whether 'a certificate was correct in its own factual averments', what purpose is being served by it? Would anyone, and if so, who, be able to bring an action in negligence against the applicant who, let it be assumed, negligently put in an erroneous certificate? The court seemed to be saying: since nobody did anything really wrong, i.e. fraudulent, and since the decision was not influenced by the error anyway, there is no reason to quash the decision. Is this approach to the planning process to be applauded as a non-legalistic common-sense one or condemned as an example of the courts being more administration-minded than the administration?

How far does this decision extend? Are all the obligations imposed by regulations discussed in this section likely to be treated in the same way by the courts? If not, where is the dividing line to be drawn and why?

Consider the following problem:[23] X applied for permission to the Oldtown BC to put in a back entrance to his builder's yard. To be able to use the back entrance X would have to cross a piece of land owned by Y. In addition, the plans showed that the gates to the back entrance would swing outwards and thereby cross Y's land. X put in a certificate in terms of section 27(1)(a) and obtained permission. Subsequently, Y learned of the application and the grant of permission and complained to the Council that since X had not put in a certificate about Y's land which was 'land to which the application relates' the Council had been without jurisdiction to deal with the application. The Clerk to the Council advised that the matter was covered by *Boulton* and the Council thereupon refused to reopen the case. Was the clerk right? Assume Y is an ordinary member of the public, with an average salary, a mortgage and a family and remains dissatisfied with the situation. Advise him as to his best course of action.

(d) OUTLINE APPLICATIONS

Town and Country Planning General Development Orders
1973 to 1974

5. (2). Where an applicant so desires, an application may be made for outline planning permission for the erection of a building, and where such permission is granted, the subsequent approval of the local planning authority shall be required to such matters (being reserved matters as defined) as may be reserved by condition. . . .

Provided that where, in Greater London, the local planning authority, and elsewhere, either the authority to whom the application is made or the authority by whom the function of determining the application is exercisable are of the opinion that in the circumstances of the case the application ought not to be considered separately from the siting or the design or external appearance of the building, or the means of access thereto or the landscaping of the site, they shall within the period of one month from receipt of the application notify the applicant that they are unable to entertain it unless further details are submitted, specifying the matters as to which they require further information for the purpose of arriving at a decision in respect of the proposed development; and the applicant may either furnish the information so required or appeal to the Secretary of State . . . as if his application had been refused by the authority.

2 (1) . . . 'reserved matters' in relation to an outline planning permission or an application for such permission means any matters in respect of which details have not been given in the application and which concern the siting, design, or external appearance of the building to which the planning permission or the application relates or the means of access to the building, or the landscaping of the site in respect of which the application was made.

The rationale of outline applications is fairly clear: a developer and/ or a prospective purchaser of land may wish to discover whether a local planning authority will agree in principle to a particular development, and not wish to incur the expense or waste the time of preparing detailed plans until such agreement has been obtained. Inevitably however, over the years, the clear rationale has been clouded over by the evolution of law and practice, particularly in the areas of (i) how much detail has to go into the outline, (ii) what can be reserved by the local planning authority for approval at the 'detailed' stage, and (iii) at what point an application for detailed approval may be treated as a fresh application because of changes between outline and details.

On the first matter, there are two circulars of relevance:

Ministry of Town and Country Planning Circular 87/50

. . . Since consideration at the approval stage is limited by the terms of the initial permission, it is essential that the permission should not take the form of a blank cheque, and, correspondingly, the authority must be furnished with sufficient information to enable them to form a proper judgment of what is proposed: there can be no question of entertaining propositions which are still in embryo. The application should indicate the character and approximate size of the building to be erected, and the use to which it is to be put. . . .

In practice many developers went further and submitted sketch plans of some of the details without intending that they should form part of the outline application. In order to clarify the difficulties to which this could give rise – i.e. some local authorities might take these to be part of the application, and the Minister ruled in one appeal that that approach was correct unless the applicant indicated to the contrary – the 1969 Amendment to the General Development Order introduced a definition of 'reserved matters' (reprinted above) and indicated its import in the circular below:

MHLG Circular No. 12/69

. . . It follows from this definition that if details of any matters of siting, design, external appearance or means of access are included in an application for planning permission, then unless the details submitted are purely illustrative that matter cannot be treated as reserved for subsequent approval and the local planning authority must take those details fully into account in reaching its decision on the application. If, whilst not objecting to the proposed development in principle, the authority are unable to accept the details, it is open to them to invite the applicant to amend his application so as to exclude them and leave them for subsequent approval. Where there is room for doubt as to the applicant's intentions in including the details the authority would do well to make inquiries on the point before deciding the application.

On this matter Hamilton comments as follows: '. . . the author sees no reason why the authority should not, if they wish to, reserve by condition, consideration of submitted details if they do not like them, and he believes this has often been done.'[24]

As cases set out below show, a developer would be wise either to submit as few details as possible, thus giving himself room for manoeuvre at the detailed stage, or to make quite clear that details are by way of illustration only and not part of the application. More details can always be supplied on request; it is on the other hand difficult to alter or withdraw details once approval has been given, without in effect submitting a fresh application.

What then are the powers of the local authority at the approval stage; when may they reject the details on the grounds of difference from the outline?

Circular No. 87/50, op. cit.

It is important if this arrangement (outline applications) is to work smoothly that there should be no doubt as to the relation between the permission and the approval. The scope of consideration at the approval stage is limited to the matters specifically reserved in the initial permission, and the only conditions which can be attached to the approval are conditions relevant to those matters. . . . All aspects of the proposed development other than those reserved must therefore be considered before permission is granted in response to the outline application, and any conditions necessary in this connection (for example, to regulate the use of the building) must be attached to the permission.

Shemara Ltd v. *Luton Corporation* (1967) 18 P. & C.R. 520

DIPLOCK LJ: In this action the plaintiffs seek a declaration against Luton Corporation as planning authority, the declaration sought being, so far as is relevant, that the planning authority were not entitled to reject some plans which the plaintiffs submitted in March 1966 on the grounds on which the planning authority did reject the plans, and secondly, and even more boldly, that as a necessary inference from the grounds of refusal given by the planning authority they should be deemed to have approved the plans. . . .

The facts start with an application by or on-behalf of the plaintiffs for outline planning permission to develop some land at Fairholme, Hart Hill, Luton. The land was about 0·7 of an acre in extent and the development for which they sought permission was to erect upon it sixty one-room flatlets and sixty-four garages. That application was made under what is now regulation 5 of the Town and Country Planning General Development Order 1963. . . .

The development proposed was sixty one-room flatlets at occupational ratio 1:4 and sixty-four garages. Details of the buildings to be erected were: five-storey blocks with garaging under plus common room over garaging, and the application was accompanied by a sketch plan which put a number of further details as to the development proposed. The development there disclosed showed three blocks of flats centrally placed in the site on a north-south axis which was up the slope of the land. There was provision for three blocks of five storeys each and provision for sixty-four lock-up garages, that is in the sense of individual separated garages, thirty-two of them under the flats and the common room, sixteen down the west boundary and sixteen down the east boundary. Between the block of flats and the boundary garages there were two access roads of 24 feet wide.

The local authority, having considered the application for outline permission, gave it on January 26, 1962, and it is necessary to see what matters were reserved for further approval in that permission. The permitted use or change of use was described as 'Use of land for erection of sixty one-roomed flatlets and sixty-four garages,' and the conditions subject to which the permission was granted were these:

This permission is granted subject to compliance with the by-laws and general statutory provisions in force in the district and to the following conditions: (1) Detailed plans and particulars incorporating the principles shown in the sketch details submitted with this application for outline permission shall be submitted to and approved by the council before construction is commenced. (2) (a) A landscape layout scheme shall be submitted to and approved by the council before construction is commenced, indicating which of the existing trees (which are the subject of a proposed Tree Preservation Order now in course of preparation) it is proposed to retain and the planting of new trees and shrubs where necessary. (b) The planting scheme as approved shall be carried out during the first planting season following the completion of the dwellings and thereafter the trees and shrubs and the land on which they are planted shall be maintained to the satisfaction of the council. (c) No trees standing on the land shall be felled without the prior consent of the council pending the confirmation of the Trees Preservation Order.

As I read that permission it is, of course, an outline permission and it reserves to the subsequent approval of the council any matters relating to the siting, design or external appearance of the buildings or the means of access thereto; but I think it restricts the right of the council to object to proposals as to the siting, design or access to the buildings. They may not require siting, design or access inconsistent with the principles which I have already enumerated and which are apparent in the sketch and the plans put forward in the application.

Now it appears, although we do not know the details of it, that a number of negotiations and other applications of one kind or another went on between the plaintiffs and the planning authority. The one with which this case is concerned is a letter of March 8, 1966, which was written by the plaintiffs to the planning authority, and it reads as follows:

I enclose herewith three copies of the survey of the above site edged in yellow showing the existing levels. This site plan also shows the land which would be available for the comprehensive development. In addition I also enclose three copies indicating how the sixty flats are to be accommodated on the site. This plan is submitted in general principle for your approval and relates to the outline planning permission granted on January 26, 1962. . . . If there are any queries arising on the drawings perhaps you would be good enough to telephone my office.

The first question that arises is: What was the nature of this application? It does not appear to be an application for approval under paragraph (3) of regulation 5, because it does not contain such particulars as are necessary to deal with matters reserved in the permission. It does not, for example, contain any reference to a landscape layout scheme indicating which of the existing trees are to be approved. It contains no greater detail than the original outline plan save that it does include the internal arrangements of the one-room flatlets and indicates the fenestration of the blocks of flats which have ceased to be three blocks and have now become four blocks and four-storey blocks instead of five-storey blocks. It is difficult to say at that stage what this letter was unless it was a friendly negotiation outside the ambit of the statutory provisions.

The planning authority, on April 12, answered that letter, saying:

[I am] enclosing plans showing land available for comprehensive development and how sixty flats are to be accommodated on the site and your recent telephone conversation with the borough engineer. At the present time detailed consideration of this proposal has not been completed, but the scheme will be placed before the planning committee at their next meeting on May 2, 1966. I should be pleased if you would complete the enclosed application forms and return them to me.

The enclosures with that letter were the ordinary forms for application for planning permission under regulation 5 (1), the planning authority taking the view at that time that the letter of March 8 was a fresh application for planning permission *ab initio*.

The plaintiffs' reply to that was as follows, and it is important to read the heading:

Re: Fairholme, Hart Hill, Luton. Town and Country Planning Act 1962, s. 43. We acknowledge receipt of your letter of April 12, 1966. The drawings which were forwarded to you on March 8, 1966, and to which your letter of April 12 refers, were forwarded to you as further and better particulars of the planning consent already given. We are of the opinion that under section 43 it is unnecessary to complete further planning application forms as this would be construed as a further application. What is required is approval to the better particulars already referred to so that detail drawings may be prepared for approval under your by-laws. We note that consideration is being given to our proposals and that they are to be placed before the planning committee at their next meeting on May 2, 1966. We have been requested to state that should there be any difficulty in reaching a decision on May 2, 1966, an extension of further time will not be entertained.

That letter appears to be saying, 'The application we are making is not an application for planning permission or an application for approval of the matter left over in an outline application, but an application under section 43 of the Act of 1962.' . . .[25]

Whatever the nature of the application made in these two highly confused and confusing letters, the planning authority did deal with the matter at their meeting on May 2, and they accepted a recommendation by Mr. Rees, the planning officer, which was in these terms:

Refused. (1) The proposed development would prejudice the development of adjoining and surrounding sites which should be developed comprehensively. (2) Parking provision in accordance with the council's standards cannot be provided satisfactorily within the site for the density proposed. (3) The submitted layout does not provide adequate vehicular road access arrangements.

Mr. Rees and no doubt the committee taking the view that this was really a fresh application because it differed so widely in important planning characteristics from that which had previously been put in.

However that may be, on May 6, the planning officer wrote the plaintiffs a letter in these terms: 'Fairholme, Hart Hill, Luton. Your proposals to develop the above site were considered by the planning committee at their meeting on May 2, and refused on the grounds that the scheme submitted would prejudice the development of adjoining and surrounding sites which should be considered comprehensively.' That, I take it, is the first reason. The letter goes on:

It is apparent that the layout submitted does not provide for an adequate vehicular access from Crescent Rise both to the site and adjoining property. A width of at least 25 feet 6 inches, comprising an 18-foot carriageway, 6-foot footpath on the north side and a 1-foot 6-inch safety kerb on the south side should be provided and the same requirements would apply to the proposed new road giving direct access to the site in a northerly direction. The turning facilities on this road are completely inadequate as are the curve radii. The flat development should be at least 35 feet from all site and road boundaries and, if this is complied with, it is evident that four blocks of flats cannot be accommodated in the manner suggested, neither is it apparent how the council's standards for parking provision can be provided satisfactorily within the site for the density proposal. I must draw your attention to the fact that no application forms were received in connection with this application and these should now be forwarded forthwith (forms enclosed).

That is a reference to the requirement of regulation 5 (1) and shows, as Mr Rees confirmed in the witness-box, that the committee regarded this application as so different from the development in respect of which outline planning permission had been given that it was in effect a fresh application and treated it as such. But before in fact receiving any forms from the plaintiffs, on May 13, the planning authority issued a formal notice refusing permission for development of land situate at Fairholme, Hart Hill Drive, in respect of the erection of sixty flats, and they set out the reasons for the council's refusal to grant permission. The reasons set out are those which I have already read, those recommended by the planning officer. . . .

In those circumstances it really does not seem to me that this effort to appeal to the court against the dislike of the planning authority for this new plan can possibly succeed. There seem to me to be four possibilities. One is that the letter of March 8 is not an application either for planning permission under regulation 5 (1) or for approval of matters left over for approval in outline permission under paragraph (3) or an application to decide a question under section 43. It is merely a piece of informal negotiation between the planning authority and the applicants, and it has no legal effect except that the plaintiffs do know that their proposals will be most unlikely to be accepted if they put them forward formally.

The next possibility which I think has to be rejected is that which was accepted by the planning authority, or was thought to be the plaintiffs' intention by the planning authority, that this was an application for planning permission under regulation 5 (1). As the forms under paragraph (1) were not filled in and it was not a formal application, the intimation by the planning authority in their letter of May 6 was nothing more than an intimation that if a formal application for a fresh planning permission was put in, then it was unlikely in its present form to receive the approval of the council.

The next one which Mr Blundell has urged, although I see grave difficulty in it, is that the letters of March 8 and April 16, although the former was said to be submitted in general principle and the latter referred to section 43, must nevertheless be treated as if they were an application under paragraph (3) for approval of the matters left over for subsequent approval in the outline planning permission of January 1962.

I have explained the difficulty that there is about bringing that within paragraph (3) because it fails to deal with the matters which were left over. It in fact contains no more details except the minor ones I have mentioned and the original application and it gave nothing in the nature of a landscaping scheme; but assuming that those difficulties can be overcome and it is treated as an application for approval, it seems to me to have been rejected or refused by the letter of May 6, the grounds of refusal being first that the siting of the blocks would prejudice the development of adjoining and surrounding sites, because as we now know it is not a development central to the site on the north-south axis; the second being that it does not provide for adequate vehicular access and the third that it does not provide for sufficient parking and garaging facilities. All three seem to me to be proper planning grounds which it is for the local planning authority to decide, and that this is a refusal of permission.

The fourth possibility is that this was an application under section 43. Again, I see great difficulties in that, but, if it is, then the local authority, by their letter of May 6, have at any rate answered it by saying that this proposed development does not fall within the provisions of the outline permission because it does not incorporate the principles shown in the sketch details of 1962.

Finally I should say that if the planning authority have mistakenly thought that it was a fresh application and dealt with it on that basis and it is really an application for approval of matters left over from outline permission, it seems to me the only possible answer is that they had not made the determination sought within the time limited, and if they had not done so the effect of section 24 is that they are deemed to have refused. That indeed is one of the difficulties I find about the decision in *Hamilton* v. *West Sussex County Council. Application dismissed.*

In *Hamilton* v. *West Sussex CC*[26] referred to in *Shemara* the defendant county council approved an outline application to build a cottage and a garage. When the detailed application was made, the defendants purported to reject the whole development on the grounds *inter alia* that the detailed plans showed a different form of access from the cottage to the road than that contained in the outline application, and there was therefore a new application before them which they could reject. On this DONOVAN J said:

The defendants, however, in their outline permission of 1955, made no reservations whatever on the subject of access. Moreover, in any event as the plaintiffs say without contradiction, the new access merely connects with the same road at a different point, and the road itself is a private road on the farm and not a public road at all. Obviously where a public road is concerned, matters of access from new buildings concern the planning authority very much; but they hardly do so where the access is simply to a private road on the same land and I do not think that art. 5 (2) of the Order of 1950, has any application to such a road. . . .

. . . From start to finish no objection has ever been raised to the design or siting of the cottage, or to the details as shown on the plan submitted with the application of October, 1956. The defendants in their defence refer to the different siting of the cottage not as something that still awaits approval but simply as a fact supporting the argument that the application of October, 1956, was a new application altogether.

On these facts I draw the conclusion that the defendants, when the 1956 application was before them, did consider through their officers those matters which had been reserved in the 1955 outline permission – as indeed was their duty – and found nothing to which they wished to object. The attitude which they took was that though the applicant's proposals were unobjectionable with regard to reserved matters, the work of converting the two old cottages into one had not been done and that this entitled them to consider the whole matter afresh, and to refuse permission on grounds of principle. As soon as the defendants came into court this claim was abandoned. They are not now entitled to consider the reserved matters a second time. It is true that they have not formally said, 'We approve', but there is nothing which obliges them to use any such particular expression. If they could find no objection after examining the applicant's proposals they could not properly withhold approval.

In these circumstances I grant the second declaration* asked for by the plaintiffs, which seems to me to cover the whole matter.

* This was 'that the outline permission dated April 27th 1955, was a good and valid permission within the Town and Country Planning Act 1947, which entitled the plaintiffs to proceed with the erection of the cottage and garage'. Was Diplock LJ (as he then was) right to be concerned about 'the step taken' (i.e. granting a declaration) in *Hamilton*?

Chelmsford Corporation v. *Secretary of State for the Environment* (1971) 22 P. & C. R. 880

BROWNE J: This is in substance an appeal by the Chelmsford Borough Council as planning authority against a decision of the Minister, as he then was, allowing an appeal by Homes (East Anglia) Ltd., the developers, against conditions sought to be imposed by the planning authority. . .

On March 23, 1965, outline permission was granted by the Essex County Council. . . . By that outline permission the county council said:

'In pursuance of the powers exercised by them as local planning authority the county council of Essex, . . . do hereby give notice of their decision to grant permission for the said development subject to compliance with the following conditions.'

The conditions are set out in a schedule and there are five of them. The vital one for the purposes of the present case is no. 1:

> The development hereby permitted may only be carried out in accordance with plans and particulars which shall previously have been submitted to and approved by the local planning authority showing the lay-out of the development, which shall include children's play spaces and which shall make provision for at least one garage or car parking space within the curtilage of each dwelling; the siting, including the disposition of all dwelling types, design and external appearance of each building and a schedule of the external materials to be used, the means of access thereto and the means of foul and surface water drainage. . . .

Apparently there were various applications and negotiations about the detailed approval, and eventually, on January 31, 1966, the Chelmsford Borough Council gave an approval. . . . there are a number of conditions but the only two which are relevant in this case are nos. 5 and 6.

Condition 5 is 'close-boarded fences not less than six feet high of a type to be agreed in writing with the local planning authority shall be erected along the lines marked in brown on the attached plan before the dwellings are occupied.'

Condition 6 is 'decorative screen walls of a height not less than six feet shall be erected along the lines marked in purple on the attached plan the details of which shall be submitted to and approved in writing by the local planning authority before any work is commenced. . . .'

On April 3, 1969, the developers gave notice of appeal against those conditions. . . .

The grounds of appeal were:

> 1. The conditions as to fencing on this estate are *ultra vires*. . . .

The Minister's decision letter is dated April 7, 1970. It sets out the conditions and the issue, and the decision, in paragraph 5, is as follows:

> The legal arguments have been considered. The view is held that as the outline planning permission granted by Essex County Council contained no specific requirement that there should be screen walls and fences then the Chelmsford Borough Council had no power to impose such a condition in the approval of details. If it was thought that conditions relating to screen walls and fences were necessary then these matters should have been reserved in the outline planning permission, or alternatively the council could have refused to approve the submitted detailed plan because it failed to make provisions on the lines they had in mind. It has been decided therefore that as the two conditions under appeal go beyond the matters which were reserved for subsequent approval the Minister has no alternative but to discharge

those conditions. Accordingly he allows your clients' appeal and hereby discharges conditions nos. 5 and 6 attached to the notice of approval . . . dated January 31, 1966.

. . . This case raises, I think, two questions. First, did the outline permission of March 23, 1965, reserve to the planning authority the right or power to lay down in their detailed approval what walls and fences were to be provided and in what positions and of what nature they were to be? Secondly, if the planning authority did reserve that power, had they power to impose further conditions as to the walls and fences at the detailed approval stage or had they then only power to approve or reject the detailed proposals outright?

On the first point the main argument of Mr Spence, who appears for the Chelmsford Corporation, is that the power was reserved by condition 1 by the provision that the development was only to be carried out in accordance with the plans submitted to and approved by the local planning authority showing the lay-out of the development. . . .

Mr Spence says that 'the development' in the phrase 'the lay-out of the development' refers to the residential development of the 23·65 acres for which outline permission was given by this document, and I agree with this approach.

Mr Spence then says that 'the development' means *all* the development, not only the houses but also everything which can fairly be said to be part of the residential development, including the children's play spaces and the garages which are expressly mentioned in the condition and also, for example, the gardens, walls and fences.

He says that 'the lay-out of the development' includes the positions in which walls and fences are to be put and that, if it includes their positions, it must also include the type of walls or fences which are to be put in them.

Mr Anderson, for the developers, and Mr Slynn, for the Ministry, say that the phrase 'the lay-out of the development' is neither wide enough nor specific enough to cover the provision and position of walls and fences, still less walls and fences for the purposes of decoration or of protecting privacy. It will be remembered, of course, that the reason for conditions 5 and 6 was 'to ensure privacy to the rear garden areas of the proposed development and to adjoining owners' and that the screen walls referred to in condition 6 are described as 'decorative screen walls.'

Mr Anderson and Mr Slynn say that the word 'lay-out' in ordinary language means the broad physical arrangement of the scheme as a whole. They accept that, of course, the lay-out will have to show the position of some boundaries – for example, between houses or between houses and children's play spaces – but they say that it will not show anything about the physical nature of the boundaries – for example, whether they will be walls or fences or what they will be. . . .

In the end, I think that the question what 'the lay-out of the development' means in condition 1 is a matter of impression, and I confess that my mind has fluctuated in the course of argument. I have, however, come to the conclusion that Mr Anderson and Mr Slynn are right and that these words did not reserve to the planning authority power to decide whether walls and fences for decorative purposes and to protect privacy should be provided and, if so, where. In my view, 'the lay-out of the development' means the arrangement of the various parts of the development – the roads, the houses, the shops – I think there are some shops in this development – play spaces and so on – and does not include the methods by which the boundaries and divisions within and round the development are to be marked or screened.

It follows that, in my view, the Minister was right in deciding that conditions 5 and 6 of the detailed approval were *ultra vires*.

Assume that the court decided that the Minister was wrong. What would have been the answer to the second question posed by the court?

(ii) The determination
(a) WHO DETERMINES?

The question of who determines has to some extent been considered in an earlier section of this chapter, and in Chapter 2 in general terms. What is considered here is the question of delegation of decision-making powers to officers and the way a planning committee works. The former matter was first formally recommended by the *Management Study on Development Control* in 1967, was provided for in the Town and Country Planning Act 1968[27], is provided for in respect of a wide range of matters by the Local Government Act 1972[28], is a cornerstone of the Bains Report, and is strongly stressed in Circular No. 142/73. Problems arising from delegation which have come before the courts will be looked at in the next section on communication; here the terms of the Act are set out, followed by an extract from Bains and the circular.

Local Government Act 1972

101.—(1) Subject to any express provision contained in this Act or any Act passed after this Act, a local authority may arrange for the discharge of any of their functions—

    (*a*) by a committee, a sub-committee or an officer of the authority; or
    (*b*) by any other local authority.

(2) Where by virtue of this section any functions of a local authority may be discharged by a committee of theirs, then, unless the local authority otherwise direct, the committee may arrange for the discharge of any of those functions by a sub-committee or an officer of the authority and where by virtue of this section any functions of a local authority may

be discharged by a sub-committee of the authority, then, unless the local authority or the committee otherwise direct, the sub-committee may arrange for the discharge of any of those functions by an officer of the authority.

(3) Where arrangements are in force under this section for the discharge of any functions of a local authority by another local authority, then, subject to the terms of the arrangements, that other authority may arrange for the discharge of those functions by a committee, sub-committee or officer of theirs and subsection (2) above shall apply in relation to those functions as it applies in relation to the functions of that other authority.

(4) Any arrangements made by a local authority or committee under this section for the discharge of any functions by a committee, sub-committee, officer or local authority shall not prevent the authority or committee by whom the arrangements are made from exercising those functions.

The New Local Authorities: Management and Structure
op. cit.

3.38. It has been suggested that extensive delegation to officers is in some way undemocratic, but we do not accept this, provided that the terms of delegation are clear and specific.

The democratic principle is, in our view, protected by the right of members to withdraw or amend the powers given to the officer. . . .

3.39. It is a basic principle of management that responsibility and authority must coincide and it follows that if officers are given the authority to take decisions they must also accept the responsibility for the consequences of those decisions. We have found that many committee agendas are liberally sprinkled with matters which seem to us to be manifestly suitable for decision at officer level, though whether this is as a result of pressure from the members or a reluctance on the part of the officers to act decisively is a matter which requires closer analysis at local level than we have been able to give. What is clear is that as a result there is often too little time available in committee to give the really important matters the attention which they warrant.

3.40. We do not believe that delegated authority, once given, requires a constant stream of reports back to the delegating committee. The officer's task is to get on with the job which he has been given to do and having given him the necessary powers the committee should allow him to exercise them according to his own judgment. He is, of course, accountable for the decisions which he takes, but such accountability, in our view, should be checked by review and investigation techniques, where the decision as to the subject of review rests with the reviewing body and is not decided by what is, or is not, included in routine written reports.

3.41. An officer working under delegated power needs, nevertheless, to keep in close touch with the committee responsible for the function which he is performing. We have deliberately avoided using the phrase 'his committee' despite its admirable brevity because we do not believe that such a phrase is compatible with the concept of a corporate approach; the officer is responsible to the Council for his actions, through the agency of the appropriate committee(s). It is in this area of informal contact between committee meetings that there is a need for a source of advice on the sensitive issues which inevitably arise in the course of day to day administration and which the officer must recognise as requiring member participation.

DoE Circular No. 142/73: 'Streamlining the Planning Machine'

7 (ii) Full use should also be made of the powers available to authorities to authorise officers to take decisions on planning applications. The Bains Report made a very strong recommendation in favour of extensive delegation (paragraphs 3.38 to 3.42). This recommendation is particularly relevant to planning decisions. In some authorities half the planning decisions are taken by officers. But in many there is no delegation. The Secretaries of State consider that only in exceptional circumstances is such an absence of delegation justifiable. Examples of decisions which should normally be delegated to officers are: small scale development (not simply confined to extensions) clearly in accord with the authority's policies: development just beyond the limits permitted under the General Development Order; some applications for approval of reserved matters; works under a scheme for a general improvement area; Section 53 determinations and certificates of established use; and, in the field of advertisement control, at least applications relating to advertisements nearly within the specified class. Each authority which has not already done so should draw up a list of classes to be delegated, reserving to themselves the right to deal with any application (either upon its merits or by way of spot check) and giving clear directions on the policies to be followed. Although comparatively minor applications can often arouse the strongest feelings locally it is important that committees should as far as possible concentrate on cases with a substantial policy content. This will mean that officers acting under delegated powers will sometimes be called upon to give decisions in accordance with a policy which may itself be unpopular. This must be accepted where it is the policy and not the particular application of the policy which is the cause. Good working relationships between officers and committees will ensure that sensitive applications are drawn to the attention of committees. The Bains Report indicates ways in which officers working under delegated powers can keep in close touch with the committee responsible for the function.[29]

How will officers 'accept the responsibility for the consequences of (the) decisions' they make in respect of planning applications? To take the case of the cement-mixing plant at Leamington Spa discussed on pages 364–5, if the officers had been empowered to make decisions and had approved that application instead of merely recommending approval, how, as a matter of practical politics and administration, could those officers have been made to accept the consequences of their decisions if two or three years later, once the plant was operating, it created traffic and pollution problems?

One of the committees Bains suggests should be established is a Performance Review Sub-Committee . . .

— [a] form of independent review process . . . what we have in mind is a body of members within each authority, rather like the Public Accounts Committee. We believe that a watchdog body of this sort, with the standing and formal authority to make detailed investigation into any project, department or area of activity would provide an extremely useful service to management. . . . Service upon such a body would provide an excellent opportunity for the development and involvement of some of the younger members.[30]

A typical term of reference for such a sub-committee is 'to review the performance by committees and departments of the programmes and objectives assigned to them'.[31] Could such a sub-committee, given such terms of reference, exercise any meaningful supervision over the decisions made by officers on planning applications? If so, how?

It is clear that the vast majority of local authorities have been recommended by their officers to adopt and have adopted Bains-type management structures[32]. It would follow, of course, that officers will have greatly increased delegated powers in the field of development control and in other fields, planning and non-planning. It must seriously be doubted whether this will make for more responsive local government in general or a more publicly acceptable system of development control in particular.

(b) HOW IS DETERMINING DONE?

The alternative to officers deciding is councillors deciding. Is that better? We have seen in an earlier section how officers arrive at a recommendation; their method of decision making would be little different. But how do councillors decide? What information is placed before them; what use do they make of that information? By giving decision-making powers to councillors, would one be doing anything else than giving them the time-wasting trappings of power leaving the realities of powers vested in the officers?[33]

Extracted below is a typical planning application as it appeared on the papers for the Leamington Spa Plans Sub-Committee, a body which exercised some delegated authority for the Warwickshire County Council. It is followed by a Borough Engineer's report on an application which he, the Borough Engineer, thought merited further information for the committee.

No.	Development	Suggested Resolution
15879	52–58a, The Parade, Leamington Spa. Redevelopment of existing retail premises as new retail store, for Debenhams Ltd, 1 Welbeck Street, London W1A 1DF	Defer for further information. Refer to WCC

Plan 15801 – Proposed youth centre and gymnasium, The Maltings, Clapham Terrace

At the meeting on the 20th November, the Committee recommended that planning permission for a period of one year be given for the above development. The County Planning Officer has now left the decision to the Committee.

I have received a letter from the architect acting for St. Mary's Parochial Church Council in which he asks that further consideration be given to this application with a view to granting permission without a time limit since otherwise it would not be possible to obtain the appropriate grant from the County Council. Without this grant the project cannot proceed.

The Town Clerk has received a letter from the County Education Officer supporting the application for permanent permission. The County Youth Service Sub-Committee are in favour of giving assistance with the purchase and adoption of the premises since they consider them to be in an area where there is urgent need.

I have again written to the three objectors to the original scheme explaining the change in circumstances and will report further at the meeting.

The Sub-Committee met every three weeks and had before it about sixty applications set out as above, with four or five Borough Engineer's reports as set out above, attached. The papers for the meeting would arrive on a Friday; the meeting was on a Tuesday evening. Often it lasted no more than one hour; rarely would it go beyond two hours. The Borough Engineer would comment on any application in respect of which he was recommending refusal or recommending a different resolution from that which was on the agenda paper under 'suggested resolution'. In respect of other applications, the onus was on individual councillors to raise them for discussion or ask questions about them. Plans were available for inspection and some of them were pinned up on the walls of the committee room.

So much for the facts of one out of over 1,000 local planning authorities which existed under the old local government system. What follows is my comment. As the length of meetings indicates, discussion was very selective. It most often arose on items which were the subject of a report from the Borough Engineer and became most vigorous when it appeared that the committee wished to depart from the Borough Engineer's recommendation. The Borough Engineer himself took a full and active part in discussions – the chairman rarely did. When objections to proposals had been made, either by residents or by amenity groups, they were either reported in summary form or read out verbatim. Occasionally objections were circulated in advance to members, but it was rare for members to have done much independent homework on the applications. On balance, my impression of the committee was that, in most cases, it attempted to apply planning considerations to those applications it discussed: conservation policy, traffic problems, back development, non-conforming uses, 'unneighbourly' extensions to houses, were the kinds of considerations the committee would take into account. It was rare for the Warwickshire Development Plan to be mentioned; it was rare too for totally irrelevant considerations to be raised, though which of two planning arguments to adopt – one for, one against – might be decided on non-planning grounds. It was rarer still for legal considerations to be raised. This last point was one of particular interest to me. The average planning application could be disposed of without any reference to the *law* of town and country planning at all. Where the law was raised was in respect of powers under the conservation part of planning legislation, and more occasionally conditions. Was a condition lawful? Could it be enforced? The legal representative from the Town Clerk's Department who attended every meeting of the committee was more concerned to explain the practical limits of enforcement of planning law than explain what that law was and how it limited the powers of the committee. His main concern was that when we refused permission to an application, we had a sound planning reason that would stand up

on an appeal to the Minister. I would calculate that the Borough
Engineer's recommendations prevailed on at least 90 per cent of the
applications.

What advantages, if any, were there then in the committee 'deciding planning applications?' Overwhelmingly, they lay in factors
outside the quality and quantity of discussion at such meetings. Objectors, whether neighbours or amenity groups, had a wide range of
access to the decision-making process by being able to contact one
of a number of councillors. There was much more chance that, if
there were objections, they would be aired. Councillors at least had
the opportunity to investigate and/or delay an application so that a
further investigation could be carried out into it. This was not used
frequently, but it would have disappeared completely if applications never came before councillors at all. This was particularly
important in respect of applications for which there were sound
planning reasons both for and against; the decision as to which set
of reasons to adopt might well turn on factors as much political as
planning, i.e. not that a proposed use was totally non-conforming
but that it would create such a wide measure of concern in the area
that it could be denominated, with some plausibility, as unneighbourly. In short, the use of a committee went some way towards
ensuring that development control was seen as a problem of people
living with each other and making use of the facilities of the town,
and not just a problem of the guidance of change through the application of 'objective' planning principles.

Notwithstanding the emphasis on streamlining the planning
machine, the DoE considers that planning committees still have a
role to play in decision making.

DoE Circular No. 142/73

(i) *Planning committee arrangements*
(a) Planning committees, or joint or area committees, or sub-committees,
should all have executive powers to decide planning applications within
wide and clearly defined terms of delegation designed to serve, among
other things, the rapid despatch of the simpler applications.
(c) There may sometimes be advantage in members of a committee
interviewing applicants before an adverse decision is taken. If, as a result,
major amendments are made it will usually be necessary to require a new
application; and sometimes even comparatively minor changes may effect
the interests of third parties and make it desirable that they should be
informed. But substantial savings of time and effort on subsequent appeals
can sometimes be achieved by face to face meetings of this kind; though
applicants must appreciate that it is for the planning authority to decide

in which case the procedure can be adopted. It should, of course, never be regarded as a substitute for the normal consultation with officers.

(d) It may even be helpful, on occasions, for a planning committee to appoint an outside person of standing to conduct an examination of proposals contained in the application and to invite the applicant and any third parties who have expressed an interest to make their representation to him orally (in public if this is thought expedient). There is of course always the possibility that an application which would warrant this treatment might eventually go on appeal to the Secretary of State and a further public inquiry then be necessary; so on balance this course is only to be recommended where both planning authority and applicant agree that it would be an advantage.

(c) WHAT MAY OR MUST BE TAKEN INTO ACCOUNT WHEN DETERMINING?

Town and Country Planning Act 1971

29 (1). Subject to the provisions of sections 26 to 28 of this Act, and to the following provisions of this Act, where an application is made to a local planning authority for planning permission, that authority in dealing with the application, shall have regard to the provisions of the development plan, so far as material to the application, and to any other material considerations. . . .

(2) In determining any application for planning permission for development of a class to which section 26 of this Act applies, the local planning authority shall take into account any representations relating to that application which are received by them before the end of the period of twenty-one days beginning with the date of the application.

[(3) Requirement to consider representations made by owners and/or agricultural tenants named in a section 27 certificate.]

Of the three matters thus specifically set out, two call for consideration here: the provisions of the development plan; and other material considerations.

1. The provisions of the development plan: the caveat 'so far as material to the application' is important as the vast majority of applications do not affect the development plan. Equally, where the development plan is out of date, and until the first generation of structure and local plans are approved, as virtually all of them are, the development plan does not affect the vast majority of applications. There are however inevitably major applications which, if granted, would represent departures from the development plan. To what extent may these be granted either at all or without reference to the DoE? The position is set out in a Circular and Direction of 1965, which in liberalising the previous position reflected the fact that by

that date more and more development plans were becoming out of date and generating major applications which represented departures from the plan.

MHLG Circular No. 70/65: 'The Town and Country
Planning (Development Plans) Direction 1965'

7. In considering whether or not an individual planning application affects the whole of a neighbourhood, planning authorities might find it helpful to note the following examples of proposals which should be brought to the Minister's attention:

(*a*)   any proposals for a large industrial installation or a major new shopping centre;

(*b*)   any proposal that would produce a substantial increase in employment or population above that provided for in the plan;

(*c*)   any proposal for development of significance in a national park, a green belt, or an area of great landscape, scientific or historic value; and

(*d*)   any proposal that might adversely affect areas containing buildings of special architectural or historic interest.

The Town and Country Planning (Development Plans)
Direction 1965

The Minister of Housing and Local Government (hereinafter called 'the Minister'), in exercise of the powers conferred on him by articles 5, 10 and 15 of the Town and Country Planning General Development Order 1963, and of all other powers enabling him in that behalf, hereby gives the following direction:—

2. An application for such development which, in the opinion of the local planning authority, would involve a substantial departure from the provisions of the development plan or would affect the whole of a neighbourhood shall, before the grant of permission thereon, be subject to the following procedure:—

(*a*)   it shall be advertised in a local newspaper circulating in the locality as an application in relation to development which does not accord with the provisions of the development plan, and the advertisement shall state that any objections to the grant of permission for the development in question should be sent to the local planning authority within a specified period, being not less than 21 days from the date of the advertisement;

(*b*)   the local planning authority shall forthwith send a copy of such advertisement and of the application and any accompanying plans to the Minister, together with any statement required under sub-paragraph (*c*) hereof, and, in a case where objections are received within the period specified in the advertisement, the local planning authority shall consider the objections and decide whether the development may properly be permitted having regard to those objections;

(c) where the application is one to which this sub-paragraph applies, the local planning authority shall (i) furnish to the Minister a statement to that effect indicating the issues involved, and (ii) at the expiration of the period for objections, notify the Minister whether any have been received and, if so, send copies of them to the Minister.

3. Paragraph 2 (c) of this direction applies to any application which relates to or includes development which would be:—

(i) not in accord with a provision of the development plan inserted by the Minister pursuant to his power of modification; or

(ii) contrary to views expressed on the proposed development by a government department; or

(iii) such as would, in the opinion of the local planning authority, affect the whole of a neighbourhood.

4.—(1) Where, after carrying out this procedure, the local planning authority remain of opinion that planning permission should be granted, with or without conditions, and they have not, within the appropriate period, received a direction from the Minister restricting the grant of such permission or requiring the reference of the application to him, they are authorised to grant permission.

(2) The appropriate period, for the purposes of this paragraph, is: —

(a) where the application is one to which paragraph 2 (c) of this direction applies, 21 days from the date when the Minister receives from the local planning authority copies of objections to the grant of permission, or notification that there are no objections, as the case may be;

(b) in any other case, 21 days from the date when the Minister receives the documents specified in paragraph 2 (b) of this direction.

5. Permission for development to which this direction applies may be granted by a local planning authority without compliance with the requirements of paragraph 2 of this direction in any case where in their opinion the development authorised by the permission, if carried out in accordance with the conditions, if any, to be imposed, would neither involve a substantial departure from the provisions of the development plan nor affect the whole of a neighbourhood.

DoE Circular No. 142/73

9. The Development Plans Directions will be recast to take account of the new structure and local plan system and local government reorganisation. In the meantime, local planning authorities are asked to interpret the expression 'substantial departure' in the Directions on the basis that the Secretaries of State would concern themselves primarily with the 'structure plan element' of development plans, the 'local plan element'

being regarded in all but exceptional cases as a matter for the discretion
of the local planning authority. An interim amendment to the Directions
is being made and will be promulgated under a separate circular. This
will contain no reference to departures affecting the whole of a neighbourhood. Local planning authorities should, however, continue to advertise such departures and to arrange for the posting of site notices. . . .

2. Material considerations: material considerations are planning
considerations of the kind mentioned in the previous section. Even
if non-material considerations find their way into a discussion of an
application at the local planning authority, they are usually absent
from a statement of reasons for refusal of an application; while a
grant of permission does not give rise to an appeal to the Minister
so that the question of non-materiality of considerations would not
often be debated. A recent case did however raise the question at
ministerial level though the comments made by the court would
apply equally at the local planning authority level. In *J. Murphy
& Sons* v. *Secretary of State for the Environment*[34], the applicants, public
works contractors, sought to quash the decision of the Secretary of
State to permit the London Borough of Camden to build houses on a
piece of land adjoining their depot (contrary to the recommendations of the inspector who held a public local inquiry into the application) on the ground, *inter alia*, that the Secretary of State in his
decision letter had failed to have regard to a material consideration
namely the cost of developing the site, a matter which the inspector
had had regard to. Ackner J was in no doubt that the Minister was
right: '. . . This point was abandoned before me and in my judgment rightly so abandoned. . . . I hold that as a matter of law the
Minister is not entitled to have regard to the cost of developing a
site in determining whether planning permission under the Planning
Acts should be granted. . . .'[35]

Do you agree with that ruling? Do you think it is either possible
or desirable to divorce considerations of cost from considerations of
planning? How do you reconcile the approach of Ackner J with the
approach of Cooke J in *Stringer* v. *Minister of Housing and Local
Government* [1971] 1 All E.R. 65:

> The arguments before me in support of the application to quash the
> Minister's decision may be classified under three heads. First, there were
> arguments based on the general nature and effect of the planning legis-
> lation. These arguments were designed to show that the Minister was
> not entitled to have regard to the interests of the telescope in reaching
> his decision on the appeal.

The interests of the telescope, it is said, are interests of a private character. It is said that the purpose of the planning legislation is to protect only the public interest, and indeed only the public interest in a particular sphere, namely the sphere of amenity.

It may be conceded at once that the material considerations to which the Minister is entitled and bound to have regard in deciding the appeal must be considerations of a planning nature. I find it impossible, however, to accept the view that such considerations are limited to matters relating to amenity. So far as I am aware, there is no authority for such a proposition, and it seems to me to be wrong in principle. In principle, it seems to me that any consideration which relates to the use and development of land is capable of being a planning consideration. Whether a particular consideration falling within that broad class is material in any given case will depend on the circumstances. However, it seems to me that in considering an appeal the Minister is entitled to ask himself whether the proposed development is compatible with the proper and desirable use of other land in the area. For example, if permission is sought to erect an explosives factory adjacent to a school, the Minister must surely be entitled and bound to consider the question of safety. That plainly is not an amenity consideration. The broad nature of the duties of planning authorities in dealing with an application is indicated in the judgment of WIDGERY J in *Fitzpatrick Development Ltd* v. *Minister of Housing and Local Government and Finchley Borough Council*[36]. WIDGERY J said: 'It is the duty of the local planning authority in the first instance and the Minister if the matter comes to him by way of appeal, to plan the area concerned, and an essential feature of planning must be the separation of different uses or activities which are incompatible the one with the other'.

The general statutory duty of the Minister is laid down in s.1 of the Minister of Town and Country Planning Act 1943 in these terms: '. . . securing consistency and continuity in the framing and execution of a national policy with respect to the use and development of land throughout England and Wales. . . .'

It seems to me that all considerations relating to the use and development of land are considerations which may, in a proper case, be regarded as planning considerations. In this case, it seems to me that the likelihood of interference with the work of the telescope is both a planning consideration and a material consideration within the meaning of s. 17.

I find it equally difficult to accept that the local planning authority and the Minister on appeal must have regard only to public interests as opposed to private interests. It is, of course, true, as Salmon J pointed out in the *Buxton* case, that the scheme of the legislation is to restrict development for the benefit of the public at large. But it seems to me that it would be impossible for the Minister and local planning authorities to carry out their duties as custodians of the public interest if they were precluded from considering the effect of a proposed development on a particular use of land by a particular occupier in the neighbourhood. The public interest, as I see it, may require that the interests of individual occupiers should be considered. The protection of the interests of individual occupiers is one aspect, and an important one, of the public interest as a whole. The distinction between public and private interests appears to me to be a false distinction in this context. . . .

McLoughlin, op. cit., pp. 54–6

. . . When a private developer is proposing new premises or a private renewal scheme it is senseless not to consider the economic feasibility of the project in terms of its location and the nature of the proposed uses. Most authorities no doubt do this. The Ministry recognizes this to some extent in its guidance on redevelopment in town centres. However, it has generally been reluctant to extend this to other areas of development. . . .

Development control acts as a brake on unlimited development and it confers substantial powers on local authorities to affect the pattern of development. In the matter of out-of-town shopping centres and so-called hypermarkets, these powers have often been used to confer advantage on one set of businessmen, those in the existing town centres. The fear of declining trade in town centres and the planning problems that would involve have clearly been motivating factors in the decisions. . . .

The major issue raised in all such cases is *what is planning control for?* What are its criteria as embodied in the development plans and the 'other material considerations' which would provide a rationale for individual decisions to be made? What precisely is meant by treating each case 'on its merits'? On the specific question of financial or economic viability the official view for some considerable time has been that it is not the function of statutory town planning to interfere with the operations of market forces in e.g. deciding how many filling stations or how many square metres of shopping floorspace a town or region needs. These matters, it is argued, are the concern of the entrepreneur, not of the bureaucrat. To argue this is to limit the operation of development control and statutory planning to such matters as external appearance and land-use zoning. But at the same time, government has introduced, after lengthy discussion, legislation which calls for an explicit concern for physical and *economic* facts in urban and regional plans. Surely we cannot have it both ways. . . .

Consider the following problem: Span Developments Ltd obtained planning permission to build a new village on approximately 430 acres at New Ash Green in Kent during the 1960s. Part of their case was that they would build a new community in a style and manner which would blend in with the surrounding countryside. At the beginning of the 1970s after the collapse of negotiations with the GLC, designed to get the authority to build £750,000 worth of public housing in the village, Span Developments sold the project to Bovis Ltd. That company announced certain modifications in the plans for the village to try and make it more attractive to potential buyers. Would the Kent County Council and the Minister of Housing and

Local Government, when deciding whether to grant planning permission, have been wrong in law to have considered, both whether Span had put forward the kind of proposal likely to attract residents and had sufficient financial resources to see it through to the end?

Another and more frequent aspect of the problem of material considerations is the question of 'policy'. To what extent may a local planning authority have a policy on any particular class of applications and to what extent may that policy influence a decision on a particular application? If a policy is a material consideration, does it exclude all other possible material considerations? It is a general principle of administrative law that administrative bodies with power to make decisions on individual applications or cases must consider each case or application on its merits; equally it is accepted that administrative bodies may have policies, but those policies must not preclude consideration of individual cases.[37] These matters were the subject of discussion in the Jodrell Bank case, *Stringer* v. *Minister of Housing and Local Government* [1971] 1 All E.R. 65:

> COOKE J: In this application under s. 179 of the Town and Country Planning Act 1962, the applicant, Mr Geoffrey Harold Stringer, seeks an order quashing a decision of the Minister of Housing and Local Government dismissing an appeal by the applicant from a refusal by the Congleton rural district council, acting on behalf of the Cheshire county council, to grant him planning permission for the erection of 23 dwellings in the hamlet of Brereton Heath. . . .
>
> In September 1966, the applicant applied to the Congleton rural district council for outline planning permission to erect 23 dwellings on the appeal site. The application was refused on 18th July 1967. Three reasons were given for the refusal. For the moment I need refer to the second reason only. It was this:
>
> > The site is in close proximity to the Jodrell Bank Authority Research Station and the development, if approved, would be likely to seriously interfere with the efficient running of the Radio Telescope.
>
> From this refusal the applicant appealed to the Minister on 3rd February 1968. On 10th September 1968, Mr Metcalfe, an inspector appointed by the Minister, held a local inquiry into the appeal. Mr Metcalfe's report is dated 25th September 1968 but, before dealing with that and with the Minister's decision which followed, it is convenient to refer as briefly as I can to the history of relations between the Jodrell Bank directorate, the Minister and the local planning authorities. . . .
>
> In March 1967, a document was executed on behalf of the county council by their assistant clerk and on behalf of the University of Manchester by Mr Lascelles, Sir Bernard's special assistant. The document was

also signed by the clerk to the Congleton rural district council, who are described as an interested party. The document is headed 'Cheshire County Council'. The sub-heading is: 'Undertakings given to Manchester University in relation to future development in that part of the consultation (hatched) zone within the Congleton Rural District for the protection of the radio telescope at Jodrell Bank.'

There is then a section headed 'Goostrey village zone', and I need not read that section. The next section is headed 'Remainder of hatched zone', and I quote para (a) of that section: 'The county council will discourage development within the limits of their powers at Blackfirs Lane, Somerford, and at Brereton Heath until 1990. This undertaking not to affect infilling plots or land which already enjoys planning permission.'

This document has been referred to as an agreement, and I will adopt that description of it. . . . In para 61 of the report, which appears under the general heading of 'case for the Local Planning Authority', I find this statement about the agreement of March 1967: 'The rural district council were a party to this agreement and it is this agreement which has resulted in the second reason for refusal. . . .'

The general duties of a local planning authority in dealing with an application for planning permission are prescribed by s.17 (1) of the Town and Country Planning Act 1962. The subsection requires the authority to have regard to the provisions of the development plan, so far as material to the application, and to any other material considerations.

It seems to me that the broad intentions of this unhappy agreement are inconsistent with the performance of that duty as regards applications for planning permission at Brereton Heath and elsewhere. It is true that the county council's undertakings to discourage development at Brereton Heath is qualified by the words 'within the limits of their powers'. But Sir Bernard Lovell bluntly interprets the agreement as meaning that development at Brereton Heath and at other places was to be resisted. The planning authority admit that since the agreement was signed they do not override the Jodrell Bank objections to development in the areas in question. But it is the duty of a planning authority to deal with the individual planning application before it and to have regard to all considerations which are relevant to that application. Plainly, on an application for planning permission to build houses in a particular place, one consideration which must always be material is the need for houses in that place, and no doubt there are other considerations, totally unrelated to the requirements of the telescope, which may be material to the application. It seems to me that the intention of this agreement was to bind the authority to disregard considerations to which, under the terms of the section, it is required to have regard. I think that the agreement was ultra vires the authority for those reasons. That is a sufficient ground for treating it as without legal effect. It may well be that in any event the parties to the agreement did not intend it to give rise to obligations which would be enforceable in law. But I have no doubt that each party intended to carry out the undertakings which it in fact gave.

Coming now to the applicant's application for planning permission to develop the appeal site, it seems to me that the local planning authority made no proper determination on that application. It appears that after the application was received but before the agreement was made, the University of Manchester was consulted on the application and objected to the proposed development on the grounds that it might lead to a significant development in the sensitive southern section of the telescope. . . .

. . . It is true that the first and third reasons given for the refusal had no connection with the telescope. The first reason was that the proposal did not accord with the county development plan, in that the appeal site was within an area where existing land uses were intended for the most part to remain undisturbed. The third reason related to the absence of mains drainage. But although the inclusion of these reasons might suggest that the local planning authority had looked at all the material considerations, the fact is that they had given an undertaking to the university which, whether legally binding or not, they intended to honour. The honouring of that undertaking would necessarily lead to the refusal of the application, and in those circumstances it is difficult to believe that the examination of other considerations can have been anything more than perfunctory, or that there was any true compliance with the statutory duties of the authority under s.17. In my view there was no such compliance. . . .

I now turn to the arguments relating to the question whether the Minister has, in determining the appeal, discharged his duty to act fairly and judicially. . . .

. . . Is there some . . . ground on which it can be said that the Minister has prejudged the issues on the appeal, or tied his hands, or precluded himself from acting with fairness and impartiality both in appearance and in fact? The Minister's anxiety that proper provision should be made for protecting the interests of the telescope is clear from many years of history. He has encouraged the definition by agreement of areas in which development is likely to interfere with the work of the telescope. He has encouraged arrangements for consultation between local authorities and the Jodrell Bank directorate about applications for planning permission in those areas. All that appears to me to be perfectly proper and in no way inconsistent with the proper performance of the Minister's quasi-judicial duties when occasion arises to perform them. The matter, however, may be said to go further than that, because it appears that the Minister has a policy for the area around Jodrell Bank, and indeed the existence of such a policy is referred to in para 4 of the Minister's decision letter on the appeal of Mr Hughes. The policy is not defined in the letter, but on the evidence before me it may be said to be a policy of discouraging development which would interfere with the efficient working of the telescope. It is not, however, as it seems to me, a policy which is intended to be pursued to the disregard of other relevant considerations. The question is whether the existence of such a policy disables the Minister from acting fairly on the consideration of an appeal.

There are obviously many matters in the field of planning legislation on which the Minister is entitled and indeed bound to have a policy. The relationship between a Minister's functions in formulating and giving effect to a policy and his functions in making a decision of a quasi-judicial nature have been considered in many cases. It seems to me that the general effect of the many relevant authorities is that a Minister charged with the duty of making individual administrative decisions in a fair and impartial manner may nevertheless have a general policy in regard to matters which are relevant to those decisions, provided that the existence of that general policy does not preclude him from fairly judging all the issues which are relevant to each individual case as it comes up for decision.

I think that in this case the Minister was entitled to have a policy in regard to Jodrell Bank, and I think that his policy is not such as to preclude him from fairly considering a planning appeal on its merits. I do not think that it precluded him from fairly considering the applicant's appeal. I do not think that the Minister has prejudged the case, or tied his own hands, or abdicated any of his functions. The contention that the rules of natural justice have not been complied with in this case cannot in my view be sustained.

In the result the application fails and must be dismissed. . . .

Was the objection to what the local planning authority had done based on the grounds that it had made an agreement, not enforceable at law, to discourage development in order to protect Jodrell Bank, or that it had not or appeared not to have taken into account all material considerations? In what way was the Minister's decision different from that of the local planning authority? Suppose there had been no agreement, but the applicant could show a consistent record of refusals of planning permission within a zone of land near Jodrell Bank; would it have been permissible to make an inference that all material considerations were not being taken into account and a policy was being rigidly applied? To what extent might the court's insistence that applications be considered on their merits be a contributory factor to delay in the planning process and thus to the urgings of the DoE that planning authorities compile development control policies?

DoE Circular No. 142/73

(xi) *Development control policies*
Those authorities which have not already done so are asked to consider compiling a comprehensive guide to development control policies and to make it available as a code of practice to the public and developers. This would of course be a non-statutory document and would provide a source from which material could eventually be selected for incorporation in structure and local plans. Among points to be borne in mind are:

(a) control measures should be clearly related to the policies and proposals which they are intended to implement and (like the policies in the plan) should be grouped according to topic, sub-area or other significant parts of the plan area (eg conservation area);

(b) in all cases the objective being pursued by the development control measures should be clearly explained, giving reasons and criteria established;

(c) detail, particularly detail liable to change in course of time, should as far as possible be avoided. Where precision is necessary – particularly in relation to a specific criterion or standard – reasons should be given;

(d) vague phrases such as 'convenient' or 'adequate' should not be used; instead the considerations which would be taken into account in determining 'convenience' or 'adequacy' should be stated.

Where such development control policies do not form part of informal interim local plans (which the Departments recommended last October should be drawn up in housing pressure areas to cover the interim period before statutory plans were available), it will usually be desirable for the policies to be the subject of local consultation. It will often, however, be possible for policies for particular areas to be set out in the form of 'development briefs' in a way that will avoid the lengthy debates between officials and developers that cause frustrations on both sides. Briefs for large scale development will often be worked out jointly by planners and developers; and developers will always be well advised to seek planning briefs at an early stage to avoid later disagreements.

What advice would you give a planning authority that wished both to use its development control policy in dealing with applications and comply with the law that each application must be considered on its merits?

Over and above these legal considerations, it must be repeated that the determination is not a technical exercise of applying planning considerations – objective measuring devices – to an application, but a political decision involving values and choices between competing alternatives. A rare judicial recognition of this is contained in *Cardiff Corporation* v. *Secretary of State for Wales*[38] where Thesiger J in commenting on the 'rather odd question of the Welsh Office', as to why the corporation had granted planning permission when the planning officer had recommended refusal said:

Apparently these offices sometimes forget that local planning authorities consist of democratically elected members, and the members are, in my view, in practice constantly considering what their voters want and may on dealing with any question, deal with it in accordance with what they think will be satisfactory to those whose votes they have solicited in the past and intend to solicit in the future.

The legal requirement to have regard to material considerations is, in the final analysis, no more than a statement that local planning authorities must make that political decision sensibly and fairly. It is rare for evidence to come to light that some are not doing so.

(d) WHAT SORT OF DETERMINATIONS MAY BE MADE

Town and Country Planning Act 1971

29 (1) (a). Subject to sections 41, 42, 70 and 77 to 80 of this Act[39] [a local planning authority] may grant planning permission either unconditionally or subject to such conditions as they think fit; or (b) may refuse planning permission.

32 (1). An application for planning permission may relate to buildings or works constructed or carried out or the use instituted before the date of the application, whether:

(*a*)   the building or works were constructed or carried out, or the use instituted, without planning permission or in accordance with planning permission granted for a limited period; or

(*b*)   the application is for permission to retain the buildings or works, or continue the use of the land, without complying with some condition subject to which a previous planning permission was granted.

(2) Any power to grant planning permission to develop land under this Act shall include power to grant planning permission for the retention on land of buildings or works constructed or carried out, or for the continuance of a use of land instituted as mentioned in sub-section (1).

33. (1) Without prejudice to the provisions of this Part of the Act, as to the duration, revocation or modification of planning permission, any grant of planning permission to develop land shall (except in so far as the permission otherwise provides) enure for the benefit of the land and all persons for the time being interested therein.

(2) Where planning permission is granted for the erection of a building; the grant of permission may specify the purposes for which the building may be used: and if no purpose is so specified, the permission shall be construed as including permission to use the building for the purpose for which it is designed.

An appeal lies from a refusal, a matter to be discussed in the next part of this chapter. Of all the aspects of permissions which give rise to problems, none do so more than conditional permissions and it is that that we shall examine in this section.

Conditions attached to permissions serve the same purpose for the planning authority as do restrictive covenants on the freehold and covenants contained in long leases for private landowners. They enable the planning authority to maintain some kind of continuing control over the development of land which it has authorised. As might be expected, therefore, they are both very common, and, where regarded by a developer as possibly irksome, they can be challenged either by an appeal to the Secretary of State on planning grounds, or on application to the courts on legal grounds (namely that the conditions imposed are, for one reason or another, *ultra vires* of the local planning authority). The concerns of the DoE, therefore, are somewhat different from the concerns of the courts – how different and in what respect, the materials below will enable us to judge. Before examining them, however, a more down-to-earth matter must be considered.

Planning conditions are imposed in their thousands; how many are followed up and, if breaches are discovered, enforced? No research has been done on them[40], but in view of the fact that few planning authorities are generously staffed, a safe assumption would be that very few are. If neighbours complain, if the breach is glaring and persistent, then enforcement action might follow; but before the courts are resorted to, there would usually be a period when letters would be exchanged and persuasion attempted. This course of action may be adopted because of doubts about the enforceability or even legality of the condition, and the local planning authority's unwillingness both to spend money on appearances in court and to risk losing a case and so putting at nought a whole series of similar conditions. In the circumstances a reasonable question is: why impose conditions? It may be suggested that what is involved is in many cases a game of bluff or even something approaching a confidence trick. Developers are willing to accept the imposition of conditions which are unenforceable in practice because they know that the imposition of such conditions is one way in which planning committees can be persuaded to accept a development which they are a little uneasy about. To grant planning permission for a light industrial use in a residential area subject to a condition that the building or factory or yard 'shall not be used in any manner so as to cause a nuisance to neighbouring residents' seems much more responsible than granting such a permission unconditionally and much more reasonable than refusing permission outright. Few developers would appeal against such a condition, and few local planning authorities would try to enforce it.

Obviously this approach is not universal. Some conditions are meant to restrict the use and development of land and are appealed against. What are known as time-limit conditions are a particular case in point[41]. Some breaches are challenged and stopped, and it is for these reasons that we must look at both the DoE advice on conditions and some of the rulings of the courts. But as so often with the law of development control, it is as well to realise that we are moving in practically two separate worlds, the world of ministerial circulars and judicial decisions and the world of day-to-day practice at the level of the local planning authority. Contact between the two gives the impression of being limited to the occasional foraging expedition.

Town and Country Planning Act 1971

30 (1). Without prejudice to the generality of section 29(1) of this Act, conditions may be imposed on the grant of planning permission thereunder —

(a) for regulating the development or use of any land under the control of the applicant (whether or not it is land in respect of which the application was made) or requiring the carrying out of works on any such land, so far as appears to the local planning authority to be expedient for the purposes of or in connection with the development authorised by the permission:

(b) for requiring the removal of any buildings or works authorised by the permission, or the discontinuance of any use of land so authorised, at the end of a specified period, and the carrying out of any works required for the reinstatement of land at the end of that period.

(2) Any planning permission granted subject to such a condition as is mentioned in subsection (1) (b) of this section is in this Act referred to as 'planning permission granted for a limited period'.

MHLG Circular No. 5/68: 'The Use of Conditions in Planning Permissions'

2. The attached memorandum, based upon the experience of the Departments in dealing with applications and appeals, sets out some general principles governing the imposition of conditions and lists some forms of condition which are acceptable in appropriate cases. It is intended only as a guide to the subject and must not be taken as an authoritative interpretation of the law, since that is a matter for the courts. In particular, the list of conditions is not exhaustive and does not exclude the imposition of any other condition, conforming to the general principles, which a local planning authority consider fitting in a particular case.

3. The fact that a condition is referred to as 'acceptable' in this memo-

randum does not relieve local planning authorities of their obligation to justify its imposition on a particular permission and to adapt its form, if necessary, to the circumstances of the case. They will need still in their decision to explain why the condition is imposed, and, if the applicant is aggrieved by the decision, to defend their action on appeal. It will not be sufficient for the authority to say that the condition is one included in the memorandum: its imposition in the particular case will still have to be justified. Careful attention should therefore be given in every case to the applicability of any condition to the permission to which it is attached, particularly where the condition is one which is so frequently used that it is printed on the form of permission used by a local planning authority; the fact that a condition has been adopted as a 'standard condition' by the authority is not in itself a sufficient reason for its imposition.

When conditions should be imposed

5. When it is desired to restrict or regulate development in a planning permission in any way, it is necessary to impose a valid condition supported by good reasons. It is not sufficient to state the requirement in the description of the development being permitted. If, for example, it is intended that an office use shall be ancillary only to another use, or that definite uses in a building shall be confined to specified floors, specific conditions to that effect should be incorporated in the permission.

Useful tests when imposing a condition

6. The following tests are suggested for deciding whether to impose a condition. Is it:

(a) necessary?
(b) relevant to planning?
(c) relevant to the development to be permitted?
(d) enforceable?
(e) precise?
(f) reasonable?

7. *The need for a condition.* One good test of need is whether, without the condition, permission for the proposed development would have to be refused. If the answer to that question is 'No,' the condition needs some special justification. It is not enough to say that a condition will do no harm. If it is to be right to impose it, it ought to do some good.

8. *Is the condition relevant to the grant of a planning permission?* It is obvious that a condition which has no relevance to planning ought not to be imposed in a planning permission. Moreover, there are matters which, though of concern in the exercise of development control, are nevertheless the subject of a more specific control in the Town and Country Planning Acts themselves; for example, advertisement control (section 34 of the Act of 1962):[42] It is better to use these controls than to rely on conditions imposed on the grant of planning permission. Other matters of close concern to planning are also regulated by other statutes or by the common law. To seek to control such matters by attaching a condition to a planning permission is usually an undesirable duplication and it invites confusion

if the impact of the condition on the development permitted is different from that of the specific control and provides different penalties. . . .

9. *Is the condition relevant to the development to be permitted?* Unless it can be shown that the requirements of the condition are directly related to the development to be permitted, the condition is probably *ultra vires*. Problems are most likely to arise in connection with section 18 (1).[43] The condition must be expedient having regard to the development which is being permitted; and where the condition requires the carrying out of works, or regulates the use of land, its requirements must be connected with the development permitted on the land which forms the subject of the planning application. For instance, it may well be expedient that, on building a factory, the developer should be required to provide parking facilities for the workers in it on a piece of land which he owns adjoining the site. A condition to this effect would be in order. It would be out of order, however, to grant permission for the factory, subject to a condition requiring the applicant to provide a car park to serve an existing factory which he owns on the other side of the street. . . . A condition requiring the removal of an existing building, whether on the application site or not, will only be reasonable if the need for that removal springs directly from the fact that a new building is to be erected. It may so spring, for example, if with both buildings on it, the site would be over-developed. But the grant of permission for a new building or for a change of use cannot properly be used as a pretext for general tidying-up by means of a condition on the permission.

10. *Is the condition enforceable?* Clearly a condition should not be imposed if it cannot be made effective. It is a useful discipline to consider what means are available to secure compliance with a proposed condition having regard to the powers of section 45 of the Act.[44] Generally speaking, if a condition can only be worded in a positive form it is likely to be difficult to enforce, unless some specific act is required as part of the initial development, such as the provision of an access, fencing, or a landscaped layout.

11. *Is the condition precise?* Every condition must tell the developer from the outset just what he has to do. A condition which requires the developer to take action if and when some other event takes place, *e.g.* to improve an access 'if the growth of traffic makes it desirable' is unacceptable; so also is a condition that requires that the site 'shall be kept tidy at all times,' or that the permitted building 'shall not be used in any manner so as to cause a nuisance to neighbouring residents.' In the one case, the meaning of 'tidy' is not explained, and in the other, apart from the fact that the condition is directed to matters of behaviour which are controllable at common law, the question whether or not a particular use constitutes a nuisance is left completely at large. (See also paragraphs 12 and 33).

12. *Is the condition reasonable?* A condition may be within the powers available, but nevertheless so unreasonable that it would be in danger of rejection by the courts. For example, it would normally be lawful to restrict the hours during which an industrial use can be carried out if the

use of the premises outside those hours would affect the amenities of the neighbourhood; but it would be unreasonable to do so to such an extent as to nullify the benefit of the permission. Again it is unreasonable to make a permission subject to a condition which has the effect of deferring the permission, by requiring, for example, that the permitted development shall not be carried out until a sewerage scheme for the area has been completed. If the development is premature, the application ought to be refused. . . .

25. . . . the planning authority ought not usually to concern themselves with the question to who would occupy the proposed building if they permitted its erection.[45]

Fawcett Properties Ltd v. *Bucks. CC* [1961] A.C. 636

LORD JENKINS: My Lords, this appeal concerns the validity of a condition imposed by the respondent council, as local planning authority under the Town and Country Planning Act, 1947, in granting permission to the appellant company's predecessor in title, Mr Donald Decimus Clark, to erect a pair of farm-workers' cottages on freehold land belonging to him at Dibden Hill Lane, Chalfont St. Giles in the County of Buckinghamshire. . . .

The effective permission of December 5, 1952, was signed by the clerk to the Amersham Rural District Council as agents for the county council and omitting formal parts was in these terms:

> In pursuance of their powers under the above-mentioned Act and Order the Bucks County Council as Local Planning Authority hereby permit erection of pair of farm-worker's cottages at Dibden Hill Lane, Chalfont St. Giles in accordance with your application dated November 22, 1952, and the plans and particulars accompanying it subject to the following conditions: (1) The occupation of the houses shall be limited to persons whose employment or latest employment is or was employment in agriculture as defined by section 119 (1) of the Town and Country Planning Act, 1947, or in forestry, or in an industry mainly dependent upon agriculture and including also the dependents of such persons as aforesaid. The reasons for imposing the above conditions are: (1) Because the council would not be prepared to permit the erection of dwelling-houses on this site unconnected with the use of the adjoining land for agriculture or similar purposes. . . .

On December 31, 1956, the appellant company bought the freehold interest in the cottages, with vacant possession, from Mr Clark's mortgagees, admittedly buying with notice of the condition as registered.

The cottages being vacant, the company wanted to let them to persons not qualified as occupants by the terms of the condition. The council refused to allow this, and after considerable correspondence the present action was brought by the appellant company as plaintiffs against the council as defendants, claiming substantially as follows: (1) A declaration that the condition was ultra vires or alternatively void for uncertainty, and that the cottages might be lawfully occupied without regard to the nature of the employment of the occupants. . . .

The case was heard by ROXBURGH J, who on October 29, 1958, gave judgment for the company on the ground that the condition was 'ultra vires as not fairly or reasonably relating to any local "planning considerations".' That aspect of the ultra vires argument may be called the 'narrow' ultra vires claim, turning as it does on the terms and apparent scope of the particular condition in question. . . .

The law relating to the 'narrow' ultra vires claim is not in dispute, and may be thus summarised:

(1) Under section 14 (1) of the Act of 1947 the council as local planning authority were empowered to grant permission for the proposed development either unconditionally or subject to such conditions as they thought fit or might refuse permission, and under section 36 they were enjoined in the exercise of their functions to have regard to the provisions which in their opinion would be required to be included in the development plan for securing the proper planning of the area.

(2) The power to impose conditions though expressed in language apt to confer an absolute discretion on a local planning authority to impose any condition of any kind they may think fit is, however, conferred as an aid to the performance of the functions assigned to them by the Act as the local planning authority thereby constituted for the area in question. Accordingly the power must be construed as limited to the imposition of conditions with respect to matters relevant, or reasonably capable of being regarded as relevant, to the implementation of planning policy. This accords with the concluding passage in section 36 above referred to. As was said by LORD DENNING in *Pyx Granite Co. Ltd.* v. *Ministry of Housing and Local Government*[46]:

> The principles to be applied are not, I think, in doubt. Although the planning authorities are given very wide powers to impose such 'conditions as they think fit', nevertheless the law says that those conditions, to be valid, must fairly and reasonably relate to the permitted development. The planning authority are not at liberty to use their powers for an ulterior object, however desirable that object may seem to them to be in the public interest.

(3) This does not mean that the wisdom or merits of a condition imposed in any given case can be made the subject of an appeal to the court at the instance of a person objecting to the condition. See *Associated Provincial Picture Houses Ltd.* v. *Wednesbury Corporation.*[47] . . .

While fully accepting the principle of the *Wednesbury* case, Mr Megarry (for the appellants) submits that in the present case the persons to whom the condition purports to limit the occupation of the two houses are defined in such comprehensive terms that on the face of it the condition (though it cannot be said to be entirely unrelated to any planning considerations) bears as a whole no fair or reasonable relation to any conceivable planning policy and is therefore beyond the powers of the local planning authority, and open to review by the court under the limited jurisdiction described in the *Wednesbury* case. Moreover, the terms of the condition do not accord with the reason given for imposing it, or in other words are not related to the respondents' own statement of their planning policy as set forth in the reason. . . .

I cannot accept Mr Megarry's argument, or ROXBURGH J's conclusion, on the narrow ultra vires claim.

As I understand the position, it would have been open to the council as local planning authority simply to grant unconditional permission for the erection of the two cottages, relying on their situation and character as sufficient for practical purposes to ensure that they would in fact be occupied by agricultural workers or persons engaged in kindred employments in the locality. If the council had taken that course, so far as I can see, they would clearly have been acting within their powers. But, as stated in the reason, the council's policy was 'not to permit the erection of dwelling-houses' on the site in question 'unconnected with the use of the adjoining land for agriculture or similar purposes.' They therefore thought it expedient to impose an express condition designed to implement that policy, and accordingly did impose the condition now said to be ultra vires. The question, then, is whether (apart from the question of uncertainty, which at this stage I ignore) this condition with all its faults could fairly and reasonably be held to make it more likely that the policy stated in the reason would be implemented than it would have been if the council had simply given unconditional permission for the erection of the two cottages. In my opinion the answer to that question must clearly be in the affirmative, and if I am right in that opinion it follows in my judgment that the narrow ultra vires claim must fail. The condition, no doubt, fell short of perfection, but so far as it went it was designed to carry out, and in practice might reasonably be expected to carry out, the respondents' planning policy.

I may now turn to the argument that the condition was void for uncertainty, which seems to me to be the difficult point in the case. It is said that the condition is so imperfectly expressed and defines the persons to whom the occupation of the cottages is to be limited with such lack of precision that many cases might occur in which no owner of the cottages could tell, and no court could decide, whether by letting a given person into, or permitting him to remain in, occupation, the owner would be committing a breach of the condition. . . .

Speaking for myself, I confess I have been attracted by the view that one aspect of the argument on uncertainty could be met by construing the words 'dependent upon agriculture' in close conjunction with the statutory definition of agriculture expressly adopted by the condition. That definition defines agriculture as including a number of activities, e.g. 'horticulture, fruit growing' . . . 'the breeding and keeping of live-stock' . . . 'the use of land as grazing land meadow land osier land market gardens and nursery grounds . . .' and so forth. True it is that the definition is not exhaustive, but that only means that there are or may be other activities proper to be classed as 'agriculture.' On this view it would follow that by the expression 'an industry . . . dependent upon agriculture' the condition means an industry which depends on some one or more of these activities for its raw materials as distinct from an industry which depends on people engaged in agriculture as customers for the agricultural necessaries which it supplies, e.g., in the form of agricultural machinery or fertilisers. . . .

There remains the argument, already touched upon, that no sure line can be drawn to enable the point at which dependence on agriculture ceases in a case in which a particular agricultural product after leaving the farm is put (perhaps by several stages) into a different state, in which it is sold, or it may be, subjected to some further manufacturing process. . .

I think the answer is that the dependence on agriculture contemplated by the condition is a direct dependence. The condition is capable of that meaning, and if construed as including any degree of dependence, however remote or indirect, it would lead to manifest absurdity. . . .

It remains to consider whether, if and so far as the condition contains any element of uncertainty, the degree of uncertainty involved is sufficient in all the circumstances of the case to justify your Lordships in holding the condition void. . . .

It clearly cannot be necessary to the validity of the condition here in question that it should be possible to identify all the persons who, according to the terms of the condition, are at any given time eligible in point of employment or latest employment to be let into occupation of the cottages. The owner is under no obligation to let anyone into occupation, and, in particular, is under no obligation to any person who satisfies the condition to let such person into occupation on that account. . . .

Such being the position of the owner, I see no reason why the possible occurrence of doubtful cases, which he would be free to reject, should be held to invalidate the condition so as to entitle him to let into possession persons clearly outside the permitted limit. The question should perhaps be regarded to some extent as one of degree. . . .

The above line of argument would, of course, have no application to a condition framed in such terms that it would be ex facie impossible to attribute satisfaction of it to anyone, for in such a case the result would be to preclude the owner from letting altogether. . . .

In conclusion, I would observe that in common with the Court of Appeal and the majority of your Lordships, I attach great importance to the circumstance that the language of the condition from the words 'persons whose employment' down to the words 'the dependents of such person as aforesaid' (omitting the words from 'as defined' down to 'or in forestry') are borrowed ipsissimis verbis from the definition of the expression 'agricultural population' contained in section 34 (2) of the Housing Act, 1930, which definition is reproduced in section 115 (2) of the Housing Act, 1936, and section 114 (5) of the Housing Act, 1957. Having regard to the close similarity between the language of the condition now under consideration and that of the Housing Act definition to

which I have just referred, I think it would be very difficult for your Lordships to hold the condition void for uncertainty. . . .
Appeal dismissed.

Hall & Co Ltd v. *Shoreham-by-Sea UDC* [1964]
1 All E.R. 1

WILLMER LJ: This is an appeal by the plaintiffs against a judgment of GLYN-JONES J given on May 27, 1963, whereby he dismissed an action brought by them against the defendant councils. The plaintiffs carry on business at premises known as Lennards' Wharf, Shoreham, and are the owners of a plot of land which it is desired to develop for industrial purposes. The defendant county council is the planning authority for the area under the Town and Country Planning Acts, and has delegated certain of its powers to the defendant urban district council. By their statement of claim the plaintiffs claim a declaration that certain conditions attached to a planning permission granted to them by the defendant urban district council in respect of proposed development at Lennards' Wharf are void for uncertainty and/or ultra vires. . . .

The plaintiffs' premises are situated in a strip of land which lies between the main Brighton road on the north and the estuary of the river Adur on the south. . . .

It is accepted that a strip of land along the northern edge of the plaintiffs' land fronting the Brighton road will be required at some future date for a road widening scheme. . . .

The plaintiffs obtained from the defendant urban district council planning permission for their proposed development in terms of a document issued to them and dated July 12, 1960. The permission was expressed to be subject to certain conditions. Condition 1 refused permission for the development of the strip of land required for the proposed road widening scheme along the northern edge of the plaintiffs' land. Condition 2 required that a level landing should be constructed at the point of the proposed access to the main road. No question arises as to either of these two conditions. The dispute has arisen over conditions 3 and 4 which are in the following terms:

> 3. The applicants shall construct an ancillary road over the entire frontage of the site at their own expense, as and when required by the local planning authority, and shall give right of passage over it to and from such ancillary roads as may be constructed on the adjoining land. The ancillary road shall consist of a carriageway twenty feet wide with a margin three feet wide on each side. 4. The new access shall be temporary for a period of five years initially, but the local planning authority will not enforce its closure until the ancillary roads referred to in condition 3 shall have been constructed and alternative access to the main road is available within 150 yards of the temporary access.

The reasons for the imposition of these conditions were expressed to be as follows:

3 & 4. The local planning authority are of the opinion that in the interests of highway safety an ancillary road should be constructed along this frontage but are prepared to allow the access now proposed as a temporary expedient pending the construction of the said ancillary road. . . .

It is contended . . . that the defendants are exceeding their powers in seeking to impose these conditions on the plaintiffs.

It will be convenient to deal first with the allegation of uncertainty. The language of conditions 3 and 4 is certainly inelegant, and no doubt somewhat obscure. I do not think that the words used by a local authority in imposing conditions are to be scrutinised in the same way as the words used by a parliamentary draftsman. It seems to me that conditions imposed by a local authority, like bye-laws, should be benevolently construed, and in this connexion I would venture to follow the same approach as that of LORD RUSSELL OF KILLOWEN CJ, in *Kruse* v. *Johnson*[48]. This approach was echoed by some words of HARMAN LJ in the recent case of *Britt* v. *Buckinghamshire County Council*[49]. The duty of the court, as I see it, is to give a meaning to the words used, if that is at all possible, and the burden is, in my judgment, on those alleging uncertainty to satisfy the court as to the uncertainty complained of.

With regard to condition 4 there is, in my judgment, rather more to be said in favour of the plea of uncertainty. The further and better particulars alleged that this condition

> is vague and uncertain because (a) it does not sufficiently specify what steps are to be taken by the plaintiffs and/or when they are to be taken; and/or (b) it does not provide for any certain alternative access; and/or (c) the expression 'is available' is vague and uncertain.

The use of the word 'initially' shows that the permission is intended to continue after the expiration of five years until a specified future event takes place. I think that the condition, though inelegantly expressed, means that the access is to be temporary in the sense that it is to continue in use for five years certain, and thereafter until the ancillary roads on the adjoining land have been constructed and alternative access to the main road is available within 150 yards. That seems to me to be the common sense of the matter, and I think that the words used are capable of this construction. I certainly do not feel able to say that it is impossible to give any sensible meaning to the words used. In these circumstances, I am of opinion that conditions 3 and 4 cannot be held void for uncertainty.

I turn now to consider what I regard as the main point in the case, namely, the contention that conditions 3 and 4 are ultra vires. . . . It is said that the work required to be carried out in accordance with the conditions sought to be imposed is not such as can fairly be said to be 'for the purposes of or in connexion with the development authorised by the permission'. It is to be observed that the provisions of s. 14 (2) (a) are expressed to be without prejudice to the generality of the previous subsection. I do not think, therefore, that it is possible to construe sub-s. (2)

(a) as imposing a limitation on the wide words of sub-s(1). Quite apart from that, however, it seems to me that a planning authority, when granting a planning permission to a property owner, must necessarily take into consideration the effect of the granting of such permission on the development of adjoining properties. Bearing this in mind, it seems to me impossible to say that the conditions relating to the construction of the ancillary road sought to be imposed on the plaintiffs are not 'in connexion with the development authorised'. . . .

It remains to consider the contention that the conditions imposed are so unreasonable that they should be held to be ultra vires on that ground. In the first place, it is to be remarked that it is not sufficient merely to say that the conditions are unreasonable or unduly onerous, for that would properly be the subject for appeal to the ministry under s. 16 of the Act of 1947. In order to justify the court in granting a declaration that the conditions are ultra vires it must be shown that they are so unreasonable that no reasonable council could have imposed them. . . .

It appears to me that the object sought to be attained by the defendants in the present case is a perfectly reasonable one. I agree with the view of the learned judge that to require the construction of an ancillary road and to limit the points at which traffic may enter or leave the main road, is 'consistent with good traffic engineering'. It is said, however, that the terms of the conditions actually imposed, particularly the requirement that the plaintiffs should give right of passage to and from the ancillary roads to be constructed on the adjoining land, are so unreasonable as to go beyond anything that Parliament can have intended or that any reasonable authority could properly have imposed. It is implicit in condition 3 that a similar requirement for the construction of an ancillary road will be imposed as a condition of developing the adjoining land, and indeed any land within the strip between the main road and the harbour which is scheduled for industrial development. Two results follow from this. First, the plaintiffs will be required to give right of passage not only to the owners of the adjoining land, but to all traffic coming to their boundary from the ancillary road on the adjoining land, whether it has come from their neighbour's land or beyond, and also to all traffic proceeding to the ancillary road on the adjoining property, whatever its ultimate destination may be. As I have already indicated, this amounts in effect to a requirement that the plaintiffs shall dedicate the ancillary road when it is built to the public. If the volume of traffic is such as to choke the road, or if the weight of traffic is such as to cause damage to it involving an inordinate amount of repair, the plaintiffs will have no redress. Secondly, if when the ancillary roads on the adjoining land are built the plaintiffs' access to the main road is closed, and they are forced to rely on access to the main road over the ancillary roads on the adjoining land, they may find themselves at the mercy of the adjoining landowners, and will have no effective remedy if such access is obstructed. In such circumstances it is contended that no developer in the position of the plaintiffs could be expected to proceed with the proposed development on such onerous terms. . . .

Under the conditions now sought to be imposed . . . the plaintiff must construct the ancillary road as and when they may be required to do so over the whole of their frontage entirely at their own expense. . . . The defendants would thus obtain the benefit of having the road constructed for them at the plaintiffs' expense, on the plaintiffs' land, and without the necessity for paying any compensation in respect thereof. Bearing in mind that another and more regular course is open to the defendants it seems to me that this result would be utterly unreasonable and such as Parliament cannot possibly have intended. . . .

I can certainly find no clear and unambiguous words in the Town and Country Planning Act, 1947, authorising the defendants in effect to take away the plaintiffs' rights of property without compensation by the imposition of conditions such as those sought to be imposed. In these circumstances, although I have much sympathy with the object sought to be achieved by the defendants, I am satisfied that conditions 3 and 4 are so unreasonable that they must be held to be ultra vires.

The defendants' contention that the conditions sought to be imposed can be saved by severing such parts as are thought to be objectionable will not, I think, bear examination. In effect what the defendants invite us to do is to re-write their conditions for them. This might well be an appropriate remedy to seek on appeal to the minister under s. 16 of the Act of 1947 against conditions sought to be imposed, but, in an action for a declaration such as the present, it seems to me to be quite outside the scope of anything that the court can be required to do.

It remains to consider what is the effect in law of my conclusion that conditions 3 and 4 are ultra vires. On behalf of the plaintiffs we have been invited to say that the planning permission can now be regarded as free of these conditions, so that the plaintiffs are at liberty to proceed with their proposed development as if these conditions had never been imposed. On the other hand, we have been referred to the dictum of HODSON LJ, in *Pyx Granite Co. Ltd.* v. *Ministry of Housing and Local Government*[50] to the effect that, if conditions are held to be ultra vires, the whole planning permission must fail, since it must be assumed that without the conditions the permission would never have been granted. . . . here the conditions objected to by the plaintiffs are fundamental to the whole of the planning permission. In such circumstances I would follow the dictum of HODSON LJ and hold that the whole of the planning permission must fail. . . .

Appeal allowed.

R. v. *London Borough of Hillingdon ex parte Royco Homes Ltd*
[1974] 2 All E.R. 643

LORD WIDGERY CJ: In these proceedings counsel moves on behalf of Royco Homes Ltd for an order of certiorari to bring up into this court with a view to its being quashed a purported grant of planning permission by the London Borough of Hillingdon dated 12th December

1973 and permitting the development of a parcel of land in the borough of Hillingdon known as 'Buntings', Swakeleys Road, for residential development. . .

The permission is made subject to conditions, many of which are not controversial and raise no sort of issue before us, but within the ambit of the conditions are four which constitute the basis of counsel for the applicants' submission that this grant of permission is a nullity.

Condition 2:
The dwellings hereby approved shall be so designed as to provide space and heating standards at least to the standards (a) defined in Appendix I to Circular 36/67 dated 25th April, 1962 issued by the then Ministry of Housing and Local Government, and (b) which shall have been designated as mandatory requirements for local authority housing schemes qualifying for Government subsidy or loan sanction, and the detailed drawings required by condition No. 6 shall show compliance with such standards.

What that comes to is that the planning authority are insisting as a condition of the planning permission that the dwellings shall be designed so as to provide space and heating to the standards required for local authority housing. For myself I would not have thought this condition on its face was a departure from the functions and powers of the planning authority to which reference must later be made, but counsel for the applicants, apart from other arguments designed to show that this permission is invalid, says that it is outside the powers of a planning authority to lay down conditions as to the internal design of houses or flats the erection of which it authorises. He says, as is the fact, that once a house has been built in accordance with planning permission, its internal arrangements can be varied to any degree without further planning permission. He, therefore, contends that it would be wholly illogical if a planning authority when granting planning permission tried to dictate the internal arrangements in the detail which this condition contemplates. For my part I do not find it necessary to reach a conclusion on that argument of counsel for the applicants and I deliberately do not attempt to pursue the matter further on that particular point.

Condition 3: The dwellings hereby approved shall be constructed at a cost per dwelling which shall not exceed the relevant housing cost yardstick (as defined by Circular 36/67) . . .

The condition goes on to further detail but the essence of it is contained in the sentence which I have read. The effect of it, if it is valid, is that the houses to be erected pursuant to this planning permission must be erected to a maximum cost equivalent to that to which local authorities are subject if they seek to obtain normal housing subsidies for development which they have carried out. This is a condition then the effect of which is to restrict the maximum cost per dwelling and in fact the yardstick chosen is the yardstick appropriate to the local authorities who seek, as they naturally would, to obtain the appropriate government subsidies for the houses which they erect.

Condition 4:

> The dwellings hereby approved shall be first occupied by persons (together with their families and/or dependents) who on the qualifying date shall have been recorded on the Housing Waiting List of the Hillingdon London Borough Council (as distinct from the Council's statutory register of applications for accommodation) for a period of not less than 12 months immediately preceding the qualifying date. The qualifying date for any person shall be any date within the period of 6 months before the commencement of his occupation of one of the dwellings hereby approved.

Again cutting through the detail of the language, this is a requirement that if the houses are erected pursuant to the permission obtained by the applicants, the occupiers of those houses shall not be occupiers chosen by the developers themselves but shall be persons who are on the local authority's housing waiting list in the terms of the condition which I have read. That is on any view an extremely serious restriction on the character of the occupier who is to go into these houses if they are built pursuant to this permission.

Finally, condition 5:

> The dwellings hereby approved shall for a period of 10 years from the date of first occupation be occupied as the residence of a person who occupies by virtue of a tenure which would not be excluded from the protection of the Rent Act 1968 by any provision of Section 2 of that Act.

Again the provision with regard to the security of tenure to be enjoyed by the respective tenants is there restricted when compared with the freedom which a developer would normally have in choosing not only the tenants who occupy his property but the terms on which they should so occupy it.

The case for the applicants before us today is that those four conditions are as a matter of law ultra vires as being in excess of the power to impose conditions enjoyed by a planning authority when granting a planning permission. Counsel for the applicants further submits that those conditions being void on that account, they are fundamental to the grant of planning permission, and if they are to be held to be null and void, the whole planning permission must fall with them, hence his application for certiorari. . . .

That the planning authority has wide power to impose conditions has been a common feature of this legislation ever since 1947. . . .

Those wide words 'subject to such conditions as they think fit' confer authority for a wide range of conditions to be attached to planning permissions. However those words are clearly too wide to be given their literal meaning and a number of years ago they were restricted by a dictum of LORD DENNING, which is constantly quoted in these matters. The dictum appears in the decision of the Court of Appeal in *Pyx Granite Co. Ltd.* v. *Ministry of Housing and Local Government.* . . .[51]

Of the cases which followed *Pyx Granite* the one which is nearest to the present is *Hall & Co. Ltd.* v. *Shoreham-by-Sea Urban District Council.* . . .

I find *Hall's* case helpfully similar to the situation which is before us. In *Hall's* case the local authority, with the best of motives, wanted in effect a new extension to the public highway and thought it right to require the developer to provide it at his own expense as a condition of getting planning permission. That was rejected in the Court of Appeal because it was a fundamental departure from the rights of ownership and it was so unreasonable that no planning authority, approaching its duty and properly applying itself to the facts, could have reached it. I think exactly the same can be said of the conditions in issue in this case.

Taking nos. 4 and 5 first of all, they undoubtedly in my judgment are the equivalent of requiring the private developer to take on at his own expense a significant part of the duty of the local authority as housing authority. However well intentioned and however sensible such a desire on the part of the planning authority may have been, it seems to me that it is unreasonable in the sense in which WILLMER LJ was using the word in *Hall's* case. I, therefore, have no doubt for myself that conditions 4 and 5 are clearly ultra vires, but I have for some time thought that conditions 2 and 3 might be saved. Conditions 2 and 3, however, strange and perhaps oppressive, do not by themselves appear to me to have a clear badge of ultra vires on them, although I would expect the Secretary of State on an appeal to him to have something to say about them. By themselves, however, I doubt whether they would have justified the allegation that they were clearly in excess of jurisdiction and clearly ultra vires. But I am persuaded in the end that one must not sever conditions 2 and 3 from conditions 4 and 5 because they are all designed to the single purpose. Conditions 2 and 3 are designed to see that the houses physically should be suitable for local authority tenants and conditions 4 and 5 are designed to see that in fact they should be occupied by the local authority tenants. I think the four being different facets of the single purpose stand or fall together and with that approach they must unquestionably fall in my opinion.

On the authority of *Hall's* case, the conditions being fundamental to the planning permission, I think they bring the planning permission down with them and that means that the applicants are entitled to the order of certiorari which they seek.[52]

What is the difference, as a matter of law, between a condition which limits occupancy of a house 'to a person whose employment or latest employment is or was employment in agriculture' and a condition which limits occupation of a house to a person on a housing waiting list of a local authority? Consider the legality of the following condition:

The dwelling hereby approved shall be first occupied by persons (together with their families and/or dependents) whose latest employment is or was employment in any of the following public services:

The Post Office;
The ILEA;
The GLC including London Transport;
Any London Borough;
The National Health Service.

Do you agree with the comment of the Chairman of the Planning and Development Committee of the London Borough of Southwark, made in a letter to the *New Law Journal* of 25 July 1974, that decisions such as the one in *Royco Homes* 'yet further impinge on sensible planning and are further illustrations of the law and lawyers bedevilling the planning processes which have been achieved only too well over the years'?

Town and Country Planning Act 1971

41.—(1) Subject to the provisions of this section, every planning permission granted or deemed to be granted shall be granted or, as the case may be, be deemed to be granted, subject to the condition that the development to which it relates must be begun not later than the expiration of—

(*a*)   five years beginning with the date on which the permission is granted or, as the case may be, deemed to be granted; or

(*b*)   such other period (whether longer or shorter) beginning with the said date as the authority concerned with the terms of the planning permission may direct, being a period which the authority considers appropriate having regard to the provisions of the development plan and to any other material considerations.

(2) If planning permission is granted without the condition required by subsection (1) of this section, it shall be deemed to have been granted subject to the condition that the development to which it relates must be begun not later than the expiration of five years beginning with the date of the grant.

42.—(2) Subject to the provisions of this section, where outline planning permission is granted for development consisting in or including the carrying out of building or other operations, it shall be granted subject to conditions to the following effect—

(*a*)   that, in the case of any reserved matter, application for approval must be made not later than the expiration of three years beginning with the date of the grant of outline planning permission; and

(*b*)   that the development to which the permission relates must be begun not later than whichever is the later of the following dates—
(i) the expiration of five years from the date of the grant of outline planning permission; or
(ii) the expiration of two years from the final approval of the

reserved matters or, in the case of approval on different dates, the final approval of the last such matter to be approved.

(iii) The communication[53]

It might be thought that the communication of a determination by a local planning authority was a straightforward matter, which, errors by the Post Office excepted, could hardly give rise to problems. That this is not so is borne out by the materials below and the issues to which they give rise, the most important of which is the question of the legal effect of informal communications made to the developer. Three other matters which it is convenient to deal with here, however, are the time within which communication must be made, the construction of permissions, and what constitutes a permission and its communication.

(a) TIME OF COMMUNICATION

Town and Country Planning General Development
Orders 1973 to 1974

7. (3) The period within which the local planning authority shall give notice to an applicant of their decision or determination or of the reference of an application to the Secretary of State shall be two months or (except where the applicant has already given notice of appeal to the Secretary of State) such extended period as may be agreed upon in writing between the applicant and (a) in Greater London, the local planning authority, (b) elsewhere, the district planning authority or, in the case of an application which falls to be determined by the county planning authority, either the district planning authority or the county planning authority.

Where a decision is not given within two months or by an agreed date, permission is deemed to have been refused, and an applicant may appeal to the Minister. It was accepted by the House of Lords in *James* v. *Secretary of State for Wales*[54] that the above provision is directory and not mandatory and that a notice given after the expiry of the period is good if acted upon and may be appealed against, but if the applicant took no action in relation to it, it might be void. Why?

(b) CONSTRUCTION OF PERMISSIONS

After a certain amount of confusion and conflict in lower courts, Lord Reid, in a judgement in which three of their Lordships expressly concurred, put the position thus in *Slough Estates Ltd* v. *Slough Corporation* (1970) 68 L.G.R. 669:

. . . The appellants argued that in construing the planning permission with which we are concerned it is proper to have regard to all relevant facts known to the planning authority when the permission was given – in this case correspondence which had passed between the parties. We did look at this correspondence before deciding whether it was admissible, and in my view it does not help the appellants so it is unnecessary to reach a decision. But as the matter was argued and is of general importance I think I should state my opinion.

It is well settled that the court in construing a will or a contract must put itself in the shoes of the testator or the parties by admitting in evidence all relevant facts known at the time by the testator or by both the parties. But in my view it does not at all follow that the same applies to a public document. It could not possibly apply to a Minister making a statutory instrument. How far can it apply to a written grant of planning permission? This is available to purchasers from the person who originally obtained the permission. He may have no means of discovering what facts were known to the planning authority. It is true that the person who originally obtained the permission would be likely to know. But the question may arise after many years. And it could hardly be that the permission could mean one thing in the hands of the original owner and something different in the hands of a purchaser from him.

There is not much authority on the matter. We were referred to two cases. In *Miller-Mead* v. *Minister of Housing and Local Government*[55] the permission granted was, if its words were given their ordinary meaning, wider than what had been asked for in the owner's application. But it was held not proper to use the application to cut down the ordinary meaning of the permission. On the other hand, in *Sussex Caravan Parks* v. *Richardson*[56], there are observations by HARMAN LJ to the effect that in construing an entry in a valuation list it is permissible to have regard to extrinsic evidence and the appellants relied on them. They were not essential to the decision and are not supported by the judgment of HOLROYD PEARCE LJ.

Of course, extrinsic evidence may be required to identify a thing or place referred to, but that is a very different thing from using evidence of facts which were known to the maker of the document but which are not common knowledge to alter or qualify the apparent meaning of words or phrases used in such a document. Members of the public, entitled to rely on a public document, surely ought not to be subject to the risk of its apparent meaning being altered by the introduction of such evidence. . . .

How should the courts construe an ambiguous planning permission where the original application and correspondence relating thereto is (a) incorporated by specific reference into the permission, (b) is not so incorporated?

(c) WHAT CONSTITUTES A PERMISSION AND ITS COMMUNICATION?

R. v. Yeovil Corporation, ex parte *Trustees of
Elim Pentecostal Church, Yeovil* (1972) 70 L.G.R. 142.

LORD WIDGERY CJ: In these proceedings Mr McCulloch moves on behalf of the applicants, the trustees of the Elim Pentecostal Church, Yeovil, for an order of *mandamus* addressed to Yeovil Corporation requiring them to issue forms of conditional planning consent under the town and country planning legislation pursuant to two applications which are identified in the statement delivered in accordance with R.S.C. Ord 53. r. 1(2).

The matter arises in this way. The applicants having certain land in their ownership, decided that they would build a youth hostel on this land. For this purpose, of course, they require planning permission under the Town and Country Planning Acts, and on May 27, 1970, they submitted to the Yeovil Corporation an outline application for planning permission. The Yeovil Corporation was the proper authority to whom to submit the application because, by virtue of delegation agreements made between Yeovil Corporation and Somerset County Council, it had executive powers in this field. Without waiting for an answer on that first application, the applicants, on June 19, 1970, submitted a further and detailed application, and, understandably, thereafter the two applications were treated together. They were dealt with quite properly. On July 2, 1970, there is a minute of the meeting of the planning committee. By that time the matter had been referred to the area planning officer, a step which was necessary under the delegation agreement, and his observations had been received by the corporation. His observations, according to the planning committee's minute of July 2, 1970, were that he recommended approval of the proposal subject to a number of conditions, the only material one being: 'The parking area indicated in blue on the submitted plan shall be available for use at all times by users of the hall until such time as alternative parking provision satisfactory to the local planning authority shall be made'.

When the matter came before the planning committee on July 2, they had that recommendation in favour of approval before them. There was some discussion at the meeting as to the method by which the car parking requirement was to be met, and at the end of the meeting the decision is minuted thus: 'It is resolved that the town clerk be authorised to approve the application subject to the above conditions when evidence of an agreement about the car parking facilities has been received'.

A great deal of debate has gone on before us in this court as to just exactly what that decision, as it is described, means. Mr McCulloch's case for the applicants is that in those words the planning committee are recording their approval of the proposal under the Town and Country Planning Acts, and merely recording that the further step, namely, as to collecting evidence of an agreement about the car park, was left to the town clerk to decide. For completeness I ought to say that the two applications being dealt with together on this occasion, that decision is a decision in regard to both.

There followed two letters of some relevance. First, on July 8, the town clerk wrote to the gentleman representing the applicants reporting the meeting of July 2, in these terms:

> The council's planning committee have further considered the application for planning permission in this matter, but have not reached a final decision as confirmation of the agreement regarding the proposed car park is not yet available. I understand that negotiations in the matter are in hand and shall be pleased if you will let me know as soon as these have been concluded. I will then arrange for the application to be dealt with.

I pause to observe that the town clerk is there writing on the footing that a matter remains before the planning application can finally be disposed of, that matter being the provision of evidence about the car parking arrangements.

A further letter dated August 4, to which we were referred was written by the chief education officer to a Mr Attwell. The chief education officer comes into it because the education authority's co-operation was required in order to make the car parking land available. In the letter he records that a Mr Newsome Martin, the chairman of the sites and buildings subcommittee of the education authority, has authorised him to write to say that: '. . . he agrees in principle to a licence being granted to the youth club for use of the land as a car park'.

It is pointed out quite fairly that that letter shows that by August 4 arrangements for the use of that land as a car park were at any rate well advanced.

In fact, however, when the matter next came before the planning committee on August 13, they withdrew their previously expressed view and decided to refuse the application. . . .

It is . . . perfectly clear in my judgment that the machinery of the Act of 1962 contemplates that when the planning authority make a decision under section 17 that decision shall be notified in writing to the applicant whether it be for better or for worse. . . .

It is . . . central to Mr McCulloch's argument that the decision had been made on July 2, and the first way in which Mr Seward seeks to meet that argument is to say that what in truth happened on July 2 was that the planning authority delegated to the town clerk the authority to make the decision. True, it was a very limited and prescribed delegation, because obviously he was only to grant permission and not refuse it. Furthermore he was to grant permission if he was satisfied with the evidence as to the car park. But Mr Seward, nevertheless, argues that the true view of what happened on July 2, was that the planning authority delegated the determination of this matter to the town clerk within those limits, and he referred to section 64 of the Town and Country Planning

Act, 1968, which contains provision for delegation by a local planning authority of some of its functions to its officers. Section 64(1) provides: 'A local planning authority may delegate to any officer of the authority the function of determining all or any, or a specified class, of the following applications, that is to say – (a) an application for planning permission under Part III of the principal Act. . . .'

So there it is, as clear as could be, power for the planning authority to delegate this important decision to an officer if they think fit. Furthermore, by section 64(3): 'A delegation made by a local authority under this section to an officer of theirs . . . (b) may be made with or without restrictions or conditions'.

That, to my mind, directly authorises the kind of delegation said by Mr Seward to have occurred in this case, namely, a delegation of the final decision, but one hedged about with restrictions and conditions which the town clerk had to observe in reaching that final decision. Section 64(5) is not without interest. It provides: 'Where any functions have under this section been delegated to an officer of a local authority, any determination by him of such an application as is referred to in subsection (1) of this section shall, if it is notified in writing to the applicant, be treated for all purposes as a determination of the delegating authority'. I draw attention to the inclusion of the words 'if it is notified in writing to the applicant'.

In my judgment, Mr Seward's argument on this point should be accepted. I am quite satisfied for my own part that no determination of the application took place on July 2, and I accept the interpretation of what occurred given to us by Mr Seward as being the correct one. In other words, I accept the view that the planning authority had delegated the final determination to the town clerk, and that unless and until he made that final determination within the authority given to him, no question of planning permission having been granted could arise. It follows in my judgment that if that was the situation on July 2, and if the town clerk had not finally determined the matter before the later meeting of the committee on August 13, it was open to the committee to change their mind, withdraw the provisional approval and refuse the application. That ground, no doubt, is sufficient to dispose of the present application, but another important matter has been canvassed, and I think it appropriate to express a view on it.

Mr Seward has supported his resistance to Mr McCulloch's application in this case on a very broad ground indeed, namely, that within this legislation there is in effect no planning permission unless and until the written notice of the planning authority's decision has been given to the applicant. Of course, if that is right, that again would be a complete answer to the present claim, because here no written notice of approval was ever given; and, if this second argument of Mr Seward's is right, then it would follow that the planning authority were perfectly free to withdraw their decision prior to their issue of the formal written notice. Mr McCulloch says that they cannot because they are *functus officio*, but on this approach to the matter they would not be *functus officio* until they had issued the written notice. No doubt when that notice had gone out they would be *functus officio*, but not until then.

For my part I think this argument of Mr Seward's is well founded also. Somewhat surprisingly it has not arisen for direct decision in the 25-odd years in which the modern town planning code has been in force, but it was touched on briefly by LORD DENNING MR in *Slough Estates Ltd.* v. *Slough Borough Council (No. 2)*.[57] LORD DENNING MR, considering the permissible aids to the construction of a written planning permission, said:

> The permission must be construed together with the plan which was submitted and was incorporated into it: see *Wilson* v. *West Sussex County Council*[58]. I confine myself to the plan. I do not think it is permissible to look at the resolution of the county council or the correspondence, for neither of them was incorporated into the permission . . .

There in terms one finds LORD DENNING MR saying that it is not permissible to look at the resolution to construe the written permission. One asks oneself why not if as Mr McCulloch contends, it is the resolution and not the written permission which really matters? LORD DENNING MR (*supra*) continued:

> The reason for excluding them is this: The grant of planning permission has to be in writing (see the Town and Country Planning (General Interim Development) Order, 1945 article 12); and it runs with the land. The grant is not made when the county council resolve to give permission. It is only made when their clerk, on their authority, issues the permission to the applicant.

I respectfully think that that is entirely right, and its effect in this case is that there never has here been a planning permission granted. *Application refused.*

Norfolk County Council v. *Secretary of State for the Environment* [1973] 3 All E.R. 673

LORD WIDGERY CJ: This is an appeal under s. 246 of the Town and Country Planning Act 1971 brought by the Norfolk County Council ('the council') in respect of the decision of the Secretary of State for the Environment ('the Minister') whereby he quashed an enforcement notice served by the council on the second respondents, Pixon Food Products Ltd ('the company'). The case is extremely special and turns on a very narrow point, and I do not find it necessary to go into the factual circumstances in any detail at all.

The outline history of the matter which gives rise to this question is that on 29th July 1971 the company were minded to build an extension to their factory, which is somewhere in Norfolk under the jurisdiction of the council. They appropriately applied for planning permission under the Town and Country Planning Acts for this facility, the extension of their factory. On 7th January 1972 the matter was before the appropriate committee of the council, no doubt the planning committee, who determined that this permission should not be granted. One need not go into the circumstances of why it was not granted. The planning authority determined through the instrument of their appropriate committee that it ought not to be granted. It was then the duty, as I understand it, of the county planning officer to notify the company of the result of their application, and in view of what the planning committee had decided, it was the clear duty of the county planning officer to write to the company, whether or not in a formal document, intimating that their application had been refused, and the reasons for it.

What happened, and nobody can understand exactly why or how, was that instead of writing a letter in those terms, the county planning officer sent to the company a document which was in the form of a grant of permission. It is in the form of a grant of permission in every detail. It is on the proper prescribed form used for that purpose. It says in terms that the council hereby permits the development which has been referred to in the application, and it even contains three conditions to which it says the permission is to be subject. It is signed by the planning officer, describing himself in that capacity, a person who, as I say, undoubtedly had authority to notify the company of the result of their planning application.

How it happened is a matter of speculation; perhaps the form had been prepared in advance, in anticipation of a grant of permission which had not materialised in the event; but however that may be, this is the document which the company received in the post the following morning. No doubt they were very pleased to see it.

The planning committee met on 2nd January 1972 and the document purporting to record their decision was sent on 11th January. Of course a mistake of this kind was bound to come to light soon, and in fact it came to light on 13th January, some two days after the permission had been issued. The council realised a mistake had been made; telephone contact was made with the company's solicitors to tell them a mistake had been made, and on 14th January 1972 a letter confirming the error was sent to the company, together with a formal notice of refusal, which was precisely the document that they ought to have received in the first instance consequent on the committee's decision. Disputes then arose as to what the position was, the company maintaining that they had a valid planning permission even though it had been granted to them by mistake, and the council contending that there was no valid planning permission.

In order to bring the matter to a head, the company made a token start with the extension to their factory by digging a few feet of the foundation trench, and then invited the council to bring enforcement proceedings against them, and thus to raise the question of what this piece of paper was worth.

All this went according to plan; the council served an enforcement notice alleging that this development had been begun in breach of the planning law and requiring it to be undone, and the company then appealed to the Minister under the Act, and the Minister appointed an inspector who sat with a legal assessor, the point at issue being essentially a legal one. The inspector in due course made his report and the

Minister's decision based on that report appears under date 28th December 1972. . . .

The Minister, having set out with great clarity and some detail the history and the arguments which I have referred to, came to the conclusion that the planning permission so-called must stand, and I think he was influenced by the legal assessor into taking the view that if the company could show that it had acted on the planning permission in any way that was enough to prevent the council from setting up the mistake. However the argument put forward by counsel for the company covers other matters than that, and I should start at the beginning.

His first submission is that when a document is issued purporting to be a planning permission, it is not permissible to look at the resolution of the planning authority in order to construe or explain the terms of the permission. That was decided some years ago in *Slough Estates* v. *Slough Borough Council*, and I think has some support in the later decision of *R.* v. *Yeovil Corpn, ex parte Trustees of Elim Pentecostal Church, Yeovil*. I entirely accept, and indeed am bound to accept that the proposition as stated by counsel for the company is a sound one, but it seems to me that there s a world of difference between a situation in which a valid planning permission has been granted and one where no such permission had been granted at all. If it is to be accepted that a permission of some kind has been granted, I accept that the effect of the document must be gauged from its face without reference to the resolution which prompted it. But where, as here, no planning permission was ever granted, I do not think that the principle of the *Slough Estates* case and others of the same line of authority prevent the planning authority from showing, if they can, that that which purported to be a permission was no permission at all, and in this case it was no permission at all.

There is authority now whereby planning authorities can delegate some of these conclusions to their officers, but no one suggests that the county planning officer in this case was authorised to make a decision. All he was authorised to do was to notify the result of the decision.

Accordingly, the body which had power to make a decision, namely the planning authority, decided in the contrary sense, and against the grant of permission, and the officer who produced the document in the form of a planning permission had no authority himself to make such a decision. His ostensible authority, as far as I can see, only went to his authority to transmit the decision which had been made, so I have no hesitation in saying that here there never was planning permission, and that it is open to the planning authority to show that by reference, amongst other things, to the actual resolution on which the permission is said to have been based, and by reference to the authority or lack of authority which that particular officer had in the matter.

That being the case, I am unable to accept counsel for the company's first submission, which simply is that this was a planning permission, or must be treated as such; it was not a planning permission, and it is proper for its inadequacy in that respect to be investigated.

His next point is that even if it was not a planning permission, it contained a representation of fact, namely that planning permission had been granted; it was issued to the company in such a manner as to show that they were expected to act on it, and they did act on it. He says that is enough to entitle us to hold the document as a planning permission even if it was not truly such a document at all.

This argument is supported, and I think may have appealed to the Minister, by virtue of certain dicta in *Lever (Finance) Ltd* v. *Westminster Corpn. . . .*[59]

The importance of the case lies in this passage from the judgment of LORD DENNING MR, where he said: There are many matters which public authorities can now delegate to their officers. If an officer, acting within the scope of his ostensible authority, makes a representation on which another acts, then a public authority may be bound by it, just as much as a private concern would be.

There LORD DENNING MR did not find it necessary to amplify his reference to a decision 'on which another acts', and to indicate what kind of action is necessary in order that the representation should be applied. But for my part I have no doubt in thinking that had he considered this matter in the detail in which we have had to consider it, he would have made it perfectly clear that the sort of action of which he was speaking was an action to the detriment of the person who so acted, because he is drawing there on the general law of estoppel (although he does not use the word) as it applies to people who are not public authorities. As I understand it the mere fact that my agent has made a representation within his ostensible authority on which you act is not enough to stop me from denying his actual authority unless you have acted to your detriment. The whole point of estoppel in this situation as I understand it is that if a man has been induced to act to his detriment, he ought to be protected, but counsel for the company admits that his clients had not acted to their detriment on the documents submitted to them. What one hopes to achieve in a situation like this, where there has been an honest mistake, is that everybody shall end up in the position in which they would have been if no mistake had been made, and if we allow this appeal and recognise that the planning permission cannot be acted on that is exactly the result which we should produce.

Appeal allowed. Case remitted.

Consider the following problem: 'A' applies for permission to build ten houses on an acre of land in the ownership of B. A and B have previously agreed that A shall apply for the permission and if it is granted pay B a price for the land which reflects its development value. The Oldtown Borough Council Planning Committee agree to grant planning permission to A subject to certain conditions regarding layout and landscaping of the site. A is informed of this grant of permission by a letter sent by the chairman of the Planning Committee from his home address as follows:

> Dear A,
> I just thought I would let you know that you have got your planning permission so you can now go ahead with your purchase of the land.

A promptly signs a contract to purchase the land from B for £50,000. Subsequently, the Planning Committee at its next meeting decides that it should not have granted A permission because of a possible lack of sewerage facilities. The Town Clerk informs the Committee that since he has not communicated the first decision to A, A has not obtained planning permission and the Committee could revoke its decision without fear of having to pay compensation. The Committee thereupon revoke its first decision and A is then informed by the Town Clerk that he has been refused planning permission, as owing to lack of sewerage facilities such a development would be premature.

(d) LEGAL EFFECTS OF INFORMAL COMMUNICATION

We saw in an earlier section of this chapter that informal communications between developers and planning officers prior to an application being formally put in is an important feature of the planning process. Such informal communications continue after a permission has been obtained as developers seek clarification of ambiguously worded conditions or check that minor modifications of plans do not need another planning permission. This is a perfectly reasonable form of communication and it is doubtful whether the planning process could keep going as well as it does if it did not occur. But an inevitable problem which arises is the legal effect of these communications; can a planning officer, pressed for time, who answers a query about a development on the telephone bind the local planning authority? Should he be able to? What are the equities in a situation such as that? There are two conflicting points of view – that on the one hand a public authority cannot be stopped from performing its statutory duties by such an informal communication; and on the other, that developers who have incurred costs on the strength of such a communication should not suffer thereby. The following cases illustrate these conflicting views.

Southend Corporation v. *Hodgson* (*Wickford*) *Ltd* [1961]
2 All E.R. 47

LORD PARKER CJ: The respondents were minded to buy premises at 37 Eastwood Road North, Leigh-on-Sea, and there establish a builder's yard. Prior to purchasing the premises they wrote to the borough engineer and surveyor in these terms:

> We have been looking for a builder's yard for some time, and we now have the opportunity to purchase one, at 37 Eastwood Road North, which we understand has been a builder's yard for about twenty years, until the death of the owner. Although we hope there will be no objection to our continuing this type of business, we would be very pleased if you could let us know if this can still be used for a builder's yard. We are enclosing a rough site plan for your information.

Six days later, on Feb. 12, 1959, they received a reply, headed: 'County Borough of Southend-on-Sea', from the Borough Engineer and Surveyor's Office, Southend-on-Sea, in these terms: 'Dear Sirs, Proposed builder's yard, 37 Eastwood Road North, Leigh-on-Sea. In reply to your letter dated Feb. 6, the land you have shown on the plan accompanying your letter has an existing user right as a builder's yard, and no planning permission is therefore necessary.'

Thereupon, as the justices find, the respondents purchased the land, moved a quantity of builder's equipment and materials on to the land and used the same as a builder's yard. The justices further find that the respondents would not have bought the land if as a consequence of the letter they had not thought that no further planning permission was required. Nevertheless, on July 17, 1959, the town clerk wrote on behalf of the local planning authority to the respondents, a letter the relevant passage of which is in these terms:

> I am also given to understand that you have had correspondence with the borough engineer in which it was suggested that the land had an existing use as a builder's yard. However, the Southend-on-Sea Corporation has received many complaints about the use of this land, as a result of which a considerable amount of evidence has been presented to the corporation showing that the land has not been used as a builder's yard and has no existing use as such. I am writing, therefore, to inform you that the corporation has decided that the land cannot be used as a builder's yard without planning permission and, furthermore, that such use does not appear to them to be in keeping with the surrounding development.

In due course, on Apr. 20, 1960, the appellants served on the respondents an enforcement notice dated Apr. 19 calling on the respondents to cease that user of the land. The respondents then, as they were entitled to do under s. 23 (4) of the Act, appealed to the justices by way of complaint and, the justices having heard the complaint, found that planning permission was not required and accordingly, quashed the notice.

I confess that I have strained throughout to support the decision of the justices in this case which clearly sounds common sense, particularly when these respondents have only acted as they have done as the result of the letter which I have read from the borough engineer. It is said, nevertheless, that the action taken by the local planning authority here is justified in law and that no estoppel can be raised against them based on the letter written by the borough engineer.

The broad submission made by counsel on behalf of the appellants takes this form: estoppel cannot operate to prevent or hinder the performance of a statutory duty or the exercise of a statutory discretion which is intended to be performed or exercised for the benefit of the public or a section of the public. It is further said that the discretion of the local planning authority to serve an enforcement notice under s. 23 in respect of development in fact carried out without permission is a statutory discretion of a public character. It is, I think, perfectly clear that that proposition is sound, at any rate to this extent, that estoppel cannot operate to prevent or hinder the performance of a positive statutory duty. That, indeed, is admitted by counsel on behalf of the respondents, but he maintains that it is limited to that and that it does not extend to an estoppel which might prevent or hinder the exercise of a statutory discretion. For my part. . . .

I can see no logical distinction between a case . . . of an estoppel being sought to be raised to prevent the performance of a statutory duty and one where it is sought to be raised to hinder the exercise of a statutory discretion. After all, in a case of discretion there is a duty under the statute to exercise a free and unhindered discretion. There is a long line of cases to which we have not been specifically referred which lay down that a public authority cannot by contract fetter the exercise of its discretion. Similarly, as it seems to me, an estoppel cannot be raised to prevent or hinder the exercise of the discretion.

Having said that, it seems to me that this matter comes down to a very narrow point on the construction of the letters to which I have referred. Based on that principle, it is conceded that in so far as the letter from the borough engineer was saying that no permission was necessary, that could not be raised as an estoppel. What is said, however, is that that letter contains a representation of a fact which can operate as an estoppel against these appellants just as it could between private parties, namely, the representation that the land has an existing user right as a builder's yard. It is said that that is a pure representation of fact which does not prevent or hinder the exercise of the discretion which the local planning authority has under s. 23 in regard to enforcing breaches of planning. For my part, I am by no means certain that that letter read as a whole can be looked on as a pure representation of fact, but assuming that it can be read in that sense, the question arises whether it does not even so limit or hinder the free exercise by the planning authority of their discretion. . . .

It seems to me . . . that if the appellants are not allowed in this case to give evidence what the true position was in regard to existing user they must be prevented from exercising their free discretion under the section. It is true that it can be said, as in this case, that they have exercised their discretion. They have said that it appears to them that the development of the land has been carried out without permission, and therefore to that extent the exercise of the discretion has not been hampered; but it seems to me quite idle to say that a local authority has in fact been able to exercise its discretion and issue an enforcement notice if by reason of estoppel it is prevented from proving and showing that it is a valid enforcement notice in that amongst other things planning permission was required. I have reluctantly come to the conclusion, accordingly, that the argument for the appellants is right, and that this appeal should succeed. . . .

Appeal allowed.

Lever Finance Ltd v. *Westminster Corporation* [1970]
3 All E.R. 496

LORD DENNING MR: . . . Lever (Finance) Ltd are developers who propose to develop a piece of land. Their architect, Mr Rottenberg, made application for planning permission to the Westminster City Council. He attached a plan numbered 896SK6(c). It was not an outline plan. It was a detailed plan. It showed the site lying between Hall Road and Melina Place. It showed the proposed development as seven houses in a terrace, and seven detached houses. These 14 houses were designated by letters A B C D E F G H I J K L M and N. One of the detached houses which was lettered G, was 40 feet distant from Melina Place. On 24th March 1969, the planning authority gave permission for that development in accordance with the detailed plan submitted. . . .

But it so appears that a month later, when the architect was getting out a further site plan, he made some variations. . . . he moved house G a distance of 17 feet nearer to Melina Place. In the original plan which had been approved, house G was 40 feet away from the houses in Melina Place. In the further site plan which the architect now submitted, house G was only 23 feet away from the houses in Melina Place. This further site plan was on a scale twice as large as the original plan. The architect sent this further site plan to the planning authority's officer, who had been dealing with all these matters, a Mr Carpenter. . . .

Unfortunately, he had lost his file. He had not got before him the original plan which the planning authority had approved. After about 10 days Mr Carpenter telephoned to the architect, Mr Rottenberg, concerning the matter. There is a difference as to what took place. Both of them were perfectly honest. In the result, the judge held that Mr Rottenberg's recollection was correct. I will read, if I may, Mr Rottenberg's version as given in his affidavit. He stated:

> I pointed out the amendments in the general layout but that the most important alteration concerned the setting out of house 'G' the rear of which would now line up with the adjoining house on Plot 'F'. I told Mr Carpenter the reason for this alteration which was to achieve a better relationship between the individual houses as well as to ensure that the terraced houses complied with the daylighting code. I asked Mr Carpenter if the proposals were satisfactory and he told me quite clearly that the alterations were not material, and that he therefore had no objection and no further consent was required. I made a note on the copy of the letter of the 25th April 1969, and I expressly asked

Mr Carpenter to make a note on his file that he was satisfied with the proposals. [Then Mr Rottenberg goes on to set out the two notes.]

My note which is contained on the said letter of the 25th April 1969 states: 'Local Authority telephoned pointed out alterations to general layout – said it is O.K. Most important 'G' lines up with 'F'. Mr Carpenter's note is as follows: 'Telephoned Mr Rottenberg, who said above drawing was similar to that approved, except house G moved slightly towards house F. But relationship with s.e. boundary remains unchanged. Not material.'

In the upshot, the judge preferred Mr Rottenberg's recollection. In any case, Mr Carpenter, according to his own note, told Mr Rottenberg that the variations were not material. In this respect I fear that Mr Carpenter made a mistake. That variation was material. If Mr Carpenter had had the file before him, he would have seen it. But, not having the file, he said that it was not material.

Howsoever that may be, Mr Rottenberg acted on what he was told. He did not put in an application for further permission so as to sanction the variations. He accepted Mr Carpenter's statement that they were not material. So he proceeded to get on with the work. Some of the houses were started in June. House G itself was started in September 1969. The foundations were set out. The houses started to go up. At that point some of the residents in Melina Place were disturbed. They had, apparently, been assured by the architect in the initial stages that house G would be 40 feet away. Now, seeing that it was only 23 feet away, they made representations to the planning authority. The officers of the planning authority were concerned about the position. They suggested to Mr Rottenberg that he should apply to the planning authority for planning permission for this variation. It would then be all in order. So, on 17th March 1970, Mr Rottenberg applied for permission for the variations. The planning officers supported the application. They reported to the committee: 'Although it is unfortunate that the development has taken place in this form without the [planning authority's] prior consent it is not considered that any valid planning objection can be raised to the siting of the houses as now being constructed, and permission is recommended to regularise the position.

But the committee rejected this recommendation. It refused to sanction the variations. It did not grant the application. No doubt it felt that the residents in Melina Place had good cause for complaint.

So the position was very awkward. The house was still going up in a position that was not sanctioned. Mr Rottenberg then made another attempt to get over the difficulty. He suggested an alteration in the structure of house G. He proposed to remove the top storey over part of it. By so doing, the occupiers of house G would not overlook the houses in Melina Place. So on 29th April 1970, he made an application for this variation in house G. This application was again supported by the planning officer and by the director of architecture and planning himself. But the committee rejected this variation also. It must have felt that the neighbours had a legitimate grievance at the way things had been done. On 18th May 1970, the committee refused permission. It went further and resolved that an enforcement notice should be issued so as to prevent Mr Rottenberg and the developers going further with the house.

This put the developers in a quandary. . . . They asked for an injunction to restrain the planning authority from serving an enforcement notice. An interim injunction was obtained. The action was expedited. It was tried before Bridge J on 18th and 19th June 1970. He decided in favour of the developers. . . .

The judge made some important findings. He found that, after Mr Rottenberg submitted his further plan (which contained the variations), Mr Carpenter used language which led Mr Rottenberg to believe that the proposed variations were not material and that no further consent was required. The judge further found that, after detailed planning permission had been given, it is a common occurrence to find that minor modifications are needed; and that when the necessity does arise, the common practice—

> . . . is for the developers' architect to submit any such proposed minor modifications to the consideration of the planning officer . . . If, in that planning officer's view the modification is not material . . . he says so, and . . . [the] development goes forward in accordance with the modified plans as approved in that sense by the planning officer, and nobody on either side considers it necessary to submit a further application . . . that is an eminently sensible practice.

One of the witnesses to the practice was Mr Hirsch, who is the chief planning officer of the planning authority, and well qualified to speak of it. He told the judge that it frequently happens that there is a minor variation from the plans; that it is discussed with the planning officer; that the planning officer says 'in my opinion it is not material'; whereupon the work goes ahead without any formal application or permission. Mr Hirsch stressed that the officer should make it clear that it is only his opinion. He should always say: '*In my opinion* it is not material'; so as to make it clear that he is not committing the planning authority. I do not know whether planning officers always remember to say 'in my opinion'. But the upshot of it all is that, if the planning officer tells the architect for the developer that in his opinion the variation is not material, then the developer goes on with the work as varied. He does not apply for any further permission.

Counsel for the planning authority accepted – as he must accept – that that is the practice. But he says that it is not binding on the planning authority. He says that Parliament has entrusted these important planning decisions to the planning authority and not to the planning officer of the council; and, no matter that the planning officers tell a developer that a variation is not material, it is not binding on the planning authority. They can go back on it. Counsel says that it is for the developer's architect to shoulder the responsibility. He must make up his own mind whether it is material. He can take the opinion of the planning officer, but it is eventually the architect's own responsibility. If the variation should turn out to be a material variation, and he has not got permission for it from the planning authority, then so much the worse for him. He ought not to have relied on the planning officer's opinion. The planning authority, he said, are quite entitled to throw over the opinion of their planning officer.

I can see the force of counsel's argument, but I do not think that it should prevail. In my opinion a planning permission covers work which is specified in the detailed plans and any immaterial variation therein. I do not use the words 'de minimis' because that would be misleading. It is obvious that, as the developer proceeds with the work, there will necessarily be variations from time to time. Things may arise which were not foreseen. It should not be necessary for the developers to go back to the planning authority for every immaterial variation. The permission covers any variation which is not material. But then the question arises: who is to decide whether a variation is material or not? In practice it has been the planning officer. This is a sensible practice and I think that we should affirm it. If the planning officer tells the developer that a proposed variation is not material, and the developer acts on it, then the planning authority cannot go back on it. I know that there are authorities which say that a public authority cannot be estopped by any representations made by its officers. It cannot be estopped from doing its public duty. See, for instance, the recent decision of the Divisional Court in *Southend-on-Sea Corpn* v. *Hodgson (Wickford) Ltd.* But those statements must now be taken with considerable reserve. There are many matters which public authorities can now delegate to their officers. If an officer, acting within the scope of his ostensible authority, makes a representation on which another acts, then a public authority may be bound by it, just as much as a private concern would be. A good instance is the recent decision of this court in *Wells* v. *Minister of Housing and Local Government.* It was proved in that case that it was the practice of planning authorities, acting through their officers, to tell applicants whether or not planning permission was necessary. A letter was written by the council engineer telling the applicants that no permission was necessary. The applicants acted on it. It was held that the planning authority could not go back on it. I would like to quote what I then said: 'It has been their practice to tell applicants that no planning permission is necessary. Are they now to be allowed to say that this practice was all wrong and their letters were of no effect? I do not think so. I take the law to be that a defect in procedure can be cured, and an irregularity can be waived, even by a public authority, so as to render valid that which would otherwise be invalid.'

So here it has been the practice of the planning authority and of many others, to allow their planning officers to tell applicants whether a variation is material or not. Are they now to be allowed to say that that practice was all wrong? I do not think so. It was a matter within the ostensible authority of the planning officer; and, being acted on, it is binding on the planning authority.[60]

Appeal dismissed.

In *Wells* v. *Minister of Housing and Local Government*[61] a determination under what is now section 53 of the 1971 Act was in issue. The applicants applied for planning permission to build a $27\frac{1}{2}$-foot high cement-batching plant in a yard where they already carried on the business of making concrete blocks. The surveyor to the Leatherhead UDC – the planning authority – replied on 1 March 1963 to the letter accompanying the planning permission as follows:

> I am instructed to inform you that the works proposed can be regarded as 'permitted development' under class VIII of the Town and Country Planning Development Order and it is therefore not proposed to take any further action on your application. . . .'

The applicants later decided to erect a larger plant than had been the subject of the above letter. It accordingly needed planning permission. Neither they nor the planning authority appeared to appreciate this and the building of the larger plant went ahead without permission being applied for or granted. Following nearby residents' complaints once the plant started operation, the planning authority served an enforcement notice requiring the larger plant to be taken down. On appeal the Minister took the position that the letter of the surveyor, quoted above, was not a valid determination under what was then section 43, so that even if the smaller plant had been erected, the planning authority could have served an enforcement notice. In the Court of Appeal, before whom the issue finally came, a majority found against the Minister and the local planning authority on this point. 'A public authority . . . can be stopped from relying on technicalities, and this is a technicality to be sure'[62]. Russell LJ dissented[63]:

> Among the decisions which from time to time have to be made by the appropriate authority under the Town and Country Planning Act 1962 are two types which differ radically from each other in character. One is a decision on an application for planning permission, which involves in the main the application of policy and perhaps taste in the discretion of the decider. The other is a decision, called a determination under section 43, whether proposed operations on land, or a proposed change of its use, (a) would constitute or involve development, and, if so, (b) whether an application for planning permission in respect thereof is required having regard to the provisions of the development order. Such a determination does not involve discretion or policy or taste: it is an adjudication upon the law as applicable to determined facts, and in theory at least there is in any case only one correct determination. . . .

In this court LORD DENNING MR considers that the requirement of an application in writing for a determination can be waived by the local planning authority, which will cure a mere defect in procedure or irregularity; or alternatively that the application for planning permission contained an implied invitation to make a determination under section 43 but only (as I understand it) in a sense favourable to the applicant. For the reasons I have given, which show, it seems to me, that an actual application in writing is an essential part of the machinery for determinations, I cannot agree with this conclusion. The local planning authority is not a free agent to waive statutory requirements in favour of (so to speak) an adversary: it is the guardian of the planning system. . . .

In truth I think, with great respect, that these views stem in large measure from a natural indignation that a practice, which seems to have grown up since the system in this form was introduced in 1947, should operate merely as a trap for the unwary landowner. But the question is, I think, one of law not to be decided by a thoroughly bad administrative practice. . . .

Is *Lever Finance* an example of a 'thoroughly bad administrative practice' being elevated to the status of a rule of law? For whose benefit does planning exist and is this a relevant consideration in determining who is to suffer from the carelessness or administrative inefficiency of a planning officer in a local planning authority? Was this question considered by the courts in the above three cases?

Are *Wells* and *Lever Finance* examples of officers, given delegated authority to take decisions, accepting 'the responsibility for the consequences of those decisions' (Bains Report, para. 3.39)? What do you think happened to the officers responsible for those delegated decisions as a result of the Court of Appeal decisions in those two cases?

Which approach better advanced the purposes of the planning system, the legalistic approach of Lord Parker CJ and Russell LJ or the away-with-bureaucratic-technicalities approach of Lord Denning MR? What advice would you give a local planning authority which wished to prevent a *Lever Finance* situation arising in its administration of planning?

Southend Corporation v. *Hodgson* arose out of a reply to an inquiry made prior to any possible planning application; *Lever Finance* v. *Westminster Corporation* arose out of a reply to an inquiry made after planning permission had been obtained. Did this make any difference to the decisions in those two cases? Would it be a sensible distinction to take in future cases?

3. Control at the central government level

The pervasive influence of the central government has been stressed throughout this book. Whether through approvals of development plans, or through circulars, directions, bulletins and decisions on planning appeals, the central government influences the direction of the evolution of planning and, when all else fails, can legislate to get its way. In this chapter we have already looked at the influence on local planning departments of the literature that pours out of the DoE. This section will deal with the decision-making powers of the DoE, exercised usually on appeal from a decision of the local planning authority and by means of either written representations or a public local inquiry. Since we have looked at this latter institution in relation to public participation, we shall confine our attention here to its role in helping to reach decisions on development control: when it is used; what its procedures are; what the relationship between inspectors' reports and departmental decisions is; and how delays can be alleviated.

(a) The occasions for ministerial or departmental decision making

The following extracts set out the statutory terms of the Secretary of State's jurisdiction in relation to deciding applications for planning permission on appeal from a local planning authority. They are followed by a summary of the other development control deciding powers of the Secretary of State, all of which make reference to his having the same powers in relation to them as he has in relation to deciding appeals.

Town and Country Planning Act 1971

(i) Appeals against refusals of permission to develop

36.—(1) Where an application is made to a local planning authority for planning permission to develop land, or for any approval of that authority required under a development order, and that permission or approval is refused by that authority or is granted by them subject to conditions, the applicant, if he is aggrieved by their decision, may be notice under this section appeal to the Secretary of State.

(2) Any notice under this section shall be served within such time (not being less than twenty-eight days from the date of notification of the

decision to which it relates) and in such manner as may be prescribed by a development order.

(3) Where an appeal is brought under this section from a decision of a local planning authority, the Secretary of State, subject to the following provisions of this section, may allow or dismiss the appeal, or may reverse or vary any part of the decision of the local planning authority, whether the appeal relates to that part thereof or not, and may deal with the application as if it had been made to him in the first instance.

(4) Before determining an appeal under this section the Secretary of State shall, if either the applicant or the local planning authority so desire, afford to each of them an opportunity of appearing before, and being heard, by a person appointed by the Secretary of State for the purpose.

(ii) The call-in procedure

35.—(1) The Secretary of State may give directions requiring applications for planning permission, or for the approval of any local planning authority required under a development order, to be referred to him instead of being dealt with by a local planning authority.

This is colloquially known as the 'call-in' procedure and is used for the following kinds of developments:

(i) cases of strong political and public interest;

(ii) cases of pending disagreement between local authorities, as to whether one is to be allowed to build in another's area;

(iii) major local controversy, such as the introduction of industry to a small country town, totally altering the character of the place;

(iv) cases affecting a wide area;

(v) cases involving development in a National Park;

(vi) cases involving an infringement of major policy, e.g. Green Belt.

Wraith and Lamb say of this procedure:

The Minister may decide to determine any planning application himself, and cases may come to the Minister's notice because of acute local controversy, questions in the House, press reports, or other means. In practice, however, most cases arise from applications which local planning authorities are bound to tell the Minister about, i.e. proposed developments which constitute a substantial departure from the development plan . . . Calling-in is the major means of controlling development by local planning authorities.

From the point of view of objectors, calling-in has the great advantage that 'if the matter goes to a public inquiry, the application must be advertised and any third party may object and thus acquire the right of appearance'.[64]

(iii) Powers of revocation

The local planning authority may revoke a planning permission but unless it is unopposed such revocation must be confirmed by the Secretary of States who before doing so 'shall afford to any person on whom a notice of revocation has been served and to the local planning authority' an opportunity of appearing before and being heard by a person appointed by the Secretary of State for that purpose.[65]

Since revocations can give rise to claims for compensation, they are not very frequent. An example of a revocation which gave rise to a large claim for compensation was the case of the Avon Gorge Hotel at Bristol; the revocation by the Secretary of State, after an inquiry, of a permission to rebuild and expand the hotel cost the ratepayers of Bristol £155,000.

(iv) Discontinuance orders

A local planning authority may if it appears expedient in the interests of the proper planning of their area (including the interests of amenity) serve a discontinuance order requiring that a use of land be discontinued or be continued subject to conditions. Such an order must be confirmed by the Secretary of State.[66]

(v) Applications to determine whether planning permission is needed[67]

An example of that is Wells v. Minister of Housing and Local Government.[68]

(vi) Enforcement notices[69]

88.—(1) A person on whom an enforcement notice is served or any other person having an interest in the land may, at any time within the period specified in the notice as the period at the end of which it is to take effect, appeal to the Secretary of State against the notice. . . .

(vii) Default powers

The Secretary of State may direct a local planning authority to act, or himself to act, by making a revocation, modification or discontinuance order or by taking enforcement action. Where he proposes to make such an order or take such action, he must first provide an opportunity for representations to be made as if the order or action was first taken by the local authority and he was the confirming or appellate authority.[70]

A catalogue of the main occasions when the Secretary of State might hold or be required to hold a public local inquiry in the context of development control serves as a useful reminder that not all such inquiries are platforms for public participation. Many inquiries are small affairs, concerned as much with legal as with planning considerations, and involving both as a matter of law and of practice only the local planning authority and the appellant. For every *cause célèbre* which is the subject of a public local inquiry, there are nine humdrum little disputes, knowledge about which often does not go beyond the appellant and the local planning authority.[71]

(b) Types of ministerial or departmental hearing

To reflect the difference between major and minor planning disputes which go to appeal, there are two alternative types of hearing which may be used – the hearing by written representations and the hearing by public local inquiry.

(i) Written representations[72]

MHLG Circular No. 32/65:
'Planning Appeals Written Representations Procedure'

3. . . . The most promising way to encourage a greater use of the written procedure is to shorten the time taken still further, so as to give this procedure a more marked advantage over the inquiry procedure.

4. Experience has shown that delays occur mostly over the initial statement of case or through the prolonging of exchanges between the parties. . . .

5. In order to shorten the procedure the Minister proposes to ask local planning authorities and appellants alike to adhere to the following timetable:

(i)   if he suggests written representations, he will wish to know within fourteen days whether the parties agree;

(ii) if they do, he will notify both parties accordingly and he will expect them to submit their statements as soon as possible and in any event not later than one month from their being notified that the appeal is to be decided by means of written representations;

(iii) copies of statements will be exchanged as soon as they are received;

(iv) on the exchange of the initial statements the Minister will ask for any further comments within a fortnight;

(v)   on receipt of such further comments, if any, he will normally expect to be able to decide the appeal;

(vi) the date of an accompanied site visit will be notified to the parties while the written exchanges are going on.[73]

DoE Circular No. 142/73: 'Streamlining the Planning Machine'
14. Paragraph 7(v) of this circular stresses the importance of applicants

and planning authorities seeking to resolve their differences by consultation and negotiation. Where an applicant does appeal there is a clear saving of time in adopting the written procedure. In cases decided by the Secretaries of State the saving on inquiry cases in September 1973 was on average 19 weeks; in cases determined by Inspectors the saving was on average 16 weeks. It has always been the policy of the Secretaries of State to encourage the maximum use of written representations. Recently about one half of cases decided by the Secretaries of State and four fifths of those decided by Inspectors have been dealt with in this way. There is scope for even further use of this method.[74]

15. Provided the reasons for the decision are fully set out in the decision notice (see paragraph 7(x) above) it should be possible for the authority's written statement to be confined to additional explanation in the light of the appellant's grounds of appeal. Detailed descriptions of the proposals, and the site and its history, should not as a rule be necessary. The planning position can often be clarified by a short, clear statement of the policies under which the decision was taken and a brief evaluation of the bearing of those policies on the appeal. Full advantage of the written representation procedure will only be gained if the timetable set out in Circular 32/65 is strictly observed. The Secretaries of State will press the parties to observe that timetable.

What redress would an aggrieved person have if the Secretary of State refused to consider further comments that arrived after the fortnight allowed for them?

(ii) Public local inquiries

The same pressures that have caused the Minister to encourage a greater use of the written representation procedure in 1965, led to a further division of responsibilities in 1968. By the Town and Country Planning Act of that year, inspectors were empowered to make decisions and not merely recommendations in certain classes of cases specified by order by the Minister. In 1969 he specified cases involving development not exceeding ten houses; in 1970 this was raised to development not exceeding thirty houses and, in 1972, this was again raised to development not exceeding sixty houses.[75] More than 70 per cent of planning appeals are, as a result of this delegation of power, decided by the inspectorate.

This change in the law and administrative practice raises a general issue which may be discussed briefly before the procedures followed by an inspector holding an inquiry are examined. What manner of man is an inspector?

(a) WHO ARE THE INSPECTORS?

The Housing and Planning Inspectorate was created in 1909 as a result of the Housing Town Planning, etc. Act of that year. There were four inspectors.[76] By 1974 the number of inspectors had risen to over 250.

Wraith and Lamb, op. cit., pp. 181–3, 192–4

They are recruited (by the normal methods of advertisement) almost wholly from outside government service, at a point when they have established themselves in other careers; no one would be recruited before his late thirties and a more usual age would be over 45. The requirement, apart from personal qualities, has normally been a professional qualification in surveying, town planning, architecture or civil engineering and the main sources of recruitment have been from local government service and private professional practice. . . .

There is some degree of specialisation in an inspector's work. The broad distinction between housing and planning continues, and within the planning category certain inspectors deal, so far as may be practicable, with inquiries where it would be helpful to have expert knowledge of, for example, building design, the extraction of minerals or trees and woodlands; currently an attempt is made to divert particular inspectors to appeals against enforcement notices, which have characteristics of their own and where knowledge is required of a growing body of case law. . . .

. . . His work is of the highest importance in that it is helping to determine whether the environment in which we live will continue to be worth living in. . . . The effect of tens of thousands of decisions on haphazard building, filling stations, advertisements and the rest, combined with the major decisions on new towns, airports and motorways, has enabled us to avoid the worst mistakes of our Victorian ancestors; while the judicious balancing of factors which is characteristic of inspectors' reports has gone some way to reconciling progress and conservation. Credit for the policies and the decisions belong of course to the Minister but inspectors' recommendations have been accepted in over 97% of the cases heard. . . .

Many people who have attended planning inquiries as observers have thought that the inspector plays too passive a role. . . . For example, he should moderate the length of counsel's speeches. . . . Alternatively, that he should assist the appellant who may be speaking for himself. . . .

. . . This is almost certainly to under-rate the good sense of the inspector, who is not without experience and who develops an instinctive appreciation of where the heart of a planning problem lies. . . . There is however, some evidence, notably from amenity organizations, that they are happier with the professional inspector than with the 'independent' however eminent. The professional inspectorate, they feel 'knows its way around' and will not be over-impressed when the weight of forensic talent is unequal.

(b) PROBLEMS OF INQUIRY AND DECISION-MAKING PROCEDURES

Inspectors and officials within the DoE must be at least as conscious of legal procedures as they have to be of planning policies, so the problems and procedures we are now to look at must be seen as part of the total system of planning, and as such we must at all times ask ourselves whether the interaction between law and planning at this point is satisfactory and makes for a better planning system, or is unsatisfactory, a contributory factor to disillusion and delay.

The Town and Country Planning (Inquiries Procedure)
Rules S.I. 1974, No. 419

Notification of inquiry

5.—(1) A date, time and place for the holding of the inquiry shall be fixed and may be varied by the Secretary of State who shall give not less than 42 days' notice in writing of such date, time and place to the applicant and to the local planning authority and to all section 29 parties at the addresses furnished by them. . . .

Statements to be served before inquiry

6.—(1) In the case of a referred application, the Secretary of State shall (where this has not already been done), not later than 28 days before the date of the inquiry (or such later date as he may specify under proviso (i) to paragraph (1) of rule (5), serve or cause to be served on the applicant, on the local planning authority and on the section 29 parties a written statement of the reasons for his direction that the application be referred to him and of any points which seem to him to be likely to be relevant to his consideration of the application; and where a government department has expressed in writing to the Secretary of State the view that the application should not be granted either wholly or in part, or should be granted only subject to conditions, or, in the case of an application for consent under a tree preservation order, should be granted together with a direction requiring the replanting of trees, the Secretary of State shall include this expression of view in his statement and shall supply a copy of the statement to the government department concerned.

(2) Not later than 28 days before the date of the inquiry (or such later date as the Secretary of State may specify under proviso (i) to paragraph (1) of rule (5), the local planning authority shall—

(a) serve on the applicant and on the section 29 parties a written statement of any submission which the local planning authority propose to put forward at the inquiry, and

(b) supply a copy of the statement to the Secretary of State.

(4) Where the local planning authority intend to refer to, or put in evidence, at the inquiry documents (including maps and plans), the authority's statement shall be accompanied by a list of such documents, together with a notice stating the times and place at which the documents may be inspected by the applicant and the section 29 parties; and the local planning authority shall afford them a reasonable opportunity to inspect and, where practicable, to take copies of the documents.

(5) The local planning authority shall afford any other person interested

a reasonable opportunity to inspect and, where practicable, to take copies of any statement served by the Secretary of State under paragraph (1) or by the authority under paragraph (2) and of the other documents referred to in paragraph (4) as well as of any statement served on the authority by the applicant under paragraph (6) of this rule.

(6) The applicant shall, if so required by the Secretary of State, serve on the local planning authority, on the section 29 parties and on the Secretary of State, within such time before the inquiry as the Secretary of State may specify, a written statement of the submissions which he proposes to put forward at the inquiry; and such statement shall be accompanied by a list of any documents (including maps and plans) which the applicant intends to refer to or put in evidence at the inquiry, and he shall, if so required by the Secretary of State, afford the local planning authority and the section 29 parties a reasonable opportunity to inspect, and, where practicable, to take copies of such documents.

Appearances at inquiry

7.—(1) The persons entitled to appear at the inquiry shall be—

(a) the applicant;

(b) the local planning authority;

(c) where the land is not in Greater London, the council of the administrative county in which the land is situated, if not the local planning authority;

(d) where the land is not in Greater London, the council of the district in which the land is situated (or the Council of the Isles of Scilly, as the case may be), if not the local planning authority; . . .

(h) section 29 parties;

(i) the council of the parish or community in which the land is situated, if that council has made representations to the local planning authority in respect of the application in pursuance of a provision of a development order made under section 24 of the Act;

(j) any persons on whom the Secretary of State has required notice to be served under rule 5(2)(b).

(2) Any other person may appear at the inquiry at the discretion of the appointed person.

(3) A local authority may appear by their clerk or by any other officer appointed for the purpose by the local authority, or by counsel or solicitor; and any other person may appear on his own behalf or be represented by counsel, solicitor or any other person.

Representatives of government departments at inquiry

8.—(1) Where either—

(a) the Secretary of State has given a direction restricting the grant of permission for the development for which application was made, or

(b) a government department has expressed in writing the view that the application should not be granted either wholly or in part or should be granted only subject to conditions or, in the case of an application under a tree preservation order, should be granted together with a direction requiring the replanting of trees, and the Secretary of State or the local planning authority have included this view in their statement as required by paragraph (1) or (3) of rule 6.

the applicant may, not later than 14 days before the date of the inquiry apply in writing to the Secretary of State for a representative of his department or of the other government department concerned to be made available at the inquiry.

(3) A representative of a government department who, in pursuance of this rule, attends an inquiry into a referred application shall state the reasons for the Secretary of State's direction restricting the grant of permission or, as the case may be, the reasons for the view expressed by his department and included in the Secretary of State's statement under rule 6 (1) or the local planning authority's statement under rule 6 (3) and shall give evidence and be subject to cross-examination to the same extent as any other witness.

(4) A representative of a government department who, in pursuance of this rule, attends an inquiry on an appeal, shall be called as a witness by the local planning authority and shall state the reasons for the Secretary of State's direction or, as the case may be, the reasons for the view expressed by his department and included in the authority's statement under rule 6 (3), and shall give evidence and be subject to cross-examination to the same extent as any other witness.

(5) Nothing in either of the last two foregoing paragraphs shall require a representative of a government department to answer any question which in the opinion of the appointed person is directed to the merits of government policy and the appointed person shall disallow any such question.

Representatives of local authorities at inquiry

9.—(1) Where any local authority has—

(a) given to the local planning authority a direction restricting the grant of planning permission or a direction as to how an application for planning permission was to be determined; or

(b) expressed in writing the view that an application for planning permission should not be granted wholly or in part or should be granted only subject to conditions, and the local planning authority have included this view in their statement, as required under rule 6 (3).

(3) A representative of a local authority who, in pursuance of this rule, attends an inquiry shall be called as a witness by the local planning authority and shall state the reasons for the authority's direction or, as the case may be, the reasons for the view expressed by them and included in the local planning authority's statement under rule 6 (3) and shall give evidence and be subject to cross-examination to the same extent as any other witness.

Procedure at inquiry

10.—(1) Except as otherwise provided in these Rules, the procedure at the inquiry shall be such as the appointed person shall in his discretion determine.

(2) Unless in any particular case the appointed person with the consent of the applicant otherwise determines, the applicant shall begin and shall have the right of final reply; and the other persons entitled or permitted to appear shall be heard in such order as the appointed person may determine.

(3) The applicant, the local planning authority and the section 29 parties shall be entitled to call evidence and cross-examine persons giving evidence, but any other person appearing at the inquiry may do so only to the extent permitted by the appointed person.

(4) The appointed person shall not require or permit the giving or production of any evidence, whether written or oral, which would be contrary to the public interest; but save as aforesaid and without prejudice to the provisions of rule 8 (5) any evidence may be admitted at the discretion of the appointed person, who may direct that documents tendered in evidence may be inspected by any person entitled or permitted to appear at the inquiry and that facilities be afforded him to take or obtain copies thereof.

(7) The appointed person shall be entitled (subject to disclosure thereof at the inquiry) to take into account any written representations or statements received by him before the inquiry from any person.

Site inspections

11.—(1) The appointed person may make an unaccompanied inspection of the land before or during the inquiry without giving notice of his intention to the persons entitled to appear at the inquiry.

(2) The appointed person may, and shall if so requested by the applicant or the local planning authority before or during the inquiry, inspect the land after the close of the inquiry and shall, in all cases where he intends to make such an inspection, announce during the inquiry the date and time at which he proposes to do so.

(3) The applicant, the local planning authority and the section 29 parties shall be entitled to accompany the appointed person on any inspection after the close of the inquiry.

'Position of Planning Officers at Public Inquiries'
[1961], *J.P.L.*, 94

[A statement made by the Council of the Town Planning Institute and published with their kind permission.]

There has recently been considerable discussion[77] and correspondence regarding the position of a planning officer called as a witness at a public inquiry, where the decision of his employing authority was contrary to his advice. Mr H. Heathcote-Williams, QC, in his letter published in *The Times* of April 9, 1960, maintained that an expert witness should give evidence in reliance upon his own professional skill, judgment and experience and that no party, whether local authority or otherwise, should be entitled to require him to give as his expert evidence opinions which he does not share. The arguments in support of this view may be summarised as follows:

(a) The proceedings at Public Inquiries should – as emphasised by the Franks Committee – be characterised by openness, fairness and impartiality.

(b) It is the task of the county clerk, town clerk or other advocate to present the case for the authority and in cases where the planning officer cannot honestly and with integrity support the case then it is for the advocate to decide whether to call the planning officer at all or whether to call a member of the authority or some other person.

(c) The witness is morally and legally obliged to tell the truth. Moreover, under section 104 of the Town and Country Planning Act, 1947, an inspector may put the witness on oath – indeed, in Scotland this is the normal practice.

The contrary view which was expressed in the correspondence, was that if the practice of planning officers putting forward their own views and not those of the authority were general, then it would be of little use for a planning committee ever to differ from the recommendations of their officials.

The Town Planning Institute, as the chartered body representing the planning profession, has considered these issues. . . .

In a great many town planning issues there are pros and cons which have to be weighed and judged, and decisions one way or the other will often be finely balanced. Investigations, meetings and discussions between the applicant, planning officials, other local authority staffs or other official bodies will normally reveal different points of view. In meetings of officials, members, sub-committees, committees, and the council, cases will be debated and decisions arrived at which will be loyally supported by the planning officer and/or his staff at a public inquiry. Few cases are entirely black or white and in marshalling his case the wise planning officer in the witness box will concede as well as make points. In many border-line cases the planning officer, having weighed all the facts and recommended approval on a knife-edged balance, may ultimately be able to support a decision of his committee contrary to his first recommendation. There will, however, be other cases where the planning officer feels quite genuinely that his professional integrity would not allow him to support in evidence a refusal contrary to his advice.

The Institute does not consider that in such cases there is any question of disloyalty by the planning officer to his employers. He is engaged by them in a professional capacity and the case for the local authority can still be made by the advocate and other witnesses. The Institute would go further and say that it is important to the local authority that the integrity of their planning officials should be recognised by the public. Planning officers are constantly in touch with members of the public, advising them on the prospects of applications. Frequently individuals will not proceed with an application or the purchase of a property or carry out some other transaction after taking the advice of the planning officer. They come to rely upon this advice which is given in full recognition of his authority's policies and practice and his own judgment.

Moreover, the planning officer contributes in a large measure to the creation of the Development Plan and the planning policies of his authority. In the light of this it is clear that his recommendations on particular issues will of necessity be identified with such policies.

It must be borne in mind that the planning profession, probably more than any other, has its decisions subject to appeal at every turn. The rigour of this discipline therefore enters into the planning officer's thinking to a greater extent than is commonly appreciated. His frequent statements, made in public, are often taken down verbatim and can be readily quoted on subsequent occasions. They are also reported, often very fully, in the local press or in technical journals and on occasion in the national press. It is important therefore to the planning authority and to the respect in which he is held by the public that the planning officer should be seen to be a public officer of professional integrity. For this reason his views should be consistent and coherent when under cross-examination.

In the opinion of the Institute the maintenance of this point of view does not in any way undermine the loyalty of the planning officer to his authority. The value of the planning officer to his authority rests upon his professional skill, integrity and judgment.

Where the officer feels genuinely that the maintenance of his professional integrity must preclude his supporting at a public inquiry the decision of the planning authority, he should advise the authority in order that they and their legal officers may consider the alternatives open to them. Amongst these will be the possibility of the planning officer giving evidence of the policy of his committee and the reasons for it, while not concealing that it is at variance with his own views. The opinion of the officer is only one of the factors which will be taken into account by the Inspector and the Minister, and there is no reason to suppose that the Minister will not give full weight to the authority's contentions despite the fact that the planning officer has expressed contrary views.

'Notes of Planning Decisions' [1968], *J.P.L.*, 708

The following is an extract from the letter (Ref. APP/1375/A/27066) of the Minister of Housing and Local Government dated September 9, 1968, allowing an appeal against the decision of the Manchester County Borough Council to refuse planning permission for the conversion of premises at Whalley Range, Manchester, into an extension to the adjoining residential hotel.

'... The Minister is advised that the Inspector acted quite properly in refusing to press the witness for the Council to disclose his own professional opinion on the matter, since the views of individual officers of the Council are not considered to be relevant to the issue before the Minister.' The relevant passage from the Inspector's report is as follows:

> During the course of his cross-examination of the witness for the local planning authority counsel for the appellant asked him for his personal opinion on the issue in this appeal. Mr Millar was not prepared to go beyond the facts and considerations which led the committee to their decision and was reluctant to express his own professional opinion. I stated that I was not prepared to oblige him to do so in the circumstances. Mr Glidewell then expressed the view, and asked me to record it, that a professional witness, albeit giving evidence as a witness for a local planning authority, should be required, and by the Inspector, to give his expert opinion even if this should disagree with that of his authority.

An editorial comment on this decision at [1968] *J.P.L.*, 661 was as follows:

> The statement that 'the views of individual officers of the council are not considered to be relevant to the issue before the Minister' must surely be one of the most extraordinary ever to appear in a planning appeal decision. Is then the planning officer not put forward as an expert witness, to provide the inquiry with his expert views on the matter under consideration? Is he really there merely to state what the council decided, and the reasons they took into account? The difficulties and dangers of him endeavouring to do so are obvious. A planning committee may reach a decision by a narrow majority: in such case is the 'witness' supposed to give a balanced account as to the various views of members of the council or committee? What if they merely decided the application without expressing any reasons – is the council's officer-witness then precluded from saying anything? – or may he give 'evidence' as to what he supposes to have been in their minds?
>
> If the views of individual officers of the council are not considered relevant to the planning appeal, as the Minister says, why is a planning officer ever a witness at all at a planning inquiry? Is it only when a council employ an outside expert as witness that the evidence put forward on their account is to be accepted as having any expert value? If not, is the Minister really saying that the witness's expert views are only relevant to the matter under consideration when they happen to support the case of the party who have called him as a witness? Any such proposition is an affront to logic as well as to elementary principles of law.

The Town and Country Planning (Inquiries Procedure)
Rules 1974

Procedure after inquiry

12.—(1) The appointed person shall after the close of the inquiry make a report in writing to the Secretary of State which shall include the appointed person's findings of fact and his recommendations, if any, or his reason for not making any recommendations.

(2) Where the Secretary of State—

(a) differs from the appointed person on a finding of fact, or
(b) after the close of the inquiry takes into consideration any new evidence (including expert opinion on a matter of fact) or any new issue of fact (not being a matter of government policy) which was not raised at the inquiry,

and by reason thereof is disposed to disagree with a recommendation made by the appointed person, he shall not come to a decision which is at variance with any such recommendation without first notifying the applicant, the local planning authority and any section 29 party who appeared at the inquiry of his disagreement and the reasons for it and affording them an opportunity of making representations in writing within 21 days or (if the Secretary of State has taken into consideration any new evidence or any new issue of fact, not being a matter of government policy) of asking within 21 days for the re-opening of the inquiry.

(3) The Secretary of State may in any case if he thinks fit cause the inquiry to be re-opened, and shall cause it to be re-opened if asked to do so in accordance with the last foregoing paragraph. . . .

Notification of decision

13.—(1) The Secretary of State shall notify his decision, and his reasons therefore, in writing to the applicant, the local planning authority and the section 29 parties and to any person who, having appeared at the inquiry, has asked to be notified of the decision.

(2) Where a copy of the appointed person's report is not sent with the notification of the decision, the notification shall be accompanied by a summary of the appointed person's conclusions and recommendations; and if any person entitled to be notified of the Secretary of State's decision under the last foregoing paragraph has not received a copy of the appointed person's report, he shall be supplied with a copy thereof on written application made to the Secretary of State within one month from the date of his decision.

Lord Luke of Pavenham v. *Minister of Housing and Local Government* [1967] 2 All E.R. 1066

LORD DENNING MR: There is a small village in Bedfordshire called Pavenham. There used to be a mansion house there, but it has been demolished and is being replaced by other houses. On the other side of the road there is an old walled garden. It used to be the kitchen garden of the mansion house. It is about one acre in extent. It is owned by Lord Luke of Pavenham and he seeks permission to build a house there. The local planning authority refused permission for this reason: 'The proposal would constitute an undesirable form of isolated and sporadic development outside the limits of the village of Pavenham in an area where no further development should be permittted other than that which is essential for agricultural purposes.'

In other words, the proposed building was outside the village 'envelope' and should not be permitted. Lord Luke appealed to the Minister of Housing and Local Government under s. 23 of the Town and Country Planning Act, 1962. The Minister appointed an inspector to hold an inquiry. It was held. The inspector made his report. He recommended that permission be granted. The Minister, however, disagreed with the inspector's recommendation. The Minister thought that Lord Luke's proposal was undesirable. He, therefore, confirmed the decision of the local planning authority and dismissed the appeal.

Prima facie the decision of the Minister was final (see s. 23 (5) of the Act of 1962); but it was open to Lord Luke to question the Minister's decision if he could show that any of the relevant requirements had not been complied with (see s. 179 (1) of the Act of 1962). Lord Luke did question the validity of the Minister's decision. He said that the relevant requirements had not been complied with in that the Minister had differed from the inspector on findings of fact and that the Minister ought to have notified him (Lord Luke) of the difference and given him an opportunity of making representations to him; and had not done so. LAWTON J upheld this contention and quashed the Minister's decision. The Minister appeals to this court. . . .

Did the Minister differ from the inspector on a finding of fact? In answering this question it is essential to draw a distinction between findings of fact by the inspector and an expression of opinion by him on the planning merits. If the Minister differs from the inspector on a finding of fact, he must notify the applicant, in accordance with the rules, before coming to his decision; but if the Minister differs from the inspector on the planning merits, he can announce his decision straight away without notifying the applicant beforehand.

In the present case the inspector has divided his report into sections headed 'Findings of fact', 'Inspector's conclusions' and 'Recommendation'; but I do not think that this division is sacrosanct. We must look into them and see which of his findings are truly findings of fact and which are expressions of opinion on planning merits. All the findings which are headed 'Findings of fact' numbered 1 to 12 are undoubtedly findings of fact. So also the finding 13 which states the intention of the planning authority. The inspector's 'Conclusions' in para. 39 are partly findings of fact and partly expressions of opinion. The inspector stated a *finding of fact* when he said: 'The site is exceptional in that it is clearly defined by a tall and fine-looking wall and forms part of a long established group of buildings which contribute to the attractive character of the village independent of distance'.

The inspector expressed his *opinion on planning merits* when he stated: 'A well designed house with the walled garden would, far from harming the countryside, add to the existing charm of its setting and could not be said to create a precedent for allowing development on farmland to the north or south.'

Now turning to the Minister's decision letter, the question is whether he differed from the inspector on a finding of fact. The decision letter is not happily expressed. The Minister said that he was unable to agree with the 'conclusions' drawn by the inspector. At one time I thought that the Minister was disagreeing with the whole of para. 39. If he disagreed with the first sentence that 'the site is exceptional in that it is clearly defined', etc., I should have thought that he was differing on a finding of fact; but I do not think that he was really differing from it. That sentence is only a summary of the previous findings of fact. The Minister's difference was only on the second sentence that 'a well-designed house would . . .', etc. He was differing from that expression of opinion by the inspector. The Minister took the view that a house would be 'sporadic development' which would harm the countryside. That was a difference of opinion on a planning matter. The Minister was entitled to come to a different conclusion on such a matter without the necessity of notifying Lord Luke, or giving him an opportunity of making representations.

I must say that I have considerable sympathy with Lord Luke. The inspector's report was very much in his favour; but it must be remembered that the Minister has the responsibility for planning policy. . . . The courts have no authority to interfere with the way in which the Minister carries it out.

I do not think that the Minister was in breach of the relevant requirements. I would, therefore, allow this appeal and restore the Minister's decision.[78]

Appeal allowed.

Givaudan & Co Ltd v. *Minister of Housing and Local Government* [1966] 3 All E.R. 696

Givaudan & Co Ltd applied to the Caterham and Warlingham UDC for permission to erect an office and stores building in the grounds of their factory. They were refused permission and appealed to the Minister. A local inquiry was held and the inspector recommended that the appeal be dismissed. The Minister notified the applicants' solicitors by letter that he had dismissed the appeal, and he made an order accordingly. The applicants, being aggrieved by the order, applied to the court to have it quashed.

MEGAW J: The applicants . . . contend, by para. 3 (e) of their amended notice of motion, that the Minister has not given good and sufficient reasons for his decision in compliance with r. 11 (1) of the Town and Country Planning Appeals (Inquiries Procedure) Rules, 1962, to which I shall refer as 'the Rules'. . . .

I have come to the conclusion that the Minister's letter of Aug. 6, 1965, is so obscure, and would leave in the mind of an informed reader such real and substantial doubt as to the reasons for his decision and as to the matters which he did and did not take into account, that it does not comply with the requirements of r. 11 (1); and that, therefore, on that ground the Minister's order must be quashed. It is not here a question of a minor or trivial error or obscurity, or a mere failure to give reasons relating to every particular point which may have been raised at the hearing. It is, I think, right that I should read the Minister's letter in its entirety:

I am directed by the Minister of Housing and Local Government to say that he has considered the report of his inspector, Mr S. T. Bramble, MTPI, Dip.TP, who held a local inquiry into your client's appeal against the refusal of the Caterham and Warlingham Urban District Council, acting on behalf of the Surrey County Council, to permit the erection of an office, flavours and stores building on land being part of the grounds of the appellant's existing factory, Godstone Road, Whyteleafe.

2. A copy of the inspector's report is enclosed.

3. The inspector says that the effect of the provisions of the Control of Office and Industrial Development Bill (now enacted) on the proposed new offices in the proposed building might require consideration.

He reports that there is considerable evidence that smells from the factory are apparent in the surrounding area and that they are objectionable and cause inconvenience to the occupiers of nearby dwelling-houses. Although the intended uses of the proposed building might not of themselves add to the smells emitted, they would make available space for increased manufactory processes which would be likely to result in an increase in the amount of smell, contrary to the condition in the permission granted for the establishment of the factory in 1950. The inspector is not satisfied that it is impracticable to reduce the amount of smell from all parts of the factory to a level which would not give rise to justifiable complaint, and unless this could be done he considers it would be undesirable, if not improper, to allow the proposed building. In the inspector's view the proposed building in itself would not have any great impact on nearby dwellings.

The inspector reports that the condition relating to the storage of containers within buildings imposed in the permission granted in 1950 has not been carried out and apart from untidiness the space available for parking cars is much less than it could otherwise be. . . .

The inspector recommends that the appeal be dismissed.

4. The Minister agrees with his inspector's conclusions and accepts his recommendation. Accordingly he hereby dismisses the appeal.

At first sight, para 4 of the letter might appear to be clear and unambiguous. There can be no objection to the inclusion, by reference, in the Minister's statement of reasons, of the inspector's conclusions, provided that those conclusions are, in themselves, sufficiently clearly and unambiguously expressed. Unfortunately in this case, in my view, it is impossible to be certain – indeed, it is impossible even to form a judgment on mere balance of probabilities – to what 'conclusions' of the inspector the Minister is referring: i.e., to be certain what conclusions of the inspector the Minister is adopting as his own, and thus relying on as his reasons for dismissing the appeal. . . .

Therefore it must be assumed, for the purposes of this application at least, that everything contained in para. 3 of the letter was regarded by the Minister as having a bearing, one way or another, on the reasons for his decision: as indicating what were the relevant 'inspector's conclusions' with which the Minister agreed and on the basis of which he accepted the inspector's recommendation. . . .

Now, the first sub-paragraph of para. 3 of the Minister's letter records, with sufficient accuracy, that 'The inspector says that the effect of the provisions of the Control of Office and Industrial Development Bill (now enacted) on the proposed new offices in the proposed building might require consideration.'

It is conceded on behalf of the Minister, at least for the purposes of this application, that the provisions of the Control of Office and Industrial Development Act 1965, and of its antecedent Bill, were irrelevant to the matter which he had to decide. It is said on behalf of the Minister that no inference can properly be drawn, from this letter, that the Minister did take the Bill or the Act into account; but, if not, what conceivable purpose was there in the express reference in the letter to the inspector's statement on this topic? If the Minister indeed regarded it as irrelevant to his decision, why did he not, in summarising what he regarded as relevant in the inspector's report, either ignore this statement, as being irrelevant, or, preferably, indicate his dissent from the inspector's expressed view as to its possible relevance? It is perhaps not without significance in this context that the ministry had this very matter much in mind before the local inquiry took place. In February, 1965, the ministry wrote to the applicants' solicitors suggesting that the local inquiry should be postponed, because, in effect, of the introduction of the Bill . . . the fact that the ministry in February, 1965, had expressed a view as to the relevance of the Bill to the holding of the inquiry, and had never retracted that view tends to give some confirmation to the suggestion that the reference in the Minister's letter may not have been, as counsel for the Minister suggests it is, a purely negative, innocuous and unnecessary reference to a matter which the Minister regarded as being totally irrelevant and which he did not take into account.

In my judgment, it is impossible to hold otherwise than that the terms of the Minister's letter either give rise to the inference that he took into account something which it is conceded he should not have taken into account, or, at the very least, leave a real and substantial doubt what was in the Minister's mind in this respect in reaching his decision to dismiss the appeal. . . .

Application granted.

Myton Ltd v. *Minister of Housing and Local Government*
(1963) 61 L.G.R. 1690

WIDGERY J: This is an appeal by the applicants, Myton Ltd, against a decision of the Minister of Housing and Local Government on appeal to him under section 16 of the Town and Country Planning Act, 1947. . . .

Putting the facts of this case in the shortest possible form, they are these. On 1st November, 1961, the applicants, who are the owners of some 24 acres of land on the outskirts of Leeds, applied to the Leeds Corporation as the local planning authority for permission to develop that land by building houses on it. The application was in the form of an outline application, that is to say, an application designed to obtain a decision in principle as to whether the proposed development should be allowed. The corporation dealt with the matter with remarkable alacrity, because on 15th November, 1961, they issued to the applicants a refusal in respect of their application. The applicants, as they were entitled to do, then appealed to the Minister and on 31st August, 1962, the Minister dismissed that appeal. . . .

Turning to the situation of Leeds with regard to the preparation and condition of development plans, the material before me shows that a development plan was approved in respect of at any rate this part of the City of Leeds on 7th April, 1955. At that time the conception of a green belt round a large city had been applied in Greater London but was not generally accepted in provincial cities, and the development plan as approved for Leeds in April, 1955, did not prescribe what we now understand as a green belt. It is true that there was some reference in the written statement forming part of the plan to the planning authority's intentions with regard to the prescription of a green belt, but no actual green belt as I understand it formed a part of the plan then approved. Consequently, in the actual plans themselves, which, in accordance with the normal method are coloured to show the planning authority's intention with regard to the future uses of land, the areas where development was intended were given their appropriate colours, and areas where no development was immediately contemplated were left uncoloured, or as is sometimes said, as white areas.

The land of the applicants with which I am concerned was on the outer edge of a substantial area of coloured land, that is to say, land intended to be developed under the terms of the plan, but it was itself a white area so that the plan contemplated that it should remain generally in its existing state, but that applications for leave to develop it would be considered on their merits as they arose.

However, the Minister for the time being was giving consideration to the setting up of green belts in other parts of the country at about the same time that the Leeds Development Plan was approved. I have been referred to a circular issued by the then Minister of Housing and Local Government dated 3rd August, 1955, which is circular No. 42/55. . . .

I understand that the invitation issued in that circular was accepted by Leeds Corporation, that in due time, namely in about 1958, a sketch plan indicating the area and approximate boundaries of a green belt around the city was prepared and approved by the Minister. It is important to bear in mind that the preparation and approval of the sketch plan was not a procedure which involved any opportunity for landowners to raise objection. The matter was done between the planning authority and the

Minister without reference to land owners. From 1958 there was in existence a sketch plan showing the proposed green belt around Leeds, and the applicants' land was shown on that plan as being part of the proposed green belt. In fact it represented part of the inner edge of the green belt.

I have now before me the full report made by the inspector appointed by the Minister to conduct the inquiry on his behalf. . . .

He reaches conclusions favourable to the applicants in that he is, as I read them, recognising that some of the obvious objections to development of this character cannot here be taken. He recognizes that the land is of little value agriculturally, that further spread of development is unlikely to follow the granting of permission in this case, and that no detriment to amenity will result.

I take it that on those findings, if no question of a green belt arose at all, the inspector would have been minded to have recommended that the appeal be allowed, because one feels that if this land had to be treated as white land without any complication of green belt proposals, the findings in those three paragraphs would indicate that the applicants had made out a case for being allowed to develop.

The inspector, however, goes on in paragraph 68 in these terms:

> The general presumption, however, in the absence of some special reason to the contrary, is against any development in a green belt area and this stricture applies also to areas in regard to which sketch plans have been submitted, as implied in circular 42/55. It is not necessary for the land included in a green belt area to be agriculturally productive. The green belt conception implies no further building except where there is a positive argument for allowing it. . . .

He states his recommendations in paragraph 72. Those recommendations are:

> That the appeal be dismissed for the following reasons:—(1) the site forms part of the green belt round the City of Leeds and no positive argument for its development has been advanced. (2) The site forms an integral part of the walk-way and green wedge system being developed within the congested urban area which forms the City of Leeds. (3) It is only possible to provide one satisfactory access to the site and this would be inadequate to serve a residential area of the extent proposed.

That report being submitted to the Minister, the Minister gave his decision on the appeal on 31st August, 1962. The decision is commendable at least for its brevity because the Minister, having referred to the inquiry having been held, and having set out the three recommendations of the inspector which I have read, simply says 'The Minister accepts his inspector's recommendations, and he accordingly dismisses the appeal.'

Mr Bridge, for the applicants, raises what seems to me to be two principal grounds for saying that in the circumstances which I have outlined the Minister has failed to comply with relevant requirements and has as a result substantially prejudiced the applicants. First of all, as I understand his argument, he said that it was the duty of the Minister in the circumstances of this case to consider whether the site, on the evidence which had been put forward at the inquiry, was of such a character and in such a situation that it could be said that it would not be required as a part of the proposed green belt. Mr Bridge fully recognizes that in cases of this kind the Minister might be quite unable on the hearing of an appeal relative to a single individual site to form a conclusion as to whether or not that site would be required as part of the green belt, but his contention is that the Minister ought to address his mind to that question, and if the circumstances justify it, the Minister ought at this stage to say that the site is inappropriate for inclusion in the green belt and in those circumstances to grant permission for development. Mr Bridge points out that if the Minister is not subject to any such duty and will refuse permission for development of a given site merely because it forms part of the proposed green belt area as shown in the sketch plan, the result will be that appeals and applications at the sketch plan stage will be quite useless and a waste of time, and that in effect they will be dealt with by means of a rubber stamp.

I accept Mr Bridge's contention that there is such a duty on the Minister. . . .

The basis of the submission that the Minister failed to give consideration to this point really springs from the fact that, in Mr Bridge's submission, there is nothing in the inspector's report to show that that stage or step in the reasoning was taken. He submits that in a case like this where the Minister has adopted the inspector's report without qualification, I ought to assume that the Minister's process of reasoning was the same as the inspector's, and he therefore invites me to look at the paragraphs of the report which I have read. It is his submission that those paragraphs show this omission on the part of the inspector. He says that the only fair way of reading this report shows that the inspector completely failed to consider whether the site ought to be excluded from the green belt, and proceeded to decide against the applicants simply because it was within the sketch plan green belt area and thus, in the view of the inspector, automatically subject to green belt restrictions.

Mr Megarry for the Minister on the other hand contends that it is implicit in the inspector's report read as a whole that the inspector had passed through this process of reasoning, and had therefore come to the conclusion that he could not recommend on the facts before him that the site be excluded from the green belt, and hence inevitably proceeded to deal with the matter on the footing that it should for the time being be regarded as subject to green belt restrictions. I think it very important when considering matters of this kind on an appeal under section 31 of the Act of 1959 to remember that the inspectors appointed by the Minister are not necessarily lawyers, and to remember that an inspector's report cannot be considered with the same precision as might be used when considering the pleadings in an action.

I am sure that it is a very important thing for inspectors to give their reasoning fully, but I would deplore any tendency on the part of the Courts to be unduly anxious to subject the words used by the inspector to a microscopic examination or to raise the kind of argument upon their interpretation which might be appropriate to documents of a different kind. I do not think that I ought to assume that a failure on the part of the inspector to refer to a particular process of his reasoning necessarily means that his mind did not pass through that particular phase. Indeed, I think that the proper way to approach this kind of question is to look at the report as a whole and ask myself whether I am satisfied that in this case I should conclude that the inspector, on a balance of probabilities, has omitted to consider the particular matter which I find he ought to have considered. It is clear enough that the issue of whether this land ought to have been included in the green belt or not was argued before the inspector. It is quite clear that the applicants, with the assistance of experienced counsel, had ranged over the whole field of argument proper and appropriate to support their application, and that amongst other matters they were urging that the proposed green belt should be adjusted at this point so as to exclude the applicants' land. I find it very hard to believe that in those circumstances the inspector would have ignored the proposition altogether. . . .

In the result, therefore, I have come to the conclusion that I cannot hold in the applicants' favour that there was a failure on the part of the inspector or the Minister to consider this aspect of the matter or any substantial prejudice to the applicants by virtue of any such omissions. Although I have reached that conclusion in this case, I am anxious to say for such value as it may be in subsequent cases that I feel most strongly that this stage of reasoning in consideration of an appeal of this kind is an important one which I hope both planning authorities and the Minister would have particular regard to in any subsequent cases.

Appeal dismissed.

Did Megaw J adopt the same approach to the Minister's decision letter in *Givaudan* as Widgery J did to the inspector's report in *Myton*? Should there be a difference of approach in the judicial consideration of inspectors' reports and Ministers' decision letters? Will and should Widgery J's approach continue to be adopted in respect of inspectors' decisions as opposed to reports and recommendations? Are the courts more willing to allow Ministers to have and apply policies to individual cases than they are local authorities? Faced with a carefully drawn decision letter which indicates that the Secretary of State considered all relevant matters and finally decided against an appellant, what remedies in law has an appellant still dissatisfied with the process? Should he have any remedies?

(c) THE INTERACTION BETWEEN LAW AND PLANNING:
SATISFACTORY OR NO?

Only a minute fraction of the many appeals decided by the Secretary of State and his inspectors finish up in the courts, yet the influence of the courts and the law on the planning process is felt here more than anywhere and has given rise to much planning anguish. Before considering whether this anguish is justified, a view from someone working in the DoE on planning appeals may be studied.

Pamela Payne,[79] 'Planning Appeals'[80] (1971)
J.R.T.P.I., 114

... The combination of the Inquiries Procedure Rules and the right of appeal to the High Court have had a profound effect on the conduct of appeals both at the inquiry itself and at decision stage. The whole process has become much more of a legal exercise – so much so that at times it is hard to remember that the main question that has to be decided on appeal is whether the development is a suitable land use for the site. . . .

Legal issues do arise and some cases, particularly those against conditions imposed, may fall to be determined solely on legal grounds. Most decisions, however, though they have to be taken within a legal framework are entirely dependent on an assessment of the planning merits of the proposal. . . .

One noticeable development in recent years is the increasing appearance of counsel at very ordinary planning appeal cases where no point of law is involved. The effect of the direct right of appeal to the High Court has had considerable repercussions on appeals work.

The publication of reports provided more scope for challenge and much time must now be spent in a painstaking checking operation to make sure that every fact has a clear source in the report and relates to a matter which has been argued at the inquiry and that the conclusions and the recommendation flow from the facts. One must be absolutely sure that an Inspector is not basing a fact or conclusion on something he has seen with his own eyes (which used to be thought the reason for his inspection of the site) which has not been discussed at the inquiry. The Minister has, in fact, submitted to judgment in a case because the decision was partly based on the fact that the Inspector noticed at the site inspection that the site was detached from the main part of a district by a busy road. No one denied that it was, but the appellants argued that they had not had the opportunity to comment on the traffic objection. The same principle also applies to plans. A challenge has been made because an Inspector, comparing two plans both handed in at the inquiry noticed discrepancies. Avoidance of this type of challenge places an added burden on decision officers who must now do a check on the 'mechanics' of the decision-taking process instead of just concentrating on the planning merits. In written representations cases care must be taken to base the decision on matters that have been argued and not on matters deduced from the representations.

... Two recent decisions have had the effect of changing the procedure. The High Court decision in the case of *Baron Luke of Pavenham* v. *the Minister* increased the number of cases referred back to the parties in cases where the Minister proposed to disagree with the Inspector because Mr Justice Lawton held that all conclusions were facts. The Court of Appeal decided that conclusions could be a mixture of fact and planning merits so every case now has to be scrutinized to see whether disagreement is on a fact, inference of fact or on an opinion on the planning merits. The case of *Wells* v. *the Minister* (a section 43 appeal) meant that the words previously used in decision letters 'that the Minister has no power to determine whether planning permission is needed in the context of an appeal under section 23' were banished overnight since the Court held that every application for planning permission has an implied invitation to the authority to consider whether it is in fact needed.

The Department is swift to act upon Court decisions. A law student who worked with me for a time said he was amazed to find how conscious we were of the powers of the Courts when so few of our cases were actually challenged. This is true, for we must behave as though every decision is going to be challenged even though only a handful of cases a year are. In the list at the moment, there is one case before the House of Lords and thirteen before the Queen's Bench Division, only two of which are being actively pursued. But their effect is profound. . . .

The various procedures introduced since 1959 have made the whole process so much more hazardous for decision officers who now have to concentrate their efforts not only on reaching a decision on the planning merits but keeping out of the Courts, away from censure by the Council on Tribunals and clear of investigation by the Commissioner of Administration. A judge recently said it was the duty of the Courts to protect the individual from oppression by the Executive. I trust that I might be forgiven if I say that this bit of the Executive sometimes feels a bit oppressed herself!

It is interesting to observe the conflicting trends that are discernible in this picture. First, there is the fettering of discretion. The Minister remains responsible for the decision on the merits of the appeal but he has now to go through extra procedural stages if he wants to substitute his own decision for that recommended by the Inspector or base it on information not argued by the parties and there are those who want to see the powers of the Courts and Commissioner extended to cover an investigation of the merits of the case. At present, the Courts rarely intervene and the Commissioner is debarred from doing so, although his powers have recently been extended to cover 'the bad rule'. Discretion has come to be regarded as a power which should not be given if it can be avoided. There is strong support for the view that every piece of new legislation should fetter the powers of the Executive. This immediately has three effects. The first is that in attempting to provide for every eventuality, the legislation becomes extremely complex. The second is that it usually results in one body of people examining cases to see if they fit in, another exerting their ingenuity to see how they can get around it while a third body is set up to arbitrate. The third effect is once it has been decided to limit discretion, there can be no choice and pleas for lenient treatment cannot be met.

Before the Inquiries Procedure Rules and the 1959 Act the Minister took his decision on the basis of the information before him and if he felt he needed more information after the inquiry in order to assess the situation more accurately, he could obtain it. If the Insepctor had recommended dismissal or allowance and he felt that an appellant or the council could be given the benefit of the doubt, he could exercise his discretion and not accept the recommendation. He can still do all these things but unless the decision is based on published Government policy (and efforts have been made to contest what is policy in the Courts) it means swinging such a cumbersome and time-consuming piece of administrative machinery into action that the case for doing so has to be much stronger than simply giving one side or other the benefit of the doubt. The number of cases in which the Minister disagreed with the Inspector has fallen from 7% in 1960 to 2–3% in recent years. If the view is taken that the Inspector's opinion is the only one that matters, it is right that it should be made extremely difficult to disagree with him but Inspectors would be the first to deny that they are infallible and there are occasions when a decision reached by an amalgam of minds is the better solution to a problem. I am not suggesting that an appeal should be decided on the basis of completely new evidence which has not been discussed. Even if it does not make the Minister wish to disagree with the Inspector, such evidence is always referred back for comment in the interests of natural justice. But the extent to which a decision can be taken on a different balancing of the facts or a different inference derived from the representations already on the file or from the plans, is becoming more and more limited. The section on the effect of the right of appeal to the High Court illustrates some of the current pitfalls. If it is believed that discretion is wrong, then it is right to limit discretion, but it is discretion that enables the balance to be corrected, the benefit of the doubt to be given, the blind eye to be turned and even the blatant exception to the rule to be made in a good cause and at the same time as it is being restricted, there are constant pleas for more compassionate, imaginative or informed decisions.

The second contradictory feature is the question of time involved. One of the greatest causes of complaint about the system is the time it takes to get a decision. Yet all the decisions taken to protect the rights of the individual usually result in more time being taken. . . .

The third contradictory feature is the greater formality involved. As already mentioned the rules must be obeyed and this makes a far more rigid framework in which to work than existed previously. . . .

The last contradictory feature is the introduction of the more complicated procedure at a time when other procedures are being streamlined for greater efficiency. It will have been seen that an inquiry has tended to become a much more formal affair than previously and both at it and during the decision taking process there is a greater emphasis on legal matters. The effect of other measures has been to create an obstacle-course for decision officers so formidable that there is a risk that through concentrating on negotiating the obstacles we will lose sight of the real object of the exercise which is to reach the best possible decision on the merits of the appeal. . . .

The thrust of the conclusions of Payne's article goes some way towards reinforcing the complaints of the planners: too many procedures lead to delay and a fettering of discretion, both of which make more difficult the reaching of 'the best possible decision on the merits of the appeal'. These views are entitled to respect, but what evidence is there that procedural due process inhibits decisions being given on the merits? Would we achieve an overall better quality of decision if a public examination procedure with its emphasis on an informal round table discussion was substituted for the public local inquiry? Layfield considered that this would be the case with inquiries into structure plans[81] and the sternest critic of public inquiries, Self, agreed on that, while showing some ambivalence on the use of the public inquiry for other purposes. Thus at one moment he admits that 'the public inquiry is a tolerable method . . . for examining specific objections to specific proposals',[82] while at another, when criticising the Roskill proceedings, he states: 'Planning decisions are not a proper subject for legal arbitration, since there is no (or little) relevant law to apply . . .'.[83] Another point of view, put by Gregory, is that the adversary procedure does often have the effect of exposing the very real weaknesses of a developer's case so that 'it may well look a good deal less impressive than at the beginning of the controversy'.[84]

This last point brings out the real difference between the protagonists and antagonists of public inquiries. How are decisions best arrived at? Is it through controversy in which opposing camps of experts or more humbly local authority and owner-occupier and architect challenge each other's case through examination and cross-examination, or through consensus where in a seminar-type procedure 'there is informal give and take and efforts towards constructive integration of diverse opinions'?[85] It is as natural that lawyers should think the former to be the best method as that civil servants and planners should think the latter to be. The compromise, after the Act of 1972, is that strategic policy questions are discussed in the seminar-type procedure – the public examination – and other questions are thrashed out at public inquiries, or settled privately by means of written representations.

A compromise is likely to satisfy no one but what has to be answered by the antagonists of public inquiries as one of the normal methods of handling planning appeals is: what should replace them or how should they be reformed so as to be less formal? Should lawyers be prevented from appearing at inquiries? Should expert witnesses? Consider Self's caustic comments: 'it should be remembered sometimes that there is plenty of cash in a public inquiry: if learned counsel and expert witnesses got a brevity bonus, the proceedings might be healthier'.[86] Should inspectors be encouraged to take a more active role, cutting off counsel and witnesses who they feel are being long-winded or irrelevant? Should all procedural rules be abolished, and inquiries run in future on the basis of the inspectors' sense of fair play supplemented by internal departmental notes for their guidance? Should inspectors be given the power to adjourn an inquiry and require the parties to try and reach a solution at a private meeting chaired by themselves? With inspectors now empowered to make decisions, is there not a possibility that more 'procedural safeguards' will be called for? Should this call, if it comes, be resisted? If not, why not?

Arguably, a much more telling criticism of the whole appellate system in development control is that it takes too long; the costs of delay outweigh the benefits of an open formal hearing. With the enormous profits to be made on land with planning permission, particularly for residential and office development, more and more refusals are being appealed against. The volume of appeals and applications was a prime cause of the appointment by the Secretary of State in October 1973 of Mr G. Dobry to review the 'system of development control, including the arrangements for appeals and to advise on the lines along which it might be improved'. Without waiting for Mr Dobry's report, the DoE put out a circular suggesting ways of streamlining the planning machine. On appeals and local inquiries the circular had this to say:

DoE Circular No. 142/73

Local inquiries

17. The immediate scope for savings of time and effort without any risk of overlooking important matters is considerable. There is no doubt that the proceedings can be shortened without detriment to the inquiry. For example, the inquiry should concentrate closely on the nature and location of the development proposed, the application of planning policies to

it, and the relevance of any public interest that may be expressed. Both the site and the character of the development proposed will normally be well-known to all parties at an inquiry. The Inspector may already have seen the site, and will in any event visit it during or after the inquiry. Detailed descriptions by successive parties and witnesses are therefore unnecessary (although it is, of course, right that important features should be referred to as they arise in the course of evidence and argument).

19. It has been customary to allow the utmost latitude to all parties in presenting their cases. This has often meant that the hearing has been prolonged by a natural desire of the parties to explore every detail of the case, however small, and to emphasise important points by repetition. Inspectors have now been asked to encourage all parties to be brief as well as relevant and in particular to confine evidence, cross-examination of witnesses and comments on evidence to essential points. It will be helpful to Inspectors if parties will, so far as possible, avoid repetition (e.g. the detailed rehearsal of evidence which witnesses are about to give or the repetition of such evidence when a party is making a closing address). It is, of course, the Inspector's duty to ensure that everyone appearing at an inquiry (whether professionally represented or not) is given a fair hearing and Inspectors will take care to ensure that the saving of time at enquiries is not done at the expense of giving everyone concerned the opportunity to put forward all of the points and evidence which are relevant to his case.

As Wraith and Lamb imply, delay is a corollary of longer procedures insisted on in the interests of justice and may also be affected by a refusal, in the interests of national economy, to increase administrative staff. Delay thus raises the same question that has appeared in other parts of this book expressly or impliedly: what sort of planning system do we want? Asked here, that question involves consideration of such issues as: the importance of consistency and quality in decision making; the costs of delay versus the costs of hasty and mistaken decisions; whether the legitimacy of the planning system is more likely to be furthered by decisions taken after anybody who feels he is interested has had a chance to contribute to them or by decisions speedily arrived at; whether fair play in planning requires or is hindered by formal procedures. These are not issues which often get discussed in the cases or in the professional journals but for lawyers and planners they lie at the heart of any consideration of the efficacy of development control.

There is, however, another set of issues involved in the question of what sort of planning system we want which has been raised in this chapter and is raised in the next. Is there a clear connection between development planning and development control? To what extent does the legal framework of planning encourage or discourage that connection or the formulation of clear, consistent and explicable planning policies? To what extent is there justice in the charge that 'The legal framework of planning control is not only tied to traditional land-use questions but it is a dual system with one set of controls dependent on the definition of development and another set of ad hoc controls *which have no clear rationale at all*?'[87]

Should there be more or less central government guidance to local planning authorities? Should legislation spell out in some detail what is meant by material considerations? Answers or partial answers to some of these questions are advanced in the report of the review of development control; but while we continue to have a comprehensive system of planning and control of land use and a constantly changing society, it must be doubted whether we shall ever reach a final answer to them.

Review of the Development Control System
Final Report by George Dobry QC (HMSO, 1975)

SUMMARY OF RECOMMENDATIONS

2.1 The report aims at:—
   (i) giving greater freedom to harmless development; but
   (ii) guarding against harmful development by retaining applications for all cases, as at present;
   (iii) separating from the main stream all applications which might cause harm;
   (iv) disposing of applications in the main stream by rapid and routine procedures; and
   (v) applying the same approach to appeals.

SECTION I: PLANNING CONTROL
Division into two categories
2.2 To achieve these objectives a division of applications into two categories, Class A and Class B, is needed.
2.3 Class A should comprise:

   (*a*) all simple cases;
   (*b*) all applications conforming with an approved development plan;
   (*c*) development which only just exceeds that permitted by the General Development Order, even when not allocated for that use in the development plan;
   (*d*) the approval of reserved matters relating to cases classed as 'A' when outline permission was sought.

Class B should comprise all other applications.

2.4 The planning officer should have the power to transfer an application between classes provided he gives reasons for the transfer. . . .

Class (A) cases

2.11 There should be a 28 day time limit for transfer to Class B.

2.12 All Class A applications must be decided in not less than 35 and not more than 42 days.

2.13 The time limit for all consultations between and within authorities should be extended from 14 to 21 days.

It must then be understood:—

    (*a*) that the time limit is to be strictly observed;

    (*b*) that if no reply is received in time the decision must be taken without it.

2.14 A Class A application should be deemed to be granted unless either:

    (*a*) the applicant has received notice of its transfer to Class B within 28 days, or

    (*b*) the applicant has received notice of a decision within 42 days. (The date of the relevant resolution or decision of a sub-committee or an officer would be treated as the decision if made 3 days before posting and duly recorded.)

2.15 For Class A there should be the following publicity:—

Compulsory	**Discretionary**
1. Site notice *or* neighbour notification	1. Notification to local societies
2. Notification of parish council.	2. Other compulsory items under Class B (see below).

2.16 Site notices should be of uniform design and size, distinctive in colour, and written in plain, non-technical language.

2.17 Neighbour notification may be more suitable in towns. A model 'Procedure for Notification of Surrounding Residents' is shown in Appendix II C i.

Class 'B' Cases

2.18 There should be a three-month *time limit* for Class B applications (a six-month limit for impact study cases). While there should be no deemed consent procedure, strict compliance with time limits would be demanded.

2.19 A Class B applicant should have a statutory right to consultation, if no decision is reached within the time specified.

2.20 For Class B there should be the following publicity:—

Compulsory	**Discretionary**
1. Site notice *or* neighbour notification	1. Notification to local societies
2. Notification of parish council	2. Advertisements for individual applications in local newspapers or on notice boards (perhaps allocated for that purpose).
3. Publication of lists of applications in local newspapers *or* on public notice boards *and* to registered local societies.	

Impact study

2.23 An applicant will be able to submit an 'impact study' in cases of special significance and in exceptional cases will be required to do this. This would not normally apply to housebuilding.

2.24 The notice requiring an impact study should be served within 14 days of application.

2.25 An impact study would describe the proposal in detail and explain the likely effects on its surroundings. The Department should publish a Bulletin giving guidance as to the form and content of an impact study.

2.26 Proposals requiring impact studies should be prominently advertised and copies of the study should be on sale to the public. . . .

Planning applications

2.35 The borderline between 'outline' and 'detailed' applications is at present unclear and the distinction is too inflexible. There should in future be four types of application:—

(a) *Outline.* These should be accompanied only by a site plan.
(b) *Illustrative.* These should be accompanied by a site plan and illustrative plans which would determine the character of the development.
(c) *Detailed.* These should be accompanied by all building plans.
(d) *Guideline.*

    (i) These should include the general likely land use within an area. A permission would be similar in effect to an allocation in an old-style development plan.

    (ii) It will be especially useful for commerce and industry's long-term development plans.

    (iii) I suggest introduction of 'Future Development Certificate' for such cases, setting out the future use likely to be permitted.

2.38 There is a strong case for introducing a stamp duty or similar standard charge for planning applications; a small charge for Class A and a substantial charge for Class B.

Rights of appeal

2.39 Applicants should have the following rights of appeal to the Secretary of State:—

(a) in Class A cases, an appeal against a refusal or the imposition of conditions upon an express consent;
(b) in Class B cases, an appeal against a refusal, the imposition of conditions or, failure to give a decision within the stipulated time limit.

2.40 There should be no appeal against a planning officer's decision to transfer a case between classes.

2.41 Where there appears, on appeal, to have been no convincing reason for a local planning authority's delay in coming to a decision an order for costs against the authority should follow as a matter of course.

2.42 In cases which raise difficult policy issues, the local planning authority and the applicant should be able to *appeal 'by reference'* to the Secretary
of State.

SECTION II: POLICY FRAMEWORK

2.64 Individual planning decisions should not be made in a vacuum. If
decisions are to be correct, fair, and, above all, consistent, they must be
made within a clear and consistently applied framework comprising:—

   (i) approved structure plans and local plans which are kept up to date,
       or
  (ii) handover statements, that is statements which set out strategic
       policies and list old-style development plans and any informal
       non-statutory plans in force, indicating to what extent these plans
       are still to be applied;
 (iii) a provisional statement of its local policies by each District Coun-
       cil;
  (iv) Local or Particular Guidelines such as proposals affecting a par-
       ticular conservation area or for a regional airport.

2.65 Speedy production of structure and local plans is crucial. There
should be a national timetable for their production and they must be
ready almost everywhere within the next five years.
2.66 A detailed procedure for the adoption of local plans should be settled
now.
2.68 There should be the following general presumptions:—

   (*a*) a strong (though always rebuttable) presumption in favour of any
        application which conforms to an up-to-date local plan;
   (*b*) a presumption (though less strong and equally rebuttable) against
        an application which does not so conform. . . .

2.72 . . . policy decisions of general importance can profitably be made
in advance of specific applications or appeals. For this purpose 'pilot
inquiries' should be convened and the public examination procedure devised for structure plan inquiries used.

Departmental guidance
2.73 Guidance from central government is essential. Such guidance
should have the following characteristics:

   (*a*) It should be clear. Guidance contained in some circulars is hedged
        with so many reservations and savings as to be capable of being
        read as meaning anything.
   (*b*) It should be comprehensive. The present welter of circulars, bul-
        letins, etc., should be pruned of obsolete material and published as
        one comprehensive and coherent whole.
   (*c*) It should be up to date. This means that the publication just men-
        tioned should be kept regularly up to date and the new policy
        should be published promptly. . . .

2.75 A Planning Control Consultative Committee should be established (with representation from local authorities, developers, the construction industry, some amenity societies and the professions) as a combined national forum for consultations between DOE and the public.

SECTION IV: PUBLIC INVOLVEMENT

2.92 The public needs to understand the nature and limits of planning control better: equally planners need a better grasp of the principles and techniques of public involvement. Public involvement must be (1) relevant, (2) more efficient, (3) constructive and selective. . . .

2.101 Voluntary organisations receive insufficient help. There is a need in due course for a central national body (British Environment Council) provided with funds.

2.102 Local authorities should adopt more widely the practice of co-opting members of amenity societies and other bodies on to planning committees. This may co-ordinate consultation and help applicants.

2.103 Parish and community councils have a vital part to play in local planning.

2.104 In the large urban areas where they do not exist, neighbourhood councils might be considered to fill the gap.

SECTION V: APPEALS

2.109 The unqualified right of appeal should not be withdrawn but the Secretaries of State should have power to exercise their discretion whether the appeal procedures should be by way of an inquiry or by way of written representations. . . .

'A' and 'B' appeals

2.113 All appeals should be divided into two classes, Class A and Class B to correspond with the class of applications.

2.114 Class A appeals should comprise:

(a) all simple cases;

(b) appeals relating to development which, within specified limits as to size, conforms to an approved up to date development plan;

(c) appeals relating to development only just exceeding the limits permitted by the General Development Order;

(d) appeals against a refusal to approve details under an 'outline' or 'illustrative' Class A application.

2.115 The decision as to which categories an appeal falls into should be that of the Department.

2.116 (1) In Class A inquiries the following simplified procedure should apply:

(a) While there should be a residual power to order Rule 6 Statements from either side such statements should not normally be required.

(b) The venue should usually be as informal as possible.

(c) The only documents to be supplied to the Secretary of State would

be the application, the grounds of refusal, the grounds of appeal
and a plan.

(d) The procedure should be as informal as possible. In particular,
persons should remain seated around a table and the Inspector
should play an active part in the proceedings.

(e) No legal representation should be allowed on either side.

(f) Where the decision was an Inspector's he should have the discretion to give an immediate oral decision with written reasons for
the decision to follow.

(2) Class A written representations should normally require the consent of
both parties but the decision could be given in about 2 months.

INQUIRIES

2.125 Members of the public make a valuable contribution to Inquiries
but some have little idea of what is relevant and Inspectors must be given
guidance on how to deal firmly with this aspect of public involvement.
2.126 There is a need for clear and well publicised central government
guidance on policy. Statistical and other information should be provided
not only for local authorities but also for appellants so that they may
judge what chance they have of success. . . .
2.135 The wider use of orders for costs is very necessary. The following
points are especially important:

(a) Costs should be awarded much more readily in cases of repetitive
appeals, last minute adjournments, etc.

(b) Inspectors should have power to award costs where the decision on
the appeal is theirs.

(c) The Inspector should make a recommendation as to costs in
Secretary of State cases.

(d) The decision letter on the appeal should generally itself deal with
the question of costs.

(e) The Secretary of State should be empowered to order costs at any
time even if there has been no inquiry. . . .

2.140 In the conduct of Class B inquiries the following changes should be
achieved:

(a) The Inspector should play a more active role, particularly in bringing out relevant facts and preventing time being wasted on irrelevant and repetitive matters.

(b) Inquiries should be less formal and legalistic.

(c) Wastage of time, for example, by cross-examination on questions
of opinion should be prevented by Inspectors. . . .

There is a need to reconcile the objectives of greater speed with the fullest
participation by the public. To this end interested parties should be encouraged to give advance written notice of their case and there should be
a power, to be used sparingly, to require them to provide and keep to a
Rule 6 Statement.

2.142 In due course a system of 'planning aid' should be available to interested persons in carefully scrutinised cases. In the meantime it should be possible for the parties to be ordered to pay the costs of interested persons who supply helpful evidence not made available by the parties.

2.147 Pre-inquiry meetings would be useful in some Class B cases.

2.148 Simple cases which raise the same question of policy and are in the same close geographical area could be dealt with at Inquiry Sessions.

2.149 The proposals in this chapter will inevitably restrict individual rights to some limited extent. The law on the review of planning decisions by the courts needs clarification. The precise grounds on which a decision may be challenged should be established. An unsuccessful party should be given an express right to apply to the High Court for an order that the decision be remitted to the Secretary of State (or an Inspector) for reconsideration on the ground that the decision was so unreasonable that no reasonable man could have come to it.

SECTION VI: ENFORCEMENT

2.150 The main problems are:

(a) the delay caused by appeals (in 65% of cases the serving of an enforcement notice leads to an appeal);

(b) the inability to serve a stop notice in respect of uses of land;

(c) reluctance to serve stop notices because of risk of liability to pay compensation;

(d) difficulties of local planning authorities (LPAs) in ascertaining facts.

2.151 The large number of appeals is not really warranted. Less than 20% of successful appeals succeed on legal grounds. On the other hand about 30% succeed on planning grounds. The same result could be achieved in a less complex way.

2.152 The L.P.A. should at the outset be required to consider whether it would grant permission (and if so subject to what conditions), and if not give reasons. If it proposes to grant permission there should first be appropriate publicity.

2.160 There should be no power to challenge the validity of enforcement notices in Magistrates' Courts in respect of Section 88 (1) of the 1971 Act (relating to the steps required to comply with an enforcement notice and time for compliance).

6

Development and its Control: Controls External to the Planning System

1. Introduction

We have hitherto been concerned with the control of development from within the planning system, either by landowners – public and private – exercising private law powers, or by public authorities exercising public law powers. Whether derived from private law or public law, the powers that are exercised are directed to creating or maintaining desirable uses of land. Unavoidably, in considering these exercises of power, we have also considered whether they have been exercised lawfully, and so we have looked at judicial decisions and considered the legal implications of exercises of power. But all along, the focus has been on how the planning system operates and how the institutions of planning function.

With this chapter the focus subtly changes. We are still concerned with exercises of power by private developers and public authorities; we are still concerned with decisions about desirable and undesirable uses of land and we are still concerned with the interaction between law and planning. But the institutions with which we are concerned are not a part of the planning system in the sense in which local planning authorities, inspectors and the DoE are. The courts, the Council on Tribunals and the Parliamentary Commissioner for Administration – the institutions featured in this chapter – are all external to the planning system, yet all (particularly to the courts) affect the way that system works and its scope, that is, whether it can operate in a particular situation at all. Thus while the institutions of control are external to the planning system, their controlling activities are very much a part of that system and must be fully taken into account in any overall assessment of it.

2. Judicial control: planning law

Judicial control may be broken down into planning law and administrative law, the former being a direct, the latter an indirect, form of control. By planning law control is meant the decisions of the courts on those substantive issues of planning that they have determined fall within their jurisdiction, *viz.* whether a particular activity can amount to 'development' as described in the Act and thus be susceptible to development control or whether a particular procedure in enforcement proceedings meets the requirements of the Act. By administrative law control is meant the decisions of the courts on the way in which planning authorities exercise their powers in which general principles of administrative law such as the rules of natural justice, the requirement that discretion be exercised fairly and the importance attached to *locus standi* are prayed in aid and regarded as applicable to the planning system. Inevitably, the two fields overlap, but the distinction, though not always easy to perceive, is one which appears to be accepted by most commentators[1] and impliedly by the courts. By adopting it here we can concentrate on two distinct issues: the legal aspects of the question of what is development and the question of how the controllers are controlled.

No part of planning has received greater attention from legal writers than that part concerned with the question: 'What is development?' It is not difficult to understand why. A determination that some activity on the land is not development both avoids the need for planning permission and negates an enforcement notice if one has been served to stop that activity. The question is therefore one of considerable moment to landowners and developers, and well worth contesting. Secondly, as Russell LJ said in *Wells* v. *Minister of Housing and Local Government*,[2] the question involves 'an adjudication upon the law as applicable to determined facts, and in theory at least there is in any case only one correct determination'. Lawyers are therefore involved in the determination of the question, both as advisers to and advocates for clients caught up in the planning process at this point. It is not my intention to add to this voluminous literature by prefacing the decisions in this section with a short essay on the question – if such is now possible – but rather to try and highlight certain trends and approaches of the courts so as to bring to the fore the overriding general issue of the interaction of law and planning.

A great number of the individual cases that come to court on this question do so because the local planning authority has issued an enforcement notice to stop activity which it considers constitutes development. The legal aspects of enforcement notices are therefore an essential prelude to a consideration of what is development.

(a) Enforcement notices

This is one area where there has been constant tension between the requirements of the courts and those of the planners. The courts have always insisted that since the effect of an enforcement notice is to stop a landowner from doing something on his land, and probably thereby incur expenditure he would not otherwise have done, there must be a certain minimum standard of procedure followed, designed to let the relevant landowner or developer or user of land know what it is he is doing which is alleged to be wrong, what he must do to stop it, how long he has to do it, and what, if anything, he must do to restore the land to its original state.

While not specifically denying that this is perfectly fair, the planners and the DoE have always chafed under what they regard as the excessive technicalities which this approach leads the courts to adopt, which in turn leads to people being able to 'get away with' breaches of the planning law. The planners' attitude is that so long as an alleged law-breaker knows broadly what it is he is doing wrong, and what he must do to put it right, fair play has been satisfied and the substantive issue should be dealt with. Technicalities should not be allowed to get in the way of the enforcement of development control in the public interest. The gulf between the two approaches may be summed up thus: a legal commentator, writing on enforcement notices in mid-1973, felt able to say: 'In planning matters the courts seem to have tried hard to avoid a legalistic approach.'[3] On the other hand, the Act of 1971 provides in section 88 (dealing with appeals to the Secretary of State against enforcement notices) : 'On an appeal under this section, the Secretary of State may correct any informality, defect or error in the enforcement notice if he is satisfied that the informality, defect or error is not material.'[4] Which approach is the better one, and from whose point of view should that question be considered? In the cases that follow consider whether the proper balance has been struck between fairness to the landowner and the local planning authority. If you think not, what needs to be done and in whose favour?

In considering these questions, it is pertinent to bear in mind that powers of enforcement were considerably increased in 1968. The four-year rule was abolished except for three specific cases.[5] This rule, which exempted from enforcement proceedings and therefore from development control, development that had commenced more than four years before the service of the enforcement notice, both allowed much 'illegal' development to continue undisturbed and gave rise to a welter of confusing and esoteric case law on when development could be said to have commenced and when a notice could be said to have been served on the peccant landowner/developer. The rule has been replaced by the 'established use certificate'[6] intended to serve as conclusive proof that specified uses of land are authorised. An addition to the armoury of enforcement is the 'stop notice'[7] which as its name suggests is designed to bring to a complete stop operations in respect of which an enforcement notice has been served but not yet determined. Compensation for losses suffered is payable in the event of the enforcement notice not being upheld.[8]

Town and Country Planning Act 1971

87.—(1) Where it appears to the local planning authority that there has been a breach of planning control after the end of 1963, then, subject to any directions given by the Secretary of State and to the following provisions of this section, the authority, if they consider it expedient to do so having regard to the provisions of the development plan and to any other material considerations, may serve a notice under this section (in this Act referred to as an 'enforcement notice') requiring the breach to be remedied.

(2) There is a breach of planning control if development has been carried out, whether before or after the commencement of this Act, without the grant of planning permission required in that behalf in accordance with Part III of the Act of 1962 or Part III of this Act, or if any conditions or limitations subject to which planning permission was granted have not been complied with.

(3) Where an enforcement notice relates to a breach of planning control consisting in—

(a) the carrying out without planning permission of building, engineering, mining or other operations in, on, over or under land; or

(b) the failure to comply with any condition or limitation which relates to the carrying out of such operations and subject to which planning permission was granted for the development of that land; or

(c) the making without planning permission of a change of use of any building to use as a single dwelling-house,

it may be served only within the period of four years from the date of the breach.

(4) An enforcement notice shall be served on the owner and on the occupier of the land to which it relates and on any other person having an interest in that land, being an interest which in the opinion of the authority is materially affected by the notice.

(6) An enforcement notice shall specify—

(a) the matters alleged to constitute a breach of planning control;

(b) the steps required by the authority to be taken in order to remedy the breach, that is to say steps for the purpose of restoring the land to its condition before the development took place or (according to the particular circumstances of the breach) of securing compliance with the conditions or limitations subject to which planning permission was granted; and

(c) the period for compliance with the notice, that is to say the period (beginning with the date when the notice takes effect) within which those steps are required to be taken.

(7) The steps which may be required by an enforcement notice to be taken include the demolition or alteration of any buildings or works, the discontinuance of any use of land, or the carrying out on land of any building or other operations.

88.—(1) A person on whom an enforcement notice is served, or any other person having an interest in the land may, at any time within the period specified in the notice as the period at the end of which it is to take effect, appeal to the Secretary of State against the notice on any of the following grounds—

(a) that planning permission ought to be granted for the development to which the notice relates or, as the case may be, that a condition or limitation alleged in the enforcement notice not to have been complied with ought to be discharged;

(b) that the matters alleged in the notice do not constitute a breach of planning control;

(c) in the case of a notice which, by virtue of section 87(3) of this Act, may be served only within the period of four years from the date of the breach of planning control to which the notice relates, that that period has elapsed at the date of service;

(d) in the case of a notice not falling within paragraph (c) of this sub-section, that the breach of planning control alleged by the notice occurred before the beginning of 1964;

(e) that the enforcement notice was not served as required by section 87(4) of this Act;

(f) that the steps required by the notice to be taken exceed what is necessary to remedy any breach of planning control;

(*g*) that the specified period for compliance with the notice falls short of what should reasonably be allowed.

(2) An appeal under this section shall be made by notice in writing to the Secretary of State, which shall indicate the grounds of the appeal and state the facts on which it is based; and on any such appeal the Secretary of State shall, if either the appellant or the local planning authority so desire, afford to each of them an opportunity of appearing before, and being heard by, a person appointed by the Secretary of State for the purpose.

(3) Where an appeal is brought under this section, the enforcement notice shall be of no effect pending the final determination or the withdrawal of the appeal.

(4) On an appeal under this section—

(*a*) the Secretary of State may correct any informality, defect or error in the enforcement notice if he is satisfied that the informality, defect or error is not material;

(*b*) in a case where it would otherwise be a ground for determining the appeal in favour of the appellant that a person required by section 87(4) of this Act to be served with the notice was not served, the Secretary of State may disregard that fact if neither the appellant nor that person has been substantially prejudiced by the failure to serve him.

90.—(1) Where in respect of any land the local planning authority have served an enforcement notice, they may at any time before the notice takes effect serve a further notice (in this Act referred to as a 'stop notice') referring to, and having annexed to it a copy of, the enforcement notice and prohibiting any person on whom the stop notice is served from carrying out or continuing any specified operations on the land, being operations either alleged in the enforcement notice to constitute a breach of planning control or so closely associated therewith as to constitute substantially the same operations.

(2) The operations which may be the subject of a stop notice shall include the deposit of refuse or waste materials on land where that is a breach of planning control alleged in the enforcement notice.

(3) A stop notice may be served by the local planning authority on any person who appears to them to have an interest in the land or to be concerned with the carrying out or continuance of any operations thereon.

Is a stop notice a deterrent to a landowner or developer who has been served with an enforcement notice which he is ignoring and challenging? If not, why not?

Miller-Mead v. *Minister of Housing and Local Government* [1963] 1 All E.R. 459

Miller-Mead owned two fields in the Green Belt at Leek Wootton in Warwickshire. On one of them – the front land – caravans had been parked for storage purposes since 1942 and no planning permission was needed for the continuance of that use. In addition, however, temporary permission had been granted in 1954 for the parking of caravans on the land. This permission expired on 31 December 1956. Miller-Mead applied each year thereafter for permission to use the land for the parking of caravans but was refused each time. He nonetheless continued to use the land for the parking of residential caravans. On 28 December, just before he could acquire existing use rights to such parking under the Caravan Sites and Control of Development Act 1960, he was served with an enforcement notice. The notice referred to the 'parking of caravans' and required Miller-Mead to 'remove the caravans from the site and discontinue the use of the site for the parking of caravans thereon'. It was argued for Miller-Mead that the notice was bad as it purported to apply to the parking for storage as well as the parking for residential use.

An enforcement notice was also served on Miller-Mead in respect of the other field – the back land – in March 1961 which he had begun to use as a caravan site in October 1960. There was no previous history of caravan use for this site. It had been used for recreational purposes by the caravan dwellers from the front land. The notice recited that there had been a change of use 'without grant of planning permission'. It was argued for Miller-Mead that as the Town and Country Planning General Development Order permitted an owner of land to use his land for recreational purposes for twenty-eight days a year, this permission made the recital incorrect and the notice bad.

Miller-Mead appealed to the Minister, who (per LORD DENNING MR):

. . . did not confirm the notices as they stood, but he gave directions to vary them. He evidently took note of the legal points which had been raised on the owner's behalf.

The minister made variations in the enforcement notice of Dec. 28, 1961, in regard to the 'front land'. Acting under the new power given to him under s. 33 (6) of the Act of 1960, he directed as follows: (i) the word 'residential' shall be inserted before the word 'caravans' where this latter word first occurs in the notice.

In other words, in the first recital instead of 'parking of caravans', he put in the word 'residential' to make it 'parking of residential caravans'. In the operative part, he went on: (ii) there shall be substituted for that part of the notice which specifies the steps required to be taken in compliance with the notice, the words— 'remove from the site all caravans used for the purposes of human habitation and discontinue the use of the site for the parking of caravans for the said purposes'.

In other words, he limited the operation of this notice so that it was no longer so wide as to include both the storage and parking of residential caravans. He only prevented the owner using the 'front land' for residential caravans; he left him free to keep storage caravans there. The minister also made variations in the enforcement notice of Mar. 24, 1961, in regard to the 'back land'. Acting under the power given in s. 33 (5) of the Act of 1960, he directed that the notice be corrected by the insertion of the words 'as part of' before the words 'a caravan site' where these latter words occur in the notice.

It was obviously more accurate to say 'part of a caravan site' instead of 'a caravan site'. No objection is taken to that variation. So the minister confirmed both notices with variations. The owner thereupon appealed to the High Court.

. . . The court dismissed the appeal in regard to the 'front land'. They held that the enforcement notice in regard to it was good. But they allowed the appeal in regard to the 'back land'.

. . . Now both sides appeal to this court. The owner appeals in regard to the 'front land' and the planning authority in regard to the 'back land'.

UPJOHN LJ: . . . . I turn, then, to the enforcement notice which was served on Dec. 28, 1960, and I deal with it, of course, before the amendments which were made by the minister. It was at one stage submitted by counsel for the minister that we must look at some application for a site licence in order to construe the enforcement notice. But I must protest in strong terms against looking at any document except the enforcement notice. This is a most important document, and the subject, who is being told that he is doing something contrary to planning permission and that he must remedy it, is entitled to say that he must find out from within the four corners of the document exactly what he is required to do or abstain from doing. For this is the prelude to a possible penal procedure. It is comparable to the grant of an injunction, and it is perfectly plain that someone against whom an injunction is granted is entitled to look only to the precise words of the injunction to interpret his duty. . . . The enforcement notice . . . . was too wide, for the planning authority had no right to require the owner to remove dead caravans from the site or to discontinue the parking of dead caravans thereon, for they were already lawfully there. The whole question, therefore, that we have to consider is: what effect has that matter on the validity of the notice? Does it invalidate the whole notice and render it inoperative of effect? At the moment I am using the word 'inoperative' as neutral language to avoid at this stage questions of nullity or invalidity and the applicability of quashing procedure.

I propose to approach this matter in the first place apart altogether from authority. It is a question of construction of s. 23 of the Act of 1947, and I deal with it first without reference to the Caravan Sites and Control of Development Act, 1960. Section 23 (1) starts by saying: 'If it appears to the local planning authority', and so, if it appears to them that the development was carried out after the appointed day without the grant of permission or that the conditions subject to which permission was granted have not been complied with, they may serve a notice. If it did not appear to the planning authority, then of course the condition precedent to the service of the notice would not be satisfied and it would be inoperative. I draw attention to the fact that the verb is that it *appears* to them, not that the planning authority must be satisfied as to a certain state of affairs. Therefore, one approaches this section with the idea in mind that a prima facie case only need be shown to satisfy the prerequisites of a valid notice. Then sub-s. (2) sets out the necessary contents of a notice. A notice has to specify certain matters. If it does not so specify, the notice is plainly in-operative as a notice under the Act. It must start by specifying one of two matters: the development alleged to have been carried out without the grant of planning permission or, as the case may be, the matters in respect of which it is alleged that any conditions subject to which permission was granted have not been complied with. Pausing there, the operative verb in each case is 'alleged'. This is hardly the right word to use if the state-ments or recitals of fact have to be substantially true and correct to ensure the validity of the notice. Then the notice may require such steps as may be specified in the notice to be taken within such period as may be specified for restoring the land to its earlier condition or for securing compliance with conditions. To be operative, therefore, the notice must specify these things, and if, for example, it does not specify what is to be done or within what period it is to be done, it will fail to have effect as an enforcement notice and the owner or occupier need not comply with it. . . .

What happens if a notice does not comply exactly with those sections? As a matter of common sense, if it does not specify the steps to be taken to remedy the alleged breach of planning permission or the alleged failure to comply with the conditions with proper and sufficient particularity, the notice will not be operative. So, too, if sub-s. (3) is not complied with. Now, I think, is the time to draw the distinction between invalidity and nullity. For example, supposing development without permission is alleged and it is found that no permission is required or that, contrary to the allegation in the notice, it is established that in fact the conditions in the planning permission have been complied with, then the notice may be quashed under s. 23 (4) (a). The notice is invalid; it is not a nullity because on the face of it it appears to be good and it is only on proof of facts aliunde that the notice is shown to be bad; the notice is invalid and, therefore, it may be quashed. But supposing that the notice on the face of it fails to specify some period required by sub-s. (2) or sub-s. (3). On the face of it the notice does not comply with the section; it is a nullity and is so much waste paper. No power was given to the justices to quash in such circumstances, for it was quite unnecessary. The notice on its face is bad. Supposing, then, on its true construction the notice was hopelessly ambiguous and uncertain, so that the owner or occupier could not tell in what respect it was alleged that he had developed the land without permission or in what respect it was alleged that he had failed to comply with a condition or, again, that he could not tell with reasonable certainty what steps he had to take to remedy the alleged breaches. The notice would be bad on its face and a nullity; the justices have no jurisdiction to quash it, for it was unnecessary to give them that power, but this court could, on application to it, declare that the notice was a nullity. That to my mind is the distinction between invalidity and nullity.

In the present case, there is no question of uncertainty or ambiguity in expression. On the face of it the notice appears to comply with the requirements of s. 23 in every particular. On investigation of the facts, however, it is proved that the allegations go too far and require the owner or occupier to do too much. . . . .

But is the notice invalid because it has alleged a breach greater than that which was in fact established? Apart from authority, to which I shall refer in a moment, I would think that the notice is not bad and invalid merely because it alleged too much. I have already stressed the importance of the words 'appear' and 'allege', and do not refer to them further. I do not think that the legislature intended the validity of the notice to depend on an entirely accurate recital of the facts. A planning authority cannot necessarily know all the relevant facts; for example, application may have been made for permission which was not required. If the officers of the planning authority see that the permission granted is not being observed, it may reasonably appear to them that it is not being complied with and they may reasonably allege that in the notice. Of course, if it is established that that is quite wrong, the justices have the power, and indeed the duty, to quash it, but I think a consideration of these facts shows that the section did not contemplate that a mere misrecital of some fact or some inaccurate allegation would necessarily be fatal to the validity of the notice. It seems to me that each case must depend on its own facts. The whole question is whether s. 23 of the Act of 1947 is complied with in the requirements that it lays down for the contents of a notice. Some mistake in the notice would not, I would think, amount to a failure to comply. Of course the failure to comply with the section may be so fundamental that the notice is bad on its face and a nullity or, while not a nullity, is proved to be so inaccurate in its recital of the facts that it would not be right to call it an enforcement notice under the Act and it ought to be quashed by the minister under s. 33 (6) of the Act of 1960. It seems to me that that must depend on the facts of each case. . . . One must remember the words of VISCOUNT SIMONDS in *East Riding County Council* v. *Park Estate (Bridlington), Ltd.*[9] that the court must insist on a strict and rigid adherence to formalities, for the rights of owners and occupiers are being subjected to interference. This interference, however, on the other hand, is for the common good and the powers are entrusted to responsible public bodies of great experience. The requirements of the section must be interpreted with reasonableness in all the circumstances of the case. With all respect to *Cater* v. *Essex County Council*[10], the function of the court is not to introduce strict rules not justified by the words of the section. I repeat, therefore, that, in my judgment, the test must be: does the notice tell him fairly what he has done wrong and what he must do to remedy it?

Before answering that question, I come to the arguments based on the

Caravan Sites and Control of Development Act, 1960. It was submitted on behalf of the minister that the Act of 1960 introduced a new code, and this view appealed to the Divisional Court, but I am unable to agree with them. The prime and all important s. 23 of the Town and Country Planning Act, 1947, remains the principal section. What has happened is that certain powers previously conferred on the justices have been enlarged and the proceedings now go to the minister. . . . I reject the notion that s. 33 constitutes anything in the nature of a code, which expression, if it means anything useful, must mean, of course, a complete, compendious and exhaustive code barring all other proceedings. That is plainly not so. Suppose a notice on its face does not comply with s. 23 (3) of the Act of 1947 or is too vague to enforce. The minister has no power to deal with that under s. 33 (1) of the Act of 1960 that I can see, and the power to come to the court for a declaration that the notice is bad on its face and is a nullity clearly remains. Indeed, the court may have jurisdiction where the order, though not a nullity, offends s. 23 but not in any respect pointed out in s. 33 (1). Direct resort to the court in such a case is not prohibited by anything in s. 33 (8). In my judgment, the Act of 1960 does no more than provide new and more comprehensive machinery to enable the subject to attack the notice and to enable the minister to correct any errors in the subject's favour and finally to quash the order on more general grounds than were formerly available to the justices.

So what is the result? It seems to me clear that s. 33 (6) of the Act of 1960 was directed to just such a case as this and that it was to enable the minister to vary the operative part of the order to accord with the facts as established before his inspector, if the original order went too far. The notice may have alleged too much. Then let it be amended in accordance with those facts, provided it is in favour of the appellant, as in this case. But, of course, the minister cannot by amendment cure a bad notice which wholly misfires and which it is his duty to quash on proof of the relevant facts, because that quite plainly would not be a variation in favour of the appellant.

I turn, then, to this notice. I think that the notice was good, although alleging too much, but it was not thereby vitiated. I think that it could have been varied under s. 23 (4) (b) of the Act of 1947 and can now be amended under s. 33 (6) of the Act of 1960. That is what the minister has done. The only power in the court to correct what the minister has done is when he has gone wrong in law. That appears from s. 34. Has he gone wrong in law in making this amendment? He took the view merely that this order was not one which ought to be quashed, but was one which went too far. That must necessarily be very much a question of fact and degree in each case. The minister thought that it was proper to amend it and I do not think that we can say that is wrong in law. . . .

LORD DENNING MR's analysis of the authorities and the changes wrought by the Act of 1960 was as follows:

. . . . As I listened to the argument and read the cases, I began to wonder whether we were not in danger of returning to the formalism of earlier days. The recitals in an enforcement notice were being treated as if they were a charge against an offender, and not only a charge, but a record of his conviction, which must be strictly accurate, else it would be a nullity and void. The reasoning employed to invalidate these enforcement notices bears a striking parallel to the reasoning which used to be employed to invalidate a conviction by justices. In the *East Riding case*, VISCOUNT SIMONDS said:

> It was in the first place contended that the Act of 1947 was highly technical and, as it encroached on private rights, the court must insist on strict and rigid adherence to formalities. This, as a general proposition, commands assent and not the less because disregard of an enforcement notice is an offence involving sufficiently serious penal consequences.

This reminds me very much of what SIR JOHN HOLT CJ said in 1702 in *R. v. Chandler*[11]: '. . . in these summary proceedings the right of an Englishman of being tried per pares suos was taken away; therefore the court was to construe them strictly, so far as to see that the fact was an offence within the Act, and that the justices proceeded accordingly.'

The result of all this strictness was that the legislature had to intervene in the case of conviction. So, also, in the case of these enforcement notices the legislature has had to intervene, and it has adopted a somewhat similar method. It has intervened, not so much by changing the substantive law, but by altering the procedure, and, in so doing, it has taken away the power of the courts to interfere on technical grounds. . . .

Appeal by the owner dismissed. Appeal by the minister allowed.

Upjohn LJ said that he agreed with Lord Denning's judgement. Did he?

Munnich v. *Godstone UDC* [1966] 1 All E.R. 930

LORD DENNING MR: In 1958, the plaintiff, Mr Munnich, and Mr Taras bought a one and a half acre property near Horley, known as 'The Laurels', Potters Field, Weatherhill Road, Smallfield. There was a rough sort of bungalow on it at the time and nothing else. About 1960 they allowed some caravan dwellers to come there. In the beginning of 1960 there were four caravans on it dwelt in by Mr Mould, Mr Billingham, Mr Ware and Mr Murray. The defendant district council, as the agent of the planning authority, on Mar. 14, 1960, served on the plaintiff and Mr Taras four documents. I will take one of them as typical. It was headed: 'To Mr Munnich and Mr Taras' describing them as 'the owners', and also 'To Mr Mould', describing him as 'the occupier' of the land described in the schedule which was the whole of the one and a half acre field. It recited that development had been carried out on the land without permission by using it for these purposes: (i) for a purpose other than as land attached to the bungalow; (ii) the placing of a moveable structure, to wit, a caravan which was used for the purpose of a dwelling. It then required them (that is, the plaintiff and Mr Taras and Mr Mould) 'To remove from the said land the said caravan thereon used or capable of being used as a dwelling'. That document was one of the four served on the plaintiff and Mr Taras. It was also served as a single document on Mr Mould. Similarly with the other three. The only difference was that, instead of Mr Mould, the names were Mr Billingham, Mr Ware and Mr Murray. All four were served on the plaintiff and Mr Taras; and one each on the caravan dwellers. None of them paid any regard to the notices. The caravans remained on the field. More came on. They increased to sixteen or eighteen caravans on the field. Meanwhile, in August, 1960, the Caravan Sites and Control of Development Act, 1960, came into operation. The plaintiff and Mr Taras, within two months, applied for a site licence. The application was duly transmitted to the planning authority. The authority did not grant a licence for the simple reason that they believed that the enforcement notices were valid and that the plaintiff and Mr Taras had no right to a site licence. If the authority were wrong, however, on this point, that is to say, if the enforcement notices were invalid, then the plaintiff and Mr Taras would be 'deemed' to have planning permission under s. 17 (3) of the Act of 1960, and thus be entitled to a site licence under s. 3 (4) of that Act. The whole point in this case is, therefore, whether the enforcement notices were valid or not. If valid, the plaintiff is entitled to nothing. If invalid, he is entitled to a site licence which would be of great value to him.

The plaintiff paid no regard to the enforcement notices. Many caravans still remained on the field. Eventually, on Apr. 16, 1962, the plaintiff was summoned before the magistrates for permitting land to be used as a caravan site in contravention of the enforcement notice. Counsel advised him that he had no defence in law. He pleaded guilty and was fined £20 and ordered to pay fifty guineas costs. A little later he received different advice. Other counsel advised him that this enforcement notice was bad in law. Solicitors wrote a letter setting up this point of law. On June 25, 1962, they issued the writ in this action claiming a declaration that the plaintiff had 'deemed permission' for this caravan site and claiming that he was entitled to a site licence under the Act of 1960. The writ did not frighten the defendant district council. They took out a summons again against the plaintiff. They charged him with continuing to permit the land to be used as a caravan site in contravention of the notice. These proceedings came before the magistrates' court on Nov. 23, 1962. This time the plaintiff was represented by counsel who argued the point of law fully, alleging that the enforcement notice was bad. The justices decided against the plaintiff. They fined him £200 and one hundred guineas costs. He asked for a Case to be stated for the Divisional Court. It was prepared by counsel; but then he abandoned it. He did not appeal to the Divisional Court; but he continued also to ignore the enforcement notice. He did not pay the fines or costs. He did not remove the caravans. They remained on the land. The defendant district council took further proceedings. On July 30, 1964, he was summoned again for continuing to permit the land to be used as a caravan site after conviction, in contravention of the enforcement notice.

This time I do not think that he was represented by counsel. He pleaded not guilty, but he was found guilty and fined £300 and one hundred guineas costs. Still he took no notice. He has not paid the fines or the costs. Then the civil action came on for hearing before MOCATTA J. The question of law was elaborately argued. MOCATTA J held that the enforcement notice was bad; that in consequence the plaintiff had a 'deemed permission' to use the land as a caravan site and in consequence was entitled to a site licence. He made a declaration to that effect. Now the defendant district council appeal to this court. . . .

The . . . point is whether these documents were a valid enforcement notice. The judge was much impressed by the cases before 1960, in one of which it was said 'that the Act . . . was highly technical and, as it encroached on private rights, the court must insist on strict and rigid adherence to formalities'. So said VISCOUNT SIMONDS in *East Riding County Council* v. *Park Estate (Bridlington), Ltd.* A good deal of water has flowed under the bridges since then. We found that many people were taking an undue advantage of that statement. Formalities were being used to defeat the public good. So we no longer favour them. *Miller-Mead* v. *Minister of Housing and Local Government, Same* v. *Same* was the turning point. We now reject technicalities and apply the simple test enunciated by UPJOHN LJ in that case 'does the notice tell him fairly what he has done wrong and what he must do to remedy it?'. Applying that test, it is plain that the plaintiff and Mr Taras, who were the 'owners' of the land and, as I think, also the 'occupiers' of the land, got full and proper notice of what was complained of, namely, that these four caravans had been brought on the site without permission. They had the four documents with the names of the caravan dwellers on them telling them what ought to be done, namely, remove those caravans from the land. I can see no difficulty whatever in holding that all four documents, coupled together and served together, constituted a perfectly valid enforcement notice. I know that Mr Mould, Mr Billington, Mr Ware and Mr Murray were described as 'occupiers'. That was erroneous. They were not occupiers within the meaning of the Act. They were simply caravan dwellers. Caravan dwellers are only licensees and are never to be regarded as occupiers unless they are granted a tenancy. It was unnecessary to serve them at all. The only persons who needed to be served were the plaintiff and Mr Taras themselves. Those two had the clearest possible notice of what was complained of and what they ought to do to remedy it.

On this short and simple ground I think that this enforcement notice was good and always has been good. Even if it were necessary to describe these caravan dwellers as occupiers and to serve them, I think that sufficient notice was given to them. I do not think that it is necessary for all the occupiers to be named in one notice. It is sufficient if each one is told what he has done wrong and what he has to do. . . .

Appeal allowed.

Were errors corrected in the subject's favour? Is that a justifiable limitation to put upon the words of the statute?

Iddenden v. Secretary of State for the Environment
[1972] 3 All E.R. 882

LORD DENNING MR: We give leave to appeal in this case and proceed to decide the appeal.

It concerns a three acre site in the Old Odiham Road near Alton, Hampshire. It was bought in 1967 by the appellant, Mr Iddenden. At that time there was on it a bungalow, a nissen hut, a lean-to workshop and storage buildings. Mr Iddenden installed some machinery in them. About nine months later, in March 1968, Mr Iddenden applied for planning permission to replace those old workshops with a new workshop and garage. That was refused. Then I am afraid he took the law into his own hands. Without obtaining any planning permission at all he put up a prefabricated asbestos building 150 ft long and 20 ft wide. He constructed a concrete base and two other prefabricated buildings. He developed in those buildings a business of manufacturing small metal components.

Thereupon in February 1971 the planning authority, the Hampshire County Council, served on him an enforcement notice. It recited the respects in which it appeared to the authority that that had been a breach of planning control; and then the notice made this requirement:

> NOW THEREFORE the [authority] in exercise of their powers under Section 15 of the Town and Country Planning Act 1968 HEREBY REQUIRE that within a period of three months from the date when this Notice first takes effect:—(i) the unauthorised buildings shall be demolished and removed from the premises (ii) the materials comprising the access and hardstanding be removed and the boundary reinstated (iii) the unauthorised uses shall be discontinued.
>
> THIS NOTICE shall take effect thirty days from the date of service thereof.

Mr Iddenden appealed against the enforcement notice to the Minister. The inspector held an inquiry. The inspector reported that these new buildings should not be allowed. He thought it was quite wrong in this area, which was residential, to allow this factory, because it meant much traffic to and fro from it. The inspector's report was accepted by the Minister. He confirmed the enforcement notice.

But Mr Iddenden took a point on the statute. He said that the enforcement notice was bad because it did not require him to restore the nissen hut or the old workshop. He said that in order to be good an enforcement notice must not only tell him to take down his new buildings but must require him to re-erect the old nissen hut, and so forth. He relied on the words of s. 15 (5) of the Town and Country Planning Act 1968 as contrasted with the words in the earlier sections, s. 23 (2) of the Town and Country Planning Act 1947 and s. 45 (4) (b) of the Town and Country Planning Act 1962.

Each of the earlier sections was in its very terms *permissive*. Each used much the same words. I take them from the 1962 Act. Section 45 (4) provided:

An enforcement notice – (a) *shall* specify the development which is alleged to have been carried out without the grant of planning permission ... (b) *may* require such steps as may be specified in the notice to be taken, within such period as may be so specified, for the purpose of restoring the land to its condition before the development took place ...

In contrast, s. 15 (5) of the 1968 Act is in its very terms *mandatory*. It provides:

An enforcement notice *shall* specify – (a) the matters alleged to constitute a breach of planning control; (b) the steps required by the authority to be taken in order to remedy the breach, that is to say steps for the purpose of restoring the land to its condition before the development took place ...

I need not read any more. Mr Iddenden says that the use of the word 'shall' in 1968 was deliberate. It means that the enforcement notice in this case must specify, not only that the new buildings must be pulled down, but also that the old buildings should be restored; that the notice must accordingly specify that the nissen hut and lean-to workshop (long since pulled down) must be replaced as near as may be. The Secretary of State rejected that contention. The Divisional Court did also. But we have been presented with an interesting argument by counsel for the appellants on which we think it proper to give leave to appeal.

The words of the section are 'to remedy the breach'. That means the breach of planning control. What was the breach in this case? If it was the pulling down of the old nissen hut or the old workshop, then it may be that, in order to remedy the breach, they would have to be restored. But I do not think their demolition was a breach of planning control. Whilst some demolition operations may be development (see *Coleshill and District Investment Co Ltd* v. *Minister of Housing and Local Government*),[12] the demolition of buildings such as these was not development. Mr Iddenden did not need planning permission so as to pull them down. No doubt the pulling down of the old and the erection of the new was all one combined operation by the workmen. But in planning law they are different operations. Mr Iddenden only required planning permission for his new buildings and their user. The only breach by him of planning control was the unauthorised erection of the new buildings, the concrete base, and the user of the factory. The enforcement notice required him to remedy that breach. It told him the steps he had to take. It was perfectly good.

There is however another point. Counsel for the authority submits that the new section in 1968 is not different from the old ones in 1947 and 1962. It says that the enforcement notice shall specify 'the steps required by the authority to be taken'. Those words give a discretion to the planning authority. They are the people to say what *they* require to be done. They need only require such steps as they think necessary. They need not do more. Indeed they must not do more. That is clear from s. 16 (1) (*f*)....[13]

Appeal dismissed.

Howard v. *Secretary of State for the Environment*
[1974] 1 All E.R. 644

LORD DENNING MR: We are here concerned with the validity of an appeal against an enforcement notice. . . .

In 1957 the appellant, Mr Howard, bought a piece of land, 6 Birkbeck Road, Romford. He was a transport contractor and he used this land for the purposes of his business. He used to park lorries and so forth. In 1970 the local planning authority (the London Borough of Havering) were of the opinion that this was contrary to planning control. So they served on him an enforcement notice. It was dated 7th October 1970. It said that it appeared to the council that the plot of land was being used as a transport contractor's depot without the grant of the required consent; that it had started after the end of 1963 and was still continuing. By the notice, the council required Mr Howard within one month to discontinue the use of it. The notice concluded with these words:

THIS NOTICE SHALL TAKE EFFECT at the expiration of a period of forty-two days after the date hereof, unless before the expiration of the said period an appeal against the notice is made to the Minister of Housing and Local Government in pursuance of Section 16 of the Town and Country Planning Act, 1968 in which event the notice will have no effect pending the final determination or withdrawal of the appeal.

So the specified period was 42 days. It was due to expire on 18th November 1970. Mr Howard had to appeal within that time. Twelve days before it expired, namely, on 6th November 1970, the solicitors for Mr Howard wrote this letter to the Ministry:

We have been instructed by our Client Mr H. Howard of 6 Birkbeck Road, Romford, regarding the Enforcement Notice herein, dated 7th October, 1970, received from the London Borough of Havering, and would ask you kindly to accept this letter as formal notice of appeal on his behalf.

The question in the case is whether that letter amounted to an 'appeal' within the specified period of 42 days. It was certainly sent and received within the 42 days, but was it a sufficient 'appeal'? The Ministry say that it was not, because it did not indicate the grounds of appeal or state the facts on which it was based. Taking that view, the Ministry sent to Mr Howard's solicitors a letter dated 10th November 1970 in these words:

You have not indicated *which of the grounds of appeal listed* in sub-section (1) of section 16 of the Act you consider apply to your case. Nor have *you stated the facts on which the appeal is based*, as required by sub-section (2) of section 16. Unless this information is provided the Minister will be unable to entertain your appeal. The grounds of appeal and statement of facts must be sent to the Minister *before the date on which the enforcement notice is to take effect.*

It is interesting to notice that the letter was printed or reproduced in multiple form. So it must be in common use by the Ministry.

Mr Howard's solicitors intended to comply with that letter. They prepared a letter dated 16th November 1970 which, if it had been posted in time, would have been within the specified period of 42 days. It was quite a long letter. In it they gave notice of the appeal. They set out the grounds of appeal in four items. They set out the facts on which the appeal was based in five items, including as one ground that the land had been used for 30 years for similar purposes. That letter would undoubtedly have been a good notice of appeal if it had reached the Ministry in time, that is, by 18th November 1970. But, unfortunately, it did not do so. Someone forgot to post it. Although it was dated 16th November, it was not actually posted until 20th November; and it did not get into the Ministry until 24th November, whereas the specified period had ended on 18th November 1970. And there is no power in anyone to extend the time.

Faced with this objection to the second letter, Mr Howard's solicitors reverted back to their previous letter of 6th November in which they said: 'We ... would ask you kindly to accept this letter as formal notice of appeal'. They submitted that this letter was sufficient to satisfy the statute; and that it was in time.

The contest is this: Mr Howard says that a simple letter saying that he 'appeals' is sufficient so long as it is within the specified period. But the Minister says that an appeal, in order to be good, must comply with s. 16 (2), which says that an appeal 'shall be made by notice in writing ... which shall indicate the grounds of the appeal and state the facts on which it is based'.

The issue depends on whether that provision is imperative or directory. ... In applying that distinction, I must draw attention to a case which was decided on s. 33 of the Caravan Sites and Control of Development Act 1960. That section was the predecessor to s. 16 of the 1968 Act. It said that an appeal shall be 'by a written notice which shall indicate the grounds on which the appeal is brought'. The case was *Chelmsford Rural District Council* v. *Powell*.[13a] A written notice of appeal was given in due time. It set out two grounds of appeal. Neither ground was substantiated. But, before the hearing, the appellant (long after the time for appeal had expired) submitted a further ground of appeal. The Minister allowed this ground to be raised and he allowed the appeal. The local planning authority urged that the Minister ought not to have considered this further ground. They said that the section was imperative. But the Divisional Court ruled that it was not imperative, but only informative, that is, directory. So it was open to the appellant to go into the further ground although it was out of time and had not been contained in the original notice.

I think that decision was perfectly correct. It is common practice in these appeals to allow new grounds of appeal to be added, and new facts to be stated. Very often the true facts do not emerge until the hearing by the inspector, and justice requires that new ground be added and new facts stated. ...

The section is no doubt imperative in that the notice of appeal must be in writing and must be made within the specified time. But I think it is only directory as to the contents. Take first the requirement as to the 'grounds' of appeal. The section is either imperative in requiring 'the grounds' to be indicated, or it is not. That must mean all or none. I cannot see any justification for the view that it is imperative as to *one* ground and not imperative as to the rest. If *one* was all that was necessary, an appellant would only have to put in one frivolous or hopeless ground and then amend later to add his real grounds. That would be a futile exercise. Then as to 'stating the facts'. It cannot be supposed that the appellant must at all costs state all the facts on which he bases his appeal. He has to state the facts, not the evidence; and the facts may depend on evidence yet to be obtained; and may not be fully or sufficiently known at the time when the notice of appeal is given.

All things considered, it seems to me that the section, insofar as the 'grounds' and 'facts' are concerned, must be construed as directory only; that is, as desiring information to be given about them. It is not to be supposed that an appeal should fail altogether simply because the grounds are not indicated, or the facts stated. Even if it is wanting in not giving them, it is not fatal. The defects can be remedied later, either before or at the hearing of the appeal, so long as an opportunity is afforded of dealing with them. . . .

I hold, therefore, that an appeal is good so long as it is made in writing and within the specified time. The grounds of appeal, and the facts, can be stated later so long as a fair opportunity (by adjournment or otherwise) is given of dealing with them. I hold that the letter of 6th November 1970 was a good appeal. I would allow this appeal, accordingly.[13b]

ROSKILL LJ: . . . It was said by counsel for the Secretary of State at one point in his argument that if we accepted counsel for the appellant's submission, there would be no way of forcing intending appellants to comply with the statute if they refused to indicate the grounds or the facts on which they relied. But in my judgment that is not so. If intending appellants seek to take that line in these cases, they will be in peril of having their appeals dismissed. There is a lot of difference between a failure to comply with statutory provisions not resulting in the notice of appeal being a nullity and the failure to comply being of no effect when it comes to consider the merits of the intended appeal. Where an intending appellant deliberately flouts the intention of Parliament and does not after one or more requests indicate his grounds or the facts on which he relies, he will be in danger of having his appeal brought on immediately by the Minister and summarily dismissed; and he will have only himself to blame if and when that happens. The Minister is and remains master of his own procedure. . . .

Appeal allowed.

What are the criteria for deciding whether a provision in the enforcement procedures of the Town and Country Planning Act is mandatory or directory?

Attorney-General v. *Smith* [1958] 2 All E.R. 557

LORD GODDARD CJ: This is an action by the Attorney-General, at the relation of the Egham Urban District Council, claiming an injunction restraining the defendants from using or causing or permitting to be used as caravan sites any land within the boundaries of the Urban District Council of Egham without previous planning permission.

The matter arises out of the provisions of the Town and Country Planning Act, 1947. Before I proceed to deal with the facts, let me say a word or two with regard to the Act itself. It is (as I think everybody knows) a somewhat difficult Act in many respects; and the procedure which is laid down under it is such that a very considerable time must very often elapse before questions whether there has been 'development' or whether permission will be granted can be finally determined. A resolute defendant can make use of that state of affairs and may very likely develop land for certain purposes – and in this case we are concerned only with caravans, which seem to continue to have a particular attraction for the provisions of the Act – and be able to take advantage of the delays which the Act permits, so as to use land, contrary to the terms of the Act, for a very considerable period before the matter is finally decided. . . .

It is perfectly obvious that the policy of the Egham Urban District Council, this district lying, as it does, within what is known as the 'Green Belt', is to prohibit the use of land for caravan sites, or caravan towns, or whatever one may like to call them, within their district. I have not the least doubt, in the circumstances of this case, that the defendants knew that perfectly well. The first defendant may not have known it when he first started, in March, 1955, to bring caravans on to the land, but I am quite sure that within a very short time he must have known that that was the deliberate policy of the district council, and he set himself out to ignore that policy. If he could legally do that, he would be entitled to, and one would not attach any moral blame to him for that. At the same time, he was taking on a very considerable risk, not only for himself but also for the people who were living in these caravans as permanent dwellings. It is a very serious thing, if planning permission is required and has not been obtained, to be letting these sites to unfortunate individuals who come there, presumably in the belief that there is power to have the caravans where they are, and then find themselves, having moved into them, in jeopardy of being turned out.

The history of the defendants' efforts to establish these caravan sites in face of the refusal of planning permission is this. The first piece of land with which we are concerned, Retreat Farm, was first used, apparently, on Mar. 28. 1955, when five caravans were brought there. On Apr. 12, 1955 – within a fortnight – an enforcement notice, to expire on May 16, 1955, was sent, requiring the removal of these caravans. Section 18 of the Town and Country Planning Act, 1947, provides that, if a person carries out any development without permission (or in ignorance, as he may easily do, of the requirements of the Act), retrospective permission can be given; so the first defendant applied, on Apr. 23, 1955, for permission to use the land, and to continue to use it, for a caravan site. On May 25, 1955, that permission was refused.

On July 18, 1955, the first defendant appealed to the Minister; and on Sept. 20 an inquiry was held. On Dec. 31, 1955, the appeal was dismissed by the Minister, who made it quite clear that he was not upholding the decision on the ground that there was some particular objection to the particular site, but that there was an objection to these caravan towns, or caravan settlements, or whatever one may call them, going up in the Egham Urban District Council's district near Chertsey because of it being in the Green Belt. The Minister, in dismissing the appeal, expressed the hope – he did not make it any condition – that the district council would act reasonably and not too precipitately, because it involved the dispersal of these unfortunate people who had taken themselves to this caravan site and found that the planning authority would not allow them to remain. The district council certainly did act with great restraint, because it was not until May 3, 1956, that they served another enforcement notice expiring on June 30, 1956. So that the first defendant had had from Dec. 31, 1955, to June 30, 1956, to comply with the notice; he had six months in which to get the land cleared of these caravans.

On June 20, 1956 (hope, I suppose, springing eternal in the human breast), he made a further application for permission. He did not know, but quite obviously he could expect, that it would be refused, as it was on Aug. 9, 1956. The district council by this time thought, no doubt, that the first defendant was simply defying them, and so they issued a summons on Aug. 14, 1956, which was returnable on Sept. 5, 1956. The magistrates imposed a fine of £25 and costs – which was certainly, I think, considering the defiance (practically) which the first defendant had shown here, a very moderate fine.

As the first defendant did not pay any attention to that at the time but still kept the caravans on his land at Retreat Farm, on Sept. 26, 1956, the district council took out a summons for the daily penalty. As the daily penalty was £20, a very considerable sum had already mounted up. So he got his caravans out. On Oct. 7, 1956, he moved them to the next-door field. That simply meant that he was going to keep the caravans. As he had been turned off one site he was going to take another site. So he moved from one field to another and there, on Oct. 7, on a site called Maindy, he installed the caravans. On Nov. 6, 1956, after they had been there for a month without permission, he applied again for permission; and on Jan. 15, 1957, it was refused. He no doubt thought (or I will assume that he thought) that he could use Maindy for a further twenty-eight days under the general permission. On Jan. 21, 1957, the direction issued by the district council under art. 4 (1) of the General Development Order came into force.

On Feb. 9, 1957, the first defendant appealed to the Minister against the refusal of planning permission in respect of the Maindy site. On Feb. 13, 1957, an enforcement notice was served, taking effect on Mar. 16, 1957. But on Mar. 23, 1957, the caravans had gone. The first defendant said that he had parted with any interest that he had in the land, because by this time, apparently, he had got the idea of going to another adjoining site which is referred to as Royal Hythe Farm. The history with regard to Royal Hythe Farm is this. The defendant company, of which the first defendant was a director, had now come into the picture, and on Jan. 26, 1957, applied for planning permission. It was here that the warning notices, saying that the site was not an authorised site, were put up. On the very day on which permission was applied for, the caravans started to move in. A very considerable number had moved in by Feb. 6, 1957, the date when planning permission was refused. That did not daunt the defendants, because, by Mar. 28, 1957, there were 119 caravans there and by Apr. 3, 1957, there were 156. By this time an appeal had been made to the Minister, and on Mar. 11, 1957, a writ had been issued, the planning authority being relators, and application had been made to the court for an interim injunction. When the summons came before the judge in chambers, no order was made, because counsel gave an undertaking that no more caravans would be moved on to this site. But there they were: there were 156. On June 14, 1957, another public inquiry was held; and on July 26, 1957, the appeal to the Minister was dismissed.

On Aug. 29, 1957, planning permission was again sought, this time to put the caravans on another part of Royal Hythe Farm, moving them quite a short distance. This really shows that it was getting to be, I might almost say, something in the nature of a scandal, because everybody knew at this time that it was not the particular field that was objected to but it was that the district council were not going to have these sites. On Sept. 18, 1957, that application was refused.

I have mentioned the matters which happened after that date as showing that the defendants intended to hold the Act at defiance as far as they could by going on making these repeated little moves from one field to another, or from one part of the farm to another part of the farm, and then applying for permission which they knew they would not get, and then appealing to the Minister and getting an inquiry, so that they could get fifteen or sixteen months' grace in which they could let caravans on the site and could take the profits for them. On Oct. 23, 1957, further enforcement notices were served. On Nov. 30, 1957, there was an appeal to the Minister, and that appeal has followed the way of all the other appeals and the Minister has refused to disturb the decision of the district council.

It has been submitted to me that, because the Act provides penalties and because no offence is committed before the enforcement notice has been disregarded, I ought not to grant an injunction. I think that the cases which have been cited, particularly *A.-G.* v. *Wimbledon House Estate Co., Ltd.*[14] and which was cited and followed by DEVLIN J in *A.-G. (on the relation of Hornchurch Urban District Council)* v. *Bastow*[15] show that, although a statute may provide a penalty for acts done in breach of it, or in respect of acts done for which it provides a penalty, if it is a matter of public right then the Attorney-General is entitled, on behalf of the public, to apply for an injunction. Of course, the Town and Country Planning Act, 1947, is an Act which is designed to confer a benefit on the public; it is for the orderly development of the countryside, to prevent unsightly development, to prevent the development of too crowded areas, to prevent the development taking place of industrial buildings and plant in what should be a residential district, and for the mapping out of residential districts and industrial districts, and so forth. It is obviously an Act which is designed for the public good, and can be used for great public advantage. Therefore, if a defendant shows by his conduct that he intends to avoid the Act and act in breach of it so far as he can and for as long as he can, then the Attorney-General is entitled to an injunction such as was granted in the cases which have been cited to me.

I think, therefore, that this is a case in which I have jurisdiction to grant an injunction; and, if I have jurisdiction to grant an injunction, I most certainly as a matter of discretion will grant it. . . .

Injunction granted.

Do you agree with the procedures used in *A.-G.* v. *Smith*? Why should a person who is merely using a defective law to his own advantage be put under threat of imprisonment for contempt of court (the penalty for failure to obey an injunction) when the original law did not provide for imprisonment as a punishment? Is it sufficient answer that 'the Act is obviously designed for the public good'?

94. – (1) For the purposes of this Part of this Act, a use of land is established if –

> (a) it was begun before the beginning of 1964 without planning permission in that behalf and has continued since the end of 1963; or
>
> (b) it was begun before the beginning of 1964 under a planning permission in that behalf granted subject to conditions or limitations, which either have never been complied with or have not been complied with since the end of 1963; or
>
> (c) it was begun after the end of 1963 as the result of a change of use not requiring planning permission and there has been, since the end of 1963, no change of use requiring planning permission.

(2) Where a person having an interest in land claims that a particular use of it has become established, he may apply to the local planning authority for a certificate (in this Act referred to as an 'established use certificate') to that effect:

Provided that no such application may be made in respect of the use of land as a single dwellinghouse, or of any use not subsisting at the time of the application.

(3) An established use certificate may be granted (either by the local authority or, under section 95 of this Act, by the Secretary of State) –

> (a) either for the whole of the land specified in the application, or for a part of it;
>
> (b) in the case of an application specifying two or more uses, either for all those uses or for some one or more of them.

(4) On an application to them under this section, the local planning authority shall, if and so far as they are satisfied that the applicant's claim is made out, grant to him an established use certificate accordingly; and if and so far as they are not so satisfied, they shall refuse the application.

(7) An established use certificate shall, as respects any matters stated therein, be conclusive for the purposes of an appeal to the Secretary of State against an enforcement notice served in respect of any land to which the certificate relates, but only where the notice is served after the date of the application on which the certificate was granted.

Bolivian Trust Ltd v. *Secretary of State for the Environment*
[1972] 3 All E.R. 918

BEAN J: This is a motion seeking an order to quash or suspend a decision of the Secretary of State for the Department of the Environment contained in a letter dated 29th March 1971, on the ground that the Secretary of State erred in law and wrongly construed s. 17 (1) (*a*) of the Town and Country Planning Act 1968. . . .

The case concerns land situated on the south-east side of York Road, the A217, at Wandsworth, SW18. The appellants are the freehold owners of the site, which they purchased on 26th January 1961. The present use of the site, as a petrol filling station, was commenced in about May 1961, without the grant of planning permission. These and other facts I take from an affidavit in the case, sworn by Oliver Alfred Sidney Cutts on 24th May 1971. On 28th June 1963 the London County Council served an enforcement notice on the appellants, alleging unauthorised use of the site as a petrol filling station; the notice was to take effect on 9th August 1963, the time for compliance being six weeks. On 16th and 17th December 1963, an inquiry was held into appeals against the enforcement notice. The inspector reported to the Minister of Housing and Local Government on 20th January 1964. . . .

The Minister, on receipt of that report, in a letter dated 25th June 1964 said this, and I start at para 4:

> The Minister has considered the submissions of the parties and his Inspector's findings of fact and conclusions. He is satisfied from the evidence that the established use of the site prior to 1961 was for general industrial purposes and that its use as a petrol filling station, which commenced in that year, constituted development for which planning permission was required and had not been granted. On the planning merits, the Minister agrees with his Inspector's view that the traffic objections at the filling station have not proved to have been such as would warrant refusing permission, but it appears to him that having regard to the possibility of redevelopment affecting the area, a temporary permission for 5 years would be appropriate, provided that the accesses to the site are satisfactory and the use strictly limited to a petrol filling station. Accordingly, the Minister had decided to allow your appeals to the extent that he hereby grants permission for the use of the appeal site as a petrol filling station subject to the following conditions

... [and I quote the third one] that the use shall cease and all plant and works installed or carried out in connection with the use hereby permitted shall be removed from the site by a date not later than five years from the date of this letter.

And he directs that the enforcement notice be quashed.

Continuing the history, in or about July 1969, the appellants applied to the London Borough of Wandsworth for renewal of the planning permission previously granted by the Minister. The borough had not, at the date of the hearing before me, made a decision on the application. On 8th October 1969 the appellants applied to the London Borough of Wandsworth for an established use certificate under Part II of the Town and Country Planning Act 1968. In about December 1969 that application for an established use certificate was referred to the Minister, pursuant to a direction given by the Minister under s. 18 of the 1968 Act. The appellants submitted written representations in support of their application for the certificate. The relevant ones I take briefly from paras 7, 8 and 9:

> There can be no doubt, therefore, that the use of the site as a petrol filling station was begun before the beginning of 1964: both the Minister's letter and the inspector's finding of fact establish the position as at the 16th and 17th December 1963. There can also be no doubt, in view of the wording of the Minister's letter and the Inspector's finding of fact, that the use of the site as a petrol filling station was begun without planning permission on that behalf. There can also be no doubt that the use of the land as a petrol filling station has continued since the end of 1963: it is still used as a petrol filling station.

Then, in para 16:

> The case falls fairly and squarely within the terms of Section 17 and the Ministry are asked to grant an established use certificate accordingly.

The Secretary of State gave his decision in a letter dated 29th March 1971, and it is sufficient if I take up his letter towards the end of the long para 5, where he says:

> ... subsection (1) (a) [i.e. of s. 17] was intended to relate only to the case where immunity from enforcement action has been acquired in respect of the material change of use because it has continued as a contravening use since before 1 January 1964. Moreover, it is considered that the phrase 'has continued' in that paragraph implies a continuance of the same state and condition as those in which the use was begun. Accordingly, the view is taken that if a grant of planning permission has been made on or after 1 January 1964 in respect of a use begun in contravention of planning control before that date, that use of the land is not established within the meaning of section 17 (1) (a) of the 1968 Act. 6. The facts in the present case show that the use of the site from 24 June 1964 until 24 June 1969 was in accordance with the grant of permission. The continuation of the use after 24 June 1969 was therefore

a new breach of planning control consisting of failure to comply with a condition subject to which planning permission was granted. Although therefore the use for which a certificate is sought began before 1964 without planning permission and subsisted at the time of your clients' application, the Secretary of State is satisfied that your clients' claim for an established use certificate has not been made out since the use has not continued as a contravening use since the end of 1963 and he therefore refuses to issue a certificate under section 17 (1) (a) of the Act.

The appellants, in the affidavit which I referred to, having recited all these matters, then say of the Secretary of State's decision in refusing the certificate that it is wrong and ultra vires.

Counsel for the appellants ... contends that the town and country planning legislation encroaches on the rights of the subject and must be construed strictly; therefore, the court ought not to accede to the interpretation of s. 17 (1) (a) sought by counsel for the Secretary of State, namely, that it deals with the use of land in respect of which (a) there was no planning permission before the beginning of 1964 and (b) there has been no planning permission since the end of 1963. Counsel for the Secretary of State invites the court to read s. 17 (1) (a) as though it were worded 'it was begun before the beginning of 1964 without planning permission in that behalf and has continued without planning permission since the end of 1963'.

Now, in my judgment, s. 17 is not a penal provision requiring narrow construction in favour of the applicant. It merely provides for a certificate to be granted in certain circumstances. But, if I am wrong, at worst there is ambiguity in part of its wording, making it possible to give s 17 (1) (a) two meanings, one of which is that which in my judgment Parliament intended it to have: see *Director of Public Prosecutions* v. *Ottewell*[16]. I believe that the whole spirit of the Town and Country Planning Acts, and in particular Part II of the 1968 Act, calls for an interpretation of s. 17 (1) (a) which would require the issue of an established use certificate only when there has not been what has been referred to as 'a contravening use'. In this present case, use of the site over five years from June 1964 to June 1969 was as the result of a grant made by the then Minister of Housing and Local Government, and since June 1969 the appellants have been in breach of planning control. I find it hard to believe that nonetheless the appellants should be entitled to an established use certificate. ...

Motion dismissed.

(b) Is it development?

Three preliminary points may be made before the case law is examined. First, although many of the cases appear to be concerned with very trivial developments, there is a point of principle of great moment at stake in all of them. It is this: local planning authorities and the Department of the Environment have an interest in keeping the ambit of development, which is not development for purposes of the Act, as narrow as possible, thus ensuring that the scope of the control of development is as wide as possible; developers on the other hand have precisely the reverse interest: the more development they can undertake which does not need permission, the freer they are from the planning system. Equally, if they have already commenced development, it is important to try and keep it going. Thus, factually trivial cases are fought through to the Court of Appeal and sometimes beyond.

Secondly, to repeat in this context a point made in other parts of the book, though the decisions of the courts are of great importance here, they are not the sole influence on the practitioners of planning at the local level where many of these decisions are made. Ministerial decisions and circulars are used in local planning offices a good deal more than are the law reports; and circulars may be used and relied upon so often that as *Coleshill Investments* v. *Minister of Housing and Local Government*[17] shows, they might influence the way the court decides. Ministerial decisions are frequently quoted in inquiries on these matters for their precedent value. Thirdly, the fact that we are in an area where the law rather than taste is a crucial factor does not mean that we have left the realm of negotiation and compromise between developer and local authority planner. It may often pay a developer not to contest a ruling of the local planning authority that what he wants to do is development; but instead, apply for permission, accept a few conditions on a grant of permission and then get started.

The concept of development is broken down by the Act into 'operations' and 'use'. This is not a distinction which is based on any inherent or fundamental difference in the use of land, for in the language of the layman all operations on land would involve the use of land and all uses of land involve operations on the land. But the distinction has been made the basis of subsidiary rules about development which does or does not require planning permission – principally the Use Classes Order reprinted below – and it has also led to a good deal of the kind of abstract conceptual reasoning which many lawyers find fascinating and other persons infuriating, taken, it seems, from the more traditional parts of the law of real property. It is this last development which has given this part of the law of planning its very distinctive flavour. To what extent this is a hindrance or a help to development control in general is a matter which should be in the forefront of our concern in this section.

(i) Operations

Cheshire County Council v. Woodward
[1962] 1 All E.R. 517

Cheshire County Council, the local planning authority, required the respondent, the occupier of a coal-yard at Green Lane, Hollingworth near Manchester, (i) to cease user of part of the land as a coal-yard and (ii) to remove a coal-hopper and conveyor equipment therefrom. The coal-hopper was some sixteen to twenty feet in height, and the conveyor was a large bit of equipment on rubber wheels which could be fed at the lower end with coal from a stack and the coal was then conveyed up and into the hopper. The occupier appealed to the Minister of Housing and Local Government. . . .

By letter dated July 5, 1961, the minister . . . directed that the enforcement notices be quashed. The local planning authority appealed to the High Court . . . against the minister's decision with regard to the coal-hopper and conveyor.

LORD PARKER CJ: . . . The question that arose was whether the installation of that equipment amounted to 'building, engineering, mining or other operations in, on, over or under land'. There is no doubt that both these bits of equipment, the hopper and the conveyor, are large and somewhat unsightly, and it is, no doubt, thought by the local planning authority that they detract from the amenities of what is in general a residential neighbourhood, and it is that which has impelled them to appeal in this case. Counsel for the planning authority, to whom the court is indebted for his argument, has contended that the Minister of Housing and Local Government has erred in law – and this is an appeal and can only be an appeal on a point of law – in holding, so it is said, that, because the hopper does not rest of its own weight on the ground or is not attached to the ground but is on four wheels, and because the conveyor is on wheels, for that reason and that reason alone the erection thereof cannot have been an operation constituting development.

The sections in question are not altogether easy to construe. Section 12 (2) of the Town and Country Planning Act, 1947, which defines 'development', does so by reference to two matters, one, a change in use of the land, and, secondly, quite regardless of change of use, whether there has been a 'carrying out of building, engineering, mining or other operations in, on, over or under [the] land'. The concept behind that definition is twofold: first, in regard to change of use, one takes the land as it is and ascertains whether it has been put to a different use, and, secondly, and this is quite regardless of use, one has to ascertain whether the land itself has been changed by certain operations. I go further and say that, having regard to the prepositions describing the operations as 'in, on, over or under land', the concept, in that limb, must be whether the physical character of the land has been changed by operations in or on it, secondly, whether the physical characteristics of what is under the land have been changed, for example by mining operations under the land, and, thirdly, whether the physical characteristics of the air above the land have been changed by operations which can be described as operations over the land. The next question is what sort of operations, in the case of operations in or on the land, can be said to change the physical characteristics of the land. I do not think that there is any one test. The mere fact that something is erected in the course of a building operation which is affixed to the land does not determine the matter. Equally, the mere fact that it can be moved and is not affixed does not determine the matter. The position is really rather analogous to the problem with which one is faced in dealing with fixtures – What fixtures pass with the freehold? There is no one test; one looks at the erection, equipment, plant, whatever it is, and asks whether in all the circumstances, it is to be treated as part of the realty. So under this Act, as it seems to me, one has to look at the whole circumstances, including what is undoubtedly extremely relevant, the degree of permanency of the erection etc. in order to see whether the operation has been such as to constitute development.

The inspector, who has reported to and whose report has been accepted by the minister, states in his conclusions:

> 32. As regards the notice which alleges development by the 'erection of a coal-hopper and conveyor equipment', both items are on wheels and movable, although having regard to the nature of the site it would be difficult to move them and their movement is unlikely whilst employed as at present. Neither item is attached to the land.

> 33. I am advised [that has reference to the fact that he was sitting with a legal assessor] that in the circumstances of the case the installation of the hopper and conveyor did not involve development within the meaning of s. 12 of the Act of 1947.

On the face of it, therefore, he has not treated the mere fact that these two bits of equipment were on wheels as conclusive, nor has he treated it as conclusive that neither of them was affixed to or attached to the land. He has looked at the whole matter and said that, in all the circumstances, the installation did not involve development. In those circumstances, I find it quite impossible to say that the minister, who accepted that finding and recommendation, erred in law. No doubt in cases where the structure is affixed to the land it will in general be part of the land and constitute development. Equally, if the structure in question is intended to move about, and can be wheeled on and off the land, in general its installation will not constitute development, but in between one can envisage many situations in which the question may be finely balanced and it may be difficult to decide on which side the scales come down.

Counsel for the planning authority has said that, owing to the very wide definition of 'building' in s. 119 (1) of the Town and Country Planning Act, 1947, each of these pieces of equipment constitutes a building, and, if that is right, I should have thought that it would be abundantly clear that their erection would be a building operation. However, approaching the matter as I do, it seems to me that when the Act defines a building as including 'any structure or erection and any part of a building so defined', the Act is referring to any structure or erection which can be said to form part of the realty, and to change the physical character of the land. In other words, that argument carries the matter no further.

Having come to the conclusion that it is impossible to say that the minister erred in law, I would dismiss this appeal.[18]

Appeal dismissed.

Coleshill and District Investment Co Ltd v. Minister of Housing and Local Government [1969] 2 All E.R. 525

LORD MORRIS OF BORTH-Y-GEST: The present case relates to certain structures which are on a site having an area of about 8¾ acres near Hampton-in-Arden. The structures themselves occupy about five acres. They consist of a number of buildings or magazines constituting, and during the last war used as, an ammunition depot. There are six separate buildings; four of them were magazines and two of them explosives stores. Around each one of them blast walls were erected which were about nine feet in height. Against these walls there were substantial sloping embankments consisting of rubble and brick and ash and soil. They extended from near the top of the walls to a distance of eight to ten feet from their base. They were all grass covered.

The War Department released the depot in 1958. In 1962 the Minister determined that user of the buildings for purposes of commercial storage (for which permission was then sought) would not constitute or involve development. In the early part of 1966 the appellants decided that they would like to remove the embankments and the walls which were felt to be unnecessary and a cause of inconvenience when the buildings were used for civilian purposes. So as a first step they set about removing the embankments. . . .

Complaints were expressed to the respondent council, the Meriden Rural District Council, and following on them the clerk of the council wrote to the appellants pointing out that the operations being undertaken constituted development and that no application for planning permission had been made. An enforcement notice dated 30th March 1966, followed. The appellants were required to discontinue their operations and to restore the land to its prior condition. The appellants took the view that their operations did not constitute development and that no planning consent had been needed. So they appealed against the enforcement notice. . . .

The Minister upheld the notice and, refusing planning permission, dismissed the appeal. The appellants exercised (see s. 180 of the Act of 1962) their right to appeal to the High Court against the decision 'on a point of law'.

The appeal which, by a notice of motion dated 12th June 1967, they lodged was related also to the kindred question whether they could without planning permission take down the walls. The removal of the embankments had only been intended to be the first stage in the operation of completely removing the embankments and walls. So when the appellants were confronted with the question whether planning permission was needed to remove the embankments it was manifest that a similar question arose or would arise in regard to the walls. Pursuant to s. 43 of the Act they asked the respondent council, as the local planning authority, to determine that question. They so asked by a letter dated 4th July 1966. There was no determination within the prescribed time and accordingly the appellants appealed to the Minister. He gave his decision in a separate letter dated 16th May 1967. Other matters were involved but the only determination that is for present purposes relevant was that the removal of the walls would constitute or involve development and that planning permission was required. The appellants claiming to be 'dissatisfied with the decision in point of law' (see s. 181) therefore appealed to the High Court on this issue also. . . .

As appears from the judgments in the Court of Appeal argument was in that court presented on behalf of the appellants to the effect that demolition of a building is not development and that no proper distinction can be drawn between demolition of a building and demolition of part of a building. Arguments to the like effect were fully and attractively developed on behalf of the appellants in support of their appeal in this House. Supported by a careful and painstaking analysis of very many sections in the Act of 1962 the contention was urged that throughout the Act there is a clear, consistent and logical distinction between demolition and alteration. The term 'alteration' when used in the Act may sometimes denote development and sometimes corrective action: the term 'demolition', on the other hand, so the argument ran, is not used in the Act as denoting development but is only used in the context of corrective action or in reference to procedures for the preservation of special buildings. It was contended that there are very many indications pointing to the conclusion that Parliament has deliberately excluded demolition (as opposed to alteration from the scope of planning control and from the concept of development. Thus, the need to protect certain buildings (such as those of historic or architectural interest) from demolition is met by special provisions. I do no more than summarise some of the steps in a very carefully constructed argument. If the contention is once accepted that demolition is not development then further steps (or jumps) in the argument run as follows: removal of the embankments or of the walls is demolition: demolition is not development: therefore, the removals are not development. Alternatively, even if the embankments and walls were parts of the buildings, since, by the definition section (s. 221), a part of a building is a building, each removal of an embankment or of a wall is removal of a building: but as removal is demolition and as demolition is not development the result is that there was not and would not be any development.

My Lords, these arguments, however persuasive, must not compel a diversion from the facts as ascertained and from the statutory terms as defined. It was for the Minister to make certain decisions. The appeals to the High Court from his decisions are only on points of law. I have already expressed the view that it is quite impossible to assert that there was an invalidity in law in the findings of the Minister to the effect that the embankments and walls were integral parts of each of the buildings. It is next necessary to consider his findings relating (a) to the removal of the embankments, and (b) to the desired removal of the walls.

The definition of 'development' is set out in s. 12 (1) and s. 221 of the Act. Subject to certain exceptions, and leaving aside the making of any material change in the use of any buildings or other land, 'development' means the carrying out of building operations (which include rebuilding operations, structural alterations of or additions to buildings, and other operations normally undertaken by a person carrying on business as a builder) or of engineering operations (which include the formation or laying out of means of access to highways) or of mining operations or of other operations in, on, over or under land. 'Land' means any corporeal hereditament, including a building (which includes any structure or erection, and any part of a building so defined but not including plant or machinery comprised in a building). 'Erection' in relation to buildings includes extension, alteration and re-erection. Wide though the definition is, it does not include any and every operation on land. In s. 43 is set out the procedure to be followed when it is desired to have a determination whether planning permission is required. Any person who proposes to carry out 'any operations' on land may apply for a ruling. Had development meant 'any' operations in, on, over or under land there would not have been included in s. 12 (1) the words 'building, engineering, mining or other'. I think that the word 'other' must denote operations which could be spoken of in the context of or in association with or as being in the nature of or as having relation to building operations or engineering operations or mining operations.

It was submitted, on the one hand, that the underlying conception of development is that of change. A rival submission was that the conception is that of positive construction. Another submission was that everything is development which is within the framework of what a 'developer' (whoever so anonymous and elusive a person might be) would understand as being development. My Lords, as Parliament has denoted what is meant by development I do not think that we should be tempted to enlarge on or to depart from the statutory definition. It may well be that some operations which could conveniently be called demolition would not come within that definition. But we must not decide hypothetical cases. Here we have actual facts and findings. The Minister had a careful report before him. No suggestion has been made that the procedure deviated from that which is laid down in the Town and Country Planning (Inquiries Procedure) Rules 1965. The question that now arises is whether the Minister erred in law. He decided that the removal of the embankments was an engineering operation clearly falling within s. 12 (1) of the Act. He had certain primary facts found for him by the inspector. He did not differ from them. His conclusion from them was one that he could reasonably and properly make. It was really a conclusion of fact, and I can see no trace of any error of law. It was contended that the Minister was giving a wider meaning to 'engineering' than it could in accepted or current use bear. I cannot accept this. The findings relating to the dimensions of the various embankments show that the task of their removal was one of some magnitude. I do not think that it can be said that the Minister erred in law in coming to the conclusion that their removal was an engineering operation.

Similar considerations apply to the Minister's decision that the removal of the blast walls would constitute or involve development and that planning permission for their removal was required. I think that it is inherent in the Minister's decision that the operation of pulling down the concrete walls (which were an integral part of the various buildings) would involve structural alterations to buildings and would therefore constitute development within the statutory definition. He then proceeded to consider s. 12 (2). That subsection does not enlarge sub-s. (1); but if an operation is covered by sub-s. (1) it may be taken out of the definition of 'development' by sub-s. (2). The Minister was, I think, amply warranted in deciding that the alterations of the buildings which would result from taking down the walls would materially affect the external appearance of the buildings. No error of law is revealed.

In my view the Court of Appeal came to the correct conclusion. I would dismiss the appeal.

LORD WILBERFORCE: . . . 'Development' is a key word in the planners' vocabulary but it is one whose meaning has evolved and is still evolving. It is impossible to ascribe to it any certain dictionary meaning, and difficult to analyse it accurately from the statutory definition. . . .

It is relevant, I think, to recall that the Act of 1947 in Part 7 provided for the levying of development charges in respect broadly of any development for which planning permission was required. But there was an exemption from these charges (by Sch. 3) of specified types of development, one of which was 'the enlargement, improvement or other alteration' of certain buildings. No mention was made, in the exemptions, of any demolition, total or partial, of any building, yet had demolition been considered to be, or possibly to be, developments such a mention would surely have been included. The development charge provisions are not repeated in the Act of 1962, but it is still legitimate to look back to that of 1947 in construing the definition of 'development'. It is on the definitions now contained in s. 12 (1) and s. 221 of the Act of 1962 that the appellants seek an answer to the question whether demolition or, as the appellants call it, demolition per se, can constitute development.

Unfortunately I do not think that the question in this form can be answered because neither in the terminology of the Act, nor in its discernible policy as regards development, is it possible to segregate some identifiable operation, for which the description or label 'demolition' is apt and to say of it that it does or does not amount to development under the Act. References, indeed, appear, in various contexts, as, for example, in the sections of the Act dealing with listed buildings, or in those which contain enforcement provisions, to demolition, removal, restoration or re-instatement, but these bear meanings which, while appropriate for their subject-matter, carry no consistent implications as regards the meaning of expressions in other contexts. The Act seems to be drafted empirically rather than logically. One must start with s. 12. It is not easy to construe, and certain negative propositions are easier to state than positive.

1. I think it is clear that the exception stated in s. 12 (2) (*a*) cannot be used to establish the meaning of 'development' in s. 12 (1). Though I endorse the result of the judgments in the Court of Appeal, I cannot agree with passages in the judgments which extract from s. 12 (2) (*a*) the words 'materially affect the external appearance of the building', say that the works in question do this, and so conclude that they are development within the meaning of s. 12 (1). Qualifying words in an exception cannot be introduced into the rule so as to enlarge the scope of the rule: so, if an operation is not one of the kinds included in s. 12 (1) it cannot be made into one merely because a condition of exemption is not complied with. Relevantly, if demolition is not included in s. 12 (1), there is nothing for the exemption in s. 12 (2) (*a*) to bite on and the question whether the external appearance is affected has no relevance or application. What is development must be ascertained from s. 12 (1) aided by s. 221.

2. I do not find it possible to identify a genus in the words 'building, engineering, mining or other operations'. It is hardly good enough, when the Minister's decision is being reviewed for error of law, to say that 'other operations' must be construed ejusdem generis: that the genus need not be defined in detail, but that it includes only operations of a certain scale. I agree with the Court of Appeal and your Lordships in thinking both that this is not an adequate test (if it is a test at all) of the genus and that in any event it led the Divisional Court to the wrong result. No more satisfactory was the test suggested by the Minister who said that the genus was identified by the word 'development' – a word which he claimed everyone understands. But since the task on which we are engaged is to ascertain what 'development', as defined, means, it hardly seems possible to interpret the words by which 'development' is defined by reference to the, ex hypothesi, unknown meaning which 'development' bears. Such a process is one of levitation by intellectual bootstrap.

Finally, there is the appellants' suggestion that the relevant operations must at least be of a constructive character, leading to an identifiable and positive result. I think that this is near the heart of the matter, and that there is an important element of truth in the argument. I would accept, and think it important to emphasise, that the planning legislation should be approached with a disposition not to bring within its ambit, unless specific words so require, operations in relation to land which do not produce results of this kind, that is to say, results (I deal only with operations, not with use) of a positive, constructive, identifiable character. In my opinion, the appellants succeed in showing that neither the development of the legislation, nor the successive descriptions of 'development', nor the policy of control and, while it lasted, of charge on development, nor common sense or common expectation, require or suggest that the mere removal of a structure, or a building, or of a part of a building should be subject to the code. And I think that they derive important support for this argument from the Minister's circular no. 67 of 15th February 1949. . . .

The Minister's circular to be fully accurate, should then have said not that it (the demolition of a building) may form part of a building operation, but that, what might be described as demolition may fall within one of the specific types of operation described in s. 12 (1) and rank as development accordingly.

The Minister has held here that the removal of the embankments was an engineering operation, and that removal of the walls would be a building operation. Neither of these conclusions appears to me to have been inevitable; he might have held that both or either would be demolition and that neither the one fell under 'engineering' nor the other under 'building'. But both were marginal decisions given in relation to a very special case, and I think were open to him to make as he did. The Act, in general, as the subject-matter probably requires, is drafted with a wide mesh; its use of expressions, particularly those relating to building, demolition, alteration and the reverse of these operations, is not precise or consistent – as to engineering or mining there is no definition at all – and the sections conferring power of decision on the Minister, in particular s. 43, show that decisions on marginal questions as to development – what it is and what it is not – are intended to be left to him through or with his expert and professional staff. I am of opinion that the decisions he reached were within his permitted field and were not wrong in law. This leads to the conclusion that the appeal must be dismissed.

Appeal dismissed

Do you agree with Lord Wilberforce that 'the planning legislation should be approached with a disposition not to bring within its ambit unless specific words so require operations in relation to land which do not produce results of this kind, that is to say results (I deal with operations, not with use) of a positive constructive identifiable character'? Why? Is Lord Wilberforce's test of an operation which amounts to development the same as Lord Parker's test of a change in the physical character of the land?

In reaching its decision in *Coleshill* did the House of Lords observe Lord Morris's admonition that 'as Parliament has denoted what is meant by development I do not think we should be tempted to enlarge on or to depart from the statutory definition'? Why did the Coleshill and District Investment Co Ltd appeal to the House of Lords? What might be included in 'other operations' in section 22 (1) of the Act? Is the legal analysis that 'operations' must involve a permanent change in the physical character of the land in line with or opposed to what a planner might consider 'operations' involved?

(ii) Use

Development means *inter alia* the making of any material change in the use of any buildings or other land. On this, Hamilton writes:

What is a material change in use? Often in practice the question assumes the form of what is the permitted or established use of a particular property? This involves consideration of whether there has been a material change in the use of the property in the relevant period, and if there has, whether there is a planning permission for that change or whether it can no longer be challenged by enforcement proceedings i.e. the new use enjoys 'existing use rights' or has become 'established' [and therefore entitled to an established use certificate].

The law on what is a material change has developed quite considerably since 1948 and in some respects is not always as clear as it might be . . . Apart from the definition of development the legislation itself provides little help.[19]

(a) USE CLASSES ORDER

The courts and the Minister have between them created a complex structure of case law. What follows concentrates on the matters in that case law which appear to give most trouble in practice or on which the law is most recondite. First, the Use Classes Order may be considered, as it is of great importance when considering changes of use. Its primary purpose is to reduce the need for planning permission by providing that certain changes of use within particular classes of use 'shall not be deemed for the purposes of the Act to involve development of the land'. As might be expected, the Order itself has given rise to a certain amount of litigation and case law, dealing principally with the scope of certain classes, which cannot however be looked at here, but an issue of general importance was raised and decided in *City of London Corporation* v. *Secretary of State for the Environment*[20] which has a potentially limiting affect on the scope of the whole Order.

The Town and Country Planning (Use Classes) Order
S.I. 1972 No. 1385

2. – (2) In this order –
'the Act' means the Town and Country Planning Act 1971 :
'shop' means a building used for the carrying on of any retail trade or retail business wherein the primary purpose is the selling of goods by retail, and includes a building used for the purposes of a hairdresser, undertaker, travel agency, ticket agency or post office or for the reception of goods to be washed, cleaned or repaired, or for any other purpose appropriate to a shopping area, but does not include a building used as a funfair, amusement arcade, pin-table saloon, garage, launderette, petrol filling station, office, betting office, hotel, restaurant, snackbar or café or

premises licensed for the sale of intoxicating liquors for consumption on the premises;

'office' includes a bank and premises occupied by an estate agency, building society or employment agency, or (for office purposes only) for the business of car hire or driving instruction but does not include a post office or betting office;

Use Classes

3. – (1) Where a building or other land is used for a purpose of any class specified in the Schedule to this order, the use of such building or other land for any other purpose of the same class shall not be deemed for the purposes of the Act to involve development of the land.

(2) Where a group of contiguous or adjacent buildings used as parts of a single undertaking includes industrial buildings used for purposes falling within two or more of the classes specified in the Schedule to this order as Classes III to IX inclusive, those particular two or more classes may, in relation to that group of buildings, and so long as the area occupied in that group by either general or special industrial buildings is not substantially increased thereby, be treated as a single class for the purposes of this order.

(3) A use which is ordinarily incidental to and included in any use specified in the Schedule to this order is not excluded from that use as an incident thereto merely by reason of its specification in the said Schedule as a separate use.

SCHEDULE

Class I. – Use as a shop for any purpose except as: –
    (i) a shop for the sale of hot food;
    (ii) a tripe shop;
    (iii) a shop for the sale of pet animals or birds;
    (iv) a cats-meat shop;
    (v) a shop for the sale of motor vehicles.

Class II. – Use as an office for any purpose.

Class III. – Use as a light industrial building for any purpose.

Class IV. – Use as a general industrial building for any purpose.

[Classes V.–IX. Special Industrial Groups A–E.]

Class X. – Use as a wholesale warehouse or repository for any purpose.

Class XI. – Use as a boarding or guest house, or an hotel providing sleeping accommodation.

Class XII. – Use as a residential or boarding school or a residential college.

Class XIII. – Use as a building for public worship or religious instruction or for the social or recreational activities of the religious body using the building.

Class XIV. – Use as a home or institution providing for the boarding, care and maintenance of children, old people or persons under disability, a convalescent home, a nursing home, a sanatorium or a hospital.

Class XV. – Use (other than residentially) as a health centre, a school treatment centre, a clinic, a creche, a day nursery or a dispensary, or use as a consulting room or surgery unattached to the residence of the consultant or practitioner.

Class XVI. – Use as an art gallery (other than for business purposes), a museum, a public library or reading room, a public hall, or an exhibition hall

Class XVII. – Use as a theatre, cinema, music hall or concert hall.

Class XVIII. – Use as a dance hall, skating rink, swimming bath, Turkish or other vapour or foam bath, or as a gymnasium or sports hall.

City of London Corporation v. *Secretary of State for the Environment* (1973) 71 L.G.R. 28

TALBOT J: This is a notice of motion to quash a decision given by the first respondent on an appeal by the second respondents and contained in a letter dated January 11, 1971, to the second respondents. The applicants are the planning authority and make this application by virtue of the provisions of sections 176 and 179 of the Town and Country Planning Act, 1962.

By his decision, the first respondent granted planning permission for the use of part of the ground floor at 44 Bow Lane, London, E.C.4, as an employment agency subject to a condition that the premises should be used as an employment agency and for no other purpose. The ground of this application is that the condition is invalid in that it prohibits the use of the premises for purposes which would not involve development whether by reason of section 12(2) (*f*) of the Act of 1962 and the Schedule to the Town and Country Planning (Use Classes) Order, 1963, or otherwise.

The facts giving rise to this application are these: (1) On January 25, 1969, the second respondents applied for planning permission to use part of the ground floor of 44 Bow Lane as an employment agency. The premises had formerly been used for textile wholesales and as a warehouse. (2) On December 11, 1969, planning permission was refused. (3) On April 15, 1970, the second respondents appealed to the Minister of Housing and Local Government. (4) On September 24, 1970, an inquiry was held by an inspector. (5) On October 24, 1970, the inspector issued his report, and the first respondent subsequently made his decision and sent the letter of January 11, 1971.

The paragraphs of particular importance in that letter are paragraphs 3 and 4, which read:

> 3. While importance is attached to the local planning authority's policy which seeks to preserve shops and restaurants in the City of London, it is noted that the former user of the appeal property was textile wholesales and warehouse, that the ground floor and basement have been vacant for over two years, and that a permission granted in October, 1968, for the restaurant use of the ground floor and basement has not been implemented. In these circumstances the inspector's view is accepted that the appeal proposal would not result in a reduction of the city's actual existing total shop floor area. As to the visual and other effects of the proposal on the surrounding area, it is noted that

the window of the appeal building at street level is only eight feet wide and occupies less than half the frontage of the building, and that Bow Lane is very narrow, with a mixture of uses at street level, including shops, eating places, public houses, storage and offices. Although no reason is seen to disagree with the inspector's conclusions about the effect upon Cheapside and upon Bow Lane itself of an office use of the appeal premises, the view is held that the particular use proposed seems less likely to present a 'dead' front to the street than the generality of offices. While, therefore, for the above reasons it has been decided to accept the inspector's recommendation to allow the appeal, it is thought desirable to impose a condition to ensure that the premises are used only as an employment agency. 4. The Secretary of State's power to impose a condition of the kind referred to above was questioned during the course of the inquiry. The view is however held that section 18 (1) of the Act of 1962 (which authorises the imposition of conditions 'for regulating the development *or use*' of land) is wide enough to allow a condition restricting the use of land even where, by reason of section 12 (2) (*f*) of the Act and the Town and Country Planning (Use Classes) Order, 1963, or otherwise, a change of use prohibited by the condition might not involve development.

The question, therefore, for determination is whether the condition imposed upon the grant of the permission is invalid because it excludes any other use. The main argument for the applicants is that by the prohibition there are excluded uses for which no permission is required either because such use would not amount to development or by reason of the Town and Country Planning (Use Classes) Order, 1963, and that such prohibition is, therefore, *ultra vires*.

It was submitted by Mr Layfield that the planning legislation, and particularly the Town and Country Planning Act, 1947, and the consolidating Act of 1962, identifies activities in relation to land and its use which come under control. Section 12 (1) of the Act of 1962 defines as development certain operations on land and any material change of use of any buildings or land. Therefore, any change of use which is not material does not amount to development and come under control. Similarly, by section 12 (2) certain operations or uses of land are not to be taken as development within the Act, and in particular I refer to section 12 (2) (*f*), which reads: 'In the case of buildings or other land which are used for a purpose of any class specified in an order made by the Minister under this section, the use thereof for any other purpose of the same class.'

Therefore, by reference to the Town and Country Planning (Use Classes) Order, 1963, made by the Minister, it can be seen that Class II in the Schedule applies to 'use as an office for any purpose' and that a change of use from an employment agency (treated for the purpose of this application as an office) may be made to any other kind of office and not constitute development for which permission is required. . . .

The point, therefore, which emerges is that the condition imposed by the first respondent prohibits any change of use even if no development within the relevant Acts may be involved. This, Mr Layfield argues, is an imposition of control by the first respondent which goes outside the Acts and seeks to do that which Parliament expressly did not do, and, if there were such a power, one would expect to find it clearly set out in the Acts or that it existed by necessary implication. . . .

I will briefly summarise Mr Silkin's and Mr Glidewell's arguments on behalf of the respondents. Mr Silkin's point was that such a condition as that imposed here was an acceptable one as local planning authorities needed the power in order to be in a position to grant permission for one particular use without letting in other uses which might be detrimental. Section 17, he argued, gave a power which was expressed as widely as it could be and there was nothing in section 18 to derogate from the wide powers in section 17. Development and use were two separate activities, and the word 'use' in section 18 should be given its ordinary and natural meaning. The final words in section 18 (1) (a) which qualified the conditions regulating the use of any land were wide enough to permit the kind of conditions imposed here.

Mr Glidewell pointed to the dilemma which local planning authorities would be in if they did not have this power. They might be quite prepared to grant permission for a particular use but not if it let in a number of other uses. Refusal on those grounds, he submitted, could hardly be supported. He drew attention to the practical distinctions between different kinds of office use and claimed that a power to limit to a particular use was a beneficial construction of the Act. The use referred to in section 18 was the use which was permitted to be made of the land in the future, and the condition in this case was precisely directed towards that. Mr Glidewell submitted the contrary to Mr Layfield, viz., that in order to take away the effect of the very wide powers given by section 17 one would expect to find clear words in the statute. . . .

I now turn to the authorities. . . .[21]

There can be no doubt that the power to subject a planning permission to a condition is clearly expressed and that the condition may be such as the planning authority thinks fit to impose. It is clear from the authorities that the conditions must fairly and reasonably relate to the permitted development and must not be unreasonable. The planning statutes enable planning authorities, for the public advantage, to restrict the development and use of land, and they lay down a code by which this may be done. It seems to me that the question which I have to decide is whether the power to impose conditions is limited to conditions which do not impose controls beyond those laid down specifically in the Acts or whether the powers are so widely expressed that in a proper case a local planning authority may add further restrictions to meet local conditions. I do not think that the powers under sections 17 and 18 to make conditions are limited or confined by the other sections in the Act. Provided that a planning authority has regard to the development plan and to other material considerations and that the conditions are reasonable and fairly and reasonably relate to the permitted development, then I consider that the conditions may impose further restrictions even if this means a restriction on a use which would not amount to development.

The power would seem to me to be necessary so that the planning authorities can meet the varied and particular circumstances of the planning of a particular area, and in my view this power does not go beyond the Acts. In this case I can see the force of giving a planning authority the power to limit a use for office purposes to the use for a particular office use and this seems to me to be of the essence of good planning. Furthermore, to limit the use to a particular office use relates directly to the development or use permitted and relates to it fairly and reasonably. To decide otherwise would, in my opinion, impose a fetter on the powers of planning authorities which is not found in the Acts.

The motion is therefore refused.

(b) CHANGE OF USE[22]

To discover whether a change of use has taken place, one must determine what use a particular unit of land was previously put to, what its use is at the time of e.g. the service of an enforcement notice, and whether the new use represents a material change from the old. While this might seem a straightforward operation to planners and laymen, it has been complicated by legal analysis, in part caused by the fact of disputes between local planning authorities and landowners, in part a product of lawyers' traditional way of looking at land. This latter aspect of the evolution of the law must be elaborated on.

Lawson has written:

One of the main difficulties the student of property law encounters at the very threshold is this presence of abstractions where he expects to find physical objects. He very soon discovers that the property lawyer takes surprisingly little interest in land . . . but a great deal in abstract things such as the fee simple of land . . . The main reason why far more attention is devoted to abstractions than to physical objects is that, since they are creations of the human mind, they can be made to conform to patterns consciously chosen for their practical utility. . . .[23]

This preference for abstractions has been carried over into planning law particularly in this area. Just as an 'estate' in the land is an abstraction used by the lawyer for the (for him) more flexible and convenient handling of transactions about land, so the lawyer has invented the 'unit of development', an abstraction which enables him to handle the problems of change of use in a (for him) flexible and imaginative way reconciling the interests of the local planning authority and the landowner in so doing. Again, just as an easement is an abstraction which confers fairly precise rights, duties, privileges and liberties on particular parties in respect of a particular plot of land, though not so precise that disputes may not arise as to the extent of the easement, so the use of the land has become more and more abstract under the lawyers' guidance, still having reference to the actual physical use of a particular piece of land – a unit of development – but involving such non-physical considerations as a time element, and intention. The result inevitably is that, in law, a use of the land might be different from its actual physical use at the time of the service of an enforcement notice, a matter of some annoyance to the planner, and the layman, but quite logical to the lawyer for whom the abstraction is the reality and the physical reality almost an irrelevance.

An understanding of this evolution of abstraction in this area of planning law is the key to understanding what would otherwise be a series of rather strange cases. It is worth repeating that for the lawyer, abstraction is designed to help him resolve difficulties and settle disputes because he is then operating within a familiar frame of reference. It is also worth noting, particularly by those planners who might be tempted to criticise the lawyers for their abstractions, that the planners too are moving in the direction of more and more abstract planning. Model building and systems analysis are as far a cry from the real world in which the planned live as is the unit of development.

What factors then are relevant in trying to determine what is the use of land and whether that use has materially changed? The old Ministry of Town and Country Planning in Circular 67/49 – a circular still regarded by the Department of the Environment and commentators as pertinent – put the matter thus:

(ii) The Minister is advised that in considering whether a change is a material change, comparison with the previous use of the land or building in question is the governing factor and the effect of the proposal on a surrounding neighbourhood is not relevant to the issue. That is to say the question to be decided at this stage is not whether the change is one which ought to be permitted, but whether it can be controlled at all . . .

(iii) The introduction for the first time of the word material into that part of the definition of development which deals with change of use . . . is to make it clear that a proposed change of use constitutes development only if the new use is *substantially* different from the old. A change in *kind* will always be material – e.g. from house to shop or from shop to factory. A change in *degree* of an 'existing use' may be 'material' but only if it is very marked. For example, the fact that lodgers are taken privately in a family dwelling house would not in the Minister's view constitute a material change of use in itself so long as the use of the house remains substantially that of a private residence. On the other hand, the change from a private residence with lodgers to a declared guest house, boarding house or 'private' hotel, would be material. In the case of a change of use involving only part of a building, which would nevertheless continue to be used as a whole, the Minister takes the view that the question whether there is a material change of use should be decided in relation to the whole premises and not merely in relation to the part i.e. the point at issue is whether the character of the whole existing use will be substantially affected by the change which is proposed in a part of the building.

Does the use of such words as 'substantially', 'degree', 'kind' to explain what is meant by the word 'material' in the Act help towards an understanding of that legal term? Brown[24] has suggested that one should ask whether the change of use affects planning considerations, e.g. does it affect zoning proposals in the development plan, does it affect the amenities of the area? This is at variance with the circular's statement that 'the effect of the proposal on a surrounding neighbourhood is not relevant to the issue' of change of use. Can the circular be right? Is not Brown's test the type of test that a local planning authority would in practice apply?

To what extent are these tests the same as those used by the courts? Consider the following cases:

(i) CHANGE OF DEGREE OF USE

Birmingham Corporation v. *MHLG*
[1963] 3 All E.R. 669

LORD PARKER CJ: These are two appeals by the Corporation of the City of Birmingham, the local planning authority, against decisions of the Minister of Housing and Local Government quashing, on the ground that there had been no material change of use of land, enforcement notices served by the appellants. The facts were as follows.

So far as the appeal in which one Habib Ullah is respondent, there were two enforcement notices concerning two separate houses, No. 33 and No. 35, Mary Road, Stechford, which I believe is just outside Birmingham. Those two enforcement notices recited that there had been development consisting of the making of a material change in use by changing the use of each house from a single dwelling-house to what is described as 'a house-let-in lodgings'. . . .

At the inquiry before one of the minister's inspectors, the inspector had the assistance of a legal assessor, and from the inspector's report it appears that the legal assessor advised him to the following effect: 'After consideration of the arguments and authorities referred to at the inquiry, on the facts found by you I advise that development for the purposes of Part 3 of the Act of 1947 is *not* involved in either case under appeal.'

He then went on in this way:

Section 12 (3) (a) of the Act of 1947 does not apply, in my view, the houses not being used as two or more separate dwelling-houses. I note that you find that in No. 33 Mary Road cooking facilities are shared and apart from an additional sink in a room on the upper floor there is only one kitchen to serve the whole house. . . .

In No. 35 Mary Road the kitchen is shared, though there is a cooker on the landing of the upper floor for the use of Mr and Mrs Arthurs. On these facts I do not think there can be said to be separate 'dwelling-houses' within the houses. An analogy is provided by the cases of *Neale* v. *Del Soto*,[25] *Llewellyn* v. *Hinson*, *Llewellyn* v. *Christmas*,[26] and other cases arising under the Rent Restrictions Acts, though I appreciate that the considerations governing planning are not identical with those under the Rent Acts.

34. Secondly, the use is still residential, by long term or permanent occupants. Class XI in the Schedule to the Town and Country Planning (Use Classes) Order, 1950, is not applicable.

35. Thirdly, while No. 33 Mary Road is, to say the least, intensively used, in the matter of residential use, intensification of use would not appear to amount per se to a material change of use. It is possible that so many persons could be members of one family. I have noted that the Housing Act, 1961, provides local authorities with wide powers to deal with mischiefs arising from the multiple occupation of houses and on the present appeals housing rather than planning considerations appear to arise.

The inspector then says: In view of the legal advice quoted above I am bound to conclude that the appellant's submissions succeed on ground (d) of s. 33 (1) of the Act of 1960, that is, on the ground 'that what is assumed in the enforcement notice to be development did not constitute or involve development for the purposes of the said Part 3' of the Town and Country Planning Act, 1947.

The minister in his decision on appeal, dated Mar. 4, 1963, recited the inspector's report and the advice which he, the inspector, had received, and then concluded in this way: 'The minister accepts his inspector's recommendation for the reasons stated and accordingly allows the appeals. He hereby directs that the two enforcement notices under appeal, served on May 1, 1962, be quashed.'

The facts in the case of the respondent Khan are slightly different. There was one house concerned there, namely 14 Vicarage Road, King's Heath, about four miles out of Birmingham. . . . The inspector found at the time of his report that in addition to the respondent Khan there were five households living in the house, as I have already described. The inspector at the inquiry in this case did not have the assistance of a legal assessor, and he found (in para. 64 of his report) this:

To my mind the degree of letting is such that the character of the building as a private residence has been changed. The appellant did not live in this house at all until this summer, and then he only occupied one room until a week before the inquiry and even now he only occupies two rooms and a kitchen. The remainder of the house is let in furnished rooms or sets of rooms to tenants who pay a weekly rent.

He concluded by saying that if he was right in thinking that this amounted to development for the purposes of Part 3 of the Town and Country Planning Act, 1947, then he did not think that it was a case in which planning permission ought to be granted.

The minister by his decision of Mar. 15, 1963, again recited the findings of the inspector, and it is to be observed that this decision was made some eleven days after the decision in the case of Habib Ullah and no doubt the minister had it well in mind. He says that he

has considered the facts of the case and the arguments adduced at the hearing. He notes that the two rooms at the back of the ground floor comprise separate living accommodation with its own cooking facilities and water supply (though with use, in common with others, of lavatory accommodation) and he considers that on an analogy with the cases decided by the courts under s. 12 (2) of the Increase of Rent and Mortgage Interest (Restrictions) Act, 1920, this is a separate dwelling-house within 12 (3) (a) of the Town and Country Planning Act, 1947. It does not seem to him, however, that the terms of the enforcement notice are apt to cover this change of use. As regards the rest of the house the minister considers that the lettings do not involve a use within Class XI in the Schedule to the Town and Country Planning (Use Classes) Order, 1950. The use is still residential; the lettings do not include separate kitchen facilities. The minister notes that the inspector considers that the character of the building as a private residence has been changed and he (the minister) appreciates that the present overcrowding has introduced a most unpleasant degree of squalor and noise into a respectable neighbourhood. But the number of persons living in the house or the way in which they behave are not in his opinion factors making for a material change of use from the previous use; both uses are residential. On the facts, therefore, the minister is satisfied that no material change of use is involved in this case. He concludes that the appeal succeeds under s. 33 (1) (d) of the Act of 1960. He directs that the enforcement notice be quashed.

Having stated those facts, it will be seen that in each of these appeals the prior use of the houses concerned was that of a single private residence. It will, however, be seen that in each case at a time admittedly within the four-year period prior to the service of the enforcement notices, those houses came into multiple occupation, being let in parts to numbers of households who paid rent. It also appears that in each case the minister considered first, whether there had been a change of use within s. 12 (3) (a) of the Act of 1947; secondly, whether the case was covered by the Use

Classes Order and thirdly, whether since the houses were originally residential and since they remained residential in the sense that they were houses in which people dwelt, there could, therefore, as a matter of law, be no material change of use.

In my judgment these cases really depend on whether the minister is right in the view which he took as to the last-mentioned consideration. . . .

The minister's approach was, I think, clearly this. If one finds a dwelling-house in the sense of a house in which people dwell, then, subject possibly to intensification of user, there can as a matter of law be no material change of use albeit the purpose for which that dwelling-house is used may be wholly different from what it was before.

Counsel for the minister argues for that contention on two grounds, if I understand him rightly. He first of all says that the minister is not concerned, as I think everybody would agree, with the characteristics of the particular people living there, whether they have more children or less children, unruly children or well-behaved children, and matters of that sort. He goes further and he says that, under this planning control, the minister is in no way concerned with the questions. How many people are occupying the house? How many families? What facilities should be provided for them? Matters of that sort, so he points out, are dealt with in other codes of legislation, Public Health Acts and Housing Acts. In particular, he refers to the Housing Act, 1936, from which, incidentally, and from other Housing Acts, this expression 'house-let-in-lodgings' which appears in the enforcement notices, is clearly lifted. Further, s. 6 (3) of the Housing Act, 1936, dealt specifically with this category, 'houses-let-in-lodgings', and enabled the local authority to provide by regulations, directions, and the like for controlling the number of persons in those houses and matters of that sort.

Again, in the Housing Act, 1957, in s. 36, reference is made to houses-let-in-lodgings and the control that can be imposed. I entirely agree with all of that, but it does not seem to me that what is sought to be done here by way of planning control in any way overlaps the control which can be exercised under the Housing Acts or the Public Health Acts. Those Acts are accepting the fact that there is a house-let-in-lodgings and they impose a control over it. The planning control, if it applies, is dealing with quite a separate thing, namely preventing a house from becoming a house-let-in-lodgings.

The other matter on which counsel for the minister relies is really based on this, that the Town and Country Planning Act, 1947, itself does not refer to anything other than dwelling-houses. He says that means houses in which people dwell, and that one cannot as it were divide up that genus into separate forms of dwelling-houses used for different purposes. In that connexion he refers to s. 12 (2) (d) of the Act of 1947 which refers to dwelling-houses, and of course to s. 12 (3) (a), with which I have already dealt. That, however, is clearly by no means conclusive. Because Parliament intended that certain considerations should apply to the whole genus of dwelling-house, it does not follow that one could not, as it were, divide up the genus into various species when considering whether there has been a change of use. For my part I feel that it would be very odd if one could not go further than merely determine that a house was residential, and that that was an end of the matter.

This sort of case has arisen not in regard to dwelling-houses but in regard to other premises in various cases. In *East Barnet UDC* v. *British Transport Commission*[27] I was considering this sort of point. In dealing there with a particular parcel of land I said:

> The question there is whether, when the second respondents went into occupation of those two parcels, there was a use of the land for a purpose which was different from the purpose for which the land was last used. The question immediately arises as to what meaning one attaches to a 'purpose different'. Does one consider the general purpose or does one have to descend to the particular and say: Was the particular purpose different?

That is exactly the point here in regard to dwelling-houses. Then I went on: To take an example, is the purpose for which a shop is occupied the purpose of a retail shop quite generally, or is it the narrower purpose of being used as a retail shop for the sale of a particular commodity? . . . I end by saying:

> It [i.e. whether there has been a material change of use] is a question of fact and degree in every case and, when the matter comes before this court by way of Case Stated, the court is unable to interfere with a finding of the justices on such a matter unless, . . ., it must be said that they could not properly have reached that conclusion.

The matter, however, is I think made clear by the Town and Country Planning (Use Classes) Order, 1950, itself. Class I of that order is dealing with use as a shop for any purpose except as a fried fish shop, etc.; that is clearly contemplating that the fact that premises remain a shop after the alleged change is not conclusive but that one must consider whether the purpose for which the shop has been used has changed. The same is to be found in Class II, 'use as an office for any purpose', and of course Class XI itself to which I have already referred, 'use as a boarding or guest house, a residential club, or a hotel providing sleeping accommodation', all of which can loosely be called residential, or houses where people dwell, and yet this contemplates that but for the Use Classes Order there would be a development of the house by a change of its use for one purpose to its use for another.

In my judgment the minister erred in law in saying that because these houses remained residential, or remained dwelling-houses in which people dwelt, there could not be a material change of use. Whether there has been in any of these cases a material change of use is, therefore, a matter of fact and degree and one for the minister. I cannot, however, fail to observe that the inspector in *Khan's* case, as it seems to me, clearly felt that what had occurred there was a material change, assuming that as a matter of law he was not debarred from considering it.

In my judgment each case must go back to the minister with the opinion of this court, and it will then be for him to find whether what had occurred in each of these houses does amount to a material change in use, albeit that they remain dwelling-houses in the sense of houses in which people dwell. He will of course take into consideration the use to which they are put, that a private dwelling-house has come into multiple paying occupation, or perhaps put another way, that a house which has been used for a private family is now being used by a man for gain by letting out rooms.

I would only say this, that I hope nothing that I have said in regard to the powers of the minister to amend the enforcement notice would suggest that, if he thinks it is necessary, he should not amend the development complained of, namely houses-let-in-lodgings, to what he may find is the true development here, the change of use to multiple paying occupation.

For these reasons I think that these appeals succeed and that the cases should be referred back to the minister for his further decision.[28]

Appeal allowed.

Was there a material change of use of the two houses involved in the above case? If so, what was it that had changed? How can the Minister's original decision – that there could not be a material change of use – be reconciled with the statement in Circular 67/49 that a change from a private residence with lodgers to a boarding house would be material when taken in conjunction with the inspector's findings of fact on the two houses?

(ii) ABANDONMENT OF USE

Hartley v. *MHLG* [1969] 3 All E.R. 1658

LORD DENNING MR: This case raises a short point under our planning legislation; it concerns a site in Cumberland between Workington and Cockermouth, the Bridgefoot petrol filling station. . . . There were three phases in the history of this site. During the *first* phase, up to 1961, the site was used for two purposes, one as a petrol filling station, the other for the display and sale of cars. Then a Mr Fisher took over the premises and continued to use the site for both purposes, but he died within a few months. After his death in 1961 his widow ran the business with the help of her son aged 19. This started the *second* phase. The widow and son did not sell cars. They continued only the business of a filling station. (The widow would not let her son sell cars, as he was not experienced in the business. One or two were sold, but there were no sales of such significance to amount to a user of the premises for the purposes of sales.) This second phase continued for some four years. During this phase the petrol filling business used the same part of the premises as it had always done; but the part which had previously been used for selling cars was not used at all. That part was disused for those four years. Then in 1965 we come to the *third* phase. Mrs Fisher sold the shop site to the appellant. He started to sell cars in a big way. He prospered exceedingly. He sold some 350 cars a year.

The planning authority thought that the appellant, by embarking on selling cars at this site, was making a material change in the use of the land, without getting planning permission. So they served on him an enforcement notice requiring him to cease to use the site for car selling, and to use it only for the petrol filling. The reason for their objection was a planning consideration. The road beside this site carried a lot of traffic and had an awkward bend. It was very undesirable to have a car selling business there on this scale. There was an inquiry before an inspector, and an appeal to the Minister who made these findings:

> It is considered on the evidence that up to the time of Mr Fisher's purchase of the petrol station in March 1961 there was a dual use of the red land as a petrol filling station and for the display and sale of cars. [Then as to the second phase:] It is considered that during this period (March 1961–February 1965) the use for car sales had ceased, the intention being to cease it indefinitely. By 1965, if not in 1961, the use for car sales had been abandoned, and the use of the site was that of a petrol filling station only.

On that ground the Minister held that the enforcement notice was good. The appellant appealed to the Divisional Court, and by leave to us.

Counsel for the appellant argued that a cessation of use is not a change of use. A man who has used a site for the business of selling cars might cease that user altogether and not use the site for any purpose. He would not have to get planning permission to stop selling cars. If, therefore a cessation of use is not a change of use, then, said counsel, neither is a resumption of use. Such a man could, he said, at any time resume the previous use for selling cars without getting planning permission. That sounds logical enough. In support of it, counsel quoted LORD PARKER CJ in *McKellen* v. *Minister of Housing and Local Government*[29]: It is of course quite plain that a change from A. to X. and then from X. to A. does not involve development, either way, if X is completely nil, no use at all. But if X. is a use, then the change from A. to X. may involve development, and the change from X. to A. may involve development.

Counsel for the appellant relied on the first sentence of that quotation. If such be the position when a man ceases a single use, said counsel, then it is the same when he ceases one of the two uses in a dual use. A cessation of one of the uses does not require planning permission. Nor, said counsel, does a subsequent resumption of that one use.

I do not accept this argument. I think that, when a man ceases to use a site for a particular purpose, and lets it remain unused for a considerable time, then the proper inference may be that he has abandoned the former use. Once abandoned, he cannot start to use the site again, unless he gets planning permission; and this is so, even though the new use is the same as the previous one.

The material time is when he starts on the new use. One has to ask at that time whether there was then a material change of use – from a non-use into a positive use. Take this very case. In 1965 the appellant started to use the site for selling cars. That was a new use. It was a change from a non-use into a use for selling cars. In needs planning permission – unless the appellant can say that the previous use was never abandoned.

The question in all such cases is simply this: has the cessation of use (followed by non-use) been merely temporary, or did it amount to an abandonment? If it was merely temporary, the previous use can be resumed without planning permission obtained. If it amounted to abandonment, it cannot be resumed unless planning permission is obtained. I said as much in *Webber* v. *Minister of Housing and Local Government*[30] and in *T. A. Miller, Ltd* v. *Minister of Housing and Local Government*[31]. Abandonment depends on the circumstances. If the land has remained unused for a considerable time, in such circumstances that a reasonable man might conclude that the previous use had been abandoned, then the tribunal may hold it to have been abandoned.

Counsel for the appellant submitted that in this case there was not sufficient grounds to find abandonment. But I think that the Minister was quite entitled to find as he did, that by 1965 the use for car selling had been abandoned. So when the appellant in that year started the car selling business again, it was a material change of use, and he needed planning permission. He had not got it, so the enforcement notice was perfectly valid. I would, therefore, dismiss the appeal.

Appeal dismissed.

What factors are or should be taken into account to determine whether a use has been abandoned? Consider the relative importance of the following factors: the intentions of the user, the length of time the use has not taken place; the reasons for the original cesser of use. Would there be any circumstances in which mere cesser of use could of itself amount to a material change of use so that planning permission was needed to continue the sole use? If a bookshop offered its customers coffee and cake and, finding that they preferred bodily to intellectual sustenance, wound up the bookshop but continued the coffee and cakes on the same scale as before, would the owner of the bookshop need planning permission? If so, and if he were then to be refused permission to use his shop for the sale of coffee and cake, would it be a correct analysis of his situation to say that he was being made to continue a bookshop which he did not wish to do in order to be able to serve coffee and cake? Could he recommence selling books without permission?

(iii) EXTINGUISHING THE USE

Petticoat Lane Rentals v. *Secretary of State for the*
Environment [1971] 2 All E.R. 793

WIDGERY LJ: This is an appeal by Petticoat Lane Rentals Ltd from a decision of what was then the Ministry of Housing and Local Government, which decision was given on 21st May 1970, upholding the validity of an enforcement notice served under the Town and Country Planning Act 1962 by the Tower Hamlets London Borough Council on the appellants. The notice referred to an area of land on the ground floor of a newly erected building called United Standard House in Middlesex Street within the borough of Tower Hamlets. It was recited that this area on the ground floor of that building had been the subject of a material change of use by using it for the purpose of siting and carrying on trade from market stalls without the grant of permission. The notice required the appellants to discontinue that allegedly irregular use.

The circumstances of the case can be quite shortly recited, and I think in the end can be narrowed to a very fine point. This newly erected building, United Standard House, is on a site in Middlesex Street which was covered with buildings before the second world war, but which buildings were very badly damaged by bombing. In due course the site was cleared and it remained as a cleared site for a substantial number of years. We are told by counsel for the appellants that during that period the appellants had a lease of the site, and that they used it by letting out stall spaces to various street traders who wished to carry on business there and that useful activity continued until a time came when the site was to be redeveloped by the erection of a new building. In 1963 planning permission was granted for such redevelopment. It was granted to Richard Costain, the builders, and the development authorised was in these terms:

> Redevelopment of the sites bounded by Middlesex Street, Goulston Street and site of Boars Head Yard, Stepney, by the erection of a building comprising office, warehousing, supermarket and car parking and loading area (to be used for market trading on Sundays), and for the formation of a new road linking Middlesex Street and Goulston Street and for the formation of a turning and loading space off Goulston Street.

... since the completion of the building and, one gathers, up to the present time, this area on the ground floor within the confines of the building, in the sense it is underneath the main development above, has been used by market traders on Sundays in accordance with the permission, and on weekdays, may I say at once, not in accordance with the permission. In these circumstances it was incumbent on the planning authority to require the discontinuance of the street trading on weekdays. Counsel for the appellants puts his case in very strong terms. His argument comes down to this. What is alleged against the appellants, he says, is that they have made a material change of the use of this land by using it for street trading. He says that that allegation is factually unsound because the area has been used for trading of this kind for many years prior to the re-development. He says that the facts do not justify the allegation that there has been any change, let alone material change, in the use to which this area has been put throughout the whole of the relevant period. The inspector's view, which was adopted by the Minister, and which is the basis of counsel for the Secretary of State's argument to us today, is that the effect in law of the erection of this new building pursuant to the planning permission to which I have referred has been to, and I quote the Minister's words: 'extinguish the former use of the site.' His argument is that on the history which I have related, one is now faced with a building which has an entirely new planning history, that is to say really a building with no planning history, starting afresh from the time when it was completed. He says that the previous use rights and activities are all extinguished by the rebuilding and that, it is submitted, is a complete answer to the appellants' case.

This question of how far existing planning rights can be lost by the occupier obtaining and implementing an inconsistent planning permission has not as yet been fully developed in the authorities. One goes first of all to a decision of this court, *Prossor* v. *Minister of Housing and Local Government*.[32] That is a case of a petrol service station on a main road where the occupier of the petrol service station sought and obtained planning permission to rebuild the petrol station. He was given such permission and an express condition was attached to the permission to the effect that no retail sales other than the sale of motor accessories should be carried out on the site. In fact, having let the establishment, the occupier began to exhibit secondhand cars for sale on the site, which was clearly a breach of the condition if the condition was effective. It was argued in favour of the occupier that he was enabled to do this because there was a continuing and unbroken use of the land for the sale of secondhand cars, and in his contention the fact that he had had a new and inconsistent planning permission and had implemented it did not destroy that right. LORD PARKER CJ having dealt with a number of arguments not relevant to the present appeal, put the matter thus:[33]

> Assuming ... that there was at all material times prior to April, 1964 [the date of the rebuilding], an existing use right running on this land for the display and sale of motor cars, yet by adopting the permission granted in April, 1964, the appellant's predecessor as it seems to me, gave up any possible existing use rights in that regard which he may have had. The planning history of this site, as it were, seems to me to have begun afresh on April 4th, 1964, with the grant of this permission, a permission which was taken up and used, and the sole question here is: has there been a breach of that condition?

Some argument has been directed to the fact that in *Prossor* v. *Minister of Housing and Local Government* the use of the land for the display of second-hand motor cars was expressly prohibited by a condition of the planning permission. For my part I do not think that that is a relevant factor at all. I think that precisely the same result would have appeared in *Prossor*'s case if, instead of granting permission for use as a garage and then attaching a condition to take out the use for secondhand car sales which would otherwise have been included in the grant, the draftsman had chosen in rather more complicated phraseology to specify precisely what could be done and had simply left out the sale of secondhand cars. I do not therefore regard the fact that there was an express prohibition as being anything more in that case than an indication of the fact that the draftsman found it easier to express his wishes in that way. . . . . The position as I see it is that although *Prossor*'s case had not been overruled or even seriously criticised, it is a case which we should apply with some little care.

For my part I also think that it was entirely correctly decided, but I think in extending and applying it we should tread warily and allow our experience to guide us as that experience is obtained. Accordingly I decline to use any general terms in saying what *Prossor*'s case decides or how it applies to the present situation, but I am quite confident that the principle of *Prossor*'s case can be applied where, as here one has a clear area of land subsequently developed by the erection of a building over the whole of that land. Where that happens, and it certainly happened in the case before us, one gets in my judgment an entirely new planning unit created by the new building. The land as such is merged in that new building and a new planning unit with no planning history is achieved. That new planning unit, the new building, starts with a nil use, that is to say immediately after it was completed it was used for nothing, and thereafter any use to which it is put is a change of use, and if that use is not authorised by the planning permission, that use is a use which can be restrained by planning control. As in *Prossor*'s case it seems to me to make no difference whether the old use sought to be restored was expressly extinguished by the new planning permission, or whether it was merely omitted from the terms of grant in that permission. The fact that it is not authorised means it is something which necessarily can be controlled because it is a change of use from the nil use which follows the erection of a new planning unit.

Counsel for the appellants has strenuously argued that notwithstanding the doctrine in *Prossor*'s case and the considerations to which I have referred, the ground floor should retain in some way the existing use to which the old building site has been put. He also seeks to obtain some assistance from the fact that the ground floor in the present case was not enclosed. With the realism which his argument shows he realised that it would be very difficult to argue that with an enclosed ground floor the pre-development use of the open space had survived, but he says that as the ground floor is not enclosed, as it is therefore still an open space in one sense, then those pre-development uses survive. I can see no substance in that argument at all. Whether the ground floor is enclosed or not enclosed, it is part of the new building. The new building embraces the land and accordingly it is a new entity; the conclusion is that to which I have referred. I would therefore dismiss the appeal.   *Appeal dismissed.*

(iv) ANCILLARY USES

Hartley raises another matter besides abandonment; ancillary or incidental uses and dual uses, a matter which Brown comments

has become increasingly prominent in the administration of planning legislation. It is a principle which results in there sometimes being development by a material change of use without there being any change in the nature of the particular use of premises, or conversely, no material change where there is an apparent change in the nature of the particular use.
. . . The case where one use is ancillary to another, and therefore is part of that other use and not a separate, independent use, is to be distinguished from the case where there are two independent uses of the same land.[34]

That in turn is to be distinguished from a situation 'where part of an area which has been used for a purpose becomes used for some distinct purpose; that part of the land can be regarded as having become a separate unit of land with a separate use, notwithstanding that the lands are still held in one ownership or management'. Why ought all these issues to be kept distinct? How are the distinctions to be discovered?

Percy Trentham v. *Gloucestershire County Council*
[1966] 1 All E.R. 701

LORD DENNING MR: In Gloucestershire there was a farmer who farmed seventy-five acres. He had a farmhouse and farm buildings. Some of the farm buildings were used for livestock, cattle and chickens; others for housing the dead stock, such as tractors and machinery, and corn and hay. This farmer bought an adjoining farm and he found that he did not need this farmhouse and outbuildings. He transferred everything to his new farmhouse and outbuildings on the other farm. He sold off this farmhouse and farm buildings to a firm of civil engineering contractors called G. Percy Trentham Ltd. The appellants applied for planning permission to turn the farm buildings over to the use of their contractors' business. They did not get permission. So they decided to use some of the buildings for their business without planning permission at all. They realised that they could not use the livestock buildings, because they did not want them for livestock; but they thought that they could use the dead stock buildings for their own dead stock – if I may use that expression. Without getting any permission at all, they used some nine of these buildings for the storage of building materials, plant and equipment. I need not pause over some of the farm buildings, which were previously used for cider and afterwards for storage. It is sufficient for the question in hand to say that there was a block of buildings which were previously used for agricultural purposes for the storage of farm machinery and equipment. Now the appellants wish to store in them building materials for their contractors' business. Similarly with the farmhouse. The farmer had had a couple of rooms which he used as an office on one or two days a week. The appellants thought that they would turn some five rooms into offices. They did so without any planning permission at all.

The planning authority in December, 1963, issued an enforcement notice against the appellants requiring them to discontinue the use of the land for offices and storage of plant and materials of building and civil engineering contractors, and requiring them to remove therefrom all office equipment and such plant and materials. The ground of that enforcement notice was that the appellants had made a material change of use by changing the use to these new purposes. On getting that enforcement notice the appellants appealed under s. 46 of the Town and Country Planning Act, 1962, to the Minister. An inquiry was held and the inspector reported against them. The Minister in his letter of decision also found against them. The Divisional Court of the Queen's Bench Division upheld the Minister. The appellants appeal to this court. They do not appeal about the use for offices. They only appeal on the use for storage.

Under the planning law if a person desires to make a material change in the use of any buildings or land, he must get permission from the planning authority unless he can bring himself within one of the exceptions. The appellants say that they do not need permission because they come within the exception in s. 12 (2) (f) of the Town and Country Planning Act, 1962. That exception says that the following use of land does not involve development, that is to say: (f) in the case of buildings or other land which are used for a purpose of any class specified in an order made by the Minister under this section, the use thereof for any other purpose of the same class. That sentence needs interpretation before anyone can understand it. To do so, you must look at the Minister's order made under it, namely, the Town and Country Planning (Use Classes) Order 1963. The order specifies in Class I 'shops'. The exception means that it is not 'development' for a person to change the use from one kind of shop to another kind of shop. A man can change it from a butcher's shop to a baker's shop without permission. He can freely switch over from one use to another so long as it is within the same class. The relevant class here is Class X. It specifies 'use as a wholesale warehouse or repository for any purpose'. It follows that if a building or other land has been used previously as a repository for any purpose, it can be used again as a repository for any purpose without permission. For instance, if it was used as a repository for storing furniture, it can be changed to a repository for storing archives.

The appellants argue that they come within Class X. I cannot agree and, for this simple reason. When the farmer used these farm buildings for his farm purposes, they were not a repository within the ordinary meaning of that word. A repository means a place where goods are stored away, to be kept for the sake of keeping them safe, as part of a storage business. It does not cover storage space which is used by a shopkeeper as merely ancillary to his shop. So here it does not cover these farm buildings, which were merely ancillary to the use of the farm. The farmer used them to house his tractors, corn or hay, but they were not a repository. On that ground alone the appellants cannot pray in aid the Use Classes Order.

Even if the appellants were able to say that these nine buildings were a 'repository', I do not think that they could sever them from the rest of the farmhouse and farm buildings. In applying the Town and Country Planning (Use Classes) Order 1963, one must consider the whole of the unit which is being used. I think that DIPLOCK LJ indicated the right test towards the end of the argument. One should look at the whole area on which a particular activity is carried on, including uses which are ordinarily incidental to or included in the activity. Thus, if there is a baker's shop with a dwelling house above and a store for flour outside, the whole is one unit. It can be switched to a butcher's shop with a dwelling house above and a cold store for meat, without getting permission.

Applying the test in this case, the unit to be considered is the whole unit which comprises the farmhouse and farm buildings, including the dead stock buildings, the livestock buildings and the yard where wagons and carts go in and out to load and unload. That is the unit to be considered. That unit was not 'a wholesale warehouse or repository' in any sense.

On both of these grounds I think that there is no ground for interfering with the decision of the Divisional Court. *Appeal dismissed.*

(v) TWO USES

Webber v. *MHLG* [1967] 3 All E.R. 981

LORD DENNING MR: Mr Webber is a farmer at Axe Farm, Axmouth, near Seaton. He has a four-acre field. Since April 1960, this field has been used extensively for camping in the summer season between Easter and the end of September. The campers bring caravans, tents and dormobiles to the field, but they are removed at the end of the summer. In the winter months the field has been used for grazing cattle, except on Saturdays, when it is used as a football pitch. It is also used on occasion for flower shows and other local events, but not frequently. On Sept. 3, 1965, the Devon County Council who are the planning authority, served on Mr Webber an enforcement notice requiring him to remove caravans, tents and dormobiles within twenty-eight days. He appealed. The Minister dismissed his appeal, and the Divisional Court upheld the Minister's decision. He now appeals, with leave, to this court.

Mr. Webber claims that he is a 'four-year man'. He says that he has used the field in the same way since 1960, for more than four years; that there has been no material change of use during that time; and that it is too late for the planning authority to serve him with an enforcement notice (see s. 45 (1) and (2) of the Town and Country Planning Act, 1962). The planning authority say that he is a 'six-months man'. There has been a material change of use, they say, every six months. In April of each year there is a change of use from agriculture to camping; in September of each year there is a change back from camping to agriculture. The latest change was in April 1965, from agriculture to camping. No permission was obtained for it. Accordingly, they say that the enforcement notice of September 1965, was given within six months of this development and was well within time.

There have been several cases on the subject of seasonal use of land. A distinction seems to have been drawn between 'non-user' and 'different user'. If a piece of land is used during the summer months as a caravan site and is *not used* at all during the winter months, then it is accepted on all hands that there is no material change of use. After it has been used for four years in that way, the occupier cannot be disturbed by an enforcement notice (see *Biss* v. *Smallburgh Rural District Council*[35] per DAVIES LJ and per RUSSELL, LJ). It is said, however, that if the occupier used it during the summer months for a caravan site and during the winter months for a *different* purpose, such as a football ground or for agriculture, then there is a material change of use. If he has not obtained planning permission, he can be disturbed by an enforcement notice. That seems to have been what was said in *Hamblett* v. *Flintshire County Council*[36] and in *Hawes* v. *Thornton Cleveleys Rural District Council*[37].

I do not think that this distinction between 'non-user' and 'different user' is valid. As I read the Act of 1962, we must look at the 'purpose' for which the land is 'normally used', or, I would add (since singular includes plural) the 'purposes' for which it is normally used, see s. 12 (4) and s. 13 (2), (3), (5), (6) and (8) of the Act of 1962. The 'normal use' of a piece of land is to be found by looking at its use from year to year over a considerable period. If you were to ask Mr. Webber: 'What do you normally use this field for?', he would reply: 'In the summer months for camping and in the winter months for grazing'. In short, for two purposes. So long as he continues that normal use from year to year, there is no material change of use. Similarly, when a shopkeeper in a seaside town has a forecourt. During the summer he places stalls on it for selling goods, but during the winter he leaves it empty. The normal use of the forecourt is for two purposes, for access to the shop throughout the year and for trading during the summer months. So long as he continues that normal use from year to year, there is no material change of use.

By way of contrast from the 'normal use', there is the 'occasional use' of a piece of land. This arises when it is used on occasions for a purpose other than its normal use, such as for a football match, a flower show or a fête. So long as these do not amount to more than twenty-eight days in the year, the occupier is covered by the general development order. If he allows it to be used for more than twenty-eight days, he would need planning permission unless it goes back to July 1, 1948, in which case he would be covered by s. 13 (3) of the Act of 1962.

Applying these considerations to the present case, it is plain on the facts that ever since 1960 the normal use of this four-acre field has been a seasonal use, camping during the summer and grazing during the winter. That normal use continued for more than four years. The enforcement notice in September, 1965, came too late. I can well understand how the Divisional Court came to an opposite conclusion. They had before them the dicta as to seasonal use in the cases of *Hamblett* and *Hawes* which drew the distinction which I have mentioned in the off season between 'non-user' and 'different user'. Once that distinction is seen to be erroneous, those dicta cannot be supported.

I would only add that if the normal use is abandoned for a time, a resumption of it afterwards would need planning permission. In this case, as I have said, the normal use has continued for more than four years. The enforcement notice came too late.

I would allow the appeal accordingly.[38] *Appeal allowed.*

Do you agree with the Court of Appeal in *Webber* that the distinction between 'non-user' and 'different user' is not valid? Why? What is there about section 22 of the Act of 1971 which would cause one to deduce that 'we must look at the "purpose" for which land is "normally used"'?

A good deal of attention is paid by the courts to the character of the use of the land. What do they mean by this? Is a change in the character of the use the same as a substantial change of use, a change of degree, or a change of kind? Why is there this constant chopping and changing in the use of language to try and describe what tests to apply to the question of change of use? In *East Barnet UDC* v. *British Transport Commission*,[39] Lord Parker CJ accepted that the question of whether there had been a material change of use 'must depend on all the circumstances and was a question almost entirely of degree and of fact for the Minister'. Does a multitude of differing tests, expressed in differing language help the Minister (now the Secretary of State) to decide that question of degree and fact? Where does the element of law come in?

On the basis of the above cases, are the courts complying with Diplock LJ's advice that: 'The Town and Country Planning Act (1971) is about how people may use their land. Words and expressions in it should be given their ordinary meaning unless it is clear that some other and esoteric meaning is intended?'[40]

(vi) THE UNIT OF DEVELOPMENT

All the commentators are agreed that the unit of development or the planning unit is a crucial factor in determining the materiality of the change of use. The unit of development refers to the geographical area to which one should apply the test of material change of use – a whole field or part of a field, the whole house or part of a house, the whole field or a particular structure within the field. A clear example is provided by *Williams-Denton* v. *Watford RDC*[41]. In this case there were four acres of orchard physically undivided in any way. On one part four caravans had been sited for many years and it was conceded that they had existing use rights to be there. On an appeal against an enforcement notice served when caravans were sited on other parts of the orchard, the appellant argued that existing use rights applied to the whole orchard. The Minister held, and the Divisional Court accepted his finding, that there were two uses of the land, an agricultural use and a caravan use, and the latter use was confined to only a part of the orchard. Its extension to the remainder of the orchard involved a change of use for that unit and an enforcement notice was rightly served.

The unit of development displays the legal approach to the question of development at its clearest. For the lawyer, brought up on a diet of estates and interests in the land, nothing is easier or perhaps more congenial, than dividing up the physical land or buildings into notional units which in turn give rise to privileges, rights, liabilities and duties. To the planner, nothing is more perplexing as the following *cri du coeur* indicates:

Journal of Planning and Environmental Law (1973),
P. 544

Dear Sir,
In April's issue of the Journal you made reference to the question of a planning unit and in particular the judgment in the case of *Burdle* and *Williams* v. *The Secretary of State and Another* (1972). I am sure I am not the only Practitioner who is constantly coming up against this problem of the planning unit and I am sure that it would be appreciated if in a future issue of the Journal you could publish a short comment on this matter and would set out the criteria for determining the planning unit which the courts set out in the *Burdle* case.

Yours faithfully,
H. G. HUCKLE & PARTNERS
Chartered Architects and Town Planners

Not only would it be difficult to oblige the planner with a short comment on the matter, but one must muddy the waters still further by considering first the question of whether the identification of the unit of development is a question of law or fact, or mixed law and fact. In the first case, the courts could always intervene and reconsider the question; in the second, they could intervene under their administrative law powers only where the decision on the facts was clearly unreasonable; and in the third case, they could intervene in somewhat uncertain circumstances which cross planning law and administrative law boundaries.

It is symptomatic of this part of the law that authority can be found both for the proposition that the unit of development is a pure question of law[42] and can therefore be decided by the courts without reference to the views of the planning authorities, and that it is a question of mixed law and fact,[43] where the courts lay down the criteria which must be applied to the evidence but the decision on the evidence and within the criteria is for the planners. Does it matter? The answer to this question turns on whether one thinks it would be advantageous to have demarcation between the role of the courts and the planners, with the planners applying their judgement to the facts and evidence within a framework of law – mixed law and fact; or whether one thinks that the concept of the unit of development is so obviously a creation of law and so vitally affects the border-line between the citizen's property rights and the public weal that the courts should have exclusive control of it – a pure question of law. The problem with the latter position is that such an argument could be applied to the whole of development control; while in the former position any such demarcation is far from clear. Palk,[44] who has studied the problem in some detail, concludes that it would be more appropriate for it to be a question of mixed law and fact because that is more consistent with the general approach of the law here and with the usual nature of the planning authority's functions. He summarises the courts' role, 'whatever the true position', as follows:

(a) Clearly the courts have a substantial power of review over the decision taken to determine the correct planning unit.

(b) They may overturn the planning authority's decision if (1) It was clearly unreasonable on the evidence, i.e. the planning authority could not possibly have reached that decision on the facts before them, (2) following Bridge J in *Burdle's* case[45], the planners have failed to consider the correct legal criteria, or following the Court of Appeal, the decision is wrong in law; (3) the planning authority fails to give good or sufficient reasons for their decision as to that particular unit. This may be deduced from Bridge J's dicta that he 'was unable to accept that the reasons as expressed by the Secretary of State in his decision letter were good reasons for concluding that the lean-to annexe was the appropriate planning unit for consideration'.

(c) As the courts have a substantial power of review, it is necessary to look at the criteria they have used to identify the planning unit. It is there that the solution to the planning unit problem lies.[46]

The tests the courts apply in determining what is the unit of development are:

(a) COMMON SENSE

S.N.L. Palk, The Planning Unit (1973), 37 *Conveyance*, 154, at p. 174

. . . This was the view of Lord Parker CJ in *East Barnet UDC* v. *British Transport Commission*[47]. Here the Lord Chief Justice, considering if one out of seven plots could be treated in isolation, said, 'Whatever the unit one considers in these cases is always a matter of difficulty, but looked at as a matter of common sense in the present case it seems to me that this was merely an unused part of the unit in question.' In other words he considered that in common sense the whole area of occupation was the correct unit to choose here.

Such a test for the identification of the planning unit has little to commend it. Since the judge only considered the whole area of occupation had to be chosen here because it was the common sense thing to do, he considered that on other occasions it would be common sense to select a smaller unit. The whole site was not to be chosen automatically. Though this is good in that it will accord with the facts of occupation, the test is hopelessly vague. One man's common sense is all too often another man's absurdity. It is hard enough to find out if development has occurred without throwing the whole matter open in this fashion. Does common sense dictate that units should be selected on the basis of fencing and curtilage? Or is in common sense an area to be divided into two units because it has two diverse activities going on there? What the planning authority find to be common sense, the developer and the courts might find to be nonsensical – not because mala fides is involved, but just because the two sides operate under different value judgments. Common sense will not do as the sole legal criterion, and it is good to see that it has not been seriously discussed in any other case. More detailed rules are necessary and fortunately it is these that have predominated in other judgments.

(b) THE WHOLE AREA OF OCCUPATION

Percy Trentham v. *Gloucestershire County Council*
[1966] 1 All E.R. 701

DIPLOCK LJ: . . . What is the unit which the local authority are entitled to look at and deal with in an enforcement notice for the purpose of determining whether or not there has been a 'material change in the use of any buildings or other land'? As I suggested in the course of the argument, I think that for that purpose what the local authority are entitled to look at is the whole of the area which was used for a particular purpose including any part of that area whose use was incidental to or ancillary to the achievement of that purpose. I think, therefore, that they were entitled here to select as the unit the whole of the hereditament acquired by the appellants, and looking at that, ask themselves: was there any material change in the use of it? It is, I should have thought, as plain as a pike-staff that there was a change of use from an agricultural use as farm buildings to a storehouse for other purposes. I agree with my brethren that on both grounds the appeal should be dismissed.[48]

Wood v. *Secretary of State for the Environment and another* [1973] 2 All E.R. 404

LORD WIDGERY CJ. This is an appeal under s. 246 of the Town and Country Planning Act 1971 which is brought before the court by the appellant, Mrs Lilian Madge Wood, against a decision of the Secretary of State for the Environment conveyed in a decision letter of 26th March 1971, whereby the Secretary of State upheld with substantial amendments one or both of two enforcement notices which had been served by the local planning authority on Mrs Wood as occupier of the appeal premises.

I turn to the notices; the first one is dated 20th April 1970 addressed to the appellant at Jades Farm, Horney Common, Maresfield, Sussex; 'it recites that she is the owner and occupier of Jades Farm House identified on the plan attached, and that the land or part or parts thereof has been used as a shop within the meaning of class 1 of the schedule to the Town and Country Planning (Use Classes) Order 1963. It recites further that it appears to the District Council that the said use of the land involves a material change of use of the land constituting development'; accordingly the notice requires the appellant to discontinue or secure the discontinuance of the use of the land as a shop. . . .

The holding in question consists of farmhouse buildings, other outbuildings including some greenhouses and about seven acres of land. It has been farmed as a smallholding producing agricultural produce for very many years; indeed at the inquiry which was held in connection with this matter, evidence showed that the use had started before the original appointed day on 1st July 1948. Since before that date agricultural produce grown on the farm and also some bought in from outside had been sold from various parts of the farmhouse and farm buildings, and the various owners and tenants of the smallholding had all bought in produce from outside for sale.

The importance of the fact that the sales included home produced produce and imported produce is, of course, that the sale of home produced produce on a holding of this kind is a use incidental to the agricultural activity, whereas the bringing in and selling of somebody else's produce is, as the Secretary of State put it in this case, a use quite separate from agricultural use of the land.

The Secretary of State says: 'The evidence showed that the sales had been made from several places in addition to the farmhouse, and the Inspector did not consider that the use could be confined to the farmhouse or the conservatory [of which more anon]. It was however necessary in his view to consider what this use amounted to.'

. . . The decision letter of the Secretary of State goes on in these terms in para 5:

The sale of goods produced elsewhere, either on other local farms or purchased from a retailer, is however considered to constitute a use for retail sales quite separate from the agricultural use of the land and the introduction of such a use is capable of involving a material change of use constituting development requiring planning permission. This depends however on the degree of the use. In this case a use for retail sales has been shown to have commenced before the appointed day but the evidence does not show that the use of the farmhouse (excluding the conservatory) (or of any of the farmhouse buildings which are, strictly, outside the scope of this present action) for this purpose has at any time been on a scale sufficient to amount to a material change of use.

Accordingly, if one looks at the premises excluding for the moment the conservatory, it is apparent that the Secretary of State is accepting that the intensity of the sale of imported goods is not sufficient to amount to a material change of use.

Now one comes to the special complication which has really brought this matter before the court, and it concerns the conservatory to which I have referred. We have been supplied with photographs which show a good looking and fairly modern looking house, and attached to it at the lefthand end as seen from the camera is a porch or conservatory which we are told measures 12 feet by eight feet. It is an extension and addition to the house; it shields the back door from the wind, and it is, on the evidence, a place where it is pleasant enough to sit out when the sun is shining. The origins of that conservatory are obscure; it is clear it was built about 1968. . . .

. . . it can, I think, safely be assumed that when this conservatory was built, it was built without express planning permission, but by virtue of the deemed permission in the General Development Order.

The conservatory having been built, it is evident from the inspector's finding that the appellant and her son, who manages these things for her, found it a convenient place in which to conduct these sales of produce. The son's evidence was that the conservatory was now mainly used for selling purposes, although it was used for sitting in from time to time. One gets, therefore, the picture that in this new addition to the house there is selling going on of a higher intensity than in other parts of the holding, but, in my understanding of the evidence in the report, still not so as to produce in the holding as a whole a material change of use within the meaning of the Act.

However, the Secretary of State has considered it right to treat the conservatory as though it were a separate unit. He has looked at it in isolation, and looking at it in isolation, I have no doubt he has correctly assessed the position in this way, that he finds that the conservatory was used primarily for selling and can quite properly in isolation be given the description of a retail shop. Accordingly he has amended the enforcement notices so as drastically to reduce their effect, indeed so as to exclude from their operation the entirety of this holding except for the conservatory, and the conservatory remains in the enforcement notice on the basis that it is a retail shop, and as things stand the appellant is required to discontinue the use of the conservatory as a retail shop.

The question for us is whether in reaching that conclusion the Secretary of State was right in law. I would approach this problem first of all by assuming that the conservatory had not been a later addition but had been a part of the original house when it was built. If that were the situation, it would seem to me abundantly clear that unless there are very special circumstances not shown in the documents before us, it would not be proper to regard the conservatory as a separate planning unit, that is to say separate from the building as a whole.

There are many cases in this court in which we have had to discuss the correct identification of a planning unit to which the planning law has to be applied, and it has been said on more than one occasion that it is difficult and dangerous to try and lay down a hard and fast principle. But in no case known to me has it been said that unless the circumstances are highly special, it is permissible to dissect a single dwelling-house into different parts and treat them as different planning units for this purpose. Indeed so far as authority goes, it all seems to me to go the other way.

The first case that we have been referred to is *Brooks* v. *Gloucestershire County Council*[49]. That was a case where a dwelling-house had been used for residential purposes, and a room in it began to be used as a shop. This did not attract the attention of the planning authority in the first instance, but in 1965, which was some three years later, two other rooms began to be used for the sale of furniture and the service of meals to customers, and this did stir the local authority into activity. They served an enforcement notice on the occupier requiring him, amongst other things, to discontinue the use of the house as a restaurant. The owner of the house appealed against the enforcement notice to this court; he contended that the mere intensification of the shop use which had been in existence for more than four years prior to the service of the notice did not amount to a material change of use of the premises. The Minister held that the shop use had in 1965 increased to such an extent that it imported a substantial second use of the building as a whole, and, having considered the merits, dismissed the appeal.

The interesting thing about that case in my judgment is that it does support the view that in that somewhat similar problem to the present, the proper approach was not to ask whether one room had become a shop and another room had become a restaurant, but to ask oneself whether the building as a whole had suffered a material change of use. That appears from my judgment where I said:[50]

> In my judgment, this is a case which the essential question for the Minister was whether there had been a material change of use in the four-year period prior to the service of the notice. He had to consider whether any such material change was one in the use of the premises as a whole, because not only was that the unit chosen by the enforcement notice, but, in my judgment, it was clearly the proper unit for consideration in this case.

Similarly, in *Williams* v. *Minister of Housing and Local Government*[51] it was a nursery garden, and in the nursery garden there was a timber building which was used as a retail shop, and this produced from the local authority an enforcement notice seeking to prohibit the use of the building as a shop except for the sale of indigenous agricultural produce. It was held in this court that the premises as a whole, namely the nursery garden together with the building thereon, was the proper unit to be considered in deciding whether there had been a material change of use. The Minister had approached it in that way, and this court upheld him, so there again one finds a disinclination to cut a holding up into penny packets and treat them as separate planning units.

There was a further decision of this court in *Burdle* v. *Secretary of State for the Environment*.[52] In that case BRIDGE J gave the leading judgment, and set out certain principles which can often be conveniently applied in deciding what is the planning unit in a given case. I do not find his particular principles really relevant to the present case because he was dealing with a rather different type of problem, but he did say[53]: 'It may be a useful working rule to assume that the unit of occupation is the appropriate planning unit, unless and until some smaller unit can be recognised as the site of activities which amount in substance to a separate use both physically and functionally.'

That authority seems to me to support the view, which I would think to be right without such assistance, that it can rarely if ever be right to dissect a single dwelling house and to regard one room in isolation as being an appropriate planning unit for present purposes.

Then the question arises: does it make any difference that this conservatory was not an original part of the house but was added later? Does that in any way justify the conclusion to treat it in isolation as a separate planning unit? The position in regard to new buildings is now covered by s. 33 of the Town and Country Planning Act 1971 which, in sub-s. (2), provides: 'Where planning permission is granted for the erection of a building, the grant of permission may specify the purposes for which the building may be used; and if no purpose is so specified, the permission shall be construed as including permission to use the building for the purpose for which it is designed.'

Counsel for the Secretary of State argues that this conservatory was erected under deemed planning permission derived from the General Development Order, that that permission was possible only because it was a dwelling-house which was being extended and improved, and therefore he says under s. 33 (2) the only permitted use of this new part of the building, namely the conservatory, is for residential purposes. The argument is attractive, and no doubt s. 33 applies strictly in accordance with its terms in the more common example of a case where a new separate building is erected, but it seems to me that one must have regard to the fact that where an addition is made to a building under the General Development Order, that addition is part of the original building. It is permitted only because it is an extension to or addition to the original building, and it seems to me that it would be almost unarguable that it did not take on itself the characteristic of the original building in all respects, and I think that that is so.

Accordingly it seems to me that the permitted uses in the conservatory are the same as the permitted uses in the house, and since it has been found that since 1948 the uses in the house have included the sale of imported horticultural produce, well, so does the conservatory[54]. . . .

Appeal allowed. Case remitted to the Secretary of State for reconsideration.

(c) SELECTIVE CHOICE OF WHOLE UNIT

Burdle v. *Secretary of State for the Environment*
[1972] 3 All E.R. 240

BRIDGE J: This is an appeal under s. 180 of the Town and Country Planning Act 1962 from a decision of the Secretary of State for the Environment given in a letter dated 7th January 1972 upholding, subject to variation, an enforcement notice which had been served by the New Forest Rural District Council as delegate of the local planning authority on the present appellants. The appellants occupy a site at Ringwood Road, Netley Marsh in the New Forest area, which has a frontage of 75 feet and a depth of 190 feet, and on which there stand a dwelling-house to which is attached a lean-to annexe and a number of buildings which it is not necessary to describe.

The relevant history of the matter is that before the end of 1963, which of course in relation to changes of use is the critical date under the Town and Country Planning Act 1968, the appellants' predecessor in title, a Mr Andrews, carried on, on the site, within the open curtilage, the business of a scrap yard and a car breakers' yard. As an incident of that business he effected from time to time on the site retail sales of car parts arising from the cars broken up on the site. There was some evidence at the inquiry at which this history emerged of a very limited scale of retail sales of car parts arising from sources other than the break-up of vehicles in the course of the breakers' yard business.

The lean-to annexe adjoining the dwelling-house was used by Mr Andrews as an office in connection with the scrap yard business. In 1965 the present appellants purchased the property; whereas Mr Andrews had carried on business under the modest title of 'New Forest Scrap Metals', the present appellants promptly changed the title to the more grandiose 'New Forest Autos'. They found the lean-to annexe in a somewhat decrepit state, and effected a substantial reconstruction and alteration of it which clearly materially altered its appearance. Inter alia they provided it with two external display windows. They started to use that building for retail sales on a substantial scale for vehicle spare parts not arising from the break-up of vehicles as part of the scrap yard business, but new spares of which the appellants had themselves been appointed stockists by the manufacturers. They also embarked on retail sale of camping equipment and the goods to be sold by retail from the annexe lean-to were displayed both in the new shop windows if one could so call them, and on shelves within the buildings. Finally it is to be observed that as well as advertising themselves as stockists of spare parts for all makes of motor cars, they included in the advertising material the phrase 'New accessories and spares shop now open'.

Those activities prompted the local planning authority to serve on 3rd February 1971 the enforcement notice which is the subject of the appeal to this court. That notice recites:

> ... that it appears to the Council: That a breach of planning control has taken place namely the use of premises at New Forest Scrap Metals, Ringwood Road, Netley Marsh, as a shop for the purpose of the sale inter alia of motor-car accessories and spare parts without the grant of planning permission required in that behalf in accordance with Part III of the Town and Country Planning Act, 1962.

The steps required to be taken by the notice are the discontinuance of the use of the premises as a shop and the restoration of the premises to their condition before the development took place. Concurrently with that notice with which the court is concerned, it is to be observed merely as a matter of history that there was also served an enforcement notice directed at the building alterations which had been effected to the lean-to annexe, but as the Secretary of State allowed an appeal against that enforcement notice, it is unnecessary for us to consider it.

The enforcement notice alleging a change of use, be it observed, uses the perhaps ambiguous expression 'premises' to indicate the unit of land to which it was intended to apply. We were told in the course of argument by counsel for the authority that the authority's intention was to direct this notice at the whole of the appellants' site; it alleged a material change of use of the whole site. It seems to have been so understood by the appellants, and when the matter came before an inspector of the Department of the Environment following the appeal to the Secretary of State by the appellants against the notice, both parties presented their cases on the footing that the whole site was the planning unit with which the inquiry was concerned.

The authority's case was that the change in the character and degree of retail sales from the site, as a matter of fact and degree, effected a material change of use of the whole site which had taken place since the beginning of 1964. Indeed, in these proceedings, counsel for the authority has submitted before us that that is still the proper approach which the Secretary of State should adopt if the matter goes back to him. On that view, so counsel said, the notice as applied to the whole site should be upheld subject to any necessary reservation to preserve to the appellants their right to effect retail sales in the manner and to the extent that such sales were effected by their predecessor before the beginning of 1964.

The appellants' case at the inquiry was in essence that, as a matter of fact and degree, looking at the site as a whole, the intensification of retail sales had not been sufficient to amount to a material change of use.

The inspector, after indicating his findings of primary fact, expressed his conclusions thus:

The legal implications of the above facts are matters for the consideration of the Secretary of State and his legal advisers but it appears to me,
from the almost complete absence of reference to wholesale deliveries,
that the original business was based on the scrapyard, grew out of the
then proprietor's specialisation in the Austin 'Seven', an obsolete
vehicle, and would not have survived as a mainly retail business. In
contrast, while sales of salvaged spares survive, the combination of
advertising with improved facilities for display, and the emphasis on
new items in that display, all now support the appellants' claim that the
annexe is a shop. But in becoming a shop a material change has taken
place, without planning permission and later than 1 January 1964.
Whether or not notice A [which is the use notice] is properly directed
to the whole property or to the annexe, the appeal should therefore
fail on ground (d).

I read that conclusion as indicating first that the inspector was aware,
although it does not appear from the report that it was raised by the
parties, that there was an issue for consideration as to what was the appropriate planning unit to be considered, either the whole site on the one
hand, or on the other hand the lean-to annexe, but he took the view that
whichever unit one considered, there had been a material change of use,
and accordingly he thought the notice could be upheld on that footing.
Speaking for myself, if the Secretary of State had adopted and endorsed
that view, I do not see that such a conclusion could have been faulted in
this court as being erroneous in point of law.

But the Secretary of State did not simply endorse his inspector's conclusion; what he said in the decision letter was this:

Both enforcement notices allege development associated with a shop.
It is clear that enforcement notice B [that is the notice relating to the
building operations] relates to the building called variously the annexe
or lean-to. Enforcement notice A refers to the use of premises as a shop
and at the inquiry it was argued for your clients that the whole site was
used for sales and should be regarded as a long established shop. This
is not an argument that can be accepted in the light of the clearly established definition of a shop for the purposes of the Town and Country
Planning Acts as a building used for the carrying on of any retail trade
etc. The view is taken that enforcement notice A as worded can relate
only to the lean-to or annexe. It is proposed to amend the notice to
make this clear. The appeal against enforcement notice A has been
considered on that limited basis.

The Secretary of State then went on to ask himself the question: has
there been a material change of use of the lean-to annexe? and on the
facts, as it seems to me inevitably, he answered that question in the
affirmative. Given that the lean-to annexe was the appropriate planning
unit for consideration, the decision of the Secretary of State that there
had been a material change of use of it was, as I think, clearly right, and,
in spite of the argument of counsel for the appellants, I cannot accept that

the Minister in any way exceeded his jurisdiction in ordering that the scope of the notice be cut down if it was originally intended to apply to the whole site, so as to limit the ambit of its operation to the lean-to annexe. As such, that was a variation of the notice in favour of the appellants.

But the real complaint and grievance of the appellants is that the Secretary of State has for insufficient or incorrect reasons directed his mind to the wrong planning unit and thereby deprived them of a consideration and decision by the Secretary of State, as opposed to the inspector, of the real question which the appellants say should have been considered, namely: has the change of activities on the whole site effected a change of use of the whole site which is the appropriate planning unit to be considered?

For my part I am unable to accept that the reasons as expressed by the Secretary of State in his decision letter were good reasons for concluding that the lean-to annexe was the appropriate planning unit for consideration. ... What, then, are the appropriate criteria to determine the planning unit which should be considered in deciding whether there has been a material change of use? Without presuming to propound exhaustive tests apt to cover every situation, it may be helpful to sketch out some broad categories of distinction.

First, whenever it is possible to recognise a single main purpose of the occupier's use of his land to which secondary activities are incidental or ancillary, the whole unit of occupation should be considered. That proposition emerges clearly from the case of *G. Percy Trentham Ltd* v. *Gloucestershire County Council*[55]. ...

But, secondly, it may equally be apt to consider the entire unit of occupation even though the occupier carries on a variety of activities and it is not possible to say that one is incidental or ancillary to another. This is well settled in the case of a composite use where the component activities fluctuate in their intensity from time to time, but the different activities are not confined within separate and physically distinct areas of land.

Thirdly, however, it may frequently occur that within a single unit of occupation two or more physically separate and distinct areas are occupied for substantially different and unrelated purposes. In such a case each area used for a different main purpose (together with its incidental and ancillary activities) ought to be considered as a separate planning unit.

To decide which of these three categories apply to the circumstances of any particular case at any given time may be difficult. Like the question of material change of use, it must be a question of fact and degree. There may indeed be an almost imperceptible change from one category to another. Thus, for example, activities initially incidental to the main use of an area of land may grow in scale to a point where they convert the single use to a composite use and produce a material change of use of the whole. Again, activities once properly regarded as incidental to another use or as part of a composite use may be so intensified in scale and physically concentrated in a recognisably separate area that they produce a new planning unit the use of which is materially changed. It may be a useful working rule to assume that the unit of occupation is the appropriate planning unit, unless and until some smaller unit can be recognised as the site of activities which amount in substance to a separate use both physically and functionally.

It may well be that if the Secretary of State had applied those criteria to the question: what was the proper planning unit which fell for consideration in the instant case? he would have concluded on the material before him that the use of the lean-to annexe for purposes appropriate to a shop had become so predominant and the connection between that use and the scrap yard business carried on from the open parts of the curtilage had become so tenuous that the lean-to annexe ought to be regarded as a separate planning unit.

But for myself I do not think it is possible on the factual and evidential material which is before this court for us to say that that was by any means an inevitable conclusion at which the Secretary of State was bound to arrive, and that being so I do not think it would be appropriate for us to usurp his function of deciding the question: what is the appropriate planning unit here? to be considered as a matter of fact and degree. Accordingly I reach the conclusion that this appeal should be allowed and that we should send the case back to the Secretary of State with a direction to reconsider his decision in the light of the judgment of this court.[56]

Appeal allowed.

S. N. L. Palk, 'The Planning Unit' op. cit. p. 178

BRIDGE J has taken the test of the Court of Appeal, namely the unit of activity or 'particular purpose' and added to it a demand for physical distinctiveness. This will prevent planners trying to divide up land whose uses are spread about in a spasmodic fashion. Moreover the legal criteria here correspond well with the facts of occupation. It is now, for instance, possible to divide buildings from their open cutilage, field from field, and fenced off area from fenced off area. Doubtless problems will still remain. What degree of physical distinctness is required? When is a use separate from its neighbours and not ancillary? How far indeed does the fact of separate usage lead to a conclusion of physical detachment? By and large however, BRIDGE J's tests are more than adequate. They are precise enough to stop the determination of the unit being hopelessly vague. They are broad enough to cover the situation where it will be suitable to sever off a smaller unit from the whole area of occupation. The courts have responded to the call that the importance of the need to identify the planning unit warranted a clear and ready solution. If, as suggested by the decisions of the Court of Appeal, the selection of the unit is a matter of law, then the criteria provided a sound legal solution. If, on the other hand, as suggested by *Burdle's* case, the decision as to the unit is at the end of the day a determination of fact, then the criteria provide an adequate base for the planners to frame their decision[57]. . . .

(c) Permitted development

Town and Country Planning General Development Orders
1973–1974

Permitted development

3. – (1) Subject to the subsequent provisions of this order, development of any class specified in Schedule 1 to this order is permitted by this order and may be undertaken upon land to which this order applies, without the permission of the local planning authority or of the Secretary of State:

Provided that the permission granted by this order in respect of any such class of development shall be defined by any limitation and be subject to any condition imposed in the said Schedule 1 in relation to that class.

(2) Nothing in this article or in Schedule 1 to this Order shall operate so as to permit any development contrary to a condition imposed in any permission granted or deemed to be granted under Part III of the Act otherwise than by this order.

Directions restricting permitted development

4. – (1) If either the Secretary of State or the local planning authority is satisfied that it is expedient that development of any of the classes specified in Schedule 1 to this order should not be carried out in any particular area, or that any particular development of any of those classes should not be carried out, unless permission is granted on an application in that behalf, the Secretary of State or the local planning authority may direct that the permission granted by article 3 of this order shall not apply to: –

>   (*a*) all or any development of all or any of those classes in any par-
>   ticular area specified in the direction, or
>   (*b*) any particular development, specified in the direction, falling
>   within any of those classes.

Provided that, in the case of development of class XII, no such direction shall have effect in relation to development authorised by any Act passed after 1st July 1948, or by any order requiring the approval of both Houses of Parliament approved after that date.

(2) Except in the cases specified in the next succeeding paragraph a direction by a local planning authority under this article shall require the approval of the Secretary of State and the Secretary of State may approve the direction with or without modifications.

(3) The approval of the Secretary of State shall not be required in the following cases: . . .

>   (*b*) a direction relating only to development in any particular area
>   of any classes I to IV specified in Schedule 1 to this order if in
>   the opinion of the local planning authority the development
>   would be prejudicial to the proper planning of their area or
>   constitute a threat to the amenities of their area:

Provided that: –

(i) any direction made in pursuance of sub-paragraph (*b*) hereof shall remain in force for six months from the date on which it was made and shall then expire unless it has before the termination of the said six months been approved by the Secretary of State; and

(ii) any second or subsequent direction made in pursuance of sub-paragraph (*b*) which relates to the same development or to development of the same class or classes or any of them in the same area or part of the same area shall require the approval of the Secretary of State.

(4) A copy of any direction made in pursuance of paragraph (3) (*b*) of this article shall be sent by the local planning authority to the Secretary of State not later than the date on which notice is given as provided by paragraphs (5) or (6) of this article; and the Secretary of State may at any time during the period of six months referred to in paragraph 3 (*b*) hereof disallow the direction which shall thereupon cease to have effect. . . .

SCHEDULE 1

The following development is permitted under article 3 of this order subject to the limitations contained in the description of that development in column (1) and subject to the conditions set out opposite that description in column (2).

Column (1) Description of Development	Column (2) Conditions
Class I. – Development within the curtilage of a dwelling-house 1. The enlargement improvement or other alteration of a dwellinghouse so long as: (*a*) the cubic content of the original dwellinghouse (as ascertained by external measurement) is not exceeded by more than 50 cubic metres or one-tenth whichever is the greater, subject to a maximum of 115 cubic metres; (*b*) the height of the building as so enlarged altered or improved does not exceed the height or the highest part of the roof of the original dwellinghouse; (*c*) no part of the building as so enlarged altered or improved projects beyond the forwardmost part of any wall of the original dwellinghouse which fronts on a highway. Provided that the erection of a garage, stable, loosebox or coach-house within the curtilage of the dwellinghouse shall be treated as the enlargement	

of the dwellinghouse for all purposes of this permission including the calculation of cubic contents.

Class II. – Sundry minor operations
Class III. – Changes of use

Development consisting of a change of use to: –

(a) use as a light industrial building as defined by the Town and Country Planning (Use Classes) Order 1972 from use as a general industrial building as so defined;

(b) use as a shop for any purpose included in Class I of the Schedule to the Town and Country Planning (Use Classes) Order 1972 from use as: –

(i) a shop for the sale of hot food;
(ii) a tripe shop;
(iii) a shop for the sale of pet animals or birds;
(iv) a cats meat shop; or
(v) a shop for the sale of motor vehicles.

Class IV. – Temporary buildings and uses
Class V. – Uses by members of recreational organisations
Class VI. – Agricultural buildings, works and uses
Class VII. – Forestry buildings and works
Class VIII. – Development for industrial purposes
Class IX. – Repairs to unadopted streets and private ways
Class X. – Repairs to services
Class XI. – War damaged buildings, works and plant
Class XII. – Development under local or Private Acts, or orders
Classes XIII–XVIII. – Development by various public authorities
Class XIX. – Development by mineral undertakers
Class XX. – Development by the NCB
Class XXI. – Uses of aerodrome buildings
Class XXII. – Use as a caravan site
Class XXIII. – Development on licensed caravan sites

J. B. McLoughlin, Control and Urban Planning
pp. 40–43

The provisions of the Act and these two important Orders taken together with a number of legal decisions constitute a full definition of development. They spell out for the planning authority what applications it will receive and in what categories of application it will have to decide whether or not to allow development to proceed. We have said above that such legal definitions and their amplification are necessary to the functioning of the planning Acts. That this is so does not mean that these definitions are without policy implication. . . .

There are two important implications to the narrowing of the definition of development. One, that the local authority is not in a position to evaluate all of the real pressures which arise for development in its area since many of them do not need its permission to proceed. Two, that a number of changes in the use of land and existing buildings with important local consequences, can take place outside of the control of the planning authority.

An example of the type of restraint on a local authority through the Use Classes Order is provided by changes of use from shops to launderettes. The authority may believe that the traffic generation potential and the hours of business of the two were materially different and hence affected the local environment in different ways. But under the provisions of the Use Classes Order most shops and launderettes are in the same use class and, therefore, change from one to the other is not considered a material change of use, therefore no application for planning permission needs to be made. . . .

At present the planning authority is only notified of changes of use in industry if the proposal is to change the industrial use from one industrial use class to another, e.g. light to heavy industry. The implications for labour intensity, the density of traffic on nearby roads, etc. in a change within a single industrial category and in some cases from general to light industry can never be formally considered by the planning authority.

The lack of general principles
It is our contention here that within the confines of the local development plan based on what are considered to be local problems, the planning authority should be in a freer position to look at the kinds of development it believes are relevant to local problems. This does not mean that the use classes and the areas of permitted development need to be abolished but perhaps that the terms in which the uses are designated be more relevant to current planning problems so that industrial classifications would be based on relevant criteria like noise levels, worker intensity, traffic, etc. rather than on the nature of the product produced and noxious odours which seem to have been the traditional criteria. . . .

The classes of permitted development are again stated in terms of *the nature of the use rather than of its impact on the environment.* Unlike the Use Classes Order certain of these categories relate to the developer apparently on the assumption that certain developments by public and quasi-public agencies require less scrutiny by planning authorities than the undertakings of private developers. It does seem a bit niggling to have a class of permitted development for fences up to a certain *height* rather than permitting all those fences which do not obstruct view on the highway. Changes in use class from general industrial to light industrial, from restaurants to most types of shop, and from excepted shops (fish and chips, etc.) to general shops are permitted under class III. These permitted changes meet with the same criticism as the use classes, that *they disregard some of the potential planning problems attendant upon these changes.*

The present categories of permitted development and the use classes do perform their intended simplifying function in that they reduce the number of applications received by and the administrative burden on the local planning authority. However, they are not altogether appropriate in that they do not match the planning problems facing the authority. They do not necessarily facilitate dealing with the environmental problems raised by industrial development and by solid waste disposal, or with problems of traffic generating in older town centres.

Do you agree with these criticisms? Would it be possible to redraft the Use Classes Order and the General Development Order so that they both met these criticisms and continued to give reasonably clear guidance to developers as to what they could do on their land without first having to obtain planning permission?

3. Judicial control: administrative law

This section will not attempt to duplicate texts on administrative law dealing with general principles of judicial review.[58] What it is designed to do is to draw out the administrative law implications of many of the cases set out in previous chapters, relating them to the general principles of judicial review, and to deal specifically and briefly with the topic of *locus standi*.

(a) General principles of judicial review

In many of the judicial decisions set out or discussed in previous chapters, the courts have been concerned to determine whether a public authority has complied with the terms of a statute. Often the statute is phrased in very broad language – for instance a local planning authority may grant planning permission 'subject to such conditions as they think fit'[59] – so that in interpreting it, the courts are inevitably doing something more than just giving a meaning to certain words; they are applying to those words their own notions and ideas of the proper way to make decisions and the proper way to conduct the administrative process. Usually these ideas are derived from previous cases, but occasionally they are derived from the particular deciding judge's notion of what is fair or reasonable, and that in turn may be influenced by such factors as his socio-political views and the attitudes and beliefs of his profession. The sum total adds up to the general principles of judicial review which are applied to the individual problems with which the judges have to deal. 'The fundamental principle of administrative law is the doctrine of *ultra vires* and the source of this principle is the common law as laid down in decided cases by the judges. . . .'[60]

Although the doctrine of *ultra vires* is the 'fundamental principle' of administrative law, it is customarily divided into certain heads, that is, an administrative body may be held to have acted beyond its powers *because* it failed to observe the rules of natural justice, or it acted in so unreasonable a manner that its decision cannot be supported, or it took jurisdiction over a matter in respect of which it had no jurisdiction, or it acted in the wrong manner. Examples of discussions of all these heads of *ultra vires* are contained in this book and will be mentioned here.

Take first the rules of natural justice. There are two fundamental rules of natural justice: no one shall be condemned unheard (the *audi alteram partem* rule) and no man shall be a judge in his own cause (the no bias or *nemo iudex in sua causa* rule). The application of and philosophy behind the first rule have played a major part in the evolution of the modern law and practice of planning and compulsory acquisition inquiries. It was the lawyers' constant complaint that appellants did not know what case they had to meet at inquiries as the 'official' point of view was rarely expounded either before or at the inquiry. Moreover, the relevant Ministry was wont to engage in 'official consultations' with interested official parties after the inquiry without giving appellants or objectors an opportunity to participate in those consultations. Complaints about these practices helped lead both to the Franks Committee, to the kind of report it produced and to the action that was taken on the report. From the planners' perspective, inquiries are too judicialised and formal; from the lawyers' perspective they now comply much more closely to the *audi alteram partem* rule of natural justice. As Wade puts it: 'Instead of taking the view that statutory inquiry procedures are intended to supplant the rules of the common law, the courts have held rather that they are a framework within which the traditional concept of natural justice should continue to operate. The statutory procedure and the common law supplement each other harmoniously.'[61] It is interesting to note that while Wade appears to be satisfied with the influence natural justice has had on inquiries and ministerial decisions taken thereafter, he notes that 'it is an open question whether a local planning authority ought to give an applicant an opportunity to make representations before planning permission is refused. There is a right of appeal to the Minister, but in principle that is no reason for not requiring the procedure to be fair at the initial stage. The Act itself is silent.'[61a]

If an applicant aggrieved by a refusal of permission to develop, applied for an order from the court to quash the decision of the local planning authority on the grounds of failure to hear him before it reached its decision, how do you think the court would decide and why? Consider in particular the cases of *R* v. *Bradford-on-Avon RDC* ex parte *Boulton*[62] page 381 and *R* v. *Hendon RDC* ex parte *Chorley*[63] (page 561 below).

One area where the *audi alteram partem* rule has not made much headway is in respect of consultations within the department, between departments, or between the department and a local authority involved in the issue the subject of an inquiry, after an inquiry has taken place. The courts themselves have not been entirely consistent in their handling of this issue. In *Errington* v. *Minister of Health*[64] they upset the confirmation of a clearance order because after the inquiry into it, Ministry officials consulted with and received further evidence from the sponsoring local authority, without the objectors being informed or being given an opportunity to comment on the further evidence. But they have rejected attempts to overthrow clearance orders where, before formal publication of the order, there had been extensive consultations between the Ministry and the local authority.[65] This is to invest the formal publication of an official proposal with a spurious importance, likely to be misleading to objectors. At the same time, as even Wade admits, *Errington*

makes it difficult for the Ministry to fulfil their functions. . . . What makes the position seem artificial is the idea that the local authority is a party to a dispute, and that the Minister is an independent judge. In fact the two authorities are working – or should be working – hand in glove, one at the local, one at the national level. Both are wielding administrative powers, and there is no real difference in the nature of their activities. The notion of the *lis* is therefore fallacious. If the scheme had been promoted by a local office of the Ministry, instead of by the local corporation, any amount of subsequent consultation might have taken place and have been passed over as ordinary departmental work.[66]

Errington has never been overruled, but its application has been restricted in the planning field in the case of development plans by a provision, first introduced in the Act of 1947,[67] permitting the Minister to consult with the local authority or anyone else at any stage without any obligation to allow further objections or hold a further inquiry. The power is retained in a revised form even in the more permissive regime of the public examination into a structure plan and in respect of a ministerial approval of a local plan.[68] In addition, in changed circumstances its philosophy did not find so ready an acceptance in the courts after the Second World War as Lord Greene MR's judgement in *Johnson & Co (Builders)* v. *Minister of Health*[69] indicates. But the difficult distinctions and problems with which *Errington* was trying to grapple have been raised again in a slightly different context in the field of planning appeals. The debate, within and without the courts, on the questions as to when the Secretary of State should re-open an inquiry, and what is the nature of the advice which is received by the decision-officer from other officials within his own and other departments, can be the more easily understood from an administrative law perspective if the background of *Errington* and the other Housing Act cases is borne in mind. The difficulties of the court in *Lord Luke of Pavenham* v. *Minister of Housing and Local Government*,[70] the dispute between the Council on Tribunals and the government over the *Chalkpit* case[71] are modern manifestations of the continued tension between the judicial and the administrative way of doing things. The rule of *audi alteram partem* indicates the judicial approach to the problem: it does not of itself provide a solution to the problem.

There have been similar difficulties of application in the planning process of the no bias rule of natural justice. Where the bias is of the 'straightforward' pecuniary or conflict of interest kind, there are few problems. A good example of this kind of bias is the case of *R* v. *Hendon UDC* ex parte *Chorley*[72] decided under the Town Planning Act 1925. An application to develop some land was considered by the Plans and Highways Committee of the Hendon RDC in its capacity as the town planning authority under the Hendon Rural Town Planning Scheme (Interim Development) Order 1925. One member of that Committee, Councillor Cross, was an estate agent acting for the vendor of the property, the subject of the application. Objections were made to the proposed development and these objections were submitted to the Committee which, however, unanimously carried a resolution that the development be permitted. Councillor Cross was present at the meeting which approved the issuing of the permit, but took no part in the discussion. He was also present at another meeting of the Committee where a motion to rescind the resolution was defeated. Chorley, a neighbouring landowner, applied for an order from the court to quash the decision of the Committee on the ground, *inter alia*, of bias. The Divisional Court granted the order,

AVORY J saying[73]: There is really no dispute that Councillor F. H. Cross was, in fact, biased in the sense that he had such an interest in the matter as to disqualify him from taking part or voting, and there is no question that he did vote in the sense in which the word is understood . . . it is clear that the resolution was passed, and it can only have been passed by the votes of those who were present. The fact that the votes were given silently and not by any oral expression of sound seems to me to make no difference. . . .

The problems that have arisen surround the issues of 'departmental bias' and the application of 'policy' to an individual decision. If the Minister and his officials or a local planning authority are committed to a particular policy, how can they adopt an unbiased approach to a dispute where one party is arguing, in effect, against that policy? Yet surely Ministers are expected to have policies and try to get them carried out, as are local planning authorities? The cases on the application of policy and the need, notwithstanding its existence, to consider each case on its merits show the difficulties the courts have had in reconciling conflicting principles and priorities. They apply rules devised for the supervision of inferior judges by the High Court to the vastly different world of ministerial and local planning authority decision making. Can one say that here 'the statutory procedure and the common law supplement each other harmoniously'?[74]

No discussion of bias within the planning system would be complete without reference to the case of *Franklin* v. *Minister of Town and Country Planning*.[75] Although the case arose out of the establishment of Stevenage New Town under the New Towns Act 1946, it raises the issue of bias in its most acute form, where the Minister himself is responsible both for initiating a major policy and its implementation and has the duty to consider objections to that policy. The language of Lord Thankerton who delivered the unanimous opinion of the House of Lords has also provoked controversy in so far as it sought to suggest that the issue of bias raised in the case was irrelevant in view of the nature of the Minister's function.

In the Stevenage case, as it is generally referred to, the Minister of Town and Country Planning had made a speech in Stevenage (before the second reading of the New Towns Bill in the House of Commons) in which he had made it clear that the Bill would become law, that Stevenage would be the first new town under the new Act and that 'while I will consult as far as possible all the local authorities, at the end, if people become fractious and unreasonable I shall have to carry out my duty. . . .'[76] The Act as finally passed laid a duty on the Minister to cause a public local inquiry to be held into objections to a draft order designating an area as a proposed new town, and to 'consider the report of the person by whom the inquiry was held'. The Minister published the draft Stevenage New Town (Designation) Order five days after the New Towns Act received the Royal Assent; an inquiry into objections was held by an inspector two months later, and a report was sent to the Minister shortly afterwards. A fortnight after receiving the report, the Minister, in letters sent to all objectors, stated that after giving careful considera- tion to all submissions made, he had decided to confirm the Order. It was alleged by Franklin and other objectors that the Minister had not carried out his duty to consider the inspector's report because he had in effect already made up his mind on the matter, and was therefore biased. The objectors won their case at first instance, but lost in both the Court of Appeal and the House of Lords ([1947] 2 All E.R. 289):

LORD THANKERTON: . . . In my opinion, no judicial, or quasi-judicial, duty was imposed on the respondent, and any reference to judicial duty, or bias, is irrelevant in the present case. The respondent's duties under s. 1 of the Act and sched. I thereto are, in my opinion, purely administrative, but the Act prescribes certain methods of, or steps in, the discharge of that duty. It is obvious that, before making the draft order, which must contain a definite proposal to designate the area concerned as the site of a new town, the respondent must have made elaborate inquiry into the matter, and have consulted any local authorities who appear to him to be con- cerned, and, obviously, other departments of the government, such as the Ministry of Health, would naturally require to be consulted It would seem, accordingly, that the respondent was required to satisfy himself that it was a sound scheme before he took the serious step of issuing a draft order. It seems clear also, that the purpose of inviting objections, and, where they are not withdrawn, of having a public inquiry, to be held by someone other than the respondent, to whom that person reports, was for the further information of the respondent, in order to the final consideration of the soundness of the scheme of the designation, and it is important to note that the development of the site, after the order is made, is primarily the duty of the development corporation established under s. 2 of the Act. I am of opinion that no judicial duty is laid on the respondent in discharge of these statutory duties, and that the only question is whether he has complied with the statutory directions to appoint a person to hold the public inquiry, and to consider that person's report. On this contention of the appellants no suggestion is made that the public inquiry was not properly conducted, nor is there any criticism of the report by Mr Morris.

In such a case the only ground of challenge must be either that the respondent did not, in fact, consider the report and the objections, of which there is here no evidence, or that his mind was so foreclosed that he gave no genuine consideration to them, which is the case made by the appellants. Although I am unable to agree exactly with the view of the respondent's duty expressed by the learned judge, or with some of the expressions used by the Court of Appeal in regard to that matter, it does appear to me that the issue was treated in both courts as being whether the respondent had genuinely considered the objections and the report, as directed by the Act.

My Lords, I could wish that the use of the word 'bias' should be confined to its proper sphere. Its proper significance, in my opinion, is to denote a departure from the standard of even-handed justice which the law requires from those who occupy judicial office, or those who are commonly regarded as holding a quasi-judicial office, such as an arbitrator. The reason for this clearly is that, having to adjudicate as between two or more parties, he must come to his adjudication with an independent mind, without any inclination or bias towards one side or other in the dispute. . . .

It seems probable that the learned judge's mind was influenced by his having already held that the respondent's function was quasi-judicial, which would raise the question of bias, but, in any view, I am clearly of opinion that nothing said by the respondent was inconsistent with the discharge of his statutory duty, when subsequently objections were lodged, and the local public inquiry took place, followed by the report of that inquiry, genuinely to consider the report and the objections. . . .

My Lords, these passages in a speech[77], which was of a political nature, and of the kind familiar in a speech on second reading, demonstrate (1) the speaker's view that the Bill would become law, that Stevenage was a most suitable site and should be the first scheme in the operation, and that the Stevenage project would go forward, and (2) the speaker's reaction to the hostile interruptions of a section of the audience. In my opinion, these passages are not inconsistent with an intention to carry out any statutory duty imposed on him by Parliament, although he intended to press for the enactment of the Bill, and thereafter to carry out the duties thereby involved, including the consideration of objections which were neither fractious nor unreasonable. I am, therefore, of opinion that the first contention of the appellants fails, in that they have not established either that in the respondent's speech he had forejudged any genuine consideration of the objections or that he had not genuinely considered the objections at the later stage when they were submitted to him. . . .

Appeal dismissed[78].

On this Wade has commented:

'(T)he House of Lords (held) that the law did not require impartial consideration at all, the Minister could be as biased as he liked provided that he observed the procedure laid down by the Act. . . . Lord Thankterton . . . treats "judicial duty" and statutory functions as two mutually exclusive things. But there were many cases then in the law reports in which it had been held that a minister considering the report of a public inquiry had a quasi-judicial duty, meaning that although his decision was a purely administrative act, he was bound by the rules of natural justice so far as they could reasonably apply to the case. . . . This case therefore endangered the "basic English" of administrative law.'[79]

Did Lord Thankerton accept that a proper challenge to what the Minister did could be mounted on the basis that his mind was so foreclosed that he did not genuinely consider the report of the inspector? What is the Minister doing when he comes to consider whether to confirm a draft order on a matter which his department originally initiated? Are you helped or hindered in answering that question by discussing it in terms of 'judicial', 'quasi-judicial' and 'administrative'?[80] Ought a Minister to be subject to control by the courts in situations similar to those posed by *Franklin?*

Procedural *ultra vires* or acting in the wrong manner is the major head of administrative law control of planning authorities, and it is this concern about acting in the wrong manner which also finds expression in complaints to the Council on Tribunals and the Parliamentary Commissioner for Administration. The fettering of statutory powers by contract is not allowed, and *Stringer* v. *Minister of Housing and Local Government*[81] was following a long line of authority in holding that the agreement between Cheshire County Council and the University of Manchester that the county council would discourage development in the area of Jodrell Bank was *ultra vires* and of no legal effect. The limitations on this principle were, however, well illustrated by *Earl of Leicester* v. *Wells-next-the-sea UDC*[82] where an agreement entered into by the local authority (that land which it purchased for allotments would be used only for allotments) was held not to fetter its power to purchase land for allotments but rather to assist it to carry out that purpose.

A particularly vexing area of procedural *ultra vires* is the extent to which individual officers of public authorities may, in giving advice to members of the public, bind the public authority to act or not act in a particular way. Cases from the planning process going both ways reflect the division of opinion generally in administrative law cases. In *Southend-on-Sea Corporation* v. *Hodgson*[83] the local planning authority was not bound by a statement made by a planning officer that a certain use of land did not need planning permission. In *Lever Finance Co* v. *Westminster LBC*[84] a local planning authority was bound by a statement by a planning officer that significant alterations to a row of houses in course of building did not need planning permission. The conflicting pressures on the courts in these situations are well summed up by Wade. On the one hand: 'Sympathy for persons misled in this way has compelled the courts to strain the law.' On the other: 'There must be serious objections to giving the force of law to wrong advice from officials.'[85] The general issues raised by these quotations are further complicated in planning law, firstly by the power to delegate the making of decisions to officers – a contributory factor in the decision in *Lever Finance* – and secondly by the courts' constant oscillation between seeing planning as being for the public good and therefore necessary to support even at the cost of individual hardship – *Hodgson* – and seeing it as an imposition upon individuals and therefore to be confined and limited as far as possible – *Lever Finance*.

Finally, on this aspect of the general principles of judicial review, the exercise by the Minister of his powers to decide appeals in planning applications must be mentioned here. The rules require the Minister to give reasons: *Givaudan & Co Ltd* v. *Minister of Housing and Local Government*[86] decided that the reasons must be set out clearly and a letter from the Minister that was so obscure as 'would leave in the mind of an informed reader such real and substantial doubt as to the reasons for his decision and as to the matters which he did and did not take into account'[87] did not comply with the rules, and the Minister's order should be quashed. Another case on a ministerial decision, this time involving, *inter alia*, wrongful delegation of the power to decide, is *Lavender and Son* v. *Minister of Housing and Local Government*.[88] The Minister's decision letter was held by the court to indicate that he was not prepared to allow development within a particular area unless the Minister of Agriculture agreed to waive his objections to such development; this amounted both to improper fettering of discretion and 'while purporting to be that of the Minister [of Housing and Local Government, the decision] was in fact, and improperly, that of the Minister of Agriculture'.[89]

(b) Locus standi[90]

Who may sue a planning authority alleging that it has failed to comply with the law? The answer given by the 1971 Act is any person 'aggrieved'[91] by any order, decision, direction, plan, etc. To the layman this may appear to mean that any person who objected to the order, etc. of the local planning authority and/or the Minister by e.g. sending a letter of objection to the local planning authority or appearing as a third party objector at the public local inquiry may sue the local planning authority or the Minister on the grounds that 'the order is not within the powers of the Act, or that any of the relevant requirements have not been complied with in relation to that order. . . .'[92] Whether the courts adopt this position is more open to doubt. Until *Turner* v. *Secretary of State for the Environment* the answer was 'probably not' – aggrieved person was given a restrictive interpretation in the relevant planning cases. That case, however, suggests that a change of position is now on the way.

Turner v. *Secretary of State for Environment*
(1974) 28 P. & C.R. 123

By notice of motion dated February 27, 1973, the applicants, Elstan Grey Turner, being the chairman, and James Gibson, being the secretary, acting for and on behalf of the Petersham Society, applied for 1. an order declaring that the decision of the first respondent, the Secretary of State for the Environment, in a letter from him to the second respondents, the Richmond-upon-Thames London Borough Council, the local planning authority, dated January 16, 1973, that he approved the details in an application No. 71/1744 for the erection of two single-storey dwellings with integral garages at the rear of Rutland Lodge, River Lane, Petersham, Richmond, Surrey, which had been submitted in accordance with an outline permission No. 66/2149, was and had been untrue and *ultra vires*, alternatively was and had been void for uncertainty and of no effect. . . .

ACKNER J: . . . The applicants in this motion, the Petersham Society, are a local preservation society whose objection to the proposed development was supported by the Ham and Petersham Ratepayers' and Residents' Association, the National Trust, the Council for the Preservation of Rural England, the Richmond Hill Committee and the Georgian Group. They were given by the inspector the right to be present at and to make representations at the inquiry. . . .

Both Mr Frank on behalf of the Secretary of State and Mr Rich on behalf of Mr Hill who was the applicant for the planning approval and who was added as a respondent at my direction, have taken two preliminary objections going essentially to my jurisdiction to entertain this appeal. . . .

The first point taken by Mr Frank and Mr Rich is the familiar one, that the applicants are not persons aggrieved by any action on the part of the Secretary of State. Both counsel rely, essentially, on the decision of this Court in *Buxton* v. *Minister of Housing and Local Government*[93], being a decision of SALMON J. In that case

... D. Heath & Sons Ltd ('the operators') were the owners and occupiers of certain land in Cambridge Road, Stansted Mount Fitchet, in the county of Essex. On December 10, 1957, the operators applied under section 16 of the Town and Country Planning Act 1947 to Saffron Walden Rural District Council for permission to develop their land by digging chalk. The rural district council were the local authority to whom the local planning authority had delegated its powers in accordance with Part III of the Act of 1947. On April 1, [1958], the [local authority] refused the application. Thereafter the operators appealed against this refusal to the Minister of Housing and Local Government pursuant to section 16 of the Act of 1947. The Minister caused a local inquiry to be held by an inspector appointed by him under sections 15 and 16 of the Act into the refusal of permission by the [local authority]. Amongst those who appeared at this inquiry, called evidence and were heard, were the operators, the local authority, and four substantial landowners, the present applicants, whose land was adjacent to that of the operators and was being used for agricultural and residential purposes.

The inspector in his report recommended that the operators' appeal should be dismissed. The Minister rejected the inspector's report and allowed the appeal, hence the application by the landowners whose land was adjacent to that of the operators against the decision.

In that case the preliminary point was taken on behalf of the Minister that those landowners were not persons aggrieved within the meaning of section 31 of the Act of 1947, which was in identical terms to section 245 of the Act of 1971 so far as is relevant to this case. In his judgment SALMON J stated that the case raised the perennial question as to what the legislature meant when it used the words 'aggrieved person.' ...

Later in his judgment SALMON J said: ... If I could approach this problem free from authority, without regard to the scheme of the Town and Country Planning legislation and its historical background, the arguments in favour of the applicants on the preliminary point would be most persuasive, if not compelling, for in the widest sense of the word the applicants are undoubtedly aggrieved. In my judgment, however, I am compelled to restrict the meaning of the words 'person aggrieved' to a person with a legal grievance.

SALMON J then dealt in some detail with the legislation, and ended by saying:

The Minister's action which these applicants seek to challenge infringed none of their common law rights. They have no rights as individuals under the statutes. Accordingly, in my judgment, none of their legal rights has been infringed, and in these circumstances it could not, in my view, have been the intention of the legislature to enable them to challenge the Minister's decision in the courts. Ever since the judgment of JAMES LJ in the well-known case of *Re Sidebotham*,[94] it has been generally accepted that the words 'person aggrieved' in statute connote the person with a legal grievance, that is to say, someone whose legal rights have been infringed. JAMES LJ said: 'the words "person aggrieved" do not really mean a man who is disappointed of a benefit which he might have received if some other order had been made. A "person aggrieved" must be a man who has suffered a legal grievance, a man against whom a decision has been pronounced which has wrongfully deprived him of something, or wrongfully refused him something, or wrongfully affected his title to something.'

SALMON J considered that the guiding principle was that laid down by JAMES LJ in *Re Sidebotham*, which, as far as he knew, had never been challenged.

At the time when that decision was made, that is, July 1960, there were not in existence the Town and Country Planning Appeals (Inquiries Procedure) Rules 1962, which have been re-enacted with various amendments until they are now to be found in the Town and Country Planning (Inquiries Procedure) Rules 1969. The Rules of 1962, as continuing to be provided, made provision for appearances at the inquiry, and in their present form they are to be found in rule 5 of the Rules of 1969, which deals with notification of inquiry, and rule 7, which deals with appearances at the inquiry. Rule 7 (1) provides: 'The persons entitled to appear at the inquiry shall be — . . .,' and then it sets out obvious categories of persons such as the applicant and the local planning authority and ends with '. . . (g) any persons on whom the [Secretary of State] has required notice to be served under rule 5 (2) (b).' Then rule 7 (2) provides: 'Any other person may appear at the inquiry at the discretion of the appointed person.' Part of the judgment of SALMON J in the *Buxton* case on which the respondents, including, of course, Mr Hill, relied is that part which reads as follows:

> In my judgment, anyone given a statutory right to have his representations considered by the Minister impliedly has the right that the Minister, in considering those representations, shall act within the powers conferred upon him by the statute and shall comply with the relevant requirements of the statute.

It is accepted by Mr Frank and Mr Rich that a rule 7 (1) (g) person is a person given a statutory right to have his representations considered by the Secretary of State and is covered by what follows in that part of the judgment, but they each contend that a rule 7 (2) person, a person who appears at the inquiry at the discretion of the appointed person, is a 'second-class citizen' for the purpose of rights of appeal, from which it must follow that SALMON J's judgment should be adapted in relation to them to read as follows: 'In my judgment, anyone given a right to appear at the inquiry at the discretion of the appointed person has impliedly no right that the Minister, in considering his representations, shall act within the powers conferred upon him by the statute and shall comply with the relevant requirements of the statute.' I must say that I find that a particularly unattractive proposition and I am sure that SALMON J would have felt the same if the submission had been made to him. . . . two recent authorities clearly have a direct bearing on the extent to which SALMON J's decision should now be followed. The first of these two cases is *Att.-Gen. of the Gambia* v. *N'Jie*[95].

LORD DENNING, in giving the judgment of the Board, made a specific reference to JAMES LJ's judgment in *Ex p. Sidebotham* which was much relied on by SALMON J in *Buxton* v. *Minister of Housing and Local Government* in the manner which I have already indicated. LORD DENNING said

> If this definition were to be regarded as exhaustive, it would mean that the only person who could be aggrieved would be a person who was a party to a lis, a controversy *inter partes*, and had had a decision given against him. The Attorney-General does not come within this definition, because, as their Lordships have already pointed out, in these disciplinary proceedings there is no suit between parties, but only action taken by the judge, *ex mero motu* or at the instance of the Attorney General or someone else, against a delinquent practitioner. But the definition of JAMES LJ is not to be regarded as exhaustive. Lord Esher MR pointed that out in *Ex p. Official Receiver, Re Reed, Bowen & Co.*[96] The words 'person aggrieved' are of wide import and should not be subjected to a restrictive interpretation. They do not include, of course, a mere busybody who is interfering in things which do not concern him: but they do include a person who has a genuine grievance because an order has been made which prejudicially affects his interests.

N'Jie's case was referred to in a decision of the Court of Appeal in *Maurice* v. *London County Council*.[97] In that case:

> The owner of premises in London, situated within 100 yards of a proposed block of flats more than 100 feet high, appealed under section 52 (2) (a) of the London Building Act 1930 as a person who deemed herself aggrieved, against a consent granted to themselves by the London County Council under section 51 of the Act of 1930 as amended by section 5 of the London County Council (General Powers) Act 1954.

In the course of his judgment LORD DENNING MR said this on the subject of 'person aggrieved':[98]

> Miss Maurice now appeals to this court. The first point argued before us is whether she can complain of loss of amenity. On this point I am afraid I have come to a decision different from that of the Divisional Court. The material words in section 52 (2) (a) give a right of appeal 'to the owner or lessee of any land within 100 yards who may deem himself aggrieved' by the grant of consent. It is quite clear that the person must be aggrieved in respect of his interest in a building or land within 100 yards. But there is no limitation whatever as to the kind of grievance. I can see no reason whatever for excluding loss of amenities. I know that at one time the words 'person aggrieved' (which I regard as the same as 'person who shall deem himself aggrieved') were given in these courts a very narrow and restricted interpretation. It was said

that the words 'person aggrieved' in a statute only meant a person who had suffered a legal grievance. Indeed in *Buxton* v. *Minister of Housing and Local Government*, which I mentioned in the course of the argument, SALMON J declined to go into the question of loss of amenities. But that narrow view should now be rejected. In the more recent case of *Att.-Gen. of the Gambia* v. *N'Jie*, the Privy Council had to consider these words 'person aggrieved' once again. On behalf of the Board, I ventured to say there: . . .

and LORD DENNING MR set out that part of the opinion of the Board to which I have just referred.

So here in this case they do include a person who has a genuine grievance because a consent has been given which prejudicially affects his interests. His interests may be prejudicially affected, not only in regard to light and air, but in regard to amenities also. The one requisite must be in respect of his interest as an owner or lessee of a building within 100 yards.

PEARSON LJ agreed with the judgment of LORD DENNING MR. . . . WILBER-FORCE J said: 'I entirely agree with the judgments which have been delivered.' SALMON J's imprecations were ignored when the planning legislation was re-enacted in 1962. Nine years later, in 1971, after LORD DENNING MR's *obiter dicta* to which I have just referred that the narrow view that a person aggrieved in a statute only meant a person who had suffered a legal grievance should be rejected, the section was again re-enacted in identical terms. Parliament's intentions remained inscrutable.

There is a firm, fixed, immutable time limit provided in the appeal provisions. The appeal can only be based on very limited and restricted grounds, as section 245 of the Town and Country Planning Act 1971 clearly reveals. I see no merit in the proposition that a person who has merely been given notice of the existence of the inquiry at the request of and not by the requirement of the Secretary of State and whose right to attend and make his representations has resulted from the exercise of the inspector's discretion should be obliged to sit by and accept the decision, which, *ex hypothesi*, is bad in law. I can see no compelling matter of policy which requires this form of silence to be imposed on a person who has, again *ex hypothesi*, a clear grievance in law. On the other hand I see good reason, so long as the grounds of appeal are so restricted, for ensuring that any person who, in the ordinary sense of the word, is aggrieved by the decision, and certainly any person who has attended and made represen-tations at the inquiry, should have the right to establish in the courts that the decision is bad in law because it is *ultra vires* or for some other good reason. It is true that the would-be developer may be held up while the appeal is made, but, as the dates in this case indicate, the procedure is a reasonably expeditious one and I have no doubt that an application for special expedition, where justified, would be listened to sympathetically by the court.

In his report the inspector classifies the applicants, *inter alios*, as 'interes-ted persons,' a classification which is clearly justified by the facts. They were persons whom the appointed person in his discretion had allowed to appear at the inquiry and make representations in relation to the subject-matter of the inquiry, which representations had to be recorded by the inspector and transmitted with his, the inspector's, findings of fact and conclusions to the Secretary of State with a view to the Secretary of State accepting or rejecting those findings of fact and conclusions. Such persons have, in my judgment, impliedly the right that the Secretary of State in considering those representations shall act within the powers conferred on him by the statute and shall comply with the relevant requirements of the statute, in just the same way (as is conceded to be the case) as has a person who makes representations at the inquiry being a person on whom the Secretary of State has required notice of the inquiry to be served. I thus conclude that no valid differentiation can be made between a person who appears at an inquiry and makes his representations having had notice of the inquiry at the insistence of the Secretary of State and a person who appears and makes his representations by permission of the appointed person. This question was not before SALMON J in *Buxton* v. *Minister of Housing and Local Government*, the Town and Country Planning Appeals (Inquiries Procedure) Rules 1962 not having then been made. Moreover, I derive from the recommendation of the Court of Appeal in *Maurice* v. *London County Council* that the narrow construction should now be rejected just sufficient fortitude for not following the decision in the *Buxton* case so reluctantly reached by the very learned judge. I therefore reject the respondents' first proposition that there is no jurisdiction in this Court because I am obliged to impose a very restricted meaning on the words 'aggrieved person.' . . . [There was, however, a second ground relied upon by counsel for both respondents,[99] and after discussing it his Lordship reached the conclusion that he had no jurisdiction under the Town and Country Planning Act 1971 to entertain the appeal, and for that reason it had to be dismissed.] *Appeal dismissed.*

Which authority – *Buxton* or *Turner* – is to be preferred? Why? In the course of his judgement in *Buxton* Salmon J referred to the pre-rogative writ of certiorari and suggested that an objector who was not a person with a legal grievance under the Act might none the less be able to get a planning decision before the courts by a different route. Certiorari thus merits investigation.

Wade discusses certiorari as follows:

Certiorari is used to bring up into the High Court the decision of some inferior tribunal or authority in order that it may be investigated. If the decision does not pass the test (of being *intra vires*) it is quashed – that is to say it is declared completely invalid, so that no one need respect it. This is therefore a remedy of public rather than of private law. . . .

It follows that an applicant for certiorari . . . does not have to show that some legal right of his is at stake. If the action is an excess or abuse of power, the court will quash it at the instance of a mere stranger, though it retains discretion to refuse to do so if it thinks that no good would be done to the public. In other words, these remedies are not restricted by the notion of *locus standi*. . . . The wide scope of these remedies may be of crucial importance where the applicant is in fact genuinely aggrieved but has no grievance in the eye of the law. He may, for example, object strongly to a building for which his neighbour has been granted planning permission, although legally this is no concern of his. If he can show that the permission is void . . . he may have it quashed by certiorari. . . .[100]

The authority Wade quotes for his example of certiorari to quash a planning permission is *R* v. *Hendon RDC* ex parte *Chorley*[101] where, it will be recalled, the court quashed a permission because of bias within the committee granting it. The court accepted the argument that certiorari lay where 'the rights and obligations of persons may be affected'[102] and since the resolution to grant permission conferred on the applicant for permission 'a right, in certain events to compensation . . . the Council was therefore dealing with a matter which affected the rights of an individual. . . .'[102]

A later authority, however, specifically on the terms of a forerunner of the present Act, cast some doubt on the continued authority of *Chorley*. This was the case of *R* v. *Bradford-upon-Avon UDC* ex parte *Boulton*, the facts of which are given above at page 381.   [1964] 2 All E.R. 492 at pp. 494–5

WIDGERY J [After discussing the first question]: . . . The second question . . . is whether certiorari does lie to bring up and quash the decision of a planning authority in a case of this kind. As far as I know, no such application has been granted since the passing of the Town and Country Planning Act, 1947, and, again, I find it unnecessary to make a decision on this important point of considerable general significance. Again I will assume without deciding it, that the court has power to supervise decisions of planning authorities by virtue of an order of certiorari; but I do emphasise that I would not wish to decide it, because I think that there may be a great deal to be said on both sides, and it may be that the court will be faced with that problem another day.

That other day came ten years later in *R* v. *London Borough of Hillingdon* ex parte *Royco Homes Ltd* ([1974] 2 All E.R. 643), the facts of which are given on pp. 426–7.

LORD WIDGERY CJ: . . . This case involves a number of important and interesting points. The first one to be considered, strangely enough for the first time since the passing of the Town and Country Planning Act 1947, is whether certiorari will go at all to control the exercise by a planning authority of its jurisdiction under the planning Acts. In other words, the first question which we have to face squarely for the first time is whether the procedure of the prerogative orders goes to a planning authority exercising its jurisdiction under the Acts. There is, as I have said, no authority on this point on the modern town planning legislation, but there is a case on the earlier Acts which really stands alone as the only authority for the assistance of this court. It is *R* v. *Hendon Rural District Council. . . .*

In the course of the judgments in this court in the *Hendon* case reference was made to a frequently quoted observation of ATKIN LJ in *R* v. *Electricity Comrs*[103]. What ATKIN LJ said was: 'Wherever any body of persons having legal authority to determine questions affecting the rights of subjects, and having the duty to act judicially, act in excess of their legal authority they are subject to the controlling jurisdiction of the King's Bench Division . . . In view of that clear dictum from ATKIN LJ it is surprising that so little use has been made of the prerogative orders in this particular field, and I think that counsel for the planning authority may have put his finger on the explanation when he referred to the fact that ATKIN LJ's dictum required not only that the body to whom certiorari was to go had legal authority to determine questions affecting the rights of subjects, but also required that that body should have the duty to act judicially, a phrase which is rather less clear and indeed very difficult of definition. Accordingly it may be that previous efforts to use certiorari in this field have been deterred by ATKIN LJ's reference to it being necessary for the body affected to have the duty to act judicially. If that is so, that reason for reticence on the part of applicants was, I think, put an end to in the House of Lords in *Ridge* v. *Baldwin*[104]. It is a case the facts of which are very far from the present and indeed have nothing to do with planning at all. But in the course of his speech LORD REID made reference to that oft-quoted dictum of ATKIN LJ and pointed out that the additional requirement of the body being under a duty to act judicially was not supported by authority. Accordingly it seems to me now that that obstacle, if obstacle it were, has been cleared away and I can see no reason for this court holding otherwise than that there is power in appropriate cases for the use of the prerogative orders to control the activity of a local planning authority. To put it the other way round, I see no general legal inhibition on the use of such orders, although no doubt they must be exercised only in the clearest cases and with a good deal of care on the part of the court.

In particular, it has always been a principle that certiorari will go only where there is no other equally effective and convenient remedy. In the planning field there are very often, if not in an almost overwhelming number of cases, equally effective and convenient remedies. As is well known, there is now under the Town and Country Planning Act 1971 a comprehensive system of appeals from decisions of local planning authorities. In the instant case the applicants could, had they wished, have gone to the Secretary of State for the Environment in the form of a statutory appeal under the Act instead of coming to this court. There would, if they had taken that course, have been open to them a further appeal to this court on a point of law following on the decision of the Secretary of State.

It seems to me that in a very large number of instances it will be found that the statutory system of appeals is more effective and more convenient than an application for certiorari, and the principal reason why it may prove itself to be more convenient and more effective is that an appeal to the Secretary of State on all issues arising between the parties can be disposed of at one hearing. Whether the issue between them is a matter of law or fact, or policy or opinion, or a combination of some or all of those, one hearing before the Minister has jurisdiction to deal with them all, whereas of course an application for certiorari is limited to cases where the issue is a matter of law and then only when it is a matter of law appearing on the face of the order.

Furthermore of course there are in some instances reasons for saying that an action for a declaration is more appropriate and more convenient than an order of certiorari, and in cases where such an argument can be used certiorari should not in my opinion go because to allow it to go would be contrary to the necessary restrictions on its use. But an application for certiorari has this advantage that it is speedier and cheaper than the other methods, and in a proper case, therefore, it may well be right to allow it to be used in preference to them. But I would define a proper case as being a case where the decision in question is liable to be upset as a matter of law because on its face it is clearly made without jurisdiction or made in consequence of an error of law.

Given those facts I can well see that it may be more efficient, cheaper and quicker to proceed by certiorari, and in those cases when they arise it seems to me proper that remedy should be available. . . .

Ridge v. *Baldwin* had been decided and reported at the time Lord Widgery CJ gave his earlier judgement in *Boulton*. What factors in the intervening period of ten years or in the two cases might have contributed to the allaying of Lord Widgery's doubts on the use of certiorari to control the activities of local planning authorities? Would the decisions have been the same if *Royco Homes* had been decided in 1964 and *Boulton* in 1974? Lord Widgery CJ suggests that the declaration might be a more appropriate and convenient remedy than an order for certiorari. What is a declaration and how might it help an objector?

Wade, *Administrative Law*, pp. 118–19, 123

The right to ask the court to declare the law in some doubtful point is a very useful remedy, for it enables disputes to be settled before they reach the stage where a right is infringed. . . . In administrative law, the great merit of a declaration is that it is an efficient remedy against *ultra vires* action by governmental authorities of all kinds, including the Crown. If the court will declare that some action, either taken or proposed, is unauthorised by law, that concludes the point as between the plaintiff and the authority. If then . . . an order is made against him, he can ignore it with impunity. . . . but there are limits to its efficacy. . . . First, the object of a declaratory judgement is to declare the legal position of the plaintiff.

In a case where he has no legal rights or no legal standing this remedy is therefore useless to him.

This last sentence is based on the case of *Gregory* v. *London Borough of Camden* [1966] 2 All E.R. 196.

The defendants had granted planning permission to the Westminster Diocese Roman Catholic Trustees to build a school in the grounds of a convent. The school was to be on land allocated under the County of London Development Plan primarily for residential use, so that the application represented a substantial departure from the provisions of the Development Plan. Notwithstanding that, no copy of the application was sent to the Minister as it should have been under the Town and Country Planning (Development Plan) Direction 1965. The court was prepared to assume that the grant of planning permission was, in these circumstances, *ultra vires* the defendants. The plaintiff was the owner of a house adjoining a new access to the new school and overlooking former open space within the convent grounds on which the school was being built. He asked the court for a declaration that the permission was *ultra vires* the defendants. After stating the facts and considering the *Hendon* case Paull J went on:

... That, as far as I know, is the only case under the Act of 1925 which bears on this matter. It bears on this matter only in this way, that, this being an action for a declaration, counsel for the plaintiffs argues that as his clients would have had an action for certiorari, therefore, they have a right to a declaration. I am not quite satisfied that that is quite right. When one is dealing with certiorari, one is quashing. When one is dealing with a declaration, one is not quashing; all that one is doing is to declare the rights of the particular individual who brings the action. One has to look at the matter a little differently, because, in a matter of a declaration, only the rights of the plaintiff and the defendant are involved, and not the rights of all persons who might be governed by the order made.

Looking at the general position in law in this case, I start with this. Building on the convent land raises the question of a loss of amenity by the plaintiffs, the occupiers of a piece of land, because of acts of an adjoining occupier of the land. I will refer to that adjoining occupier as 'the trustees', because this building was in fact being erected under the aegis of trustees, who in fact are the trustees of the lands of the convent. Apart from having to get permission from the planning authority, the trustees have the absolute right in law to do what they are doing, namely, to build a school on that land and to make the access to the school over those pieces of their land for which permission was given to have access. That might hit the plaintiffs hard, but things done by an occupier may hit hard the occupier of adjoining land. To give two examples: I own a house, and on the next plot to my house, which I thought was going to be part of a large garden, there is erected another house. It is erected within two or three feet of my house, just over the border. The effect of that is to block out the light from my windows. Unless I have the right of ancient lights, no legal right of mine has been affected. It is to be noticed that, all the way through in the case to which I have referred, the words 'legal rights' are used. One has to consider the legal rights of someone. Again, next to my land there may be built a school. I may be very much affected by the noise of the children coming out to play, by the shouts, by the laughter and everything else; but unless I can establish that it is a nuisance, I have lost no legal right. I have lost amenities, but no legal rights. My legal rights are exactly as they were before the building was built and the noise arose.

In this case, no question of public rights is involved, as where there is interference with the highway. There is a long series of cases on this, and my attention has been drawn to a number of them, ranging from *R. v. Surrey Justices*[105] to *R. v. Bradford-on-Avon Urban District Council, Ex. p Boulter*[106]. All those cases involve rights over public roadways in one shape or another; in other words, places where the public have rights. In this case, I have merely to consider the right of one landowner in relation to the acts of another landowner, and in relation to the fact that the adjoining landowner is putting up a building to be used in a certain way.

The question that I would ask on this matter is: I am concerned with the rights of adjoining occupiers so far as the building is concerned, and if there is no cause of action against a neighbour because he is putting up that building, or because he is proposing to use it for a certain purpose, then is there any right to step in if the adjoining occupier has to ask a third party for permission before he can begin? Let me take the case of contract. I occupy land next door to B. So far as I am concerned, B has a perfect right to build right up to my border; but suppose B cannot do that because he has a contract with X whereby he has to get the permission of X to build. B starts to build, not having got the permission of X. Am I entitled to enjoin him? Or is B entitled to say that that is nothing to do with me, it is a matter between X and himself? In my view, quite clearly B is so entitled. I, as occupier, although affected by what B is doing, must put up with the consequences unless B is in some way affecting my legal rights, and I have no legal right to object to the building which he is putting up. Therefore, if this were a case of contract between the defendants and the trustees, the plaintiffs would have no rights at all.

If that is how the matter stands in contract, does it make any difference that the matter is not one of contract but of statute? That may well depend on the purpose for which the statute was passed. There are certain statutes which were passed to protect a certain class of people; and, if a statute is passed to protect a class of persons, then anyone in that class who is affected by a breach of the statute may bring an action for damages in respect thereof. The Town Planning Acts, however, have been passed to give rights to the public only, and not to any particular class of the public. On that I am assisted by SALMON J in *Buxton v. Minister of Housing and Local Government* . . . .[107]

In this case, as I see it, the plaintiffs are really saying that in effect they have a right which they would not have had but for the passing of the Town and Country Planning Act, viz., a right to look and see if the Minister or the town planning authority has made an order which is not a good order, and, if they find that this is so, then they can take steps whereby this building may possibly be stopped. That is essentially what the plaintiffs are saying for this action is no use to them whatsoever unless in some way it will influence the question whether the trustees can or cannot go on with their building. Looking at it in that rather simple way, it seems to me that the answer to the question which I have to determine is that the plaintiffs have no legal right to step in at all. They may have suffered damnum, that is to say, loss in one way or another, but they have not suffered injuria, that is to say, any legal wrong. There are many acts which cause loss which give no legal rights. Before one can come to a court of law, one must suffer an injuria as well as damnum; one must have suffered a legal wrong as well as an actual loss of money or amenity or something else. What is taking place on this land behind Nos. 51 and 53 is something in respect of which, as between the plaintiffs and the trustees, there are no legal rights whatsoever, and the plaintiffs cannot interfere by maintaining that a third party's permission must be got before the building can be built. This may be a simple way of looking at this matter, but it seems to me that that is the way by which one can find the solution which seems to fit in with legal principles and with the purposes for which these Acts have been passed. . . .

My conclusion, therefore, is that, on this point of law, the defendants are right. There is no status for the plaintiffs to claim a declaration, which is what they are doing, not asking that the order should be set aside, but asking that, as between themselves and the defendants, they should have a declaration that the defendants acted ultra vires. I think that they have no standing for that purpose, and, therefore, my decision is in favour of the defendants.

If an affirmative decision of a local planning authority cannot be appealed to the Secretary of State, why should the courts make themselves available so that it can be appealed to them? Does not the decision in *Gregory* indicate that something is wrong with the law? What should be done to set it right? Consider the following: (i) the proposal of the Law Commission that:

any person who is or will be adversely affected by administrative action should have sufficient standing to challenge the legality of that action, and therefore be able to obtain the form of relief requested.[108]

(ii) The statement by the Law Commission that:

Whether the formulae (on *locus standi*) in the Town and Country Planning Acts . . . should be looked at in the light of our general proposals for *locus standi* is obviously a delicate policy question. . . . It may well be that it is possible to justify a more restrictive criterion of *locus standi* in these special areas just as it is possible to justify shorter time limits. It may be that to allow neighbours and third parties to challenge grants of planning permission would endanger the whole system of planning machinery. . . . But against this it should be said that when planning permission has been granted by the local planning authority there have been very few applications by neighbours on certiorari to quash these orders. The threat of intervention by a large number of third parties may be more imaginary than real.[109]

4. Administrative controls

The two institutions to be discussed in this part of the chapter – the Council on Tribunals and the Parliamentary Commissioner for Administration – have in common the fact that they were both created to oversee parts of the administrative machine which it was widely felt could not be adequately controlled by any other means, be those means judicial control or the parliamentary question. They have in common also the fact that, in the final analysis, their ability to check the administration depends upon two things: first, the willingness of the administration to be checked, and second, where it is not willing, the pressure that Parliament and the press can bring to bear on it to force it to submit to being checked. It is a matter for consideration here whether such a system of control is, or is likely to be, very effective.

(a) The Council on Tribunals[110]

Established in 1958, the Council's task is to supervise the workings of tribunals and inquiries. It was not originally envisaged that it would receive individual complaints on the operation of these institutions, but when it began to receive them it was prepared to investigate them. On this aspect of the Council's work Wraith and Lamb write as follows (op. cit. p. 230):

The volume of complaints received direct from the public either as individuals or through firms of solicitors, professional organisations or the press, has imposed a considerable burden on the Council. At the same time it has shown perhaps better than anything else could have done where the shoe was pinching and what were the real issues between the public and the administration. Complaints about inquiries have, over the years, exceeded those about tribunals, they rose to a peak (57) in 1961, and thereafter receded, probably as a result of the procedural rules of 1962;

a resurgence to forty-eight in 1968 was misleading, as thirty-two of the forty-eight complaints concerned Stansted Airport, but over ten years they have averaged thirty a year.

. . . Some (complaints) of a kind which would now be referred to the Parliamentary Commissioner for Administration, have arisen through genuine and admitted mistakes and complainants have been satisfied without much difficulty; others have alleged errors of judgement as in the actual conduct of an inquiry by an inspector or a decision about the award of costs; others have raised matters of fact or principle which have proved to be obscure . . . a few have given rise to *causes célèbres*, and have become the subject of Special Reports to the Lord Chancellor.

Except in the last-named instances, when the Council has been forced into the open, its method has been to consult the relevant government department, to engage in informal discussion, and to pour oil on troubled waters.

The Council does, however, later give an account of the complaint and its handling of it in its annual report.

More important from the point of view of judging its effectiveness as a device for the control of the planning process is to consider the *causes célèbres* when it has been forced into the open and clashed with the government of the day. There have been two such clashes, the *Chalkpit* case in 1961[111] and the *Packington Estate* case in 1965. The latter will be examined here.

Like the *Chalkpit* case, this case involved procedure after an inquiry and the rights of third parties. As with *Chalkpit* the Council's intervention sparked off a political dispute in the Houses of Parliament, this time principally in the House of Commons where the government of the day was defending a very small majority, and an election was widely regarded as imminent. Inevitably, therefore, the important issues of procedure were to some extent overlaid with political posturing and this no doubt contributed to the Minister's refusal to admit to anything other than an apparent discourtesy to the Council. But as the extracts from the debate in the House of Commons show, there were valid arguments on both sides of the question. Is it so clear that the Council were in the right as most commentators have assumed?[112] How should the fundamental issue of delay versus participation be solved? Have any of the reforms introduced into the planning process since 1965 pointed the way towards a better solution of the problem than occurred in this case?

Annual Report of the Council on Tribunals (1965)
pp. 24–8

APPENDIX A

Special Report made to the Lord Chancellor on the 2nd February 1966 by the Council on Tribunals under section 1(1)(c) of the Tribunals and Inquiries Act 1958

THE PACKINGTON ESTATE, ISLINGTON

1. Complaints have been made to the Council about the procedure followed by the Minister of Housing and Local Government in connection with proposals for the redevelopment of the Packington Estate, Islington which were the subject of a public local inquiry last year. As a result of their investigation of these complaints the Council have decided that the matter is of sufficient importance to justify a special report to the Lord Chancellor under section 1(1)(c) of the Tribunals and Inquiries Act 1958.

The first planning application
2. In August 1964 the Islington Metropolitan Borough Council applied to the London County Council (which was then the local planning authority) for planning permission for the redevelopment for residential purposes of certain land on the Packington Estate, Islington. For reasons which are not material, no such permission was granted within a period of two months from the date of the application. The application was accordingly deemed to have been refused (see section 24 of the Town and Country Planning Act 1962).

The Appeal and Inquiry
3. The Borough Council exercised its right to appeal to the Minister of Housing and Local Government (section 23 of the Town and Country Planning Act 1962) and the Minister appointed an inspector from his Department to hold a public local inquiry.

4. This inquiry was held in February 1965. Only the applicant and the local planning authority have a legal right to be heard at such an inquiry, but by administrative concession it is customary for the inspector to allow all persons who have a genuine interest in the application to appear and be heard. Such persons are known as 'third parties'. The inspector followed the usual practice and the following 'third parties' were permitted to appear either in support of or in opposition to the proposed development: –

In support: Islington Tenants' Association
In opposition: London and Manchester Assurance Company Ltd.
A group of 425 residents of surrounding properties
The Islington Society
London and Counties Tenants Federation (Islington Branch)
Beaconsfield Buildings Tenants' Association
Popham Street Tenants' Association

Two individual members of the Appellant Borough Council

Two other private individuals.

5. The Borough Council's application had been accompanied by detailed plans of its proposals, but at the inquiry it sought leave to proceed on the basis of an application for outline approval only and no objection was raised to this course.

6. The opposition to the Borough Council's application was based upon the proposition that the site should be rehabilitated and not redeveloped. This view was endorsed by the local planning authority, but the main burden of the opposition was borne by the third parties and, in particular, by the London and Manchester Insurance Company Ltd., owners of an adjoining estate. This company put forward a very detailed case in favour of rehabilitation and supported it with expert evidence. The inquiry lasted for six days.

7. On 12th April 1965 the inspector submitted his report to the Minister. In it he recorded that the application had been considered as if it were one for outline permission and stated that the issue at the inquiry had been whether the properties on the appeal site should be rehabilitated with some in-filling development or should be redeveloped. His recommendation to the Minister was that the appeal be allowed, subject to certain conditions. In other words he was in favour of redevelopment rather than rehabilitation.

The Minister's decision on the first application

8. By a letter dated 23rd July 1965 those concerned, including the third parties, were informed of the substance of the inspector's report and that the Minister had noted the views of the inspector. The letter recorded that by the London Government Act 1963 the functions of the appellant Council had been taken over by the Council of the new London Borough of Islington and that this Council was now the local planning authority. The letter went on to give the Minister's decision in the following terms:

But [the Minister] is not satisfied on the details submitted that the Council's proposals would result in a scheme of the quality to compensate for destroying an estate of the type that many people still find attractive in layout and design. Any scheme which is to be acceptable must produce an environment which would justify the loss of the existing buildings; and it must not prejudice the amenities of the surrounding area. The Minister would want to be satisfied that this result would be obtained before he would feel able to decide in favour of redevelopment against rehabilitation. He has therefore decided to dismiss the present appeal though without prejudice to the submission to him of another application subsequently; and he proposes to arrange a discussion with the Council about how the kind of layout and design which seem to him to be required here might best be achieved. It would be right that the Greater London Council should be represented at the discussion.

The first complaint

9. On 23rd August 1965 the secretary of the group of 425 residents of surrounding properties forwarded to this Council a copy of the decision letter and sought its assistance. He expressed the view that the procedure proposed by the Minister was likely to result in the formulation of proposals which would be supported by the Islington Council, the Greater London Council, and the Minister, but that there was a grave risk that they would be unacceptable to his group or to the London and Manchester Insurance Company. He felt that, bearing in mind that the Minister had upheld the parties' objections to the original scheme, it would be particularly regrettable if the procedure adopted made it impossible for any further effective representation to be made by them.

10. A copy of this letter was sent to the Ministry by the Council on 24th August 1965 with a request for the Ministry's comments.

11. On 16th September 1965 the secretary of the residents' group wrote to the Town Clerk of the Islington Borough Council concerning a newspaper report that the Borough Council were submitting "new proposals" to the Minister and stated that his group would be grateful for an opportunity of examining the new proposals in view of their direct interest in the matter and in the light of the Minister's decision following the public inquiry. The Town Clerk replied on 17th September 1965 that:

> Amended proposals have been submitted to the Minister but as long as they are under reconsideration by the Minister it would not be proper for the Council to publish details. I am, however, sure that they will do so as soon as the Minister gives his clearance.

It seemed to the Council on Tribunals to be important that the Ministry should be aware of this correspondence and copies were forwarded to the Ministry as soon as it became available to the Council, namely on 21st September 1965.

12. By a letter dated 24th September 1965 the Ministry furnished this Council with their comments on the first complaint. They may be summarised as follows:

> (*a*) The rights of the objectors to state their views arose out of the exercise by the Inspector of his discretion to allow them to appear at the inquiry into the appeal and their rights did not continue beyond the inquiry.
> (*b*) If the London County Council had approved the application, the objectors would have had no opportunity of stating their views.
> (*c*) It did not follow from the fact that the inspector allowed the objectors to state their views that a resubmission of their views would still have been of value.
> (*d*) The objectors would have preferred that the properties be rehabilitated, but that issue had been decided against them.

(*e*) A discussion of proposals with a prospective applicant was not itself a part of the appeals procedure, but was a proper part of planning.

13.   It seemed to the Council that though the Ministry might not be technically at fault in the procedure adopted, the complainants had good grounds for feeling that they had not been fairly treated. Furthermore the Council was unable to reconcile the terms of the decision letter (paragraph 8 above), and in particular the statement therein that *before the Minister would feel able to decide in favour of redevelopment against rehabilitation* certain conditions would have to be satisfied, with the statement in the Ministry's letter of 24th September 1965 that the issue of rehabilitation versus redevelopment had been decided by the Minister against the objectors.

The second complaint

14.   This was received on 27th September 1965 from a firm of surveyors which had been concerned in the inquiry on behalf of the London and Manchester Insurance Company. It appeared that following the issue of the decision letter the firm had written to the Ministry complaining of their clients' exclusion from further discussion of the future of the Packington Estate. Whilst they acknowledged that the Minister was acting *intra vires*, they considered that this procedure was unfair. They expressed the view that if public confidence was to be maintained the various procedures should be as open as possible and that the obvious way of achieving this was to invite their clients and any necessary technical advisers to attend the meetings to discuss the future of the estate. They added that their clients had a vast fund of valuable information pertaining to the possibility of rehabilitation, only a part of which had been put before the inquiry, and they expressed the view that this was a matter on which neither the Borough Council nor the London County Council had shown themselves to be well informed at the inquiry.

15.   The Ministry had replied to the complainants that the Minister appreciated the offer of further information about the possibility of rehabilitation. However, the case for and against rehabilitation had been argued at the inquiry, the Minister had had the benefit of the inspector's conclusions in the light of these arguments and he was no longer concerned with the issue of the advantages or disadvantages of rehabilitation as compared with redevelopment.

16.   The Council were still unable to reconcile this view with the terms of the decision letter (paragraph 8 above) and invited the Ministry to comment on this second complaint. At a meeting of the Council on 27th October 1965 the matter was further considered and it was resolved that representatives of the Ministry be invited to attend the next meeting of the Council on 24th November 1965 for an informal discussion of both complaints. Such an invitation was accordingly sent to the Ministry on 29th October 1965.

The second planning application

17. Meanwhile, unknown to this Council or, it is believed, to the complainants, the discussions between the Islington Borough Council and the Ministry had been concluded and on 13th October 1965 a fresh application had been made for planning permission for the redevelopment of the Packington Estate. News of this application reached this Council in the circumstances set out in the succeeding paragraph of this report.

The Minister's decision on the second application

18. On 23rd November 1965, the day before the Council were to have discussions with representatives of the Ministry, the Council received from the Ministry a copy of a letter dated 22nd November 1965 addressed to the Town Clerk of the Islington Council. This letter referred to the application of 13th October 1965, to the earlier inquiry and to the subsequent discussions with the Islington Council and the Greater London Council. It continued:

> In these circumstances the Minister is no longer concerned with the advantages and disadvantages of rehabilitation as compared with redevelopment, but only with the quality of the redevelopment scheme. He has not therefore considered it necessary to invite representations from those who previously objected to the redevelopment.

The letter concluded by granting planning permission for redevelopment, save in so far as the relevant plans concerned two shops planning permission for which was refused.

The third complaint

19. Both the secretary of the group of 425 residents and the firm of surveyors who acted for the insurance company received copies of the Minister's letter of decision on the second application and both made further complaint to this Council. Both expressed the view that the scheme for which planning permission was given in November 1965 was substantially the same as that for which planning permission had been refused in July 1965.

Discussion with the Ministry

20. On 24th November 1965 representatives of the Ministry attended a meeting of the Council. They were told that the Council considered that the Ministry had shown some discourtesy in bringing the matter to a conclusion two days before it was due to be discussed at that meeting. In reply the representatives expressed regret that the Council should take this view and explained that the case had proceeded in the ordinary way after the second application had been found to be satisfactory. The substance of the first and second complaints was discussed but no additional information or explanation emerged. The Council were informed that the Ministry would have had no objection to the objectors being informed of the revised scheme which the Islington Council proposed to submit to the Minister (see paragraph 11 above).

Conclusions

21.   The Council do not suggest that at any stage the Minister exceeded his powers. Nevertheless they consider that the complainants have real reason to feel aggrieved.

22.   It will be seen that in seeking to justify the procedure adopted the Ministry contend, and the complainants deny, that the Minister upon consideration of the inspector's report decided that the future of the area must lie in redevelopment rather than in rehabilitation.

23.   The Ministry's contention involves the proposition that the issue was decided without regard to any specific acceptable scheme of redevelopment. This is unconvincing since the Minister's letter recognized that the decision must depend upon a balance of advantages and disadvantages – 'Any scheme which is to be acceptable must produce an environment which would justify the loss of the existing buildings; and it must not prejudice the amenities of the surrounding area.'

24.   If the Minister did intend to decide initially in favour of redevelopment the Council consider that the decision letter of 23rd July 1965 was ineptly expressed and likely to mislead the complainants. In particular they draw attention to the passage in which it was stated that certain conditions would have to be satisfied before the Minister would feel able to decide in favour of redevelopment against rehabilitation. The Council, for their part, can only read the letter as meaning that (i) the scheme proposed was not preferable to rehabilitation; (ii) other schemes of redevelopment might be preferable to rehabilitation and (iii) the Minister intended to have discussions with the Islington Council and the Greater London Council concerning alternative schemes of redevelopment which might form the subject matter of a subsequent application for planning permission.

25.   But the real grievance of the complainants is, as it appears to the Council, that they were denied the opportunity of taking any part in the proceedings on the second application. They were rightly allowed to contest the first application and secured its rejection; and the second application was so closely connected with the first that it was, in substance, a further stage in the same proceedings. By being excluded at that stage altogether the complainants were, as the Council think, less than fairly treated.

26.   The Council have assumed that the Ministry are correct in suggesting that the second application was substantially different from the first. If, as the complainants maintain, the two applications were substantially the same, the complainants have the further grievance that one or other of the decisions must have been wrong.

27.   Whatever the truth of the matter, there has been apparent unfairness to the complainants. Openness, fairness and impartiality – the hall-marks of good administration – are not enough, if they are not all apparent.

House of Commons Debate, Vol. 725, cols 1367–75.
'Packington Estate, Islington (Council on Tribunals'
Report)'

MR R. H. S. CROSSMAN (Minister for Housing and Local Government): . . . we on this side of the House who are Ministers take seriously the work of the Council on Tribunals. Indeed, I take it seriously enough.

Immediately Lord Tenby wrote his letter in the *Daily Telegraph*,[113] I wrote to him saying that I should like to hear very much what he thought I should have done, and asking whether I could see him, and whether we could arrange a meeting and have a discussion of the Packington case and the issues arising out of it. . . . it is ridiculous to say that there is any question of our not taking the Council's criticism seriously.

I have reflected on it, and studied it ever since. In what I have to say I shall obviously be partly agreeing with it and partly disagreeing with it, but, above all, I shall be saying, and repeating, that I think that the question of the semi-judicial status of the Minister is one of the most difficult that he has to face. Any Minister will tell one that he will sometimes be right and sometimes wrong. Having listened to a collection of lawyers, as we have done this afternoon – my hon. Friend and I have been the only non-lawyers who have spoken – discussing and arguing the rights and wrongs here, I feel grateful that I am instructed to do my job alone, with nobody to advise me. . . .

The second issue – this is one about which I feel distressed – was the Council's sense that I had committed an act of discourtesy in taking a decision two days before my officials were due to meet it. . . .

I wonder whether the Council realises that, while it certainly put me in a position where I seemed deliberately discourteous, it by its own action put the Minister in an extremely difficult position. It is one thing when the Council on Tribunals comments on procedure adopted when a decision has already been taken in a case. This process enables the responsible Minister to have the benefit of the Council's advice and to consider with it whether the system needs improvement, and how.

. . . It is quite another thing for a Minister to be faced with a complaint which the Council on Tribunals is taking cognisance of while he is still considering his decision on the case. This is a very different position for the Minister. . . .

The difficulty was that while we were still proceeding the Council on Tribunals took cognisance of the objectors and began to take a keen interest and to question my officials. As my hon, and learned Friend the Member for Warrington (Mr W. T. Williams) pointed out, if this were to happen often, if it were the regular thing for a kind of interim injunction to be applied to a Minister by the Council, all any objector would have to do would be to put his case to the Council and the Minister would automatically be banned from proceeding with the case. That would be very serious, and I am sure that nobody wants that. In this case, the objection had started weeks before and if I had done what was asked of me, I should have had to have suspended the case pending clearing it with the Council.

However, on reflection it is quite clear to me that issuing the judgment as we did two days before the Council was meeting my officials was something which could be interpreted as discourteous. I regret that it happened. . . .

I now turn to the second charge which is levelled by the Council and which concerns the drafting of the vital sentences in the decision letter. Perhaps I can let out a secret of Ministries. I do not disguise the fact that this part of the letter was written in my own fair hand and I bear full and total and personal responsibility for those sentences which I believe one could almost recognise to be mine by the fact that it was not a lawyer but a layman who wrote them – they were so intelligent, they were so intelligible, they were so sensible. They were blatantly those of someone trying to be, using the Council's own words, fair and impartial and above board.

What they did was to spell out precisely what was in my mind, to say that this was not a simple issue and that Islington Council, which saw nothing but the redevelopment of council houses, must not lose sight of what rehabilitation could make of Canonbury. Equally, the developers, the property companies and the residents said that they wanted Packington to be like Chelsea or Canonbury, which must mean *de facto* that not one single person among the residents could live there, because the rents would be raised.

An important social issue is thus raised in Islington. The social issue is simple. In Islington there are thousands of people on the housing list and there is very little room for houses. The council's job is to build houses for those on the housing list, and every time a part of Islington is turned into Canonbury, the area on which to build for those on the housing list is reduced. That is the real issue. It has not been thought about outside of the House, as here, by lawyers. . . . That was the issue which I tried to express when I wrote these words into the letter: Any scheme which is to be acceptable must produce an environment which would justify the loss of the existing buildings. That was to say that the council should redevelop, but must not be ruthless about it, must not put into the area the iron edifices of industrialised building, but must build so that the environment of the area could be a proper mixture between redevelopment and rehabilitation and not be hopelessly onesided.

I added on the other side: The Minister would want to be satisfied that this result would be obtained before he would feel able to decide in favour of redevelopment against rehabilitation. Those are the key sentences which the Council on Tribunals selected to describe as badly drafted.

With hindsight, I now understand what the Council meant. The right hon. Member for Kingston-upon-Thames[114] knows the problems of Ministers. Of course, it is true that if I had simply taken the inspector's report in favour of redevelopment and had signed on the dotted line and had told Islington to go ahead, no one could have challenged me. There would have been no debate today if I had been completely onesided and safely black and white and if I had not tried to indicate that this was a genuinely finely balanced judgment. I would not have had any problem and the Council on Tribunals, which asks me to be fair and impartial and open, would not have accused me of failing to be those things if I had just closed my mind and suppressed by own doubts and had simply told the objectors that Islington Council was to go ahead and not told Islington Council that it would have to be careful. . . .

What happened after that? Exactly what I said would happen. The council had the plans rejected and I said we would have consultations and we did. . . .

My officials went down and talked to the authority. Up till now we had not seen any plans or models so I had them brought into my office. We had our architects in and we made absolutely sure that all that we would require in Islington would be incorporated in the new plans when they were put up to us. There was a wonderful moment in the discussion when I was being challenged from the Opposition benches. Was this second plan a new plan or an old plan? It was new and it was old. It was the old plan revised precisely in the way I asked for it to be revised. . . .

I turn now to the substantial question of the right of the objectors. We had had a six-day inquiry in which thousands of words were spoken and which produced a report of some 25,000 words. The inquiry had been conducted extremely well. The case for rehabilitation was put by the insurance company and by the residents in an extremely able fashion. I have no doubt that they know much more about rehabilitation than Islington Borough Council. The case was powerfully put and there were no further facts for me to learn. They had all been established in the first inquiry.

The facts were out. The second question was, if the facts are out, is there a right for the objectors to have a second round of protest and delay? Let us be honest about this – it is delay. I had to decide this. Nobody said that I had to give it to the objectors, everybody said it was within my discretion to give it to them. Now nobody says that I ought to have held an inquiry.

I return to the point, if there is to be no inquiry, what do I do? If I choose the main objectors and exclude others I should be violating every kind of principle. I cannot pick and choose. If I have any objectors then the borough council must be allowed to come in and give its case, and before one knows it, one has an inquiry. This is the central point. I have been thinking about this ever since. How could I have done what the Council asked?

How effective is the Council? Is its practice of informal discussion and occasional forays into the public and political arena the best way to achieve results? Is it the only way? Commentators have been guarded. Garner states that 'as a general observation it may be said that the Council's views have always been received appreciatively by Government Departments, although there have been a few cases of disagreement with them'.[115] Wraith and Lamb however state that 'in its first ten years it has suffered a good deal of frustration, through being ignored or suspected; it has not always been popular with departments. . . .'[116] Wade, who was a member of the Council from its inception to 1971, declines to comment on its effectiveness beyond saying that it may be thought that both institutions (the Council and the Parliamentary Commissioner) are in need of greater resources of legal expertise.[117] De Smith noted that there have been conflicts between the Council and Ministers of Housing and Local Government and that 'when conflicts arise the Council is handicapped by its lack of political power base'.[118]

These last two quotations point in different directions and assume two very different kinds of administrative system: the first one where greater legal expertise will bring greater effectiveness *vis-à-vis* the bureaucracy; the second where greater political power will bring greater effectiveness. It may well be that while the first assumption reflects the ideal to which we should aim, the second reflects the reality of the world around us. What would greater legal expertise have contributed to the Council's role in the *Packington Estate* case?

(b) The Parliamentary Commissioner for Administration[119]

The Parliamentary Commissioner for Administration (PCA) was established by the Parliamentary Commissioner Act 1967. De Smith summarises his functions and mode of operation as follows (*Constitutional Law*, pp. 628–30):

His terms of reference are to investigate complaints by individuals and bodies corporate (other than local authorities and other public corporations) who claim to have 'sustained injustice in consequence of maladministration' while they were in the United Kingdom, at the hands of scheduled central government departments or persons or bodies acting on their behalf, performing or failing to person administrative functions.

He cannot act on his own initiative nor can he be approached directly by a member of the public. He can act only in pursuance of a written complaint to an M.P. forwarded to him by an M.P. with the consent of the complainant. His investigations must be conducted in private, and the official head of the Department concerned and any other official implicated in the complaint must be notified and given the opportunity of commenting on the allegations. No set form of inquiry is prescribed but the P.C.A. has adequate powers to compel the attendance of witnesses and documents. Wilful obstruction of his investigations is punishable as if it were a contempt of court. His reports on investigations, and communications with M.P.'s on the subject matter of a complaint are protected by absolute privilege in the law of defamation. . . .

The P.C.A. has no power to alter or rescind decisions. His statutory powers are confined to making reports on his investigations, or giving to the M.P. who referred the complaint his reasons for not investigating. . . .

If it appears to the P.C.A. that an injustice has been caused by maladministration and has not been rectified, he may make a special report to both Houses, he may make other special reports and must make an annual report to each House. His special and annual reports are considered by a small Select Committee of the House of Commons on the Parliamentary Commissioner for Administration. . . .

'Injustice' and 'maladministration' were deliberately left undefined. 'Injustice' means something wider than legally redressible damage; it includes hardship and a sense of grievance which ought not to have arisen. 'Maladministration' covers a multitude of administrative sins, sins of commission and omission. . . . The Commissioner is not allowed to question 'the merits of a decision taken without maladministration . . . in the exercise of a discretion. . . .' He interpreted this limitation as meaning that he could not consider whether a decision was manifestly unreasonable or even apparently based on a clear mistake of fact, if the appropriate procedures had been followed and there was no evidence of impropriety. He was persuaded by the Select Committee that in an extreme case he ought to infer maladministration from the 'thoroughly bad' *quality* of a decision; but he has shown extreme circumspection in this matter. . . .

He has his own office and appoints his own staff, subject to Treasury approval. By 1972 he had a staff of over sixty, drawn from the civil service, none of them, astonishingly, was a professional lawyer.

As might be expected, the Department of the Environment and its predecessors have attracted a fair number of complaints, several of them involving the planning process as it affects both private and public developments. An example of the PCA's handling of complaints follows.

> *Fourth Report of the Parliamentary Commissioner for Administration*, Session 1972–3

Case No. 241/G – Planning permission for building of a supermarket

1. The complaint concerns the actions of the Department of the Environment about a planning permission given by the County Council which allowed a supermarket to be built well in front of a long-standing improvement line for a main road on the outskirts of a town.

2. The complainants (a local group of Residents) say that this mistake has not only caused them serious loss of amenity but will result in the loss of some of their land for road widening which cannot now be done on the other side as planned. They maintain that it is unjust that they should have thus to suffer because of the County Council's mistake. They say that the inspector who held the inquiry into the matter strongly recommended that the building should be set back, and that they were led to believe by a letter issued by the Department that the Secretary of State accepted that this should happen. However, 7 months later, and without giving them the

opportunity to make further representations, the Department announced that the Secretary of State had decided not to require action to be taken to set back the building at all, because of the high cost of compensation that would fall on the County Council and the disturbance involved for established traders.

3. The Residents, who point out that they brought the mistake to notice when the building was still in its early stages, say that those factors would not have arisen had the Department not taken an inordinate time to consider the matter. They also question the circumstances in which the Secretary of State's decision was reversed without their being given an opportunity to make further representations.

4. The Residents also complain that they have still not had a decision about reimbursement of the costs they incurred in defending their interests at the inquiry, although it is two years since that inquiry was held.

Background
5. In 1968, the County Council ('the CC') gave planning permission for a shopping precinct, including the supermarket, on land fronting the main road in question. The road hereabouts marks the boundary between the County and the County Borough, the road itself being in the Borough. For many years the County Borough Council ('the CBC') have had plans for widening the road on the County (supermarket) side and by agreement between the two Councils development along that side has been kept behind a defined building line to allow for the future widening of the road.

6. Work on the shopping precinct site began in August 1969 and by November it was apparent that the supermarket building was being erected well in front of the road improvement line. Local residents brought this to the notice of the CC and the CBC. It was then discovered that due to an oversight on the CC's part when they had considered the plans and a failure to consult the CBC about the proposal, as they had a statutory obligation to do under the Planning Acts, the permission they had given allowed the supermarket to be sited where it was being built. Local residents and the CBC made representations to the CC that they should exercise powers available to them under the planning Acts and make an order revoking or modifying the permission so as to require the building to be set back to the line observed by the existing development along that side of the main road. But the CC, who estimated that the compensation cost of such action, at that stage of building, would be in the region of £50,000, were not prepared to do that. In their view a still satisfactory widening of the road was possible without moving the supermarket or taking land from properties on the other side of the road.

Action by the Department
7. In view of the CC's refusal, local residents (in January 1970) and the CBC (in February 1970) brought the situation to the Department's notice and asked that the Secretary of State ('the S of S)' should use his

default powers under Section 207 of the Town and Country Planning Act 1962 to direct the CC to take action to remedy their mistake. The Department first sought information and comments from the CC. In the light of the CC's reply and the representations by then received from the CBC, the Department, on 11th March, formally consulted the CC about making an order and sought further information from the CBC. They had replies from both Councils by the middle of April and on 19th May announced that, in view of the apparently irreconcilable views of the two Councils, a public local inquiry would be held to obtain all the facts for the purpose of deciding whether the S of S should exercise his default powers.

The inspector's report following the inquiry

8. The inquiry opened on 23rd July, 1970 and ended on 7th August. The inspector presented his 40 page report on 17th September. He reported that construction of the building had gone ahead and was nearly finished and that the prospective lessees of the supermarket hoped to open for business in November. Also they and the developers of the precinct estimated that compensation of the order of £200,000 to £270,000 would be payable, depending on whether the building was set back 20 feet (which would just clear the road improvement line) or 65 feet (which was the whole depth of the supermarket from the road frontage wall to the next shop in the precinct). The inspector was in no doubt that the road would need to be widened in the foreseeable future to cope with increasing traffic. On the basis of an overall width of 60 feet (including safety and amenity verges), which seemed to him to be necessary and reasonable, that widening could only be achieved, if the supermarket remained where it was, by taking land from about 12 properties and demolishing a building on the other side of the road bringing it so close to some of the houses that their amenities would be seriously affected. And the inspector considered that, apart from the question of the road widening, in its present forward position the supermarket building injuriously affected the amenity of those who lived opposite it in particular and the surroundings in general. Noting that the positioning of the supermarket stemmed from a gross error on the part of the CC, he concluded that, although it would involve a considerable sum of public money and delay in the provision of the shopping facilities to rectify it, those serious consequences did not outweigh the importance of the highway and amenity considerations which, in his opinion, warranted setting back the supermarket at least 50 feet. Accordingly he recommended that orders should be made to secure that this was done.

9. The Department's papers show that they weighed the pros and cons at length in the light of the inspector's report. Some doubts were expressed whether, notwithstanding that the situation had arisen from palpable errors by the CC which they could have rectified at lesser cost had they acted immediately, the consequences of leaving the supermarket where it had been built justified expenditure of upwards of £200,000 and the loss of materials involved in setting it back now. However, the conclusion

reached was that, despite that cost, there were no really sufficient grounds for disagreeing with the inspector's recommendation that the building should be set back; but that there should be further discussion with the CC and CBC to see whether a satisfactory solution to the road and amenity problems could be achieved by a less drastic solution than the 50 feet set back recommended by the inspector, e.g. a set back limited to 20 feet. The Department were advised that this could be done without re-opening the inquiry and on 5th April, 1971 they sent a letter to the CC which enclosed a copy of the inspector's report and said –

> The Secretary of State is disposed to accept the inspector's recommendation that there is a need to set back the building from the line of the highway, but he wishes to consider whether a lesser distance of setting back than that recommended by the inspector would be appropriate and also what conditions (such as architectural treatment and landscaping) should be imposed.
>
> He therefore proposes to continue his consultations with the County Council under Section 207 of the Act of 1962 on these aspects alone and at the same time to seek the views of the County Borough Council. His decision will be issued after these consultations have taken place.

Copies of this letter and the inspector's report were sent to the CBC and to the other interested parties, including the residents, who had attended the inquiry.

10. After some discussion within the Department, a meeting was held with officials of the CC and the CBC on 18th June to examine the technical possibilities of a number of schemes which would have involved set backs of the supermarket ranging from 6 feet to 44 feet, in two cases involving the complete resiting of the supermarket on part of the adjacent copse and parking area. The result of this meeting was that there did appear to be some feasible alternatives to what the inspector had recommended, involving a lesser set back and less disturbance of the shopping precinct development, but that there was little to choose between them on cost grounds, which according to the estimates made would still be in the region of £200,000 which had been put forward at the inquiry. However, it appears from the Department's note of the meeting that the CC remained strongly opposed to taking any action to set back the supermarket and that the CBC's officials did not altogether rule out the alternative possibility of widening the road on its other side, if the S of S decided that the supermarket should not be moved.

11. The Department then reappraised the situation in the light of that examination of the possible schemes, and after further debate came to the conclusion that it would be possible to obtain the minimum width needed for a satisfactory improvement of the road without moving the supermarket, even though this would mean taking land from the properties on the other side of it. In the circumstances they decided that, after all, there was not sufficient justification for the cost and disturbance that any set back of the supermarket would involve. Accordingly, on 9th November,

1971 they issued a letter stating that the S of S had carefully considered the whole case afresh in the light of the inspector's report and the further consultations the Department had had with officials of the CC and the CBC about possible schemes for setting back the supermarket a lesser distance than that proposed by the inspector, all of which would entail very large claims for compensation which would fall on the [County] ratepayers. Although the S of S accepted, for the road and amenity reasons indicated by the inspector, that the supermarket should never have been allowed to be built so close to the road, the situation was that planning permission for this had been given and the supermarket and some of the shops were already in business. What had to be considered therefore was whether the demerits of the development were of such an overriding character that they required the supermarket to be set back despite the cost burden on ratepayers and the disturbance to established traders and users of the shopping facilities. In the S of S's view, although the development had significant defects in the unneighbourliness of the building and the extent to which its position restricted future options for improving the road, these were not so serious as to warrant the exercise of his default powers to require the CC to take action.

FINDINGS

The Department's change of mind

12. The Residents say that they understood the letter of 5th April, 1971 to mean that the fundamental decision that the supermarket should be set back had been taken and that all that remained to be settled was whether the set back needed to be as much as 50 feet.

13. The Department agree that it did carry such an implication but they point out that it was cautiously worded – it said that the S of S was disposed to accept, not that he had accepted (even in principle) the inspector's recommendation – and that it made it clear that a decision had yet to be taken. In their view, the reference to further consultations with the two Councils to consider whether a lesser set back would be appropriate meant that, if a lesser set back was not found to be appropriate, the whole question of setting back the building at all would be reviewed. But my reading of the Department's papers is that a decision that the supermarket should be set back had in fact been taken and the only aspect left open for further consideration was the amount of the set back. And my interpretation of the letter is that, if a lesser set back was not found to be appropriate, it would be the Department's intention to require the full set back recommended by the inspector. Moreover, it appears to me that the subsequent change of mind derived not from the evidence that was obtained about the implications of different degrees of set back, but from a reassessment of the situation on a further, closer look at the issues involved. I accept that the letter of 5th April did not, in terms, commit the S of S as to his decision on the matter; and I accept that the decision he finally came to, hard though it is on the Residents, was one it was open to him to reach in the exercise of his discretion. But I consider the Residents have every cause to feel aggrieved about the decision in the face of the acknowledged

implications of the earlier letter the Department had issued, after long and close consideration of the matter in the light of the inspector's report.

Residents given no opportunity of further representations before the decision was taken

14. The Residents believe that the reversal of the S of S's decision was the result of further representations made by the CC 'in private' after the inquiry. They also make the point that, had they not been lulled into a false sense of security by the letter of 5th April 1971, they would have put forward further evidence that had not been available to them at the inquiry which, they say, suggested that there would only be a minimal difference in cost between, on the one hand, setting back the supermarket and widening the road on that side, and on the other, acquiring land from properties to widen it on the opposite side. I have seen that the Minister for Local Government and Development refused to see a deputation from the CC to argue their case further after the letter of 5th April was issued and the Department have assured me that the only discussion they had with the CC was the meeting with officials, at which the CBC were also represented, in June 1971, to examine the possibilities of schemes involving a lesser set back of the supermarket (paragraph 10). However, while I accept that the Department were entitled to have these further consultations with the CC in coming to a decision about the exercise of the S of S's default powers, and were under no obligation to give the Residents the opportunity to make further representations, I consider that, in the circumstances of this case, it would have been reasonable to have provided such an opportunity before coming to that eventual decision which was so much at variance with the implications of the Department's letter of 5th April, 1971. In this connection, I have noted that in the interval between that letter and the decision in November 1971, they had letters which clearly showed that the Residents believed that a decision in principle had been taken but which also asked for an opportunity to make further representations in the light of any developments as a result of the further consultations with the CC; but that the Department neither explained that the whole issue still remained open nor invited further representations.

Delay

15. The Residents complain that the high cost of compensation and the question of disturbance of established traders and shopping facilities which played a large part in the S of S's final decision, arose from the inordinate time the Department took to consider the matter. The Residents make the point that 7 months passed from the time they brought the situation to the Department's notice (when building was still at a fairly early stage) before the inquiry was held; and that 16 months then elapsed before the final decision was given, making a total time of nearly two years during which they were kept in a state of stress and uncertainty about a matter of great concern to them.

16. Although the Department's papers do not reveal appreciable periods when no action was being taken, I consider it took them unreason-

ably long to consider and reach a decision on the matter, albeit it was a difficult one to make; and I think there is some substance in the Residents' complaint about being kept waiting so long before they knew the outcome.

17. The Department acknowledge that their consideration of the matter was protracted but they do not accept that the final decision was affected by that delay, as the Residents suggest it was. They explain that since the development was in accordance with the permission that had been granted, there was no way of halting it except by making an order revoking or modifying that permission, and that such action involved procedures, including the holding of an inquiry if the developers so requested, which inevitably took a fair amount of time. While the cost of compensation would no doubt have been lower if the CC had submitted an order to the S of S for confirmation as soon as the mistake had been noticed, the Department tell me there was no likelihood, having regard to the stage of building when the matter was brought to their notice, that the necessary procedures involved in invoking the S of S's default powers and then getting an order to the point where it became effective could have been achieved in time to prevent construction of the building being completed. I accept this assessment of the position. My study of the Department's papers also satisfies me that the final decision, not to require the building to be set back, was not attributable to any significant hardening of the cost and disturbance factors in the interval between the presentation of the inspector's report and when that decision was taken.

19. As to the delay, I appreciated that there were difficulties in the way of settling the question of costs until a decision on the supermarket was finally made in November 1971. But it seemed to me that for some time after that the Department had allowed the matter to drift unnecessarily. But what occasioned me more cause for concern than the delay in deciding the applications was the Department's view that they would not be justified in awarding costs to the Residents. I was aware from my study of the papers that the Department had sanctioned payment by the CC of the costs incurred by the supermarket developers and lessees and I asked them to explain why they did not think that the Residents too should have their costs paid.

20. The Department told me that their established policy on costs, formulated in the light of a report by the Council on Tribunals on the subject, is that third parties, whether or not they are successful and however much they contribute to the inquiry proceedings, are awarded costs only in special circumstances where they have been put to additional expense by adjournment or postponement of an inquiry. This was not so here and the Department had no evidence that the Residents' costs had increased because of the circumstances that gave rise to their complaint.

21. I told the Department that I did not question the generality of their policy on awarding costs but it did seem to me that this case presented an unusual combination of circumstances which could not be easily fitted

into the frame of the normal policy. At the cost of adding to the delay in settling the applications, I asked them to review the whole matter, taking into consideration those features which seemed to me to merit exceptional consideration – including the fact that this inquiry would not have taken place but for the mistake by the CC in the first place. The Department agreed to do this and I am glad to report that they now tell me they accept that there are grounds for treating this as an exceptional case and paying the Residents' costs. They are so informing the Residents.

Conclusions

22. It is clear that the building of the supermarket in a position where it should not have been allowed has caused injustice to the Residents. Not only are they suffering an unnecessary loss of amenity but some of them will be adversely affected when the improvement of the road, which is foreseen as necessary within the next few years, takes place. Instead of the road being widened on the supermarket side as intended, it will have to be improved on the other side where the Residents face the prospect of loss of at least part of their property and damage to their use and enjoyment of the remainder.

23. The origin of this injustice is the admitted mistake of the CC in granting permission for the building of the supermarket on that site, and the subsequent refusal of the CC to take action to rescind that permission. The actions of the CC are not within my jurisdiction. But it lay within the power of the Department to initiate action to remedy that error when the CC refused to do so, and my investigation has been concerned with the question whether there was maladministration by the Department in reaching their decision not to take that action.

24. In their consideration of the difficult situation which had arisen as a result of the error by the CC the Department had to balance a number of conflicting issues. And I have found serious shortcomings in the way they handled the problem. Initially they decided to accept the inquiry inspector's recommendation that they should take steps to secure a set back of the supermarket further from the Residents' homes; and they issued a letter which (as the Department themselves acknowledge) clearly implied that they had so decided and that the only question outstanding, on which further enquiries were to be made, was the extent of the set back. Having made those further enquiries, they decided to set aside completely their earlier decision, to reject the inspector's recommendation and to allow the CC's permission to stand. They were in part influenced, when coming to their new decision, by the fact that their letter had been so worded that it did not, in terms, commit them to the original decision; and they did not, in my view, at that time attach sufficient weight to the acknowledged implication of the letter as a whole. And in the interval between the two decisions they neither explained the position in reply to letters from the Residents which made it clear that they took the view that the Department had decided to take steps to secure a set back of the supermarket and in which they asked to be consulted about any developments, nor gave the

Residents an opportunity to submit further comments (as in my view would, in the particular circumstances, have been reasonable) before taking their final decision.

25. I cannot say that the Department's mishandling of the case means that their final decision was necessarily wrong. It was a decision which lay within their discretion, after proper consideration of all the relevant facts, arguments and representation; and, having carefully reviewed the matter in detail once more in the light of all those factors, they have reaffirmed that decision. But I understand, and sympathise with, the Residents' dissatisfaction with a procedure which (though there had been no actual change of circumstances) produced two contrary decisions by the Department within a few months and failed to give them the opportunity to represent their own views further before the Department's change of mind. It is not surprising that they are convinced that they have suffered an injustice.

P. Payne, 'Planning Appeals', (1971), *J.R.T.P.I.*, 114

... The Second Report of the Select Committee on the Parliamentary Commissioner for Administration records the evidence given by the Permanent Secretary to the Department, Sir Matthew Stevenson (page 55, paragraph 197). He pointed out the widespread effect of an investigation into a case and added:

> But this is not the total impact of the Commissioner on the Department. There was a noticeable tendency, in the very early stages for the work to proceed more slowly and, I do not doubt, more carefully. This, at the same time as we had a very big backlog, was a matter of very great concern because other complaints will relate to delay. . . . You also find that there is a tendency for officers who think they might be criticized to pass things upwards on the grounds that the best thing to do if you are going to be criticized, is not to be the man to take the decision.

I would confess that on my first case it was not a question of going more slowly; I stopped completely for a few hours! Recovery from this initial traumatic experience was fairly swift though it has left its mark. There had been a question of maladministration by omission (happily not eventually upheld) because I, writing to a colleague, had used a piece of internal shorthand that meant a lot to us but nothing to the Commissioner's staff. I think what affected my morale so badly was the thought that my career could be blighted by the fact that although I had read and digested all the papers on the file and looked at the plans, because this was something I did every time, it did not occur to me to record the fact. It seemed to me for a while, that no decision I took could be good enough. It requires a certain amount of nerve to take any type of decision and appeal decisions sometimes take a considerable amount of it. Unless you are reasonably confident that you know what you are doing and that those above you normally regard your judgment as sound, you cannot act alone. The initial impact of the Commissioner's investigations caused a crisis of confidence and it was this more than anything, that caused cases to be put upwards for decision. However, cold common-sense (which dictated that one had to carry on) and bracing messages from above, helped to redress the damage. . . .

From the point of view of the student of the planning process or of bureaucracy, the PCA's report and other similar ones are a mine of information about how decisions actually get taken, and confirm the point made in Chapter 2 that the making of a decision is a process where it is almost impossible to say that such and such an event was decisive, or at such and such a point in time the decision was taken. But that is not the perspective from which the PCA should be judged. Does case No. 241/G suggest that he is an effective controlling device on the planning process? Should he have the power to award damages or compensation? Does he need more legal expertise or more political backing? Is it an adequate conclusion to reach in any case that 'I regard the apologies as sufficient remedy for the Ministry's shortcomings in dealing with the post-inquiry letters'?[120]

In a case he considered in 1969, where the complaints centred on the Ministry of Housing and Local Government's inactivity and misleading statements by the Ministry of Transport about the possibility of holding an inquiry into road building proposals in a possible conservation area, the PCA concluded:

While I do not consider that the Ministry of Housing and Local Government were inactive in this case, it is my opinion that much of the activity was misdirected, and so not conducive to settling the issues with reasonable clarity and despatch. Their handling of the case was protracted, and their administrative performance was faulty in that over a considerable period they failed to communicate their decisions and intentions at all effectively to the parties concerned. As the buildings involved have already been demolished there is, unfortunately, no longer an opportunity for the C.P.R.E. to express further views on the merits of the Scheme. In my opinion the Ministry might have been more helpful in their communications to the C.P.R.E. in view of the latter's particular interest in the conservation aspects of this case.[121]

What would your reactions be to such a conclusion if you were (a) a developer, (b) an official in a Ministry, (c) a member of a complainant amenity group?

This chapter has been concerned with institutions of control external to the planning process. Having considered them in some detail, are you satisfied that overall they provide an adequate system of external control? Do these institutions and their operation reinforce or render over-dramatic the insistent demands for more public participation in planning, more community involvement in decision making, and more controls on the process, such as have been provided for by the establishment of the Commission for Local Administration in England and Wales?[122]

7

Land Values and Compensation

1. Introduction

Hitherto, we have considered the problems of the planning system in terms of decision making and public participation and the inter-relationship between different groups of people and institutions, specifically planners and planning institutions on the one hand, and lawyers and legal institutions on the other. In this last chapter the focus shifts to the other overarching problem area of planning – that of land values. To be understood properly in the planning context, land values must be considered together with compensation for compulsory acquisition of land and for planning restrictions. They are general and specific aspects of the same issue of how the financial costs and benefits of planning shall be determined and parcelled out. At the general level of land values, we shall be concerned with the effect a comprehensive system of planning has on the market value of land, the problems to which this is thought to give rise, the various solutions that have been tried in the past and are being proposed for the present or future. At the specific level, we shall be concerned to explore the meaning of 'market value' as it operates in practice in respect of compensation for the compulsory acquisition of land, the effect the planning system has had on the concept, and the attempts made by the courts and the legislature to 'soften the blow' of compulsory acquisition by certain additions to market value.

The key link between the general and the specific is, as the Uth-watt Report[1] indicated, the operation of the market for land. At the general level the problems are caused by the lack of any adequate or long-lasting legal connection between planning permissions and the financial benefits created by them. At the specific level the problems are caused by basing compensation on market value when, as Davies[2] points out, the factual situation is the very opposite of a market for the land in question and in any event this hypothetical market value has to be worked out by reference to assumptions about equally hypothetical planning permissions.

This key link also highlights the connection between the whole problem of land values and positive planning. 'The key to "positive planning" as distinct from "negative planning" has to be compulsory purchase.'[3] Yet a system of land-use planning that tries to live with and leave as untouched as possible a free market for land is almost inevitably forced into accepting only a residual role for positive planning conducted on terms largely dictated by private enterprise; compulsory purchase for planning purposes is the exception rather than the rule and is a great burden on the public purse. On the other hand a system of planning that is geared to a high level of public development will give the public authorities sufficient power over the financial aspects of planning to ensure that they call the tune on all development and that compulsory purchase is a normal and not an exceptional exercise of planning powers. Thus a consideration of the problem of land values in an age of comprehensive planning is a consideration of the waxing and waning of the emphasis placed on public development and positive planning.

2. Land values and planning[4]

(a) The problem stated

H. R. Parker[5], 'The History of Compensation and Betterment Since 1900', in *Land Values*, ed. P. Hall, p. 53

The problems of compensation and betterment referred to in this paper arise out of the intervention by the state in the market for building land. They concern the changes in development values which occur as a result of the operation of town planning provisions. When public authorities take decisions with regard to the use of land these decisions upset market expectations; some owners receive more for their land than they anticipated, others receive less. The question arises of how these gains and losses should be handled. This has proved to be one of the most difficult problems of the past fifty years.

Historically, the problems have been dealt with in two main ways. The first method is called a 'continuing' solution, because it attempts to deal with the gains and losses of development value as they arise. The gains and losses, it is argued, occur because of decisions taken in the public interest; therefore, if owners who lose development value feel entitled to claim compensation for their loss, by the same token the public authority is entitled to deprive the benefited owners of their gains. Accordingly provision is made to tax the gains when they occur by means of a betterment levy and to pay compensation out of the proceeds to those owners whose property values are held down. This method of dealing with the problems was attempted from 1909 to 1939.

The second approach involves what is called a 'once-for-all' solution. It attempts to resolve the problems finally by a single operation at a given date. In this case the argument is based on the view that all increases in urban site values derive from the natural growth of society and can therefore properly be appropriated by the state. Accordingly provision is made to vest the development rights of land, at least, in the public authority and compensation is paid only for the development values that exist on the enacting date. In this way all development values in future accrue to the state and the gains and losses caused by planning decisions do not matter for wherever they occur only the public purse is affected. The solution recommended by the Uthwatt Committee in 1942 and the one incorporated in the Town and Country Planning Act of 1947 were of this kind. . . .

First it should be understood that the problems of compensation and betterment form part of a much broader economic issue which has not so far been resolved in any particular detail. This issue lies at the heart of the mixed economy: how can the government exercise control over the allocation of resources and at the same time secure that these resources are allocated to their determined ends through the medium of the market?

In the case of compensation and betterment the conflict is between taking away the gains of development value from benefited owners on the one hand, and keeping the market working on the other. An owner will only sell his land for development provided he obtains for it more than it is worth to him in its existing use. If for reasons of equity, or saving in cost to the public, or on any other grounds, the extra value is taken away from him he will not be willing to make his land available and the market will break down. This means that the choice of solution to the problems depends in the first place upon how much importance is attached to the continued satisfactory working of the market. If the market is held to be indispensable to the allocative process a very different kind of solution is likely to result from that where the market is deemed to have outlived its usefulness. . . .

Final Report of the Expert Committee on Compensation and Betterment, Cmd. 6386 (HMSO, 1942)

6. The object of our enquiry is twofold. First, to make an objective analysis of the subject of the payment of compensation and recovery of betterment in respect of public control of the use of land. . . .

8. Historically, the first part of our terms of reference dealing with the subject of compensation and betterment arose out of the deliberations of the Barlow Commission which was appointed in 1937. Evidence placed before the Commission revealed that 'the difficulties that are encountered by planning authorities under the existing system of compensation and betterment are so great as seriously to hamper the progress of planning throughout the country'. It was clear to the Commission that their enquiry and their recommendations would be of little effective value if these difficulties were not removed.

22. It is clear that under a system of well-conceived planning the resolution of competing claims and the allocation of land for the various requirements must proceed on the basis of selecting the most suitable land for the particular purpose, irrespective of the existing values which may attach to individual parcels of land. A coastal area, a beauty spot, the fringe land round existing towns, may all have a high building value for residential or industrial development, yet it may be in the national interest to forbid building whether for reasons of amenity or because the soil is highly fertile and suited for agriculture. Similarly it may be in the national interest to prevent some of our existing large cities from expanding further. This will involve sterilisation from building of much land which, if unrestricted, would continue to command a high price for development.

. . . In this connection two well-recognised facts must be borne in mind. The first is that potential development value created by the expectation of future development is spread over many more acres than are actually required for development in the near future or are ever likely to be developed. The second is that wisely imposed planning control does not diminish the total sum of land values, but merely redistributes them, by increasing the value of some land and decreasing the value of other land. These principles of 'floating value' and 'shifting value' respectively are of prime importance in connection with the amount of compensation payable, both in respect of the imposition of restrictions on the use of land and also in respect of its acquisition, for the result is not only that compensation has, in the aggregate, to be paid far in excess of the real loss but that payment has to be made for land values that are not really destroyed at all.

Floating Value

23. Potential development value is by nature speculative. The hoped-for building may take place on the particular piece of land in question, or it may take place elsewhere; it may come within five years, or it may be twenty-five years or more before the turn of the particular piece of land to be built upon arrives. . . .

24. Potential value is necessarily a 'floating value,' and it is impossible to predict with certainty where the 'float' will settle as sites are actually required for purposes of development. When a piece of undeveloped land is compulsorily acquired, or development upon it is prohibited, the owner receives compensation for the loss of the value of a probability of the floating demand settling upon his piece of land. The probability is not capable

of arithmetical quantification. In practice where this process is repeated indefinitely over a large area the sum of the probabilities as estimated greatly exceeds the actual possibilities, because the 'float,' limited as it is to actually occurring demands, can only settle on a proportion of the whole area. There is therefore over-valuation.

Shifting Value

26. The public control of the use of land, whether it is operated by means of the existing planning legislation or by other means, necessarily has the effect of shifting land values: in other words, it increases the value of some land and decreases the value of other land, but it does not destroy land values. Neither the total demand for development nor its average annual rate is materially affected, if at all, by planning ordinances. If, for instance, part of the land on the fringe of a town is taken out of the market for building purposes by the prohibition of development upon it, the potential building value is merely shifted to other land and aggregate values are not substantially affected, if at all. Nevertheless, the loss to the owner of the land prohibited from development is obvious, and he will claim compensation for the full potential development value of his land on the footing that, but for the action of the public authority in deciding that development should not be permitted upon it, it would in fact have been used for development. The value which formerly attached to his land is transferred and becomes attached to other land whose owners enjoy a corresponding gain by reason of the increased chance that their land will be required for development at an earlier date.

A similar shift of value takes place if part of the land is taken out of the market for building purposes by being purchased for a public open space or other public purpose.

27. In theory, in view of these considerations, it should be possible to compensate all owners whose land is decreased in value by restrictions on development out of a 'betterment' fund levied from owners the value of whose land is thereby increased. No scheme has, however, yet been devised under which in actual practice compensation and betterment can be equated in this way. . . .

38. On the problem of compensation and betterment, the main conclusions we have drawn in the course of our analysis may now be summarised as follows: . . .

(*b*) The existence of the compensation-betterment problem can be traced to two root causes: –

(i) The fact that land in private ownership is a marketable commodity with varying values according to location and the purposes for which it is capable of use.

(ii) The fact that land is held by a large number of owners whose individual interests lie in putting their own particular piece of land to the most profitable use for which they can find a market, whereas the need of the State and of the community is to ensure the best use of all land of the country irrespective of financial return. If planning is a necessity and an advantage to the community, as is undoubtedly the case, a means must be found for removing the conflict between private and public interest.

(c) It is in the sphere of 'development value', whether attaching to land already developed by building, as in urban areas, or to land suitable for development in the predictable future, as in the case of fringe land around towns and cities, that the compensation difficulty is acute. Development values as a whole, however, are dependent on the economic factors that determine the *quantum* of development of various types required throughout the country, and as planning does not reduce this *quantum* it does not destroy land values but merely redistributes them over a different area. Planning control may reduce the value of a particular piece of land, but over the country as a whole there is no loss.

(d) In theory, therefore, compensation and betterment should balance each other. In practice they do not. The present statutory code is limited in operation and is not designed to secure balance, and we are convinced that within the framework of the existing system of land ownership it is not possible to devise any scheme for making the principle of balance effective. It is only if all the land in the country were in the ownership of a single person or body that the necessity for paying compensation and collecting betterment on account of shifts in value due to planning would disappear altogether.

It is evident from these conclusions that an adequate solution to the problem must lie in such a measure of unification of existing rights in land as will enable shifts of value to operate within the same ownership, coupled with a land system that does not contain within it contradictions provoking a conflict between private and public interest and hindering the proper operation of planning machinery. We do not imagine that this theoretical conclusion leaves much room for dispute; any difference of opinion that may arise is more likely to be in regard to the most suitable method of translating theory into practice.

(b) Solutions officially proposed or attempted 1942–71

(i) *Expert Committee on Compensation and Betterment.*

47. . . . the solution of the compensation-betterment difficulty can only lie in a degree of unification of existing rights in land carried out on a national scale and involving their national ownership. If we were to regard the problem provided by our terms of reference as an academic exercise without regard to administrative or other consequences, immediate transfer to public ownership of all land would present the logical solution; but we have no doubt that land nationalisation is not practicable as an immediate measure and we reject it on that ground alone. We state our objections to its immediate practicability shortly. *First.* Land nationalisation is not a policy to be embarked upon lightly, and it would arouse keen political controversy. A change of view upon the topic of land nationalisation calls for more than a rearrangement of prejudices. Delay, to say the

least, would result. *Second*. It would involve financial operations which in the immediate post-war period might, as we see the matter, be entirely out of the question. *Third*. Land nationalisation would involve the establishment of a complicated administrative machinery equipped to deal with the whole of the land of the country.

(4) OUTLINE OF RECOMMENDATIONS

48. That conclusion makes it desirable to consider whether there is any method, short of immediate nationalisation, which will effectively solve the compensation-betterment problem of the present system and provide an adequate basis on which the post-war reconstruction will be able to proceed.

The only method which answers this test in regard to undeveloped land is the proposal made to the Barlow Commission[6] for the acquisition by the State of the development rights in undeveloped land. This scheme, which for convenience we refer to as the 'development rights scheme', does in our view provide a solution which is both practicable and equitable. Different considerations apply in the case of developed land and it seems to us that piecemeal transfer of urban land to public ownership, as and when required for planning or other public purposes, would be less cumbersome and less onerous a task than that involved in immediate wholesale nationalisation. . . .

I. Measures for Land Outside Built-up Areas

49. We recommend the immediate vesting in the State of the rights of development in all land lying outside built-up areas (subject to certain exceptions) on payment of fair compensation, such vesting to be secured by the imposition of a prohibition against development otherwise than with the consent of the State accompanied by the grant of compulsory powers of acquiring the land itself when wanted for public purposes or approved private development.

This measure of unification in the State of the development rights attaching to undeveloped land outside built-up areas is an essential minimum necessary to remove the conflict between public and private interest to which we have referred. As regards the area to which it applies, it is a complete solution of the hoary and vexing problem of shifting values. The development value for all time will have been acquired, and paid for. Compensation will no longer be a factor hindering the preparation and execution of proper planning schemes. The scheme will thus facilitate the operation of a positive policy for agriculture, the improvement of road systems and public services, the preservation of beauty spots and coastal areas, the reservation of green belts and National Parks, the control over the expansion of existing towns and cities, the establishment of satellite towns and the planned location of industry in new areas.

Shortly the scheme we recommend involves four points: –

(*a*) The placing of a general prohibition against development on undeveloped land outside built-up areas and immediate payment to owners of the land affected of compensation for the loss of development value.

(*b*) Unfettered determination through planning machinery of the areas in which public or private development is to take place, the amount and type of development being determined as regards development for public purposes by national needs and, as regards private development, by private demand.

(*c*) Purchase by the State of the land itself if and when required for approved development whether for public purposes or for private purposes.

(*d*) In the case of approved development for private purposes the leasing of such land by the State to the person or body undertaking the development.

A scheme on these lines has been much canvassed and has been commonly described as a purchase by the State of the development rights. That is not, in truth, the transaction: it is the result of the transaction. For, when the land itself is purchased for development purposes, the price then payable excludes the development value. It is, indeed, valuable to describe the scheme as a purchase of the development rights as emphasising that the object of the scheme is to secure development, not to prevent development, and for purposes of statement it is a convenient phrase which we use. The control of development passes from the individual to the State. Just as a prohibition against dishonesty finds its real meaning as an inspiration to honesty, so a prohibition against uncontrolled development should inspire ordered development. . . .

II. *Measures for Built-up Areas*

50. We recommend the conferment upon public authorities of powers of purchase, much wider and simpler in operation than under existing legislation.

If it is accepted, as we think it has to be, that fair compensation must be paid to an owner whose existing interest in land is required for planning purposes, it must be recognised that, in so far as the difficulties of the past arose merely from the necessity of paying this compensation, there is no remedy. Values have attached to land on the basis of the existing system of ownership and, short of confiscatory measures, it will always be costly to make land in private ownership available for planning purposes.

From the point of view of planning, the ideal is that the best plans should be prepared, unhampered by financial considerations. As matters stand the cost falls on the local authority and the plans suffer accordingly. It lies outside our terms of reference to consider to what extent the cost of planning should fall upon national funds, but we are satisfied that it is necessary, both from the point of view of avoiding delay in the preparation and execution of schemes, and from the point of view of cost, that planning authorities should have every facility for purchasing whatever land may be required for fulfilling their schemes. Suitable financial arrangements are therefore imperative.

51. Inasmuch as sound planning does not destroy total land values but

merely redistributes them, the ultimate cost may be reduced by recoupment elsewhere. The 'development rights scheme' will enable the State to secure the benefit of any shift of values to undeveloped land. Purchase of other land for recoupment, which we recommend in Chapter IX, will enable much of the shift within the area of towns to be collected for the public purse. The main defect in the structure of our scheme is that increased values may still accrue in part to land which for the time being remains to the full in private ownership.

We therefore recommend a scheme for the imposition of a periodic levy on increases in annual site value, with the object of securing such betterment for the community as and when it is realised, enjoyed or realisable.

The method we suggest is, in our view, the only effective way of collecting betterment without hampering individual enterprise in the development of land. The levy will not be payable in respect of land, the development rights in which are to be acquired under the 'development rights scheme', so long as such land remains undeveloped. . . .

Parker, op. cit., p. 64

[The recommendations] were not well received politically and certain administrative flaws were found in them.

Right-wing politicians took exception to the report on the grounds that it represented the thin end of the wedge of land nationalisation. Ultimately all developed land would belong to the state. The main practical objection was to dividing the land into three categories. It was pointed out that this distinction was very difficult to observe in many cases and endless litigation would result. Objection was taken also to the betterment levy. It was argued that this had nothing to do with the problems of compensation and betterment in town planning, and the Committee was accused of exceeding its terms of reference.

(ii) *Town and Country Planning Act 1947:*

Land, Cmnd. 5730

7. The Town and Country Planning Act 1947 drew substantially on the work of the Uthwatt Committee, which dealt specifically with compensation and betterment, without precisely following its recommendations. The Act represented the first comprehensive approach to the related problems of planning, compensation, and betterment. The key – as under the Uthwatt proposals – was the effective transfer to the state of all development rights in land.

8. State ownership of development rights had three inter-connected effects:

(*a*) *planning permission* was required for all development throughout the country;

(*b*) no *compensation* was payable where planning permission was refused (except for development defined as being within 'existing use' for compensation purposes); and

(*c*) *betterment* accrued to the state through the imposition of a development charge which was payable to a Central Land Board before development commenced.

9. One consequence of the nationalisation of development value was that all land was supposed to change hands at existing use value. This meant that local authorities could acquire land cheaply for their own purposes. But the system was criticised as removing any incentive for owners to bring forward land for development, because developers who were going to have to pay development charge should, in theory, not have paid more than existing use value when they bought the land. (In practice, land changed hands at more than existing use value, though at less than full market value.) It is as likely that with-holding of land from the market may have arisen from the expectation that the system would be abandoned if there were a change of Government. A second difficulty about the development charge system was that the basic principle on which it was based was inadequately understood. It is probable that, given time to settle down, the 1947 Act system could have been made to work. But it was abolished before this could be tested.

10. Two of the three basic principles of the 1947 Act have, however, survived. The planning system introduced by the Act remains virtually untouched. Planning control still operates as under the 1947 Act; and the development plan system remains (though changed by the introduction of structure and local plans in the Town and Country Planning Act 1968). And one of the most important aspects of the 1947 nationalisation of development value – the principle that in general compensation is not payable where planning permission is refused – remains, with the result that the ability to prevent the realisation of development value still rests with public authorities.

11. Although the provisions of the 1947 Act dealing with betterment were repealed following the change of Government in 1951, the Town and Country Planning Acts of 1953 and 1954 left untouched the provisions under which public authorities acquired land at a price largely excluding development value.

But as the development charge had been abolished, sales between private persons reflected the full market value including development value. Pressure against this two-price system led to its abolition. Under the Town and Country Planning Act 1959 full open-market value, including development value, was reinstated as the basis on which public authorities paid for land.

(iii) *Land Commission Act 1967*

12. Concern about rising land prices and large unearned gains led the 1966 Labour Government to set up the Land Commission. Under the Land Commission Act 1967 development gains on land were subject to a special flat rate tax – the betterment levy – set at 40%. The Act, however, did not bring about any changes in the planning system. Broadly speaking, the Commission operated within the framework laid down by local planning authorities – in general, the Commission could buy land

compulsorily only where it had been allocated or in some other way accepted as ready for development. Nor did the system allow public authorities, other than the Commission, to acquire land more cheaply.

13. The 1967 Act did not have as significant an effect on the land market as the 1947 Act system. There were transitional provisions in the Act which helped to avoid major disruption while the system was being introduced. But the betterment levy scheme did not make adequate provision for exemption of small cases or for flexibility in operation.

14. As with the 1947 Act system, it is probable that, given time and some extra flexibility (such as that introduced by the Finance Act 1969), the system would have been workable. But, like the 1947 Act, the 1967 Act was repealed, this time following the change of Government in 1970. This repeal came before the Land Commission had been given the wider powers of land acquisition which the legislation provided should be available to them after a 'second appointed day', so that the Commission were unable to buy land on the scale originally envisaged.

(c) Solutions proposed since 1971

The demise of the Land Commission and the transformation of betterment levy into capital gains tax in 1971 did nothing to still the quest for a solution to the problem of betterment. Indeed the final ending of that particular solution took place at the same time as a dramatic increase in the value of land, both urban and agricultural, a falling-away of the building of new houses and, inevitably, well-publicised newspaper stories of the few property speculators who were making, or were alleged to be making, fortunes out of the shortage of residential accommodation in towns and cities and out of the shortage of land with planning permission for development. This in turn sparked off renewed demands from all shades of the political spectrum for 'something to be done' about the problem of the rising price of land and its apparent shortage.

The Conservative Government's solution was multi-faceted: some local authorities in 'stress' areas were allowed to borrow additional money to purchase and assemble lands for private development;[7] Circular 122/73 urged local planning authorities to release more land for residential development and adopt a presumption in favour of development in respect of applications for development on 'white land'. In addition, the White Paper *Widening the Choice: The Next steps in Housing*[8] indicated that some Green Belt land would be released for residential development and all statutory undertakers were urged to review their landholdings and release land not wanted for their own future developments for housing development. From the perspective of this chapter, however, the most interesting of the proposed solutions was the Land Hoarding Charge, the principle of which was set out in the same White Paper (Cmnd. 5280) as follows:

26. .... The purpose of this charge is to ensure that land with planning permission for housing is developed promptly, and to penalise the speculative hoarding of such land. ...

27. The charge will be levied for failure to complete development within a specified period from the grant of planning permission. Legislation will prescribe a normal completion period of 4 years from the grant of outline permission or 3 years from the grant of full permission where no outline application was made in the first instance. Local planning authorities will be empowered to authorise longer completion periods on application where this seems reasonable in the light of the particular circumstances; the legislation will set out the kinds of considerations to which authorities may have regard. These will include the size of the development, its relationship to programmes for services, and the general state of the housing market. Authorities will also be empowered to extend the period if this is justified by any change in circumstances, in particular those outside the developer's control, including any delay in approval of detailed plans following a grant of outline permission.

29. The charge will be levied on the full market value of the property on the day after which the relevant planning permission is granted or, in the case of land with permission granted before the date of the White Paper, the value on the date of the White Paper. This value will be assessed by the District Valuer, subject to appeal to the Lands Tribunal. The charge will accrue from the end of the completion period by reference to a fixed percentage of that value for each year's delay, the charge to be levied for the actual year of completion being based on the proportion of that year which has elapsed before completion. The charge will be due and payable for the first time either on the date of completion or on the expiry of a year from the end of the completion period, whichever is the earlier, and on the same day in each subsequent year during which the delay continues until the completion date. Interest will be payable for any period of delay in payment after the due date.

30. The Government's present intention is that the charge should be at a rate of 30 per cent for each full year of delay. A final decision on the rate will be taken in the light of the circumstances prevailing when the legislation is introduced. But on the basis of an annual rate of 30 per cent a person who had three years in which to complete development and was allowed no extension of the period would become liable to the charge if, on the first day of the fourth year, the development was incomplete. The amount of the charge would increase day by day until at the end of the fourth year it would be 30 per cent of the value at the beginning of the first year, at the end of the fifth year it would be 60 per cent of that value and so on. Where part of the land is completely developed, the charge

would apply only to so much of the site as had not been completely developed.

31. The charge will not be deductible for tax purposes i.e. it will not be treated either as a trading expense for builders and developers or as an addition to cost for those liable to capital gains tax.[9]

Various proposals for more radical action were put forward and discussed by different people, groups and publications within the Labour movement.[10] The Labour Government elected in 1974, after considering these ideas, published its proposals for solving the problem in September 1974.

Land, Cmnd. 5730

20. Public ownership of development land puts control of our scarcest resource in the hands of the community, and enables it thereby to take an overall perspective. In addition, by having this land available at the value of its current use, rather than at a value based on speculation as to its possible development, the community will be able to provide, in the places that it needs them, the public facilities it needs, but cannot now afford because of the inflated price it has to pay to the private owner.

24. The Government therefore believe that in England and Scotland the acquisition and disposal of development land is best left in the main to local authorities – which term throughout this White Paper includes new town development corporations. They will be supported by a back-up organisation to help and advise them and to act on the Secretary of State's behalf in default. In Wales, however, the acquisition and disposal of land for private development will be the responsibility of an all-Wales body, which will also be able to provide local authorities with an advisory service.

25. These proposals relate to land which is to be developed or re-developed – for houses, shops, factories, for example. They are not concerned with land which is to remain in use for agriculture or forestry; and no change is proposed in the existing arrangements relating to such land. The land to be acquired will be land which the community accepts as requiring development or redevelopment generally not more than ten years ahead. The acquisitions will be monitored as part of a rolling pro-gramme as local authorities build up their land banks. Ten years is the maximum period needed to ensure orderly development and create the requisite degree of certainty in the development industry and in agricul-ture and forestry. Care will continue to be taken to avoid the acquisition of good quality agricultural land wherever possible.

27. . . . it is the Government's intention to lay a duty on local authorities to acquire all land required for private development. From the date that

the duty is brought in, no development will be allowed to begin save on land owned by a public authority, or made available by them for this purpose. Local authorities will therefore buy land which in their opinion is suitable for development and will also be required to buy where the need for development (e.g. as indicated in a planning application) is accepted even though it may be a departure from the plan. The general vesting declaration procedure set out in the Town and Country Planning Act 1968 can apply to such acquisitions to secure speedy disposal for development.

28. The new local authority acquisition powers and duties in respect of private development in England will, so far as possible, follow the split of planning functions between county and district. Both councils will as a result of land ownership have new and positive roles in ensuring the proper development of their areas. The tiers of local government already agree their respective fields of operation (within the broad context of legislation) through development plan schemes and development control schemes. It may be that community land acquisition schemes would be an appropriate technique for defining their respective spheres of interest in relation to acquisition. . . .

30. The principle that all development land should be acquired by the community will have important implications. Given the acceptance of this approach by Parliament, objection to the principle of public acquisition will no longer be an appropriate ground of objection to an individual compulsory purchase order, and the Secretary of State will be enabled to disregard objections put forward on this basis (as he can already do in relation to compulsory purchase orders made by new town development corporations). Special consideration will need to be given to the implications of a situation in which the grant of planning permission may make land subject to compulsory acquisition, and the legislation will contain appropriate provisions to safeguard the position of owners and others with an interest in land.

32. . . . The Government propose that the ultimate basis on which the community will buy all land will be current use value – that is to say the market value of land for its current use without including any additional value representing the hope that it might be developed for any other purpose, except those covered by the permanent exemptions referred to in paragraphs 34–35. The Government also propose to amend at the earliest possible moment the provision whereby an owner of land can require a certificate of appropriate alternative development even though the owner (for example of a sports field which the authority wish to acquire for public open space) has no possibility of getting planning permission for the development set out in the certificate.

34. The Government propose to exclude from the scheme the building of a house for owner-occupation on a single plot which was owned by the prospective owner-occupier on the date of this White Paper (12 September 1974).

35. Other permanent exemptions from acquisition under the scheme will be set out in due course but they will include alterations and extensions to dwelling houses; the building, within the curtilage of a dwelling occupied by the owner at the date of this White Paper, of a single house for occupation by the owner or a member of his family; buildings used in agriculture and forestry; and development related to the extraction of minerals.

46. When all acquistions by local authorities come to be made at current use value there may arise individual cases of financial hardship of the sort that can occur in any large scheme. The Government therefore propose to set up at the appropriate time tribunals throughout the country, which will have authority to consider such cases and to award an additional payment.

55. The terms on which local authorities dispose of land acquired under these arrangements will need in general to ensure that the local community retains a share of future increases in value. The disposal of land for commercial or industrial development therefore will be on a leasehold basis with provision for rent revisions. In general disposals, whether on a freehold or a leasehold basis, will be at the market value at the time.

56. The Government have made it clear that their public ownership proposals do not seek to affect the provision of land on which houses can be built for owner-occupation. Land for housing can be disposed of in a variety of ways. Local authorities will be encouraged to offer it to builders on licence, with the plots being conveyed direct to the house purchasers. Plots for owner-occupation will also be made available freehold.

57. The operation of the scheme will require close co-operation between local authorities and developers, and the Government wish to see the skills and initiative of private developers contribute to the needs of the community in a positive way. Local authorities will be encouraged to involve developers in their plans, and the method of disposal should encourage developers to make a contribution towards the overall design of each scheme.

59. The effect of these proposals will be that the community will enjoy the full value created when land is developed. The community in general, i.e. the taxpayer, will have made a contribution towards the acquisition of land and the Government propose therefore that the benefits from the scheme should be shared between central and local government. The major part of the benefit will accrue to the taxpayer in general through the Exchequer; but a part will remain with the local community and a part will be distributed amongst local authorities to help equalise the benefits of the scheme between ratepayers at large. The Government will consult with the local authority associations in order to arrive at a rational distribution of benefits. It is the Government's intention that those buying

their first homes should share in the benefits of the scheme. It must be recognised that because of the timelag between acquisition and disposal it will be some time before benefits accrue generally.

60. Transfers of land between local authorities and the valuation of appropriations within a local authority will be on terms which ensure that the local community will benefit directly from the new proposals. Land to be used by them for council housing or other purposes will therefore be transferred or appropriated at the cost of acquisition. Adjustments will be made as appropriate in Exchequer financial arrangements.

What are the relative merits of these proposals and solutions? The first thing to be said is that they are not particularly original; in one way or another they can be traced back to some suggestion or proposal discussed in the Uthwatt Report. The point made by Parker in 1965 that 'the Uthwatt Report is the most authoritative statement on the problems we have'[11] is still true, at least at the official and party-political level. This leads on to a second point. There appears to be an assumption that the more radical the solution to the problem, the less complicated the legislation and administration will have to be. But one has only to refer back to the financial provisions of the Town and Country Planning Act 1947 and the Land Commission Act 1967 to see that any legislation concerned with land tenure and land values (whether for a total or a partial solution to the problems) is immensely complex.[12] Until the proposals for action recognise that, one will remain doubtful whether they are feasible.

A third point is: what are the problems that the solutions are trying to deal with? Is the problem seen as a short-term one of 'doing something about the politically embarrassing figure of the land speculator'? Or is it seen as part of the problem of the failures of the system of development control in not ensuring that enough land is available at the right place at the right time for residential development? Or is it seen as a particularly glaring example of the general failure and lack of social responsibility of the capitalist system? Or is it seen as a taxing problem? Or a bit of each, or none of these at all? All the suggested solutions seem to see the problem in a different light so that in asking which is best we might not be comparing like with like.

Even when we turn from political nostrums to academic or specialist diagnosis, the problem of finding the problem remains.

Statement of the Town and Country Planning
Association: Development Values and Land
Assembly, *T. & C.P.*, May 1973, p. 258

2. ... (I)t is not planning as such that has brought about the recent
phenomenal increase in the cost of development land; there have been no
changes in the way planning is practised that could account for this. The
making of eccentric private fortunes out of development values, therefore
is as much symptom as cause of some fundamental failing in a planning
system that, now put to the test, is allowing such diversion of values to
occur. ...

3. These tensions over development land serve to remind us that planning is after all a political function; but, by the same token, planning can
operate only within certain agreed limits ... the problem of development
values cannot be treated in abstract; it can only be solved as part of a
viable planning system – a system such as we are now being brought to
admit the country lacks. ...

4. The argument is becoming daily more tenable, then, that we are
witnessing the breakdown of the comprehensive planning system created in
Britain by the 1947 Act. It is a breakdown, central to which lies the divorce
of planning from any responsibility for development values. ...

R. Drewett, 'Land Values and the Suburban
Land Market', in P. Hall *et al.*, *The Containment
of Urban England*, pp. 242–5

[discussing the influence and attitudes of the Land Commission during
its short life as a solution to the problem] ... during its early surveys in
the first year (the Commission) discovered that *the shortage of land for immediate development was due to insufficient land being allocated in local authority
Development Plans.* ... By the time the Commission published its second
Annual Report it recognised that its contribution to the steady flow of
land on to the market had been modest but its explanation of the cause
was now more pointed. It was: *'largely due to planning policies which are
directed to the containment of urban growth and the preservation of open country.'*
For various reasons ... the contribution by the Land Commission to
land release was modest and in global terms was a failure. After three
years of its existence, the *basic problem of land supply remained.* ... Both the
previous Labour Government and the present Conservative Government
diagnosed the problem correctly, but the incoming Government's prog-
nosis was to scrap the only *type* of legislation likely to assess demand for land
objectively and overcome the intransigence of many planning authorities.
Leaving the onus of land release in the hands of individual planning
authorities was a return to the status quo of the early sixties which created
the shortage in land that brought the need of a Land Commission into
being.
The irony of this land and housing dilemma is that *planning decisions* are

mainly creating the economic and social costs which are borne in the main by one sector of the private housing market, the sector whose price elasticity of demand is so high.

[Earlier in the same chapter[13] Drewett makes the important point that] . . . whenever one has to attempt to answer a few apparently simple questions in the field of land values, one is made to realize that all one can do is to scratch the surface of an immensely complex subject – a subject in which there are *remarkably few cut and dried facts and where, because of market forces, so much depends on the negotiating position between buyer and seller.*

Drewett's approach to the question of land values was a behavioural one, adopted through a detailed survey of actual transactions, in which one conclusion was 'that the need to obtain *planning permission* to develop land substantially affects the value of that land',[14] developers considering that high land values were largely attributable to a scarcity of supply in turn caused by various public policy decisions.

Drewett's work is part of the most thorough survey of the system of town and country planning in England that has been attempted since it was introduced in 1947 and his conclusions that the system of development control – planning permissions, the need to obtain them, the policies behind them and implemented through them – is a, if not the, major contributory factor to scarcity of land and high land values is entitled to a great deal of respect. Conversely, the view of the Town and Country Planning Association that 'it is not planning as such that has brought about'[15] increases in the cost of development land is difficult to support, notwithstanding that it was made by a working party which numbered planners and developers among its members.

Given the different diagnoses of the problem it is significant that both Drewett and the T & CPA suggest similar sorts of solutions: Drewett, 'A new formula of land assembly and release may be under another name [to the Land Commission] will have to be instituted soon if the needs of the building industry and the housing programme are to be met';[16] the T & CPA 'The magnitude of the problem of development values is now such that it demands the creation of a public land bank. By this we mean that land must be acquired by the public in advance of development, just as developers have long since built up private land banks, generally in conjunction with land owners.'[17] The T & CPA would link the land bank to rising development values by providing that the bank would buy at existing (agricultural) use value only.

We think it just to use such a principle. We have already suggested this particular figure (£1,000 per acre) is greatly inflated precisely by the factors (i.e. the reinvestment of development values in agricultural land) our policy would eliminate. In allowing the figure to stand in the present calculation therefore, we are reinsured against any underestimation of the cost of our policy. . . . Perhaps, more to the point, however, would be an objection that, by not allowing for the public banking of all land for development, we would be encouraging the existence of two markets in land, side by side. We doubt, however, whether perfectionism in this respect would be worth its cost. It is here, perhaps, that site-value rating, or the proposed land hoarding charge, could play an important part. For if there were inequity between, on the one hand, profits on land hoarded in small amounts for developments outside the public land bank, and, on the other, the price paid for land by the bank, a charge on the former (more marginal) transactions would be a redress – yet without endangering planning at large, as we have suggested such a more generalized charge could do. Crucial to all these propositions however, is a requirement that land publicly banked should be expeditiously assembled and duly brought forward for development.[18]

Drewett does not link his suggestion to any proposal for the transfer of development values from the private to the public purse. This too is significant for it brings out the point that there are two problems here: the problem of the supply of land, and the problem of development values. There is no necessary logical connection between the two; the supply of land problem could be solved by vigorous public assembling and releasing of land, with development values going to the erstwhile private landowners. Likewise, the development value problem could be solved – in theory at any rate – by nationalising development values as was done in 1947, though the effect of such a policy on the supply of land might be counter-productive.

The problem *behind* the problems is that while land supply has been seen as a problem by both major political parties, development values have not. The Labour Party, taking its cue from the Uthwatt Report, has always been of the opinion (i) that it is neither possible nor desirable to continue to preserve 'the purely individualistic approach to land ownership',[19] (ii) that there is a problem of development values caused by 'the fact that land is held by a large number of owners whose individual interests lie in putting their own particular piece of land to the most profitable use for which they can find a market, whereas the need of the state and of the community is to ensure the best use of all land of the country irrespective of financial return',[20] and (iii) 'that an adequate solution to the problem must lie in such a measure of unification of existing rights in land as will enable shifts of value to operate within the same ownership, coupled with a land system that does not contain within it contradictions provoking a conflict between private and public interest and hindering the proper operation of planning machinery'.[21]

The Conservative Party, on the other hand, subscribes to very different views about land and the individual's rights to enjoy it to the full. A modern statement of the Conservative position is as follows:

T. Raison[22], *Why Conservative?* (1964), p. 39

The essence of the modern Tory view of property should be found in the distinction between the economic and social spheres. The right of ownership – subject to the payment of taxes and the observance of the law – is one of the essential bases of the economic sphere where the economic laws should prevail. In the social sphere however, other considerations may be more important; and though social considerations should always be clearly distinguished from economic considerations they must nevertheless on occasion be allowed to override the strictly economic.

It is for this reason that Conservatives must accept a degree of town and country planning – perhaps a greater degree of it than exists today. . . . Yet although many Conservatives are appalled at the squalid way in which many British towns are evolving . . . they are too impressed by the rights of property to be able to accept nationalisation or municipalization of land or the view that the community, rather than the individual owner, should benefit from rise in property values. The emphasis therefore, is on finding ways by which development or redevelopment may take place through a sacrifice of some of the rights of ownership, but not of ownership itself.

While such incompatible views exist, and are acted upon, it is extremely unlikely that the 'problem' of development values of land is anywhere near solution. One of two things will have to happen: either one or other of the two main political parties will have to do an about-turn on their position on the issue, or accept that expediency must triumph over principle, and (if Labour) abandon proposals to tackle the problem on the grounds that they are bound to be reversed by the next Conservative Government, and (if Conservative) abandon proposals to undo what a Labour Government has done on the grounds that the resulting upheaval and complications in the land tenure and allocation system are not in the best interest of the country. During the period that the Conservative–Labour two-party system has been in existence, the Conservative

Party has shown a willingness to accept Labour-inspired changes to property relations via nationalisation legislation, while the Labour Party has shown an equal willingness to tone down its more radical proposals once it gains power. This accommodation has not yet been applied to land values, though with the Leasehold Reform Act it has been applied to land tenure. The political embarrassment of rapidly rising land values and the small number of people who appeared to be making large profits from that in the early 1970s led to a real possibility that an accommodation would be achieved here too with the Conservatives accepting that there is a problem of land values and who gets them and Labour accepting that a lasting solution must stop short of full nationalisation.

A further point may be made; the problems discussed in this part of this chapter are political and contentious, a far cry from the problems discussed in Chapter 6. They are, notwithstanding that, just as much problems with which lawyers should grapple as are those in Chapter 6.

By way of conclusion to this part, consider the following problem: The Warwickshire County Draft Structure Plan published in mid-1972 indicated in general terms that the area of Leamington Spa–Warwick could accommodate an increase in population. This was in line with a sub-regional survey (which included Warwickshire) which had been published in May 1971. The draft plan was the subject of some public participation and after the results of that exercise had been digested and some second thoughts discussed the structure plan was published in April 1973 with the suggestion of growth for Leamington Spa–Warwick modified in the light of the returns of the 1971 population census but still intact as a principle. That structure plan was the subject of a public examination in November and December 1973.

At the same time as the county structure plan was slowly going through the planning process, the county planning authorities were working on an urban structure plan for the Leamington Spa–Warwick area. The results of both an exercise in public participation and what was called a 'technical' exercise[23] indicated that an area in the south of Leamington Spa called Heathcote, which consists of good agricultural land and is an open space dividing Leamington Spa from neighbouring residential areas, was one most favoured for development for up to 10,000 people. The results of these exercises were published in mid-1973 and there began to emerge feelings of hostility and concern within the Leamington Spa–Warwick area at the possibility of so large a development at Heathcote. In October 1973 a member of the Warwick Council Planning Committee reported that eighty-one acres of land at Heathcote had been advertised for sale in a national newspaper, and had been described as an 'area proposed by the Coventry–Solihull–Warwickshire sub-regional planning study as being suitable for the expansion of Leamington Spa and Warwick during the period 1976–1991'.[24] At that date it was reasonable to suppose that it would be *at least* fifteen months before the urban structure plan was approved by the Secretary of State after a public examination.

Assuming that an approved urban structure plan indicates that Heathcote should be developed so as to accommodate 10,000 people, what kind of mechanisms, and at what point in time using what kind of procedures, paying what kind of price, could be used or should have been available to be used so as to enable the public authorities to acquire the necessary land in advance of development, but not so as to prejudge the processes of public participation?

3. Compensation[25]

From the policy issues in section 2 above, we turn now to what may seem to be down-to-earth matters – how is market value determined when a public authority wishes to, or, in respect of inverse compulsory purchase, is compelled to acquire land? What kinds of factors can be taken into account to boost or limit the compensation payable? What effect does a system of planning have on the calculation of compensation and, equally important, what effect does a system of planning have on the payment of compensation? Can compensation be claimed in respect of planning decisions that can be shown to have adversely affected the value of land? Even in this more down-to-earth part of the chapter, however, we cannot ignore policy issues; they arise in the section immediately following, when we consider such questions as whether there is or should be a right to compensation for loss of value due to planning restrictions; they arise also when we consider whether market value is too small or too generous a measure of compensation, and the relationship between compensation and public participation in so far as they affect the acceptance of public development. In this as in other areas of planning, therefore, policy and law are intimately entwined.

(a) Is there a right to compensation?

There is no Bill of Rights for England and Wales and there is, therefore, no constitutional guarantee that persons will not be deprived of their property except on prompt payment of fair, adequate or full compensation. The general rule is that a person seeking compensation for the expropriation of his property must be able to point to a statutory provision which requires that compensation be paid; in the absence of such a provision no compensation is payable. Such a person's task is facilitated by a general judicial presumption that 'a statute should not be held to take away private rights of property without compensation unless the intention to do so is expressed in clear and unambiguous terms'.[26] It is this presumption that has sometimes misled people into thinking that there is, in English law, a right to compensation for interference with private property. In practice it is almost inconceivable, in times of peace, that property would be expropriated without compensation, so the debate on whether there is or should be a right to compensation has revolved round the restrictions imposed on the use of land by the planning law, which do not give rise to any compensation. Even the one constitutional case that has arisen on the general question of a right to compensation – from Northern Ireland – concerned the deprivation of property rights without compensation via planning restrictions. The issue also arose sharply in an important English decision of the House of Lords.

Belfast Corporation v. *O.D. Cars Ltd* [1960] 1 All E.R. 65

The respondent had been refused permission to develop its land in accordance with the planning legislation of Northern Ireland. It claimed compensation for injurious affection, arguing, *inter alia*, that the Government of Ireland Act 1920, which prevented public authorities from taking property without compensation, applied to its case.

LORD RADCLIFFE: . . . The fundamental question, as I see it, is whether the prohibition of taking any property without compensation contained in s. 5 (1) of the Government of Ireland Act, 1920, bars the enactment by law of such restrictions on the user or development of property as are referred to in s. 10 (2) of the Planning and Housing Act (Northern Ireland), 1931, unless compensation is provided. In my opinion, it does not, because it seems to me that the word 'taking', when used in this context, does not extend to cover the act of imposing restrictions of that kind.

I do not see how you can give a meaning to this phrase, 'taking without compensation', except by reference to the general treatment of the subject in the law of England and Ireland before 1920. A survey would, I think, discern two divergent lines of approach. On the one hand, there would be the general principle, accepted by the legislature and scrupulously defended by the courts. that the title to property or the enjoyment of its possession was not to be compulsorily acquired from a subject unless full compensation was afforded in its place. Acquisition of title or possession was 'taking'. Aspects of this principle are found in the rules of statutory interpretation devised by the courts which required the presence of the most explicit words before an acquisition could be held to be sanctioned by an Act of Parliament without full compensation being provided or imported an intention to give compensation and machinery for assessing it into any Act of Parliament that did not positively exclude it. This vigilance to see that the subject's rights to property were protected, so far as was consistent with the requirements of expropriation of what was previously enjoyed in specie, was regarded as an important guarantee of individual liberty. It would be a mistake to look on it as representing any conflict between the legislature and the courts. The principle was, generally speaking, common to both. Side by side with this, however, and developing with increasing range and authority during the second half of the nineteenth century, came the great movement for the regulation of life in cities and towns in the interests of public health and amenity. It is not an adequate description of the powers involved, so far at any rate as the United Kingdom is concerned, to speak of them as 'police powers'. They went far beyond that. Their chief sphere was in the delegated legislation conceded to local authorities, though in some cases they arose from the direct legislation of Parliament itself. Achieved by one means or the other, there is no doubt at all that the effect of them was to impose obligations and restrictions on the owner of town land which impaired his right of development, prohibited or restricted his rights of user and in some cases imposed monetary charges on him or compelled him to expend money on altering his property. Generally speaking, though not without exception, these obligations and restrictions were treated as not requiring compensation, though, of course, in a sense they expropriated certain rights of property. A perusal of the Public Health Act, 1875, will be sufficient to make the point. It shows how extensive interference could be, even at that date. Only in a few special cases is compensation provided for the consequence of interference. No one, so far as I know, spoke of this as a 'taking of property' or treated the general principle of 'no taking without compensation' as applicable to the case. For instance, bye-laws, which have to be 'reasonable', i.e., not manifestly unjust, if the courts are to sustain them, were upheld, even though seriously restricting the user of property without affording any compensation for the restriction (see *Slattery* v. *Naylor*[27], a case from Australia).

When town planning legislation came in eo nomine in 1909, the emphasis had, no doubt, shifted from considerations of public health to the wider and more debatable ground of public amenity. It may possibly have been for this reason. I do not know, that the Act of 1909 included a comprehensive, though not exhaustive 'injurious affection' section, the effect of which was to give property owners whose rights were interfered with in the cause of town planning, a right to compensation for any damage that they suffered, subject to counter-claims for betterment and certain exclusions. This 'injurious affection' embraced an altogether wider category of injury than the 'injurious affection' that had been the subject of compensation under the Lands Clauses Consolidation Act, 1845. In fact, as we know, s. 59 (2) of the Housing, Town Planning, etc. Act, 1909 (which did not itself extend to Ireland), excluded compensation for injurious affection in respect of several of the same heads of restriction as those which are found in s. 10 (2) of the Act of 1931 in Northern Ireland. I do not think that this last circumstance has any bearing on the present issue; the Westminster legislature with its full sovereignty might be able to exclude compensation in cases where the Northern Ireland Parliament under its constitutional limitations could not. What is important, I think, is to recognise that, though interference with rights of development and user had come to be a recognised element of the regulation and planning of towns in the interest of public health and amenity, the consequent control, impairment or diminution of those rights was not treated as a 'taking' of property nor, when compensation was provided, was it provided on the basis that property or property rights had been 'taken' but on the basis that property, itself retained, had been injuriously affected.

These considerations lead me to the following conclusions: (i) The taking of property referred to in s. 5 (1) of the Government of Ireland Act, 1920, ought not to be treated as applying to the imposition of restrictions on user and development under town-planning powers. (ii) It is within the competence of the Parliament of Northern Ireland to decide on what occasions and to what extent compensation is to be afforded for injury suffered under such restrictions. (iii) Section 10 (2) of the Act of 1931 is, accordingly, a valid enactment. . . .

I do not imply by what I have said that I regard it as out of the question that, on a particular occasion, there might not be a restriction of user so extreme that in substance, though not in form, it amounted to a 'taking' of the land affected for the benefit of the public. It is not very easy to imagine such a restriction being imposed by a responsible authority or surviving the test of the Ministry's approval, the more so as the Act deals separately with open spaces as a subject of acquisition, not without compensation. But given that such a case might hypothetically occur, the question for us is whether that possibility in itself is sufficient to invalidate s. 10 (2), the natural subject of which is restrictions and not 'takings'. I do not think that it is. It seems to me the wrong way to treat the constitutional provision. To my mind, it does more justice to its intent if a restriction which is in substance a taking, should one ever occur, is attacked ad hoc as not within the true meaning and scope of s. 10 (2) than that the whole subsection should be thrown on the scrap-heap as constitutionally an outlaw[28]. . . . *Appeal allowed.*

Westminster Bank Ltd. v. *M. H. L. G.* [1970] 1 All ER 734

LORD REID: My Lords, the appellants have a branch of their bank on a site between Saturday Market and Lairgate, Beverley. The site has frontages of some 30 feet and a depth of 90 feet. They wished to increase their accommodation by some alterations of the existing building and by building a new strongroom on that part of the site on Lairgate which is at present an open space. They applied for planning permission in 1964. This was refused with regard to the new strongroom on the grounds that 'the proposed development might prejudice the possible future widening of Lairgate'.

The appellant bank appealed and a public local inquiry was held. The Minister's inspector reported on 22nd April 1965 recommending that the appeal should be allowed. The report narrated the contention of the appellant bank that the machinery of the Highway Act 1959, s. 72, should have been but had not been invoked, and the contention of the local planning authority –

> The fact that the improvement line has not been prescribed under Section 72 of the Highways Act is irrelevant. The authority has the duty and the power to safeguard future provisions of a development scheme by refusing permissions which might have the effect of placing new and substantial burdens on the public purse. There are no plans in hand for the implementation of the road widening proposal. . . .

The Minister held up his decision until 10th March 1966. Then a letter was sent saying that he was 'disposed, in the light of fresh expert evidence, to disagree with the recommendation of his Inspector'. . . .

This letter then enquired whether the appellant bank wished the inquiry to be re-opened and stated that the scope of the further inquiry would be limited to an examination of the new evidence and any evidence which might be put forward to rebut it. . . .

For some reason not stated a different inspector was appointed to conduct the re-opened inquiry. He made his report on 23rd November 1966. . . .

This second inspector rightly made no recommendation because, as he says, the re-opened inquiry and his report related only to one aspect of the matters considered at the previous inquiry.

Then, on 31st January 1967, the Minister issued his decision letter which concluded:

> It is considered that the evidence given at the reopened inquiry by the representatives of the Ministry of Transport and the local planning authority made it clear that, as a result of proposals for the town centre generally, Lairgate would become a main internal traffic road and would require to be widened. . . . There seems to be no doubt that the appeal site will eventually be required for road widening, and it is considered that it would not be right to prejudice the local planning authority's scheme by permitting further development in front of their

improvement line. The Minister is therefore unable to accept Mr Deans' recommendation that the appeal should be allowed.

I am inclined to think that the Minister is here going beyond the findings of the inspector for I do not find there ground for saying that there is no doubt that the appeal site will be eventually required for road widening. But apparently there is in the rules[29] governing this matter a curious distinction. Where an inspector makes a recommendation the Minister cannot alter his findings without giving to the applicant an opportunity to be heard. But, for some reason which counsel could not explain, the Minister can, without hearing the applicant, make new findings and even receive fresh evidence if the inspector has made no recommendation – even in a case such as the present where it would not have been proper for the inspector to make any recommendation. If this is so then the point will no doubt be examined when the rules come to be revised. But here on any view we must accept the Minister's view of the facts as authoritative.

It seems unfortunate that this long and costly procedure should be required before the Minister is in a position to give his decision. But a court can do no more than draw attention to the financial burdens which property owners, perhaps of moderate means, must face if they wish to pursue their statutory rights.

The appellant bank's main argument arises out of the provisions of s. 72 of the Highways Act 1959 which re-enacted pre-war legislation. This section entitles a highway authority to prescribe an 'improvement line' where in its opinion it is necessary or desirable that a street should be widened. When that is done the owner of property adjoining the street is no longer permitted to build on that part of his property which lies between the street and the improvement line. But he is given an immediate right to claim from the highway authority compensation for the injurious affection so caused to his land.

The appellant bank's argument is that this is the only lawful way of preventing a frontager from building on his land adjoining a street, and that, unless and until such a line has been prescribed, it is ultra vires of a planning authority to refuse to grant planning permission on the ground that the land will or may be required for street widening. Where a planning authority refuses permission no compensation is payable except in special circumstances. So the appellant bank says that Parliament cannot be supposed to have authorised public authorities to defeat a frontager's immediate right to compensation by allowing something to be done by way of refusal of planning permission which can and should be done by the prescription of an improvement line.

There is no reference to this alternative method of procedure in the Town and Country Planning Act 1947 (or indeed in any of the planning legislation). . . .

There are many indications that the planning authority must have a free hand – subject always to appeal to the Minister – with regard to roads and streets. But I shall not expand this matter because I think that it is covered by s. 118[30] which for the avoidance of doubt declares that the provisions of this Act apply in relation to any land notwithstanding that provision is made by any enactment in force at the passing of this Act for regulating any development of the land. An enactment in force at the passing of the Act must I think include a later re-enactment of the same provisions and s. 72 of the Highways Act is a provision regulating the development of land. So I cannot accept the argument that planning authorities' powers under the Town and Country Planning Act are insufficient to entitle them to give effect to their views about street widening where no improvement line has been prescribed.

The appellant bank's argument is really founded on the principle that '. . . a statute should not be held to take away private rights of property without compensation unless the intention to do so is expressed in clear and unambiguous terms', per Lord Warrington of Clyffe, in *Colonial Sugar Refining Co Ltd* v. *Melbourne Harbour Trust Comrs.*[31] I entirely accept the principle. It flows from the fact that Parliament seldom intends to do that and therefore before attributing such an intention to Parliament we should be sure that that was really intended. I would only query the last words of the quotation. When we are seeking the intention of Parliament that may appear from the express words but it may also appear by irresistible inference from the statute read as a whole. But I would agree that, if there is reasonable doubt, the subject should be given the benefit of the doubt.

It would be possible to distinguish this statement of the principle on the ground that planning legislation does not take away private rights of property; it merely prevents them from being exercised if planning permission is refused. But that would in my view be too meticulous a distinction. Even in such a case I think we must be sure that it was intended that this should be done without compensation.

But it is quite clear that when planning permission is refused the general rule is that the unsuccessful applicant does not receive any compensation. There are certain exceptions but they have no special connection with street widening. If planning permission is refused on the ground that the proposed development conflicts with a scheme for street widening, the unsuccessful applicant is in exactly the same position as other applicants whose applications are refused on other grounds. None of them gets any compensation. So absence of any right to compensation is no ground for arguing that it is not within the power of planning authorities to refuse planning permission for this reason.

The appellant bank next relies on a different argument. In the present case the same authority is both the local planning authority and the highway authority for Lairgate. So they could if they had so chosen have achieved their object by the alternative method of prescribing an improvement line and thereby entitling the appellant bank to compensation. At one stage the appellant bank put its case so high as to say that the only reason they proceeded by way of refusal of planning permission was in order to avoid having to pay compensation. This is denied by the local authority. . . .

But even if the sole reason for the authority proceeding in the way it did had been the desire to save public money, it does not follow that they were not entitled to do that. The appellant bank says that this was 'unreasonable'. The authority generally referred to in this connection is the judgment of LORD GREENE MR in *Associated Provincial Picture Houses Ltd* v. *Wednesbury Corpn*.[32] The word 'unreasonable' as there used requires I think a little expansion. The decision of any authority can be attacked on the ground that it is in excess of its powers or on the ground that it is an abuse of its powers. The word unreasonable is not at all an apt description of action in excess of power, and it is not a very satisfactory description of action in abuse of power. So in this chapter of the law the word has come to acquire a rather artificial meaning. Here the authority did not act in excess of power in deciding to proceed by way of refusal of planning permission rather than by way of prescribing an improvement line. Did it then act in abuse of power? I do not think so.

Parliament has chosen to set up two different ways of preventing development which would interfere with schemes for street widening. It must have been aware that one involved paying compensation but the other did not. Nevertheless it expressed no preference, and imposed no limit on the use of either. No doubt there might be special circumstances which make it unreasonable or an abuse of power to use one of these methods but here there were none. Even if the appellant bank's view of the facts is right, the authority had to choose whether to leave the appellant bank without compensation or to impose a burden on its ratepayers. One may think that it would be most equitable that the burden should be shared. But the Minister of Transport had made it clear in a circular sent to local authorities in 1954[33] that there would be no grant if a local authority proceeded in such a way that compensation would be payable, and there is nothing to indicate any disapproval of this policy by Parliament and nothing in any of the legislation to indicate that Parliament disapproved of depriving the subject of compensation. I cannot in these circumstances find any abuse of power in the local authority deciding that the appellant bank and not its ratepayers should bear the burden[34]. . . .

Appeal dismissed.

Do you agree with Lord Reid's statement that in the circumstances of the existing legislation and Circular 696/54, he could not find any abuse of power in the local authority in deciding that the bank and not the local ratepayers should bear the burden of loss of use of the land? Did the Minister abuse his power in issuing the circular he did?

Is it realistic to assume that because Parliament had not disapproved of the circular, it must be taken to be satisfied with the law and its administration on compensation? Do you approve of this decision? Would you still approve of the decision if, instead of a bank, the appellant had been the owner of a local corner shop? If not, why not? If yes, at what point should the community be prepared to shoulder the cost of its own restrictions on private property?

Are there any other remedies open to either the bank or the local corner shop in a situation such as this?

Why did the Ministry not alter the rules relating to inquiries to remove the 'curious distinction' to which Lord Reid drew attention with the pointed comment that 'the point will no doubt be examined when the rules come to be revised'?

'... It is quite clear that when planning permission is refused the general rule is that the unsuccessful applicant does not receive any compensation. There are certain exceptions....'[35] What is the reason for the general rule and what are the exceptions? The exceptions may be dealt with first to see if they throw any light on the reasons for the general rule.

There are occasions when planning restrictions or proposals are held to be so drastic that the owner of the land affected is entitled to require the local planning authority to purchase his land. It may be suggested that the broad ground on which such inverse compulsory purchase is admitted into the law is that the economic value of the land to the owner has been so substantially reduced that it would be inequitable to insist that he bore the total loss involved. The restrictions or proposals are made in the public interest and the owner should not be required to bear more of their cost than any other tax- or ratepayer. In so far as this principle is not carried to its logical conclusion – that is, not all owners affected by planning proposals may require the local planning authority to purchase their land, and not all planning restrictions which, to the layman, would render the land incapable of reasonably beneficial use give rise to inverse compulsory purchase – the reason is that the more compensation is payable, the more reluctant the local planning authority may become to exercise its powers on planning grounds, and this is thought to be undesirable. In other words, two principles come into conflict here: on the one hand, private landowners should not be made to bear the whole cost of public restrictions on the use of their land; and on the other, socially desirable public restrictions on the use of land should not give rise to a claim for compensation any more than do many other state-imposed restrictions on one's freedom to do what one likes with one's own property. The question that may be posed here is: are the other exceptions to the general rule explicable by reference to the attempt to strike a balance between these two competing principles, and if not, how are they explicable?

JUSTICE, *Compensation for Compulsory Acquisition and Remedies for Planning Restrictions*, (1969)[36]

64. The ability or otherwise of an owner of an interest in land to claim compensation in respect of any loss he has suffered as a result of the exercise by a local planning authority of its power to control the development of land can be explained historically but not logically. If an adverse planning decision is made in respect of an application for development of land other than for 'new development', i.e. in respect of an application for the development specified in Schedule 8 of the Town and Country Planning Act 1971, compensation for any loss suffered is available in cases falling within Part II of the Schedule. If an adverse planning decision is made in respect of an application for development of land not within Schedule 8 to the Act ('new development') a condition precedent to the payment of compensation is that the owner or his predecessor in title should have made in 1948 a claim for loss of the development value of his land which the Town and Country Planning Act 1947 had sought to appropriate and transfer to the state. . . .

65. The present right to receive payment of compensation for restriction on 'new development' depends on a claim having been made more than twenty years ago in respect of loss of development value which existed at that time, resulting in there being in respect of the land an 'unexpended balance of established development value'. It is questionable whether there is any fairness in distinguishing between the development value of land as it existed in 1948, upon which, provided a claim for its loss had been made compensation might be available, and the development value of land arising since 1948, when it is not. One result of this distinction is that in many cases no compensation is payable at all in respect of restrictions on 'new development'. The present position is quite absurd. . . .

66. It may well be that the real anomaly in this area of law is not that many people receive no compensation, but that a few people receive some in the shape of the 'unexpended balance of established development value' attached to the land . . . it is difficult to escape from the fact that transactions in land have, for the past twenty years, been undertaken with full knowledge that compensation for restrictions on new development is in the main non-existent, or, at the most, extremely limited. We believe that the community has now accepted that there should in general be no payment of compensation for such restrictions.

67. . . . We propose . . . that where there is an 'unexpended balance of established development value' in respect of land, the right to claim compensation should be redeemed over a fixed and limited period of time. . . . We believe that this proposal, if accepted, . . . would provide a fair, logical and acceptable principle free from the historical influences which at present plague this area of law.

68. Since 1948, when planning control was universally imposed on the development of land, compensation has been payable in respect of any

restriction on development where the development might be regarded as part of the existing use of land. We refer to development other than 'new development', i.e., the development set out in Schedule 8 to the Town and Country Planning Act 1971. Any restriction on development falling within Part I of the Schedule may allow the owner to serve a purchase notice on the local planning authority requiring it to purchase his interest. Any restriction on development falling within Part II of the Schedule may also give rise to a claim for compensation, under section 169 of the Act, of an amount equal to the depreciation in the value of the interest caused by the restriction.

73. Irrespective of the kind of development authorised by a planning permission, . . . if that permission is subsequently revoked or modified, compensation is payable under section 164 of the 1971 Act in respect of loss directly attributable to that revocation or modification. As mentioned in the Report of the Chartered Land Societies Committee (para. 100), section 164 (4) appears to exclude payment of compensation for development falling within Schedule 8, as it is provided that in calculating the compensation payable it is to be assumed that permission for such development would be granted. We have no knowledge of the section being applied this way. If the question were to come before the courts, we doubt whether they would accept this interpretation. . . .

Of the three situations in which compensation is payable, the first is an historical anomaly: what are the other two? Can they both be brought under the same head of 'existing use': once one has a permission to develop, the value of the land has changed upwards; if that is then modified, the value changes downwards: if one is restricted in one's existing use, the value of the land may well change downwards. In each case it may plausibly be argued that if circumstances outside the control of the landowner cause a public authority to decide to stop that landowner doing either what he has hitherto been doing or doing what he has been given permission to do, the losses caused thereby should fall on the public purse. Can this approach be justified on a modern equitable basis?

Expert Committee on Compensation and Betterment,
op. cit.

32. . . . Ownership of land involves duties to the community as well as rights in the individual owner. It may involve complete surrender of the land to the State or it may involve submission to a limitation of rights of user of the land without surrender of ownership or possession being required. There is a difference in principle between these two types of public interference with the rights of private ownership. Where property is taken over, the intention is to use those rights, and the common law of England

does not recognise any right of requisitioning property by the State without liability to pay compensation to the individual for the loss of his property. The basis of compensation rests with the State to prescribe. In the second type of case, where the regulatory power of the State limits the use which an owner may make of his property, but does not deprive him of owner-ship, whatever rights he may lose are not taken over by the State; they are destroyed on the grounds that their existence is contrary to the national interest. In such circumstances no claim for compensation lies at common law. . . .

35. The difference in treatment as regards compensation may be rested on the difference between expropriation of property on the one hand and restriction on user while leaving ownership and possession undisturbed on the other. If the question be asked 'Does ownership of land necessarily carry with it the right to turn it to any use which happens to be most profitable to the owner?', a negative answer must clearly be given. As we have seen, some restrictions may clearly be imposed – and would be ac-cepted unquestionably by any landowner – without any suggestion of hardship or of giving rise to any just claim for compensation. They are both reasonable and necessary in order that other persons should not be injured in the legitimate enjoyment of their own rights. The principle is at its lowest that of 'live and let live' and advances so as to comprehend all the obligations which according to the social standards of the day are regarded as due to neighbours and fellow citizens. But, as the scope of these restric-tions increases by the operation of planning, a stage is reached at which the restrictions imposed will be said to go beyond the claims of 'good neigh-bourliness' and general considerations of regional or national policy require so great a restriction on the landowner's use of his land as to amount to a taking away from him of a proprietary interest in the land. When this point has been reached, the landowner will claim to be fairly entitled to compensation, such compensation to be computed upon the principles applicable where other rights of property are taken away from him.

Thus we may state five propositions: –
(1) Ownership of land does not carry with it an unqualified right of user.
(2) Therefore restrictions based on the duties of neighbourliness may be imposed without involving the conception that the landowner is being deprived of any property or interest.
(3) Therefore such restrictions can be imposed without liability to pay compensation.
(4) But the point may be reached when the restrictions imposed extend beyond the obligations of neighbourliness.
(5) At this stage the restrictions become equivalent to an expropria-tion of a proprietary right or interest and therefore (it will be claimed) should carry a right to compensation as such.
It will always be a matter of difficulty to draw the line with any satis-factory logic, i.e., to determine the point at which the accepted obligations of neighbourliness or citizenship are exceeded and an expropriation is

suffered – particularly as the standard of obligation will vary with the political theory of the day. . . .

Can the legal extension of categories of planning blight by the Land Compensation Act 1973 be related to this shifting line between compensable and non-compensable restrictions? Why should not the owners of land within the recently designated Coventry Green Belt be compensated? Is this not a case of 'general considerations of regional or national policy (requiring) so great a restriction on the landowner's use of his land as to amount to a taking away from him of a proprietary interest in the land'?[37] Does the requirement that land must no longer be capable of reasonably beneficial use before a purchase notice may be served represent an application of or a derogation from the principles spelt out by the Uthwatt Report? If a derogation, on what grounds is it justifiable? Assuming that these are the principles on which the law is based, do you agree with them? If not, what would you put in their place? To what extent must any system of compensation, designed to be fair, be matched by a system of collection of betterment in respect of planning decisions which greatly increase the value of land? Consider in this connection the following:

(i) '. . . the compensation difficulty exists because planning, which is directed to securing the best social use of land, tries to operate within a system of land ownership under which there is attached to land a development value depending on the prospects of its profitable use. If there is to be a completely satisfactory basis for planning which gets rid of the difficulty, that system itself must be revised for difficulties which arise out of a system are not solved by framing a new code for assessing compensation and collecting betterment which operates within that system.' (The Uthwatt Report, para. 37.)

(ii) The 38-acre Hays Wharf site in the Borough of Southwark is to be developed by private developers who plan to put in at least 2,000,000 square feet of office accommodation. The cost of the development of the whole site has been put at £300 million and one published City of London estimate put the profit of the scheme at £160 million. If Southwark Council had wished to develop the land and so reap the profits itself, it would clearly have had to pay a very large sum by way of compensation for compulsory purchase. Are the principles governing compensation justifiable if they produce a result by which the private developer cannot lose and the public authority cannot gain unless the private developer voluntarily foregoes some or all of his profit?

(b) When is compensation assessed?

Procedures relating to compulsory acquisition are not directly dealt with in this chapter.[38] However, there are some matters which cross the boundary between procedure and substance. One of the most important of these concerns the time at which assessment of compensation takes place. Procedurally this involves a consideration of the notice to treat; the substantive issue is that in an age of inflation the benefits and burdens of choosing a particular time will be or may be dramatically different for compulsory vendor and purchaser. Should the time of assessment be when the notice to treat is served or should it be when the actual taking occurs if there is a substantial interval of time between the notice and the taking? Should the principle to be followed be different for different types of compensation? What effect might different rules have on actual practices of local authorities? These issues are raised by the important House of Lords decision of *Birmingham Corporation* v. *West Midland Baptist (Trust) Association (Incorporated)* [1969] 3 All E.R. 172:

LORD REID: My Lords, in 1947 the appellants obtained a compulsory purchase order covering an area of 981 acres in the centre of Birmingham. Within this area was a site belonging to the respondents, on which was 'The People's Chapel'. By statute registration of this order on 14th August 1947 had the effect that notice to treat was deemed to have been served on that date on the respondents and on the numerous other owners of land within that area. It was obvious that redevelopment of this area would take a long time. The respondents wished to continue to use their chapel and it was understood that in due course the appellants would make another site available for rebuilding it, although they may not have been under a legal obligation to do this. In 1958 a site for a new chapel was offered to the respondents and they accepted it in 1959. The property of the old site was not vested in the appellants until 24th June 1963. The determination of the amount of compensation due to the respondents was referred to the Lands Tribunal in 1965.

The assessment of compensation for compulsory acquisition of land is now regulated by six rules set out in s. 2 of the Acquisition of Land (Assessment of Compensation) Act 1919. . . .

It was agreed that in this case compensation falls to be assessed under r. (5) and r. (6). And it was further agreed that £5,025 should be awarded under r. (6). The question at issue in this case is the meaning of 'the basis of the reasonable cost of equivalent reinstatement' in r. (5). The appellants argue that we are required to assume that equivalent re-instatement took place at the date of the notice to treat in 1947 and that r. (5) requires an assessment of what the cost of such re-instatement would have been at that date. If that is right it is agreed that that cost would have been £50,025. The respondents argue that the proper date for assessing that cost is the date at which re-instatement might reasonably have begun. If that is right, that date is agreed to have been 30th April 1961 and it is agreed that the cost would then have been £89,575. The difference between these two figures is accounted for by the steady rise of costs of all kinds since the last war. In fact rebuilding of the chapel was only begun in 1965 but apparently the date in 1961 has been agreed because there was some unnecessary delay on the part of the respondents. . . .

The substance of r. (2), r. (5) and r. (6) was not new in 1919 and these rules must be interpreted in light of the provisions of the Lands Clauses Consolidation Act 1845, and of later decisions of the courts. In 1845 and for many years thereafter compulsory purchase of land was generally authorised by private Acts of Parliament. Before 1845 these Acts generally contained a number of sections regulating procedure and the Act of 1845 enacted a standard code which would apply except insofar as varied by a particular Act. Broadly speaking, the position was that each Act conferred on the promoters power to take specified lands. . . .

If the promoters decided to take particular land the first step they had to take was to serve notice to treat on persons who had interests in that land. By s. 18 of the Act of 1845 the notice to treat had to require the person on whom it was served to state particulars of his interest and of his claims, but it has been held that he can amend this claim later. The notice to treat did not give to the promoters any right, title or interest in the land. It enabled the promoters to proceed to have compensation assessed, to take possession if certain requirements were fulfilled and ultimately to obtain a title to the land taken. And it enabled the person on whom it was served to take action himself to compel the owners to pay for and take the land if he did not wish to wait for the promoters to act. And it was soon decided that it had another effect; the owner of the land could not, after receiving the notice to treat, increase the burden of compensation on the promoters by creating new interests in the land or by making improvements on it. He was not prevented from creating a new interest or making an improvement but if he did so the promoters did not have to pay for it. . . .

Apart from severance and injurious affection there is only one subject for compensation – the value of the land. . . .

But it came to be recognised that this method did not always produce a fair result and in certain classes of cases the cost of re-instatement was adopted as giving a better assessment of the value of the land to the owner who was being dispossessed. . . .

In the 5th edition of CRIPPS ON COMPENSATION (the last I think to be edited by LORD PARMOOR) it is said:[39]

> There are some cases in which the income derived, or probably to be derived, from land would not constitute a fair basis in assessing the value to the owner, and then the principle of reinstatement should be applied.

This principle is that the owner cannot be placed in as favourable a position as he was in before the exercise of compulsory powers, unless such a sum is assessed as will enable him to replace the premises or lands taken by premises or lands which would be to him of the same value. It is not possible to give an exhaustive catalogue of all cases to which the principle of reinstatement is applicable. But we may instance churches, schools, hospitals, houses of an exceptional character, and business premises in which the business can only be carried on under special conditions or by means of special licences.

and this is substantially repeated in the 8th edition of 1938.

These passages show clearly that their authors were assuming that the assessed cost of re-instatement would be sufficient to enable the owner to re-instate himself if he acted reasonably. But the appellants maintain that long before any of them was written it had become a rule of law that the value of land to the owner must always be assessed as at the date of the notice to treat, whether or not that was in fact sufficient to enable the owner to re-instate himself as soon as that was reasonably practicable. It appears to me to be self evident that, if anything is taken, compensation should be assessed as at the date when it is taken. But taking or acquisition under the Lands Clauses Consolidation Act 1845 involves a series of steps spread over a period of time and so it is necessary to determine at what stage the promoters can properly be regarded as having taken the land and the owner can properly be regarded as having had it taken from him.

In the nineteenth century the purchasing power of money remained fairly constant over long periods, otherwise consols would not have been held to be the safest possible investment. And there was seldom any long delay by the promoters in completing the acquisition of land after notice to treat had been served; counsel could not find any case in which the delay had exceeded two or three years. So from a practical point of view it did not much matter which stage in the process of acquisition was taken as the time as at which compensation should be assessed. It was convenient to take the date of the notice to treat, and from at least 1870 onwards it was generally assumed that this was the right date to take.

The first authority generally cited for the proposition that interests must be valued as at the date of the notice to treat is the judgment of SIR WILLIAM PAGE WOOD VC in *Penny* v. *Penny*[40]. . . .

The essence of this decision was that the extent or quality of an interest to be compensated cannot be altered or increased by the giving of the notice to treat or the compulsory acquisition of that interest. No one would now doubt that. But this does not imply that the interest must be valued as at the date of the notice to treat, and it is to be observed that SIR WILLIAM PAGE WOOD VC did not say that serving the notice is or must be regarded as a taking of the property. He treated as identical 'the time when the house was about to be taken' and the 'moment when the notice to treat was given'. If he had foreseen present conditions I think he would have used rather different language.

There is no indication in the later authorities of anyone having contended that any other date should be taken than that of the notice to treat. . . .

I can find no substantial reason given for taking the date of the notice to treat other than that it was the most convenient date to take, and that it was so near to the date of the actual taking that assessment as at the date of the notice to treat would do no substantial injustice to either party. Moreover this so-called principle does not appear to have been applied to every element of the value of the land to the owner. . . .

And it could not be right to value one element of the value to the owner, the market value of the land, as at one date, and to value the other elements, consequential losses, as at a different date. So it appears to me that the so-called principle rests on very unstable foundations.

We have to construe r. (5) of the Act of 1919. I think it clear that the natural meaning of 'the basis of the reasonable cost of equivalent rein-statement' is that one envisages a reasonable owner re-instating himself in premises reasonably equivalent for his purpose as soon as, in all the circumstances, that is reasonably practicable, and awards to him as compensation such sum as will enable him to do that. But if it had been clearly established before 1919 that the proper basis for assessing the cost of re-instatement was the hypothetical cost as at the date of the notice to treat, then I would find it somewhat difficult to hold that r. (5) had altered the law, because I doubt whether it can be said that the words of r. (5) are incapable of having this meaning. I am therefore unwilling to decide this case without coming to some conclusion as to what the pre-existing law was.

If we are to consider the law as it was before 1919 I do not think that we can take re-instatement in isolation. On the one hand, the rule that the date of the notice to treat must be taken was generally stated as applying to all compensation, e.g.: The principle of compensation is indemnity to the owner, and the basis on which all compensation for lands required or taken should be assessed, is their value to the owner as at the date of the notice to treat . . . (*Cripps on Compensation* (5th Edn.)

On the other hand, the principle underlying the rule was that the owner was to be compensated for his expulsion from the land taken. . . .

The principle and the rule cannot be reconciled except on the basis that the total value to the owner at the date of the notice to treat is always substantially the same as the value at the date of the expulsion. For it cannot be said that the owner is in any way expelled from his land by the notice to treat. So the question is whether it is proper for this House to re-examine a judge-made rule of law based on an assumption of fact which was true when the rule was formulated but which is no longer true and which now in many cases causes serious injustice.

The appellants argue that we cannot do this because, in at least three fairly recent Acts, Parliament has recognised the validity of the existing rule[41]. . . .

These provisions do show that Parliament (or the draftsman) must have thought that the law was that compensation was assessable on the basis of value as at the date of notice to treat. But the mere fact that an enactment shows that Parliament must have thought that the law was one thing does not preclude the courts from deciding that the law was in fact something different. This has been stated in a number of cases including *Inland Revenue Comrs. v. Dowdall, O'Mahoney & Co. Ltd*[42]. No doubt the position would be different if the provisions of the enactment were such that they would only be workable if the law was as Parliament supposed it to be. But in my view all that can be said here is that these enactments would have a narrower scope if the law was found to be that compensation must be assessed at a date later than that of the notice to treat. I do not think that that is sufficient to preclude your Lordships from re-examining the whole matter.

Then there is the importance of not upsetting existing proprietary or contractual rights. We cannot say that the law was one thing yesterday but is to be something different tomorrow. If we decide that the rule as to the date of the notice to treat is wrong we must decide that it always has been wrong, and that would mean that in many completed transactions owners have received too little compensation. But that often happens when an existing decision is reversed. Here there appears to me to be little or no chance that by re-opening the whole matter we would alter the future operation of existing vested rights.

The only other difficulty is to find the right date for the assessment of compensation. No stage can be singled out as the date of expropriation in every case. Sometimes possession is taken before compensation is assessed. Then it would seem logical to fix the market value of the land as at that date and to take actual consequential losses as they occurred then or thereafter provided that the dispossessed owner had acted reasonably. But if compensation is assessed before possession is taken, taking the date of assessment can I think be justified because then either party can sue for specific performance and the promoters obtain a right to the land, as if there had been a contract of sale at that date. In cases under r. (5) I have already said that that rule appears to point to assessment of the cost of re-instatement at the date when that became reasonably practicable. . . .

If the views which I have expressed are accepted the result is that the present practice with regard to r. (2) is wrong, that what I understand to be the present practice with regard to r. (6) is correct, and that under r. (5) the respondents are entitled to the larger agreed sum. I would dismiss the appeal.

Appeal dismissed.

Davies sums up the discussion on date of valuation as follows: 'There was general agreement with this proposition that the date of taking possession, or the date of the assessment itself, whichever is the sooner, should be the date of valuation.' Do you agree with this proposition? Why not adopt a principle of 'whichever is the later date'?

What advice would you give to a local authority contemplating the compulsory purchase of an area of development land that wished to limit as much as possible the amount of compensation it paid?

Contrast Lord Reid's judgement in this case with his judgement in *Westminster Bank Ltd* v. *Minister of Housing and Local Government* (*supra* p. 627). What were the crucial factors in each case which caused him to decide the way he did?

(c) The assessment of market value

Davies, op. cit., pp. 111, 128–9

The question of market value is a paradox which lies at the heart of the law of compulsory purchase of land. The nature of the paradox is this. 'Market value' as a concept means a purely natural phenomenon, namely a price-level reached between buyers and sellers bargaining with the minimum of artificial constraints: in theory without any constraints. But this condition of the 'free market' is the very opposite of the condition of a compulsory purchase, which is ex hypothesi a situation of constraint. Therefore to say that compulsory purchase compensation is to be assessed at 'market value' is to say that a state of affairs is to be visualised in terms of its direct opposite.

. . . [The] 'market value' of land is comprised of more than one element – 'development value' as well as 'existing use value' – and . . . development value in turn depends on the co-existence of two things, market demand for the land for development purposes and planning permission, actual or assumed for such development. . . .

The legal approach is no doubt an over simplification in the eyes of valuers; but as far as the law is concerned, the proper analysis of land value seems to be threefold. There are in other words, three elements of value which, when aggregated in a proper case go to make up the market price of land. But not all three elements are present every time. They can be expressed as the 'existing use' value of land, the value of the prospect of development over and above the existing use, and the total cost of such development if carried out (including the developer's profit). . . .

The process can be expressed diagrammatically:

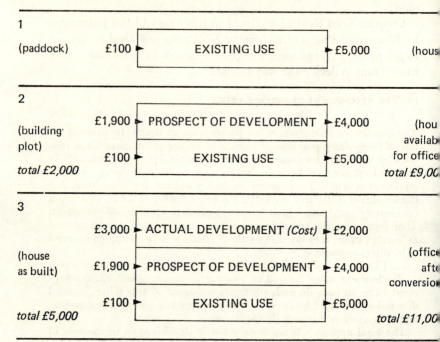

1

(paddock) £100 ► EXISTING USE ► £5,000 (hous

2

(building·
plot)

£1,900 ► PROSPECT OF DEVELOPMENT ► £4,000 (hou
availab

£100 ► EXISTING USE ► £5,000 for office

total £2,000 total £9,00

3

(house
as built)

£3,000 ► ACTUAL DEVELOPMENT *(Cost)* ► £2,000 (office

£1,900 ► PROSPECT OF DEVELOPMENT ► £4,000 afte
conversio

£100 ► EXISTING USE ► £5,000

total £5,000 total £11,00

It will be noticed that stage (3) in the first process of development is at the same time stage (1) in a subsequent process of development. But it will be noticed also that stage (2) in any process of development sees the property in exactly the same physical state as stage (1). It is this lack of difference in physical terms that presents the most teasing problem in the assessment of compulsory purchase compensation, namely, should land be treated as having an 'existing use' value only, or should it be treated as having a 'prospective development' value on top of 'existing use' value to give an over-all development value? If the latter is right, what prospective development should be taken into account?

No doubt, as Davies implies, valuers do not assess the value of land in that way, nor is the relevant law set out in that way, but the Land Compensation Act 1961, the basic statute on assessment, does distinguish between 'Rules for assessing Compensation' contained in section 5 and 'Assumption as to planning permission and allied matters' contained in sections 14–22. Artificial though it may be, therefore, the distinction will be followed here.

(i) *Rules for assessing compensation*

The basic rules are set out in section 5 of the Land Compensation Act with additional rules set out in sections 6–9. In addition, certain principles have been grafted onto, or developed alongside, the statutory rules by the courts and they may be considered under this head as well.

(a) THE POINTE GOURDE PRINCIPLE

Pointe Gourde Quarrying and Transport Co Ltd v. *Sub-Intendent of Crown Lands* [1947] A.C. 565

The United States required for the establishment of a naval base in Trinidad certain lands owned by the appellants at Pointe Gourde in that Island. . . . The Crown acquired those lands in the exercise of its compulsory powers. . . .

On part of the lands so acquired there was a large quantity of good limestone. The appellants had quarried and sold stone and lime from that part for many years before the acquisition. . . .

The appellants' claim for compensation was heard, pursuant to the provisions of the Ordinance, by a tribunal. . . .

[which awarded, *inter alia*, a sum of $15,000] described by the tribunal as being 'for special adaptibility'. But, despite the similarity of description, it was clear that that item was intended to be quite different and distinct from any other in the compensation allowed. It was meant to cover . . . not the special suitability or adaptability of the land for the purpose of quarrying, which existed before acquisition, but the special adaptability (to follow the language of the tribunal) which the quarry land possessed after acquisition, in that its proximity to the naval base under construction made it specially suited to the special needs of the United States. . . .

The point for determination was whether or not that $15,000 item was allowable in law as part of the compensation payable to the appellants.

LORD MACDERMOTT: . . . It is well settled that compensation for the compulsory acquisition of land cannot include an increase in value which is entirely due to the scheme underlying the acquisition. As it was put by EVE J in *South Eastern Ry. Co.* v. *London County Council*[43]: 'Increase in value consequent on the execution of the undertaking for or in connexion with which the purchase is made must be disregarded.' This rule was recognized by the Full Court and, indeed, appears to be the basis of its main conclusion.

On behalf of the appellants it was said that the relevant scheme in this matter was the acquisition of the quarry land and not the construction of the naval base in its vicinity. Their Lordships are unable to accede to this argument. The case stated finds that the lands acquired were 'required by the United States for the establishment of a naval base in Trinidad.' That being so, the nature of the scheme of this acquisition is clear and the award of $15,000 can only be related to the additional value which it gave to the quarry land. For these reasons their Lordships consider that the Full Court was right in disallowing the item in question.

Appeal dismissed.

Wilson v. *Liverpool City Council* [1971] 1 All E.R. 628

LORD DENNING MR: . . . In 1960 the council was very much pressed to provide housing accommodation. It could only find one area suitable for housing development. It was some 391 acres between two golf courses. It was in private ownership. The council managed to buy some 305 acres of it by agreement. But there was quite a large area which it was unable to acquire by agreement. It took steps to obtain compulsory powers over it. I will not go into details, but I may say that on 14th November 1963 the Minister of Housing and Local Government himself granted the council permission to develop the whole of the land. On 28th February 1964, the council made a compulsory purchase order for the remaining portion which it wanted to acquire. There was a public inquiry. The inspector made recommendations suggesting that some should be left for private development, but those were overruled by the Minister. On 27th January 1965, the Minister confirmed the compulsory purchase order without modification. He felt that the council's urgent housing needs and its slum-clearance problems should take precedence over other considerations. We are only concerned with 74 acres belonging to one owner. On 2nd May 1965, the council gave notice to treat. The Lands Tribunal assessed the value of the land as at that date. In making its calculations, it made a deduction on account of an increase in value which was due to the scheme underlying the acquisition. The tribunal applied the principle which was stated by Lord MacDermott in *Pointe Gourde Quarrying and Transport Co. Ltd* v. *Sub-Intendent of Crown Lands.* . . .

The question has arisen whether that principle applies to cases under the Land Compensation Act 1961. That Act contains an elaborate provision about prospective development. It sets out in a schedule the circumstances in which no account is to be taken of any increase in value due to the prospect of development: see s. 6 (1) and Part I of Sch. 1. It is suggested that that provision contains a code which defines exhaustively the increases which are *not* to be taken into account, so that any other increase *is* to be taken into account; and, accordingly, there is no room for the *Pointe Gourde* principle. But this court has rejected that argument. In *Viscount Camrose* v. *Basingstoke Corpn*[44] we held that the *Pointe Gourde* principle still applies to development which is not mentioned in Sch. 1 to the 1961 Act. Counsel for the claimants recognises that that decision is binding on this court but he may desire to challenge it in the House of Lords. Accepting the decision, however, he says that the *Pointe Gourde* principle does not apply here. The principle only applies, he says, when the scheme is precise and definite; and is made known to all the world. . . .

I do not accept counsel's submission. A scheme is a progressive thing. It starts vague and known to few. It becomes more precise and better known as time goes on. Eventually it becomes precise and definite, and known to all. Correspondingly, its impact has a progressive effect on values. At first it has little effect because it is so vague and uncertain. As it becomes more precise and better known, so its impact increases until it has an important effect. It is this increase, whether big or small, which is to be disregarded as at the time when the value is to be assessed.

The tribunal gave an excellent reasoned decision. I find no fault in it. . . . Applying the *Pointe Gourde* principle, the tribunal made its valuation in this way. It took some comparable land, next door to these 74 acres, which was sold in 1965 for £6,700 an acre. It was sold by a private owner to a private developer. That was the dead ripe value. That value was an enhanced value because seller and purchaser knew of the scheme; and knew that the council would install sewage works, and so forth, of which the developer could take advantage; and it was two years in advance of the land the subject of this inquiry. Making all allowances, and deducting the increase owing to the scheme, it arrived at a value of £343,500. I think that the tribunal was quite right to deduct the increase owing to the scheme. I would dismiss this appeal accordingly[45].

Appeal dismissed.

The converse of this principle is provided for by statute:

Land Compensation Act 1961

9. No account shall be taken of any depreciation of the value of the relevant interest which is attributable to the fact that (whether by way of designation, allocation or other particulars contained in the current development plan, or by any other means) an indication has been given that the relevant land is, or is likely, to be acquired by an authority possessing compulsory purchase powers.

(b) SECTION 5, LAND COMPENSATION ACT[46]

5. Compensation in respect of any compulsory acquisition shall be assessed in accordance with the following rules:

(1) No allowance shall be made on account of the acquisition being compulsory:

(2) The value of land shall, subject as hereinafter provided, be taken to be the amount which the land if sold in the open market by a willing seller might be expected to realise:

(3) The special suitability or adaptability of the land for any purpose shall not be taken into account if that purpose is a purpose to which it could be applied only in pursuance of statutory powers, or for which there is no market apart from the special needs of a particular purchaser or the requirements of any authority possessing compulsory purchase powers:

(4) Where the value of the land is increased by reason of the use thereof or of any premises thereon in a manner which could be restrained by any Court, or is contrary to law, or is detrimental to the health of the occupants of the premises or to the public health, the amount of that increase shall not be taken into account:

(5) Where land is, and but for the compulsory acquisition would continue to be, devoted to a purpose of such a nature that there is no general demand or market for land for that purpose, the compensation may, if the Lands Tribunal is satisfied that reinstatement in some other place is bona fide intended, be assessed on the basis of the reasonable cost of equivalent reinstatement:

(6) The provisions of Rule 2 shall not affect the assessment of compensation for disturbance or any other matter not directly based on the value of land.

(c) SECTION 6, LAND COMPENSATION ACT[47]

Davy v. Leeds Corporation [1965] 1 All E.R. 753

LORD GUEST: My Lords, at the end of counsel's arguments the decision in this case turned on a very narrow point of construction. The broad question was whether in assessing the compensation payable to the appellants for the compulsory purchase of their unfit houses which were in a clearance area under the Housing Act, 1957, the valuation should be on the basis that the area adjoining and surrounding the appellants' houses should be treated as being clear of houses, as the appellants contend, or should be treated as being in an area of houses which were themselves unfit for human habitation, as the respondents contend. In other words, for the purposes of valuation should the clearance area be considered or ignored? . . . In the end the problem is, in my view, to be solved by an interpretation of s. 9 of the latter Act[48]. The relevant portions of that Act are in the following terms. Section 9 (1) provides:

(1) In addition to the rules applicable in accordance with s. 2 of the Act of 1919 (which prescribes rules for the assessment of compensation), the following provisions of this section shall have effect for the purpose of assessing the compensation payable in respect of compulsory acquisitions to which s. 1 of this Act applies:

Provided that, in cases falling within Pt. 1 of Sch. 1 to this Act, those provisions shall have effect subject to the provisions of that part of that schedule.

Section 9 (2) provides:

In each of the cases mentioned in the first column of the following table, no account shall be taken of any increase or diminution of the value of the relevant interest which is attributable –

(a) to the carrying out of any such development as is mentioned in relation thereto in the second column of that table, or

(b) to the prospect that any such development will or may be carried out,

in so far as any such development (whether actual or prospective) is or would be development arising from the circumstances of that case.

TABLE

Case	Development
1. In the case of every acquisition for pupuses involving development of any of the land authorised to be acquired.	Development of any of the land authorised to be acquired, other than the relevant land, being development for any of the purposes for which any part of the first-mentioned land (including any part of the relevant land) is to be acquired.

Section 9 (7) provides as follows:

Any reference in this section to development (whether actual or prospective) which is or would be development arising from the circumstances of a case mentioned in the first column of the table set out in sub-s. (2) of this section –

(*a*) in relation to any acquisition for purposes involving development of any of the land authorised to be acquired, shall (subject to the next following paragraph) be construed as a reference to development (whether actual or prospective) which would not have been likely to be carried out if the acquiring authority had not acquired, and did not propose to acquire, any of that land, and

(*b*) in relation to any acquisition falling within one or more of paras. 2 to 5 in the said first column,

shall be construed as including (or, if the acquisition is not for purposes involving development of any of the land authorised to be acquired, shall be construed as) a reference to any development (whether actual or prospective) which would not have been likely to be carried out if the area or areas referred to in that paragraph or those paragraphs had not been defined or designated as therein mentioned or (in a case falling within para. 5) if the scheme therein mentioned had not come into operation.

By s. 9 (8) 'any . . . development of any land' includes clearing of that land. Counsel were agreed that in the circumstances of the case the combined interpretation of s. 9 (2) and (7) was as follows:

No increase or decrease of value due to the clearing of the surrounding land (whether actual or prospective) is to be taken into account if this clearing would not have been likely to be carried out if the acquiring authority had not acquired and did not propose to acquire any of the surrounding land.

The history of events is that on Nov. 6, 1957, the respondents declared the Albert Grove district in Leeds to be a clearance area within which were the appellants' unfit houses. On Dec. 4, 1957, the respondents resolved to deal with the whole clearance area by making a compulsory purchase order pursuant to their powers under s. 43 (3) of the Housing Act, 1957. On July 30, 1958, the respondents made the necessary compulsory purchase order. The appellants' sites were within the area the subject of the order. On Nov. 2, 1959, notice to treat was served on the appellants. This is the date at which the compensation falls to be assessed.

The appellants contended that the question under s. 9 (2) and (7) of the Act of 1959 – would clearance have been likely if the respondents had not proposed to acquire – permitted of only one answer, namely that if the respondents did not themselves acquire, clearance must have taken place because that was the only alternative open to them under s. 43 of the Housing Act, 1957. If they did not acquire compulsorily, their statutory duty was to clear, which duty they could have been compelled to fulfil by the Minister under default powers. The respondents, on the other hand, contended that if they had not proposed to acquire, no private developer would ever have cleared the area. The clearance declaration and compulsory purchase orders were so inextricably bound together that, although the resolution to make compulsory purchase orders did not follow till nearly a month after the clearance declaration, it was implicit that the respondents would never have made the clearance declaration unless they had proposed to follow it up with compulsory purchase orders. In considering the likelihood or otherwise of clearance it was impossible to isolate the clearance declaration, and consider what would have been the situation if that had stood alone without the proposal to acquire. The question was therefore whether, if the respondents had not proposed to acquire, there was any likelihood of a private individual developing the area.

In my view, the interpretation of the respondents of s. 9 (2) read with s. 9 (7) of the Town and Country Planning Act, 1959, is correct and follows more closely the policy of Parliament in regard to the basis of compensation for houses unfit for human habitation. Case 1 provides in effect that if the clearing would have been likely to have been carried out with government intervention then the owner is not to receive any benefit or disadvantage from that intervention. Section 9 (7) safeguards the case where the clearing would have come about without government intervention and provides for the owner being entitled to an enhanced value if it was due to that development.

The question therefore resolves itself into one of fact. If the respondents had not proposed to acquire would redevelopment have taken place by any private developer? This question was, however, never before the Lands Tribunal. They fell into an error of law, which was put right in the Court of Appeal. . . .

They have said that the inevitable inference from the Case Stated by the Lands Tribunal is that no private developer would ever have developed the area if the respondents had not proposed to acquire. I agree. The appellants' basis of compensation therefore falls to the ground and the respondents' basis must be sustained.

For these reasons I would dismiss the appeal.

Appeal dismissed.

(ii) *Assumptions as to planning permission: prospective development value*
Section 14 of the Land Compensation Act 1961 provides that for the purpose of assessing compensation one or more assumptions contained in sections 15 and 16 'shall be made in ascertaining the value of the relevant interest' in the land, that these assumptions are in addition to any planning permissions that might be in force at the date of the notice to treat, and that it is not to be assumed that other planning permissions might be refused; 'but in determining whether planning permission for any development could in any particular circumstances reasonably have been expected to be granted in respect of any land, regard shall be had to any contrary opinion expressed in relation to that land in any certificate of appropriate alternative development'.

As summarised by Heap, section 15 provides that

it will assume that
(1) planning permission will be granted for the development which brings about the need for the compulsory purchase . . .
(2) planning permission will be granted for all development falling within the ambit of the 'existing use of land' . . . but not, of course, if the existing use value of the land has already been realised by the payment to the landowner of compensation; and
(3) planning permission will be granted for 'certificated development' that is to say, development in respect of which a certificate [certificate of appropriate alternative development] is issued under Part III of the 1961 Act.[49]

Section 16 deals with planning assumptions, based on the local planning authorities' development plans. It must be read together with section 17, which introduces the certificate of appropriate alternative development. The principles behind the sections and their interrelation is explained by Davies (op. cit., pp. 134–7):

Section 16 provides that planning permission may be assumed for proposed development which, in the current development plan, is specifically indicated for the relevant land or is a reasonable project of development for some use within a *general* category 'zoned' for an area which includes the relevant land. . . . the general categories of development for which land is customarily 'zoned' in development plans comprise, in broad terms, the following: residential, commercial and industrial development. These are varieties of development which do attract appreciable market demand among private developers; and they can therefore be regarded collectively as lucrative development. They can also be regarded as being virtually the only categories of land *use* (whether involving development or not) which can be thought of as having a wide and general market value. . . .

Section 16 authorises planning permission to be assumed for development, 'lucrative' or otherwise, if the relevant land is in an area 'zoned' for one or more uses and the proposed development is for such a use. But the test which must be satisfied is specific as well as general. Not only must the land be in a 'zone' for the particular use for which development is proposed, but in addition it must be 'development for which planning permission might reasonably have been expected to be granted in respect of the relevant land. . . .'

If the relevant land is in an area 'zoned' for any 'lucrative' use or uses . . . or an area of comprehensive development, which in this context almost certainly amounts to the same thing, then the way is open for the owner to lay claim to an appreciable element of prospective development value, subject of course to the reasonable suitability of the particular land to particular development suggested. But the current development plan may not be so favourable to the owner's land. It may indicate the land as . . . 'white' on the map. 'White land' is most likely to be farmland or other rural land which the local planning authority wishes to remain in its undeveloped state. . . .

If this is the case Part III of the 1961 Act (sections 17 to 22) gives an owner of any interest in land being compulsorily acquired a sporting chance none the less to lay claim to prospective development value. He does this by applying to the local planning authority for a 'certificate of appropriate alternative development' . . . .

Any application for one of these certificates must itself 'specify one or more classes of development appearing to the applicant to be . . . appropriate to the land in question if it were not proposed to be acquired by any authority possessing compulsory purchase powers . . . .' . . . . The local planning authority must, between 21 days and two months after (the date of the service of the notice) issue the certificate specifying the class or classes of development for which permission might, in their opinion, 'reasonably have been expected to be granted' in the absence of compulsory purchase . . . or alternatively that no development, other than any involved in the acquiring authority's project, could be envisaged. Any class or classes of development approved in a certificate need not be the same as specified by the applicant; nor need they necessarily be in accordance with the development plan.

. . . Appeal may be made against an unfavourable certificate either by the owner of an interest in land to which it relates, or by the acquiring authority. . . . It is made to the Secretary of State for the Environment . . . who . . . is to consider the matter entirely de novo. Accordingly he 'shall either confirm the certificate, or vary it, or cancel it and issue a different certificate in its place, as he may consider appropriate'.

Persons aggrieved by the decision of the Secretary of State may apply to the High Court for an order suspending the operation of or quashing the decision.

These principles and rules are complex: how have the courts interpreted them and have their interpretations helped or hindered the valuers in arriving at 'the only question at stake . . . what should be the amount of compensation payable'?[50]

Jelson Ltd v. *MHLG* [1969] 3 All E.R. 147

LORD DENNING MR: Leicester is expanding. It has reached Blaby in the outskirts. Before the war there was a proposal that there should be a ring road round Leicester. In 1951 the county development plan showed a proposed ring road and showed the land on either side of the proposed ring road as being allocated primarily for residential purposes. In 1954 the applicants George Wimpey & Co. Ltd bought a good deal of the land there, which included part of the site of the proposed ring road. A family called Jelson owned much of the land, which also included part of the proposed ring road. In 1954 Jelsons themselves became a limited company, Jelson Ltd, soon afterwards Wimpeys and Jelsons ('the applicants') applied for planning permission for residential development of the land they owned. They were granted permission to build housing estates on the land allocated for residential purposes; but they were refused permission to develop the site of the proposed ring road. In pursuance of that permission, both applicants built great housing estates adjoining the proposed ring road. There remained a long narrow strip of land, about 146 feet wide, awaiting the proposed ring road.

But in 1962 the proposal for the ring road was abandoned. The reason was because a big motorway, the M1, was built in the neighbourhood. In consequence, there was no need for the ring road. Thereupon both applicants applied for permission to develop the site of the proposed ring road for residential purposes. It was a long narrow strip, of which the applicants Wimpeys had some 2½ acres and the applicants Jelsons 5½ acres. On 31st December 1964 the Minister refused both of them permission to develop this long narrow strip. . . . Seeing the strip thus rendered sterile, both applicants sought to compel the local authority to buy the land. They served a notice under s. 129 of the Town and Country Planning Act 1962, requiring, the respondents, the Blaby Rural District Council to purchase the strip on the ground that permission had been refused and that the land had become incapable of reasonable beneficial use in its existing state. There was an inquiry by an Inspector who recommended that the purchase notice should be confirmed. On 28th September 1965 the Minister accepted the inspector's recommendation. . . . The effect of that decision is prescribed by s. 133 (1) of the Act. Its effect was that on 29th September 1965, the respondent council was deemed to have served notice to treat in respect of this strip of land so as to acquire it compulsorily.

The question now is; what compensation is to be paid for the deemed compulsory acquisition? For this purpose we have to turn to the Land Compensation Act 1961. We then find that the amount of compensation depends on whether (if there had been no deemed compulsory acquisition) both applicants might reasonably have expected to get permission to build residential houses on this strip. If they might reasonably have expected permission for residential development, the local authority should issue to them a valuable certificate within s. 17 (4) (*a*) of the Act of 1961 on which they would get large compensation. But, if they could not reasonably have expected permission for residential development, the local authority would only issue to them a nil certificate within s. 17 (4) (*b*) of the Act of 1961, on which they would get little compensation. . . .

Both applicants applied for a valuable certificate. The respondent council refused and issued a nil certificate. Both applicants appealed to the Minister under s. 18. On 23rd June 1967 the Minister confirmed the nil certificate. His letter of decision stated:

The Minister agrees that it is a fair assumption that had it not been for the Outer Ring Road proposal the land in question would have been included as part of the housing estates which flank it. However, in view of its shape and the disposition of adjoining houses, the Minister is satisfied that planning permission could not reasonably have been expected to be granted for residential development of the land, if it had not been acquired by an authority possessing compulsory purchase power. . . . The Minister having considered all forms of development for which permission might reasonably have been granted has decided to issue a 'nil' certificate. . . .

After the discussion we have had, I think the decision depends on this one short point under s. 17 (4); what is the date at which it must be decided whether planning permission 'might reasonably have been expected to be granted'. The Minister says it must be decided as at the date of the deemed notice to treat, that is, on 29th September 1965. At that date there was this long narrow strip of land bordered by great housing estates on either side. At that date planning permission would not be granted for any beneficial purpose. So there should be a nil certificate. But both applicants say that that is not that date at all. They say that the date should be some time in the distant past before there was any proposal for a ring road. At that time they might reasonably have expected planning permission to be granted, not only for the housing estates, but also for this long narrow strip for residential development.

Whichever date is taken, there are anomalies. . . . I will . . . come straight to s. 17 (4). It provides:

Where an application is made to the local planning authority for a certificate under this section in respect of an interest in land, the local planning authority shall . . . issue to the applicant a certificate stating either of the following to be the opinion of the local planning authority regarding the planning permission that might have been expected to be granted in respect of the land in question, if it were not *proposed* to be acquired by any authority possessing compulsory purchase powers, that is to say – (*a*) that planning permission for development of one or more classes specified in the certificate (whether specified in the application or not) might reasonably have been expected to be granted; or (*b*) that planning permission could not reasonably have been expected to be granted for any development other than the development (if any) which is proposed to be carried out by the authority by whom the interest is *proposed* to be acquired.

The crucial word in that subsection is the word 'proposed', which is defined in s. 22 (2):

For the purposes of sections seventeen and eighteen of this Act, an interest in land shall be taken to be an interest *proposed* to be acquired by an authority possessing compulsory purchase powers in the following (but no other) circumstances, that is to say – (*a*) [(put shortly) where there is an *actual* notice to treat; (*b*) (put shortly) where there is a *deemed* notice to treat; (*c*) (put shortly) where there is an offer to negotiate to purchase.]

That definition shows that the word 'proposed' refers to the proposal contained in an actual or deemed notice to treat or in an offer to purchase. that gives a good clue to the *date* of the proposal. It is the date of the actual or deemed notice to treat or of the offer to purchase, as the case may be.

In the light of that definition, s. 17 (4) means that the planning authority must form an opinion as to what planning permission might reasonably have been expected to be granted at the date of the *actual* notice to treat, or the *deemed* notice to treat, or the *offer* to purchase, as the case may be. In the present case, therefore, which is a case of a *deemed* notice to treat, s. 17 (4) must be read: 'that might have been expected to be granted [at the date of the service of the deemed notice to treat] in respect of the land in question, if it were not proposed [at that date] to be acquired'. The planning authority must form an opinion as to what planning permission might reasonably be expected at that date, namely, 29th September 1965. It must look at the position as at that date and see, in the circumstances then existing, whether planning permission might reasonably be expected to be granted.

Looking at this long narrow strip as at 29th September 1965 I think that the Minister was entitled to find that planning permission could not reasonably be expected for residential development. There was no profitable development open to it. He was, therefore, right to issue a nil certificate. And the judge was right to affirm his decision. . . .

Appeal dismissed.

What are or might be the anomalies to which Lord Denning refers.

Margate Corporation v. *Devotwill Investments* [1970] 3 All E.R. 864

LORD MORRIS OF BORTH-Y-GEST: My Lords, on 2nd September 1965 the respondents, as owners of a piece of land in Birchington in the borough of Margate, applied to the appellants (as the local planning authority) for outline planning permission to develop the land for residential use. The land has an area of approximately 1·35 acres; in part it fronts on to a road called Canterbury Road and in part it extends to the rear of numbers 245 to 249 Canterbury Road. The land has no buildings on it. It formed part of an area allocated for residential use in the Thanet town map which was part of the current development plan for the county of Kent and which was approved by the Minister of Housing and Local Government in 1958. On 1st October 1965 the appellants refused permission. The refusal was stated to be on the ground that part of the land would be required for road improvement works to Canterbury Road (designed to by-pass Birchington Square) and that residential development of the land would be premature until it was possible 'to finalise details of the improvement scheme'. No such road improvement works to Canterbury Road were shown on the development plan. . . . On 26th November 1965 the respondents served . . . [a purchase] notice. On 24th February 1966 the appellants served a notice (see s. 130 (1)) stating that they were agreeable to purchase the land and stating that the district valuer had been asked to negotiate the terms of the acquisition. The result of this was (see s. 130 (2) of the Town and Country Planning Act 1962) that the appellants were deemed to be authorised to acquire the respondents' interest compulsorily (in accordance with the provisions of Part V of the Act) and to have served a notice to treat in respect thereof on the date of service of their notice. The respondents became entitled to receive compensation on the basis that there was compulsory acquisition of their land. The amount of the compensation was for the Lands Tribunal to determine. . . . in accordance with the provisions of the Land Compensation Act 1961. . . . It is common ground that certain assumptions which are set out in s. 16 are applicable in this case. By s. 16 it is provided as follows:

(2) If the relevant land or any part thereof (not being land subject to comprehensive development) consists or forms part of an area shown in the current development plan as an area allocated primarily for a use specified in the plan in relation to that area, it shall be assumed that planning permission would be granted, in respect of the relevant land or that part thereof, as the case may be, for any development which – (a) is development for the purposes of that use of the relevant land or that part thereof, and (b) is development for which planning permission might reasonably have been expected to be granted in respect of the relevant land or that part thereof, as the case may be. . . .

(6) Where in accordance with any of the preceding subsections it is to be assumed that planning permission would be granted as therein mentioned – (a) the assumption shall be that planning permission would be so granted subject to such conditions (if any) as, in the circumstances mentioned in the subsection in question, might reasonably be expected to be imposed by the authority granting the permission, and (b) if, in accordance with any map or statement comprised in the current development plan, it is indicated that any such planning permission would be granted only at a future time, then (without prejudice to the preceding paragraph) the assumption shall be that the planning

permission in question would be granted at the time when, in accordance with the indications in the plan, that permission might reasonably be expected to be granted.

(7) Any reference in this section to development for which planning permission might reasonably have been expected to be granted is a reference to development for which planning permission might reasonably have been expected to be granted if no part of the relevant land were proposed to be acquired by any authority possessing compulsory purchase powers. . . .

. . . The Lands Tribunal had to proceed on the footing that the respondents' land had been available for residential use. Beyond this they had to assume (by reason of what was shown on the current development plan) that planning permission would have been granted for development for residential use. They had to decide what planning permission for such development might reasonably have been expected to be granted. In assuming that planning permission for residential use would have been granted they had to assume that such permission might have been granted subject to conditions and, if that were so, that the conditions would have been such as it might reasonably have been expected would have been imposed.

The task of the Lands Tribunal was therefore to give consideration to all the relevant facts and circumstances concerning the locality and on the footing that the respondents' land would have been available for and would have been the subject of planning permission for residential use (and would not be taken for a by-pass) to decide what planning permission (and subject to what, if any, conditions) the respondents might reasonably have expected to receive. Having reached decision on that matter the task of the Lands Tribunal was to assess the fair and reasonable compensation that the respondents should receive for the compulsory acquisition of their land endowed with such planning permission. . . .

The decisions to be made by the Lands Tribunal were decisions in the field of fact. Some of the witnesses appear to have felt that they were asked to apply their minds to situations having an unreality only to be expected in fairyland. I do not think that their approach should have been so hesitant. Their evidence had to be directed to the realities of the conditions that existed and to the actual facts of the period so that the Lands Tribunal should be assisted to reach decision on the basis of the assumptions that had to be made. Even if the appellants had concluded that the problem of road congestion was to be solved by their projected by-pass they were not precluded from expressing an informed view on the question whether if that by-pass could not be constructed there were or were not any other ways of dealing with the problem of road congestion and if so what they were.

The question that arises is whether the decision of the Lands Tribunal was erroneous in point of law. It would be so if based and founded on an erroneous legal proposition. The actual decision was that: '. . . at the date of the deemed notice to treat planning permission might reasonably have been expected for immediate development of the whole of the subject land.' But it is essential to see what were the steps which led to this decision or the propositions on which it was founded.

In the decision of the Lands Tribunal reference was made to a dictum of Lord Asquith of Bishopstone in *East End Dwellings Co Ltd* v. *Finsbury Borough Council*[51]. In the course of his speech in that case Lord Asquith made the general observation: 'If one is bidden to treat an imaginary state of affairs as real, one must surely, unless prohibited from doing so, also imagine as real the consequences and incidents which, if the putative state of affairs had in fact existed, must inevitably have flowed from or accompanied it.'

My Lords, even apart from the respect which knowledge of the authorship of the words would command I cannot imagine that anyone would question their soundness. After a quotation of the words the decision of the Lands Tribunal contained the following passage:

> Lord Asquith was there dealing with quite different legislation, but the dictum I have quoted seems to me to be apposite in the present case. I am bidden to assume that the subject land is not proposed to be acquired by an authority having compulsory powers. The inevitable corollaries of this seem to me to be as follows: 1. There can be no by-pass on the subject land; 2. There can therefore be no by-pass on the line at present proposed; 3. But since there is urgent need to take the traffic out of Birchington Square, it must be assumed that a by-pass is proposed on some other line; 4. This other line can only be a line which leaves the subject land inside the by-passed area, for I am satisfied that the position of the subject land in relation to Birchington Square and existing development south of the square makes any other conclusion impossible. . . .

My Lords, in my view these passages reveal an error of approach. An assumption had to be made that the respondents' land was not going to be acquired so that a by-pass should there be constructed – but it was in no way an inevitable corollary that there would be a by-pass on some other line and in some different position. If there was not to be a by-pass on the respondants' land it by no means followed that there would inevitably be a by-pass somewhere else. There might be or there might not be. It might have been possible to have another route for a by-pass; it might have been quite impossible. It would be a question depending on topographical and various and many other factors whether there could be a by-pass somewhere else. It would be for consideration whether any alternative by-pass was or was not possible or probable and further whether its construction was or was not likely. These matters could not rest on any assumptions but rather on an examination of all the evidence. Nor could the enquiry (as to what planning permission might reasonably have been expected) depend only on the view taken as to one or other or some only of the relevant factors. Although I consider that it was erroneous to assume positively that a by-pass on an alternative site would have been constructed I think that it would be wrong to proceed on the basis that if the appellants were denied the opportunity of dealing with their road problem in the way that they had planned and thought best they would abandon all hope of solving their problem and give it no further consideration. I cannot accept the submission that as a matter of law the Lands Tribunal had to proceed on the basis that any relief of traffic congestion in Canterbury Road in the foreseeable future was to be ruled out. It would, however, be very relevant to enquire whether the initiation and carrying out of any alternative plan would or would not have been likely.

The requirement that the possibility of a by-pass on the site of the respondents' land was to be eliminated had the consequence that the enquiry had to be on the basis that one expected way of dealing with road congestion problems must be ruled out. There would have to be new examination of the problem. Were there then some other ways? If so what were they – and how effective would they be? Would it have been practicable to effect some road-widening? Could some traffic regulatory adjustments have been made? Within what period of time might some improvement of road conditions have been made? Even if the problem of relieving traffic congestion proved to be baffling – what planning permission for house building might reasonably have been expected? Was there a housing shortage which presented an urgent and serious problem? If the need for homes was pressing, might permission for house building on the basis desired by the respondents have been given even at the cost of adding or adding temporarily to traffic congestion and traffic hazards? How considerable would the added traffic volume be? Was it reasonably to have been expected (on the basis that the respondents' land was not to be taken for a by-pass) that the Minister would have granted unqualified permission for the development as planned and at the time as planned by the respondents or was it reasonably to have been expected that there would be some, and if so what, different permission for development – the difference being in relation to the location of the houses and the time of their erection? All the many relevant facts and circumstances would have to be considered before answer could be given. The amount of compensation to be awarded would depend on the value of the permission that might reasonably have been expected.

The matter must in my view be remitted to the Lands Tribunal for new consideration on the lines that I have indicated. It will still be open to the respondents to contend that in the light of all the actual facts of the situation (but on the basis that there was to be no by-pass on the line as projected by the appellants) it was reasonably to be expected that planning permission to build houses in accordance with their plan would have been forthcoming. It will still be open to the appellants to contend that no planning permission to do more than was covered by their suggestions would reasonably have been expected or would have been forthcoming.[52]

Appeal allowed.

Davies, op. cit., p. 141, comments on this decision as follows:

LORD MORRIS remitted the case to the Lands Tribunal 'for new consideration of the lines that I have indicated'. These lines were set out in some detail. But it is submitted that, lacking statutory authority, they could only be suggestions. Any choice of them, or others, by the Tribunal would have to be made on the basis of reasonable expert valuation opinion; and although factual evidence would have to be considered, a great many assumptions would have to be made as well – especially as the basic exercise must, by virtue of section 16, be a notional one. In addition, the matters suggested by LORD MORRIS involve complex and extensive planning questions, such as it might well be necessary to consider before reaching a planning decision on an actual project of development, but hardly before reaching a notional one for the purposes of assessing compensation. 'Were there some other ways (of dealing with traffic congestion)? . . . Was there a housing shortage which presented an urgent and serious problem? . . . All the many relevant facts and circumstances would have to be considered before answer could be given.' The conclusion cannot be escaped that LORD MORRIS has in effect given the Lands Tribunal the task of making a great many more extra-statutory valuation assumptions than before.[53]

Assume the Lands Tribunal attempted to reconsider the case along the lines suggested by Lord Morris. What decision would it have reached and why?

Myers v. *Milton Keynes Development Corporation*
[1974] 2 All E.R. 1096

LORD DENNING MR: . . . In April 1966 the Minister was satisfied that it was expedient in the national interest that the area [north of Bletchley] should be developed as a new town. He made an order designating it as the site of a new town under the New Towns Act 1965. Under it a development corporation was established with powers to acquire land compulsorily. It was called the Milton Keynes Development Corporation. The designated area covered 22,000 acres. It included the towns of Bletchley, Wolverton and Stony Stratford. Also many villages. In particular it included the whole of the Walton Manor estate owned by Mr Myers.

On 17th March 1970 the development corporation published a master plan which contained its proposals for the development of the area. It included the compulsory acquisition of the Walton Manor estate. On the next day, 18th March 1970, the corporation gave a notice to treat to Mr Myers for the purchase of the estate; or rather, by agreement, a notice to treat was deemed to be served on that day. On the same day, 18th March 1970, vacant possession was given. The value is to be assessed as at that date: see *Birmingham City Corpn* v. *West Midland Baptist (Trust) Association (Inc)*.

In assessing the value, it is important to consider what would have happened if there had been *no scheme*, but instead the area had been allowed to develop without it. This was a matter of controversy. But it would seem likely that Bletchley would have developed as the major town in the area, and that the surrounding villages would have developed into modest satellite towns around Bletchley. But that there would be stretches of open countryside in between. The Walton Manor estate would have been fortunately placed. It would have been in an open stretch of land between the two villages of Wavendon and Simpson. 'The foregone outcome', said the Lands Tribunal, 'would have been to remain as it is, as open country-side'.

In contrast, however, we must see what had really happened by 18th March 1970. The new corporation had already done, or allowed to be done, considerable development in Bletchley itself. But nothing much in the neighbourhood of Walton. It had, however, prepared the master plan which it showed on two maps. One map showed 'The First Ten Years plan'. This showed that during the first ten years the development corporation proposed to develop a strip about eight miles long and two miles wide from Bletchley northwards; but to leave the whole of the Walton Manor estate untouched. The estate was situate next to the Open University, and it was proposed to be kept as open countryside for ten years. The other map showed 'The Strategic Plan'. This showed the final development, when completed, more than ten years hence, of the whole of the 22,000 acres of the new town. In this map it was proposed that the Walton Manor estate would become a residential area between the Open University and the further education colleges.

Those maps, of course, showed only the proposals at 18th March 1970. . . .

Such being the facts, the question for the Lands Tribunal was: what was the compensation payable by the Milton Keynes Development Corporation for the Walton Manor estate? . . .

[His Lordship then discussed the genesis of the Land Compensation Act 1961 and in particular sections 14–16. He then continued:] . . . the Walton Manor estate did not have any actual permission. It was not in a zone that was *allocated* for residential use in any development plan. So it did not come within s. 16 (2). It was in an area where nothing was zoned or allocated: but where *proposals* had been made by the acquiring authority. These proposals had been made by the development corporation under s. 6 of the New Towns Act 1965, and approved by the Minister. So far as Walton Manor estate is concerned, the proposals were not for immediate development, but for it to be a residential area after ten years.

That is the setting in which we have to interpret s. 15 (1) of the Land Compensation Act 1961, which says:

> In a case where – (*a*) the relevant interest is to be acquired for purposes which involve the carrying out of proposals of the acquiring authority for development of the relevant land or part thereof, and (*b*) on the date of service of the notice to treat there is not in force planning permission for that development, it shall be assumed that planning permission would be granted, in respect of the relevant land or that part thereof, as the case may be, such as would permit development thereof in accordance with the proposals of the acquiring authority.

That section gives rise to these questions. *First*: what is to be assumed about the *rest* of the designated area of the new town of Milton Keynes? One thing is quite clear. You are not to assume that it would have been developed in the way it had *already* been developed by the development corporation, or that there was the prospect of it being developed in the *future* in the way proposed by the development corporation. You are only to assume such development as would have been likely to take place if the development corporation had *never* come into being: see s. 6 (1) of the 1961 Act and Sch 1, Part I, Case 3. *Second*: what is to be assumed about the Walton Manor estate itself? Here again one thing is clear. You are not to assume that it would have been developed in accordance with the proposals of the development corporation. You are to disregard any increase by reason of the estate itself being developed in accordance with their proposals: see *Viscount Camrose* v. *Basingstoke Corpn*[54]. But you are to assume that after ten years planning permission would be available for development as a residential area.

It comes to this: in valuing the estate, you are to disregard the effect of the scheme. But you are to assume the availability of planning permission. This is best explained by taking an imaginary instance. A scheme is proposed for building a motorway across Dartmoor with a service station every five miles. Suppose that land is taken on which a service station is to be built as soon as possible. In assessing compensation, you are to disregard any increase due to the proposed motorway, or service stations. But, if the landowner had already been granted *actual* permission for that piece of land for commercial purposes (e.g. as a cafe), you are to have regard to it: see s. 14 (2). Even if he had no such permission already, you are to assume that he would have been granted planning permission for a service station: see s. 15 (1). And you are to value that land with that permission in the setting in which it would have been if there had been no scheme. If it would have been a good site for a service station, there would be a great increase in value. If it would have been in an inaccessible spot on the wild moor, there would be little, if any, increase in value, because there would be no demand for it. A further complication arises when the proposals are not to be put into effect for ten years. Planning permissions are not in practice granted so far ahead. They are only granted for immediate development. In the illustration you are, therefore, to assume that, after ten years, planning permission would be granted for development of a service station – in a setting where there had been no scheme.

4 *Application in this case*

It is apparent, therefore, that the valuation has to be done in an imaginary state of affairs in which there is no scheme. The valuer must cast aside his knowledge of what has in fact happened in the past eight years due to the scheme. He must ignore the developments which will in all probability take place in the future ten years owing to the scheme. Instead, he must let his imagination take flight to the clouds. He must conjure up a land of make-believe, where there has not been, nor will be, a brave new town, but where there is to be supposed the old order of things continuing – a county planning authority which will grant planning permission of various kinds at such times and in such parcels as it thinks best, but with an assurance that in March 1980 planning permission would be available for the residential development of the Walton Manor estate.

In this imaginary state of affairs, the valuer has then to ask himself: what is the appropriate way of valuing the land with this assumed planning permission? He would do well, we think, to follow the course set by Mr Hobbs, that most experienced member of the Lands Tribunal, in *Viscount Camrose* v. *Basingstoke Corpn*. If the land, apart from the scheme, would be virtually certain to be developed in a reasonable time, then it would be appropriate to take the present value of the land with planning permission now, but then make a deduction for the period during which the development would be deferred and also for the risk that it might not take place. That is the method Mr Hobbs adopted for the 150 acres. But, if the land, apart from the scheme, was unlikely to be developed for a long time (indeed so far ahead that it would not be realistic to use a method of deferring a present value), then it would be appropriate to value it at a 'hope' value. That is the value which it has for its existing use as agricultural land, but with an addition on account of the 'hope' that it would at some time in the foreseeable future be profitable to develop it – in accordance with the assumed planning permission. That is the method Mr Hobbs adopted for the 233 acres. Perhaps we may quote what was said there:

> Even though the 233 acres are assumed to have planning permission, it does not follow that there would be a demand for it. It is not planning permission by itself which increases value. It is planning permission coupled with demand. The tribunal thought that the demand for these 233 acres was so far distant as to warrant only a 'hope' of development, and valued them accordingly. I see nothing wrong with this method of calculation.

But these are valuation questions, not questions of law. Different valuers may take different views about the best method of valuing the land in the hypothetical circumstances which have to be imagined. In the event of any divergence of views of valuers called to give expert evidence, the tribunal must decide whose evidence it prefers and determine the value as a question of fact.

In the present case the question of fact to be answered can, we think, be best formulated in this way: on 18th March 1970 what price would a willing seller be prepared to accept, and a willing purchaser to pay, for the Walton Manor estate, if there had been no proposal for a new town at Milton Keynes; and if the prospects of development on and in the neighbourhood of the Walton Manor estate had then been such as they would have been if there had been no proposals for a new town; but with this one additional circumstance, that the purchaser had an assurance that in March 1980 or thereafter, if he applied for planning permission to develop the Walton Manor estate or any part of it for residential purposes – in a manner not inconsistent with the development corporation's proposals – he would be granted it.

In the circumstances, we think that the case must go back to the Lands Tribunal for reconsideration in the light of the law as we have tried to expound it. It will be for the member of the Lands Tribunal to decide whether he wants further evidence or argument. . . .[55]

(d) Depreciation and injurious affection[56]

Development and Compensation: Putting People First
Cmnd. 5124

Most development, whether public or private, affects other property in its vicinity, sometimes beneficially and sometimes adversely. This is one of the normal hazards of property ownership. Where the development and its use cause a nuisance the remedy generally open to those affected is an action at common law. But substantial injurious affection can be caused by the use of public developments where the landowner has no redress because the use is immune from such action. This is particularly true when the use is for a road or an aerodrome. . . .

The importance of this passage is two-fold: first, it highlights the close connection between the action for nuisance and the claim for injurious affection; second, it heralded the introduction into the law of a new head of claim for injurious affection, a head which in effect overrules the case of *Hammersmith and City Railway Co. v. Brand.*[57] In that case, premises were depreciated in value because of vibrations caused by trains using a newly constructed railway nearby. A claim in nuisance was rejected by the House of Lords on the ground that statutory authorisation to carry out a particular purpose implicitly carried with it statutory authorisation to commit a nuisance if that was the unavoidable consequence of carrying out the particular purpose. From then on, while the courts developed certain claims for injurious affection out of the provisions of the Lands Clauses Consolidation Act 1845, that arising out of use of the land once the public works were constructed was barred. The claims under the Land Clauses Consolidation Act, and its successor, the Compulsory Purchase Act 1965, will be dealt with before those created by the Land Compensation Act 1973.

'Injurious affection . . . is depreciation of land caused by what happens on the other hand.'[58] There are two heads of claim under the Compulsory Purchase Act 1965.

(i) *Depreciation resulting from taking the claimant's land*

Compulsory Purchase Act 1965, s. 7

In assessing the compensation to be paid by the acquiring authority under this Act regard shall be had not only to the value of the land to be purchased by the acquiring authority, but also to the damage, if any, to be sustained by the owner of the land by reason of the severing of the land purchased from the other land of the owner, or otherwise injuriously affecting that other land by the exercise of the powers conferred by this or the special Act.

Lawrence and Moore, *Compulsory Purchase and Compensation*, 5th ed., p. 144

To establish the right to compensation it must be shown that the land affected, was, at the time of acquisition, held with the land taken. This does not necessarily mean that it was immediately contiguous to such land, or held under the same title or for the same estate – although this will usually be the case.

In *Cowper Essex* v. *Acton Local Board*,[59] the claimant's land – a building estate – was compulsorily purchased for a sewage farm. He claimed compensation both for the land taken and for land separated from the land taken by a railway on which he would have built houses before the local board's project made it less desirable to do so. The House of Lords allowed the claim, Lord Watson saying:

Where several pieces of land owned by the same person are, though not adjoining, so near together and so situated that the possession and control of each gives an enhanced value to all of them, they are lands held together within the meaning of the Act, so that if one piece is compulsorily taken and converted to uses which depreciate the value of the rest, the owner has a right to compensation for the depreciation.

The nature of the injurious affection for which owners may claim is illustrated by the old case of *Duke of Buccleuch* v. *Metropolitan Board of Works* (1872) L.R. 5 H.L. 518.

LORD CHELMSFORD: The Duke of Buccleuch is tenant to the Crown of Montagu House in Whitehall Place. . . .

Montagu House and premises were bounded on the river side by a wall, along the whole length of which, at high water, the river flowed. There was a gate in this wall, usually kept locked, which led from some stairs in the garden of the house to a causeway or pier which ran out into the river to low water-mark. The causeway had been used for more than forty years for landing coals from barges, and for bringing vegetables, &., for the use of the tenants of Montague House, who always repaired the causeway at their own expense when it needed repair.

By the Thames Embankment Act, 25 & 26 Vict. c. 93, the Metropolitan Board of Works was authorized to construct an embankment on the north side of the Thames from Westminster Bridge to Blackfriars Bridge. In the course of performing the necessary works it became necessary to remove the causeway and the landing-place connected therewith, and also entirely to shut off Montagu House and premises from direct access to the river. In the place where the water had previously flowed a solid embankment was made, which has since become a public high-way.

The Plaintiff gave the Defendants notice that he claimed compensation as well for the entering upon and taking by them of the causeway, pier, or jetty, as for the removal and obstruction of the use and enjoyment of the landing-place, and for all other damage sustained or to be sustained by him by such injurious affecting of his said messuage or dwelling-house, and other lands, premises, and hereditaments. . . .

Arbitrators were named by the respective parties, who nominated Mr Charles Pollock, Queen's Counsel, as umpire. Mr Pollock, having taken upon himself the reference, ultimately made an award in the following terms: – 'I award, order, and determine that there is due from the said Metropolitan Board of Works to the said Duke of Buccleuch and Queens-berry the sum of £8325 as and for compensation for the interest of the said Duke of Buccleuch and Queensberry in the said causeway, pier, and jetty; and for the shutting up of the said landing-place, and for the damage by the depreciation of the said mansion-house, lands, tenements, and heredita-ments, by the otherwise injuriously affecting the same by the execution by the said Board of their said works, and by the exercise of the powers of the said Act.' . . .

I now proceed to consider whether the umpire has included in his award any head of damage not properly the subject of compensation.

It appears to me that the notice of claim is rather imperfectly framed, as it does not point distinctly to the injury to Montagu House arising from the construction and use of the embankment. It requires the Metropolitan Board of Works to pay the Duke of Buccleuch compensation, as well for the entering upon and taking of the causeway, pier, or jetty, as for the removal and obstruction of the use and enjoyment of the said landing-place, and for all other damage sustained and to be sustained by him by *such* injurious affecting of his said messuage and dwelling-house, the word 'such' referring to the taking of the causeway and removing of the landing-place. However, it has never been questioned that the umpire had authority to take into his consideration the injury to Montagu House arising from the construction and use of the embankment. There can be no doubt, and none has been entertained, that the Plaintiff is entitled to compensation in respect of the taking away the causeway and landing-place, and the injury arising to his house and premises by depriving him of access to the river. The only question upon which there has been a difference of opinion among the Judges is, whether the umpire was authorized to give compensation in respect of the depreciation of Montagu House by the conversion of the land between it and the river into a high-way, and the consequent public use of it. This question partly depends upon the 63rd section of the *Lands Clauses Consolidation Act*, 1845, which is incorporated with the *Thames Embankment Act*. . . .

The Plaintiff was the owner of lands within the meaning of this clause in respect of the causeway which was taken away from him. . . . the 27th section of the [*Thames Embankment Act*,] contemplates two descriptions of damage likely to be sustained by the owners of lands on the bank and river frontage of the Thames – one by loss of the river frontage; the other in any other manner, by reason of the embankment or other the exercise of any of the powers of the Act.

It seems to me to be quite clear that the umpire was entitled to consider not only the damage which the Plaintiff sustained by being deprived of the causeway, but also whether he was entitled to compensation in respect of damage otherwise sustained by reason of the embankment. Now, if he was of opinion that Montagu House was depreciated in value as a residence by reason of the proximity of the embankment, and of all the consequences of its use as a public highway, he was bound to give the Plaintiff some compensation, and the amount proper to be awarded was entirely for him to determine.

It can hardly be doubted that in addition to the damage sustained by the loss of the river frontage the house must have been 'injuriously affected' – i.e., depreciated in value – by the interposition between it and the river of an embankment to be used as a public highway; and this seems to bring the right to compensation within the very words of the 27th section of the special Act, because it is a damage otherwise than by loss of the river frontage by reason of the embankment or roadway.

The only question then arises upon the award itself – whether the umpire had any power to give compensation for the damage by the depreciation of the mansion-house, lands, tenements, and hereditaments, by the otherwise injuriously affecting the same by the execution by the Defendants of the said works and by the exercise of the powers of the Act. Now, he was authorized, both by the special Act and by the *Lands Clauses Act*, to give compensation if the premises were injuriously affected – a fact which it was the duty of the umpire to ascertain and determine.

He had determined it, and awarded compensation in respect of the damage thereby sustained by the Plaintiff; and I see nothing in the case to impeach the correctness of his award.

Appeal allowed.

Davies comments on this case as follows (at p. 152):

Although injurious affection greatly resembles private nuisance, it should be noted from this case that it extends to loss of privacy, which is not a matter for which damages may be awarded in tort. This in turn points to the fact that the governing consideration here is not an identification with the law of tort, but the making up in full of the claimant's loss in land value. It is fundamentally a valuation approach, not a legal approach. This kind of injurious affection is, so to speak, 'tort plus'.

Do you agree? If a private non-statutory body built and used a road adjacent to the Duke's land and created the same dust and noise, would he have a claim in nuisance against the body and would it affect either his chances of success or his remedy that he could not claim specifically for loss of privacy? *See Halsey* v. *Esso Petroleum*[60] at pp. 53–61.

(ii) *Depreciation not resulting from taking the claimant's land*

Compulsory Purchase Act 1965, s. 10

(1) If any person claims compensation in respect of any land, or any interest in land, which has been taken for or injuriously affected by the execution of the works, and for which the acquiring authority have not made satisfaction under the provisions of this Act or of the special Act, any dispute arising in relation to the compensation shall be referred to and determined by the Lands Tribunal.

(2) This section shall be constructed as affording in all cases a right to compensation for injurious affection to land which is the same as the right which section sixty-eight of the Lands Clauses Consolidation Act 1845 has been construed as affording in cases where the amount claimed exceeds fifty pounds.

The limits of this provision were fixed by another old case arising out of the construction of the Victoria Embankment in London, *Metropolitan Board of Works* v. *McCarthy*,[61] which decided that

Where by the construction of the works there is a physical interference with any right, public or private, which owners or occupiers of property are by law entitled to make use of in connection with such property, and which gives an additional market value to such property, apart from the uses to which any particular occupier or owner might put it, there is a title to compensation if, by reason of such interference, the property, as a property, is lessened in value.[62]

A modern discussion of the limits of this principle is contained in the following case.

Argyle Motors v. *Birkenhead Corporation*
[1974] 1 All E.R. 201

LORD WILBERFORCE: My Lords, this appeal arises out of some extensive works of reconstruction to the approaches to the Mersey Tunnel. They were carried out by the corporation of Birkenhead under statutory powers conferred by the Birkenhead Corporation (Mersey Tunnel Approaches) Act 1965 ('the local Act'). The appellants, dealers in motor cars, are lessees from year to year of premises abutting on Conway Street, which was one of the streets to be reconstructed. As a result of the works, access to their premises from Conway Street was interfered with, first temporarily while the work was being executed and, secondly, permanently, through the new Conway Street being so constructed that direct access from it to their premises is no longer possible. Under each head they claim to have suffered loss of business and consequently loss of profit. The proceedings were started by the appellants by action in the Chancery Division claiming declarations that they were entitled to compensation for these losses, and on 30th July 1971, certain preliminary issues were ordered to be tried before the trial. These were whether, on the basis of specified paragraphs in their statement of claim, i.e. assuming the facts were pleaded to be established, the appellants were entitled to compensation in respect of loss of profits arising from (a) the temporary obstruction (b) the permanent obstruction of access. Both questions have been answered in the negative by Foster J at first instance and by the Court of Appeal, though on slightly differing bases.

The answers to these questions are stated to depend on the construction of the local Act, together with certain well-known sections of the Lands Clauses Consolidation Act 1845 which it incorporates, a process which, in this case, cannot be carried out with any judicial satisfaction. The relevant section of the 1845 Act (s. 68) has, over 100 years, received through a number of decisions, some in this House, and by no means easy to reconcile, an interpretation which fixes on it a meaning having little perceptible relation to the words used. This represents a century of judicial effort to keep the primitive wording – which itself has an earlier history, in some sort of accord with the realities of the industrial age. The local Act, as is common with land acquisition and works legislation, contains a farrago of sections, loosely pinned together from various precedents, which have neither internal clarity nor mutual consistency.

I start with the fact that, by s. 4 of the local Act, the 1845 Act is incorporated. The value of this provision is reduced by the words 'so far as . . . not inconsistent with the provisions of this Act' but there is at least a starting point. There is no doubt that this section introduces s. 68 of the 1845 Act.

It is not disputed that, in spite of its apparent form, this subsection is, by the force of judicial interpretation, a compensation section and not merely procedural, i.e. it authorises the payment of compensation 'in respect of any lands, or of any interest therein which shall have been . . . injuriously affected by the execution of the works'. Its incorporation into the local Act, which contains a works part (Part III), must provide a strong indication that injurious affection by the authorised works is to be compensated under this provision.

The next point, which may be vital to this appeal, is that by a series of judicial observations of high authority it is well established that the only compensation which can be obtained under this section is 'in respect of lands', i.e. in respect of some loss of value of land, or (what is a branch under this same heading) in respect of some damage to lands and that compensation cannot be obtained for any loss which is personal to the owner, or which is related to some particular user of the land. The first clear statement to this effect was made by LORD CRANWORTH in *Ricket* v. *Directors, etc, of Metropolitan Railway Co*[63]. In *Metropolitan Board of Works* v. *McCarthy*, LORD CHELMSFORD, in effect, adopted LORD CRANWORTH'S proposition.

In the third case in this House, *Caledonian Railway Co* v. *Walker's Trustees*[64], a case on the similar Scottish Act, the rule was again stated, in firm language by LORD SELBORNE LC and by LORD BLACKBURN.

My Lords, it is fair comment that *Ricket's* case was really decided on remoteness, and that in the two other cases it does not appear that a claim for loss of profits was actually in issue. But the pronouncements by the eminent members of this House are in such explicit terms that only a clear conviction of their error or, possibly, the most powerful considerations of policy would need to be present before so strong a current of authority could be turned back. As a matter of language, though language is an uncertain guide in this statute, it must be said that the words I have quoted 'in respect of any lands . . .' support the exclusion of claims for personal loss. And, though it might be said that a generous policy of compensation would favour compensation for losses caused to individuals through works of social benefit, a policy to this effect, however just it might appear in a particular case, involves too great a shift in financial burden, and too many adjustments or qualifications (if it were to be workable) to be suitable for introduction by judicial decision.

I must, therefore, agree with both courts below, that if the right to compensation in the present case depends on s. 68, the appellants cannot succeed in obtaining compensation for business losses as such. I make it clear, as did the Court of Appeal, that if they can prove that a loss of profitability affects the value of their interest in the land, they can recover compensation for this loss of value.[65] . . .

Appeal dismissed.

A formal justification for the exclusion of compensation for loss of profit is that injurious affection deals with depreciation in the value of land and not with what goes on on the land. Is there any other justification? Is it sufficient to provide that trade loss may be compensated for by disturbance payments, which are payable only when the land itself is compulsorily purchased? Could there be any circumstances in which a person might suffer significant trade loss yet find that the value of the land on which his particular trade was being carried on either remained the same or rose, with the consequence that his rates and, where relevant, rent also rose? What advice would you give to a person seeking a remedy in such a situation?

(iii) *Depreciation caused by use of public works*

Land Compensation Act 1973, Part I

1. – (1) Where the value of an interest in land is depreciated by physical factors caused by the use of public works, then, if –

    (*a*) the interest qualifies for compensation under this Part of this Act; and

    (*b*) the person entitled to the interest makes a claim within the time limited by and otherwise in accordance with this Part of this Act,

compensation for that depreciation shall, subject to the provisions of this Part of this Act, be payable by the responsible authority to the person making the claim (hereafter referred to as 'the claimant').

(2) The physical factors mentioned in subsection (1) above are noise, vibration, smell, fumes, smoke and artificial lighting and the discharge on to the land in respect of which the claim is made of any solid or liquid substance.

(3) The public works mentioned in subsection (1) above are –

    (a) any highway;

    (b) any aerodrome; and

    (c) any works or land (not being a highway or aerodrome) provided or used in the exercise of statutory powers.

(4) The responsible authority mentioned in subsection (1) above is, in relation to a highway, the appropriate highway authority and, in relation to other public works, the person managing those works.

(5) Physical factors caused by an aircraft arriving at or departing from an aerodrome shall be treated as caused by the use of the aerodrome whether or not the aircraft is within the boundaries of the aerodrome; but, save as aforesaid, the source of the physical factors must be situated on or in the public works the use of which is alleged to be their cause.

(6) Compensation shall not be payable under this Part of this Act in respect of the physical factors caused by the use of any public works other than a highway unless immunity from actions for nuisance in respect of that use is conferred (whether expressly or by implication) by an enactment relating to those works or, in the case of an aerodrome and physical factors caused by aircraft, the aerodrome is one to which section 41 (2) of the Civil Aviation Act 1949 (immunity from actions for nuisance) for the time being applies.

2. Interests qualifying for compensation (summary).

Interests are those of an occupier of a dwelling house, which he is occupying as his residence, of a hereditament other than a residence, or an agricultural unit. In the case of the dwelling-house the occupier-claimant must own either the legal fee simply or a tenancy with at least three years to run. In the case of the hereditament and agricultural unit, the interest must be that of an owner-occupier, defined as for the occupier-claimant of a dwelling-house, with the addition that the claimant must occupy the whole or a substantial part of the hereditament or the whole of the agricultural unit.

3. (2) Subject to the provisions of this section and of sections 12 and 14 below, no claim shall be made otherwise than in the claim period, that is to say, the period of two years beginning on the expiration of twelve months from the relevant date.

(5) Where compensation is payable by a responsible authority on a claim there shall be payable by the authority, in addition to the compensation, any reasonable valuation or legal expenses incurred by the claimant for the purposes of the preparation and prosecution of the claim; but this subsection is without prejudice to the powers of the Lands Tribunal for Scotland in respect of the costs or expenses of proceedings before the Tribunal by virtue of section 16 below.

4. – (1) The compensations payable on any claim shall be assessed by reference to prices current on the first day of the claim period.

(2) In assessing depreciation due to the physical factors caused by the use of any public works, account shall be taken of the use of those works as it exists on the first day of the claim period and of any intensification that may then be reasonably expected of the use of those works in the state in which they are on that date.

(4) The value of the interest in respect of which the claim is made shall be assessed –

(a) ... by reference to the nature of the interest and the condition of the land as it subsisted on the date of service of notice of the claim;

(b) subject to section 5 below, in accordance with rules (2) to (4) of the rules set out in section 5 of the Land Compensation Act 1961. . . .

5. Assessment of compensation: assumptions as to planning permission (summary). In assessing compensation the value of the interest will be its 'existing use value'. Planning permission will be assumed to be granted only in respect of the limited 'Part II of Eighth Schedule' (formerly Third Schedule) classes of development regarded as comprised in the existing use of the property for general compensation purposes. Even if within those classes it is to be disregarded if compensation has been paid or is payable in respect of the development value.

It will be assumed that planning permission would not be granted in respect of any other development, even if it has actually been granted.

6. – (1) The compensation payable on a claim shall be reduced by an amount equal to any increase in the value of –

(a) the claimant's interest in the land in respect of which the claim is made; and

(b) any interest in other land contiguous or adjacent to the land mentioned in paragraph (a) above to which the claimant was entitled in the same capacity on the relevant date,

which is attributable to the existence of or the use or prospective use of the public works to which the claim relates.

(3) Where, for the purpose of assessing compensation on a claim in respect of any interest in land, an increase in the value of an interest in other land has been taken into account under subsection (1) above, then, in connection with any subsequent acquisition to which this sub-section applies, that increase shall not be left out of account by virtue of section 6 of the Land Compensation Act 1961 or taken into account by virtue of section 7 of that Act or any corresponding enactment, in so far as it was taken into account in connection with that claim.

7. Compensation shall not be payable on any claim unless the amount of the compensation exceeds £50.

8. – (1) Where a claim has been made in respect of depreciation of the value of an interest in land cause by the use of any public works and compensation has been paid or is payable on that claim, compensation shall not be payable on any subsequent claim in relation to the same works and the same land or any part thereof (whether in respect of the same or a different interest) except that, in the case of land which is a dwelling, this subsection shall not preclude the payment of compensation both on a claim in respect of the fee simple and on a claim in respect of a tenancy.

9. Alterations to public works and changes of use (summary). Claims for compensation may be made in respect of depreciation cause by alterations or changes of use but not for intensification of use.

15. (Summary). The authority responsible for the works shall keep a record and – on demand – furnish a statement in writing of the date on which the highway or other public works were first used after completion.

17. Where, in resisting a claim under this Part of this Act, a responsible authority contend that no enactment relating to the works in question confers immunity from actions for nuisance in respect of the use to which the claim relates, then if –

(a) compensation is not paid on the claim; and
(b) an action for nuisance in respect of the matters which were the subject of the claim is subsequently brought by the claimant against the authority,

no enactment relating to those works, being an enactment in force when the contention was made, shall afford a defence to that action in so far as it relates to those matters.

26. – (1) Subject to the provisions of this section, a responsible authority may acquire land by agreement for the purpose of mitigating any adverse effect which the existence or use of any public works has or will have on the surroundings of the works.

(2) Subject to the provisions of this section, a responsible authority may acquire by agreement –

(a) land the enjoyment of which is seriously affected by the carrying out of works by the authority for the construction or alteration of any public works;
(b) land the enjoyment of which is seriously affected by the use of any public works, if the interest of the vendor is of the kind mentioned in section 22 (2) above.

These provisions represent a fundamental shift in the law of compensation. On a narrow technical level it could be said that the law of nuisance, inapplicable to nuisance caused by public works since *Brand's* case, has been introduced or re-introduced into the area of public works. On a broader level it may be seen as part of the implementation by the government of its decision that whereas 'hitherto some of the wider results of development, such as severance of communities and loss of amenity, have been paid for by the people whose properties have been adversely affected, [in] future more of these costs must fall on the community at large through the authorities responsible for the development . . . as they more fully compensate those whose land they take, or whose property is depreciated as a result of their activities'.[66] These provisions cannot then be seen as just an overdue amendment to the law of injurious affection; they are part of the total package of making public development more acceptable to the public for whose supposed benefit it takes place. The extent to which the package, and particularly the financial parts of it, might succeed in its aims will be looked at in a later section of this chapter.

One general question may however be raised here. The JUSTICE *Report* was an influential factor in bringing about changes in the law relating to compensation. The Committee made recommendations to extend injurious affection to user of land acquired by public authorities and acknowledged that if their recommendations were accepted.

> ... we realise that it would place in juxtaposition the status of persons who suffer damage to an interest in land through the user of land acquired by an authority, and persons who suffer damage to an interest in land through the exercise of regulatory powers as occurs with the imposition of traffic management schemes or 'no parking' restrictions. We believe that compensation through the compensation code ought to be limited to the former situation and that compensation for injury caused by the exercise of regulatory powers should continue to be governed by the particular code of law which grants such powers. In making these recommendations we recognise that we are drawing an artificial line between damage caused to land by the taking and use of other land and damage caused to land by the user of other land without any taking.[67]

The Act accepts this broad distinction and indeed goes further by confining a right to compensation to depreciation caused by physical factors and excluding an intensification of use from giving rise to compensation. Do you agree with such an exclusion and the maintenance of the distinction discussed by the JUSTICE *Report*? On what grounds may the distinction be justified?

(e) Disturbance

Davies, op. cit., pp. 161–3

In an ordinary free sale on the open market, it is unlikely that the purchaser will pay the vendor's removal expenses, or incur any other incidental costs for the vendor's benefit. ... On the whole ... market conditions will apply to sales of land. The purchaser either agrees to pay a price acceptable to the vendor, or he does not, and the vendor has no way of jockeying him into payment of extras without giving corresponding benefits in return. ...

But in compulsory purchase both practice and law diverge here from free market transactions. The acquiring body is required to pay to the expropriated owner compensation for 'disturbance' over and above purchase price compensation. There are circumstances, expressly provided for by statute, in which authorities are given a *discretion* to pay compensation for disturbance. But these do not apply to expropriated owners, who are entitled to such compensation as of right. The right is regarded as statutory yet it is not expressly laid down in any statutory provision. It would be more accurate to say that 'disturbance' is compensatable in so far as it can be shown to be a part of an expropriated owner's 'true loss', the latter being greater in such a case than the mere market value purchase price of the land. In fact the true loss may well extend even beyond disturbance: there is no logical reason why it should be so confined, and there are particular reasons why it should not. Rule (vi) of section 5 of the Land Compensation Act expresses this well enough when it states that, 'the provisions of Rule (ii) shall not affect the assessment of compensation for disturbance *or any other matter* not directly based on the value of land'.

. . . Disturbance . . . seems to have originated in a general feeling that the statutory provisions for compensation must be interpreted as favourably to owners as possible.

Although disturbance compensation was first approved by the court in 1846,[68] the leading authority on the question of what can be compensated for under this heading is the following case:

Horn v. *Sunderland Corporation* [1941] 1 All E.R. 480

SIR WILFRID GREENE MR: On Aug. 20, 1936, the appellants, the Sunderland Corporation, served on the respondent a notice to treat in respect of 102·123 acres of freehold land known as Springwell Farm and owned by the respondent. On May 13, 1937, the appellants served on the respondent another notice to treat in respect of the sand and gravel and the upper stratum of limestone lying within and under the same land. These notices were served in connection with a compulsory purchase by the appellants under the Housing Act, 1925, s. 64, and they were preceded by the usual order made by the corporation and confirmed by the Minister of Health in accordance with the provisions of the Housing Act, 1925, Sched. III. Para. 3 of that schedule provides that the order of the Minister: . . . shall incorporate, subject to the necessary adaptations, the Lands Clauses Acts (except the Lands Clauses Consolidation Act, 1845, s. 127) as modified by the Acquisition of Land (Assessment of Compensation) Act, 1919.

The respondent, who is a farmer, occupied the land in question as farmland. . . . By his award, dated Apr. 8, 1940, the arbitrator assessed the compensation payable to the respondent in respect of the subject-matter comprised in both notices to treat at the sum of £22,700. No separate assessment was made in respect of the sand, gravel and limestone. The evidence on both sides was to the effect that, if they had to be considered as likely to be worked, it would be impossible to get building value for the surface of the farm. The award contained the following paragraph:

The said sum of £22,700 does not include any sum as compensation for the disturbance of the claimant's business by reason of his dispossession of the land. I find that the sum so assessed could not be realised by a willing seller in the open market unless vacant possession were given to the purchaser for the purpose of building development. . . .

It is not disputed that the sum of £22,700, which is at the rate of £220 per acre, was arrived at upon the footing that the land was building land, and is far in excess of the value of the land considered as agricultural land. As I have already stated, the respondent claimed that the land should be valued on the footing that it was building land, and this was accepted by the appellants.

The basic argument on behalf of the appellants may best be summarised by quoting an extract from the points submitted by the acquiring authority in *Mizen Bros.* v. *Mitcham Urban District Council*[69]. . . . In that case, a similar point to that now in issue arose with regard to a market-garden business, and the language of the extract is as follows:

> That the claimants were not entitled to combine in the same claim a valuation of the claimants' land upon the footing of an immediate sale for building purposes with vacant possession and a claim for disturbance and consequential damage upon the footing of interference with a continuing market-garden business.

This argument was accepted by the Divisional Court, but it is argued on behalf of the respondent that the decision was in that respect wrong in law. . . .

The Act of 1919 provides in sect. 1 (1) for the reference of 'any question of disputed compensation' in cases to which the Act applies, and sect. 2 lays down certain rules in accordance with which the arbitrator is to act 'in assessing compensation.' . . .

Rule (6) does not confer a right to claim compensation for disturbance. It merely leaves unaffected the right which, before the Act of 1919, the owner would have had in a proper case to claim that the compensation to be paid for the land should be increased on the ground that he had been disturbed. It is true that the arbitrator now cannot well avoid doing what a jury under the Lands Clauses Acts was not bound to do – namely, arrive at one figure for the value of the land and (in a proper case) another figure for disturbance – but these two figures are still, in my opinion, merely the elements which go to build up the global figure of price or compensation payable. The sum of them would be the proper figure to be inserted in a conveyance. . . . It is a mistake to construe rr. (2) and (6) as though they conferred two separate and independent rights, one to receive the market value of the land and the other to receive compensation for disturbance, each of which must be ascertained in isolation.

In the present case, the respondent was occupying for farming purposes land which had a value far higher than that of agricultural land. In other words, he was putting the land to a use which, economically speaking, was not its best use, a thing which he was, of course, perfectly entitled to do. The result of the compulsory purchase will be to give him a sum equal to the true economic value of the land as building land, and he thus will realise from the land a sum which never could have been realised on the basis of agricultural user. Now he is claiming that the land from which he is being expropriated is to be treated, for the purpose of valuation, as building land, and, for the purpose of disturbance, as agricultural land, and he says that the sum properly payable to him for the loss of his land is (i) its value as building land, plus (ii) sum for disturbance of his farming business. It appears to me that . . . these claims are inconsistent with one another. He can realise the building value in the market only if he is willing to abandon his farming business in order to obtain the higher price. If he claims compensation for disturbance of his farming business, he is saying that he is not willing to abandon his farming business – that is to say, that he ought to be treated as a man who, but for the compulsory purchase, would have continued to farm the land, and, therefore, could not have realised the building value. . . .

Case referred back to the arbitrator.

Harvey v. *Crawley Development Corporation*
[1957] 1 All E.R. 504

DENNING LJ: The freeholder, Mrs Harvey, used to own a house, 'St Raphael's,' Three Bridges Road, Crawley, Sussex. The acquiring authority, Crawley Development Corporation, decided to acquire that house compulsorily. When the freeholder was faced with the request for acquisition, she agreed to let the acquiring authority have the house at a price to be settled by the Lands Tribunal in accordance with the statutory provisions. The question before us is as to the way in which the compensation should be assessed. The agreed total sum which she has been awarded is £4,148 1s.

The question in the case arises in this way. The freeholder tried to find another house for herself to go into. She saw a house which she liked and was proposing to buy it, but she had a surveyors' report for it and when she got the surveyors' report she discovered it was an unsatisfactory house and she did not go on with the purchase of it. Afterwards she did find a house which suited her and she bought it. She had to pay the solicitors costs and the surveyors' fees when she bought it; she had some travelling expenses, and so on. The total expense to which she was put for travelling expenses, surveyors' fees and legal costs (on the proposed house and the house she bought) comes altogether to £241 10s. 1d.; and the question is whether she is entitled by way of compensation to have that sum in addition to the £4,148 1s. which I have already mentioned. It has been found by the Lands Tribunal that those expenses were all reasonably incurred by her in finding another house, and the tribunal has awarded that sum to her as compensation. The acquiring authority appeal to this court and say that in point of law such compensation is not to be granted to the freeholder.

It seems to me that, as these costs of £241 10s. 1d. were reasonably incurred by the freeholder in getting another house, they can fairly be regarded as a direct consequence of the compulsory acquisition. Prima facie, therefore, they fall within the heading of compensation for disturbance. It is said, however, that they are not properly compensation for disturbance, but only compensation for reinstatement: and that the cost of reinstatement of a person in other premises can never be the subject of compensation; and s. 2 (5) of the Act of 1919 was relied on. I do not think that sub-s. (5) supports that proposition. It is only dealing with the value of land when there is no market for it. Take, for instance, a church, for which there is no market. Under sub-s. (5) the owners can sometimes get the cost of buying another piece of land and putting up a church on it. The fact that the cost of reinstatement is there specifically allowed does not mean that in every other case anything in the nature of reinstatement is to be disallowed. It all depends on whether it comes properly within 'compensation for disturbance'.

Next it was said that the freeholder was really seeking compensation for the acquisition being compulsory, and sub-s. (1) was referred to, which says that no allowance shall be made on account of the acquisition being compulsory. Sub-section (1) is, however, directed only to the added sop of ten per cent. which in the old days was always given in these cases to soften the blow of compulsory acquisition. Sub-section (1) disallows that ten per cent. It leaves untouched the rule that everything which is a direct consequence of the compulsory acquisition can be recovered under the head of 'compensation for disturbance'. Instances were given in this very case. The freeholder gets compensation for having to move out her furniture and put it into the new house: she gets compensation for having to alter the curtains and carpets and remake them to fit the new windows and floors. Take business premises where fixtures and fittings have to be moved; or there is loss of business through being turned out; or loss of goodwill. All that loss and expense is the proper subject of 'compensation for disturbance' in addition to the open market value of the land.

I would therefore say that the £241 10s. 1d., which has been expended and is the direct consequence of the freeholder being turned out of her house, is properly to be regarded as compensation for disturbance. I would not, however, like this to be taken too far. Cases were put in the course of the argument. Supposing a man did not occupy a house himself but simply owned it as an investment. His compensation would be the value of the house. If he chose to put the money into stocks and shares, he could not claim the brokerage as compensation. That would be much too remote. It would not be the consequence of the compulsory acquisition but the result of his own choice in putting the money into stocks and shares instead of putting it on deposit at the bank. If he chose to buy another house as an investment, he would not get the solicitors' costs on the purchase. Those costs would be the result of his own choice of investment and not the result of the compulsory acquisition. Another case was put in the course of the argument. If an elderly man and wife owned and occupied a house which was compulsorily acquired and they thought to themselves: 'We do not think we need to get another house; we will go into a guest house', they would not get the costs of moving into a new house when they had not incurred them. Nor would they be able to claim the cost of living in a boarding house for the rest of their days. They would only get the market value of their former home. These illustrations show that the owner only recovers costs of the present kind in a case where a house is occupied by an owner, living there, who is forced out and reasonably finds a house elsewhere in which to live. If he pays a higher price for the new house, he would not get compensation on that account, because he would be presumed to have got value for his money: but he does get the costs that he has to pay a surveyor and lawyer to get it. The costs are then the subject of compensation under the heading of 'disturbance' as specified in s. 2 (6).

For these reasons, I think that the decision of the Lands Tribunal was correct and I would dismiss the appeal.

Appeal dismissed.

Davies suggests that in principle higher loan charges *bona fide* incurred for a necessary purchase of dearer premises ought to be recoverable under the heading of 'disturbance'. Do you agree? How could one determine whether the purchase of dearer premises was 'necessary', or whether the higher loan charges were imposed because of the purchase of the particular premises? Consider whether disturbance compensation would or ought to be payable in the following circumstances:

(i) A has a mortgage with a large national building society. His house is compulsorily purchased during a period of 'mortgage famine' and the large national society declines to give him a loan on mortgage to purchase a new house. He is forced to borrow from a small local building society whose interest rates are always fixed at ½ per cent above those of the large national society with which he used to have a mortgage.

(ii) B obtained a thirty-year mortgage on his house when he bought it in 1955. B was then twenty-five. The house is compulsorily purchased. B finds another house suitable for his needs, but because of his age is only able to obtain a twenty-year mortgage for the same size loan as his previous thirty-year one. His monthly repayments are therefore substantially higher.

The Land Compensation Act 1973 has introduced a new category of disturbance payments as follows:

37. – (1) Where a person is displaced from any land in consequence of –
(*a*) the acquisition of the land by an authority possessing compulsory purchase powers;
(*b*) the making, passing or acceptance of a housing order, resolution or undertaking in respect of a house or building on the land; or the service of an improvement notice, within the meaning of Part VIII of the Housing Act 1974, in respect of a house on the land
(*c*) where the land has been previously acquired by an authority

possessing compulsory purchase powers or appropriated by a local authority and is for the time being held by the authority for the purposes for which it was acquired or appropriated, the carrying out of any improvement to a house or building on the land or of redevelopment on the land, he shall, subject to the provisions of this section, be entitled to receive a payment (hereafter referred to as a 'disturbance payment') from the acquiring authority, the authority who made the order, passed the resolution or accepted the undertaking or the authority carrying out the redevelopment, as the case may be.

(2) A person shall not be entitled to a disturbance payment –

(*a*) in any case, unless he is in lawful possession of the land from which he is displaced;

(*b*) in a case within subsection (1) (*a*) above, unless either –

(i) he has no interest in the land for the acquisition or extinguishment of which he is (or if the acquisition or extinguishment were compulsory would be) entitled to compensation under any other enactment. . . .

38. – (1) The amount of a disturbance payment shall be equal to –

(*a*) the reasonable expenses of the person entitled to the payment in removing from the land from which he is displaced; and

(*b*) if he was carrying on a trade or business on that land, the loss he will sustain by reason of the disturbance of that trade or business consequent upon his having to quit the land.

(2) In estimating the loss of any person for the purposes of subsection (1) (*b*) above, regard shall be had to the period for which the land occupied by him may reasonably have been expected to be available for the purpose of his trade or business and to the availability of other land suitable for that purpose. . . .

Section 39 may be seen as a somewhat similar concession in similar situations to those set out in section 37 (i) (a) (b) and (c). It provides that:

Where a person is displaced from residential accommodation on any land . . . and suitable alternative residential accommodation on reasonable terms is not otherwise available to that person, then, subject to the provisions of this section, it shall be the duty of the relevant authority to secure that he will be provided with such other accommodation.[70]

(f) Defects of market value as a basis of compensation[71]

Disturbance compensation reflects the fact that market value might not be the true loss to the expropriated owner. The necessity to take into account hypothetical planning permissions when assessing market value points to the difficulties of assessment in an age of planning. Both of these matters show up defects in the principle of basing compensation on market value. The main plank of the case for market value is that it is 'objective'; it can be assessed by valuers by reference to impartial and impersonal factors. This case becomes somewhat shaky when it is admitted that there can be optimistic and pessimistic assessments of the market,[72] but marketeers can legitimately ask anti-marketeers: what is the alternative?

The answer to this question can only be approached by first attempting to answer another question: what are the purposes of the state in providing compensation for compulsory purchase in the first place? This in turn involves asking: what is meant by 'compensation' in this context? Is compensation awarded as an equivalent for what has been lost or as a solace for what has happened? Concentrating on the 'purposes' question, it is suggested that the models developed by Michelman[73] to answer the question of when compensation should be paid are of great assistance here, for both models regard as fundamental considerations the expectations and valuations of those who are being deprived of their property. Thus according to the utilitarian model, compensation is due whenever 'demoralisation costs' exceed 'settlement costs' and, when it comes to calculating the former, 'we are compelled . . . to frame the question about demoralisation costs in terms of responses we must impute to ordinarily cognisant and sensitive members of society'.[74] Similarly, when we turn to the fairness model we find that 'a decision not to compensate is not unfair as long as the disappointed claimant ought to be able to appreciate how such decisions might fit into a consistent practice which holds forth a lesser long-run risk to people like him than would any consistent practice which is naturally suggested by the opposite decision'.[75]

Personal considerations such as these are incompatible with assessment based on market value. How incompatible particularly in relation to compulsory purchases of dwelling houses may be judged from the following:

House of Commons Debate, Vol. 847, col 88:
Second Reading, Land Compensation Bill

R. B. CANT MP: I wish to take up a great deficiency in the Bill, namely, the continued acceptance of market value and disturbance payment as a basis of compensation. If there is anything which seems 100% correct in theory or principle it is that compensation should be related to market value plus disturbance. It borders almost on generosity. However, one finds from talking to people who are victims of what is happening as a consequence, for example, of the building of motorways in towns, that in many cases the results are nothing less than a travesty of social justice, personal agony and sometimes tragedy for the people concerned.

The same point had been made in less dramatic terms below:

Report of the Urban Motorways Committee
(HMSO July 1972)

12.18 . . . It will not be sufficient to assume that in the case of those who have to move, the cost of compensation or rehousing fully reflects the burden that is put on them. Many individuals are attached to their particular house or their particular neighbourhood and would not freely move simply for the market value of their property. They suffer an additional loss – sometimes called loss of householders surplus – which is real for them but for practical purposes very difficult to value in specific cases.

12.19. The present compensation rules make no provision for any payment in respect of this additional loss. . . . Most of the non-Departmental members of the Committee recommend *the establishment of an additional head of compensation, payable to the occupiers of dwellings, in recognition of the real personal disturbance that is inflicted on them when they are required to move. . . .* To attempt to tailor such payments to individual circumstances would be a matter of considerable complexity for which no sufficient basis of relevant evidence at present exists. Though further studies in this field might well influence future practice, the amounts will at present therefore have to be set by some general and fairly arbitrary formula. . . .

The Government accepted this recommendation and the argument that the amounts of compensation would have to be set by 'some general and fairly arbitrary formula'.

Land Compensation Act 1973

Home loss payments. Right to home loss payment where person displaced from dwelling.

29. – (1) Where a person is displaced from a dwelling on any land in consequence of –

(*a*) the compulsory acquisition of an interest in the dwelling;

(*b*) the making, passing or acceptance of a housing order, resolution or undertaking in respect of the dwelling; or the service of an improvement notice, within the meaning of Part VIII of the Housing Act 1974, in respect of the dwelling;

(*c*) where the land has been previously acquired by an authority possessing compulsory purchase powers or appropriated by a local authority and is for the time being held by the authority for the purposes for which it was acquired or appropriated, the carrying out of any improvement to the dwelling or of redevelopment on the land, he shall, subject to the provisions of this section and section 32 below, be entitled to receive a payment (hereafter referred to as a 'home loss payment') from the acquiring authority who made the order, passed the resolution or accepted the undertaking or the authority carrying out the redevelopment, as the case may be.

(2) A person shall not be entitled to a home loss payment unless throughout a period of not less than five years ending with the date of displacement –

(a) he has been in occupation of the dwelling, or a substantial part of it, as his only or main residence; and

(b) he has been in occupation as aforesaid by virtue of an interest or right to which this section applies.

(3) For the purpose of this section a person shall not be treated as displaced from a dwelling in consequence of the compulsory acquisition of an interest therein if he gives up his occupation thereof before the date on which the acquiring authority were authorised to acquire that interest, but, subject to that, it shall not be necessary for the acquiring authority to have required him to give up his occupation of the dwelling.

(5) No home loss payment shall be made to any person displaced from a dwelling in consequence of the compulsory acquisition of an interest therein if the acquisition is in pursuance of the service by him of a blight notice within the meaning of section 192 of the Town and Country Planning Act 1971.

Amount of home loss payment in England and Wales

30. – (1) Subject to subsection (2) below, the amount of a home loss payment in England and Wales shall be:

(a) where the date of displacement is before 1st April 1973, an amount equal to the rateable value of the dwelling multiplied by seven;

(b) where the date of displacement is on or after 1st April 1973, an amount equal to the rateable value of the dwelling multiplied by three; subject in either case, to a maximum of £1,500 and a minimum of £150.

(2) The secretary of State may from time to time by order prescribe different multipliers and a different maximum or minimum for the purposes of subsection (1) above, . . .

32. – (1) . . . no home loss payment shall be made except on a claim in that behalf made by a person entitled thereto ('the claimant') before the expiration of the period of six months beginning with the date of displacement; . . .

It would not be profitable to debate the reasons why the particular multipliers and maximum and minimum amounts found a place in the Act as finally passed; a general and fairly arbitrary formula is, after all, just that. More to the point is to ask why the possibility of tailoring amounts of compensation to individual circumstances was rejected. Is it 'a matter of considerable complexity' as the Urban Motorways Committee thought? Would it lead to large amounts of compensation being payable? Is home loss payment solace or equivalence? What would personalised compensation be?

It is pertinent to note that personalised compensation has found its way into English statute law, albeit only a local Act.

Devon River Authority (General Powers) Act 1972, s. 6 (7)

The Authority may pay to the occupier of any land used for the purposes of agriculture which has been acquired by the Authority under the Act of 1963 for any purpose in connection with the performance of any of their new functions such reasonable allowances as they think fit towards any loss or in respect of any personal hardship which in their opinion he will sustain or be put to by reason of his having to quit the land.

Other local Acts in the early 1970s that attempted to incorporate such a provision were prevented from doing so by the government. Could this Act be part of the 'further studies in the field' which the Urban Motorways Committee thought necessary before personalised compensation could be made general? If so, why not allow a local Act having application in an urban environment to incorporate such a provision? If not, why allow the provision at all? Quite apart from a local Act, personalised compensation would not be such a shot in the dark as the Urban Motorways Committee seemed to think.

Report of the Commission of Inquiry into the siting of the Third London Airport[76], *1971*

1.13 The estimation of consumers' surplus is important in the evaluation of the impact of the airport on the lives and on the environment of local residents. There is a clear distinction between what things cost, or what they could be sold for, and their subjective value to the person concerned. An inhabitant of a house on the site of the airport will receive financial compensation for the freehold of his property in accordance with statutory practice. This sum may be sufficient for him to buy a comparable property elsewhere. But over the years, he and his family may have invested much time and effort in adapting the house to their particular requirements. They may also have built up a circle of friends and local activities, which they might find it difficult or impossible to build up again in some other locality. These factors are not necessarily reflected in either market prices or compensation values; to the extent that they are not, they may be defined as consumer surplus.

20.3 (b) S- the difference between the householder's subjective value of his house and the market value. This corresponds to consumer surplus as defined in chapter 1. The subjective value in this case is the sum which the householder would consider just sufficient to compensate him for loss of the property, assuming he had to leave the noisy area altogether . . .

20.27 The value of S will tend to rise as the resident develops contacts with the local community but may fall if the contacts are with a distant urban community. If the resident's family increases in size and the house becomes too small, the value of S would fall. It would also fall if the resident acquired the means to enable him to move to a more expensive neighbourhood or if he found that familiarity did not increase his satisfaction. On the other hand the value of S might increase continuously over the years for a middle-aged couple as the prospect of moving to a completely new area becomes less inviting. Relatively high values of S are therefore likely to be found among the middle-aged and retired and lower values among the young and more mobile.

20.28 The value of S for the population resident around the four sites might have been estimated by a deductive process similar to that used for estimating the value of other disbenefits. In principle situations could be examined where nuisance had been imposed and the movement rate observed but in practice it is difficult to find comparable situations. Therefore, the consumer surplus could be valued only on the basis of people's own estimates derived by social survey methods. In the survey which was undertaken people were asked what sum of money would be just high enough to persuade them to part with their existing house, on the assumption that they had to make a move of at least ten miles. This price was defined to include all costs of removal both financial and psychic. . . .

20.30 Of the 615 interviews completed, 570 answered the basic question on consumer surplus. It was impossible to distinguish any differences in the amount of surplus due to factors such as present market value of property, length of residence, etc. . . .

DISTRIBUTION OF CONSUMER SURPLUS VALUES

Consumer surplus (% excess of market price)	% of sample
0	11
1–15	16
16–25	19
26–35	11
36–45	9
46–55	9
Over 55	17
Would not sell	8
Total	**100**

Note: The average excess over market price for those respondents quoting a figure is 39%.

Is this average excess over market price too high to warrant moving towards personalised compensation? How could one ensure that householders did not constantly raise the value of their householders' surplus as they became aware that the acquiring authority was prepared to pay for the whole or a part of that surplus?

(g) Inverse compulsory purchase

Compulsory purchase by a local authority may occur for a variety of reasons and therefore covers a wider field than purely planning matters. Inverse compulsory purchase, on the other hand, largely owes its existence to the system of planning, and is contained primarily within the Town and Country Planning Act. The term refers to the power conferred upon an owner of land to require a public authority to purchase his land either because as a result of a planning decision 'the land has become incapable of reasonably beneficial use in its existing state'[77] and cannot be rendered capable of reasonably beneficial use by the carrying out of development for which planning permission has been or may be granted, or because, as a result of certain specified planning proposals, the owner 'has been unable to sell it (the land) except at a price substantially lower than that for which it might reasonably have been expected to sell if no part'[78] of the land was comprised in land of any of the specified descriptions. In the first case the owner serves a purchase notice; in the second he serves a blight notice. The procedures governing each may be briefly outlined.

(i) Purchase notices[79]

When a purchase notice has been served on a local authority under section 180 of the Act, it must notify the landowner within three months

(a) that it (or some other local authority or statutory undertaker) is prepared to purchase the land, in which case the relevant local authority is empowered to purchase it and is deemed to have served a notice to treat which cannot be withdrawn, or

(b) that no authority is prepared to purchase the land, in which case it must notify the Secretary of State, who after providing an opportunity for both parties to appear before and be heard by an inspector must either

(i) confirm the notice with or without modifications in which case (a) above applies or

(ii) grant the planning permission which was originally applied for or with less restrictive conditions than originally imposed so that the land does then become capable of reasonably beneficial use, or

(iii) direct that any planning permission shall be granted for any other development which he considers could render the land capable of reasonably beneficial use within a reasonable time.

If the Secretary of State does not take any of the above action within either six months of when the notice was transmitted to him or nine months of its original service, whichever is the earlier, or does not within that period notify the owner that he does not propose to confirm the notice, he is then deemed to have confirmed it.

These provisions also apply in the following cases:

1. Revocation or modification of planning permission.
2. An order requiring discontinuance of a use, or alteration or removal of buildings or works.
3. A tree preservation order if the order so applies them.
4. Where an application for listed building consent is refused or granted conditionally, or any such consent is revoked or modified.
5. To advertisements if applied by the Control of Advertisement Regulations.

Just as the date of valuation crossed the boundary between procedure and compensation, so does the concept of 'reasonably beneficial use'. If there is such use, there is no compensation (compensation is based on the market value of the property). Does the use also have to be 'market use' – i.e. the use that gives the land its maximum market value? How are local planning authorities to determine these questions? They may derive assistance from both the courts and ministerial circulars and decisions.

R. v. *Minister of Housing and Local Government*
ex parte Chichester RDC [1960] 2 All E.R. 407

The Minister had upheld a purchase notice served on the Chichester RDC after an adverse planning decision on the ground that 'the land in its existing state and with its existing permissions is substantially less useful to the server (of the notice) than it would be with permission for the permanent redevelopment for residential purposes'. The Council sought an order of certiorari to quash the Minister's decision and obtained one in the Divisional Court.

LORD PARKER CJ: It is quite clear that that of itself (the Minister's reasons) is not the test. I suppose that in every case where land is worth developing and permission to develop is refused, the existing use of the land will be of less beneficial use, it will be less useful to the owner, than if it were developed. The test is whether it has become incapable of reasonably beneficial use in its existing state.

It may be that the word 'reasonably' invokes some comparison, but the fact that the land is less useful . . . in its present state than if developed is clearly not the test . . . and it is a non-sequitur to say that because it is of substantially less use than if developed, therefore the conditions specified . . . are fulfilled.

Brookdene Investments Ltd v. *MHLG* (1970)
21 P. & C.R. 545

July 30. FISHER J: This case concerns five blocks of property in Manchester owned by the applicants.

On September 25, 1967, they applied for planning permission to demolish the existing properties and to build warehouses, showrooms and shops. On November 1, 1967, permission was refused. On November 24, 1967, the applicants served purchase notices on the council, claiming that the land had become incapable of reasonably beneficial use in its existing state. On February 8, 1968, the council gave notice that they were not willing to comply with the purchase notices. . . .

On July 16, 1968, an inquiry was held by an inspector appointed by the Minister into both the purchase notices and the appeal against refusal of planning permission. . . .

On September 5, 1968, the Minister wrote to the applicants enclosing a copy of the inspector's report. In his letter, the Minister said:

The Inspector recommended that the purchase notices be not confirmed. The Minister accepts the validity of the comparison with Third Schedule values as being relevant to the question of whether the purchase notice sites have become incapable of reasonably beneficial use in their existing state . . . the Minister is not satisfied on the information before him that the sites, or any of them, have become incapable of reasonably beneficial use in their existing state and for this reason he accepts the inspector's recommendation. He does not, therefore, propose to confirm any of the purchase notices concerned, and the notices are not confirmed because he is not satisfied that the conditions specified in paragraphs (*a*) and (*c*) of subsection (1) of section 129 of the Act of 1962 are fulfilled.

On October 16, 1968, the applicants gave notice of motion for an order quashing the Minister's decision. . . .

In order to understand the arguments, it is necessary to say something about the evidence which was called at the inquiry. I refer to the paragraphs in the inspector's report. Mr Westbrook, a surveyor, gave evidence that the total annual value of the premises in their existing state was £10,000, but that the total annual value of development not constituting 'new development' (*i.e.* if Third Schedule development had been carried out) would be £53,415 after providing for the cost of the development – that is, over five times as much. . . .

The first point taken by Mr Dobry is that the statute requires a comparison of this kind to be made in every case in order to determine whether the land has become incapable of reasonably beneficial use in its existing state, and that, in a case where the difference is substantial, the Minister must necessarily find that it has, even though there may be other evidence pointing to the opposite conclusion.

Mr Slynn accepts that the Minister has not treated the comparison test as paramount or over-riding, and that, if the statutory requirement is as stated by Mr Dobry, the decision must be quashed. He submits, however, that the question whether or not land has become incapable of reasonably beneficial use in its existing state is a question of fact and degree to be decided by the Minister on all the evidence before him, and that, although a comparison of the value in existing state with the value after Third Schedule development may in certain cases be relevant, it is merely one of the matters to be taken into consideration along with the other evidence and that it is open to the Minister to decide on other evidence that land is capable of a reasonably beneficial use in its existing state even though the difference between the two values is considerable. . . .

What does section 129 (2) say? It says that, in determining a certain question for a certain purpose, no account shall be taken of a certain matter, *i.e.* it is negative in form and a positive obligation can be spelled out of it (if at all) only as a matter of necessary inference. The *purpose* (so far as is relevant to this case) is that of determining whether the land has become incapable of reasonably beneficial use. The *question* is: what is a reasonably beneficial use of the land? The *matter of which no account is to be taken* is any prospective use of that land which would involve the carrying out of 'new development.'

How can a use which would involve the carrying out of development be relevant to an inquiry as to whether land has become incapable of reasonably beneficial use *in its existing state*? It might be relevant if the development consisted merely of change of user (see section 12 (1) of the Town and Country Planning Act 1962) and did not involve an alteration in the state of the land. In such a case, the effect of section 129 (2) would be to enlarge the category of uses which might be taken into account in answering the question: 'has the land become incapable of reasonably beneficial use in its existing state?' to include in addition to the existing use any change of user falling within the Third Schedule, but no other change of user. If the existing use of land were reasonably beneficial, then one would need to look no further. If the existing use were not reasonably beneficial, then you could look for prospective uses of which the land was capable which involved a change of user within the Third Schedule, but no other user – and if you found one, and it was reasonably beneficial, then the condition under section 129 (1) (*a*) would not be fulfilled. This construction of the section seems to me to be supported by what LORD PARKER CJ said in *R. v. Minister of Housing and Local Government, ex p. Rank Organisation Ltd.* . . .[79a]

Does section 129 also provide that, in considering whether the use of which land in its existing state is capable is 'reasonably beneficial,' one is entitled to take into account some other use to which *after its existing state had been altered by Third Schedule development* the land could be put?

Obviously, by altering its state you may render the land capable of a *more* beneficial use whether the alteration does or does not consist of 'new development.' Does the section provide that, if the land can be rendered capable of more beneficial use by Third Schedule development, one is entitled to take that fact into account in deciding whether the use of which it is capable in its existing state is reasonably beneficial? I have doubts about this (for the reasons given by LORD PARKER CJ in the *Rank* case), but the Minister has accepted that it is so and I am prepared to assume, in deciding this case, that he is correct.

I am, however, satisfied that the section does not expressly or by necessary inference provide that one *must* in every case treat that fact as conclusive. The highest at which the implication from the negative provision of section 129 (2) can be put is that one *may* take it into account and that, if one does so, it must be considered along with other relevant facts. It is for the Minister to decide in each case how much weight to give to it in deciding whether land has become incapable of reasonably beneficial use in its existing state.

I do not accept that, as a matter of definition, a use cannot be 'reasonably beneficial' if the land can be rendered capable of a more beneficial use by Third Schedule development. . . .

In my judgment, the first point taken by the applicants is a bad one.

MHLG Circular No. 26/69: Appendix 1

4. The question to be considered in every case is whether the land in its existing state taking into account operations and uses for which planning permission (or listed building consent) is not required is incapable of reasonably beneficial use. No account may be taken of any prospective use of the land which would involve the carrying out of new development (see section 12 of the 1962 Act) nor of any works which require listed building consent, other than works for which the local planning authority or the Minister have undertaken to grant such consent. In considering what capacity for use the land has, relevant factors are the physical state of the land, its size, shape and surroundings, and the general pattern of uses in the area. A use of relatively low value may be reasonably beneficial if such a use is common for similar land in the neighbourhood: it may be possible for a small area of land in certain circumstances to be rendered capable of reasonably beneficial use by being used in conjunction with a wider area, provided, in most cases, that the wider area is owned by the owner or prospective owner of the purchase notice land. Profit may be a useful test in certain circumstances but the absence of profit is not necessarily material: the notion of reasonably beneficial use is not specifically identifiable with profit. It should be noted that a use which is reasonably beneficial to someone other than the owner or prospective owner of the land to which a purchase notice relates cannot be taken into account.

5. In determining whether the land has become incapable of reasonably beneficial use in its existing state it is relevant, where appropriate, to con-

sider the difference (if any) between the annual value of the land in its existing state and the annual value of the land if development of a class specified in Part I or Part II of Schedule 3 to the 1962 Act were carried out thereon. Development of any class not specified in Schedule 3 must not be taken into account. The reason is that the remedy by way of a purchase notice is not intended for the case where the owner shows merely that he is unable to realise the full development value of his land.

Davies writes of purchase notices and their rationale as follows (at p. 196):

It should be emphasised that a great deal of the trouble experienced with this part of the law arises from failure to take proper account of the distinction between actual use or development of land, and the value of such use or development. Since owners are not now deprived of prospective development value (except by adverse planning decisions) but merely taxed in respect of it, the rationale of purchase notice procedure can be both clear and acceptable: namely that *existing use* of land is nil in all cases where this procedure applies; that development is prohibited; that the valuelessness of the existing use justifies 'inverse compulsory purchase', and that development value can be realised in the compensation for the acquisition by virtue of the 'assumptions as to planning permission' . . . .

If a purchase notice is not accepted, it is because some reasonably beneficial use can be made of the land; if it is accepted, compensation is paid at a rate which includes development value, a sum which will almost certainly greatly exceed reasonably beneficial use value. Is the rationale of this 'both clear and acceptable'?

(ii) *Blight notices*[80]

Planning blight was a layman's term before it received the official imprimatur of the Town and Country Planning Act 1968. As used in the Act (now the Act of 1971) and the Land Compensation Act 1973 it refers to the depreciation which the existing use value of land suffers because of the existence of proposals for certain classes of public development. As such, it has close affinities with injurious affection.

In theory, it would be possible to confine compensation for planning blight to the difference between the market value for the unblighted existing use and the price which the owner of the land was ultimately able to obtain for it or an officially determined new blighted existing use value. In practice this has not happened, partly because proposals for public development are assumed to be likely to take place so that blighted property might ultimately need to be compulsorily acquired and partly because the blighted property provisions have always been confined primarily to residential or small business property in respect of which there is virtually no market of any kind at all. In those situations blight compensation would almost equal existing use value. In the circumstances it was both fairer and administratively easier to allow inverse compulsory purchase. Why are blight provisions confined to the 'small working proprietor' and designed to exclude the 'very large business organisations'?[81]

The classes of land in respect of which a blight notice may be served are as follows:

(a) SECTION 192 THE TOWN AND COUNTRY PLANNING ACT 1971

Davies, op. cit., pp. 206–7

Section 192 of the 1971 Act sets out ten kinds of 'specified description'.

(1) The land is shown in a valid structure plan as being required for the functions of some public body, or for an 'action area'; unless there is also a local plan for the district which specifies any land in that district as being so required.

(2) The land is shown in a valid local plan as being so required.

(3) The land is shown in a development plan, otherwise than in either of the above categories, as the site or part of the site of a highway as it will be constructed or altered.

(4) The land is liable to be compulsorily purchased by virtue of a valid order or scheme under the Highways Acts 1959 and 1971, as the site or part of the site of a trunk or special road, or a road joining a classified road, as it will be constructed or altered.

(5) The land is shown on plans approved by a resolution of a local highway authority as the site or part of the site of a highway as it will be constructed or altered.

(6) The land is the site or part of the site of a trunk or special road which the Secretary of State, by written notice to the local planning authority 'together with maps or plans sufficient to identify the proposed route of the road', states that he 'proposes to provide'.

(7) The land is subject to a compulsory purchase order empowering a highway authority to acquire rights over it under section 47 of the Highways Act 1971 but notice to treat has not been served.

(8) The land is subject to a local authority's published intention to acquire it as part of a 'general improvement area' under Part II of the Housing Act 1969.

(9) The land is liable to be compulsorily purchased under a 'special enactment', which means private legislation or subordinate legislation specifically referring to the land.

(10) The land is covered by an effective compulsory purchase order, but is not yet subject of a notice to treat.

(b) LAND COMPENSATION ACT 1973

DoE Circular No. 73/73

64. Sections 68 to 76 extend the classes of land in respect of which blight notices may be served under the 1971 Act requiring the acquisition by certain authorities of interests in land which cannot otherwise be disposed of, except possibly at a depreciated price, because of the existence of proposals for public development of the land. Generally these sections give statutory effect to the advice given to local authorities in Ministry of Housing and Local Government Circular 46/70 (Welsh Office Circular 48/70) and enable blight notices to be served at an earlier stage.

65. The extensions cover land affected –

    (a) by proposals in structure plans and alterations thereto where the plan or alteration has been submitted to the Secretary of State but has not come into force (section 68 (1) (*a*) and (*b*));

    (b) by modifications proposed to be made by the Secretary of State in a submitted structure plan (section 68 (1) (*c*));

    (c) by proposals in a local plan or proposals for alterations to such a plan where the plan or proposed alterations have been made available for inspection under the publicity arrangements in the 1971 Act (section 68 (2) (*a*) and (*b*));

    (d) by modifications proposed to be made by the Secretary of State or the local planning authority in a local plan (section 68 (2) (*c*));

    (e) by proposals submitted to the Secretary of State for alterations to an 'old style' development plan (in force until superseded by the new style of development plan) and by modifications proposed to be made by the Secretary of State in such proposals (section 68 (3));

    (f) by highway orders or schemes submitted for confirmation to or prepared in draft by the Secretary of State where notice of the order has been published (section 69);

    (g) by compulsory purchase orders submitted for confirmation to or prepared in draft by a Minister where notice of the order has been published, including orders providing for the acquisition of rights over land (sections 70 and 75);

    (h) by an indication in a plan (other than a development plan) approved by the local planning authority for development control purposes that the land may be required for the purposes of a government department, local authority or statutory undertakers (section 71 (1)(*a*));

    (i) by action which the local planning authority have resolved to take to safeguard the land for the purposes of development by such bodies, or by directions of the Secretary of State restricting the grant of planning permission in order to safeguard the land for such development (section 71 (1) (*b*));

(j) by the proposed exercise of powers under section 22 (1) of the Land Compensation Act 1973 to acquire land for the purpose of mitigating any adverse effect which the existence or use of a new or improved highway may have on the surroundings of the highway (section 74).

The persons who may serve a blight notice are: (i) a resident owner-occupier of the whole or a substantial part of an hereditament, defined as 'the aggregate of the land which forms the subject of a single entry in the valuation list for the time being in force for a rating area'; (ii) a non-resident owner-occupier if the premises are small business or other premises including dwelling houses not exceeding a rateable value to be fixed by the Secretary of State. The limit was fixed at £2,250 as from 1 April 1973, and takes account of the revaluation for rates effective from that date; (iii) a resident or non-resident owner-occupier of an agricultural unit, defined as 'land which is occupied as a unit for agricultural purposes, including any dwelling-house or other building occupied by the same person for the purpose of farming the land'.

Owner occupation requires physical occupation for at least six months up to the date of the service of the blight notice or up to any date not more than twelve months before service of the notice, provided that in the intervening period before service the land (other than a farm) was unoccupied.

The circumstances under which a qualified person (usually an owner-occupier) may serve a blight notice are that he has made reasonable endeavours to sell his land and that 'in consequence of the fact that the hereditament or unit or a part of it was, or was likely to be comprised in land of any of the specified descriptions, he has been unable to sell that interest except at a price substantially lower than that for which it might reasonably have been expected to sell if no part of the hereditament or unit were, or were likely to be, comprised in such land.'[82]

What are reasonable endeavours?

Stubbs v. *West Hartlepool Corporation* (1961)
12 P. & C.R. 365 (Lands Tribunal)

Ten persons had been to view Stubbs's house and two offers to purchase at the asking price of £850 had been made. One offer was not proceeded with and the other by a Mr Campbell withdrawn when the offeror discovered that the house was in a redevelopment area and subject to a possible compulsory purchase order eleven years from the date of his buying it. Mr Stonehouse [the estate agent who had acted for Stubbs] said:

R. C. G. FENNELL F.R.I.C.S. . . . He could not think of any further steps he could have taken to compel the market. He considered his price had been justified by the two offers, and the 88 per cent mortgage awarded. He would not have recommended an offer of £750 but would have referred one of £800 for his client's personal decision.

In his experience offers 'went off' very seldom and the 1 per cent suggested in evidence by Mr Wilson as the proportion 'going off' on account of an intending purchaser's second thoughts might well be right. He said that planning blight produces some strange anomalies of effect which were unpredictable. Sales take place regularly in some affected areas; building society mortgages are often the crux; public diffidence comes in spasms and local waves of gossip affect the market, but he did not know how such gossip came or where it went.

He also said that the amount of compensation to be received when the time came would remain open to doubt. Market conditions could be affected and one could not foretell the trend of legislation between now and then. Many people would not want to be compelled to remove at some indefinite time after ten years, and if they wanted to move for some reason after, say, five years, the shorter potential life would increase the difficulty of finding a purchaser. . . .

The questions I am required to answer in order to determine (to quote the notice of reference) 'whether the notice served on the local authority under section 39 (2) of the Town and Country Planning Act, 1959, is a valid notice and that the local authority is required to purchase my interest in the said land or property' are:

(i) Has the claimant made reasonable endeavours to sell that interest since the relevant date?

Having regard to Mr Stonehouse's opinion of the figure asked, to the offers quickly received, to the later advertisement effected and the interest shown, and to the state of activity of the cottage market as disclosed by the corporation's evidence, the endeavours were, in my view, reasonable in extent, and not lacking in proper quality as suggested by Mr Waggott. The section does not say that reasonable endeavours must be made to sell the property at a substantially lower figure than that at which it was reasonably expected to sell.

(ii) Has the claimant been unable to sell it except at a price substantially lower than that for which it might reasonably have been expected to sell if no part of the hereditament or unit were comprised in land of any of the specified descriptions?

Dealing first with the second part of the paragraph, I am satisfied that Mr Campbell withdrew his offer of £850, fortified by the deposit, on account of what he had heard about the development plan – that officially he might be deprived of his property at any time after twenty years from 1951, that is, after eleven years from his intended date of purchase.

I am also satisfied that as no more than the two original offers have been forthcoming, the claimant has not neglected any substantially lower offers which the purchasing public were at liberty to, but did not, make.

I consider that I should, in the circumstances of this case, accept the lack of offers and of response (apart from inspections) to advertisements as a practical disappearance of the market and as satisfying the expression 'unable to sell except at a price substantially lower than that for which it might reasonably have been expected to sell.'

Consequently, I find that the objections by the corporation to Mrs Stubbs's notice were not well founded, and that the notice is a valid notice.

Lade and Lade v. *Brighton Corporation* (1971)
22 P. & C.R. 737 (Lands Tribunal)

H. P. HOBBS Esq., FRICS: This reference concerns a blight notice served pursuant to section 139 of the Town and Country Planning Act 1962 on behalf of Mr and Mrs D. V. W. Lade on January 13, 1970, and a counter-notice served by Brighton Corporation on February 3, 1970, pursuant to section 141 of the Act. The premises concerned are the shop and living accommodation known as 15–16 Church Street, Brighton. . . .

In the development plan of 1958 these premises are in an area scheduled for industrial use but subsequently there have been proposals to use Church Street as a principal traffic route and it is known that it is intended to erect a multi-storey car park to replace the present temporary car park.

Mrs Lade told me that early in 1969 she decided that she wanted to sell the property but rather than putting out a board and advertising in the press, which she considered would be bad for the business, she put a notice in the window and let it be known to those in the trade who visited the shop. She said some people had been interested but once the intentions of the Corporation became known any interest ceased. . . .

The issue between the parties in this case can be set out quite shortly. Is the expression 'reasonable endeavours to sell' satisfied by the owner trying to sell privately by a notice in the window and by telling those in the trade who visit the shop, or is it necessary to advertise in the local press and circulate to the trade generally?

This is a shop in a very second-rate street selling antiques and bric-a-brac not only to the public at large but also to dealers in the trade and whilst generally I would agree with the corporation that the normal procedure for sale should be carried out, in the particular circumstances of this case I take the view that potential purchasers would be more likely to be drawn from visiting dealers than from the more impersonal circularising of particulars and advertising in the local press and I am satisfied that the requirement that the owner shall have made reasonable endeavours to sell has been fulfilled. Accordingly I find that the counter-notice is not well-founded and that the notice given by the claimants is a valid notice, and a notice to treat shall be deemed to have been served on January 13, 1970.

The blight notice is served on the appropriate authority, i.e. the authority which would at some later date have come to acquire the property compulsorily in accordance with the planning proposals which are bringing about the blight. The appropriate authority may either accept the notice, in which case the normal compulsory purchase procedure goes forward, or they may challenge it by serving a counter-notice within two months of the date of service of the blight notice. The counter-notice

must state one or more grounds for objection. . . . There are seven main grounds but they come down in effect to four, as follows:
   (1) No part of the land comes within 'the specified descriptions'
   (2) The claimant, when serving the blight notice, was not entitled to an interest 'qualifying for protection' in any part of the land
   (3) He has not genuinely tried and failed to sell the land for a reasonable price on the open market.
   (4) They do not in fact intend to acquire any of the land; or they intend to acquire only a specified part of the land.[83]

One particular ground of objection may be considered in more detail. Section 194 (2) (d) provides that in respect of land earmarked for a public purpose in a structure plan or for a highway in a development, the authority may object to the blight notice on the ground that they 'do not propose to acquire . . . any part of the affected area during the period of fifteen years from the date of the counter-notice or such longer period from that date as may be specified in the counter-notice'. A claimant under a blight notice may require an objection made in a counter-notice to be referred to the Lands Tribunal. In respect of most objections the onus is on the claimant to show that the objection is not well founded, but in the case of an objection made under section 194(2) (d) the onus is on the appropriate authority to show that the objection is well founded.

What is the rationale and justification of the 'fifteen-year' provision? Davies says roundly that 'its basic morality seems highly doubtful. Land is unsaleable in any reasonable sense if the freehold cannot be offered to purchasers in an unthreatened state. Here, all that can be so offered is a leasehold for 15 years'.[84] If the provision does not exist to protect owner-occupiers, whom *does* it protect? Is its rationale a 'political' one (that it serves to prevent public authorities acquiring too much land) or an 'economic' one (that it serves to prevent public authorities having to acquire too much land)? What is the value of an undertaking given in the House of Commons during the passage of the provision that 'the Minister will attach very great weight to the counter-notice in considering any subsequent purchase order that may be brought before him . . . the local authority . . . will be bound by it unless it can make out a very strong case why it should not be bound by it'?[85] Is it a sufficient safeguard for the owner that he can serve successive blight notices constantly to extend the fifteen-year period?

(h) Compensation and participation

At first sight it might seem strange to link these two topics: compensation is technical and comes at the end of a process of decision making; participation is political and comes at the beginning and during a process of decision making. The link however exists; it was commented on both by the Skeffington Committee and DoE circular 52/72 on the Committee's report in relation to participation and planning blight, and was highlighted by the process of reform of the compensation code culminating in the Land Compensation Act 1973.

(i) *The conflict between blight and participation*

The conflict and the Committee's conclusion thereon were stated thus by the Skeffington Committee:

212 There is thus a conflict between, on the one hand, the desirability of giving full publicity at an early stage to proposals the planning authority are considering, so as to stimulate informed public discussion and, on the other hand, the need to avoid causing hardship to individuals by the casting of blight over land or property that may not be acquired for many years or, indeed, at all.

213 . . . Some increase in planning blight may have to be accepted if there is to be increased participation by the public.

The Department of the Environment in effect agreed (Circular 52/72):

If, and at whatever stage, authorities decide to present alternatives, however, they should do so in a way which will cause the least possible danger of blight. It may be that in some cases the authority will reach the conclusion that blight is being increased by rumours in the absence of publicity upon feasible options. The danger can never be entirely eliminated whatever publicity course is adopted since it is inseparable from forward planning, publicity and public participation; it is one of the prices to be paid for them; but it should be minimised.

Blight can be minimised both by a decrease in participation and an increase in the possibility of compensation payable where blight can be shown to have occurred. Both have been attempted.

To what extent have the provisions of the Land Compensation Act 1973, which extend the classes of blighted land, met the problem of increased blight caused by increased public participation?

Do you agree with Circular 52/72 that in order to minimise blight 'only realistic alternatives should be published and where the local planning authority have a preference they should indicate this'? To what extent will such a suggestion, if acted upon, so fix blight on a particular area that meaningful public participation, i.e. participation that might result in blight being shifted to another area, will be impossible?

Is a property-owning democracy compatible with participatory planning?

(ii) *Will increased compensation increase public acceptance of development?*
The first official suggestion that there was a connection between increased compensation and decreased public complaints about development came in the Franks Report.

One final point of great importance needs to be made. The evidence which we have received shows that much of the dissatisfaction with the procedures relating to land arises from the basis of compensation. It is clear that objections to compulsory purchase would be far fewer if compensation were always assessed at not less than market value. . . . we cannot emphasise too strongly the extent to which these financial considerations affect the matters with which we have to deal.[86]

Two years after the Report was published market value was restored as the basis of compensation for compulsory acquisition of land. Notwithstanding that fact, the 1960s saw the public participation explosion in planning and an increase in organised opposition to major public developments. Yet the same assumption of connection was voiced by the Secretary of State for the Environment in introducing the Land Compensation Bill to its second reading in the House of Commons:

One cause of hardship has been the absence of a statutory right to compensation where land and property are depreciated in value by public schemes although no part of them is taken by the scheme. This gap is closed by the provisions of the Bill.
All this may mean more work for those who plan roads, and more initial expense. But I believe that it will also have the beneficial effect of

speeding up the administration of development projects. There will, I believe, be less incentive for those affected to obstruct good public schemes by using every legal means at their command.[87]

Is there any basis for this assumption? Would the villagers of Cublington have been less opposed to the siting of the third London airport at Cublington if the Land Compensation Act 1973 had been law in 1971?

There was no noticeable falling away of vigour or enthusiasm of the opponents of the M40 when a public local inquiry into the Birmingham–Warwick part of it opened at Kenilworth in September 1973. Rather the reverse, as they sought to widen the scope of the inquiry to embrace the policy of having a network of motorways in the first place.[88] Is this surprising?

A reason for the likely continuance of opposition to public development was put in the same debate by Mr W. Whitlock:

[The Bill] does not go far enough to bring about a fair balance between provision for the community as a whole and the mitigation of harmful effects on individual citizens, and it does not, as the White Paper claimed it would, put people first. They will still have the same upsetting impact on all our lives. Noises, smells, danger and visual pollution will still be there, even though a little more money changes hands. The loss of a beloved home in a cherished spot will still be just as hard to bear under the Bill's proposals.[89]

The two positions may be summed up thus: in every debate or public inquiry on a proposed public development there is a 'hidden' issue: one school of thought would argue that that issue is the amount of compensation payable and the solution is to increase the amount of compensation payable; the other school would argue that the issue is whether the development is essential or needed and the solution is to increase public participation so that those matters may be debated at large before too many options are foreclosed. Are these two positions irreconcilable? Is it impossible to combine both more compensation for the ultimate losers in the debate on public development and more debate? How does the Land Compensation Act 1973 fit into the picture?

These questions raise once again, in a slightly different context, the issues with which we have been grappling throughout this book. What is and what should be emphasised by the system of planning that we have? Is it more important to get development off the ground, or to allow everybody likely to be affected by it an opportunity to have their say before it gets off the ground? Are the various attempts at holding a balance between these two positions credible or successful? Upon whom and in what proportions should the costs of a system of planning be placed? Is it right to assume that absence of legislation and legally imposed duties on public authorities in respect of particular planning matters betoken absence of commitment by governments on those matters, or are there advantages, not always perceived by lawyers, in non-legal flexibility and broad discretions? Are we any nearer to solutions of these problems now than in 1947?

A more general and fundamental question is raised by this last section, as indeed it has been raised by other parts of the book; it is appropriate, however, to broach it here. What can we learn of the state of relations between governed and government in England and Wales from this study of the planning process – its problems and attempted solutions? Do we see a system of administration too impersonal and uncontrolled to realise that the concerns of ordinary people are not being adequately attended to, or do we see an administration attempting to be responsible to these concerns and trying to balance them against national considerations? Is planning an advertisement for democratic government and the rule of law as those terms are customarily understood in e.g. Western Europe and North America, or is it, as Hayek believes, incompatible with them? How have lawyers adapted one of their traditional roles of standing between state and citizen to the complex world of planning, where the state claims to be acting on behalf of the citizen and for his own good and citizen is often pitted against citizen in an argument about what the public good requires? In short, has planning, besides increasing the powers of government to solve problems, increased its perceptions of what the problems are? Has it, while imposing limitations on our property rights, increased the opportunity for the exercise of our political rights and furthered our social and economic well-being?

Notes

CHAPTER I

1 See Chapter 2 for a discussion of this.
2 *Report of the Committee on Intermediate Areas* (The Hunt Committee), Cmnd. 3998/1969.
3 *Royal Commission on the Distribution of the Industrial Population*, Cmnd. 6153/1940.
4 See Chapter 3 for details.
5 E.g. Civic Amenities Act 1967; Town and Country Planning Act 1968; Town and Country Planning (Amendment) Act 1972; Town and Country Amenities Act 1974.
6 Housing Act 1969; Housing Act 1974.
7 E.g. the establishment of the standing Royal Commission on Environmental Pollution in 1970, and the Control of Pollution Act 1974.
8 Land Commission Act 1967; Land Compensation Act 1973.
9 Senior Tutor in Countryside Planning, Wye College, University of London.
10 S. M. Lipset, 'Some Social Requisites of Democracy: Economic Development and Political Legitimacy', *American Political Science Review*, vol. 53, 1959, p. 86.
11 On this, see Chapter 3, section 4 (d).
12 On this, see Chapter 2, Chapter 3, section 4 (d) and Chapter 5, section 3 (b).
13 *The Road to Serfdom*, 1944.
14 (1848) 2 Ph. 774.
15 (1866) L.R.I. Ex.265 affd. (1868) L.R.3 H.L.330.
16 (1915) A.C. 120.
17 The Town Planning Institute was founded in 1914; it received a Royal Charter in 1970.
18 Professor of City and Regional Planning, University of California, Berkeley.
19 Footnotes omitted.
20 Poet Laureate.
21 Lecturer in Sociology, University College, London.
22 Footnotes omitted.
23 Of Centre Point fame.
24 Euston Centre is (to date) their most famous development. See O. Marriott, *The Property Boom* (1967), chapter 11.
25 '. . . in 1963, he became the first knighted developer'. Ibid., p. 50. Chairman of Land Securities Investment Trust. Raised to the Life Peerage 1972.

26 M. Pye, *Sunday Times*, 12 December 1971, p. 56.
27 Headquarters of the National Westminster Bank.
28 Quoted in Mariott, op.cit., p. 5.
29 Cmnd. 5280, cit., para 25.
30 Ibid., para 26.
31 Marriott, op.cit., picture facing p. 87.
32 Chairman's Report, Annual Meeting 1973.
33 McAuslan, 'The Plan, The Planners and The Lawyers' (1971), *P.L.*, 247; and 'Planning Law's Contribution to the Problems of an Urban Society' (1974), *M.L.R.*, 134.
34 Visiting Professor of Economics, University of Salzburg; formerly Professor of Economic Science and Statistics, University of London.
35 Two non-legal works to which reference may be made are: W. Ashworth, *The Genesis of Modern British Town Planning* (1954), and C. and R. Bell, *City Fathers, the Early History of Town Planning in Britain* (1969).
36 C.13. 12 Ric. 2., *Statutes at Large*, vol. 2., p. 306.
37 C.7. 29 Eliz., *Statutes at Large*, vol. 6, p. 409.
38 C.3. 19 Chas. 2., *Statutes at Large*, vol. 8, p. 233.
39 (1960) 3 All E.R. 503.
40 Ashworth, op.cit., p. 167.
41 Ibid., p. 188.
42 The question of what is development is taken up in Chapter 6.
43 E.g. The Clyde Valley Regional Plan 1946.
44 On this, see Chapter 3, sections 4 (a) and (b).
45 *Luby* v. *Newcastle-under-Lyme Corporation* (1964) 3 All E.R. 169; *Evans* v. *Collins* (1964) 1 All E.R. 808.
46 MHLG Circular 46/67.
47 Rent (Control of Increases) Act 1969.
48 W. O. Hart and J. F. Garner, *Introduction to the Law of Local Government and Administration*, 9th edn (1973), pp. 538–546. The Act was repealed by the Housing Rents and Subsidies Act 1975.
49 P.4.
50 For a general discussion of the whole question of partnership, see the *Report of the Working Party on Local Authority/Private Enterprise Partnership Schemes* (DoE 1972: HMSO).
51 The Alkali Act 1863 established the inspectorate and armed it with powers. The Alkali Code, based on the Alkali etc. Works Regulation Act 1906, as extended from time to time by statutory instruments, now controls processes which consume nearly three-quarters of the fuel used in England and Wales (E. Sharp, op.cit., pp. 126–7).
52 There are some interesting comments on the work of the Public Health Inspectorate in Birmingham in J. Rex and R. Moore, *Race, Community and Conflict* (1967), especially at pp. 32–3 and 135–7.
53 Public Health Act 1848.
54 Housing Act 1969.
55 S.1. 1972, No. 1385. On this, see Chapter 6, section 2 (a).
56 (1723).
57 (1868) L.R. 3 H.L.330. The law of waste is also an example of judicial attempts to regulate conflicting land uses, but between generations rather than between neighbours. Space forbids a discussion of the subject in this book. See R. H. Maudsley and E. H. Burn, *Land Law, Cases and Materials*, 2nd edn (1970) pp. 19–24, and the interesting case of *West Ham Central Charity Board* v. *East London Waterworks Co.* [1900] 1 Ch.624.

58 The law and practice summarised in this paragraph are taken up in more detail in Chapters 5 and 6.

59 See particularly s.65 Town and Country Planning Act, which empowers a local planning authority to serve a notice on the owner or occupier of any garden, vacant site or other open space, requiring them to abate an injury to the amenities of the area if it appears to that local planning authority that the amenities of the area have suffered by the condition of the land. See *Britt* v. *Bucks CC* [1963] 2 All E.R. 175.

60 Amenity 'appears to mean pleasant circumstances, features, advantages' per Scrutton LJ in *Re Ellis and Ruislip-Northwood UDC* [1920] 1 K.B. 343. See further on a possible establishment of an amenity right, Mishan, pp. 71–3 *infra*.

61 *Buxton* v. *MHLG* [1960] 3 All E.R. 408.

62 (1865) 11 H.L.C. 642.

63 [1961] 2 All E.R. 145.

64 (1909) 25 T.L.R. 262. *Aliter* if they had been crying because they were neglected.

65 [1968] 3 All E.R. 545.

66 *Report of the Commission on the Third London Airport*, Chapter 12.

67 Written Statement, p. 50, para. 4.s(20).

68 Thesiger L.J in *Sturges* v. *Bridgman* (1879) 11 Ch. D. 852 at p. 865.

69 C. M. Haar, *Land Use Planning*, 1st edn (1959), pp. 95–6.

70 (1868) L.R. 3 H.L. 330.

71 (1867) L.R. 3 Eq. 409 at p. 412.

72 (1872) 8 Ch. App. 8. at pp. 11–12.

73 (1851) 4 De G. & Sm. 315 at p. 322.

74 [1914] 2 Ch. 47. at p. 57.

75 (1851) 4 De G. & Sm. 315.

76 (1880) 40 Ch. D. 80.

77 [1961] 2 All E.R. 145.

78 [1953] 1 All E.R. 181.

79 [1955] 1 All E.R. 481.

80 'The law relating to the rights of riparian proprietors is well settled. A riparian proprietor is entitled to have the water of the stream, on the banks of which his property lies, flow down as it has been accustomed to flow down to his property, subject to the ordinary use of the flowing water by upper proprietors, and to such further use, if any, on their part in connection with their property as may be reasonable under the circumstances. Every riparian proprietor is thus entitled to the water of his stream, in its natural flow, without sensible diminution or increase and without sensible alteration in its character or quality. Any invasion of this right causing actual damage or calculated to found a claim which may ripen into an adverse right entitles the party injured to the intervention of the court.' *John Young & Co.* v. *Bankier Distillery Co.* [1893] A.C. 691 at p. 698.

81 A similar conclusion was reached by the *Committee on Salmon and Freshwater Fisheries*, Cmnd. 1350 (HMSO 1961), para. 159.

82 Reader in Economics, London School of Economics.

83 (1851) 4 De G. & Sm. 315 at p. 322.

84 (1878) 3 App. Cas. 430.

85 (1881) 6 App. Cas. 193.

86 [1930] A.C. 171.

CHAPTER 2

1 Ministry of Town and Country Planning 1942–51; Ministry of Local Government and Planning 1951; Ministry of Housing and Local Government 1951–69; Ministry of Land and Natural Resources 1965–7; Department of Local Government and Regional Planning 1969–70. Only under the last reorganisation were the fields of transport and public works – up to that point separate ministries undergoing their own constant reorganisations – brought within the purview of the Minister who had control of planning. Prior to 1942 however planning and public works had been yoked together. Housing was the responsibility of the Ministry of Health between 1919–51. E. Sharp, *The Ministry of Housing and Local Government* (1969), pp. 14–15, 23, 232–6.

2 T. Aldous, *Battle for the Environment* (1972), p. 13.

3 Sharp, op.cit., p. 22.

4 Aldous, op.cit., p. 20.

5 Quoted in Aldous, pp. 18–19.

6 *The Reorganisation of Central Government*, Cmnd. 4506/1970 para. 3 (ii).

7 Ibid., para. 31.

8 A. Toffler, *Future Shock* (1970), pp. 122–6.

9 The tensions exist, because, at its simplest, the DTI is concerned to get development going in some areas by e.g. issuing an industrial development certificate while the DoE, concerned with judgements about balance of types of development within particular areas or towns, might refuse planning permission for a development for which an IDC had been issued, or in interdepartmental bargaining appear to be 'dragging its feet' on environmental grounds over a major project the DTI is pushing.

10 Sharp, op.cit., pp. 21–2.

11 Aldous, op.cit., is a good general description of the workings of the DoE.

12 S.I. 1974, No. 1486.

13 *The Deeplish Study, improvement possibilities in a district of Rochdale* (HMSO 1966). The studies have increasingly become more ambitious. See the *Making Towns Better* studies on Oldham, Rotherham and Sunderland (DoE 1973: HMSO) originating 'from a concern that conventional planning and management procedures in local government have, in general, failed sufficiently to improve the conditions of the urban environment'. (Oldham: Vol. 1, para. 1.1.).

14 Cmnd. 3602.

15 E.g. s. 8 (3–5) (withdrawal of structure plan at direction of the Secretary of State owing to inadequate pre-submission publicity). This takes place without a hearing and does not imply rejection of the plan. It is meant to act as a stimulus to ensure adequate public participation. S.10(c) 4 (submission of development plan scheme to the Secretary of State).

16 S. 276.

17 As it does, in theory, in relation to public participation.

18 Chapters 5 and 6.

19 Wolverhampton, Walsall, Dudley, Sandwell, Birmingham, Solihull, Coventry.

20 P. Self, 'The new planning system takes shape', December 1971, *T. & C.P.*, p. 533. D. Senior, 'Memo. of Dissent to Royal Commission on Local Government', Cmnd. 4040–1, p. 100.

21 Districts may petition Her Majesty for a charter conferring on them the status of a borough. Where a petition is granted, the council becomes a borough council and the chairman of the council becomes a mayor. Where a charter is not petitioned for, or not granted, then any former borough wholly comprised in a district finds itself with Charter Trustees, able, *inter alia*, to elect a mayor. Charter Trustees consist of the serving district councillors from the former

borough. Parish/town councillors on the other hand, who are entitled to exercise more powers than Charter Trustees, consist initially of the members of the old local authority (ss. 245–6, Local Government Act 1972). It is hard to see much sense in provisions which give some former local authorities powers and status by right and others status without power dependent on which way a district council votes on the question of borough status. In the upshot, some areas will have embryo neighbourhood or community councils as a third tier, some will not, and others may have them to begin with, then lose them at some indeterminate date in the future.

22 If any authorities are unable to reach an agreement on arrangements, resort may be had to a Minister who may be requested to give a direction on the matter. No direction so given can extend beyond 1 April 1979, s. 110.

23 J. A. G. Griffiths, *Central Departments and Local Authorities* (1966) p. 54.

24 1969. Prepared by a Sub-Committee of the Committee on Administrative Law.

25 *Blackpool Corporation* v. *Lockyer* [1948] 1 All E.R. 85. *Patchett* v. *Leathem* (1949) 65 T.L.R. 69.

26 S. 276 (1).

27 S. 101 (1).

28 H. W. R. Wade, *Administrative Law*, 3rd ed. (1971), p. 340.

29 D. Hall, 'A poor invitation to participation', (November 1971) *T. & C.P.*, p. 484. See too, 'The Participation Swindle', *Community Action*, No. 1, February 1972.

30 Griffith, op.cit., p. 62.

31 Sharp, op.cit., p. 32.

32 For a judicial discussion of the meaning of consultation in relation to the designation of a new town see *Rollo* v. *Minister of Town and Country Planning* [1948] 1 All E.R. 13, and *infra* Chapter 5, section 2.

33 S. 183 Local Government Act adds s.10c to the Town and Country Planning Act; 10c (7) confers these adjudicatory functions.

34 H. A. Simon, *Administrative Behaviour*, 2nd ed. (1957), pp. 12–14.

35 R. G. S. Brown, *The Administrative Process in Britain*, Chapter 7.

36 *Local Government and Strategic Choice* (Tavistock 1969).

37 MHLG 1967: HMSO.

38 At the time of writing this I had served on a local authority for eighteen months.

39 J. Buxton, *Local Government*, 1st ed. (1970) did, in my view. See his rather pessimistic description of local councillors at work at pp. 178–183.

40 *The New Local Authorities: management and structure*, Report of a Working Group (Chairman M. A. Bains), DoE 1972: HMSO.

41 In a paper given at the annual conference of the Town and Country Planning Association, November 1969.

42 The same councillor also made the fair point that all illustrations in the Skeffington Report of participators in action were of *objectors* and not of constructive participators.

43 Senior Lecturer, Extra-Mural Studies, University of Sheffield.

44 *The New Local Authorities, management and structure*, op.cit.

45 Examples from Leamington Spa will be used from time to time in this book. I cannot claim that it was a standard type of local planning authority but I was a member of the borough council for the last two years of its existence and in that capacity had a hand in deciding or debating all the examples used. They were some of the more contentious to arise. Leamington Spa has a population of approximately 45,000 and, when it was a separate unit of local government, exercised power to decide planning applications on a delegated

basis from Warwickshire County Council. On some matters Leamington could decide; on others it could only recommend and the county would decide.

46 *Commission of Inquiry into the siting of the Third London Airport*, Chairman: Mr Justice Roskill.

47 *Special Report from the Select Committee on the Maplin Development Bill* (HMSO, 1973).

48 One could also argue that the opportunities provided for public participation by Warwickshire County Council were too few, but that point is not in issue here.

49 See pp. 110 *infra*.

50 For a good example of the use of technical considerations to try and disguise a political judgement, see the extract from the public examination into the Warwickshire, Coventry and Solihull Structure Plans, Chapter 3, pp. 198–9.

51 Mr A. M. Skeffington was, at the time, Joint Parliamentary Secretary, Ministry of Housing and Local Government.

52 Sometime Comptroller, City of London, Past President Royal Town Planning Institute and The Law Society. Author of *An Outline of Planning Law*, 6th edn (1973).

53 Lecturer in Sociology, University of Strathclyde.

54 Lecturer in Town and Country Planning, Heriot Watt University.

55 Footnotes omitted.

56 The Skeffington Report.

57 See R. E. Wraith and G. B. Lamb, *Public Inquiries as an Instrument of Government* (1971) for a good survey.

58 This is the subject of DoE circulars. See 71/73 reproduced in Chapter 5, section 2 (c).

59 S. Jenkins, 'The Press as Politician in Local Planning' (1973), 44 *Pol. Q.*, 47.

60 In the first clash however – the *Chalkpit* case, 1961 (Griffith and Street, *Cases on Administrative Law*, pp. 142–74) – the Council lost the battle but arguably won that particular phase of the war, for the verbal formula on the extent of the Minister's powers to consult with and take advice from officials after the inquiry over which the Council had been in dispute with the government was, in the following year, incorporated into the inquiry regulations and so made subject to a judicial rather than a ministerial final interpretation.

61 However, second thoughts about the desirability of third-party rights were implicit in some of the questions posed for consideration and discussion by Mr G. Dobry in his review of development control.

62 *Sunday Times*, 2 September 1973, reporting that the DoE had conceded that the question of the need for a motorway could be raised at a public inquiry into the Warwick extension of the M40 Birmingham–Oxford–London motorway.

63 A. M. Potter, 'Attitude Groups' (1958) 29 *Pol. Q.*, 72.

64 The fortunes of this group have been discussed from time to time in *The Times* on Saturdays by Halladora Blair. The series started in mid-1972.

65 H. E. Bracey, *People and the Countryside* (1970), p. 219.

66 Professor of Local Government Studies, University of Birmingham.

67 Skeffington, op.cit., para. 59.

68 Para. 7.

69 Harrison, *New Society*, 12 April 1973.

70 The Government published a consultation paper in July 1974 in which it stated that it was 'favourably inclined' to legislate for the establishment of neighbourhood councils in England. It recognised, however, that diversity and local initiative were the key features of existing successful neighbourhood councils and that any legislation should have full regard to those considerations.

Thus neighbourhood councils would not be imposed on all urban areas regardless of need and local wishes.

71 Lock, 'To balance the scales', *T. & C. P.*, March 1973, p. 163.

72 White, *New Society*, 29 June 1972. The problems that these more radical community action groups encounter and cause are summed up in the above article as follows: '. . . at the Covent Garden public inquiry, Austen Williams (Chairman of the C.G.C.A.) agreed with counsel for the GLC that the Community's campaign was part of a "world-wide struggle against giantism and authority." And Jim Monahan agrees: Covent Garden is "part of a national problem, whereby local and national government have lost touch with the people."

'This concept of a macrocosm of inhuman planning, related to the microcosm of Covent Garden, is shared by most of the architects and planners in central London community action. Hence the "spawning" of new barricades. The Piccadilly group is encouraging the people of Soho to prepare to resist development. The CGCA is taking up the plight of Cambridge Circus, and young activists are spreading the gospel of Covent Garden as far away as Liverpool.

'Small wonder that at Westminster City hall, all hope of a "dialogue" between the radicals and the planners has vanished. How, say the planners, can there be any discussion when the radicals want to change not merely the plans but the society we live in? Why so negative an attitude on the part of the young people towards comprehensive redevelopment? Why so reactionary? For it denies the process of urban regeneration that created Bloomsbury and Regent Street.

'"There is a danger of architects and planners turning into Fabian luddites," observes Cedric Price, an architect who lives and works nearby. "They forget the opportunism of people. Would a dirty-book seller want to stay in Soho if it became a fey conservation area of their kind? A dimension, the time being, is missing from their thinking. And the opportunity for people to be able to change their minds.'

CHAPTER 3

1 For a general analysis of the problems in the UK in the 1960s see G. McCrone, *Regional Policy in Britain* (1969). On this point, p. 92.

2 Chairman: Sir Montague Barlow.

3 Fellow, Brasenose College, Oxford.

4 See P. Hall, *The Theory and Practice of Regional Planning* (1970), p. 74.

5 DoE Circular No. 85/71 – Reorganisation of Regional Offices of the DoE.

6 DoE Circular No. 48/72 – Decentralisation of the DoE's administrative work on planning matters.

7 HMSO 1965.

8 *The West Midlands: A Pattern of Growth*, Introduction.

9 Ibid.

10 Quoted in B. Cullingworth, *Problems of an Urban Society*, vol. 1 (1973), p. 78, from an unpublished document.

11 'The Report has been called "highly indecisive": the "strategy" proposal is "plaint in terms of its breadth of response and the range of its dimensions". A critic has referred to it as "a cotton wool report" which is "feminine in its submissiveness. . . ." The Report rapidly ran into the opposition of Birmingham City Council who complained of the inadequate relief that the plan would provide for the city's housing problems and – to the extent that relief was provided – of the serious damage which would be suffered if the city were

drained of its population and industry. Thus the essentially political nature of the whole process is demonstrated.' Cullingworth, op.cit., pp. 78–9.

12 s. 4(2)(3), Sched. 1 Pt. 1 Town and Country Planning Act 1947.

13 HMSO 1970.

14 In a private communication afterwards, members of the study team indicated that they had welcomed that line of questioning but had not encountered it in any of the other meetings.

15 Past President RTPI. Chief Planner: DoE Member: PAG.

16 Committee on Administrative Tribunals and Enquiries, Cmnd. 218.

17 Chairman: Lord Redcliffe-Maud.

18 McAuslan, 'The Plan, the Planners and the Lawyers' (1971), *P.L.*, 247.

19 *The Future of Development Plans*, para. 1. 46. The word 'better' appears constantly in the Report in relation to plans, planners, public participation and results. The Report radiates a kind of mechanistic optimism which was obviously very persuasive.

20 What does that mean?

21 Past President RTPI. Past President ILA, FRIBA. A paper delivered of a meeting of the RTPI.

22 Cf. Town and Country Planning (Amendment) Act 1972, discussed at pp. 225–33.

23 Cf. the establishment by the DoE of the Review of Development Control by Mr G. Dobry in October 1973 largely owing to a very rapid rise in the number of planning applications and appeals and a widespread realisation that the system of development control was in danger of breaking down.

24 In the debate that took place on this paper Dr W. Burns defended the Report against 'some of the really mischievous things' said.

25 See s. 8(1) Town and Country Planning Act. Mr MacDermot is referring to the words 'the local authority shall take such steps *as will in their opinion* secure'. (italics added). Is he right?

26 This is now 8(3).

27 See now s. 9 of the Act amended by the Town and Country Planning (Amendment) Act 1972, discussed on pp. 225–33.

28 The first order was made in July 1971. Town and Country Planning Act 1968 (Commencement No. 6) (Teeside etc.) Order 51. 1971 No. 1108.

29 S.I. 1971, No. 1109.

30 Italics added. An order was made bringing the relevant parts of the Act into operation in Warwickshire on 25 July 1972. Town and Country Planning Act 1971 (Commencement No. 1) (West Midlands) Order S.I. 1972, No. 1060. Another order brought amendments made by the Town and Country Planning (Amendment) Act 1972 into operation in Warwickshire on 11 September 1972. Town and Country Planning Act 1971 (Commencement No. 5) (West Midlands) Order S.I. 1972 No. 1314.

31 As a district in a metropolitan county, Coventry would retain control of education, whereas if it became a district of Warwickshire it would lose control of education to Warwickshire. Neither political party in Coventry wanted to see the city lose control of its education service.

32 Parl. Deb., H. of L., Vol. 316, cols 1120–31. 'My main criticism of the Government's proposals is that in some areas they simply do not apply their own criteria. . . . If I may give another example where it seems to me that politics have dictated what is proposed rather than local government it is in the suggestion that Coventry should be part of the West Midland Metropolitan area. This honestly is nonsense. There is very little connection in the sense of commuting travel to work and so forth between Coventry and the West

Midland conurbation and Coventry, as you have only to look at your map to realise it is part and parcel of Warwickshire. . . . If you want an example of the hopelessness of trying to settle the reorganisation of local government according to the wishes of individual local authorities, this is a perfect one.' What is the difference between 'politics' and 'local government'?

33 A particularly strong critic of the government's local government reforms was D. Senior, the dissenting member of the Royal Commission on Local Government. He delivered a strong attack on the Proposals for Reorganisation, Cmnd. 4584, in a paper – Strategic Planning in the New Metropolitan areas – given at the annual meeting of the Town and Country Planning Association in 1971.

34 J. R. Long, *The Wythall Inquiry: A Planning Test Case* (1961), Cullingworth, op.cit., pp. 76–9.

35 Added by s. 183 Local Government Act 1972.

36 Standing Committee B, session 1971–2, Local Government Bill 1972, col. 1901.

37 Deb. cit., col. 1903.

38 ss. 10A and 10B were added by the Town and Country Planning (Amendment) Act 1972.

39 S. 11(1)(2)(9A) were respectively amended and added by the Local Government Act 1972.

40 See p. 162.

41 Paras 3.23–26.

42 All contributions were unscripted and are unchanged apart from correcting obvious spelling errors which may be put down to defects of transcription. It would seem unfair if I 'doctored' my own contribution while others did not have the opportunity to correct or amend theirs.

43 Chairman of the panel of examination.

44 I was appearing as one of a group of individuals opposing certain parts of the Warwickshire Structure Plan.

45 The Worcestershire Structure Plan was scheduled for its public examination in early 1974.

46 I quoted Regulation 8 and Circular No. 44/71 as a background to the points then made.

47 Does it?

48 See section (d) (ii) *infra* for the public examination. Is this a fair comment on s.9 of the Act?

49 I went on to develop some more 'political' points about the way Warwickshire was handling the whole process of structure planning. When Mr Heaton asked the representative from Warwickshire if they wished to comment on what I had said, they confined their comments to answering the political points and did not deal with the question of relationships between plans.

50 Is it a matter of opinion or a matter of law as to whether the Secretary of State was right to accept the submitted structure plan?

51 Warwickshire Structure Plan, para. 3.26.

52 *The Future of Development Plans*, para. 5.16.

53 Town and Country Planning (Structure and Local Plans) Regs. 1974, Reg. 15(1).

54 Regulations, Sched. 1 P. II(i).

55 Regulations, Sched. 2 P. II(i).

56 Italics added.

57 See F. Hayek, *The Road to Serfdom* in Chapter 1, pp. 31–3 above, and P. Payne, *Planning Appeals* in Chapter 5, pp. 471–4.

58 For a survey of structure planning and the use of the manual, see (1973) J.R.T.P.I. 115 (J. B. McLoughlin).

59 *The New Local Authorities* (HMSO, 1972).

60 *supra* p. 20.

61 McLoughlin, op.cit.

62 (1973) *J.R.T.P.I.*, 121.

63 Para. 17.

64 Professor of Local Government Studies, University of Birmingham.

65 Deputy Director, Institute of Advanced Urban Studies, University of Bristol.

66 B. Cullingworth, *Problems of an Urban Society*, vol. 2, Chapter 5, from which much of this section is derived.

67 HMSO 1967.

68 Ibid., Chapter 5.

69 *Children and their Primary Schools: Report of the Central Advisory Council for Education* (England) (HMSO 1967).

70 *Report of the Committee on Local Authority and allied Personal Social Services*, Cmnd 3703.

71 Cmnd. 3703, p. 150.

72 Home Office, *Urban Needs in Britain*, 23 June 1970, cited in Cullingworth, op.cit., p. 141.

73 Director of the Planning Aid Centre, Glasgow.

74 Community Development Project: *Objectives and Strategy*, 1969.

75 S.7(4)(a).

76 para. 46.

77 McLoughlin, op.cit., p. 120.

78 This point was made by the then Deputy County Planning Officer in answer to a question put at a public meeting on the draft county structure plan in September 1972.

79 Cullingworth, op.cit., p. 143.

80 *supra*, p. 205.

81 PAG Report, op.cit., paras 1.49, 7.39.

82 Deb. cit., esp. cols. 1903–4, 1972 JRTPI, 151.

83 McLoughlin, op.cit., p. 123.

84 Ibid., p. 123.

85 *Tomorrow's London: A Background to the Greater London Development Plan* (GLC 1970) p. 44, quoted in Cullingworth, op.cit., p. 150.

86 PAG Report cit., para. 7.39.

87 Ibid., para. 2.5.

88 McLoughlin, op.cit., p. 118.

89 E.g. economists and sociologists (Report footnote).

90 Examples of these are: 'The Council's main aims are . . . and to give new inspiration to the onward development of London's genius' (WS para. 2.16); 'Development schemes throughout London should provide as many new dwellings as a good standard of environment will allow' (WS para. 3.26); 'The Plan . . . /seeks/ to provide the greatest residential capacity in London commensurate with the aims of the Plan as a whole' (WS para. 3.26); '. . . for in the face of the competition of the car, a background of good public transport service must be maintained to serve all Londoners . . .' (WS para. 5.6); 'The Council's policy is the . . . objective of improving public transport in all possible ways' (WS para. 2.9). (N.B. A GLC witness, see Transcript Day 175 p. 15B, agreed this statement was wholly imprecise, and even potentially misleading). (Report footnote.)

The same criticism could be made of many of the twenty-four objections of the Warwickshire Structure Plan. Among them were the following:

4. To locate all new development so that the safety of the public is protected from both natural and man-made hazards.

5. To locate new housing where good living conditions can be ensured.

8. To provide the best possible shopping facilities in convenient locations.

9. To ensure that social, community, educational and recreational facilities are provided in step with population growth, and are conveniently located.

10. To provide employers with suitable sites having good access to labour, markets, necessary services and transport.

11. To provide the widest choice of jobs and the maximum opportunity for all who wish to work to do so.

12. To help areas where industry is declining.

13. To avoid changes which will disturb existing development.

21. To provide a choice between the private car and public transport and to create optimum conditions for the operation of efficient and convenient bus and rail services.

22. To provide the most efficient and convenient road system.

23. To minimise the journey to work.

91 Op.cit., p. 121.

92 Unlike Coventry, Warwickshire's Project Report was not available to the general public.

93 I wrote an article for the *Leamington Spa Courier* on public participation and the plan criticising the short time during which the draft plan could be publicly discussed in view of the fact that two of the three months allowed for debate were holiday months when traditionally political and similar activity were at their lowest level of the year. I hoped that this article might spark off a reply from some planner or county councillor but none was forthcoming. A leading Leamington Spa Conservative attacked the County Council some time later on the same grounds and was answered in public by the Chairman of the County Council's Town and Country Planning Committee who defended the Council's process in a vigorous fashion.

94 It produced a 10 per cent return. Is this statistically insignificant or a triumph for public participation? Both views were advanced at a private meeting of councillors.

95 I received unofficial reports that the DoE was none too happy with the questionnaire but Warwickshire rejected the criticism and went ahead.

96 Not surprisingly, as the implications for urban expansion within the Kenilworth–Leamington Spa–Warwick area of the county structure plan began to emerge from the questionnaires and tentative draft maps of the urban structure plan, opposition began to arise to the likely urban structure plan. Almost certainly it is too late since the policies which made such urban expansion necessary lie embedded in the county structure plan, and were not adequately discussed at the public examination because the urban structure plans and policies were not available.

97 Report, Appendix 3, reprinted Coventry's evidence on how it ran participation for its Development Plan Review exercise in 1966.

98 There were 27,000 objections lodged to that plan. The inquiry took over two years.

99 Report cit., para. 1.15.

100 Para. 2.15.

101 One such concerned Coventry's need for land for housing. Coventry's figures were challenged and explained away publicly. Privately it was admitted that an error had been made in the calculations. A probing discussion would have exposed that error in public. Would anything have been gained by so doing?

102 One of the few to appear was Mr Layfield QC on behalf of a potential hyper-

market developer. He read the panel a little essay on the nature of structure planning and the role of the public examination. He was thanked in suitably deferential terms.

103 All participants were asked to write in with their comments on the procedure. These were followed up by discussions with participants where relevant.

104 *Supra* pp. 145–52.

105 'The proposals contained in this written statement are, in the Council's view, justified by the supporting Reports of Survey and by such other information as they have obtained. In particular, this is contained in the following documents:- ... (vii) "A strategy for the Sub-Region" (viii) "A Developing Strategy for the West Midlands Planning Authorities Conference".' (para. 14).

Even more explicit references are contained in the minutes of the Town and County Planning Committee of the Warwickshire County Council. Thus, after its April 1971 meeting, the Committee reported: 'It is expected that the ... Sub-Regional Planning study will be published within the next two months and will recommend the broad framework for the Structure Plans for the three constituent authorities.' And after its June 1972 meeting, the Committee reported: 'The County Structure Plan has been prepared on the basis of the report and recommendations of the ... Sub-Regional Planning Study which was adopted by the Council in November last and after full consultation with the various Committees of the Council.'

106 Minutes of the Town and County Planning Committee of the Warwickshire CC, September 1972. Co-operation and liaison were on an informal basis and had already been achieved through the sub-regional and regional studies.

107 The Schedules of the Regulations dealing with what local authorities shall, if they see fit, include in their surveys and local plans are in much the same terms as the schedules dealing with the structure plans reproduced *supra* at pp. 188–90. A possibly significant difference is highlighted at p. 200 *supra*.

108 S. 6(1) of the 1971 Act.

109 s. 14(5) of the 1971 Act as amended by the Local Government Act 1972.

110 S.I. 1974, No. 1486.

111 See Chapter 5, section (b)(ii)(c).

112 McLoughlin op.cit., p. 122.

113 Brenda White, 'Information Inside and Outside the Local Authority', T. & C.P.A. Conference on Development Control, January 1974.

114 McLoughlin, op.cit., p. 122.

115 McLoughlin, op.cit., p. 122.

116 S. 4(1) of the Town and Country Planning (Amendment) Act 1972 substituting a new s. 19 and Sched. 4 for the original provisions of the 1971 Act.

117 Evans, op.cit., p. 122.

CHAPTER 4

1 Law Commission, No. 11.

2 J. H. Beuscher, *Land Use Controls, Cases and Materials*, 3rd ed. (1964), p. 92.

3 (1848) 2 Ph. 774. On the common law position, see Cheshire's *Modern Real Property*, 11th ed. 1972, pp. 579–82.

4 (1822) 2 M. & K. 522.

4a *Mann* v. *Stephens* (1846) 15 Sim. 377.

5 (1834) 2 M. & K. 547.

6 Law Commission, No. 11.

7 See Cheshire's *Modern Law of Real Property*, op. cit., pp. 502–44, for easements.

8 (1882) 20 Ch. D. 562.

9 (1881) 6 App. Cas. 740.
10 At p. 824.
11 (1752) 2 Ves. Sen. 453.
12 (1862) 13 C.B. (N.S.) 841.
13 (1859) 7 H.L. Cas. 349.
14 1587 cited in *Aldred's Case* (1606) 9 Coke 58(a).
15 [1964] 2 All E.R. 35.
16 Pp. 37–8. It must be doubted whether in this particular case that conclusion was correct. The two houses involved were Nos 16 and 14 Market Street, Warwick. No. 14 was pulled down as a result of a demolition order served by Warwick Corporation, and the action was brought by the owner of No 16. It is at least arguable that in an old town such as Warwick, 'desirable improvement' comes about through renovation and not demolition of old buildings.
17 (1848) 2 Ph. 774 at p. 777.
18 (1858) 4 De G. & J. 276 at p. 282.
19 (1869) L.R. 4 Ch. App. 654.
20 (1877) 7 Ch. D. 227.
21 (1882) 20 Ch. D. 562 at p. 583.
22 Scrutton J. in *LCC* v. *Allen* [1914] 3 K.B. 642 at p. 667.
23 [1914] 3 K.B. 642. The quotation is at p. 672.
24 [1903] 2 Ch. 539.
25 [1906] 1 Ch. 386.
26 [1914] 2 Ch. 231.
27 D. J. Hayton, 'Restrictive Covenants as Property Interests' (1971), 87 L.Q.R. 539 at pp. 540–1.
28 Fellow of Jesus College, Cambridge. Footnotes to the article omitted.
29 [1964] Ch. 38.
30 [1966] 1 All E.R. 937.
31 [1968] Ch. 508.
32 [1962] V.R. 274 at p. 293.
33 (1789) 3 T.R. 393.
34 (1878) 9 Ch. D. 125.
35 (1882) 20 Ch. D. 562.
36 (1854) 1 Kay 560.
37 [1933] 1 Ch. 611.
38 [1952] 1 All E.R. 279.
39 [1922] 2 Ch. 309 at p. 319.
40 [1937] 2 All E.R. 691.
41 [1898] 2 Ch. 394.
42 (1877) 6 Ch. D. 521.
43 [1966] 1 All E.R. 937.
44 Megarry J in *Brunner* v. *Greenslade* [1970] 3 All E.R. 833 at p. 842.
45 D. J. Hayton, op.cit., p. 539.
46 [1908] 2 Ch. 374.
47 (1879) 11 Ch. D. 866.
48 (1888) 14 App. Cas. 12.
49 [1939] 2 All E.R. 503.
50 [1938] 1 All E.R. 546.
51 *Baxter* v. *Four Oaks Properties Ltd supra*.
52 [1914] 3 K.B. 642. The quotation is at p. 673.
53 S. 148 Housing Act 1936.
54 S. 34 of the 1932 Act.

55 *Encyclopedia*, Vol. 2, Part II, para. 2–2729.
56 Megarry J in *Brunner* v. *Greenslade* [1970] 3 All E.R. 833 at p. 842.
57 [1938] 2 All E.R. 158.
58 [1956] 3 All E.R. 802.
59 Davies and Salmon LJJ delivered concurring judgements.
60 Chairman: Lord Wilberforce.
61 Not reproduced.
62 A Working Paper – *No. 36, Appurtenant Rights* – was published in July 1971. See however Housing Act 1974 s. 126, which provides for the enforcement of covenants 'to carry out any works or do any other thing on or in relation to land' between a council and 'a person having an interest in land in their area . . . .' The council is empowered to enter on the land and do the covenanted work if there is a breach of the covenant.
63 Based on research carried out with the helpful co-operation of Wates Ltd in February and March 1971.
64 See section 6 of this chapter.
65 [1957] Ch. 169, Cmnd. 2719, para. 8(iv).
66 [1957] 3 All E.R. 164.
67 Lord Gardiner.
68 Law Commission, No. 11. Proposition 9(a).
69 [1962] 1 W.L.R. 902.
70 [1972] 3 All E.R. 77.
71 (1883) 8 App. Cas. 623.
72 [1907] 2 Ch. 366.
73 [1938] 2 All E.R. 230.
74 [1910] 2 Ch. 12.
75 Law Commission, No. 11. Proposition 9(b).
76 Newsom, op.cit., 5th ed., Appendix II, pp. 308–11. '. . . paragraph (a) (of section 165) cannot be regarded as entirely spent, as was hinted in earlier editions of this book. . . . It is submitted that notwithstanding the rather narrow wording of paragraph (a) this section could be very much more useful than it in fact is . . . it is admirably adapted to be employed in an epoch when people want smaller places to live in. The real trouble is that few practitioners have any idea how it works, or how it could work . . . If [the jurisdiction] was transferred to the Lands Tribunal and thus focused, the reported cases of a year or two could transform the situation and make this jurisdiction really useful.'
77 [1904] A.C. at p. 775.
78 (1930) 37 O.W.N. 392.
79 (1931) 40 O.W.N. 572.
80 [1945] 2 D.L.R. 244.
81 Secretary of State for Home Affairs.
82 Carried out in 1971. Some of the information in the following pages also comes from the reports of the inspectors who held inquiries in accordance with s. 19 of the Act into the question of whether a certificate should be granted by the Minister allowing the owners of the estate to retain certain management powers notwithstanding enfranchisement. See the text of s.19, on pp. 338–42.
83 Cmd. 7982.
84 However, one of the major complaints of residents opposing the grant of a certificate to the Trustees of the Calthorpe Estate at the public inquiry was that the management was not efficient or vigorous about enforcing the covenants and did not welcome tenants' complaints about its failures. The answer given

was that the management tended not to enforce covenants very vigorously in areas where leases were about to fall in. Does such an answer support or counter the case for enfranchisement?

85 *The Bournville Estate*, op. cit.
86 Set out in some detail in paras 22–34 of the inspector's report.
87 This may seem harsh but it was an essential part of the case of the Trustees before the inspector that the estate did enjoy good relations with the Birmingham planning authorities and that Birmingham's civic leaders supported what the estate was trying to do. The chief witness for the estate, Mr Greening, the resident agent, quoted an approving statement made by Alderman Sir Frank Price, ex-Lord Mayor and Chairman of the Public Works and Planning Committee of the city council at a time when the estate's development proposals were being formulated. Also called on behalf of the estate was Mr A. G. S. Fidler, city architect of Birmingham between 1952–64 and a resident of the estate during his tenure of that office. His evidence was reported by the inspector as follows: '. . . many influential citizens who have the interest of the city at heart live there and have not moved outside the city boundaries . . . As an expert planner he would be very sorry indeed to see an area such as Edgbaston lose its unique character. . . . In the witness' experience the Calthorpe Estate had always administered its land ownership in a responsible manner. . . . It had been concerned with the retention of those features and those controlling factors that contribute to civilised living.'
88 Landlord and Tenant Act 1954.
89 Leasehold Reform in England and Wales, Cmnd. 2916/1966, which set out the case for enfranchisement.
90 Sixteen of the estates joined together to put forward a memorandum on the Bill. It was extensively referred to in the debates in the House of Commons, particularly by Mr Graham Page, the official opposition spokesman on the Bill.
91 At the time Parliamentary Secretary, Ministry of Housing and Local Government.
92 A former Minister of Housing and Local Government.
93 H.C. Stndg. Cmte. B., Vol. IV, Session 1966–7, cols 589–90.
94 Secretary of the Association.
95 [1971] 3 All E.R. 1283.
96 [1972] 2 All E.R. 177.

CHAPTER 5
1 J. B. McLoughlin, *Control and Urban Planning*, Faber 1973.
2 paras (a) (b) and (c) refer to mineral workings, (e) to operations in a National Park and (f) prescribed operations.
3 Italics added.
4 Circular No. 74/73.
5 Part II of the Town and Country Planning General Development Regulations S.I. 1969 No. 286 required a county council, on notice served by a county district council with a population of 60,000 or more, to delegate most of their development control functions to that county district council on terms set out in the Regulations. Delegation to other district councils was settled by individual agreement.
6 HMSO 1967.
7 Planners' slang for non-statutory informal plans, e.g. town centre maps; McLoughlin pp. 124–6.
8 s. 101 applying the principle of delegation contained in the (now repealed)

s. 4 of the Town and Country Planning Act 1971 to most of the field of local government.

9 R. & Co's letter of reply to SLAM caused one officer to come to the next meeting of the Plans Sub-Committee to deny what he took to be an implication in the letter that he had agreed to R & Co's suggestions for certain measures of pollution control. The Sub-Committee eventually reversed its recommendation to the County Council, who were not, in any event, going to grant permission.

10 Up to the end of 1974, fourteen policy notes had been issued on the following topics: 1. General Principles 1969; 2. Development in residential areas 1969; 3. Industrial and commercial development 1969; 4. Development in rural areas 1969; 5. Development in town centres 1969; 6. Road Safety and traffic requirements 1969; 7. Preservation of historic buildings and areas 1969; 8. Caravan sites 1969; 9. Petrol filling stations and motels 1969; 10. Design 1969; 11. Amusement Centres 1970; 12. Hotels and Motels 1972; 13. Out of Town Shops and Shopping Centres 1972; 14. Warehouses – wholesale, cash and carry, etc.

11 McLoughlin, op,cit., goes some way towards giving us information on the matter but only in rather general terms.

12 Brown, 'Town Maps or Town Centre Maps' [1965] J.P.L. 413.

13 J. G. Buxton, *Local Government*, 1st edn (1970).

14 N. Dennis, *People and Planning* (1969); *Public Participation and Planner's Blight* (1972).

15 It may be doubted whether the pathway will change very much in the re-formed local authority structure.

16 *Wilson* v. *Secretary of State for the Environment* [1974] 1 All E.R. 428 discusses the various methods of giving public notice of a particular action to be taken in relation to land where no specific provision is made by the legislation. In that case, a notice was held inadequate because of the misdescription of the piece of land to which it referred and applicants were held to have been substantially prejudiced by that misdescription because they had thereby been deprived of the opportunity to make representations against an application to appropriate common land for highway improvement.

17 *Report of the Working Party on Local Authority/Private Enterprise Partnership Schemes* (HMSO 1972).

18 J. F. Garner, *Administrative Law*, 3rd edn (1970) p. 74.

19 *Rollo* v. *Minister of Town and Country Planning* [1948] 1 All. E.R. 13.

20 A possible case in point here is *Agricultural, Horticultural and Forestry Industry Training Board* v. *Aylesbury Mushrooms Ltd* [1972] 1 All. E.R. 280. Under the Industrial Training Act 1964, section 4(1) 'Before making an industrial training order, the Minister shall consult any organisation or association of organisations appearing to him to be representative of substantial numbers of employers engaging in the activities concerned. . . .') the Minister was minded to establish a training board for the agricultural etc. industry. A draft order was prepared and circulated to *inter alia* the Mushroom Growers' Association, a specialist branch of the NFU with whom preliminary consultations had taken place. No comments were received from the MGA and the order was ultimately made. It subsequently transpired that the Ministry had dealt primarily with the NFU and although the MGA had been sent copies of relevant documents, they had never received them. The court held that the MGA, though small (180 members out of 150,000 in the NFU), was an organisation which had to be consulted, that consultation had not taken place vicariously via the NFU and that on the facts the Minister had not discharged his duty of consultation, i.e. the fact that the communication from the Ministry had not been received

by the MGA meant that no consultation had taken place. 'In truth the mere sending of a letter constitutes but an attempt to consult and this does not suffice. The essence of consultation is the communication of a genuine invitation, extended with a receptive mind, to give advice' [p. 284]. Would it be possible to argue that no 'genuine invitation' had taken place if it was issued so late in the process that advice received was extremely unlikely to influence the final outcome of the decision?

21 That part of his judgement is reproduced in Chapter 6, section 3, p. 573.

22 Lord Parker CJ and John Stephenson J agreed with this judgement.

23 With slight variations, this problem came before the Warwick Borough Council.

24 R. N. D. Hamilton, *A Guide to Development and Planning*, 5th ed. (1970) p. 109. The author was at the time Deputy Clerk of the Buckinghamshire CC.

25 Now s. 53 of the 1971 Act. The section deals with applications to determine whether planning permission is necessary.

26 [1958] 2 All. E.R. 174.

27 s. 64.

28 Replacing s. 4 of the Town and Country Planning Act 1971.

29 Does it?

30 Para. 4.20.

31 These were proposed to the Policy and Resources Committee of the Warwick District Council to which such a sub-committee would report.

32 See J. D. Stewart, *Developments in Corporate Planning in British Local Government* (1973), Loc. Govt. Studies 13.

33 There are many studies of local authorities in action in the planning and allied fields. Some have been quoted or referred to already, reference may also be made to P. Hall *et al*, *The Containment of Urban England* (1973), especially Vol. 2, for a general survey of the effects of planning. See too S. Crowther's, *Making Planning Decisions: The Councillor and his officers*, T & CPA Conference on Development Control, 1974.

34 [1973] 2 All E.R. 26.

35 At p. 32.

36 1965 (unreported).

37 See *Sagnata Investments* v. *Norwich Corporation* [1971] 2 All E.R. 1441 at pp. 1447–8 per Lord Denning MR.

38 (1971) 22 P. & C.R. 718 at p. 726. The whole case is worth reading for a good description of the planning process in action in relation to an obviously contentious issue. It is too long to reprint in full and too detailed to reprint only an extract.

39 These sections deal with time limit conditions (41,42 reprinted in part on pp. 430–1 *infra*), industrial development (70), and office development (77–80) certificates.

40 McLoughlin's did not research into them during his investigations into development control. This is an area where the planner often takes second place to the lawyer in practice; it would seem pre-eminently to be an area where the lawyer could investigate and report on the practice.

41 *Kent CC* v. *Kingsway Investments (Kent) Ltd* [1970] 1 All E.R. 70. Now provided for by ss. 41–44 of the 1971 Act.

42 Now s. 63 of the 1971 Act.

43 Now s. 30 of the 1971 Act.

44 Repealed by the 1968 Act.

45 Cf. *R.* v. *London Borough of Hillingdon ex. parte Royco Homes Ltd* [1974] 2 All E.R. 643.

46 [1958] 1 All E.R. 625 at p. 633.
47 [1947] 2 All E.R. 680.
48 [1898] 2 Q.B. 91.
49 [1963] 2 All E.R. 175.
50 [1958] 1 All E.R. 625 at p. 637. The dictum was approved by a majority of the House of Lords in *Kent CC* v. *Kingsway Investments (Kent) Ltd.*
51 [1958] 1 All E.R. 625 at p. 633.
52 Melford Stevenson and Bridge JJ agreed with this judgement.
53 M. Albery: What and when is a planning decision (1974) 90 L.Q.R. 351.
54 [1966] 3 All E.R. 964.
55 [1963] 2 Q.B. 196.
56 [1961] 1 W.L.R. 561.
57 [1969] 2 Ch. 305 at p. 315.
58 [1963] 2 Q.B. 764.
59 [1970] 3 All E.R. 496 See p. 443 *infra*.
60 Megaw LJ agreed with the judgement of Lord Denning MR.
61 [1967] 2 All E.R. 1041.
62 Lord Denning MR at p. 1044.
63 Pp. 1047, 1050.
64 Wraith and Lamb, op.cit., p. 61. Circular No. 142/73 the Secretary of State announced that in future he intended 'to be more selective about calling in applications . . . for [his] decision. Applications will in general only be called in if planning issues of more than local importance are involved; they will not be called in merely on grounds of local controversy.' para. 11.
65 Sec. 45 (3)
66 S. 51.
67 S. 53.
68 [1967] 2 All. E.R. 1041.
69 Chapter 6, section 2 for details.
70 S. 276.
71 Although all local inquiries are public, the local press does not always give good coverage either of an impending inquiry or of the progress of one. When there is an issue of importance, the press can be a potent force for alerting the public to it, but what is important to the press and what to sections of the public can differ. For a good discussion on the role of the press in planning see Jenkins, op.cit., Chapter 2, footnote 59.
72 Wraith and Lamb, op.cit., pp. 198–200.
73 'At some stage during these communications, a site visit is carried out by an official from the Ministry (not necessarily in the presence of the parties). The "official" need not necessarily be an inspector – he could, for example, be an executive officer – since site visits in these simpler cases may not call for professional knowledge. On the other hand, since 1 January 1969 most written representations cases would normally be transferred to an inspector for decision and he would make the site visit himself.' Wraith and Lamb, op. cit., p. 199.
74 'The written representations procedure is now believed in the Ministry to be approaching "saturation point". The Ministry has always had discretion whether or not to offer a written appeal, or indeed whether to order an inquiry even if both parties wished to use the written method, but the percentage of appeals probably cannot be raised very much more without endangering the interests of third parties, or else reaching decisions on information which is not as complete as that which would be furnished by the inquiry method. In other words, not much more than 50 per cent of cases can be called simple enough to be dealt with in writing.' Wraith and Lamb, op. cit., p. 200. If the authors

are right, what is meant by saying that there is 'scope' for even further use of this method?

75 Town and Country Planning (Determination of appeals by appointed persons) (Prescribed classes) Order S.I. 1972, No. 1652. For statutory provisions governing the exercise of the power see Sched. 9, paras 1 and 2 of the 1971 Act; and Town and Country Planning (Determination by Appointed Persons) (Inquiries Procedure) Rules S.I. 1974, No. 420.

76 Wraith and Lamb, op. cit., p. 181.

77 In an article at [1960] J.P.L. 384, Mr Desmond Heap advanced the view that where a planning officer does not agree with the decision of his authority, someone acting as advocate should put forward the local authority's view and that some other representative for the authority (not the planning officer) should act as witness to support that case.

78 In *Coleen Properties Ltd* v. *MHLG* [1971] 1 All E.R. 1049, a case on compulsory acquisition under s. 43 (2) Housing Act 1957, Lord Denning MR said: '[the inspector] was clearly of the opinion that the acquisition of Clark House [the property in question] was not reasonably necessary. I can see no possible justification for the Minister in overruling the inspector . . . . The question of what is reasonably necessary is not planning policy. It is an inference of fact on which Ministers should not overrule inspectors' recommendations unless there is material sufficient for the purpose. There was none here.' Do you agree with this statement?

79 Pamela Payne MBE is a Principal in the Department of the Environment. The views expressed in the paper are her personal views and not those of the DoE.

80 Prize-winning essay in the Haldane Essay Competition 1968.

81 See Chapter 3, section 4(b) pp. 226–7.

82 P. Self, 'A Planning Charade', *T. & C.P.*, September 1970, p. 366. He went on: 'It is a rotten instrument for arguing generally about planning policies.'

83 P. Self, 'The Lessons of the Airport Saga', *T. & C.P.*, June 1971, p. 292 at p. 294.

84 R. Gregory, *The Price of Amenity* (1972), p. 27.

85 Self, *T. & C.P.*, September 1970, p. 367.

86 *Ibid.* p. 367.

87 McLoughlin (Solomon), op. cit., p. 56.

CHAPTER 6

1 Thus books on administrative law do not discuss cases dealing with such questions as the unit of development and the meaning of an 'operation' on land. Similarly, books on planning law do not discuss, though they may briefly mention, the general principles of administrative law.

2 [1967] 2 All E.R. 1041 at p. 1047.

3 H. W. Wilkinson, 'Wording an Enforcement Notice', 117 Sol. J. 496 at p. 497.

4 Sub. s. 4(a). This repeats a provision first put into the law in 1960.

5 S. 87(3) Town and Country Planning Act 1971 below.

6 S. 94; see pp. 506–9 below.

7 S. 90; see p. 489 below.

8 S. 177.

9 [1955] 2 All E.R. 269.

10 [1959] 2 All E.R. 213.

11 (1702) 1 Salk. 377; 91 E.R. 378.

12 [1969] 2 All E.R. 525; see below pp. 513–18.

13 Buckley LJ agreed with this judgement.

13(a) [1963] 1 All E.R. 150.

13(b) Stamp and Roskill LJJ agreed with this judgement.

14 [1904] 2 Ch. 34.

15 [1957] 1 All E.R. 497.

16 [1968] 3 All E.R. 153.

17 [1969] 2 All E.R. 525.

18 Ashworth and MacKenna JJ agreed with this judgement.

19 R. N. D. Hamilton, *A Guide to Development and Planning*, 5th edn, p. 65.

20 (1973) 71 L.G.R. 28. On the question with which this case dealt, see J. E. Alder, *Planning Conditions and Existing Rights* (1972), 36 Conv. 421.

21 He referred to *Pyx Granite* v. *MHLG* [1958] 1 All E.R. 625, *Fawcett Properties* v. *Bucks CC* [1960] 3 All E.R. 503, *Hall & Co. Ltd.* v. *Shoreham-by-Sea UDC* [1964] 1 All E.R. 1, *Allnatt London Properties* v. *Middlesex CC* (1964) 15 P. & C.R. 288, and *Kent CC* v. *Kingsway Investments (Kent) Ltd* [1970] 1 All E.R. 70.

22 H. J. J. Brown, 'Material Change of Use within the definition of Development', (1974) *J.P.L.*, 180.

23 F. H. Lawson, *An Introduction to the Law of Property*, p. 16.

24 H. J. J. Brown, *Planning Law and Practice from the Decisions*, Encyclopedia of Planning Law and Practice Vol. III Pt. VI, para. 6–085.

25 [1945] 1 All E.R. 191.

26 [1948] 2 All E.R. 95.

27 [1961] 3 All E.R. 878. The quotations come from pp. 884–5.

28 Ashworth and Hinchcliffe JJ agreed with this judgement.

29 *Estates Gazette*, 6 May 1966.

30 [1967] 3 All E.R. 981. *infra* pp. 539–41.

31 [1968] 2 All E.R. 633.

32 (1969) 67 L.G.R. 109.

33 At p. 113.

34 Brown, op. cit., para. 6–058.

35 [1964] 2 All E.R. 543.

36 (1961) 11 P. & C.R. 284.

37 (1965) 17 P. & C.R. 22.

38 Edmund Davies LJ agreed with this judgement.

39 [1961] 3 All E.R. 878.

40 *Webber* v. *MHLG* [1967] 3 All E.R. 981, at p. 984.

41 (1963) 61 L.G.R. 423.

42 *Bendles Motors Ltd* v. *Bristol Corporation* [1963] 1 All E.R. 578.

43 *Burdle* v. *Secretary of State for the Environment* [1972] 3 All E.R. 240.

44 S. N. L. Palk, 'The Planning Unit', (1973) 37 *Conveyancer*, 154.

45 [1972] 3 All E.R. 240.

46 Op. cit., pp. 173–4; footnotes omitted.

47 [1961] 3 All E.R. 878.

48 See, too, Lord Denning MR's judgement on p. 539 *supra*.

49 (1967) 19 P. & C.R. 90.

50 At p. 97.

51 (1967) 65 L.G.R. 495.

52 [1972] 3 All E.R. 240.

53 At p. 244.

54 Cusack and Croom–Johnson JJ agreed with this judgement.

55 [1966] 1 All E.R. 701.

56 Lord Widgery CJ and Willis J agreed with this judgement.

57 But see *De Mulder* v. *Secretary of State for the Environment* [1974] 1 All E.R. 776, which shows that the position might not be as easy as Palk suggests.

58 As to which, see S. A. de Smith, *Judicial Review of Administrative Action*, 3rd ed.;

J. F. Garner, *Administrative Law*, 4th ed. Chapter 6; H. W. R. Wade, *Administrative Law*, 3rd ed.; J. A. G. Griffith and H. Street, *Principles of Administrative Law*, 5th ed., Chapters 4 and 5. See too J. E. Trice, 'Administrative Law Reform and Planning Law', (1972) 36 Conv. 375.

59 s.29(i)(a) Town and Country Planning Act 1971.
60 H. W. R. Wade, *Administrative Law*, 3rd ed. p. 51.
61 Wade, op. cit., p. 198.
61a op. cit. p. 210.
62 [1964] 2 All E.R. 492.
63 [1933] 2 K.B. 696., All E.R. Rep. 21.
64 [1935] 1 K.B. 249.
65 *Offer* v. *Minister of Health* [1936] 1 K.B. 40.
66 Wade, op. cit., p. 196.
67 S. 10 (3).
68 S. 9 (7), 14 (4)(e), Town and Country Planning Act 1971.
69 [1947] 2 All E.R. 395.
70 [1967] 2 All E.R. 1066.
71 J. A. G. Griffith and H. Street, *A Casebook on Administrative Law*, pp. 142–174. The case is also briefly discussed in McAuslan, 'The Plan, the Planners and the Lawyers', (1971) *P.L.*, 247, at pp. 253–4.
72 [1933] 2 K.B. 696.
73 At p. 703.
74 Wade, op. cit., p. 198.
75 [1947] 2 All E.R. 289.
76 As quoted in Lord Thankerton's judgement at p. 296.
77 He quoted passages from the speech, one of which is set out above.
78 This speech was agreed to by the other Law Lords hearing the case.
79 Wade, op. cit., p. 185.
80 See P. H. Levin, 'Towards Decision-making Rules for Planners', (1967) *J.T.P.I.*, 437.
81 [1971] 1 All E.R. 65, pp. 409–12 *supra*.
82 [1972] 3 All E.R. 77, pp. 316–18 *supra*.
83 [1961] 2 All E.R. 46, pp. 440–3 *supra*.
84 [1970] 3 All E.R. 496, pp. 443–6 *supra*.
85 Wade, op. cit., pp. 68–9.
86 [1966] 3 All E.R. 696, pp. 464–6 *supra*.
87 At. p. 698.
88 [1970] 3 All E.R. 871.
89 At. p. 880.
90 J. E. Trice, 'The Problem of Locus Standi in Planning Law' (1973) *J.P.L.* 580.
91 ss. 244, 245 Town and Country Planning Act.
92 s. 245 (1) (a).
93 [1960] 3 All E.R. 408; the case was part of the *Chalkpit* case.
94 (1880) 14 Ch. D. 458.
95 [1961] 2 All E.R. 504.
96 (1887) 19 Q.B.D. 174.
97 [1964] 1 All E.R. 779.
98 At p. 782.
99 This was that, probably through an oversight, an appeal to the court under s. 245 of the Town and Country Planning Act 1971 did not lie from the Secretary of State's decision given under call-in powers in respect of an application for approval of any local planning authority required under a development order, which it was accepted this decision was.

100 Wade, op. cit., pp. 128, 138–9.
101 [1933] 2 K.B. 696.
102 Per Avory J at p. 704.
103 [1924] 1 K.B. 171.
104 [1963] 2 All E.R. 66.
105 (1870) L.R. 5 Q.B. 466.
106 [1964] 2 All E.R. 492.
107 [1960] 3 All E.R. 408.
108 Published Working Paper No. 40, *Remedies in Administrative Law*, para. 125.
109 Ibid., para. 131.
110 R. E. Wraith and G. B. Lamb, *Public Inquiries as an Instrument of Government*, chapter 6; J. F. Garner, 'The Council on Tribunals' (1965) *P.L.*, 321.
111 J. A. G. Griffith and H. Street, *A Casebook on Administration Law*, pp. 142–174.
112 'Comment', (1966) *P.L.*, 1. See too the Crossman Diaries, *S.T.*, 9/3/75.
113 10 February 1966, in reply to a statement made by Mr Crossman on 9 February in the House of Commons on the Special Report of the Council.
114 Mr J. Boyd-Carpenter, an ex-Minister who had introduced the motion of censure on Mr Crossman.
115 Garner, *Administrative Law*, 3rd ed., p. 192.
116 Wraith and Lamb, op. cit., p. 236.
117 Wade, op. cit., p. 276.
118 De Smith, *Constitutional and Administrative Law*, 2nd ed, p. 560.
119 P. Jackson, 'Work of the Parliamentary Commissioner for Administration' (1971) P.L. 39; H. W. R. Wade, 'The British Ombudsman, a lawyer's view' (1972) 24 Adm. Law Rev. 137; D. Foulkes, 'The Discretionary Provisions of the Parliamentary Commissioner for Administration Act 1967' (1971) 34 M.L.R. 377.
120 *Second Report of the PCA*, Session 1971–2, Case C.414/s, para. 17.
121 Case 245/L, *Second Report of the PCA*, session 1971–2, p. 71.
122 Local Government Act 1974, Part III. The Commissions consist of full-time or part-time Local Commissioners. They must submit annual reports to bodies designated by the Secretary of State as being representative of local authorities in England and Wales. Complaints alleging maladministration must be made in writing to a member of a local authority who may then refer it to the Local Commissioner for his investigation. Before proceeding to investigate a complaint, a Local Commissioner must satisfy himself that the complaint has been brought to the notice of the local authority and that that authority has been afforded a reasonable opportunity to investigate and reply to the complaint. No investigations shall be made in respect of matters that the complainant had a right of appeal in relation thereto to a tribunal or a Minister or a remedy by way of proceedings in any court. In addition 'a Local Commissioner shall not conduct an investigation in respect of any action which in his opinion affects all or most of the inhabitants of the area of the authority concerned'. [s.26(7)] Would this rule out complaints about the lack of public participation in the making of a structure or local plan?

CHAPTER 7

1 *Report of the Expert Committee on Compensation and Betterment*, Cmd. 6386/1942.
2 K. Davies, *Law of Compulsory Purchase and Compensation* (1972) p. 111.
3 Ibid., p. 180.
4 This section does not purport to deal with all the difficult economic questions involved in land values and the effect planning has on them. For these, see

B. Goodall, *The Economics of Urban Areas* (1972); and R. Drewett (Chapters 6 and 7) in P. Hall *et al.*, *The Containment of Urban England* (1973), vol. 2.

5 Senior Lecturer, Department of Economics, University of Liverpool.

6 Royal Commission on the Distribution of the Industrial Population Cmd. 6153, paras. 250–256.

7 DoE Circular No. 102/73, paras. 16–23.

8 Cmnd. 5280.

9 This proposal had not been enacted into law by the time the then government was defeated in the general election of February 1974. The government had also proposed taxation of development gains on the disposition of land (H.C. Deb., Vol. 866, col. 952) and this was taken over by the incoming government and enacted in the Finance Act 1974 Pt. II and Schs. 3–10. It was made clear, however, that this was an interim measure pending more radical changes in relation to development land (Cmnd. 5730, paras 39–45).

10 D. Massey, R. Barras and A. Broadbent, 'Labour must take over land', *Socialist Commentary*, 21 June 1973. D. Lipsey, *Labour and Land*, Fabian Tract No. 422; J. Brocklebank, N. Kaldor, J. Maynard, R. Neild and O. Stutchbury, 'The Case for Nationalising Land' (1973). Public Enterprise No. 7 Aug./Sept. 1974, 'Public Ownership of Land'.

11 Porter, op. cit., p. 62.

12 Tanzania is the only country I know of that changed all freehold into leasehold titles. The legislation that achieved this – Freehold Titles (Conversion and Government Leases) Act 1963 – is far and away the most complex piece of legislation passed by the legislature of Tanzania since independence. The draftsman of it told me he regarded it as one of his most challenging tasks. On the Act see R. James, *Land Tenure and Policy in Tanzania* (1970), Chapter 6.

13 Drewett in P. Hall *et al.*, op. cit., pp. 209–10.

14 Ibid., p. 222.

15 T. & C.P.Assoc., op. cit., para 9(a).

16 Drewett in P. Hall *et al.*, op. cit., p. 244.

17 Op. cit. para. 12.

18 Ibid., para 14. On the general question of the market for land see Drewett in P. Hall *et al.*, op. cit., Chapter 7.

19 Cmd. 6386, para. 17.

20 Ibid., para. 38(b)(ii).

21 Ibid., para. 38.

22 Conservative MP.

23 This consisted of an examination of such things as location of sewage facilities, merits of the land from an agricultural and landscaping points of view, ease of access to public transport, etc.

24 *Coventry Evening Telegraph*, 24 October 1973.

25 K. Davies, *Law of Compulsory Purchase and Compensation* (1972) on which this part heavily relies. J. F. Garner (ed.), *Compensation for Compulsory Purchase* (UKNCCL series No. 2) 1975.

26 Per Lord Warrington of Clyffe in *Colonial Sugar Refining Co Ltd* v. *Melbourne Harbour Trust Commissioners* [1927] A.C. 343 at p. 359.

27 (1888) 13 App. Cas. 446.

28 Lord Cohen and Lord Keith of Avonholm agreed with this judgement.

29 The relevant rules were the Town and Country Planning (Inquiries Procedure) Rules 1965 (S.I. 1965, No. 473); see now the Town and Country Planning (Inquiries Procedure) Rules S.I. 1974, No. 1486, particularly r. 12 (2).

30 Now s. 289, Town and Country Planning Act 1971.

31 [1927] A.C. 343 at p. 359.

32 [1947] 2 All E.R. 680 at p. 685.
33 Circular 696/1954.
34 Lord Morris of Borth-y-Gest and Lord Guest agreed with this judgement.
35 Per Lord Reid *supra*.
36 Prepared by a Sub-Committee of the Committee on Administrative Law; Chairman: D. Widdicombe QC.
37 Cmnd. 6386, para. 35.
38 Davies, op. cit., Part I, for a full account of the procedures.
39 At p. 118.
40 (1868) L.R.5 Eq. 227.
41 s. 57, Town and Country Planning Act 1944; s. 55(2), Town and Country Planning Act 1947; s.14, Town and Country Planning Act 1959.
42 [1952] 1 All E.R. 531.
43 [1915] 2 Ch. 252, at p. 258.
44 [1966] 3 All E.R. 161.
45 Megaw LJ agreed with this judgement.
46 Some of the rules here set out are discussed in cases in this chapter; Rule 5 was discussed in the *West Midland Baptist Trust* case; Rule 6 – disturbance – is discussed under that heading *infra* p. 672; Rule 2 cannot be discussed in isolation from the planning assumptions surrounding market value. Rule 1 prevents any *solatium* being paid over and above market value as was the case before the Act of 1919. Rule 4 it is suggested is self-evident. Rule 3 is slightly different to the *Pointe Gourde* principle. It refers to the land and not the products of the land. For a discussion of this Rule see *Lambe* v. *Secretary of State for War* [1955] 2 All E.R. 386.
47 For ss. 7 and 8, see Davies, op. cit., pp. 123–5.
48 Town and Country Planning Act 1959. Though slightly reworded, the section corresponds to s. 6 and Sched. 1 of the Land Compensation Act 1961.
49 D. Heap, *Outline of Planning Law*, 6th edn, p. 260.
50 Davies, op. cit., p. 138.
51 [1951] 2 All E.R. 587, at p. 599.
52 Lords Reid, Hodson, Guest and Diplock agreed with this judgement.
53 Davies comments in a footnote at p. 141: 'There is a hidden distinction at the root of this difficult matter. It is between an assumption as to planning permission, which is highly artificial and utterly dependent on the statutory provisions, and an assumption as to factual occurrences. Valuers must continually make assumptions as to facts, particularly future facts, because that is what "the market" is all about. This distinction, though hidden, in fact gave the Lands Tribunal no trouble: but it led the House of Lords into treating valuers' assumptions as to relevant facts as if they were not a question of expertise but a question of law.'
54 [1966] 3 All E.R. 161.
55 Buckley and Roskill LJJ agreed with this judgement.
56 Davies, op. cit., Chapter 9; and 'Injurious Affection and the Land Compensation Act 1973', (1974) 90 *L.Q.R.*, 361.
57 (1869) L.R. 4 H.L. 171.
58 Davies, op. cit., p. 151.
59 (1889) 14 App. Cas. 153. The quotation from Lord Watson is at p. 167.
60 [1961] 2 All E.R. 145.
61 (1874) L.R. 7 H.L. 243. It is sometimes said that the *McCarthy* case laid down 'four rules' governing this head of compensation but 'it would be truer to say that the rules are derived from cases generally on this question'. (Davies, op. cit., p. 156). In any event, the fourth 'rule' – that loss should be caused by the

execution and not by the use of the works – has been largely abrogated in respect of works first used on or after 17 October 1969 by the Land Compensation Act 1973.

62 D. M. Lawrence, *Compulsory Purchase and Compensation*, 4th edn, p. 133.

63 (1867) L.R. 2 H.L. 175.

64 (1882) 7 App. Cas. 259.

65 Lord Hodson and Lord Diplock agreed with this judgement.

66 Cmnd. 5124.

67 Op. cit., para. 59.

68 *Jubb* v. *Hull Dock Co.* (1846) 9 Q.B. 443.

69 (1929) Unreported.

70 The value of this provision may have been somewhat reduced by the decision of the Court of Appeal in *Hendy* v. *Bristol Corporation* (1974) 72 L.G.R. 405. The Court decided that the section does not require that a displaced person be given priority over all other persons on a council's housing list, or that, if the person was previously in accommodation protected under the Rent Act, that he must be given equivalent security of tenure.

71 I would like to thank my colleague David Farrier for allowing me to use in this section and section (h) extracts from a first draft of an article we wrote jointly for the UK National Committee on Comparative Law's colloquium on 'Compensation for Compulsory Acquisition and Planning Blight' in August 1973. For the full text, see Garner (ed.), *Compensation for Compulsory Purchase*, chap. 2.

72 A point conceded under questioning by an experienced valuer attending the colloquium on compensation.

73 F. I. Michelman, 'Property, Utility and Fairness', 80, 1165.

74 Ibid., pp. 1215–6.

75 Ibid., p. 1223.

76 The question of consumer surplus is taken up again in Appendix 23 to the Report under the heading, 'Householders' Surplus'. The Appendix reports on two other surveys done, one by the Commission's Research Team, the other by the British Airport Authority. Their methods and results were as follows:
9. The Research Team's survey used a direct approach. After some introductory questions respondents were asked what they thought was the market value of their house or flat. They were then asked to suppose that a developer was willing to make an offer and to say what price would be sufficient to compensate them for leaving. Householders' surplus was measured by the percentage increase of the latter sum over the former. In both cases removal expenses and any taxes or levies were expressly excluded.
10. There is no reason to suppose that all answers accurately measured such a surplus. . . .
12. . . . . The questionnaire for the British Airports Authority's survey did not require market price to be estimated nor mention a development and so is free of the distortions which these might have introduced. The interview started with questions about the local area and then asked respondents if they would move to an area five or more miles away if they found the comparable house price there was so much lower that a profit of £100 could be made after paying all expenses. If £100 were said to be insufficient this was followed by two further questions, the first asking how much would be required and secondly, if no figure were then named, whether a sum equal to the value of the respondents' present house would be sufficient.
13. The results of these questions can be compared with those derived from the Research Team's survey by multiplying the percentages calculated from the

latter by its average price. The comparison is given in Table 1 below and shows that up to £2,500 the distributions are closely similar.

TABLE 1   Inducement required to give up house (Cumulative percentage of respondents)

BAA survey		Research Team survey	
Inducement	%	Inducement	%
Up to £150	12	Up to £150	11
„ „ £450	16	„ „ £450	13
„ „ £950	29	„ „ £950	27
„ „ £1,500	49	„ „ £1,500	46
„ „ £2,500	55	„ „ £2,500	57
£2,500+	62	Up to £4,500	75
Would not sell and		„ „ £10,000	87
sum not stated	38	£10,000+	92
		Would not sell	8

77 S. 180. Town and Country Planning Act 1971.
78 Ibid., s. 193.
79 Ibid., ss. 180–91.
79a [1958] 3 All, E.R. 322.
80 Ibid., ss. 192–207.
81 H.L. Deb., Vol. 215, col. 1043, quoted in the notes to s. 192 Town and Country Planning Act 1971, *Encyclopedia of Planning Law and Practice*, para. 2–3185.
82 S. 77(2) L.C.A. 1973.
83 Davies, op. cit., p. 210.
84 Ibid., p. 211.
85 H.C. Stand. Comm. G, 28 March 1968, col. 729, quoted in Hamilton, op. cit., p. 47.
86 Cmnd. 218, para. 278.
87 H.C. Deb., Vol. 847, col. 39 (Mr Rippon).
88 Cf. the comment of Mr B. Douglas-Mann in the same debate: (Deb. cit., col. 40): 'When we had the proposals for Westway, running through North Kensington, the objections were not based on financial factors but on the effects of the road on the community.' But see DoE Circular No. 30/73 – *Participation in Road Planning*. This provides for increased publicity and participation in respect of road proposals but states that the Department of the Environment does not think it appropriate for the general underlying policy of road building to be brought into question in relation to the various stages of development of individual schemes. It is always possible for anyone to raise the need for a particular road policy at any time with the Department but (para. 15): 'it is not really appropriate to attempt to crystallise opinion on it at the public participation stage because there is not at that stage a specific proposal worked out in detail in relation to which the question can be determined'.
89 Deb. cit., col. 73.

Index

Abandonment of use, case illustrating, 531–3
Acquisition of land, compulsory *see* Compulsory purchase
Action area, 167, 168, 186, 187
  plans relating to, 163, 196, 200
Administrative controls, 579–601
Administrative law
  defined, 485
  fundamental principle of, 558–66
  judicial control, 558–601
  a principle of, 409
Afforestation, 3–5
Agriculture, use of land productivity in, 5–6
Amenity groups
  and costs of inquiries, 120–1
  growth of, 127
  local effectiveness of, 130–6, 364
  role of, in planning, 126–36, 481
Ancillary uses, cases illustrating, 537–41
Annexation
  and restrictive covenants, 254–5
  cases of, 255–8
  defined, 254–5
Anti-planning view, 22
Appeal(s) 436–9, 466–9, 481–2
  and the principle of judicial review, 556
  cases of, 490–5, 503–6
  impact of in planning, 471–4
  rights of, 479–80
  time aspect of, 500–2

Assignment of restrictive covenants
  cases of, 258–9
  defined, 259–72
Atmosphere, pollution of (case), 53–61
  see also 'Nuisance'
Audi alteram partem rule, 559–61

Barlow Commission (Royal Commission on the Distribution of the Industrial Population) (1940), 143, 144, 605, 608
Bath, replanning of, 131–6
Battersea corruption, 30
Betterment, compensation and, 2, 606, 607–12, 633–6
Betterment levy, 611
  changed into capital gains tax, 612
Bias, aspects of, 573
Blight and participation, conflict between, 696–7
Blight and planning, 168, 220, 228, 635, 689–96
Blight notices, 689–96
Borough Engineer, say in planning applications in Leamington Spa, 401–2
Boundary disputes, during local government reorganization, 177–8
Bourneville Estate, management of, 332
Breach of planning control, 487–9
Building Regulations, 41
Built-up areas, measures for, 609

'Call-in' procedure concerning
planning permission, 449–50
Calthorpe Estate
application for certificate, 341–6
development plan, 334
management of, 332, 344–6
Capital gains tax, enforced in 1971,
612
Caravan sites and planning
permission, 490–7, 539–41, 563–6
Casework carried out by planners,
361–3
Central Government circulars, 366–7,
373–7
control at the level of, 449–82
general constraints, 365–8
guidance in planning, 480–1
influence on planning, 379
nature of, 92
specific constraints, 365–6
Centre for Environmental Studies, 17,
22
Certificate of appropriate alternative
development, 650
Certificate
'valuable', 652
'nil', 652
Certification of local plan, 182–3
Certiorari
action for, 381–4
an order of, 426–8, 685
discussed by Wade, 572–8
Change of use, 541–58
a material, 534
of degree of use (cases), 526–31
permitted development, 556
Civic Trust, 127, 128
Claim for injurious affection, 662–72
Commencement orders, 175–6
Communications
for planning permission, 431–48
legal effects of informal, 440–8
Community Councils, role in
planning, 140–1
Community Development Project,
role in planning of, 139–40
Community governance, analysis of,
18–19
Community life
and development officer, 138–9,
220
and estate management, 333–5
and recent planning, 16

Compensable and non-compensable
restrictions, 634–5
Compensation, 2, 623–41
and betterment outline of
recommendations, 608–10
solutions as regard to (1942–71),
607–12
and disturbance, 672–8
and home loss payments, 680–2
and participation, 696–9
as regards to depreciation and
injurious affection, 662–72
assessing, 605
assessment of (case), 636–40
assessment of, shift in the law of,
670–2
case referred back to the arbitrator,
675–8
cases regarding, 624–30, 651–3
land values and, 602–99
no legal right to, 624–35
personalised, 682
restriction of on 'new development',
632–3
rules for assessing, 642
time factor in assessment, 636–41
Compulsory purchase of land, 603
Acts in connection with, 316
and compensation, 45, 602, 646,
651–3, 663
cases illustrating, 624–30
inverse, 684–96
procedures relating to, 636
proposal on, 614–17
Conservation
affect on local government, 87
legislation and, 1
Conservative position on property and
ownership, 621–2
Corporate Planning, 17
and structure planning, 202–7
area of concern in, 204–5
Bain's Report, 96–7, 203
Costs
and amenity groups at inquiries,
120–1
arising at inquiries, 125–6
awarding of, in public local
inquiries, 115–26
Council for the Protection of Rural
England, 30, 127, 128
activities of, 129
Council on Tribunals, 484

effectiveness of, 590
function of, 579–90
Councillors *see* Elected members
Countryside Commission, 81
County Councils, functions of, 84–7
Coventry
  experience in, 99, 140, 233
  public examination of structure
    plans, 197–9, 234

Decision-making, 7–8
  changes in planning, 7
  effect of law and politics on, 97
  in planning, 94–101
  powers of Department of the
    Environment, 449–82
  public participation in, 97–111
  role of Minister in, 96
Default powers, 451–2, 593
Demolition, 23, 46–8, 92, 513–18
Department of the Environment,
  decision making powers of, 449–82
Depreciation and injurious affection,
  662–72
  caused by use of public works, 668–
    72
  not resulting from taking the
    claimants land, 666–8
  resulting from taking the claimants
    land, 662–5
Developers, 26–30
  acceptance of conditions, 415
  declining status of, 29–35
Development
  by the Crown, 375–82
  control of, 509–44
  depreciation and injurious affection,
    662–72
  directions restricting permitted,
    554–7
  in built-up areas, 609–10
  lay-out of, 395–6
  outside built-up areas, 608–9
  permitted, 554–8
  procedure on departure from plan,
    404–5
  unit of, 541–2
  within the curtilage of a dwelling-
    house, 555–6
Development control
  important sources of advice, 366
  introduction of policy notes, 367

policies, 412–31
power of local authorities in, 356–
  69
public law on, 350–483
recommendations by Dobry, 477–83
Development land, increases in the
  cost of, 619
Development order, 353, 371
Development plans, 154–67, 334
Development plan scheme, 178, 179,
  182, 184–7, 243
  objections to, 180
  see also District plan *and* Structure
    plan
Development Plan System, 222
Development Plans, costs of appeals
  against, 121–4
Development rights scheme,
  recommendation with regards to,
  608–10
Development value, 607
  consequence of nationalisation, 610
Discontinuance orders, 451
District Councils
  functions of, 84–7
  plan-making powers of, 178–81
District plan *see* Local plan
Disturbance
  and compensation, 672–8
  new category of payments (1973),
    677–8

Educational needs
  of elected members, 20
  of planners, 18–21, 210–11, 481
  of public, 97, 110–12, 114, 139,
    220–1, 481
Effect of the common law principle of
  nuisance on planning law,
  48–65
Elected member, 368–9
  at public examinations, 232
  attitude of caseworkers towards, 363
  decision delegation to officers, 397–8
  function of, 108–10
  functional relations with others,
    103–4, 364
  role in decision making, 96–7, 99,
    399
  training opportunity needs, 20
Enforcement notices, 451, 483, 486–
  518
  as seen from the courts, 486–7

Enforcement–*cont.*
   as seen from the Department of the
      Environment, 486–7
   stop notice, 487, 489
Environment, Department of the, 8,
      77–82
   adjucatory functions of, 94
   creation of, 77–80
   consultation with local authorities,
      93–4
   planning responsibilities and power
      of, 80–3
   relations with local authorities, 87–
      90
Environmental Pollution, Royal Com-
      mission on, 129
Estates, control over by long lease,
      329–49
'Established use certificate', 487, 506–9
Estoppel, use of, 43–9, 442

Flats
   planning permission for, 388–92
   positive covenants on, 292–8
   restrictive covenants, 273, 279, 308–
      14
Floating value, defined, 605–6
Franks Committee (Committee on
      Administrative Tribunals and
      Inquiries), 114, 116, 124, 154,
      231, 350, 459, 697

Garden Cities Association, 11
Government circulars, 84–6, 116–17,
      152–3, 181–4, 190–1, 194–6, 206–
      7, 218–21, 358–9, 367–8, 373–5,
      375, 375–6, 381, 386, 387, 396,
      398, 402–3, 405–6, 412–14, 416–
      17, 427, 452–3, 475–6, 688–9
   functions of, 90–3
   list of other communications, 80
Greater London Development Plan
      (Layfield Report), 8, 24, 213–16,
      226
Green Belt Land released for
      development, 612–13

Home loss payments,
   right to, 680
   amount of, in England and Wales,
      681
Houses-let-in-lodgings, case cited,
      526–31

Ideology
   and public policy in planning,
      13–16
   a statement on a social issue, 588
   upper class, 25–6
Improvement line (cases involving),
      592, 627–30
Inquiry *see* Public local inquiry
Inspectorates
   alkali, 44
   for housing and planning, 452–3,
      459, 463–70, 482
   Public Health, 44, 134
Inverse Compulsory Purchase, 684–96
   see also Compulsory purchase,
      Planning restrictions
Issues of departmental bias, 562–5

Judicial control
   administrative law, 558–601
   planning law, 489–558
Judicial regulation of land use via
      nuisance, 48–65
   case studies, 51–65

Land
   intensity of competition for, 2–6
   seasonal use of (case), 539–41
   use of referred to in 1971 Act, 351–3
Land-use control
   common law of nuisance issue, 48–
      65
   exercised by counties, county
      boroughs, and regions, 40
   'modern' legislation, 46
   since the 1875 Act, 39–40
Land-use planning
   and control, changes in laws dealing
      with, 1
   control and development since the
      1840s, 37–48
   decisive legal cases in, 11
   function of, 7–8
   function of inspectorates in, 44
   increase in public power in, 41
   influence of socio-economic changes
      in, 43
   legislative history of, 34–38
   public local inquiry in, 9
   reforms and innovations in, 1–3
Land Hoarding Charge, 613–17
Land Nationalisation, points on, 607–8

Land outside built-up areas,
measures for, 608–9
Land Values
and compensation, 602–99
and planning, 603–7
Lands Tribunal, 290, 291, 292, 297,
303, 304, 306, 307, 308, 314, 315,
336, 613
role of, 655–6
Law Commission, 298, 314, 318
Lawyers in the administration of
planning, 30–3
Leasehold estates
control by the ground landlord,
329–33
enfrachisement of, 336
redevelopment of, 342
relationship with local authorities,
334–5
Legislation
post-industrial revolution, 37–48
pre-industrial revolution, 34–7
Lettings and planning permission
(case), 526–31
Local Administration in England and
Wales, Commission for, 601
Local Authorities
central government constraints on,
365–9
conflicting plan-making powers,
171–4
consultation and informing between,
377–8
consultation with Department of
Environment, 93–4
control over planning, 354–69
co-operation between, 181–2
loan sanctions against, 89
necessary consultation in preparing
structure plans, 201
planning disputes, ministerial
intervention, 183–4
power of, 11, 41, 43, 45, 387
relations with Department of
Environment, 87–90
restrictive covenants and, 315–21
see also County Council, District
councils, Parish councils
Local authority housing, fixing of
rents, 41
Local Government
area committees, 137–8
creation of metropolitan areas, 83–4
division of responsibilities in, 156–7
functions of, 84–7
reorganization of, 79–80, 96–7, 104,
137–8
reforms in the system of, 171–4
Local inquiries, 475–6
see also Inquiries
Local plan, 173, 180, 183, 184, 194,
196, 236
and public participation, 216–33,
234–41
approval by Secretary of State,
238–9
certification of, 180, 182–3
directions and creation of, 187
future of, 241–4
rejection or recommendation of by
inspector, 239–41
relationship with structure plan,
199–200
Locus standi, 566–90
London Airport
action against a third, 105
report on (1971), 682–3

Management of Local Government
(Maud Report), 96
Management schemes and positive
covenants, 299–302
Market value
and property, 602
assessment of, 641–62
defects of basis of compensation, 678
definition of, 641
Material change, question of, 544
Metropolitan areas, creation of, 83–4
see also Local Government
Metropolitan county councils see
County Councils
Metropolitan district council see
District Council
Ministerial or departmental hearing,
452
written representations, 452–3

Natural Justice, rules of, 559–61
National Parks, 178, 356, 357, 378, 608
and 'call-in' procedure, 450
National Trust, and enforcement of
restrictive covenants, 286
necessity to ask opinion of, 23
Nature Conservancy, control of land
development, 378

Negative easements, examples of, 249,
    250, 251
Neighbourhood, nature of discussed,
    319–21
New Town Development Corporations
    81, 82
New Urban developments, 4
Noise, case of excessive, 61–5
Noise and nuisance in law, case of,
    53–61
'Nuisance', 662
    and amenity, 71–4
    and public development, 74
    action regarding, 74–6
    in law (cases of), 51–65
    legal actions in pollution control, 2,
        65–71
    legal aspects dealing with cases,
        48–65
    noise and, 53–61
    see also Pollution

Official Arbitrators, 303, 304
Operations, in relation to land and
    planning, 511–18
Outline applications, rationale of, 385,
    96
Ownerships Certificates, 380–5

'Packington Estate' Islington
    report on proposals for
        redevelopment in, 581–90
Parish Councils
    functions of, 86
    functions of new, 84
Performance Review Sub-Committee,
    399
Permissions, communications of, 431–2
Permitted development, 554–8
    directions restricting, 554–7
Physical planning
    characteristic of, 25
    failures of, 23–6
    relationship to regional economic
        planning, 144
Planners, 17
    and control, 360–5
    and the law, xxv
    attitude of caseworkers, 362–3
    attitude towards planning, 243, 361
    consideration and casework of, 361–
        3
    decision making, 362–4

knowledge and training of, 18–21,
    210–15
lack of skill of, 212–15
power of, 360–3, 396–9
role of, 12–26, 81, 111, 360, 361
shortage of, 210–12
Planning
    approach to systems, 11
    article on London, 27–8
    and land values, 603–7
    case-study in, 364–4
    casework in, 361–4
    central government policy in, 80–1
    conditional permissions, 414–31
    conditions imposed on, 417–19
    control at local authority level, 354–
        69
    control external to the system, 484–
        601
    debate on public participation in,
        97–107
    decision making process in, 94–101,
        396–9
    defined, 18–19
    development control policies in,
        412–31
    governmental reorganisation of, 78–
        80
    ideology and public policy in, 13–16
    interaction between law and, 471–
        83
    public participation in, 96
    publicity issue in, 371–80
    regional and sub-regional growth of,
        233, 234
    social, 207–9, 236
    systems, problems, and reform of,
        2, 158–70
    types of decision, 447–8
    see also Corporate, Regional, Town,
        Social, Sub-regional, and Urban
        planning
Planning appeal
    public local inquiry following appeal
        to Minister, 8, 454–8
    third party involvement, 114–15
Planning application
    communications regarding, 431–48
    function of local authorities on, 356–
        9
    large-scale, 8–9
    outline and detailed, 479
    procedure for, 371–7

small-scale, 9
statistics on, 354–5
Planning Authority
enforcing conditions of internal
design (case), 426–8
legal actions against, 566–90
Planning blight, 168, 220, 228, 635,
689
Planning committee
advantages of, 402
arrangements, 402–3
legal advice, in, 401
working of, 396–9
Planning Control
breach of, 487–9
categorization of, 477
purpose of, 408
Planning law, judicial control, 485–
558
Planning of urban development, 36–7
Planning officers
power of, 478
views of, 458–60, 460–1
Planning organization, function of,
18–20
Planning permission, 8–9
and aspects of communication, 431–
48
and cessation of use (case), 531–3
and conditions imposed by, 521–4
and controversial cases, 380–95
and estoppel (case), 440–3
and prospective development value,
649–62
and the certificate of ownership,
380–5
application for, 369–80
'call in' procedure, 449–50
change of character made on
buildings (case), 549–53
consideration of policies in, 409–12
default powers, 451–2
discontinuance orders, 451
early Act (1589), 34–5
effect of delays in, 471–83
enforcement notices, 451
for alterations in building (case),
513–18
for building and supermarket (case),
591–9
for factory extension (case), 436–9
for the City of London (1667), 35–6
framework of policy, 450–1
guidance of government in, 480–1
irregular use of buildings (case),
534–6
law cases regarding, 431–48
ministerial or departmental
hearings, 452–3
minor variations from plan, 443–6
occasions for ministerial or
departmental decisions, 449–52
points in determining, 403–31
powers of revocation, 451
procedure of inquiries, 452–70
refusal of and compensation for,
624–36
time factor as regards to
applications, 431–2
when to restrict, 417–19
working procedure for, 385–432
Planning, public involvement in, 97–
101
Planning register, 374
Planning restrictions
and inverse compulsory purchase,
631, 684–96
case of, 651–3
Plowden Committee, 207
Pointe Gourde Principle, 643–5
Policy
permission, 409–12
consideration of in planning
framework of in planning
permission, 480–1
Pollution of atmosphere (case), 53–61
see also 'Nuisance'
Positive covenants, 290–302
cases of, 252, 253
covenants between neighbours, 292
enforcement of, 298–302, 332–3
in cases, 331–2
non-enforceability of, 290–302
power to enforce end of life of
building, 298
problems arising over blocks of
flats, 294–8
Strata Titles system and, 296–8
see also Restrictive covenants
Poulson and corruption, 30
Private property, theme of judicial
protection of, 43, 46–84
Professional bodies, attitude of towards
planning, 128, 172, 201
Property development and corruption
in local government, 30

Public development, nuisance and,
    74
    see also disturbance
Public involvement in planning, 97–
    101
    opinion against, 108–10
    see also Public local inquiries
Publicity concerning planning
    permission, 371–80, 478
Public local inquiry, 174, 243, 453,
    459, 482
    and the planning advisory group,
        165–6
    and third parties, 114–15, 119, 121
    appearances at inquiry, 456
    attitudes to, 113
    awarding of costs in, 115–26
    example of, 581–2
    following appeal to Minister, 8,
        236–7
    following residents complaint (case),
        592
    function of, 10
    in connection with structure plans,
        170, 218
    in land-use planning, 9
    notification of inquiry, 455
    problems of inquiry and decision-
        making procedures, 454–70
    notification of decision of, 462
    procedure after inquiry, 461–2
    procedure at, 458
    presentation of government
        departments at, 456–7
    representation of local authorities at,
        457
    statements to be served before
        inquiry, 455–6
    site inspectors concern with, 458
    when to reopen, 561
    see also Public involvement in
        planning
Public participation, 2, 9, 10
    and compensation, 696–9
    at public local enquiry of district
        plans, 236–41
    before submission of district plans,
        234–6
    causes of activation, 112
    examples of in decision making,
        105–6
    implications and drawbacks of,
        101–11

in consultation with local authority,
    97–101, 102–4, 137, 219–20
in planning, 96, 151–2, 481
in planning application, 371–80
in planning, debate on, 101–111
'Packington Estate' (case), 581–90
residents complaint against
    development, 591–9
social consequences of, 112–13, 139
Public participation in structure plans,
    216–33
    at public examination, 225–33
    before submission of plans, 216–25
    in district plans, 234–41
Public Roadways, rights over, 577
Purchase notices, 684–5

Redevelopment on break-up of
    leasehold estates, 342
Regional Planning, 143–54, 207
    decentralization of, 145
    public participation in, 233
    relationship to statutory development
        planning, 143–8
    relationship with local structure
        plans, 152–3
    see also Sub-regional planning
Regional strategic plans, 145–8
Residential estates, control over by
    long lease, 329–49
Resident Type Scheme, 300
Restrictive covenant(s), 247–92
    and annexations, 254–8
    and assignment, 257–72
    and development schemes, 273–83
    and erection of flats (cases), 308–12,
        312–14
    and local authorities (case), 280–3
    and variation in lease, 319–21
    compulsory acquisition of, 315
    description of, 246
    discharging of, 303, 306–8
    enforcement of, 283–6, 332–3
    enforcement by National Trust
        (cases), 286–9, 389–92
    exemption from under statutory
        powers, 289
    in leases, 331
    legal basis for, 247–9
    methods of enforcement, 299–302
    modification of, 303–15
    racial, 321–9
    removal of, case judgements, 273–83

suspension by local authorities, 315–21
transfer of (case), 247–9
wording when land is sold, 254
see also Positive covenants
Revocation, powers of in planning permission, 451
Roskill Inquiry into third London airport, 105
Royal Commission on 'Housing for the Working Classes' (1884–5), 43
Rule of Law, Principles of, 31–3

Seasonal use of land (case), 539–41
Secretary of State's jurisdiction, Statutory terms of, 449–50
Seebohm Committee (on Personal and Allied Social Services), 207
Shifting value, defined, 606
Skeffington Report, The (*People and Planning*), 104–8, 111, 112, 138–9, 141
Slum clearance, early legislation on, 38
Social functions of planning *see* Ideology, Planning
Social planning, 4–5, 24–6, 210
Social Science Research Council, 5
State ownership of development rights, 610–11
Statutory model scheme, 296, 297, 298
'Stop Notice', 487, 489
Strata Titles system, 296–8
Structure and local plan regulations, 201
Structure planning, 202–7
 and local government, 211
 and social planning, 207, 209, 236
 difficulties in implementing the P.A.G. report, 212–14
 relationship with corporate planning, 205–7
Structure plan(s), 167, 168, 169–71, 178, 179, 183, 190, 191, 194–6, 213, 214, 215, 234, 240
 aims of, 193
 and public participation, 216–33
 boundaries of, 168
 consultation on, 201, 227
 development of, 172, 173
 directions on and creation of, 184–7, 195–6
 functions of, 192–3, 194–5, 204
 future of, 241–4

preparation of, 174–7
public examination of, 225–33
regulations of, 188–90
relationship of various types of, 197–200
relationship with district plan, 191
Warwickshire example, Heathcote, 622–3
written statement on, 188–90, 191, 202
urban, 196, 197, 198, 200, 224, 225
see also Development plans, Development plan scheme
Sub-regional planning, 148–51
 public participation in, 151, 233
 strategies of, 149
Supermarket, planning permission for building, 591
Surplus
 consumer, 682–3
 household, 600–3

Time-limit conditions in planning, 416, 478
Town and Country Planning Association, 141, 619
Tree preservation, 309–10, 332, 343
 order for, 388, 389, 685
 provisional, 309
Tripe, disliked by some, 49
Trust Instrument Scheme, 299

Ultra vires, declaration against, 575–9
Unit of development
 problem of defining, 541–4
 selective choice of whole, 549–53
Urban area
 altered patterns of growth, 4–5
 growth of, 3–4
 population density in, 6
Urban planning
 bulletin on, 367–8
 process of in the future, 17–19
 report of planning advisory group, 162
Urban Structure Plans *see* Structure Plans
Use
 abandonment of (case), 531–3
 ancillary, 537–41
 cessation of, 532
 change of, 541–58, 524
 change of degree of (cases), 526–31

Use – *cont.*
  change of in building or land,
    518–19, 544–9
Uthwatt Report (*Expert Committee on
  Compensation and Betterment*), 602,
  604, 610, 617, 620, 635

Warwickshire County Council (Town
  and Country Planning
  Committee)

Minutes of October 1970 meeting,
  175–6
Minutes of April 1971 meeting, 175
Report of, for September 1972
  meeting, 223
Warwickshire County Draft Structure
  Plan (1972), 622
Wilberforce Committee Report
  (*Committee on Positive Covenants*),
  298